FORD

*Georgia Voices*

# Georgia Voices

## Volume Two: Nonfiction

### Edited by Hugh Ruppersburg

The University of Georgia Press   Athens and London

© 1994 by the University of Georgia Press
Athens, Georgia 30602
All rights reserved

Set in Stemple Garamond by Tseng Information Systems, Inc.
The paper in this book meets the guidelines
for permanence and durability of the Committee on
Production Guidelines for Book Longevity
of the Council on Library Resources.

Printed in the United States of America

98  97  96  95  94  C  5  4  3  2  1
98  97  96  95  94  P  5  4  3  2  1

Library of Congress Cataloging in Publication Data
Georgia voices.

Includes bibliographical references.
Contents: v. 1. Fiction—v. 2. Non-fiction.
1. American literature—Georgia.   2. Georgia—Literary collections.
I. Ruppersburg, Hugh M.
PS558.G4G44        1992        813.008'09758        91-36688
ISBN 0-8203-1432-3   (v. 1: alk. paper)
ISBN 0-8203-1433-1   (v. 1: pbk.: alk. paper)
ISBN 0-8203-1625-3   (v. 2: alk. paper)
ISBN 0-8203-1626-1   (v. 2: pbk.: alk. paper)

British Library Cataloging in Publication Data available

# Contents

*Part Four*
Contemporary Georgia, 1970 to the Present

# Contents

# *Preface*

The first volume of *Georgia Voices* collected some of the best fiction by writers from this state. This second volume, an anthology of non-fiction, is somewhat different. It still seeks to present a wide range of writing consistently high in quality, but it also seeks to convey a portrait of the state as a product of both its history and geography. My reason for making it so is simple. The state's history tells a story. Its characters are the native Americans, blacks, and whites who lived and fought for survival here, some perishing, some enduring. The themes of this story are manifold: the struggle of early settlers against the wilderness, the plight of the Cherokee and Creek, slavery and emancipation, war and defeat, reconstruction, the struggle toward and against modernity, the civil rights movement, the global community. It is a dramatic story— often sad and pathetic, sometimes comic, frequently moving, on occasion ennobling. It is a story this anthology cannot hope to tell fully, but at the least the writings included here may suggest its outlines.

Although most of the writers in this volume are native Georgians or long-term residents, a few are not. James Oglethorpe, Francis Moore, and Frances Kemble were natives of England. Emily Burke was from Ohio. In each case, however, the perspective they and other nonnative Georgians bring to the state merited their inclusion. Many writers of the state do not appear here, especially modern and contemporary writers. To present a genuinely comprehensive selection of the worthy nonfiction written in Georgia over the course of its history would require many volumes. The best this anthology can do is to attempt to provide a representative sampling. That one writer or another does not appear does not necessarily indicate a low opinion of his or her work. Some writers simply did not fit the design of the anthology and had to be left out. Others were omitted because the kind of writing they produced was already represented: Henry Grady and Ralph McGill are two of a significant number of newspaper editors from the state, while the diaries of Alexander Stephens, Mary A. H. Gay, and Fanny Kemble provide noteworthy examples of a kind of writing frequently practiced in the nineteenth century. Admittedly, a few writers may fail to appear through oversight that later editions will correct.

A number of people provided invaluable assistance during the preparation of this volume. Sheri Joseph and David Peterson were especially helpful in gathering books, tracking down disparate bits of information, and conducting general research. I thank as well David Aiken, Edwin T. Arnold, Rodney Baine, Lisa Barnett, Darren Thomas Felty, Jean Friedman, Tony Grooms, Phyllis Gussler, Mary Hembree, James Kilgo, Alice Kinman, Edward Krickel, Stanley Lindberg, Hubert McAlexander, Lisa McNair, Charlotte Marshall, Rayburn Moore, Tony Murphy, Beaté Oertel, Charles and Sue Smith, and Coburn Freer, former head of the University of Georgia English department, and my wife, Patricia. My sons, Michael, Charles and Max, were as always a profound inspiration. I found much useful information in the Georgia Room of the University of Georgia Library, and I am indebted to that facility and its staff for its wonderful collection. I thank the University of Georgia Press, especially editorial assistants Diana Schuh, Kelly Caudle, and Laura Sutton and executive editor Karen Orchard, for their help and encouragement. To my mother, Margaret Caruthers Ruppersburg, and to the people of Georgia, this second volume of *Georgia Voices* is dedicated.

# Acknowledgments

The Press and I would like to acknowledge the authors and publishers who gave us permission to reprint material in this volume. They are:

From *Ushant: An Essay* by Conrad Aiken. Reprinted by permission of Little, Brown.

From *The Last Radio Baby* by Raymond Andrews. Reprinted by permission of Peachtree Publishers.

"Being from Georgia" from *Crackers* by Roy Blount, Jr. Copyright 1977, 1978, 1980 by Roy Blount, Jr. Reprinted by permission of Alfred A. Knopf, Inc.

From *Turning Point: A Candidate, a State, and a Nation Come of Age* by Jimmy Carter. Copyright 1992 by Jimmy Carter. Reprinted by permission of Times Books, a division of Random House, Inc.

From *A Childhood: The Biography of a Place* by Harry Crews. Copyright 1978 by Harry Crews. Reprinted by permission of John Hawkins & Associates, Inc.

From *Fatal Flowers: On Sin, Sex, and Suicide in the Deep South* by Rosemary Daniell. Copyright 1980 by Rosemary Daniell. Reprinted by permission of Henry Holt and Company, Inc.

From *Praying for Sheetrock* by Melissa Fay Greene. Copyright 1991 by Melissa Fay Greene. Reprinted by permission of Addison-Wesley Publishing Company.

"Grits Billy Bob" from *Won't You Come Home, Billy Bob Bailey?* by Lewis Grizzard. Reprinted by permission of Peachtree Publishers.

From "Mountain Spirits" by James Kilgo. Reprinted by permission of the author.

"The American Dream" by Martin Luther King, Jr. Reprinted by permission of the Joan Daves Agency.

" 'My Old Mule Is Gone' " and "Hatred Reaps Its Harvest" from *The Best of Ralph McGill* edited by Michael Strickland, Harry Davis, and Jeff Strickland. Reprinted by permission of Cherokee Publishing Company.

"It Has Happened Here" from *No Place to Hide* by Ralph McGill, edited by Calvin Logue. Reprinted by permission of Mary Lynn Morgan and Ralph E. McGill, Jr.

"The King of the Birds" from *Mystery and Manners* by Flannery O'Connor. Copyright 1961, renewal copyright 1989 by the Estate of Mary Flannery O'Connor. Reprinted by permission of Farrar, Straus & Giroux, Inc.

From *At Home on St. Simons* by Eugenia Price. Reprinted by permission of Peachtree Publishers.

From *Killers of the Dream* by Lillian Smith. Copyright 1949, 1961 by Lillian Smith. Copyright renewed 1977, 1989 by Paula Snelling. Reprinted by permission of W. W. Norton & Company, Inc.

From "Growing Up in Georgia and Tennessee: The Letters of John E. Talmadge and William Wallace Davidson." Reprinted by permission of the *Georgia Review.*

"Beyond the Peacock: The Reconstruction of Flannery O'Connor" from *In Search of Our Mothers' Gardens* by Alice Walker. Copyright 1975 by Alice Walker. Reprinted by permission of Harcourt Brace Jovanovich, Inc.

From *A Man Called White* by Walter White. Copyright 1948 by Walter White, renewed 1976 by the Estate of Walter White. Reprinted by permission of Viking Penguin, a division of Penguin Books USA Inc.

"Some Things You Can't Pave Over" by Philip Lee Williams. Reprinted by permission of the author.

"Gentian" from *Emblems of Conduct* by Donald Windham. Copyright 1963 by Donald Windham. Reprinted by permission of the author.

The publication of this volume was supported by
The Friends of the University of Georgia Press

# Introduction

The word *nonfiction* names a broad and indistinct category of writing that includes essays, autobiographies, personal narratives, travelogues, journalism, and other forms of expression clearly intended for a public audience. It can also refer to kinds of writing not intended for the public. Most letters, for example, are written between private individuals who have no thought of another audience. Such writing does not usually make exciting reading since it often dwells on day-to-day details. On occasion, however, a particularly effective writer can bring mundane details to life. Or the dramatic context of a historical situation—the Civil War, for instance—will empower private letters to speak directly and poignantly to a public audience that years later comes to read them. This is the case with the letters of the Charles Colcock Jones family in *Children of Pride*. There individuals and families caught in the struggle and uncertainty of the Civil War speak with a poignancy that transcends time and place. Their words bring us as readers into intimate contact with the reality of sweeping historical events that otherwise exist only as a litany of dry facts and figures.

Less affecting, but still interesting, are diaries, journals, and other writings by early settlers of the state. James Oglethorpe, founder of the British Colony of Georgia, recorded his activities in a private journal and wrote reports not merely for his own satisfaction but to inform his sponsors and the public in Britain about the progress of the new colony. John Wesley, the founder of Methodism, spent a brief period in the early Georgia colony, and he wrote with a similar purpose in his journal, though he also probably regarded it as a record of his struggle to do God's will. Both Oglethorpe and Wesley probably knew, or at least hoped, that their writings would one day see publication. Other, more private writers did not ever imagine that their journals and diaries would be published, although a few of them, long years after the fact, revised their diaries for a public audience.[1]

The distinctions between fiction and nonfiction are not always clear. We associate fiction with the craft of writing: finely drawn characters, vivid prose, plots, and themes. Yet these elements are no less important in nonfiction. The fictionist who neglects the importance of portraying the world as it is, of exploring realistic problems and situations, is not likely to meet with much success. Writers of nonfiction—who are clearly interested in real problems and situations—are not always above stretching the facts or even creating them out of thin air. The nineteenth-century newspaper letters of Charles Henry Smith, or "Bill Arp," are written in the tradition of tall-tale Southern humor. On occasion they warp and stretch the truth for comic or satiric effect. In more recent years, such humorists as Lewis Grizzard and Roy Blount have shown a similar disregard for mere facts in their nonfiction when a heightened and exaggerated truth can result in more humor. Some might argue that such writers as Arp, Grizzard, and Blount are indeed writing a peculiar brand of fiction, but almost always their letters and columns concern topical issues of their contemporary world.

Writers may toy with the facts for other reasons as well. A natural shyness apparently led Joel Chandler Harris to cloak the story of his early life on the plantation of editor Joseph Addison Turner under the guise of fiction, though in the introduction to his novel *On the Plantation* (1892) he admits its autobiographical character. In a much different autobiography entitled *Ushant* (1952) the poet Conrad Aiken similarly camouflaged his life, but he did so for artistic effect, to embellish and objectify the story he had to tell.[2] John Donald Wade, in his 1930 essay "The Life and Death of Cousin Lucius," writes about a man who never existed, but in

---

1. The most famous Civil War diarist was a South Carolinian, Mary Boykin Chesnut, who extensively revised and rewrote her diary in the 1880s prior to her death in 1888.

2. T. S. Eliot, for instance, with whom Aiken roomed at Harvard, is named Tsetse, while Ezra Pound is Rabbi Ben Ezra.

doing so he chronicles fifty years of history that radically transformed the Southern landscape.

As the potential readership for Georgia writers increased in both North and South toward the end of the nineteenth century and into the twentieth, the nonfiction that Georgians produced grew less varied, more self-conscious and artful. For the most part, twentieth-century nonfiction came in the form of writing conceived and produced for a public audience. Autobiography grew in importance, as did newspaper writing. One type of writing that has remained significant throughout Georgia history has been what we might call descriptive place writing. Even such early writers as Oglethorpe and Francis Moore were much concerned with describing the flora and fauna of the new colony, or the ways of the Cherokee and Creek, or the habits of the colonists. In her *Letters from the South* (1850) Emily Burke described with great care for her mostly Northern readers the lives of blacks and whites in Savannah and on south Georgia plantations. Pre–Civil-War slave narratives served a similar purpose, but with a moral and political objective. They were written by escaped slaves, sometimes with the aid of their abolitionist editors, for the sake of convincing Northern readers of the horrors of slavery and winning support for the abolitionist cause. Frequently the results were not literary in quality. Sometimes, however, as with the famous narratives of Frederick Douglass, or the narrative of the Georgia slave John Brown, the results are riveting and heartrending. In whatever form—slave narrative or private letter or plantation journal—such writing was in one sense a kind of travel writing, usually directed toward non-Georgian, non-Southern readers. Much the same is true of Frances Kemble's diary, or of Frances Butler Leigh's post–Civil-War journal about her experiences on a coastal Georgia plantation.

As the civil rights movement intensified in the 1950s, focusing national attention on the South, the market for articles and books about Southern life grew. In the 1970s the South became for a time the focus of popular culture, partially because of the popularity of country music, partially also because of the 1976 election of Jimmy Carter to the presidency. Throughout the latter half of this century writers have sought in various ways to address and satisfy interest in the American South. Yet they have also continued to try to explain the South to themselves and to their Southern readers as well. Such writers as Lillian Smith in *Killers of the Dream* (1949), Erskine Caldwell in *Deep South* (1968), and Rosemary Daniell in *Fatal Flowers* (1980) seem to address a non-Southern audience, while such writers as Harry Crews in *A Childhood: The Biography of a Place* (1978) and Raymond Andrews in *The Last Radio Baby* (1991) record their memories of a Southern tradition and way of life to insure their survival for posterity. The best of such writing is accessible to any audience, but for Southern readers these memories of the past, of vanished ways of life, may hold special poignancy.

# Part One

---

*Early Georgia, 1733–1830*

The colony of Georgia was founded not merely as a commercial enter-prise but also as a utopian settlement where people who had found little success in Britain, or had suffered religious persecution in Europe, might make a fresh start and enjoy better opportunities on a new continent. In *The History of Georgia* Phinizy Spalding explains that the colony "was not created simply to be another Maryland or South Carolina. Georgia must be something new and refreshing—a kind of Holy Experiment. Like Pennsylvania, Georgia was to be a refuge for European Protestants who suffered injustices at the hands of their overlords. The charter of Georgia also anticipated that the colony would help relieve the prob-lem of unemployment at home by providing unfortunates with 'a com-fortable sustenance' in America."[1] To prevent the development of large plantations, the Georgia charter forbade individual land grants of more than five hundred acres. The first Trustees of Georgia, themselves pre-vented by the charter from acquiring property in the colony, forbade the importation of slaves. Primogeniture was recognized only in a limited fashion, land ownership was regulated (the renting and leasing of land was prohibited), and the use of alcohol stronger than beer or ale was ille-gal. Oglethorpe did not want Georgia to become a province like South Carolina, whose plantation system "favored the few."[2] The leaders of the colony also sought to establish good relations with the coastal Indians. In short, Georgia was founded on noble principles, not merely in hope of profit but from a desire to serve the unfortunate.

1. *A History of Georgia*, Kenneth Coleman, ed., "Colonial Period" by Phinizy Spalding (Athens: Univ. of Georgia Press, 1977), p. 17.
2. Ibid., pp. 17, 22.

Few Georgians, and fewer Americans, are aware of these facts.[3] But by
1740 the laws restricting land ownership and primogeniture were repealed
and the law forbidding whiskey was widely ignored. In 1752 slavery became legal. In general, most of the noble intentions of Oglethorpe and
the Trustees came to naught. It is significant, however, that they tried to
establish what Spalding has described as a "novel province that would act
as a future guidepost for colonial America."[4] The state's writing reflects
the struggle between the pull of these founding ideals and the practicali-
ties of everyday life, which finally brought those ideals down.

Much of the earliest writing in Georgia came not from the deliberate
effort of the settlers to record their experiences, but as the by-product
of their normal activities. Eighteenth-century colonial Americans had no
means of communication with England other than the slow and uncer-
tain ships that sailed back and forth across the Atlantic. A man such as
Sir James Oglethorpe would naturally be concerned that the Trustees of
Georgia in England be made aware of the colony's progress. To that end,
he wrote a number of reports on the early affairs of the coastal settlers.
He wrote to assure the Trustees that the colony was commercially and
politically viable, that he was acting responsibly, and that he was providing the Carolina colonies with a defensive buffer against Spanish invasion
from the south. He wrote also to satisfy the curiosity of British citizens,
whose approval could only improve his chances for continued financial
support from the British government. One senses in his writings another
motive as well: a compulsion to express his own sense of wonder and
pride at the enterprise he had helped organize, and at the natural wealth
and beauty of the Georgia landscape.

Of course, the first British settlers in Georgia were not the first Georgians. The Spanish had tried to colonize coastal Georgia, and the French
had made an appearance as well. A few settlers from South Carolina had

3. By present-day standards the laws governing the state were not egalitarian. The
charter forbade the presence of Roman Catholics in the colony, and the Trustees, while
outlawing slavery, also outlawed the immigration of blacks (in general they felt that slavery
would encourage laziness among the white colonists). When a shipload of Jewish families
arrived, Oglethorpe allowed them to settle, over the objections of the Trustees.

4. *A History of Georgia,* p. 24.

already drifted into northeastern portions of the state by the time of Oglethorpe's arrival. But the first true Georgians came long before any of these. The Creek and Cherokee Indians whom Oglethorpe, Moore, and others described in their writings had been living in the state for centuries. These native Americans did not possess writing (though the Cherokee eventually developed this skill), but they did have a vigorous oral tradition that survived well into the nineteenth century. James Mooney compiled an extensive record of it, though by then the coherence of the Cherokee mythology had disappeared. The myths of the Cherokee are the efforts of a people to make sense of their world, to explain its origins, and to identify their place within it. They are the work of a people who liked to tell and listen to stories and who felt eminently secure in their surroundings. But by the time Mooney recorded their stories, the Cherokee had long been displaced, along with the Creek, to reservations in Arkansas and Oklahoma. Early Georgia colonists made genuine efforts to coexist peacefully with the Indians. Although displacement of the Indians was not at first one of their goals, it soon became so. Tension mounted as the white settlers became increasingly frustrated with the presence of the Indians, who themselves felt threatened by the settlers moving in to take over their lands. Bloody conflict ensued. Hugh McCall's *History of Georgia,* a lively account of the first fifty years of the state, describes a number of harrowing encounters and battles between the settlers and Indians. George Gilmer, a governor who during the 1830s fiercely argued for the removal of the Indians, writes of his own encounter with the Cherokee in his sketches of early Georgia life. In a more lighthearted vein, Henry Hull, in his *Annals of Athens* describes how the threat of a Cherokee raid on Athens during the War of 1812 prompted students and faculty of the University of Georgia to mobilize in defense of the town. Indian attack was a frequent cause for concern among early Georgians, even well into the nineteenth century, when the danger was more perceived than real.

In 1826 Elias Boudinot, a thoroughly civilized, even Europeanized chief of the Georgia Cherokee, pleaded eloquently before the state legislature, asking that his people be allowed to remain in the state, citing their industry, their accomplishments, and their desire to be a part of the state and its community. His pleas went unheeded. It should be dis-heartening for modern Georgians to discover in the early documents of the state's history the fervor with which the state's leaders sought to be rid of the Cherokee and Creek. Modern Americans tend to think of the fate of the American Indian in terms of the wars between the U.S. army and various western tribes during the last thirty years of the nineteenth century. But the conquest of the Indians began much earlier, from the moment of the first settlement of the colonies. The Creek began ceding land to the Georgia settlers a short time after their arrival. By 1840, in Georgia and most of the rest of the southeast, the Indian presence was a fading memory. Yet in place names, some history books, and in the memories of some of the state's writers, the Cherokee and Creek heritage faintly survives.

# James Mooney

## From *Myths of the Cherokee*

### HOW THE WORLD WAS MADE

The earth is a great island floating in a sea of water, and suspended at each of the four cardinal points by a cord hanging down from the sky vault, which is of solid rock. When the world grows old and worn out, the people will die and the cords will break and let the earth sink down into the ocean, and all will be water again. The Indians are afraid of this.

When all was water, the animals were above in Gălûñ'lătĭ, beyond the arch; but it was very much crowded, and they were wanting more room. They wondered what was below the water, and at last Dâyuni'sĭ, "Beaver's Grandchild," the little Water-beetle, offered to go and see if it could learn. It darted in every direction over the surface of the water, but could find no firm place to rest. Then it dived to the bottom and came up with some soft mud, which began to grow and spread on every side until it became the island which we call the earth. It was afterward fastened to the sky with four cords, but no one remembers who did this.

At first the earth was flat and very soft and wet. The animals were anxious to get down, and sent out different birds to see if it was yet dry, but they found no place to alight and came back again to Gălûñ'lătĭ. At last it seemed to be time, and they sent out the Buzzard and told him to go and make ready for them. This was the Great Buzzard, the father of all the buzzards we see now. He flew all over the earth, low down near the ground, and it was still soft. When he reached the Cherokee country, he was very tired, and his wings began to flap and strike the ground, and wherever they struck the earth there was a valley, and where they turned up again there was a mountain. When the animals above saw this, they were afraid that the whole world would be mountains, so they called him back, but the Cherokee country remains full of mountains to this day.

When the earth was dry and the animals came down, it was still dark, so they got the sun and set it in a track to go every day across the island from east to west, just overhead. It was too hot this way, and Tsiska'gĭlĭ, the Red Crawfish, had his shell scorched a bright red, so that his meat was spoiled; and the Cherokee do not eat it. The conjurers put the sun another hand-breadth higher in the air, but it was still too hot. They raised it another time, and another, until it was seven handbreadths high and just under the sky arch. Then it was right, and they left it so. This is why the conjurers call the highest place Gûlkwâ'gine Di'gălûñ'lătiyûñ', "the seventh height," because it is seven hand-breadths above the earth. Every day the sun goes along under this arch, and returns at night on the upper side to the starting place.

There is another world under this, and it is like ours in everything—animals, plants, and people—save that the seasons are different. The streams that come down from the mountains are the trails by which we reach this underworld, and the springs at their heads are the doorways by which we enter it, but to do this one must fast and go to water and have one of the underground people for a guide. We know that the seasons in the underworld are different from ours, because the water in the springs is always warmer in winter and cooler in summer than the outer air.

When the animals and plants were first made—we do not know by whom—they were told to watch and keep awake for seven nights, just as young men now fast and keep awake when they pray to their medicine. They tried to do this, and nearly all were awake through the first night, but the next night several dropped off to sleep, and the third night others were asleep, and then others, until, on the seventh night, of all the animals only the owl, the panther, and one or two more were still awake. To these were given the power to see and to go about in the dark, and to make prey of the birds and animals which must sleep at night. Of the trees only the cedar, the pine, the spruce, the holly, and the laurel were awake to the end, and to them it was given to be always green and to be greatest for medicine, but to the others it was said: "Because you have not endured to the end you shall lose your hair every winter."

Men came after the animals and plants. At first there were only a brother and sister until he struck her with a fish and told her to multiply, and so it was. In seven days a child was born to her, and thereafter every seven days another, and they increased very fast until there was danger that the world could not keep them. Then it was made that a woman should have only one child in a year, and it has been so ever since.

### THE FIRST FIRE

In the beginning there was no fire, and the world was cold, until the Thunders (Ani'-Hyûñ'tĭkwălâ'skĭ), who lived up in Gălûñ'lătĭ, sent their lightning and put fire into the bottom of a hollow sycamore tree which grew on an island. The animals knew it was there, because they could see the smoke coming out at the top, but they could not get to it on account of the water, so they held a council to decide what to do. This was a long time ago.

Every animal that could fly or swim was anxious to go after the fire. The Raven offered, and because he was so large and strong they thought he could surely do the work, so he was sent first. He flew high and far across the water and alighted on the sycamore tree, but while he was wondering what to do next, the heat had scorched all his feathers black, and he was frightened and came back without the fire. The little Screech-owl (*Wa'huhu'*) volunteered to go, and reached the place safely, but while he was looking down into the hollow tree a blast of hot air came up and nearly burned out his eyes. He managed to fly home as best he could, but it was a long time before he could see well, and his eyes are red to this day. Then the Hooting Owl (*U'guku'*) and the Horned Owl (*Tskĭlĭ'*) went, but by the time they got to the hollow tree the fire was burning so fiercely that the smoke nearly blinded them, and the ashes carried up by the wind made white rings about their eyes. They had to come home again without the fire, but with all their rubbing they were never able to get rid of the white rings.

Now no more of the birds would venture, and so the little Uksu'hĭ snake, the black racer, said he would go through the water and bring back some fire. He swam across to the island and crawled through the grass to the tree, and went in by a small hole at the bottom. The heat and smoke were too much for him, too, and after dodging about blindly over the hot ashes until he was almost on fire himself he managed by good luck to get out again at the same hole, but his body had been scorched black, and he has ever since had the habit of darting and doubling on his track as if trying to escape from close quarters. He came back, and the great blacksnake, Gûle'gĭ, "The Climber," offered to go for fire. He swam over to the island and climbed up the tree on the outside, as the blacksnake always does, but when he put his head down into the hole the smoke choked him so that he fell into the burning stump, and before he could climb out again he was as black as the Uksu'hĭ.

Now they held another council, for still there was no fire, and the world was cold, but birds, snakes, and four-footed animals, all had some excuse for not going, because they were all afraid to venture near the burning sycamore, until at last Kănăne'skĭ Amai'yĕhĭ (the Water Spider) said she would go. This is not the water spider that looks like a mosquito, but the other one, with black downy hair and red stripes on her body. She can run on top of the water or dive to the bottom, so there would be no trouble to get over to the island, but the question was, How could she bring back the fire? "I'll manage that," said the Water Spider; so she spun a thread from her body and wove it into a *tusti* bowl, which she fastened on her back. Then she crossed over to the island and through the grass to where the fire was still burning. She put one little coal of fire into her bowl, and came back with it, and ever since we have had fire, and the Water Spider still keeps her tusti bowl.

# James Oglethorpe

## "An Account of Carolina and Georgia"

Carolina is part of that territory which was originally discovered by Sir Sebastian Cabot. The English now possess the sea-coast, from the river St. John's, in 30 degrees 21 minutes north latitude. Westward the King's charter declares to be bounded by the Pacifick Ocean.

Carolina is divided into North Carolina, South Carolina, and Georgia; the latter is a province which his Majesty has taken out of Carolina, and is the southern and western frontier of that province, lying between it, and the French, Spaniards, and Indians.

The part of Carolina that is settled, is for the most part a flat country: all near the sea, is a range of islands, which breaks the fury of the ocean: within is generally low-land for twenty or twenty five miles, where the country begins to rise in gentle swellings. At seventy or eighty miles from the sea, the hills grow higher, till they terminate in mountains.

The coast of Georgia is also defended from the rage of the sea by a range of islands. Those islands are divided from the main by canals of salt water, navigable for the largest boats, and even for small sloops. The lofty woods growing on each side of the canals make very pleasant land-scapes. The land at about seven or eight miles from the sea, is tolerably high; and the farther you go westward the more it rises, till at about 150 miles distance from the sea, to the west, the Cherikees or Apellachean mountains begin, which are so high that the snow lies upon some of them all the year.

This ridge of mountains runs in a line from north to south, on the back of the English colonies of Carolina and Virginia; beginning at the great lakes of Canada, and extending south, it ends in the province of Georgia, at about two hundred miles from the bay of Appellachee, which is part of the gulph of Mexico. There is a plain country from the foot of these mountains to that sea.

The face of the country is mostly covered with woods; the banks of the rivers are in some places low, and form a kind of natural meadows, where the floods prevent trees from growing. In other places, in the hollows, between the hillocks, the brooks and streams being stopt by falls of trees, or other obstructions, the water is penn'd back: these places are often covered with canes and thickets, and are called in the corrupted American dialect, swamps. The sides of the hills are generally covered with oaks and hiccary, or wild walnuts, cedar, sassafras, and the famous laurel tulip, which is esteemed one of the most beautiful trees in the world: the flat tops of the hillocks are all covered with groves of pine-trees, with plenty of grass growing under them; and free from underwood, that you may gallop a horse for forty or fifty miles an end. In the low grounds, and islands of the river, there are cypress, bay-trees, poplar, plane, frank-incense, or gum-trees, and other aquaticks. All parts of the province are well watered; and in digging a moderate depth, you never miss a fine spring.

What we call the Atlantic Ocean, washes the east and southeast coasts of these provinces. The gulph stream of Florida sets with a tide in the ocean to the east of the province; and it is very remarkable, that the banks and soundings of the coast extend twenty or twenty-five miles to the east of the coast. To explain this, we will mention the manner of the voyage from Europe. You set out with variable winds, and having got enough to the west of Europe, you stand southerly till you meet with the trade winds; which you do, on this side the 20th degree north latitude. Those winds blowing generally eastwardly, and moderately brisk, soon drive you over the greatest part of the Atlantick ocean: you keep the same latitude, till you think you are near the Bahamas, and then you steer northwardly, to avoid falling in with them, till you come into 29 degrees, and then you run in to make the shore. You cross the gulph stream of Florida, which is a rapid tide, that sets out from between the island of Cuba and Bahama, on the one side, and Florida on the other. It is upwards of twenty leagues wide, and so rapid that it runs to the northward, at the rate of three miles an hour. When you are past the gulph stream, you throw the lead, and if you find the ground at twenty five leagues of the coast of Georgia or Carolina, these they call the banks, and the water shoals gradually to shore, till you come within two leagues, where the banks are so shoaly that they bar all further passage, excepting in the channels which lie between the bars. These bars are the defence of the coast against enemies fleets, and the reason that it has laid so long undiscovered; for without good pilots you cannot come into any harbour, the shoaliness of the coast frightened ships so from coming to make discoveries upon it: till Mr. Oglethorpe had the entries on the coast of Georgia sounded in the year 1733, no ship attempted to go into ports in Georgia, nor did the merchants believe there were any ports upon that coast. Though now they find the river Savannah an excellent harbour; and upon the worst of the bar, three fathom at dead low water. There is also a noble harbour to the southward, called Teky-Sound, where there is anchoring for a large squadron in ten or fourteen fathom water land-locked, and a good and safe entry through the bar.

Between these harbours on the one side, and the Bahamas on the other, the Spanish ships must come home with all the treasures of Mexico; and a squadron here in time of war, can hardly miss intercepting them, and at the same time have safe harbours under their lee, and a healthy climate; have all Georgia, Carolina, and North-America, a plentiful country, to supply them with fresh provisions; so that they would be under none of those inconveniences from want and sickness, which those squadrons suffered who lay at Porto Bello.

The tides upon this coast flow generally seven foot: the soundings are sand, or ooze, and some oyster banks, but no rocks: the coast appears low from the sea, and covered with woods.

Cape Fear is a point which runs with dreadful shoals far into the sea from the mouth of Clarendon river, in North Carolina. Sulivan's Island, and the Coffin-land, are the marks of the entry into Charles-Town harbour: Hilton-head upon Trenches Island, shews the entry into Port-Royal; and the point of Tybee Island, marks the entry of the Savannah river. Upon that point the trustees for Georgia have erected a noble final or lighthouse, 90 foot high, and 25 foot wide; it is an octagon, and upon the top there is a flagstaff 30 foot high.

The province of Georgia is watered by three great rivers, which rise in the mountains, viz. the Alatamaha, the Ogechee, and the Savannah, the last of which is navigable six hundred miles for canoes, and three hundred miles for boats. The British dominions are divided from the Spanish Florida by a noble river called St. John's. These rivers fall into the Atlantick ocean; but there are besides them, the Flint, the Catooche, and even the Missisippi river, which pass through part of Carolina, or Georgia, and fall into the gulph of Apellachee or Mexico.

All Carolina is divided into three parts: North Carolina, which is divided from South Carolina by Clarendon river, and of late by a line marked out by order of the council; South Carolina; which on the south is divided from Georgia by the river Savannah. Carolina is divided into several counties; but in Georgia there is but one yet erected, viz. the county of Savannah: it is bounded on the one side by the river Savannah, on the other by the sea, on the third by the river Ogechee, on the fourth by the river Ebenezer, and a line drawn from the Ebenezer to the Ogechee. In this country are the rivers of Vernon, Little Ogechee, and of Westbrook. There is the town of Savannah, where there is a seat of judicature, consisting of three bailiffs and a recorder. It is situated upon the banks of the river of the same name. It consists of about two hundred houses, and lies upon a plain of about a mile wide, the bank steep to the river, forty five foot perpendicularly high: the streets are laid out regular. There are near Savannah, in the same country, the villages of Hampstead, Highgate, Skydoway, and Thunderbolt; the latter of which is a translation of a name: their fables say, that a thunderbolt fell, and a spring thereupon arose in that place, which still smells of the thunder. This spring is impregnated with a mixture of sulphur and steel, and from this smell probably the story arose. In the same county is Joseph's Town, and the town of Ebenezer, both upon the river Savannah, and the villages of Abercorn and Westbrook. There are saw-mills erecting on the river Ebenezer, and the fort Argyle lies upon the pass of this county over the Ogechee. In the southern divisions of the province lies the town of Frederica, with its district, where there is a court with three bailiffs and a recorder. It lies on one of the branches of the Alatamaha. There is also the town of Darien, upon the same river, and several forts, upon the proper passes, some of four bastions, some are only redoubts; besides which there are villages in different parts of Georgia. At Savannah there is a publick store-house built of large square timbers; there is also a handsome court-house, guard-house, and work-house: their church is not yet begun, but materials are collecting, and it is designed to be a handsome edifice. The private houses are generally sawed timber, framed and covered with shingles; many of them are painted, and most have chimneys of brick. At Frederica, some of the houses are built of brick; the rest of the province is mostly wood. They are not got into luxury yet in their furniture, hewing only what is plain and needful; the winters being mild, there are yet but few houses with glass-windows.

The Indians are a manly well-shaped race; the men tall, the women little: they, as the antient Greeks did, anoint with oil, and expose themselves to the sun, which occasions their skins to be brown of colour. The men paint themselves of various colours, red, blue, yellow and black: the men wear generally a girdle, with a piece of cloth drawn through their legs, and turned over the girdle both before and behind, so as to hide their nakedness. The women wear a kind of petticoat to their knees. Both men and women in the winter wear mantles, something less than two yards square, which they wrap round their bodies, as the Romans did their toga, generally keeping their arms bare: they are sometimes of woollen, bought of the English; sometimes of furs, which they dress themselves. They wear a kind of pumps, which they call morgisons, made of deer skins, which they dress for that purpose. They are a generous good-natured people, very humane to strangers; patient of want and pain; slow to anger, and not easily provoked; but when they are thoroughly incensed, they are implacable; very quick of apprehension, and gay of temper. Their publick conferences shew them to be men of genius, and they have a natural eloquence, they never having had the use of letters. They love eating, and the English have taught many of them to drink strong liquors, which, when they do, they are miserable sights. They have no manufactures but what each family makes for its own use; they seem to despise working for hire, and spend their time chiefly in hunting and war; but plant corn enough for the support of their families, and of the strangers that come to visit them. Their food, instead of bread, is flour of Indian corn boiled, and seasoned like hasty-pudding; and this is called homminy. They also boil venison and make broth: they also roast or rather broil their meat. The flesh they feed on is buffaloe, deer, wild-turkeys, and other game; so that hunting is necessary, to provide flesh, and planting for corn. The land belongs to the women, and the corn that grows upon it; but meat must be got by the men, because it is they only that hunt. This makes marriage necessary, that the women may furnish corn, and the men meat. They have also fruit-trees in their gardens, viz. peaches, nectarines and locusts, melons and water-melons; potatoes, pumpkins, and onions, &c. in plenty, and many wild kinds of fruits; as parsimonies, grapes, chinquepins, and hickary-nuts, of which they make oil. The bees make their combs in the hollow trees, and the Indians find plenty of honey there, which they use instead of sugar. They make what answers salt of wood-ashes, and long-pepper which grows in their gardens; and bay-leaves supply their want of spice. Their exercises are a kind of ball-playing, hunting, and running; and they are very fond of dancing: their musick is a kind of a drum, as also hollow cocoa-nut shells. They have a square in the middle of their towns, in which the warriors sit, converse, and smoke together; but in rainy weather they meet in the King's house.

They are very healthy people, and have hardly any diseases, except those occasioned by the drinking of rum, and the small pox: those who do not drink rum are exceeding long-lived. Old Brim, Emperor of the Creeks, who died but a few years ago, lived to one hundred and thirty years; and he was neither blind nor bed-rid, till some months before his death. They have sometimes pleurisies and fevers, but no chronical distempers. They know of several herbs that have great virtues in physick, particularly for the cure of venomous bites and wounds.

The native animals are, first the urus or zorax, described by Caesar, which the English very ignorantly and improperly call the buffaloe. They have deer of several kinds, and plenty of roe-bucks and rabbits. There are bears and wolves, which are very small and timerous; and a brown wild-cat, without spots, which they very improperly call a tyger; otters, beavers, foxes, and a species of badgers, which they call racoons. There is great abundance of wild fowls, viz. the wild turkey, the partridge, doves of various kinds; wild geese, wild ducks, teal, cranes, herons of many kinds, not known in Europe: there are great variety of eagles and hawks, and great numbers of small birds, particularly the rice bird, which is very like the ortelan. There are also some rattle snakes, but not near so frequent as is generally reported. There are several species of snakes, some of which are not venomous. There are crocodiles, porpoises, sturgeon, mullets, catfish, bass, drum, devil-fish, and many species of fresh water fish, that we have not in Europe; oysters upon the sea islands in great abundance. But what is most troublesome here, is flies and gnats, which are very troublesome near the rivers; but as the country is cleared, they disperse and go away. Besides the animals that are natives, there are all the same animals as in Europe, cows, sheep, hogs, &c.

The vegetables are innumerable; for all that grow in Europe grow there; and many that cannot stand in our winters thrive there.

# Francis Moore

## From *A Voyage to Georgia*

Mr. Oglethorpe spoke to the people to prevent their being terrified with false reports. There seemed to be little need of it, for they were all zealous to settle a town of their own, and trusting entirely to him, were not at all apprehensive of any danger, but were fearful of staying and losing their time at Savannah.

After three hours stay, he set out for Savannah and took me along with him. About midnight we arrived there, but being then high-water, and the German ministers who were to go with him to Ebenezer, not caring to go by night, he could not go forward as he intended, some of the boatmen being ill, and the freshes strong. He lay that night at a house which he hires at Savannah; it is the same as the common freeholders' houses are, a frame of sawed timber twenty-four by sixteen foot, floored with rough deals, the sides with feather-edged boards unplaned, and the roof shingled.

On the 9th, I heard that the Saltzburghers at Ebenezer were very discontended; that they demanded to leave their old town, and to settle upon the lands which the Indians had reserved for their own use; and this was the occasion of Mr. Oglethorpe's going up in such haste at a time when he could be ill spared from the ships. He set out this morning tide, with several gentlemen, and the Saltzburghers' ministers, and went by water to Sir Francis Bathurst's, where part of Captain Mackay's troops of horsemen, lately come out of the Indian country, lay; there he took horse for Ebenezer.

When he was gone, I took a view of the town of Savannah. It is about a mile and a quarter in circumference; it stands upon the flat of a hill, the bank of the river (which they in barbarous English call a bluff) is steep and about forty-five foot perpendicular, so that all heavy goods are brought up by a crane, an inconvenience designed to be remedied by a bridged wharf, and an easy ascent, which in laying out the town, care was taken to allow room for, there being a very wide strand between the first row of houses and the river. From this strand there is a very pleasant prospect; you see the river wash the foot of the hill, which is a hard, clear, sandy beach, a mile in length; the water is fresh, and the river one thousand foot wide. Eastward you see the river increased by the northern branch, which runs round Hutchinson's island, and the Carolina shore beyond it, and the woody islands at the sea, which close the prospect at ten or twelve miles distance. Over against it is Hutchinson's island, great part of which is open ground, where they mow hay for the Trust's horses and cattle. The rest is woods in which there are many bay trees eighty foot high. Westward you see the river winding between the woods, with little islands in it for many miles, and Toma Chi Chi's Indian town standing upon the southern banks, between three and four miles distance.

The town of Savannah is built of wood; all the houses of the first forty freeholders are of the same size with that Mr. Oglethorpe lives in, but there are great numbers built since, I believe one hundred or one hundred and fifty, many of these are much larger; some of two or three stories high, the boards plained and painted. The houses stand on large lots, sixty foot in front by ninety foot in depth; each lot has a fore and back street to it; the lots are fenced in with split pales; some few people have palisades of turned wood before their doors, but the generality have been wise enough not to throw away their money, which in this country laid out in husbandry is capable of great improvements, though there are several people of good substance in the town, who came at their own expense, and also several of those who came over on the Charity, are in a very thriving way; but this is observed that the most substantial people are the most frugal, and make the least show, and live at the lease expense. There are some also who have made but little or bad use of the benefits they

received, idling away their times, whilst they had their provisions from
the public store, or else working for hire, earning from two shillings,
the price of a laborer, to four or five shillings, the price of a carpenter, per diem, and spending that money in rum and good living, thereby
neglecting to improve their lands, so that when their time of receiving
their provisions from the public ceased, they were in no forwardness to
maintain themselves out of their own lands. As they chose to be hirelings
when they might have improved for themselves, the consequence of that
folly forces them now to work for the daily bread. These are generally
discontented with the country; and if they have run themselves in debt,
their creditors will not let them go away till they have paid. Considering
the number of people, there are but very few of these. The industrious
ones have throve beyond expectation; most of them that have been there
three years, and many others have houses in the town, which those that
let, have for the worst ten pounds per annum, and the best for thirty
pounds.

Those who have cleared their five acre lots, have made very great profit
out of them by greens, roots, and corn. Several have improved the cattle
they had at first, and have now five or six tame cows; others who, to
save the trouble of feeding them, let them go into the woods, can rarely
find them, and when they are brought up, one of them will not give
half the quantity of milk, which another cow fed near home will give.
Their houses are built at a pretty large distance from one another, for
fear of fire; the streets are very wide, and there are great squares left at
proper distances, for markets and other conveniences. Near the river side
there is a guard house inclosed with palisades a foot thick where there are
nineteen or twenty cannons mounted, and a continual guard kept by the
freeholders. This town is governed by three bailiffs, and has a recorder,
register, and a town-court, which is holden every six weeks, where all
matters civil and criminal are decided by grand and petty juries, as in
England; but there are no lawyers allowed to plead for hire, nor no attor-
neys to take money, but (as in old times in England) every man pleads
his own cause. In case it should be an orphan, or one that cannot speak
for themselves, there are persons of the best substance in the town, appointed by the Trustees to take care of the orphans, and to defend the

helpless, and that without fee or reward, it being a service that each that is capable must perform in his turn. They have some laws and customs peculiar to Georgia; one is, that all brandies and distilled liquors are prohibited under severe penalties; another is, that no slavery is allowed, nor negroes; a third that all persons who go among the Indians must give security for their good behavior; because the Indians, if any injury is done to them, and they cannot kill the man who does it, expect satisfaction from the government, which if not procured, they break out into war, by killing the first white man they conveniently can. No victualler or ale-house keeper can give any credit, so consequently cannot recover any debt. The freeholds are all entailed, which has been very fortunate for the place. If people could have sold, the greatest part, before they knew the value of their lots, would have parted with them for a trifling condition, and there were not wanting rich men who employed agents to monopolize the whole town; and if they had got numbers of lots into their own hands, the other freeholders would have had no benefit by letting their houses, and hardly of trade, since the rich, by means of a large capital, would underlet and undersell, and the town must have been almost without inhabitants, as Port Royal in Carolina, is by the best lots being got into a few hands.

The mentioning the laws and customs leads me to take notice that Georgia is founded upon maxims different from those on which other colonies have been begun. The intention of that colony was an asylum to receive the distressed. This was the charitable design, and the governmental view besides that, was with numbers of free white people, well settled to strengthen the southern part of the English settlements on the continent of America of which this is the frontier. It is necessary, therefore, not to permit slaves in such a country, for slaves starve the poor laborer. For if the gentleman can have this work done by a slave who is a carpenter or a brick-layer, the carpenter or brick-layers of that country must starve for want of employment, and so of other trades.

In order to maintain many people, it was proper that the land should be divided into small portions, and to prevent the uniting them by marriage or purchase. For everytime that two lots are united, the town loses a family, and the inconveniency of this shows itself at Savannah, notwithstanding the care of the Trustees to prevent it. They suffered the moiety of the lots to descend to the widows during their lives: those who re-married to men who had lots of their own, by uniting two lots made one be neglected; for the strength of hands who could take care of one, was not sufficient to look to and improve two. These uncleared lots are a nui-sance to their neighbors. The trees which grow upon them shade the lots, the beasts take shelter in them, and for want of clearing the brooks which pass through them, the lands above are often prejudiced by floods. To prevent all these inconveniences, the first regulation of the Trustees was a strict Agrarian law, by which all the lands near towns should be divided, fifty acres to each freeholder. The quantity of land by experience seems rather too much, since it is impossible that one poor family can tend so much land. If this allotment is too much, how much more inconvenient would the uniting of two be? To prevent it, the Trustees grant the lands in tail male, that on the expiring of a male line they may regrant it to such man, having no other lot, as shall be married to the next female heir of the deceased, as is of good character. This manner of dividing prevents also the sale of lands, and the rich thereby monopolizing the country.

Each freeholder has a lot in town sixty foot by ninety foot, besides which he has a lot beyond the common, of five acres for a garden. Every ten houses make a tithing, and to every tithing there is a mile square, which is divided into twelve lots, besides roads: each freeholder of the tithing has a lot or farm of forty-five acres there, and two lots are reserved by the Trustees in order to defray the charge of the public. The town is laid out for two hundred and forty freeholds; the quantity of lands nec-essary for that number is twenty-four square miles; every forty houses in town make a ward, to which four square miles in the country belong; each ward has a constable, and under him four tithing men. Where the town lands end, the villages begin; four villages make a ward without, which depends upon one of the wards within the town. The use of this is, in case a war should happen, the villages without may have places in the town, to bring their cattle and families into for refuge, and to that pur-pose there is a square left in every ward, big enough for the outwards to encamp in. There is ground also kept round about the town ungranted, in order for the fortifications whenever occasion shall require. Beyond the villages, commence lots of five hundred acres: these are granted upon terms of keeping ten servants, &c. Several gentlemen who have settled on such grants have succeeded very well, and have been of great service to the colony. Above the town is a parcel of land called Indian lands; these are those reserved by king Toma Chi Chi for his people. There is near the town, to the east, a garden belonging to the Trustees, consisting of ten acres; the situation is delightful, one half of it is upon the top of the hill, the foot of which the river Savannah washes, and from it you see the woody islands in the sea. The remainder of the garden is the side and some plain low ground at the foot of the hill, where several fine springs break out. In the garden is variety of soils; the top is sandy and dry, the sides of the hill are clay, and the bottom is a black, rich garden mould well watered. On the north part of the garden is left standing a grove of part of the old wood, as it was before the arrival of the colony there. The trees in the grove are mostly bay, sassafras, evergreen oak, pellitory, hickory, American ash, and the laurel tulip. This last is looked upon as one of the most beautiful trees in the world; it grows straight-bodied to forty or fifty foot high; the bark smooth and whitish, the top spreads regular like an orange tree in English gardens, only larger; the leaf is like that of a common laurel, but bigger, and the under side of a greenish brown; it blooms about the month of June; the flowers are white, fragrant like the orange, and perfume all the air around it; the flower is round, eight or ten inches diameter, thick like the orange flower, and a little yellow near the heart. As the flowers drop, the fruit which is a cone with red berries succeeds them. There are also some bay trees that have flowers like the laurel, only less.

The garden is laid out with cross-walks planted with orange trees, but the last winter, a good deal of snow having fallen, had killed those upon the top of the hill down to their roots, but they being cut down sprouted again, as I saw when I returned to Savannah. In the squares between the walks, were vast quantities of mulberry trees, this being a nursery for all the province, and every planter that desires it has young trees given him gratis from this nursery. These white mulberry trees were planted in order to raise silk, for which purpose several Italians were brought at the Trustees' expense, from Piedmont by Mr. Amatis; they have fed

worms, and wound silk to as great perfection as any that ever came out of
Italy; but the Italians falling out, one of them stole away the machines for
winding, broke the coppers and spoiled all the eggs which he could not
steal, and fled to South Carolina. The others who continued faithful, had
saved but a few eggs when Mr. Oglethorpe arrived; therefore he forbade
any silk should be wound, but that all the worms should be suffered to
eat through their balls, in order to have more eggs against next year. The
Italian women are obliged to take English girls apprentices, whom they
teach to wind and feed; and the men have taught our English gardeners
to tend the mulberry trees, and our joiners have learned how to make
the machines for winding. As the mulberry trees increase, there will be
a great quantity of silk made here.

Besides the mulberry trees, there are in some of the quarters in the
coldest part of the garden all kinds of fruit trees usual in England, such
as apples, pears, &c. In another quarter are olives, figs, vines, pomegranates and such fruits as are natural to the warmest parts of Europe. At the
bottom of the hill, well sheltered from the north wind and in the warmest part of the garden, there was a collection of West India plants and
trees, some coffee, some cocoa-nuts, cotton, Palma-christi, and several
West Indian physical plants, some sent up by Mr. Eveleigh, a public-
spirited merchant at Charlestown, and some by Dr. Houston, from the
Spanish West Indies, where he was sent at the expense of a collection
raised by that curious physician, Sir Hans Sloan, for to collect and send
them to Georgia, where the climate was capable of making a garden
which might contain all kinds of plants to which design, his Grace, the
Duke of Richmond, the Earl of Derby, the Lord Peters, and the Apothe-
cary's Company contributed very generously; as did Sir Hans himself.
The quarrels among the Italians proved fatal to most of these plants, and
they were laboring to repair that loss when I was there, Mr. Miller being
employed in the room of Dr. Houston, who died in Jamaica. We heard
he had wrote an account of his having obtained the plant from whence
the true Balsamum Capivi is drawn; and that he was in hopes of getting
that from whence the Jesuits' Bark is taken, he designing for that purpose
to send to the Spanish West Indies.

There is a plant of Bamboo cane brought from the East Indies, and sent over by Mr. Towers which thrives well. There was also some tea seeds, which came from the same place; but the latter, though great care was taken, did not grow.

Three miles from Savannah, within land, that is to say to the south, are two pretty villages, Hampstead and Highgate, where the planters are very forward, having built neat huts, and cleared and planted a great deal of land. Up the river also there are several other villages and two towns, not much better than villages, on the Georgia side, the one called Joseph's town, which some Scotch gentlemen are building at their own expense, and where they have already cleared a great deal of ground. Above that is Ebenezer, a town of the Saltzburghers. On the Carolina side is Purysburgh, chiefly inhabited by Swiss. There are also a party of rangers under the command of Capt. McPherson, and another under the command of Capt. Æneas M'Intosh; the one lying upon the Savannah river, the other upon the Ogeechee. These are horsemen and patrol the woods to see that no enemy Indians, nor other lawless persons, shelter themselves there.

There were no public buildings in the town, besides a storehouse; for the courts were held in a hut thirty foot long, and twelve foot wide, made of split boards, and erected on Mr. Oglethorpe's first arrival in the colony. In this hut also divine service was performed; but upon his arrival this time Mr. Oglethorpe ordered a house to be erected in the upper square, which might serve for a court house, and for divine service till a church could be built, and a work house over against it; for as yet there was no prison here.

Two ships lay close to the town, the James, Capt. Yokely, in the Trustees' service, waiting for our arrival (with provisions) and another ship from Bristol, Capt. Dickens, commander, loaded with passengers. The water is not only deep, but thoroughly sheltered from hurricanes, and, being fresh, there are no worms, an advantage few ports have in America.

\* \* \*

On the 17th we set sail with the morning tide, in company with the Symond and London Merchant. As soon as we were over the bar we parted, they for Charlestown, and we for Frederica. In the evening the wind shifted, and we came to an anchor, the sea being very smooth, and but little wind.

On the 18th, the wind came about, and we stood to the southward two days; at which time we stood in for the land, and made a woody island. The land seemed high about the middle. We stood in within two miles: it looked pleasant, the beach being white sand, the woods lofty, and the land hilly. We daily saw several smokes and fires all along the shore, which were made by the friendly Indians, by Mr. Oglethorpe's order. At noon we had an observation, and found we were in 31 deg. 20 min., being twenty miles to the southward of Frederica, for the entrance of Jekyl sound, is in 31 deg. 0 min. We turned to the northward, and on the 22d in the evening, we made the opening between Jekyl island and St. Simons. We came to an anchor that evening, and the next morning, being the 23d, we stood into the opening, and found a good channel between the breakers all the way to Jekyl sound, at the entrance of which, Captain Yokely's boat came off to us. We ran directly up to Frederica, and anchored close to the shore in three fathom water, where lay the James, Captain Yokely.

I went on shore, where I found Mr. Oglethorpe was gone to the Spanish frontiers, and I was surprised to find that there was a battery of cannon mounted, which commanded the river, and the fort almost built, the ditches being dug round, though not to their width, and the rampart raised with green sod. Within the fort a very large and convenient storehouse, sixty foot in front, and to be three stories high, was begun, with a cellar of the same size underneath, and one story already raised above ground. The town was building, the streets were all laid out, the main street that went from the front into the country, was twenty-five yards wide. Each freeholder had sixty foot in front, by ninety foot in depth, upon the high street, for their house and garden; but those which fronted the river had but thirty foot in front by sixty foot in depth. Each family had a bower of palmetto leaves, finished upon the back street in their own lands; the side towards the front street was set out for their houses. These palmetto bowers were very convenient shelters, being tight in the hardest rains; they were about twenty foot long, and fourteen foot wide, and in regular rows, looked very pretty, the palmetto leaves lying smooth and handsome, and of a good color. The whole appeared something like a camp; for the bowers looked like tents, only being larger, and covered with palmetto leaves instead of canvass. There were three large tents, two belonging to Mr. Oglethorpe, and one to Mr. Horton, pitched upon the parade near the river.

Mr. Oglethorpe had divided the colony into parties, one cut forks, poles, and laths for building the bowers, another set them up, a third fetched palmetto leaves, a fourth thatched, and a Jew workman, bred in the Brazil, and had come from Savannah, taught them to do this nimbly, and in a neat manner. Mr. Oglethorpe had appointed some men who knew the country to instruct the colony in hoeing and planting; and as soon as the bowers were finished, a party was set to that work, and the rest were hired by him to work at the fort, by reason that a great part of the workmen were not yet come up. It was so late in the year, he hoped little from any planting, therefore what he ordered to be done, was rather to teach the colony against another season, than from any advantage likely to arise from it, and he employed the men of the colony to work at the fort that they might get something to help to subsist themselves the next year. There was potatoes and Indian corn in the ground, and they were planting more; there was some flax and hempseed, which came to little, being too late set. And it is an observation that all Europe grains should be sowed rather before winter, that they may shoot and cover the ground, for if they are sowed in spring, the weather coming hot upon them, the blades shoot at once into height, and not shading the roots the heat of the sun dries them up. But when the winter has checked the growth of the blade, the plant spreads, and covering the ground thick, shades it from the parching sun, and thereby keeps a moisture underneath, which prevents the roots from being dried up. There was barley, turnips, lucerne grass, pumpkins, water-melons and several other seeds sown or sowing daily; all was for the whole colony, the labor was in common, though they were assisted by several workmen hired from Savannah. I was the more surprised to see a team and six horses ploughing, not having heard any thing of it before; but it was thus: Messieurs Walter Augustine and Tolme, escorted by Mr. Hugh Mackay, had, pursuant to their orders, surveyed from Savannah to Darien, and had made a plan of it, and Mr. Hugh Mackay had brought these horses then with him, which were embarked in periaguas from Darien to Frederica. They reported that the Indians had accompanied, assisted, and hunted for them in their survey; and that they had met some camps of friendly Indians, besides those which Toma Chi Chi Mico sent with them; that they had found the country passable for horses, but to keep the horse road they were obliged to go round about, and head several valleys which were too rich and wet to be passable, therefore that road was ninety miles round; but that the road might be carried so as to make it but seventy; that there were two rivers to be swam over; and some boggy places. The news they brought had been no small joy to the people of Frederica, since they had a communication from the Darien by land, open to Savannah, and consequently to all the English colonies of North America.

Frederica is situated in the island of St. Simons, in the middle of an Indian field, where our people found thirty or forty acres of land cleared by them. The ground is about nine or ten foot above high water mark, and level for about a mile into the island; the bank is steep to the river, which is here narrow but deep and makes an elbow, so that the fort commands two reaches. The woods on the other side this branch of the Alatamaha are about three miles distance. All that three miles is a plain marsh, which by small banks might easily be made meadow: when I was upon it, it was so hard that a horse might gallop, but most part of it is flooded at very high tides. The open ground on which the town stands, is bounded by a little wood to the east, on the other side of which is a large Savannah of above two hundred acres, where there is fine food for cattle. To the South, is a little wood of red bay trees, live oaks, and other useful timber, which is reserved for the public service. In the fort also are some fine large oaks preserved for shade. To the north are woods, where the people have leave to cut for fire and building, for all that side is intended to be cleared. To the west is the river, and the marshes beyond it as I said before. The soil is a rich sand mixed with garden mould, the marshes are clay. In all places where they have tried, they find fresh water within nine foot of the surface. The grass in the Indian old field was good to cut into turf which was useful in sodding the fort.

The woods on the island are chiefly live-oak, water-oak, laurel, bay, cedar, gum and sassafras, and some pines. There are also abundance of vines growing wild in the woods; one called the fox grape, from a kind of muscadine taste, is as large and round as the duke cherry, and fleshy like it, but the stones are like the grape. This kind of grape does rarely grow in clusters, but singly like cherries. The other grape is black in clusters, small, thick skinned, big stoned, but pleasant enough; it seems to be the Bourdeaux grape, wild and unimproved; they are ripe about September, but a quantity sufficient to make a true experiment of wine (which can hardly be done under sixty gallons) is hard to be got, because the bears, raccoons and squirrels eat them before they are ripe, and as they run up very high trees, it is difficult, or almost impossible to get to the tops of them where the best grow. These grapes are common to the woods in most parts of America. But there is on St. Simons, a wild grape much nearer the Europe vine, the fruit being exactly the same as the common white grape, though the leaf is something different. The birds and wild animals like it so well that they suffer it seldom to ripen. All the vine kinds seem natural to the country. The China root produces a kind of bind or briar; and the melon, the water-melon, cucumber, kidney bean, pumpkin and gourd, all thrive wonderfully.

The island abounds with deer and rabbits; there are no buffaloes in it, though there are large herds upon the main. There are also a good many raccoons, a creature something like a badger, but somewhat less, with a bushy tail like a squirrel, tabbied with rings of brown and black. They are very destructive to the poultry.

# Hugh McCall

## From *The History of Georgia: Containing Brief Sketches of the Most Remarkable Events up to the Present Day*

In April, 1760, colonel Montgomery landed in Carolina: great was the joy in the province of Georgia upon the arrival of this gallant officer; but as the conquest of Canada was the grand object of this year's campaign in America, he had orders to strike a sudden blow for the relief of the southern provinces, and return to head quarters at Albany without loss of time; nothing was therefore omitted that was judged necessary to forward the expedition. Soon after his arrival he marched to the Congarees in South Carolina, where he was joined by the military strength of that province, and immediately put his little army in motion for the Cherokee country. Having but little time allowed him, his march was uncommonly spirited and expeditious: after reaching Twelve Mile river, he encamped on an advantageous ground, and marched with a party of his men in the night, to surprise Estatoe, an Indian town about twenty miles from his camp: the first noise he heard by the way, was the barking of a dog before his men, where he was informed there was an Indian town called little Keowee, which he ordered his light infantry to surround, and, except women and children, to put every Indian in it to the sword. Having done this piece of service, he proceeded to Estatoe, which he found abandoned by all the savages, excepting a few who had not time to make their escape. The town which consisted of two hundred houses, and was well provided with corn, hogs and poultry, was reduced to ashes. Sugar-town, and every other settlement eastward of the Blue Ridge, afterwards shared the same fate. In these lower towns about sixty Indians were killed, forty made prisoners, and the rest driven to seek for shelter among the mountains. Having finished this business with the loss of only three or four men, he marched to the relief of fort Prince-George, which had been for some time infested by savages, insomuch that no soldier durst venture beyond the bounds of the fort, and where the garrison was in distress, not so much for the want of provisions, as fuel to prepare them.

While the army rested at fort Prince-George, Edmund Atkins, agent of Indian affairs, despatched two Indian chiefs to the middle settlements, to inform the Cherokees, that by suing for peace they might obtain it, as the former friends and allies of Britain: at the same time they sent a message to fort Loudon, requesting captains Demere and Steuart, the commanding officers at that place, to use their best endeavors for obtaining peace with the Cherokees in the upper towns. Colonel Montgomery finding that the savages were not yet disposed to listen to terms of accommodation, determined to carry the chastisement a little farther. Dismal was the wilderness into which he entered, and many were the hardships and dangers he had to encounter, from dark thickets, rugged paths and narrow passes; in which a small body of men, properly posted, might harass and tire out the bravest army that ever took the field. Having on every side suspicious grounds, he found occasion for the exercise of constant vigilance and circumspection. On the 27th of June, when he had advanced within five miles of Etchoe, the nearest town in the middle settlements, he found there a low valley, covered so thick with brush, that a soldier could scarcely see the length of his body, and in the middle of which, there was a muddy river, with steep clay banks; through this dark place, where it was impossible for any number of men to act together, the army must necessarily march; and therefore captain Morison, who commanded a company of rangers, had orders to advance and scour the thicket: they had scarcely entered it, when a number of savages sprang from their ambuscade, fired on them, killed the captain and wounded several of his party: upon which the light infantry and grenadiers were ordered to advance and charge the enemy, which they did with great courage and alacrity. A heavy fire then began on both sides, and during some time the soldiers could only discover the places where the savages were hid by the report of their guns. Colonel Montgomery finding that the number of Indians that guarded this place was considerable, and that they were determined obstinately to dispute it, ordered the royal Scots, who were in the rear, to advance between the savages and a rising ground on the right, while the Highlanders marched towards the left to support the light infantry and grenadiers: the woods resounded with the war-whoop and horrible yells of the savages; but these, instead of intimidating the troops, seemed rather to inspire them with more firmness and resolution. At length the Indians gave way, and in their retreat falling in with the royal Scots, suffered considerably before they got out of their reach. By this time, the royals being in the front, and the Highlanders in the rear, the enemy keeping up a retreating fire took possession of a hill, apparently disposed to remain at a distance, but continued to retreat as the army advanced: colonel Montgomery perceiving that they kept aloof, gave orders to the line to face about, and march directly for the town of Etchoe. The enemy no sooner observed this movement, than they got behind the hill, and ran to alarm their wives and children. In this action, which lasted about an hour, colonel Montgomery who made several narrow escapes, had twenty men killed and seventy-six wounded: what number the enemy lost was not ascertained. Upon viewing the ground, all were astonished to see with what judgment and skill it was chosen; the most experienced officer could not have fixed upon a spot more advantageous for way-laying and attacking an enemy, according to the method of fighting practised among the Indians. This action, though it terminated in favor of the British army, had reduced it to such a situation as made it very imprudent, if not impracticable, to penetrate farther into those woods; as the repulse of the enemy was far from being decisive, for they had only retired from one advantageous situation to another, in order to renew the attack when the army should again advance. The humanity of the commander would not suffer him to leave so many wounded men exposed to the vengeance of savages, without a strong-hold in which he might lodge them, or some detachment to protect them, and which he now could not spare; should he proceed further, he saw plainly that he must expect frequent skirmishes, which would increase the number; and the burning of so many Indian towns would be a poor compensation for the great risk, and perhaps sacrifice of so many valuable troops. To furnish horses for the men already wounded, he was obliged to throw away many bags of flour into the river, and what remained was no more than sufficient for his army on their return to fort Prince-George. Under these circumstances therefore, orders were given for a retreat, which was made with great regularity, although the enemy continued hovering around and annoying them to the utmost of their power. A large train of wounded men was brought above sixty miles through a hazardous country in safety, for which no small share of honor and credit was due to the officer who conducted the retreat.

The dangers which threatened the frontiers, induced colonel Montgomery to leave four companies of the royal regiment under the command of major Frederick Hamilton for their protection, while he embarked with the battalion of Highlanders, and sailed for New York. In the mean time, the distant garrison of fort Loudon, consisting of two hundred men, was reduced to the dreadful alternative of perishing by hunger, or submitting to the mercy of the enraged Cherokees. Having received information that the Virginians had undertaken to relieve them, for a while they seemed satisfied, anxiously waiting for the realization of their hopes. The Virginians however, were equally disqualified with their neighbors of Carolina, from rendering them any assistance. So remote was the fort from every settlement, and so difficult was it to march an army through a barren wilderness, where the passes and thickets were ambuscaded by the enemy, and to carry at the same time sufficient supplies, that the Virginians had given over all thoughts of the attempt. The provisions in the mean time being entirely exhausted at the fort, the garrison was reduced to the most deplorable situation: for a whole month they had no other subsistence but the flesh of lean horses and dogs, and a small supply of Indian beans. Long had the officers animated and encouraged the men with the hopes of relief; but now being blockaded night and day by the enemy, and having no resource left, they threatened to leave the fort, and die at once by the hands of the savages, rather than perish slowly by famine. In this extremity, the commander was obliged to call a council of war, to consider what was proper to be done; the officers were all of opinion that it was impossible to hold out any longer, and therefore agreed to surrender the fort to the Cherokees on the best terms that could be obtained from them. For this purpose captain Steuart, an officer of great sagacity and address, and much beloved by all the Indians who remained in the British interest, procured leave to go to Chote, one of the principal towns in that neighborhood, where he obtained the following terms of capitulation, which were signed by the commanding officer and two chiefs: "That the garrison of fort Loudon march out with their arms and drums, each soldier having as much powder and ball as their officer shall think necessary for their march, and all the baggage they may choose to carry: that the garrison be permitted to march to Virginia, or fort Prince-George, as the commanding officer shall think proper, unmolested; and that a number of Indians be appointed to escort them, and hunt for provisions during the march: that such soldiers as are lame, or by sickness disabled from marching, be received into the Indian towns, and kindly used until they recover, and then be allowed to proceed to fort Prince-George: that the Indians do provide for the garrison as many horses as they conveniently can for their march, agreeing with the officers and soldiers for the payment: that the fort's great guns, powder, ball, and spare arms, be delivered to the Indians without fraud or further delay, on the day appointed for the march of the troops."

Agreeably to the terms stipulated, the garrison delivered up the fort, on the 7th of August, and marched out with their arms, accompanied by Occonostota the prince of Chote, and several other Indians, and that day marched fifteen miles on their way to fort Prince-George. At night they encamped on a plain about two miles from Taliquo an Indian town, when all their Indian attendants, upon some pretence or other, left them; which the officers considered as an unfavorable omen, and thereforce placed a strict guard round their camp. During the night they remained unmolested, but next morning at the dawn of day, a soldier from an outpost came running in, and informed them, that he saw a vast number of Indians, armed and painted in a warlike manner, creeping among the bushes, and advancing in order to surround the camp: scarcely had the commanding officer time to order his men under arms, when the savages poured in upon them a heavy fire from different directions, accompanied by the most hideous yells, which struck a panic into the soldiers, who were so much enfeebled and dispirited that they were incapable of making any effectual resistance. Captain Paul Demere the commander, and three other officers, with twenty-six men, fell at the first onset; some fled into the woods and were afterwards taken prisoners; captain Steuart, and those who remained, were seized, pinioned, and carried back to fort Loudon. No sooner had Attakullakulla heard that his friend captain Steuart, had escaped death, than he hastened to the fort and purchased him from the Indian who took him, giving him his rifle, clothes, and all that he could command, by way of ransom: he then took possession of captain Demere's house, where he kept his prisoner as one of his family, and humanely shared with him the little provisions his table afforded, until an opportunity should offer of rescuing him from their hands; but the poor soldiers were kept in a miserable state of captivity for some time, and then ransomed at considerable expense.

During the time these prisoners were confined at fort Loudon, Occonostota formed a design of attacking fort Prince-George, and for this purpose despatched a messenger to the Indian settlements in the valley, requesting all the warriors to join him at Stickoe-old-town. By accident a discovery was made of ten kegs of powder, and ball in proportion, which the officers had secretly buried in the fort, to prevent it from falling into the hands of the enemy: this discovery had nearly proved fatal to captain Steuart, and would certainly have cost him his life, had not the interpreter had so much presence of mind, as to assure the enemy that this ammunition had been concealed without his knowledge or consent. The Indians having now abundance of ammunition for the siege, a council was called at Chote, to which captain Steuart was brought, and put in mind of the obligations he lay under to them for sparing his life; and as they had resolved to carry six cannon and two cohorns with them against fort Prince-George, to be managed by men under his command, they told him he must go and write such letters to the commandant as they should dictate: they informed him at the same time, that if that officer should refuse to surrender, they were determined to burn the prisoners, one after another before his face, and try if he could be so obstinate as to hold out while he saw his friends expiring in the flames: captain Steuart was much alarmed at his situation, and from that moment resolved to make his escape or perish in the attempt: his design he privately communicated to his faithful friend Attakullakulla, and told him how uneasy he was at the thoughts of being compelled to bear arms against his countrymen: he acknowledged that he had always been a brother to him, and hoped he would now assist him in projecting the means of escape from this perilous situation. The old man took him by the hand, told him he might rely upon his friendship, that he had given him one proof of his esteem, and intended to give him another, so soon as his brother should return and help him to concert the measure: he said he was fully apprized of the evil designs of his countrymen, and the fatal consequences which would be the result; and should he go and persuade the garrison of fort Prince-George to surrender by capitulation, as fort Loudon had done, what could be expected but that they would share the same treacherous dismal fate.

Strong and uncultivated minds carry friendship, as well as enmity, to an astonishing length. Among the savages, family friendship is a national virtue, and civilized nations may blush, when they consider how far barbarians have often surpassed them in the practice of it. The instance I am going to relate, is as singular and memorable as many that have been recorded in the annals of history.

Attakullakulla claimed captain Steuart as his prisoner, and had resolved at every hazard to save his life, and for this purpose there was no time to be lost: accordingly he signified to his countrymen that he intended to go hunting for a few days, and carry his prisoner with him to eat venison: at the same time captain Steuart went among his soldiers, and told them that they could never expect to be ransomed by their government, if they gave the smallest assistance to the Indians against fort Prince-George. Having settled all matters, they set out on their journey accompanied by the old warrior's wife, his brother and two soldiers, who were the only persons of the garrison that knew how to convey great guns through the woods. For provisions they depended upon what they might kill by the way: the distance to the frontier settlements was great, and the utmost expedition necessary, to prevent any surprise from Indians pursuing them. Nine days and nights did they travel through a dreary wilderness, shaping their course by the sun and moon for Virginia, and traversing many hills, vallies and paths, that had never been travelled before but by savages and wild beasts. On the tenth they arrived at Holston's river, where they fortunately fell in with a party of three hundred men, sent out by colonel Bird for the relief of such soldiers as might make their escape that way from fort Loudon. On the fourteenth day the captain reached colonel Bird's camp, on the frontiers of Virginia, where having loaded his faithful friend and his party, with presents and provisions, he sent him back to protect the unhappy prisoners until they should be ransomed, and to exert his influence among the Cherokees for the restoration of peace. Captain Steuart's first reflections, after his escape from the savages, were exercised to concert ways and means for the relief and ransom of his garrison: he despatched expresses to Georgia and Carolina, informing them of the sad disaster that had happened to the garrison of fort Loudon, and of the designs of the Indians against fort Prince-George. In consequence of which, orders were given to Major Thompson, who commanded the militia on the frontiers of Georgia and Carolina, to throw in provisions for ten weeks into that fort, and warn the commanding officer of his danger. The settlers near Augusta, secured their families as well as they could in stockade forts. A messenger was sent to Attakullakulla, desiring him to inform the Cherokees, that fort Prince-George was impregnable, having vast quantities of powder buried under ground every where around it, to blow up all enemies that should attempt to come near it. Presents of considerable value were sent to ransom the prisoners at fort Loudon, a few of whom had by this time made their escape: and afterwards, not only those that were confined in the towns and in the vallies, but also all that had survived the hardships of hunger, disease and captivity, in the upper towns, were released and delivered up to the commanding officer at fort Prince-George.

# Henry Hull

## From *Annals of Athens, Georgia, 1801–1901*

In the times of which I write, the military spirit engendered by the Revolution was kept alive by the recitals of *old soldiers.*

> *"Wherein they spoke of most disastrous chances:*
> *Of moving incidents by flood and field:*
> *Of hair breadth 'scapes; the imminent and deadly breach."*

And the proximity of the two powerful Indian tribes, Creek and Cherokee, kept in check only through fear of the white man's rifle, seemed to render it indispensable to keep the militia so organized as to make it effective when the country should demand its services. In every house there were as many guns as men, and boys old enough to handle them, which were always kept in good order and in frequent if not constant use upon the bears, wolves and deer in which the forest abounded. The militia laws were enforced and a captain of a company was a dignitary of no small consideration, particularly on *muster* day. Well do I remember the respect and admiration, not unmixed with fear, which Captain Warham Easly excited among the boys when he appeared in the showy uniform of the day—cocked hat with waving plumes, tipped with red, red sash and epaulets with Continental dress. I thought him the most magnificent man in the world, and was unutterably shocked to see him after parade return to his store and sell a pound of copperas to a country woman, and that too before he had taken off his uniform!

Every body in the district came to town on muster day, but a company muster was nothing compared to a battalion muster. Six or eight companies formed a battalion, and there were five or six times as many people in town on such occasions.

Major McKigney was not so tall by six inches as Captain Easly, but then he had the advantage of parading on horseback and his horse was always the handsomest in the neighborhood. It was considered a compliment, both to the horse and his owner, for the Major to ask the loan of him for the day, and the owner thought his horse as important a factor as any officer on parade.

But the great muster was the regimental, or general muster as it was called, when all the militia of the county met at Watkinsville, commanded by the Colonel and sometimes the General of the Division, accompanied by the Inspector General, Fouche—pronounced in that day *Fosh*. It was a great advance in civilization when in after years these military parades were discontinued, for their effect on the community was only evil and that continually. On general muster days there was more drunkenness, profanity and fighting than on any other occasion of public assembly, and while the militia laws remained upon the statute book the *disregard* of them was considered their best *observance*. The last commanders of the Athens militia were Doctor William Bacon, Captain, and Doctor William B. Wells, first Lieutenant, who were elected upon the distinct understanding that the company was never to be called out, and I think they were both cashiered by the authorities after a year or two had expired for their neglect of duty.

Pack Wells was keeper of the first livery stable in Athens, and chiefly through the influence of the students, who were required to perform militia duty, and to whom he freely extended credit in his line of business, was elected Major. Much elated by his promotion, he ordered a battalion muster. The Major thought it prudent to assemble his soldiers in a retired part of the town, and drill them somewhat before marching down Broad street. Accordingly, the ranks were formed on Hancock avenue, in front of his livery stable, which then stood a little north of Mrs. Blanton Hill's front yard. It is beyond my power to give any description of the attempt to form that battalion. The students could not resist the temptation to turn the affair into ridicule. Their love of fun overcame their desire to obtain *credit* with the Major, while the citizen soldiery cheerfully contributed their aid to carry out the plan. A strange diversity of opinion prevailed in regard to *right* and *left,* and as they were equally divided on this question, the order to "face" or "wheel" resulted in inextricable confusion. It is enough to say that the battalion never got out of Hancock avenue, though the students were exceedingly anxious to prolong the fun by marching down Broad street. The Major in disgust resigned his honors immediately afterwards.

In the war of 1812, when a call was made upon the counties for volunteers, the armsbearing population of Clarke county—all males between 18 and 45—assembled at Watkinsville and were formed into a regiment. After one or two short addresses to "fire the hearts" of the men, a drum and fife starting the head marched down in front of the regiment, closely followed by Captain James Meriwether inviting all who desired to form a rifle company to *fall in* as he passed the line. The men could scarcely stand still until the music passed, and sprang into line with a leap as joyful as if joining a marriage festival. Meriwether's quota was soon full— a splendid looking company and was called into service a month afterwards. Soon after another company was formed, both joining General Taylor's command and did good service at the battles of Autosee and Calabee Swamp. These men attained a wonderful degree of accuracy in rifle practice. For the greater part of them, one of the company would not hesitate to hold the target between his knees to be fired at from the distance of 80 or 100 yards.

The Cherokee Indians, our near neighbors, were with few exceptions friendly, and although we were within fifteen miles of their territory, no anxiety was felt nor danger apprehended and consequently no means of repelling aggression, adopted. But about a year after the war had begun our town was thrown into a state of distracting alarm by a runner who brought the information that a party of Indian warriors had crossed the Apalachee and attacked a family murdering some of them, and taking whatever they could carry away, had returned across the river.

This news was received with general incredulity, but as the day advanced other persons coming from the neighborhood confirmed the report of the murder, but said the number of marauders did not exceed ten or a dozen. Later in the day rumors were current that the party consisted of a hundred warriors; that the people of the settlement were flying in all directions; that the Indians so far from retreating had visited other plantations and were advancing towards Athens and that the attack upon the town would be made that night. Some of the men and all of the women and children were in the greatest state of alarm, and the students of the College in the highest excitement. Mr. Thomas, Judge Clayton, Colonel Carnes, President Brown and others having carefully sifted the evidence came to the conclusion that a few Indians, perhaps five or six, had made an inroad, and after killing some members of a family had retreated with the plunder as rapidly as they came and were probably by that time on the west side of the Chattahoochee. They found it impossible, however, to allay the fears of the women, who of course believed that they were the special objects of the expected raid. So it was determined to invite all the women and children of the town who desired to do so, to take refuge during the night in the College, which would be cheerfully vacated by the students, who under command of a suitable captain should keep guard over the building and its precious contents.

Dr. William Green, the Professor of Mathematics, as brave an Irishman as ever left the Emerald Isle, had made the suggestion and was placed in command of the forces. But lately arrived in this country, the commander-in-chief was totally ignorant of the Indians and their mode of warfare. He was therefore very much excited and favored putting ourselves in the best possible state of defence. We had no cannon, no block house, no breastworks, no muskets; so the citizens had to depend upon the students, who armed with shot guns and a few rifles stood awaiting the fearful attack, by night, of a savage foe. But Dr. Green and the boys were masters of the situation, and the fair refugees committed themselves to their guardianship with unfaltering faith in their courage and devotion.

Some of the ladies went into the College under serious apprehensions of danger, others, and especially the younger, for a frolic. Of these refugees, I know but one who is living now—one whose character is as lovely after the frosts of seventy winters have whitened her locks as her person was beautiful and attractive when a girl. The students would have shed their blood in her defence with *infinite pleasure,* as they averred. I allude to that estimable lady, relict of Major Jacob Phinizy and mother of Thomas M. Meriwether, Esq., of Newton county. No doubt she still remembers that memorable night, the only one perhaps she ever passed in a College for boys.

Captain Green detailed a patrol around the College and established pickets at various points along the Jefferson road as far as Mr. Sam Wier's blacksmith shop, which was then where Mr. Nat Barnard lives. Between that and Mrs. Deloney's house was thick forest. The picket guards were relieved every two hours and it fell to the lot of the writer, armed with his father's shot gun, loaded with buck shot, to stand guard at Wier's shop, in company with two other boys, the last two hours of the night. We were charged to keep awake, for it was ever the habit of the Indians to make their attacks just before day, and ours was the most important post and the most dangerous time. For a very short time we gazed up the road; then the excitement and fatigue of the day, the chilly night air and the attractive warmth of a neighboring coal kiln, overcame our respect for orders and in less than ten minutes we were all asleep. Sometime after day break Mr. Wier awoke us, saying, that doubtless the Indians were afraid to attack such brave soldiers and we might as well return to camp, which advice we immediately adopted. When we reached headquarters we found no soldiers, no officer to receive our report which we had prepared with considerable care. The College was evacuated, everybody seemed asleep; and it seemed as if nobody cared whether the Indians had captured or killed us, so we dispersed to our homes in disgust. About fifty years later when the writer in company with other *Thunderbolts*, stood for five hours at the Market House awaiting the advance of Stoneman's Raiders, with a double barrelled shot gun, loaded with twenty-eight buckshot, he did not feel as much like a soldier as on that other occasion at Wier's shop.

# George R. Gilmer

## From *Sketches of Some of the First Settlers of Upper Georgia, of the Cherokees, and the Author*

## Part II.

In the part of Wilkes County below Long Creek, and extending south-wardly from Savannah River, a settlement was made before and during the revolutionary war by the Clarks, Dooleys, Murrays, Waltons, and others. They were from Bertie and the adjoining counties of North Carolina, and were all connected together by blood or intermarriages. Gen. Jackson was their countryman, and Col. Benton their kinsman.

These North Carolina settlers lived upon game and the milk of the cattle which they carried with them in their emigration. Hogs, sheep, and poultry, were not to be had, except in the fewest numbers. A sufficient supply of these indispensables for a new country could only be obtained from South Carolina, whither the settlers went for that purpose when they had sufficient money to purchase. Many years passed before they owned hogs and sheep enough for bacon and clothing. Those were hard times, when the breakfast of the family depended upon catching an opossum the over night or a rabbit in the morning. The range was so unrestricted that the cows often wandered away beyond returning or finding, so that the children had no milk to wash down their otherwise dry bread. The horses which did the ploughing had to be turned on the wild grass to get their food. They strayed beyond finding, if their legs were not fastened together, so that the art of hobbling was as important as the blacksmith's. Bells were put upon them, for the purpose of indicating their whereabouts; and then the Indians, if on the frontiers, carried them off. It was difficult to clear of its timber enough of land for corn and tobacco. The term patch was for a long time used for the land sown in wheat, because only a small quantity was allotted for that grain. Even these patches were not seen for years after the settlement began, so that flour could not be had at times for love or money. It was a long time before the children had more than a biscuit a-piece on Sunday mornings. Traps, snares, pens, and other contrivances, were resorted to for catching birds and turkeys. The end of a switch was twisted in the hair of a rabbit, to draw him from his refuge up in a hollow tree. Food was eaten then with the greatest relish, which the lady descendants of the settlers would be horrified to see on their tables now. An opossum, with its full dish of gravy, occupied the place of the sucking pig at present. There were no tanneries then to prepare leather for shoes, nor well-instructed shoemakers to manufacture them. Skins, taken from the cattle killed for beef, and those that died with the hollowhorn, were hung in running streams until the hair could be slipped off, and then put into troughs with bark until they became what was called fit for manufacture. Even this hard material could only be had in sufficient quantities to allow shoes to the children when the frost and snow made the cold too severe for their bare feet to bear. Most went without shoes the greater part of the year.

The first houses were log cabins, with dirt floors and clapboard coverings. Vile toads and venomous serpents were often found crawling over them, and occasionally on the beds. Snakes abounded, until the increase of hogs lessened their number. The rattle of the rattlesnake and the cry of a panther often sent the children home in a hurry from the woods when hunting the cows. The sheep had to be kept in inclosures about the cabins, or there was no wool for winter use. No school gave to the children an hour's play time. After working all day, they sat around the hearth at night, picking the lint from the cotton seed, to supply the material for their clothing. There was no fruit in the country to gratify their eager appetites, except wild grapes, haws, and whortleberries. The boys had no marbles nor tops, until their own labor added to their fathers' means to buy them. All work, little play, no fruit, poor eating, thin clothing, open houses, hard beds, and few blankets, made children hardy or killed them. No novels, pianos, or idleness filled the heads of the girls with vain imaginings. The singing at the meeting-houses of the primitive Baptists tempted but few to attend for the sake of the melody. The great pleasure indulged in by the young people was dancing at night. The married women sought recreation from their six days' work by visiting their neighbors on Sunday. The men went to musters, shooting matches, and horse races, on Saturdays. Housekeepers treated their friends and their own families to a pudding for dinner when company came, and the man of the house drew forth his bottle of whiskey. Many a little fellow had a hearty cry when the last piece of pudding disappeared before he got to the table. The pretty girls, dressed in striped and checked cotton cloth, spun and wove with their own hands, and their sweethearts in the sumach and walnut dyed stuff, made by their mothers. Courting was done when riding to meetings on Sunday, and walking to the spring when there. Newly-married couples went to see the old folks on Saturday, and carried home on Sunday evenings what could be spared them. There was no ennui among the women for want of something to do. If there had been leisure to read, there were but few books for the indulgence. Hollow trees supplied cradles for babies. The fine voices which are now heard in the pulpit and at the bar from the first native Georgians began their practice by crying, when infants, for the want of good nursing.

The preacher and the schoolmaster, the first to commence the onward march of civilization, were slow in reaching outskirt settlements. Most who did were drunken Irishmen or dissolute Virginians, who found the restraints of society in the old countries too binding for their comfort, and therefore moved to the new. Newspapers were confined to the select few. It appears from the record of the Court of Ordinary of Wilks County, that five out of sixteen wills had the makers' mark put to them, instead of their signatures. The proportion of those who could not write must have been still greater among those who died intestate. In the inventories of estates from 1777 to 1783, the first five had only four books, and they valued at five shillings. In the next three there is an entry of one parcel of old books, valued at five shillings. In the next eight no mention is made of books. In the next five there is an entry of a prayer book. Then there are three, in which there is one entry of an old bible and hymn book. The next has an entry of a parcel of old books, valued at seven shillings and sixpence. The next thirteen have no entry of books. The succeeding one has an entry of a tomahawk, prayer-book and testament; the next, of a bible; the next six, one bible; and the next fourteen are without any entry of books at all.

\* \* \*

## CHAPTER III.

Returning home in October, 1813, after travelling for some months, I received a commission of first lieutenant in the 43d regiment. Dr. Bibb, whose medical advice I had been following, was then in Congress. He obtained this commission for me without my knowledge, believing, as he said, that service in the army would probably produce some change in my diseased system which would kill or cure me. Col. Long, of Washington, Wilks County, was commander of the 43d. I immediately went to see him. He advised me to accept the commission, promising that he would give me an active command as soon as possible. I took quarters at the barracks near Washington, where Capt. Tatnall was then stationed. Our acquaintance, and subsequent friendship, was the happiest result of my military service. Our strong regard and intimate intercourse was never interrupted for a moment during his life.

As soon as a few recruits were collected, an order was issued by Gen. Pinckney, then in command of the Southern army, that they should be put under a suitable officer, and sent into the Indian territory, where active hostilities were going on against the Creeks. I asked for the command and received it. I marched with twenty-two recruits, without arms, except refuse drill muskets, and a small quantity of loose powder and unmoulded lead. My appointed station was on the banks of the Chatta-hoochee, about thirty or forty miles beyond the frontiers of the State, near an Indian town, not far from where the Georgia railroad now crosses the Chattahoochee River.

It was an awkward business for one who had only seen a militia muster! who had never fired a musket, and only drawn a sword to govern men who knew no part of their duty. I was ordered to build a fort. I had never seen a fort, and had no means of knowing how to obey the order but what I could get from Duane's Tactics. I went to work, and succeeded very well, so far as I know, or any one else, I suppose, as the strength and fitness of my fortification was never tested.

A few days after my arrival at the standing peach-tree, a ruffian fellow came into the camp with some fine catfish for sale. I had supplied myself with hooks and lines for catching cat in the Chattahoochee before I left home, and had baited and hung them from limbs into the water. I had noticed this fellow the day before gliding stealthily along near the bank of the river, in a small canoe, where the lines with baited hooks were hung. I intimated to him that the fish he was offering to sell were taken from my hooks. With the demoniac look of hatred and revenge, he drew his knife from his belt, and holding it for a moment in the position for striking, turned the edge to his own throat, and drew it across; expressing thus, more forcibly than he could have done by words, his desire to cut my throat. I never saw him afterwards.

One night, immediately after dark, and before any preparations for defence had been made, the Indian war-whoop was heard several times in different directions near the camp. An hour or two after I was roused from my bunk by some of the soldiers rushing into my cabin and crying out that the Indians were upon us. I found, upon jumping up, several of the Cherokee men of the town mixing with the soldiers, and endeavoring to alarm them by assuring them that a large force of hostile Creeks were close by. As soon as possible, I had a barricade constructed in front of the ditch which had been dug for the palisades of the fort. In this ditch, and between the cabins and the barricade, I stationed myself and soldiers.

The Indians went off in the direction in which they reported the hostile Creeks to be. My servant, who had been drinking and was very much alarmed, went off with them. In a short time they returned, accompanied by their women, and carrying off some of their goods to give a show of reality to their feint. From the report of my servant, and the entire conduct of those who had thus attempted to alarm me, I became convinced that their object was to make me leave the country.

At the first cry of Indians, the workmen employed in building boats loosed the horses from the wagons and fled towards the nearest frontier white settlement. To prevent the great alarm which their report would have created among the people of the adjoining territory, I despatched the fleetest runner among the soldiers after them, with orders to pass them if possible. The soldier informed those that had fled, as he passed them, that there was no danger, and then proceeded on to Jefferson, the court-house town of Jackson County, and, through the letter which he carried, prevented the depopulation of the frontier.

At the time of this attempt of the Indians to frighten me out of their country, I had not received the arms and ammunition which was designed for my command. I used bark moulds for running lead into bullets and slugs, and the paper which I carried with me for my own use, for making cartridges. A wagon with a supply of arms was within twenty miles of the encampment. The workmen in passing it so frightened the horses that they broke loose and fled, so that it was several weeks before the arms were received. Whilst I was still unprepared for making much of a fight, I heard one day, about one o'clock, the firing of volleys of rifles in the swamp across the river from my camp. After calling in the men who were in the woods felling timbers for picketing, getting the drill muskets in the best possible order, and putting the men in a position for defence, I ordered a resolute soldier to cross the river and endeavor to find out what the firing meant. He saw several warriors going from cabin to cabin of the town, and meeting the men and women with apparent joy. Soon after eleven warriors, with their town people came to the camp and described to me exultingly as well as they could the battle of the Horseshoe, where they had fought under General Jackson. They brought home eighteen scalps. The night after the day of their arrival the scalps were fastened upon the top of a pole and the men, women and children danced around it all night. I was invited to attend the rejoicing. I sent a soldier that I might be informed of its particulars.

After I had been stationed for several months at the standing peach-tree, I received one morning a visit from a young Cherokee lad, who, in the fulness of his anticipated pleasure, came to communicate to me the secret, that at twelve o'clock the chief men of the town would kill two hostile Creek Indians, who were in huts on the opposite side of the river with a family akin to them. I armed myself, took with me a well armed soldier, and set off for the hut. Upon crossing the river I met several of the members of the family with whom the Creeks intended to be killed were staying. They showed great distress. A little boy belonging to the family had overheard the Cherokees talking of their purpose, and had given information to his relations. The party were going in search of the head of their family. One of them went on; the others accompanied me back to their cabin. One of the Creeks had already left, and the other soon disappeared, I did not perceive where. After a good deal of difficulty their friends found them. All accompanied me to the fort. The soldiers were put under arms. In a few hours the Cherokee men of the town arrived at the fort. They were directed to disarm and enter. After some hesitation they did so. The chiefs were invited into my cabin, where the Creeks were. I knew the leader well. His name was George Proctor. He was one of several brothers and sisters, the children of a white man by that name, and an Indian squaw. I told Proctor that the war was at an end, and that the Creeks were not to be injured. He answered, that the Creeks had killed his brother, and that he must kill a Creek. He was the most respectable man of the town. When he entered my cabin his whole appearance was altered. His usual quiet look had become fixed, intent and demoniac. His clothes, thrown back, hung loosely about him. His knife was stuck in his belt ready for his hand. After a long conversation with the Cherokees of the town who accompanied the Creeks, Proctor consented to defer his revenge until a meeting of the chiefs of the Standing Peach-tree and two or three chiefs of the neighboring villages. Upon the chiefs assembling, the Creeks were assured that they would not be injured.

On the day after this success in saving the lives of two hostile Creeks, I took my departure from the Standing Peach-tree. Upon my arrival at the Washington barracks, where Capt. Hide then commanded, I received a furlough for some weeks. I passed the time most pleasantly with my family friends on Broad River. When I returned to the barracks, I wrote to Col. Long, reminding him of his promise to give me active service. He answered that I should go to the seaboard, then threatened by the British, as soon as I enlisted twenty men, and directed me to seek a favorable situation to effect that object. I went to Carnesville, Franklin County, carrying with me a handsome young recruit, of fine spirit to assist me. I issued circulars, and made speeches, but all in vain. The station had been previously occupied by an officer who used means fair and foul—the people said the latter oftenest—to procure men. He had marched off thirty or forty, leaving the station in bad repute for future recruiting officers. I obtained two recruits, one a maniac, and the other a deserter. My time passed most unsatisfactorily. It was once relieved by the arrival of my old schoolmate, A. Longstreet. We spent a very pleasant evening together, and separated in the morning, he looking for land, I to attend a regimental drill.

The assemblage was of the very rudest people of the country towards the mountains. I was in full dress, and soon found myself a show. The people formed a circle around me as they would have done if they had been looking at a bear or elephant. I addressed them upon the advantages of joining the regular army. Finding that I talked like other men, they soon got near enough to handle my sword and epauletes. Even my whiskers, which were very long and very red, did not escape fingering. It required all my self-command to bear up under such an infliction. But I did, and as I thought when it was over, well; certainly very much to the amusement of Longstreet when I described it to him that evening when we again met at Carnesville. I have warned him against making a Georgia scene of my recruiting efforts, at the Franklin regimental muster.

Finding myself entirely unfit for the recruiting service, I applied to Maj. King for the appointment of adjutant at Columbia, South Carolina. The duty of that office was to take care of the new recruits, and prepare them for service. The appointment was given me. I went to Washington barracks, for the purpose of marching the recruits who were there to Columbia, South Carolina. Whilst I was at Washington news of peace was received. I went to Columbia, and spent some time discharging the duties of drill adjutant, but with little interest.

War having been declared by the Government against Algiers, I applied to Dr. Bibb to procure me a commission in the marine corps. My service in the army had not improved my health. I was desirous of trying the effect of a campaign on the ocean. My application was not successful. I returned home, and remained with my father, whose health was then very bad, until he died. In the beginning of 1818, I went to Lexington and commenced the practice of law. I soon found that the excitement of business did less injury to my health than the listlessness of inaction.

# Elias Boudinot

## From *Speech of Elias Boudinot, Chief of the Cherokees, Pleading for the Rights of His Nation*

To those who are unacquainted with the manners, habits and improvements of the Aborigines of this country, the term *Indian* is pregnant with ideas the most repelling and degrading. But such impressions, originating as they frequently do, from infant prejudices although they hold too true when applied to some, do great injustice to many of this race of beings.

Some there are, perhaps even in this enlightened assembly, who at the bare sight of an Indian, or at the mention of the name, would throw back their imaginations to ancient times, to the savages of savage warfare, to the yells pronounced over the mangled bodies of women and children, thus creating an opinion, inapplicable and highly injurious to those for whose temporal interest and eternal welfare, I come to plead.

What is an Indian? Is he not formed of the same materials with yourself? For "Of one blood God created all the nations that dwell on the face of the earth." Though it be true that he is ignorant, that he is a heathen, that he is a savage; yet he is no more than all others have been under similar circumstances. Eighteen centuries ago what were the inhabitants of Great Britain?

You here behold an *Indian,* my kindred are *Indians,* and my fathers sleeping in the wilderness grave—they too were Indians. But I am not as my fathers were—broader means and nobler influences have fallen upon me. Yet I was not born as thousands are, in a stately dome and amid the congratulations of the great, for on a little hill, in a lonely cabin, overspread by the forest oak I first drew my breath; and in a language unknown to learned and polished nations, I learnt to lisp my fond mother's name. In after days, I have had greater advantages than most of my race; and I now stand before you delegated by my native country to seek her interest, to labour for her respectability, and by my public efforts to assist in raising her to an equal standing with other nations of the earth.

The time has arrived when speculations and conjectures as to the practicability of civilizing the Indians must forever cease. A period is fast approaching when the stale remark—"Do what you will, an Indian will still be an Indian," must be placed no more in speech. With whatever plausibility this popular objection may have heretofore been made, every candid mind must now be sensible that it can no longer be uttered, except by those who are uninformed with respect to us, who are strongly prejudiced against us, or who are filled with vindictive feelings towards us; for the present history of the Indians, particularly of that nation to which I belong, most incontrovertibly establishes the fallacy of this remark. I am aware of the difficulties which have ever existed to Indian civilization, I do not deny the almost insurmountable obstacles which we ourselves have thrown in the way of this improvement, nor do I say that difficulties no longer remain; but facts will permit me to declare that there are none which may not easily be overcome, by strong and continued exertions. It needs not abstract reasoning to prove this position. It needs not the display of language to prove to the minds of good men, that Indians are susceptible of attainments necessary to the formation of polished society. It needs not the power of argument on the nature of man, to silence forever the remark that "It is the purpose of the Almighty that the Indians should be exterminated." It needs only that the world should know what we have done in the few last years, to foresee what yet we may do with the assistance of our white brethren, and that of the common Parent of us all.

It is not necessary to present to you a detailed account of the various aboriginal tribes, who have been known to you only on the pages of history, and there but obscurely known. They have gone; and to revert back to their days, would be only to disturb their oblivious sleep; to darken these walls with deeds at which humanity must shudder; to place before your eyes the scenes of Muskingum Sahta-goo and the plains of Mexico, to call up the crimes of the bloody Cortes and his infernal host; and to describe the animosity and vengeance which have overthrown, and hurried into the shades of death those numerous tribes. But here let me say, that however guilty these unhappy nations may have been, yet many and unreasonable were the wrongs they suffered, many the hardships they endured, and many their wanderings through the trackless wilderness. Yes "Notwithstanding the obloquy [with] which the early historians of the colonies have overshadowed the character of the ignorant and unfortunate natives, some bright gleams will occasionally break through, that throw a melancholy lustre on their memories. Facts are occasionally to be met with in their rude annals, which though recorded with all the colouring of prejudice and bigotry, yet speak for themselves, and will be dwelt upon with applause and sympathy when prejudice shall have passed away."

Nor is it my purpose to enter largely into the consideration of the remnants of those who have fled with time and are no more. They stand as monuments of the Indian's fate. And should they ever become extinct, they must move off the earth, as did their fathers. My design is to offer a few disconnected facts relative to the present improved state, and to the ultimate prospects of that particular tribe called Cherokees to which I belong.

The Cherokee nation lies within the charted limits of the states of Georgia, Tennessee, and Alabama. Its extent as defined by treaties is about 200 miles in length from East to West, and about 120 in breadth. This country which is supposed to contain about 10,000,000 of acres exhibits great varieties of surface, the most part being hilly and mountainous, affording soil of no value. The valleys however, are well watered and afford excellent land, in many parts particularly on the large streams, that of the first quality. The climate is temperate and healthy, indeed I would not be guilty of exaggeration were I to say, that the advantages which this country possesses to render it salubrious, are many and superior. Those lofty and barren mountains, defying the labour and ingenuity of man, and supposed by some as placed there only to exhibit omnipotence, contribute to the healthiness and beauty of the surrounding plains, and give to us that free air and pure water which distinguish our country. These advantages, calculated to make the inhabitants healthy, vigorous, and intelligent, cannot fail to cause this country to become interesting. And there can be no doubt that the Cherokee Nation however obscure and trifling it may now appear, will finally become, if not under its present occupants, one of the Garden spots of America. And here, let me be indulged in the fond wish, that she may thus become under those who now possess her; and ever be fostered, regulated and protected by the generous government of the United States.

The population of the Cherokee Nation increased for the year 1810 to that of 1824, 2000 exclusive of those who emigrated in 1818 and 19 to the west of the Mississippi—of those who reside on the Arkansas the number is supposed to be about 5000.

The rise of these people in their movement toward civilization, may be traced as far back as the relinquishment of their towns; when game became incompetent to their support, by reason of the surrounding white population. They then betook themselves to the woods and commenced the opening of small clearings, and the raising of stock, still however following the chase. Game has since become so scarce that little dependence for subsistence can be placed upon it. They have gradually and I could almost say universally forsaken their ancient employment. In fact, there is not a single family in the nation, that can be said to subsist on the slender support which the wilderness would afford. The love and the practice of hunting are not now carried to a higher degree, than among all frontier people whether white or red. It cannot be doubted, however, that there are many who have commenced a life of agricultural labor from mere necessity, and if they could, would gladly resume their former course of living. But these are individual failings and ought to be passed over.

On the other hand it cannot be doubted that the nation is improving, rapidly improving in all those particulars which must finally constitute the inhabitants of an industrious and intelligent people.

It is a matter of surprise to me, and must be to all those who are properly acquainted with the condition of the Aborigines of this country, that the Cherokees have advanced so far and so rapidly in civilization. But there are yet powerful obstacles, both within and without, to be surmounted in the march of improvement. The prejudices in regard to them in the general community are strong and lasting. The evil effects of their intercourse with their immediate white neighbours, who differ from them chiefly in name, are easily to be seen, and it is evident that from this intercourse proceed those demoralizing practices which in order to surmount, peculiar and unremitting efforts are necessary. In defiance, however, of these obstacles the Cherokees have improved and are still rapidly improving. To give you a further view of their condition, I will here repeat some of the articles of the two statistical tables taken at different periods.

In 1810 there were 19,500 cattle; 6,100 horses; 19,600 swine; 1,037 sheep; 467 looms; 1600 spinning wheels; 30 wagons; 500 ploughs; 3 saw-mills; 13 grist-mills &c. At this time there are 22,000 cattle; 7,600 horses; 46,000 swine; 2,500 sheep; 762 looms; 2488 spinning wheels; 172 wagons; 2,943 ploughs; 10 saw-mills; 31 grist-mills; 62 blacksmith-shops; 8 cotton machines; 18 schools; 18 ferries; and a number of public roads. In one district there were, last winter, upwards of 1000 volumes of good books; and 11 different periodical papers both religious and political, which were taken and read. On the public roads there are many decent inns, and few houses for convenience, &c., would disgrace any country. Most of the schools are under the care and tuition of Christian missionaries, of different denominations, who have been of great service to the nation, by inculcating moral and religious principles into the minds of the rising generation. In many places the word of God is regularly preached and explained, both by missionaries and natives; and there are numbers who have publicly professed their belief in the merits of the great Savior of the world. It is worthy of remark, that in no ignorant country have the missionaries undergone less trouble and difficulty, in spreading a knowledge of the Bible than in this. Here, they have been welcomed and encouraged by the proper authorities of the nation, their persons have been protected, and in very few instances have some individual vagabonds threatened violence to them. Indeed it may be said with truth, that among no heathen people has the faithful minister of God experienced greater success, greater reward for his labour, than in this. He is surrouned by attentive hearers, the words which flow from his lips are not spent in vain. The Cherokees have had no established religion of their own, and perhaps to this circumstance we may attribute, in part, the facilities with which missionaries have pursued their ends. They cannot be called idolators; for they never worshipped Images. They believed in a Supreme Being, the Creator of all, the God of the white, the red, and the black man. They also believed in the existence of an evil spirit who resided, as they thought, in the setting sun, the future place of all who in their life time had done iniquitously. Their prayers were addressed alone to the Supreme Being, and which if written would fill a large volume, and display much sincerity, beauty and sublimity. When the ancient customs of the Cherokees were in their full force, no warrior thought himself secure, unless he had addressed his guardian angel; no hunter could hope for success, unless before the rising sun he had asked the assistance of his God, and on his return at eve he had offered his sacrifice to him.

There are three things of late occurrence, which must certainly place the Cherokee Nation in a fair light, and act as powerful argument in favor of Indian improvement.

> First. The invention of letters.
> Second. The translation of the New Testament into Cherokee.
> And third. The organization of a Government.

The Cherokee mode of writing lately invented by George Guest, who could not read any language nor speak any other than his own, consists of eighty-six characters, principally syllabic, the combinations of which form all the words of the language. Their terms may be greatly simplified, yet they answer all the purposes of writing, and already many natives use them.

The translation of the New Testament, together with Guest's mode of writing, has swept away that barrier which has long existed, and opened a spacious channel for the instruction of adult Cherokees. Persons of all ages and classes may now read the precepts of the Almighty in their own language. Before it is long, there will scarcely be an individual in the nation who can say, "I know not God, neither understand I what thou sayest," for all shall know him from the greatest to the least. The aged warrior over whom has rolled three score and ten years of savage life, will grace the temple of God with his hoary head; and the little child yet on the breast of its pious mother shall learn to lisp its Maker's name.

The shrill sound of the Savage yell shall die away as the roaring of far distant thunder; and Heaven wrought music will gladden the affrighted wilderness. "The solitary place will be glad for them, and the desert shall rejoice and blossom as a rose." Already do we see the morning star, fore-runner of approaching dawn, rising over the tops of deep forests in which for ages have echoed the warrior's whoop. But has not God said it, and will he not do it? The Almighty decrees his purposes, and man cannot with all his ingenuity and device countervail them. They are more fixed in their course than the rolling sun—more durable than the everlasting mountains.

The Government, though defective in many respects, is well suited to the condition of the inhabitants. As they rise in information and re-finement, changes in it must follow, until they arrive at that state of advancement, when I trust they will be admitted into all the privileges of the American family.

*   *   *

When before did a nation of Indians step forward and ask for the means of civilization? The Cherokee authorities have adopted the mea-sures already stated, with a sincere desire to make their nation an intel-ligent and a virtuous people, and with a full hope that those who have already pointed out to them the road of happiness, will now assist them to pursue it. With that assistance, what are the prospects of the Cherokees? Are they not indeed glorious, compared to that deep darkness in which the nobler qualities of their souls have slept. Yes, methinks I can view my native country, rising from the ashes of her degradation, wearing her purified and beautiful garments, and taking her seat with the nations of the earth. I can behold her sons bursting the fetters of ignorance and un-shackling her from the voice of heathenism. She is at this instant, risen like the first morning sun, which grows brighter and brighter, until it reaches its fullness of glory.

She will become not a great, but a faithful ally of the United States.

In time of peace she will plead the common liberties of America. In time of war her interpid sons will sacrifice their lives in your defence. And because she will be useful to you in coming time, she asks you to assist her in her present struggles. She asks not for greatness; she seeks not wealth; she pleads only for assistance to become respectable as a nation, to enlighten and ennoble her sons, and to ornament her daughters with modesty and virtue. She pleads for this assistance, too, because on her destiny hangs that of many nations. If she complete her civilization—then may we hope that all our nations will—then, indeed, may true patriots be encouraged in their efforts to make this world of the West, one continuous abode of enlightened, free, and happy people.

But if the Cherokee Nation fail in her struggle, if she die away, then all hopes are blasted, and falls the fabric of Indian civilization. Their fathers were born in darkness, and have fled in darkness; without your assistance so will their sons. You see, however, where the probability rests. Is there a soul whose narrowness will not permit the exercise of charity on such an occasion? Where is he that can hold his mite from an object so noble. Who can prefer a little of his silver and gold, to the welfare of nations of his fellow beings? Human wealth perishes with our clay, but that wealth gained in charity still remains on earth, to enrich our names, when we are gone, and will be remembered in Heaven, when the miser and his coffers have mouldered together in their kindred earth. The works of a generous mind sweeten the cup of affliction; they enlighten the dreary way to the cold tomb; they blunt the sting of death, and smooth his passage to the unknown world. When all the kingdoms of this earth shall die away and their beauty and power shall perish, his name shall live and shine as a twinkling star; those for whose benefit he did his deeds of charity shall call him blessed, and they shall add honor to his immortal head.

There are, with regard to the Cherokees and other tribes, two alternatives; they must either become civilized and happy, or sharing the fate of many kindred nations, become extinct. If the General Government continue its protection, and the American people assist them in their humble efforts, they will, they must rise. Yes, under such protection, and with such assistance, the Indian must rise like the Phoenix, after having wallowed for ages in ignorant barbarity. But should this Government withdraw its care, and the American people their aid, then, to use the words of a writer, "They will go the way that so many tribes have gone before them; for the hordes that still linger about the shores of Huron, and the tributary streams of the Mississippi, will share the fate of those tribes that once lorded it along the proud banks of the Hudson; of that gigantic race that is said to have existed on the borders of the Susquehanna; of those various nations that flourished about the Potomac and the Rhappahannoc, and that peopled the forests of the vast valley of Shenandoah. They will vanish like a vapour from the face of the earth, their very history will be lost in forgetfulness, and the places that now know them will know them no more."

There is, in Indian history, something very melancholy, and which seems to establish a mournful precedent for the future events of the few sons of the forest, now scattered over this vast continent. We have seen every where the poor aborigines melt away before the white population. I merely speak of the fact, without at all referring to the cause. We have seen, I say, one family after another, one tribe after another, nation after nation pass away; until only a few solitary creatures are left to tell the sad story of extinction.

Shall this precedent be followed? I ask you, shall red men live, or shall they be swept from the earth? With you and this public at large, the decision chiefly rests. Must they perish? Must they all, like the unfortunate Creeks, (victims of the unchristian policy of certain persons) go down in sorrow to their graves?

They hang upon your mercy as to a garment. Will you push them from you, or will you save them? Let humanity answer.

# Part Two

Antebellum Life, Civil War,
and Reconstruction, 1830–1900

Private writing in the form of diaries and personal letters remained important in Georgia well into the nineteenth century. In the absence of television, telephones, radios, and other fast and reliable means of communication, letters were the only way family members had of staying in touch over long distances. Most of the letters in this anthology were written by well-educated members of the white middle and upper classes. In often highly expressive, articulate prose husbands and wives, brothers, sisters, and friends exchanged news of their lives. Such letters could serve as more than a simple means of communication. They could and often did serve as journals. The letters of the Charles Colcock family in *Children of Pride* are vividly expressive and descriptive documents. On occasion letters are written to inform distant readers about life in the South. Emily Burke's *Letters from the South* serves this purpose, as do the letters in Frances Kemble's plantation diary.[1] Kemble, Burke, and other "private" writers of nineteenth-century Georgia give some of the most comprehensive and detailed accounts of life in the state during the nineteenth century.

The personal narratives of slaves form a more complex and difficult body of writing. Unlike the private letters of slave owners and other nineteenth-century Southern whites, slave narratives were often intended

1. Kemble did not actually mail the letters in her journal, though she did intend Elizabeth Sedgwick eventually to read them. In fact, they are not real letters at all but simply a way she chose to order her journal. See "Editor's Introduction," *Journal of a Residence on a Georgia Plantation in 1838–1839*, by Frances Anne Kemble, ed. John A. Scott (Athens: Univ. of Georgia Press, 1984), p. xlii.

for publication. Moreover, the abolitionist movement found these narratives a powerful weapon in its battle against slavery. As a result, some
narratives were heavily edited, cowritten, or even ghostwritten by aboli-
tionists who wanted to make sure that they made the appropriate point.
Literary critics and historians are just beginning to understand the full
nature of this editorial involvement and its implications. The best of the
slave narratives, such as those by Frederick Douglass and Harriet Jacobs,
are riveting documents that changed the course of American history and
influenced writers as diverse as Harriet Beecher Stowe, William Styron,
and Toni Morrison.

Two nineteenth-century slave narratives by Georgians are included
here. *Running a Thousand Miles for Freedom* was one of the last narratives
published prior to the Civil War, and it has remained popular over the
years, though it bears the clear marks of an editor's pen. This narrative
is interesting not so much for what it reveals about slavery as for the adventurous extremes to which William and Ellen Craft must go in order
to escape to freedom. Much more direct and visceral in its descriptive
impact is the *Narrative of the Life, Sufferings, and Escape of John Brown,
a Fugitive Slave,* which was dictated to an editor. Slave narratives were a
popular form of reading in the middle nineteenth century, at least in the
Northern states, just as narratives by people who had survived capture
by Indians were popular in the eighteenth century. Slave narratives were
an important means by which Northerners learned about the South and
thus an important force in the formation of Northern perceptions of the
South prior to the Civil War.

In the 1930s, writers in the Works Progress Administration (WPA)
collected a different kind of narrative: primarily oral accounts of plantation life given by surviving former slaves. These narratives are interesting
but not trustworthy. One often suspects that the personality of the inter-
viewer along with the natural tendency of the old to sentimentalize the
past, especially in a time of economic deprivation, influenced the nostalgic accounts given by many of the former slaves. The poignant force
of some of these accounts helps explain the tenacity of the myth of the
antebellum South in the memories of black and white Southerners alike.
Ironically, the WPA narrative included here is given by a woman who

had been a slave on the plantation of Alexander Stephens, vice-president of the Confederacy, whose own prison diary is excerpted here as well.

The most traumatic years of the nineteenth century in Georgia came during the Civil War. Many men were busy fighting at the fronts or engaged in other activities that left them little time for writing. Women were also busy, but some found opportunity to keep journals and diaries, perhaps as a means of solace in the absence of their husbands and sons, perhaps also as the only form of self-expression available to them. Women in the antebellum South, as in much of the rest of the nation, did not find an atmosphere receptive to female writers. Men frowned on, and even prevented, their involvement in journalism and literature. Such endeavors would strain fragile feminine brains and, perhaps more to the point for the disapproving men, take women away from their domestic duties. Frances Kemble's plantation diary appears to have been one of the only means of intellectual stimulation available to her on her husband's plantation. As she grew increasingly disenchanted with slavery and her husband, her diary became an important refuge. The Civil War diaries of such women as Eliza Andrews and Mary A. H. Gay, both excerpted here, provide a vivid account of life in Georgia during the Civil War. Gay's diary in particular deserves special note. Her account of her brazen fifteen-mile hike through enemy lines on the eve of the fall of Atlanta is a remarkable story, though the way in which she wrote the journal prior to its publication in 1892, constructing it over a period of years from her own memories, those of her sister, and from her brother's wartime letters, suggests the possibility of exaggeration.

The most notable diary by a writer of this period is Alexander Stephens's prison journal, which describes his imprisonment from the time of his arrest shortly after the Confederate defeat in 1865 to his release six months later. Stephens's diary is an intriguing example of how a writer can manipulate that most private form of writing—the diary—into a forum for addressing public issues. Yet there is no evidence that Stephens intended his journal for publication, or that he ever thought anyone would read it but himself. It provided him with diversion and intellectual stimulation while he was in prison, but he made of it considerably more than a dry exercise. It became, first of all, an apologia for his role as vice-president of the Confederacy. Stephens viewed himself as the enlightened defender of the Constitution who sided with his native state and its neighbors only after he had done all he could to preserve the Union and prevent secession. He became, in this view, a Union loyalist—though more loyal to the concept of Union than to the federal government that enforced it. (He was by no means alone in Georgia in his pre–Civil-War Unionism.) He also stressed his opposition to Jefferson Davis, with whom he disagreed on many issues, and whom he blamed in part for the South's defeat. He presented himself, further, as a man for all seasons, a man of ideas who submitted to imprisonment stoically and nobly, and who suffered nonetheless. In fact, the physical pain he suffered in prison from afflictions that had plagued him throughout his life is a minor theme of the diary. The Stephens who emerges from its pages is a figure of physical and intellectual isolation, a misunderstood defender of Union and virtue, and almost, in a modern context, an existential hero. Though he may also be, in part, a product of his own self-serving and defensive imagination, he is nonetheless an absorbing figure.

Stephens is also a remarkable experimenter in literary form and style. His diary is written in various modes: drama, philosophical meditation, political treatise, and introspective character study. Ultimately, it does not wholly cohere—it contains too much of the mundane, too many letters to government officials quoted in their entirety, too many unconnected fragments. Stephens frequently introduces an interesting thought or detail and then fails to develop it, or, worse, develops it interminably. Nonetheless, his diary is a remarkable document. An important legacy of a central Civil War leader, its varying techniques anticipate many of the experiments in literary modernism of the twentieth century, though probably none of the modernists knew the Stephens journal.

While Stephens was looking backward, assessing the disaster of the Civil War and continuing to argue issues it left unresolved, others were looking to the future. Among these was the editor of the *Atlanta Constitution*, Henry W. Grady. His 1886 "New South" address has traditionally been viewed as an important milestone in the South's recovery from the Civil War. Rather than arguing for regional separatism or longing sentimentally for an unrecoverable past, Grady insisted that the South reconcile with the North, that it look to the future and to commerce and industry as much as to agriculture for economic strength. He did not suggest that the South should abandon its traditions, but he at least implied that the South must join modern America and the modern world. Too often Grady's address has been read as a cultural pronouncement urging fellow Southerners to rethink certain basic attitudes about themselves and their region. In fact, "The New South" is really a public relations address in which a Southern newspaper editor with a canny grasp of the benefits of good business relations with the North (and who recognizes, like other New South proponents, the benefits an improved Southern economy would bring him) argues for change. The speech thus has its weaknesses. Its glib optimism underestimates the deep psychological and economic damage the South suffered in the Civil War and offers no solution for the problems of the former slaves who, now free, nonetheless lived in a society not disposed toward improving their condition. Grady also envisioned a South centered on the city rather than on rural life and agriculture—a traditional source of Southern economic strength by no means exhausted at the time of the "New South" address. What Grady advocated could substantially improve conditions in Atlanta, but for the small independent farmers and sharecroppers in south Georgia, he offered little. Some Southerners argued, in Grady's own time as well as later, that his program for the South amounted to a further surrender of the Southern position to the North. The Southern agrarians of the 1930s certainly thought so. To them, Grady did not merely advocate giving in to the enemy—he *was* the enemy.

One last form of nineteenth-century writing deserves mention. Humor has been a significant part of Georgia life since the first settlement. A notorious early satire, *A True and Historical Narrative of the Colony of Georgia* (1741), was written by three early colonists dissatisfied with policies and conditions in colonial Georgia. Their sarcastic attacks on Oglethorpe provoked considerable consternation among the Trustees. In the nineteenth century, humorous sketches of frontier Georgia life by Augustus Baldwin Longstreet and William Tappan Thompson were popular with Northern and Southern readers alike. About the time of the Civil War, Charles Henry Smith, or "Bill Arp," used a comic persona to satirize Lincoln, the North, and other enemies of the South. Late in the century, Joel Chandler Harris's Uncle Remus tales became famous throughout the world. These humorists set the stage for a number of modern writers, including Flannery O'Connor and Harry Crews, who used humor not merely to provoke laughter but to probe fundamental issues of the modern world.

# Frances Anne Kemble

## From
## *Journal of a Residence on a Georgian Plantation in 1838–1839*

### XIX
### Women in Slavery

[February 28–March 2, 1839]

Dear E[lizabeth],

I cannot give way to the bitter impatience I feel at my present position, and come back to the North without leaving my babies; and though I suppose their stay will not in any case be much prolonged in these regions of swamp and slavery, I must, for their sakes, remain where they are, and learn this dreary lesson of human suffering to the end. The record, it seems to me, must be utterly wearisome to you, as the instances themselves, I suppose, in a given time (thanks to that dreadful reconciler to all that is evil—habit), would become to me.

This morning [February 28] I had a visit from two of the women, Charlotte and Judy, who came to me for help and advice for a complaint, which it really seems to me every other woman on the estate is cursed with, and which is a direct result of the conditions of their existence; the practice of sending women to labor in the fields in the third week after their confinement is a specific for causing this infirmity, and I know no specific for curing it under these circumstances. As soon as these poor things had departed with such comfort as I could give them, and the

69

bandages they especially begged for, three other sable graces introduced themselves, Edie, Louisa, and Diana; the former told me she had had a family of seven children, but had lost them all through "ill luck," as she denominated the ignorance and ill-treatment which were answerable for the loss of these, as of so many other poor little creatures their fellows. Having dismissed her and Diana with the sugar and rice they came to beg, I detained Louisa, whom I had never seen but in the presence of her old grandmother, whose version of the poor child's escape to, and hiding in the woods, I had a desire to compare with the heroine's own story.

She told it very simply, and it was most pathetic. She had not finished her task one day, when she said she felt ill, and unable to do so, and had been severely flogged by driver Bran, in whose "gang" she then was. The next day, in spite of this encouragement to labor, she had again been unable to complete her appointed work; and Bran having told her that he'd tie her up and flog her if she did not get it done, she had left the field and run into the swamp.

"Tie you up, Louisa!" said I; "what is that?"

She then described to me that they were fastened up by their wrists to a beam or a branch of a tree, their feet barely touching the ground, so as to allow them no purchase for resistance or evasion of the lash, their clothes turned over their heads, and their backs scored with a leather thong, either by the driver himself, or, if he pleases to inflict their punishment by deputy, any of the men he may choose to summon to the office; it might be father, brother, husband, or lover, if the overseer so ordered it. I turned sick, and my blood curdled listening to these details from the slender young slip of a lassie, with her poor piteous face and murmuring, pleading voice.

"Oh," said I, "Louisa; but the rattlesnakes—the dreadful rattlesnakes in the swamps; were you not afraid of those horrible creatures?"

"Oh, missis," said the poor child, "me no tink of dem; me forget all 'bout dem for de fretting."

"Why did you come home at last?"

"Oh, missis, me starve with hunger, me most dead with hunger before me come back."

"And were you flogged, Louisa?" said I, with a shudder at what the answer might be.

"No, missis, me go to hospital; me almost dead and sick so long, 'spec driver Bran him forgot 'bout de flogging."

I am getting perfectly savage over all these doings, E[lizabeth], and really think I should consider my own throat and those of my children well cut if some night the people were to take it into their heads to clear off scores in that fashion.

The Calibanish wonderment of all my visitors at the exceedingly coarse and simple furniture and rustic means of comfort of my abode is very droll. I have never inhabited any apartment so perfectly devoid of what we should consider the common decencies of life; but to them, my rude chintz-covered sofa and common pine-wood table, with its green baize cloth, seem the adornings of a palace; and often in the evening, when my bairns are asleep, and M[argery] upstairs keeping watch over them, and I sit writing this daily history for your edification, the door of the great barnlike room is opened stealthily, and one after another, men and women come trooping silently in, their naked feet falling all but inaudibly on the bare boards as they betake themselves to the hearth, where they squat down on their hams in a circle, the bright blaze from the huge pine logs, which is the only light of this half of the room, shining on their sooty limbs and faces, and making them look like a ring of ebony idols surrounding my domestic hearth. I have had as many as fourteen at a time squatting silently there for nearly half an hour, watching me writing at the other end of the room. The candles on my table give only light enough for my own occupation, the firelight illuminates the rest of the apartment; and you cannot imagine anything stranger than the effect of all these glassy whites of eyes and grinning white teeth turned toward me, and shining in the flickering light. I very often take no notice of them at all, and they seem perfectly absorbed in contemplating me. My evening dress probably excites their wonder and admiration no less than my rapid and continuous writing, for which they have sometimes expressed compassion, as if they thought it must be more laborious than hoeing; sometimes at the end of my day's journal I look up and say suddenly:

"Well, what do you want?" when each black figure springs up at once, as if moved by machinery; they all answer: "Me come say ha do (how d'ye do), missis"; and then they troop out as noiselessly as they entered, like a procession of sable dreams, and I go off in search, if possible, of whiter ones.

Two days ago I had a visit of great interest to me from several lads from twelve to sixteen years old, who had come to beg me to give them work. To make you understand this, you must know that, wishing very much to cut some walks and drives through the very picturesque patches of woodland not far from the house, I announced, through Jack, my desire to give employment in the wood-cutting line to as many lads as chose, when their unpaid task was done, to come and do some work for me, for which I engaged to pay them. At the risk of producing a most dangerous process of reflection and calculation in their brains, I have persisted in paying what I considered wages to every slave that has been my servant; and these my laborers must, of course, be free to work or no, as they like, and if they work for me must be paid by me. The proposition met with unmingled approbation from my "gang"; but I think it might be considered dangerously suggestive of the rightful relation between work and wages; in short, very involuntarily no doubt, but, nevertheless, very effectually I am disseminating ideas among Mr. [Butler]'s dependents, the like of which have certainly never before visited their wool-thatched brains.

Last night, after writing so much to you, I felt weary, and went out into the air to refresh my spirit. The scene just beyond the house was beautiful; the moonlight slept on the broad river, which here is almost the sea, and on the masses of foliage of the great Southern oaks; the golden stars of German poetry shone in the purple curtains of the night, and the measured rush of the Atlantic unfurling its huge skirts upon the white sands of the beach (the sweetest and most awful lullaby in nature) resounded through the silent air.

I have not felt well, and have been much depressed for some days past. I think I should die if I had to live here. This morning [March 1], in order not to die yet, I thought I had better take a ride, and accordingly mounted the horse which I told you was one of the equestrian alternatives offered me here; but no sooner did he feel my weight, which, after all, is mere levity and frivolity to him, than he thought proper to rebel, and find the grasshopper a burden, and rear and otherwise demonstrate his disgust. I have not ridden for a long time now; but Montreal's opposition very presently aroused the Amazon which is both natural and acquired in me, and I made him comprehend that, though I object to slaves, I expect obedient servants; which views of mine being imparted by a due administration of both spur and whip, attended with a judicious combination of coaxing pats on his great crested neck, and endearing commendations of his beauty, produced the desired effect. Montreal accepted me as inevitable, and carried me very wisely and well up the island to another of the slave settlements on the plantation, called Jones's Creek.

On my way I passed some magnificent evergreen oaks,* and some thickets of exquisite evergreen shrubs, and one or two beautiful sites for a residence, which made me gnash my teeth when I thought of the one we had chosen. To be sure, these charming spots, instead of being conveniently in the middle of the plantation, are at an out-of-the-way end of it, and so hardly eligible for the one quality desired for the overseer's abode, viz., being central.

All the slaves' huts on St. Simons are far less solid, comfortable, and habitable than those at the rice island. I do not know whether the laborer's habitation bespeaks the alteration in the present relative importance of the crops, but certainly the cultivators of the once far-famed long-staple, sea-island cotton of St. Simons are far more miserably housed than the rice raisers of the other plantation. These ruinous shielings, that hardly keep out wind or weather, are deplorable homes for young or aged people, and poor shelters for the hard-working men and women who cultivate the fields in which they stand.

Riding home I passed some beautiful woodland, with charming pink and white blossoming peach and plum trees, which seemed to belong

---

*The only ilex trees which I have seen comparable in size and beauty with those of the seaboard of Georgia are some to be found in the Roman Campagna, at Passerano, Lunghegna, Castel Fusano, and other of its great princely farms, but especially in the magnificent woody wilderness of Valerano.

to some orchard that had been attempted, and afterward delivered over to wilderness. On inquiry, I found that no fruit worth eating was ever gathered from them. What a pity it seems! for in this warm, delicious winter climate any and every species of fruit might be cultivated with little pains and to great perfection.

As I was cantering along the side of one of the cotton fields I suddenly heard some inarticulate vehement cries, and saw what seemed to be a heap of black limbs tumbling and leaping toward me, renewing the screams at intervals as it approached. I stopped my horse, and the black ball bounded almost into the road before me, and, suddenly straightening itself up into a haggard hag of a half-naked Negress exclaimed, with panting, eager breathlessness: "Oh, missis, missis, you no hear me cry, you no hear me call. Oh, missis, me call, me cry, and me run; make me a gown like dat. Do, for massy's sake, only make me a gown like dat." This modest request for a riding habit in which to hoe the cotton fields served for an introduction to sundry other petitions for rice, and sugar, and flannel, all which I promised the petitioner, but not the "gown like dat"; whereupon I rode off, and she flung herself down in the middle of the road to get her wind and rest.

The passion for dress is curiously strong in these people, and seems as though it might be made an instrument in converting them, outwardly at any rate, to something like civilization; for, though their own native taste is decidedly both barbarous and ludicrous, it is astonishing how very soon they mitigate it in imitation of their white models. The fine figures of the mulatto women in Charleston and Savannah are frequently as elegantly and tastefully dressed as those of any of their female superiors; and here on St. Simons, owing, I suppose, to the influence of the resident lady proprietors of the various plantations, and the propensity to imitate in their black dependents, the people that I see all seem to me much tidier, cleaner, and less fantastically dressed than those on the rice plantation, where no such influences reach them.

On my return from my ride I had a visit from Captain F[raser], the manager of a neighboring plantation, with whom I had a long conversation about the present and past condition of the estate, the species of feudal magnificence in which its original owner, Major [Butler], lived, the iron rule of old overseer K[ing] which succeeded to it, and the subsequent sovereignty of his son, Mr. R[oswell] K[ing], the man for whom Mr. [Butler] entertains such a cordial esteem, and of whom every account I receive from the Negroes seems to me to indicate a merciless sternness of disposition that may be a virtue in a slave driver, but is hardly a Christian grace. Captain F[raser] was one of our earliest visitors at the rice plantation on our arrival, and I think I told you of his mentioning, in speaking to me of the orange trees which formerly grew all round the dikes there, that he had taken Basil Hall there once in their blossoming season, and that he had said the sight was as well worth crossing the Atlantic for as Niagara. Today he referred to that again. He has resided for a great many years on a plantation here, and is connected with our neighbor, old Mr. C[ouper], whose daughter, I believe, he married. He interested me extremely by his description of the house Major [Butler] had many years ago on a part of the island called Sinclair. As far as I can understand, there must have been an indefinite number of "masters'" residences on this estate in the old Major's time; for, what with the one we are building, and the ruined remains of those not quite improved off the face of the earth, and the tradition of those that have ceased to exist, even as ruins, I make out no fewer than seven. How gladly would I exchange all that remain and all that do not for the smallest tenement in your blessed Yankee mountain village!

Captain F[raser] told me that at Sinclair General Oglethorpe, the good and brave English governor of the State of Georgia in its colonial days, had his residence, and that among the magnificent live oaks which surround the site of the former settlement, there was one especially venerable and picturesque, which in his recollection always went by the name of General Oglethorpe's Oak. If you remember the history of the colony under his benevolent rule, you must recollect how absolutely he and his friend and counselor, Wesley, opposed the introduction of slavery in the colony. How wrathfully the old soldier's spirit ought to haunt these cotton fields and rice swamps of his old domain, with their population of wretched slaves! I will ride to Sinclair and see his oak; if I should see him, he cannot have much to say to me on the subject that I should not cry amen to.

I have made a gain, no doubt, in one respect in coming here, dear E[lizabeth], for, not being afraid of a rearing stallion, I can ride; but, on the other hand, my aquatic diversions are all likely, I fear, to be much curtailed. Well may you, or any other Northern abolitionist, consider this a heaven-forsaken region—why, I cannot even get worms to fish with, and was solemnly assured by Jack this morning [March 2] that the whole "Point," i.e., neighborhood of the house, had been searched in vain for these useful and agreeable animals. I must take to some more sportsmanlike species of bait; but, in my total ignorance of even the kind of fish that inhabit these waters, it is difficult for me to adapt my temptations to their taste.

Yesterday evening I had a visit that made me very sorrowful, if anything connected with these poor people can be called more especially sorrowful than their whole condition; but Mr. [Butler]'s declaration, that he will receive no more statements of grievances or petitions for redress through me, makes me as desirous now of shunning the vain appeals of these unfortunates as I used to be of receiving and listening to them. The imploring cry: "Oh missis!" that greets me whichever way I turn, makes me long to stop my ears now; for what can I say or do any more for them? The poor little favors—the rice, the sugar, the flannel—that they beg for with such eagerness, and receive with such exuberant gratitude, I can, it is true, supply, and words and looks of pity, and counsel of patience, and such instruction in womanly habits of decency and cleanliness as may enable them to better, in some degree, their own hard lot; but to the entreaty: "Oh, missis, you speak to massa for us! Oh, missis, you beg massa for us! Oh, missis, you tell massa for we, he sure do as you say!" I cannot now answer as formerly, and I turn away choking and with eyes full of tears from the poor creatures, not even daring to promise any more the faithful transmission of their prayers.

The women who visited me yesterday evening were all in the family way, and came to entreat of me to have the sentence (what else can I call it?) modified which condemns them to resume their labor of hoeing in the fields three weeks after their confinement. They knew, of course, that I cannot interfere with their appointed labor, and therefore their sole entreaty was that I would use my influence with Mr. [Butler] to obtain for them a month's respite from labor in the field after childbearing. Their principal spokeswoman, a woman with a bright sweet face, called Mary, and a very sweet voice, which is by no means an uncommon excellence among them, appealed to my own experience; and while she spoke of my babies, and my carefully tended, delicately nursed, and tenderly watched confinement and convalescence, and implored me to have a kind of labor given to them less exhausting during the month after their confinement, I held the table before me so hard in order not to cry that I think my fingers ought to have left a mark on it. At length I told them that Mr. [Butler] had forbidden me to bring him any more complaints from them, for that he thought the ease with which I received and believed their stories only tended to make them discontented, and that, therefore, I feared I could not promise to take their petitions to him; but that he would be coming down to "the Point" soon, and that they had better come then sometime when I was with him, and say what they had just been saying to me; and with this, and various small bounties, I was forced, with a heavy heart, to dismiss them; and when they were gone, with many exclamations of: "Oh yes, missis, you will, you will speak to massa for we; God bless you, missis, we sure you will!" I had my cry out for them, for myself, for *us*. All these women had had large families, and *all* of them had lost half their children, and several of them had lost more. How I do ponder upon the strange fate which has brought me here, from so far away, from surroundings so curiously different—how my own people in that blessed England of my birth would marvel if they could suddenly have a vision of me as I sit here, and how sorry some of them would be for me!

I am helped to bear all that is so very painful to me here by my constant enjoyment of the strange, wild scenery in the midst of which I live, and which my resumption of my equestrian habits gives me almost daily opportunity of observing. I rode today to some new-cleared and plowed ground that was being prepared for the precious cotton crop. I crossed a salt marsh upon a raised causeway that was perfectly alive with land crabs, whose desperately active endeavors to avoid my horse's hoofs were so ludicrous that I literally laughed alone and aloud at them. The sides of this road across the swamp were covered with a thick and close embroidery of creeping moss, or rather lichens of the most vivid green and red: the latter made my horse's path look as if it was edged with an exquisite pattern of coral; it was like a thing in a fairy tale, and delighted me extremely.

I suppose, E[lizabeth], one secret of my being able to suffer as acutely as I do, without being made either ill or absolutely miserable, is the childish excitability of my temperament, and the sort of ecstasy which any beautiful thing gives me. No day, almost no hour, passes without some enjoyment of the sort this coral-bordered road gave me, which not only charms my senses completely at the time, but returns again and again before my memory, delighting my fancy, and stimulating my imagination. I sometimes despise myself for what seems to me an inconceivable rapidity of emotion, that almost makes me doubt whether anyone who feels so many things can really be said to feel anything; but I generally recover from this perplexity by remembering whither invariably every impression of beauty leads my thoughts, and console myself for my contemptible facility of impression by the reflection that it is, upon the whole, a merciful system of compensation by which my whole nature, tortured as it was last night, can be absorbed this morning in a perfectly pleasurable contemplation of the capers of crabs and the color of mosses as if nothing else existed in creation. One thing, however, I think, is equally certain, and that is, that I need never expect much sympathy, and perhaps this special endowment will make me, to some degree, independent of it; but I have no doubt that to follow me through half a day with any species of lively participation in my feelings would be a severe breathless moral calisthenic to most of my friends—what Shakespeare calls "sweating labor." As far as I have hitherto had opportunities of observing, children and maniacs are the only creatures who would be capable of sufficiently rapid transitions of thought and feeling to keep pace with me.

And so I rode through the crabs and the coral. There is one thing, however, I beg to commend to your serious consideration as a trainer of youth, and that is, the expediency of cultivating in all the young minds you educate an equal love of the good, the beautiful, and the absurd (not an easy task, for the latter is apt in its development to interfere a little with the two others): doing this, you command all the resources of existence. The love of the good and beautiful, of course, you are prepared to cultivate—that goes without saying, as the French say; the love of the ludicrous will not appear to you as important, and yet you will be wrong to undervalue it. In the first place, I might tell you that it was almost like cherishing the love of one's fellow creatures—at which, no doubt, you shake your head reprovingly; but, leaving aside the enormous provision for the exercise of this natural faculty which we offer to each other, why should crabs scuttle from under my horse's feet in such a way as to make me laugh again every time I think of it, if there is not an inherent propriety in laughter, as the only emotion which certain objects challenge—an emotion wholesome for the soul and body of man? After all, *why* are we contrived to laugh at all, if laughter is not essentially befitting and beneficial? and most people's lives are too lead-colored to afford to lose one sparkle on them, even the smallest twinkle of light gathered from a flash of nonsense. Hereafter point out for the "appreciative" study of your pupils all that is absurd in themselves, others, and the universe in general; it is an element largely provided, of course, to meet a corresponding and grateful capacity for its enjoyment.

After my crab and coral causeway I came to the most exquisite thickets of evergreen shrubbery you can imagine. If I wanted to paint Paradise I would copy this undergrowth, passing through which I went on to the settlement at St. Annie's, traversing another swamp on another raised causeway. The thickets through which I next rode were perfectly draped with the beautiful wild jasmine of these woods. Of all the parasitical plants I ever saw, I do think it is the most exquisite in form and color, and its perfume is like the most delicate heliotrope.

I stopped for some time before a thicket of glittering evergreens, over which hung, in every direction, streaming garlands of these fragrant golden cups, fit for Oberon's banqueting service. These beautiful shrubberies were resounding with the songs of mockingbirds. I sat there on my horse in a sort of dream of enchantment, looking, listening, and inhaling the delicious atmosphere of those flowers; and suddenly my eyes opened, as if I had been asleep, on some bright red bunches of spring leaves on one of the winter-stripped trees, and I as suddenly thought of the cold Northern skies and earth, where the winter was still inflexibly tyrannizing over you all, and, in spite of the loveliness of all that was present, and the harshness of all that I seemed to see at that moment, no first tokens of the spring's return were ever more welcome to me than those bright leaves that reminded me how soon I should leave this scene of material beauty and moral degradation, where the beauty itself is of an appropriate character to the human existence it surrounds: above all, loveliness, brightness, and fragrance; but below! it gives one a sort of Melusina feeling of horror—all swamp and poisonous stagnation, which the heat will presently make alive with venomous reptiles.

I rode on, and the next object that attracted my attention was a very startling and by no means agreeable one—an enormous cypress tree which had been burned, stood charred and blackened, and leaning toward the road so as to threaten a speedy fall across it, and on one of the limbs of this great charcoal giant hung a dead rattlesnake. If I tell you that it looked to me at least six feet long, you will say you only wonder I did not say twelve; it was a hideous-looking creature, and some Negroes I met soon after told me they had found it in the swamp, and hung it dead on the burning tree. Certainly the two together made a dreadful trophy, and a curious contrast to the lovely bowers of bloom I had just been contemplating with such delight.

This settlement at St. Annie's is the remotest on the whole plantation, and I found there the wretchedest huts, and most miserably squalid, filthy, and forlorn creatures I had yet seen here—certainly the condition of the slaves on this estate is infinitely more neglected and deplorable than that on the rice plantation. Perhaps it may be that the extremely unhealthy nature of the rice cultivation makes it absolutely necessary that the physical condition of the laborers should be maintained at its best to enable them to abide it; and yet it seems to me that even the process of soaking the rice can hardly create a more dangerous miasma than the poor creatures must inhale who live in the midst of these sweltering swamps, half sea, half river slime. Perhaps it has something to do with the fact that the climate on St. Simons is generally considered peculiarly mild and favorable, and so less protection of clothes and shelter is thought necessary here for the poor residents; perhaps, too, it may be because the cotton crop is now, I believe, hardly as valuable as the rice crop, and the plantation here, which was once the chief source of its owner's wealth, is becoming a secondary one, and so not worth so much care or expense in repairing and constructing Negro huts and feeding and clothing the slaves. More pitiable objects than some of those I saw at the St. Annie's settlement today I hope never to see: there was an old crone called Hannah, a sister, as well as I could understand what she said, of old House Molly, whose face and figure, seamed with wrinkles, and bowed and twisted with age and infirmity, really hardly retained the semblance of those of a human creature, and as she crawled to me almost half her naked body was exposed through the miserable tatters that she held on with one hand, while the other eagerly clutched my hand, and her poor blear eyes wandered all over me as if she was bewildered by the strange aspect of any human being but those whose sight was familiar to her. One or two forlorn creatures like herself, too old or too infirm to be compelled to work, and the half-starved and more than half-naked children apparently left here under their charge, were the only inmates I found in these wretched hovels.

I came home without stopping to look at anything, for I had no heart any longer for what had so charmed me on my way to this place. Galloping along the road after leaving the marshes, I scared an ox who was feeding leisurely, and, to my great dismay, saw the foolish beast betake himself with lumbering speed into the "bush": the slaves will have to hunt after him, and perhaps will discover more rattlesnakes six or twelve feet long.

After reaching home I went to the house of the overseer to see his wife, a tidy, decent, kindhearted little woman, who seems to me to do her duty by the poor people she lives among as well as her limited intelligence and still more limited freedom allow. The house her husband lives in is the former residence of Major [Butler], which was the great mansion of the estate. It is now in a most ruinous and tottering condition, and they inhabit but a few rooms in it; the others are gradually moldering to pieces, and the whole edifice will, I should think, hardly stand long enough to be carried away by the river, which in its yearly inroads on the bank on which it stands has already approached within a perilous proximity to the old dilapidated planter's palace. Old Molly, of whom I have often before spoken to you, who lived here in the days of the prosperity and grandeur of "Hampton," still clings to the relics of her old master's former magnificence, and with a pride worthy of old Caleb of Ravenswood showed me through the dismantled decaying rooms and over the remains of the dairy, displaying a capacious fish box or well, where, in the good old days, the master's supply was kept in fresh salt water till required for table. Her prideful lamentations over the departure of all this quondam glory were ludicrous and pathetic; but, while listening with some amusement to the jumble of grotesque descriptions, through which her impression of the immeasurable grandeur and nobility of the house she served was the predominant feature, I could not help contrasting the present state of the estate with that which she described, and wondering why it should have become, as it undoubtedly must have done, so infinitely less productive a property than in the old Major's time.

Before closing this letter, I have a mind to transcribe to you the entries for today recorded in a sort of daybook, where I put down very succinctly the number of people who visit me, their petitions and ailments, and also such special particulars concerning them as seem to me worth recording. You will see how miserable the physical condition of many of these poor creatures is; and their physical condition, it is insisted by those who uphold this evil system, is the only part of it which is prosperous, happy, and compares well with that of Northern laborers. Judge from the details I now send you; and never forget, while reading them, that the people on this plantation are well off, and consider themselves well off, in comparison with the slaves on some of the neighboring estates.

*Fanny* has had six children; all dead but one. She came to beg to have her work in the field lightened.

*Nanny* has had three children; two of them are dead. She came to implore that the rule of sending them into the field three weeks after their confinement might be altered.

*Leah,* Caesar's wife, has had six children; three are dead.

*Sophy,* Lewis's wife, came to beg for some old linen. She is suffering fearfully; has had ten children; five of them are dead. The principal favor she asked was a piece of meat, which I gave her.

*Sally,* Scipio's wife, has had two miscarriages and three children born, one of whom is dead. She came complaining of incessant pain and weakness in her back. This woman was a mulatto daughter of a slave called Sophy, by a white man of the name of Walker, who visited the plantation.

*Charlotte,* Renty's wife, had had two miscarriages, and was with child again. She was almost crippled with rheumatism, and showed me a pair of poor swollen knees that made my heart ache. I have promised her a pair of flannel trousers, which I must forthwith set about making.

*Sarah,* Stephen's wife; this woman's case and history were alike deplorable. She had had four miscarriages, had brought seven children into the world, five of whom were dead, and was again with child. She complained of dreadful pains in the back, and an internal tumor which swells with the exertion of working in the fields; probably, I think, she is ruptured. She told me she had once been mad and had run into the woods, where she contrived to elude discovery for some time, but was at last tracked and brought back, when she was tied up by the arms, and heavy logs fastened to her feet, and was severely flogged. After this she contrived to escape again, and lived for some time skulking in the woods, and she supposes mad, for when she was taken again she was entirely naked. She subsequently recovered from this derangement, and seems now just like all the other poor creatures who come to me for help and pity. I suppose her constant childbearing and hard labor in the fields at the same time may have produced the temporary insanity.

*Sukey,* Bush's wife, only came to pay her respects. She had had four miscarriages; had brought eleven children into the world, five of whom are dead.

*Molly,* Quambo's wife, also only came to see me. Hers was the best account I have yet received; she had had nine children, and six of them were still alive.

This is only the entry for today, in my diary, of the people's complaints and visits. Can you conceive a more wretched picture than that which it exhibits of the conditions under which these women live? Their cases are in no respect singular, and though they come with pitiful entreaties that I will help them with some alleviation of their pressing physical distresses, it seems to me marvelous with what desperate patience (I write it advisedly, patience of utter despair) they endure their sorrow-laden existence. Even the poor wretch who told that miserable story of insanity, and lonely hiding in the swamps, and scourging when she was found, and of her renewed madness and flight, did so in a sort of low, plaintive, monotonous murmur of misery, as if such sufferings were "all in the day's work."

I ask these questions about their children because I think the number they bear as compared with the number they rear a fair gauge of the effect of the system on their own health and that of their offspring. There was hardly one of these women, as you will see by the details I have noted of their ailments, who might not have been a candidate for a bed in a hospital, and they had come to me after working all day in the fields.

# Emily Burke

## From *Pleasure and Pain: Reminiscences of Georgia in the 1840s*

### LETTER III

Savannah received its name, originally, from its general appearance, which was justly called a savanna, a term that signifies an open, marshy plain, without timber, as its first settlers found it. But though it still retains its first name with merely the addition of one letter, it can no longer be literally applied to it. For now it looks like a city built in a forest, so numerous are the shade trees in every part of it. Beneath these trees, the lamps are suspended that give light to the city in the evening. These lights, interspersed with the many long black shadows that fall everywhere around, heighten the romantic effect that the first sight of these streets would naturally produce in the mind of one unaccustomed to Southern scenes.

The city is laid out in squares, each of which is surrounded by a beautiful growth of ornamental trees. The Pride of India is the most common, the preference being given to these trees because they attain their full growth sooner than any others. They become large trees in six or seven years, and, when they arrive at maturity, they are as large as our oldest elms. For a long time in the summer season they are completely covered with blossoms in color like our lilac and growing in clusters like the snowball. Then the blossoms are succeeded by a yellow, dry kind of fruit about as large as our English cherry, which remains on the tree till the blossoms again appear.

Many of the squares in Savannah are left open for places of public resort and promenade and planted with beautiful shade trees of various kinds. In the midst of these grounds, wells are dug for the accommodation of the public, there being but few, if any, private wells and reservoirs of water. One of these beautiful sites is ornamented with a splendid monument erected to the memory of General Pulaski,* who lost his life near this spot in the defence of our country's liberties. As all these grounds are named from some particular circumstance, this is called the Monument square; another is called the Market square, because the city market stands upon it, and so on.

On the evening of my arrival, seeing none but white people in the streets, the fact that I was in a land where the largest proportion of its inhabitants were slaves did not occur to my mind. Neither was I forcibly reminded of this unpleasant truth till the following morning. For all the slaves in the city are obliged to retire within the precincts of their own dwellings at eight o'clock in the evening, the hour when the bell rings to summon the city patrol to their several posts. After that hour every slave who is found in the streets without a passport is taken up and confined in the guard house till he has had a trial. If then he can prove he had a reasonable excuse for being out at an unreasonable hour, he is liberated. If it is found he is a runaway slave, then he is advertised for a certain number of days and sold at public auction, if the owner of the slave does not make his appearance and prove property before the advertisement is out. A pail carried by a slave in the evening serves for a legal passport. The propriety of this law I do not understand unless it is this: that a slave, running away, would not be likely to encumber himself with so much of a burden, and, besides, the pail would naturally signify an errand.

Soon after I had taken tea, I retired to a chamber already prepared for my reception. Words cannot express how sweet it was to be once more where the creaking of masts and the eternal clattering of the ropes and

---

*General Lafayette dedicated the cornerstone of a monument at Johnson Square in 1825. This monument, completed in 1830, honored both Count Casimir Pulaski and General Nathanial Greene until a separate monument to Pulaski was erected at Monterey Square in the 1850's.

sails and the dashing of the waves against the sides of the ship could no longer reach my ears. I could not for some time sleep, I so much enjoyed the consciousness of being where I was not constantly tumbled from one side of my bed to the other, and where too I was not expecting to be thrown out of my bed if I did not exert all my strength in clinging to it all night!

In the morning, no sooner had the sky begun to look a little grey than a confused jargon of strange sounds broke upon my ear. I arose and threw aside my curtain to learn the cause that had deprived me of my morning nap, when to my surprise I saw a great many colored persons, with now and then a white man among them, and animals of various kinds, among which mules were the most numerous, all of which were assembled together under a sort of shelter. That, from the appearance of things, I soon judged to be the city market, a description of which, perhaps, will not be uninteresting to those who have not visited the South. It is not a closed building like our markets at the North but merely a roof, supported by pillars. This roof covers quite an extent of ground, laid with bricks for a floor. In the middle stands a pump, where water is obtained that is used in the market. This building is furnished with stalls, owned by individuals in the city who send produce there to sell.

In each of these stalls stands a servant woman to sell her master's property, who is careful to deck out his saleswoman in the most gaudy colors to make her as conspicuous as possible that she may be successful in trade. I once heard a gentleman, whose saleswoman had not been very successful, say, "he must get her a new handkerchief for her head and see if she would not sell more!" Bonnets are not worn by the colored people at the South, not even to church. The fashion of their headdress is a sort of turban, made by folding a cotton handkerchief in that peculiar kind of way known only to themselves. They select for this purpose the most gaudy that can be found. I never saw any of the kind before or since. During my stay in Georgia, I saw many of those red and yellow articles worn by the colored people. These turbans are so arranged, as to entirely conceal their own hair. But those who are particularly desirous to make a good external apperance wear false braids and curls as long as those that grace the face of any white lady.

The market is free for trade from five o'clock in the morning till ten. Then the bell rings and all are obliged to disperse and take with them their unsold articles, for everything that remains on the ground after ten o'clock belongs to the keeper. Trade is not allowed in the market excepting on Saturday evening, when it is more crowded than at any other time. For the people come then to purchase for the Sabbath, and many go just because they want to see a great crowd. It has been estimated that on some pleasant evenings there are no less than four thousand people in the market at one time. Here almost every eatable thing can be found. Vegetables fresh from the garden are sold the year round. All kinds of fish, both shell and finny, may be had there; birds of all kinds, both tame and wild; and the most delicious tropical fruits, as well as those which are brought from cold countries. People travel a great distance for the purpose of buying and selling in the market. I have known women to come one hundred miles to sell the products of their own industry.

* * *

## LETTER VIII

Notwithstanding the great precaution which is used to prevent the mental improvement of the slaves, many of them steal knowledge enough to enable them to read and write with ease. It is often the case that the white children of a family impart much of that information they have acquired at school to those among the black children who happen to be their favorites. For it must be understood that not only every little boy and girl has each a favorite slave, but also every young man and woman has his favorite servants, to whom he not only often imparts much useful information but confides in them more as companions than merely waiting men and women. And it is not uncommon to see the favorite slave nearly as wise as his master. A lad about eleven years of age in the family where I once visited made it his practice, unknown to the family, to spend an hour or two every day in teaching a black boy to read, an act exposing the father of the noble hearted boy to a heavy fine if found out. This fact came to my knowledge by a colored woman who had sufficient confidence in me to believe I should not betray the child.

Clerks often instruct the slaves who labor in the back stores, and many by this means acquire a decent education. I have often seen a young man belonging to one of the largest firms in Savannah who could read, write, cipher and transact business so correctly that his masters often committed important trusts to his care. The firm valued him at fifteen hundred dollars. He read with great eagerness every Northern paper that came within his reach and had by this means gained a good knowledge of the political state of our country. At the time I was there, he was deeply interested in the election of President Harrison, as were the slaves generally in the Southern states, for they were all Harrison men. And they were bold enough to assert publicly that "when William Henry Harrison became President of the United States they should have their freedom!"

I do not know that ever I was more deeply impressed with a sense of the cruelty of depriving the slaves of the means of instruction than one evening while on my way to my room I met two little colored children, apparently about eight years old, trying to find out between themselves some of the letters of the alphabet. It appeared that one of them had found an old, crumpled, soiled leaf torn from a toy-book, upon which a few of the large letters were still legible, and then they had seated themselves upon the stairs to study them out. One of the children was saying just as I reached them that she heard somebody say that the round letter was O; the other replied that she heard such a little girl say the straight letter was L; so alternately each was teacher and scholar. Oh, if the children at the North, who are almost compelled to go to school, could have witnessed that scene, it would I think have taught them a lesson not soon to be forgotten.

As a general thing the slaves in the city wear good clothing. Many even dress extravagantly and decorate their persons with a great deal of costly jewelry. I have seen colored men with no less than six or eight rings upon one finger. Many in the city have good houses and expensive furniture. I have seen ladies in the streets with such light complexions and dressed so elegantly that when told they were Negroes I could not willingly credit the assertion. I ought here to say that at the South all who have a drop of the African blood in their veins, however white their skins may be, are called Negroes. But those who dress and live in the manner above described, purchase their time, and all they can earn besides paying a certain sum per week or month to their masters they use in any manner they choose. A gentleman informed me he had a slave who accumulated more property than himself after paying nine dollars per month for his time!

It is quite common for a master to give his slave all his time, if he will take care of himself after he has become so old and worn out as to be of no service to him. It often happens that infirm old slaves are by the death or failure of their masters left without any sort of a home or means of subsistence. As a remedy for this evil in Savannah a kind of asylum has been prepared for all such helpless old people among the black population. But from what I have been able to learn respecting the institution it is next to having no home at all, and those who avail themselves of the comforts it affords only do it when every other resource for the means of subsistence fails them. I have known poor old men almost bent to the ground by hard labor, with locks which age had bleached as white as newly washed wool, rather than to go to this asylum travel from one plantation to another, begging a potato from one slave and a morsel of hominy from another, sleeping at night in some corner of an old outhouse or in the woods, till they were finally compelled by those who thought themselves doing a deed of mercy to take up their residence in a place as much dreaded by these unfortunate creatures as the almshouse is at the North by poor people.

But those among this down-trodden race of people in our country, whom I commiserated as much as any while in Savannah, were the little chimney sweeps. These were the most forlorn, half-starved, emaciated looking beings I ever beheld. Their masters always accompanied them about the city, because they could not trust them to go to their labor alone, for they were invariably obliged to beat them before they would ascend a chimney, the task was so revolting. But notwithstanding this task seemed so dreadful, extreme hunger often compelled them to climb upon the outside of the house in the nighttime and then descend the chimney to steal something to eat.

In the city it is not unusual to hear of colored boys gaining admittance to a house by descending through the chimney. An instance of this kind came under my observation while in Savannah. Two young men who boarded at one of the public houses, lodged in rooms over their office, one of which they had furnished for a parlor. It was their custom to send a servant into this room every evening to prepare a table of refreshments, which having done, he would lock the door and hand the key to his masters. At length they discovered that depredations were committed every evening upon their wines, cigars, etc. And, notwithstanding they took great pains, they were not able to get the least clue to the source of this mischief, till one evening when going into the room as usual, they found the culprit lying upon the floor in a state of intoxication. When he recovered his senses sufficiently to give an account of himself, he confessed he had been in the practice of entering the room by the way of the chimney and taking whatever he wanted. This time he had partaken too freely of champagne to escape detection.

The slaves carry all their burdens upon their heads, and to me it is quite unaccountable how they can sustain such weights as they do in this manner. They will transport from one place to another tubs of water, large, heavy, iron-bound trunks or any other burden they can raise to their heads. I have seen the man who had the care of the city lamps going from one street to another with a ladder in one hand, a large wooden box in the other and a heavy can of oil on his head. Even the white children often learn from their nurses to carry things in this way. It is quite common to see a little group of school girls with all their books on their heads going to or returning from school, and almost the first thing the little child tries to do when it begins to walk is to balance its toys upon its head. I have often heard the old washerwomen complain of pain in their necks after supporting on their heads a large tub of water or basket of wet clothes.

The dog is the Negro's favorite pet, and almost every man and woman owns one or two of these faithful animals. Consequently they are exceedingly numerous in the city. Efforts are often made to diminish their numbers, but they seldom avail much, as their owners generally succeed in concealing them. In the daytime the dogs usually left the city to seek their food in the woods, but they always returned at night to the city.

And they often collected together in such companies on moonlight nights that people could not sleep in consequence of their howling and barking. This circumstance made the poor beasts many enemies.

Just hearing the sound of martial music, I am reminded of the appearance and of the manner in which military parades are conducted at the South. In the first place all their musicians are colored men, for the white gentlemen would consider it quite beneath their dignity to perform such a piece of drudgery as to play for a company while doing military duty. These colored musicians are dressed in the full uniform of the company to which they belong, and, on the morning of the day in which the several companies are to be called out, each band in uniform, one at a time, marches through all the streets to summon all the soldiers to the parade ground. This performance also calls out all the servants that can obtain permission to attend the training, and it is not a few of them that not only follow but go before the companies wherever they march. They are excessively fond of such scenes, and crowds of men, women and children never fail of being present on all such occasions, some carrying their masters' young children on their heads and shoulders, while many are seen with large trays on their heads, loaded with fruit, sweetmeats and various kinds of drinks to sell to those who always wish to purchase on such days. In Savannah there are five of that kind of companies that exist in all the states and are called by all names, composed of all such persons as only perform military duty because they are obliged. In Savannah they are called ragamuffins, and I never heard a name more appropriately applied. Scarcely any two were dressed alike or took the same step, and, whenever I saw them approaching, some with a shoe on one foot and a boot on the other, some with their guns wrong end up and others with them on their shoulders, wearing their knapsacks bottom up and wrong side out, I could not help thinking one might suppose they were learning how to catch up their guns and knapsacks and effect the most speedy escape in time of danger instead of facing an enemy. The independent companies are a credit to the militia system. They are well disciplined and wear elegant and expensive uniforms. The Hussars are a noble and splendid company, mounted on fine spirited steeds so well-trained that they understand the word of command nearly as well as their riders.

## LETTER IX

After having spent several months in the city, I left it for a residence in the country during the summer season. As we had a journey of fifty or sixty miles to perform in one day by private conveyance, it was necessary to set out very early in the morning. Accordingly, long before the dawn of day or the morning sun began to lift the dense white fog from the tops of the trees and houses, the carriages were at the door and all things ready for our departure. One friend abundantly supplied me with the richest tropical fruits and sweetmeats for my journey, another loaded me with papers, periodicals and books, while all heaped upon me their best farewell wishes. Never did I feel sadder when taking leave of a place than I did that morning.

On leaving the city, we took a southeasterly course, and a few moments' ride carried us into the dark woods, where certainly, if I had not been traveling in a little caravan, I should have had some apprehensions concerning our safety. But our company was large and well provided with means of defence, which is always necessary when traveling in the woods of Georgia and was particularly so at that time on account of the Indians, by whom many were robbed and killed that year while traveling. Seeing that our personal safety had been cared and provided for, I endeavored to make myself as comfortable as possible. The further we went the more dark and gloomy everything grew. Trees on each side of us, heavy with moss, stretched out their limbs over our pathway, shutting out almost every cheerful ray from the sun, which at that time we greatly needed, it being the winter season, and the morning was cold and damp. In this manner we rode hour after hour, meeting with nothing to vary the scene save now and then a little country cart drawn by a mule and conducted by a woman or a slave with a swine or deer or bunch of live fowls upon his head going to market. Occasionally our approach would start a timid hare from the path or scare up some large wild bird, which then would flap its lazy wings and disappear from our sight.

Finally, about the middle of the forenoon, we passed a building in the woods by the wayside that I supposed was a barn, yet why it should be there, so far from any cultivated field or human habitation, I could not

divine. Consequently I made inquiry concerning the matter of the gentleman I was riding with. He looked quite surprised at my interrogation,
and certainly I was no less so at his answer, when he said it was a meeting
house! I then asked, as a matter of course, where the people came from
who worshipped there? He replied: "Oh, out of the woods, all around
here." But I was no more enlightened upon the subject. It was all beyond
my comprehension what the church was there for or from whence the
people could come who assembled in it, for we had then rode perhaps
twenty miles and had not before seen a single spot of cleared land or
anything that bore the least resemblance to a building, and the whole
remained a mystery to me till I had been in the country long enough to
know more of its manners and customs.

I had observed, all the way along, little dark avenues leading off into
the woods on our right and left, but never for once dreamed they were
more than paths made by lumbermen while clearing timber. But each one
of them leads to a plantation. One might travel a week on the main road
and see nothing of the plantations. To have a view of these, one must
turn off from the highway and pass through one of those narrow avenues
for two, three or four miles, then after passing a gate he will soon find
himself among luxuriant crops of corn, cotton and tobacco. So I was
much nearer the abodes of men than I supposed through all that long day
in which I thought we were all the time going farther and farther from
human habitations.

In such a path as this we traveled long after I had begun anxiously to
look out for an inn, greatly needing rest and refreshment. But just as
I began to despair of finding the desired entertainment that day, as the
woods all the time seemed to grow thicker and darker, the gentleman in
the forward carriage who took the lead of our little party stopped and
called out to the company, "if it was not time for dinner." I was not a
little surprised as well as amused and began to think this was going to
be another incomprehensible meeting-house affair. But all mystery vanished when I saw saddlebags, portmanteaus and wallets brought out and
emptied of their contents upon a cloth spread upon the ground. Then I
found, for the first time, how convenient it was to be independent of a
public house, and that our necessities could be well supplied right in the

woods and save our half dollars into the bargain. For our good host had well considered our wants before leaving the city.

After a little rest and man and beast had sufficiently partaken of their repast, we set forward on our journey again, while the plumed songsters sent forth their sweetest and most enchanting notes to cheer us on. We often passed in the course of the day wells of water by the wayside, dug for the comfort of the wayfaring man and his beast. About the middle of the forenoon we came to a river where we had a toll-bridge to pass. Here was a toll-house and blacksmith's shop, the first buildings we had seen, excepting the meeting-house, after leaving Savannah. We tarried there a little while to have one of the carriages repaired and then plunged into the dark woods again.

Near evening we reached a small settlement on a wide creek where large boats and sloops run up from South Newport River to land various kinds of merchandise. It was one of the sweetest little spots I ever saw. Weeping willows grew plentifully up and down the shores of the creek, extending their slender branches over the barges there lying upon their oars, while the sailors who manned them added the sound of the bugle and violin to the music of the surrounding forest in chanting the evening's parting lay to setting sun. Now for a short season we enjoyed the evening twilight, then the darkness of night began to close in upon us. Trees on either hand formed arches above our heads, and, though occasional openings among the boughs suffered us to get a peep at a star or two, the darkness before us the remainder of the evening appeared impenetrable, yet we always found the darkness to recede as we advanced.

At length we came to one of those dark avenues I have before spoken of. After having gone about two miles in this road, so narrow we were often obliged to make use of much adroitness in order to avoid the limbs of the trees, we came to a gate which opened upon an extensive plantation, as I rightly judged was the one to which we were bound. At the farther extremity of this wide plain we saw faint lights through the branches of a cluster of trees, when one of the company observed that when we reached the spot where those lights were we should complete our day's journey. It was grateful news to me, for then it was past eight o'clock, and, besides being chilled through by a cold December dew, I was never more faint and weary. When we arrived at the planter's house we were met at the gate by half a score of servants, who came out to take the horses and assist us from our carriages. I was then conducted beneath a beautiful growth of shade trees, then up a short flight of steps on to a broad piazza and from thence into one of the principal rooms of the house, of which in my next letter I will try to give you some description.

## LETTER X

The house stood upon four posts about five feet from the ground, allowing a free circulation of air beneath as well as forming a fine covert for the hounds, goats and all the domestic fowls. It was only one story high, though much taller than buildings of the same description at the North. It was divided into four apartments below and two in the roof and furnished with two broad piazzas, one in front of the building, where there is always the gentleman's sitting room, and one on the back of the house, where the servants await their master's orders. The building was slightly covered with boards, arranged like clapboards to shed the rain. This was the entire thickness of the walls, there being no ceiling, lathing or plastering within. The floors were all single and laid in so unwork-manlike manner I could often see the ground beneath when the carpets were not on the floor, and they are always taken up in the summer to make the apartments cooler. The roof was covered with long shingles nailed to the timbers to save the expense of boards beneath, the ends of one tier just lapping upon the next, and this executed so shammily that not only the wind but the light and rain often finds free access into the upper apartments through ten thousand holes among the shingles. Two chimneys, one upon each end, built of turfs, sticks, blocks of wood and occasionally a brick plastered over with clay, ornamented the outside of the house. The windows were furnished with panes of glass, a luxury but few enjoy. The above is as true a description as I can give of the singular fashioned house to which I was conducted on my arrival in the country.

My appearance there was altogether unexpected by the whole family, therefore there was no small stir nor little inquiry among the Negroes and the younger members of the family what I was there for, who I was and from whence the strange lady had come who had so unexpectedly dropped in among them. From the room in which I sat, I could look into all the other apartments about me, and I was not a little amused to see the many dark forms with bare feet and noiseless steps flitting about from one place to another to get a peep at the newcomer and to hear the whisperings on all sides of me, of which I well understood I was the subject. The servants would come to the windows on the outside and lift up one corner of the curtain to steal a look at me, others would creep softly up the steps of the piazza and peep into the door, while one old woman, less bashful than the others, ventured into the room, dressed in a coarse oznaburg gown extending a little below the knees with bare feet, neck and arms, and came before me and made a low curtsey, accompanied by the formal salutation, "How de Misse," and then sat down on the floor at a little distance from me and in a very respectful manner entered into conversation. She was one of the oldest women on the plantation, and, though she was one of the field hands, she had free access to her master's house, and she possessed such a good share of common sense that her master and mistress always consulted her on important matters, and she was looked up to and reverenced by the whole family as a sort of mother. While I remained on the plantation she frequently called at my room to spend an hour or two in conversation, and I never failed of obtaining some useful information from her on these occasions.

All this time I was eagerly watching to see if I could discover any preparations going on preliminary to a supper, but as I could discover none and it was then near nine o'clock, I had just summoned all my fortitude to meet my hungry fate with the most becoming resignation, when a robust young woman made her appearance up the steps of the back piazza into the room where I was and brought out two or three large tables, nearly reaching from one side of the room to the other, and began to lay them for supper. Presently another of the same description came from the same quarter, bringing the eatables. When all these preparations were complete, the tea-bell was rung from the piazza, which to my great surprise (for I had seen only two or three white persons, excepting those I came with) brought around the table a family of twenty or twenty-five persons, consisting partly of transient members and visitors. Where they all came from was as mysterious to me as where those people lived who attended the church, for I had not yet forgotten about the meeting house in the woods.

Soon after tea I was conducted to the room I was to occupy while a resident in the family, one of the chambers in the roof. Though my first impressions concerning my future comfort in it were very unfavorable, yet I found, after I had learned that my accommodations for that place were of a superior order and when I had had a view of the surrounding scenery from my windows, that it was one of the most delightful of situations. But in the darkness of evening when I first entered my apartment, shutting out from my view every object but the rough walls around me, it could not be thought strange if my forebodings were not of the most pleasing kind. Though the house was of but one story, it was so constructed that I had three windows in my chamber. These were closed with heavy board shutters. The floor was smooth and white, and the walls ceiled to the windows, the remainder being rough boards. Overhead there was nothing to be seen but the unfinished timbers and shingles, warped into all shapes. The furniture was brought from the North and consisted of all those articles usually used in furnishing such rooms and looked very natural, all but my bed. This had very high posts and was covered with a spread so small that it gave the bed the appearance of standing on stilts! My doubts concerning my future convenience did not at all diminish by taking a view of the surrounding objects. Nevertheless I made haste to avail myself of all the comforts my apartment afforded and shortly was nicely ensconced beneath the quilts and coverlets. But when I had extinguished my light I was utterly thrown into the horrors to find, instead of a close warm shelter for my head, a complete sieve was stretched out over me, and I could not shut my eyes to sleep for perfect terror at those thousands of holes in the roof, through which the light of the then rising moon was staring in upon me. They seemed to me through the greater part of that night to be so many cold and freezing eyes trying to look me out of countenance!

In the morning, on throwing open my blinds and taking a view of the surrounding scenery, I began to feel much more reconciled to my situation than on the previous evening. At the southeast the ever rolling Atlantic stretched itself out as far as the eye could reach, and where the sky and water seemed to meet now and then a sloop would lose itself to the sight or a little white speck would appear which would grow larger and larger till a ship under full sail would ride majestically over the mighty waves. On all other sides of the plantation the dark green forest of the long leafed pines completely hemmed us in, separating us from all other plantations and leaving us a little world by ourselves. As I said before, the plantation was an extensive plain, which at this season of the year was covered with the decaying stalks of the last year's crops, waiting to be gathered and burned to make room for a new harvest. The dry, black cotton stalks were still standing, and, though it was very early in the morning, the slaves were busy in pulling from the bursting burs the snow-white cotton. Here and there in different parts of the field the little curling smokes betrayed the bonfires at which the women warmed their frost-chilled fingers. The plantation was beautifully dotted with oak and mulberry trees. I found also that on this as all other plantations, it required more than one building to make up a family residence and that, instead of having all the necessary apartments under one roof as at the North, there were nearly as many roofs as rooms. In my next letter I will speak of all these separate little buildings.

# John Brown

## From *Slave Life in Georgia: A Narrative of the Life, Sufferings, and Escape of John Brown, a Fugitive Slave*

### CHAPTER III
#### *I Am Sold Again—How I Fared*

Our journey lasted six weeks, as we made a good many stoppages by the way, to enable the speculator, Finney, to buy up, and change away, and dispose of his slaves. I do not recollect the names of all the places we passed through. We crossed the Roanoke river by ferry, and went on to Halifax, and from there to Raleigh in North Carolina. Several incidents occurred on the road, of which I will relate only two.

When I joined the coffle, there was in it a negro woman named Critty, who had belonged to one Hugh Benford. She was married, in the way that slaves are, but as she had no children, she was compelled to take a second husband. Still she did not have any offspring. This displeased her master, who sold her to Finney. Her anguish was intense, and within about four days from the time I saw her first, she died of grief. It happened in the night, whilst we were encamped in the woods. We set off in the morning, leaving her body there. We noticed, however, that two of Finney's associates remained behind, as we conjectured to dispose of the corpse. They fetched up with us again about two hours after.

The other incident was the stealing of a young negro girl. An old lady whose name I do not remember, and who was going into Georgia, travelled with the drove for the sake of society. She was accompanied by her waiting-maid, a young woman about twenty years of age, and of smart appearance. When we stopped at night, the old lady would be driven to some planter's house to lodge, and her horses be sent back to feed with ours. The girl remained with us. This was cheaper for the old lady than having to pay for the keep of her horses and her maid. In the morning her horses would be sent to the place where she had lodged, and she would drive on until she overtook us on the road, and then take up her maid. Finney determined to steal this girl. One morning, we being then on our way through South Carolina, the old lady's horses were sent as usual, to the house where she had staid the night, and we went on. Instead, however, of keeping the direct road, Finney turned off and went through the woods, so that we gave the poor girl's mistress the slip. She was then forced to get up in the wagon with Finney, who brutally ill-used her, and permitted his companions to treat her in the same manner. This continued for several days, until we got to Augusta, in the state of Georgia, where Finney sold her. Our women talked about this very much, and many of them cried, and said it was a great shame.

At last we stopped at one Ben Tarver's place in Jones' County, Georgia. This man was a Methodist Minister, and had a cotton plantation, and a good many slaves. He had a great name for possessing the fastest cotton-picking negroes in the whole county, and they were frequently set to work with others against time for wagers. He had an overseer who did the best part of his flogging, but he used the cow-hide himself occasionally, and they said he hit worse than the overseer; but I cannot say if it was so, as he never flogged me. I know he did not give his slaves any thing to eat till noon-day, and then no more again until nine at night. They got corn, which they made into cake, but I never knew them to have any meat, and as far as I was able to learn, I do not think any was given to them. He was reputed to be a very bad master, but a very good preacher.

During the time I staid there, which was two weeks, Finney used to take out his slaves every day, to try and sell them, bringing those back whom he failed to dispose of. Those who did not go out with Finney, for the market, were made to work in Tarver's cotton-fields, but they did not get any thing extra to eat, though he profited by their labour. In these two weeks Finney disposed of a good many of his drove, and he became anxious to sell the rest, for he wanted to take another journey into Virginia, on a fresh speculation. One day I was dressed in a new pair of pantaloons and a new shirt, made from part of the tilt of a waggon in which we children sometimes slept. I soon found out why I was made so smart, for I was taken to Milledgeville, with some other lads, and there put up at auction.

This happened to me some time in the month of March. The sale took place in a kind of shed. The auctioneer did not like my appearance. He told Finney in private, who was holding me by the hand, that I was old and hard-looking, and not well grown, and that I should not fetch a price. In truth I was not much to look at. I was worn down by fatigue and poor living till my bones stuck up almost through my skin, and my hair was burnt to a brown red from exposure to the sun. I was not, however, very well pleased to hear myself run down. I remember Finney answered the auctioneer that I should be sure to grow a big-made man, and bade him, if he doubted his judgment, examine my feet, which were large, and proved that I would be strong and stout some day. My looks and my condition, nevertheless, did not recommend me, and I was knocked down to a man named Thomas Stevens, for three hundred and fifty dollars: so Finney made forty dollars by me. Thomas Stevens could not pay cash for me, so I went back to Ben Tarver's that night, but next morning Finney and one of his associates, Hartwell Tarver, Ben's brother, took me round to Stevens' place, and the money having been paid, I was again handed over to a new master.

Thomas Stevens' plantation was on the Clinton road, in Baldwin County, and about eight miles from Milledgeville. He was a man of middle height, with a fair skin, but had black hair. He was of Welsh origin. His countenance always wore a laughing expression, but this did not indicate his disposition, which was dreadfully savage. Still, he always laughed, even when in a passion. In fact, at such times, and they were very frequent, he laughed more than at any other. Originally he had been a poor jobbing carpenter. He then set up a still, and made some money by distilling whiskey. He next purchased a plantation and stocked it with negroes, continuing his trade as a maltster of Indian corn, and a distiller. He was a very bad and a dishonest man, and used to force his negroes to go out at night and steal corn from his neighbours. His plan was to gain their negroes over by a present of whiskey. They would then agree to have a quantity of corn ready at a specified place and by a certain hour, which he would then send his own people to fetch away. He always took good care, however, to keep out of the way himself when the stealing was going on, so that if any of his slaves should be caught, he might take sides against them, and his own dishonesty not be suspected. The stolen corn used to be carried to his mill, which was about half a mile from his still-house, where it was taken in by an old negro named Uncle Billy, who had to account for all that was brought. Stevens contrived to keep a pretty correct account himself, for as he was a great rogue, he had no confidence in anybody, and was always trying to prevent himself from being cheated.

I was sent to the still-house, and placed under Uncle Billy. I had to carry whiskey from the still-house to the store, and meal from the mill-house to the still. I also had to carry his breakfast to a slave of the name of John Glasgow, who was at that time employed up in the woods chopping billets for the still. This lasted the whole winter, during which season only, the still was worked. It could not be done in the summer, because the heat turned the malted meal sour and rendered it useless for making whiskey. When the time came for "pitching the crop," that is, for putting in seeds, I was set to labour in the fields along with the rest, clearing the ground, cutting down corn-stalks and burning them, and such like. I was not used to this heavy work; besides which my heart was heavy thinking of my mother and my relations, and I got down-hearted and discouraged, which made me forget my duties, and do what I was set about very indifferently. Then my master would flog me severely, and swear at me the most abominable oaths. I used to feel very bad, and wish to die, and only for John Glasgow I think it must have come to that soon.

I was one of the gang that worked with John Glasgow, who used to tell me not to cry after my father and mother, and relatives, for I should never see them any more. He encouraged me to try and forget them, for

my own sake, and to do what I was bidden. He said I must try, too, to
be honest and upright, and if I ever could get to England, where he came
from, and conducted myself properly, folks would respect me as much
as they did a white man. These kind words from John Glasgow, gave me
better heart, and inspired me with a longing to get to England, which I
made up my mind I would try and do some day. I got along a little better
after a while, but for all that my master would flog me for the least thing.

One day, and not long after I had been there, a sudden heavy fresh
in the river caused the mill-dam to overflow, and the mill-door being
locked, nobody could get in to raise the flood-gate. I was sent to the
house to fetch the key. The house was about a mile off, and I ran every
step of the way there. Indeed, I ran so fast, that I lost an old hat I used
to wear, for I would not stay to pick it up. My mistress made me take a
horse out of the stable to get back quicker, so I was not gone very long
in all. After the flood-gates were opened, Stevens came to me, and called
me to him from the spring-head where I was, cleaning out the leaves
from the water-troughs. This spring-head was up the side of a hill, and
troughs were laid down from it to the still-house, on tall stakes, so as to
throw the water up to the top of the still-house. Stevens was standing at
the bottom of the hill and I went down to him. He began swearing at
me directly, and asked me why I did not run when he sent me to fetch
the key.

"I did run, Sir," I said.

"You ran, did you, Sir?" said he again, with another oath.

"Yes, Sir," I answered.

"Oh, you ran, did you?" And as he said this he took out his knife and
cut a hickory rod from the hedge, with which he beat me until it was
destroyed.

"Now, Sir, you tell me you ran, eh?" he asked.

"Yes, Sir," I answered; for I would not tell him to the contrary, though
the blood was trickling down my back.

"Oh, you ran, did you?" he said again, and cut another rod, with
which he beat me as before.

I do not know how it was that the pain did not make me cry. It did
not, however, but seemed to harden me; or perhaps my feelings were

benumbed, for you may be whipped sometimes till sensation is almost gone. When he saw I did not cry, he swore at me louder, and said,

"Why don't you cry, Sir, why don't you cry?"

It was of no use his asking me, for I could not cry, and would not answer.

He cut a third rod, and repeating the same questions, "why I didn't run," when I was sent after the key, and "why I didn't cry," beat me with it till that was worn out.

In this way he cut five rods, all of which he used upon my poor back in the same way. Uncle Billy was in the still-house, whilst Stevens was punishing me in this manner, and came running up.

"Oh, Massa," he said, "don't kill the poor boy. Perhaps he hasn't got sense to cry. Don't, please, Massa; please don't kill him."

Uncle Billy usually had some influence with Stevens, because he received the stolen corn up at the meal-house, and knew a great deal about Stevens' business. But on this occasion his entreaties were all thrown away, for my master only swore the louder and hit me the harder. Uncle Billy wrung his hands and went down on his knees to him, still it was not of any use. I think he would have killed me, had not Hartwell Tarver just then rode up to tell him that Starling Finney had arrived from Virginia with a new drove of negroes, and was waiting at Ben Tarver's, to give him (Stevens) the pick of them. He was cutting another hickory rod when Hartwell Tarver came up, and took off his attention from me. I verily believe I owe my life to that accident. I was very bad after this heavy flogging, but I got over it after a while.

Another time Stevens went to see a man hanged at Milledgeville, and his wife set me to cut broomcorn during his absence. I accidentally broke the knife, in two places, in an attempt I made to cut more stalks in a handful, and so get through more work. I took the knife up to his wife, but when her husband came back she told him I had done it for devilment, that I might not have to do any more work. So he called me up and asked me about it. I told him the truth, and showed him how the accident happened. It was easy to see I was telling the truth, but he called me many horrible names, swore I was lying, and flogged me for an hour with the cowhide.

Stevens seemed to have a spite against me, especially after a particular time, when a mare in the team I used to drive died. She got overheated in the field, and would not eat her corn when I put her up at noon. I noticed it when I took her out again, in about an hour after, not knowing she was not fit to work. She dropped down and died in the plough. I was sent to tell my master to come and see the mare, and on my way, stopped in the stable, and shifted the uneaten corn out of the mare's bin into another, substituting the cobs that the other horse had left. I did this lest Stevens should go into the stable and see that the mare had not eaten her corn, and he should flog me for taking her out under those circumstances. The artifice succeeded so far, that he attributed the mare's death to her being overheated in the sun; but this did not save me from a very severe flogging.

From this time he led me a dreadful life, and became so savage to me, I used to dread to see him coming. I had only too good reason for my fears.

I was ploughing one day, some long time after the mare died, with what we call a buzzard plough. It is made so as to cut under the roots of the grass and weeds that choke the cotton, and must be used carefully, or it will go too deep, and leave the roots of the cotton-plant exposed to the sun, when the plant will wither and die. The share was loose on the helve, and would not run true, so I could not do my work quickly or well, as I had to keep stooping down to set the share true. Stevens saw me, came up, and asked me why I did not plough better. I explained to him why, and shewed him that the plough ran foul. I stooped for this purpose, and was cleaning the dirt off from the share with my hands, when he viciously raised his foot, which was heavily shod, and unexpectedly dealt me a kick with all his might. The blow struck me right between the eyes, breaking the bone of my nose, and cutting the leaders of the right eye, so that it turned quite round in its socket. I was stunned for the moment, and fell, my mouth filling with blood, which also poured from my nose and eyes. In spite of the pain, and though I could scarcely see, I got up and resumed my work, continuing it until the evening. John Glasgow then doctored my eye. He washed the blood from my face, and got a ball of tallow, and an old handkerchief from Aunt Sally, the cook up at the house. He gently pressed the ball of tallow, made warm, against the displaced eye, until he forced it back into its proper position, when he put some cotton over it, and bound it up with the handkerchief. In about a fortnight I was able to have the bandage removed, but my eye remained very bad, and it was more than two months before I could use it at all. The other eye was also seriously affected, the inflammation having extended to it. I have never been able to see so well since, and cannot now look long at print without suffering much pain. The letters seem cloudy. To this day my right eye has remained out of its proper place.

# William Craft

## From *Running a Thousand Miles for Freedom, or, The Escape of William and Ellen Craft from Slavery*

My wife was torn from her mother's embrace in childhood, and taken to a distant part of the country. She had seen so many other children separated from their parents in this cruel manner, that the mere thought of her ever becoming the mother of a child, to linger out a miserable existence under the wretched system of American slavery, appeared to fill her very soul with horror; and as she had taken what I felt to be an important view of her condition, I did not, at first, press the marriage, but agreed to assist her in trying to devise some plan by which we might escape from our unhappy condition, and then be married.

We thought of plan after plan, but they all seemed crowded with insurmountable difficulties. We knew it was unlawful for any public conveyance to take us as passengers, without our masters' consent. We were also perfectly aware of the startling fact, that had we left without this consent the professional slave-hunters would have soon had their ferocious bloodhounds baying on our track, and in a short time we should have been dragged back to slavery, not to fill the more favorable situations which we had just left, but to be separated for life, and put to the very meanest and most laborious drudgery; or else have been tortured to death as examples, in order to strike terror into the hearts of others, and thereby prevent them from even attempting to escape from their cruel taskmasters. It is a fact worthy of remark, that nothing seems to give the slaveholders so much pleasure as the catching and torturing of fugitives. They had much rather take the keen and poisonous lash, and with it cut their poor trembling victims to atoms, than allow one of them to escape to a free country, and expose the infamous system from which he fled.

The greatest excitement prevails at a slavehunt. The slaveholders and their hired ruffians appear to take more pleasure in this inhuman pursuit than English sportsmen do in chasing a fox or a stag. Therefore, knowing what we should have been compelled to suffer, if caught and taken back, we were more than anxious to hit upon a plan that would lead us safely to a land of liberty.

But, after puzzling our brains for years, we were reluctantly driven to the sad conclusion, that it was almost impossible to escape from slavery in Georgia, and travel 1,000 miles across the slave States. We therefore resolved to get the consent of our owners, be married, settle down in slavery, and endeavor to make ourselves as comfortable as possible under that system; but at the same time ever to keep our dim eyes steadily fixed upon the glimmering hope of liberty, and earnestly pray God mercifully to assist us to escape from our unjust thraldom.

We were married, and prayed and toiled on till December 1848, at which time (as I have stated) a plan suggested itself that proved quite successful, and in eight days after it was first thought of we were free from the horrible trammels of slavery, and glorifying God who had brought us safely out of a land of bondage.

Knowing that slaveholders have the privilege of taking their slaves to any part of the country they think proper, it occurred to me that, as my wife was nearly white, I might get her to disguise herself as an invalid gentleman, and assume to be my master, while I could attend as his slave, and that in this manner we might effect our escape. After I thought of the plan, I suggested it to my wife, but at first she shrank from the idea. She thought it was almost impossible for her to assume that disguise, and travel a distance of 1,000 miles across the slave States. However, on the other hand, she also thought of her condition. She saw that the laws under which we lived did not recognize her to be a woman, but a mere chattel, to be bought and sold, or otherwise dealt with as her owner might see fit. Therefore the more she contemplated her helpless condition, the more anxious she was to escape from it. So she said, "I think it is almost too much for us to undertake; however, I feel that God is on our side, and with his assistance, notwithstanding all the difficulties, we shall be able to succeed. Therefore, if you will purchase the disguise, I will try to carry out the plan."

But after I concluded to purchase the disguise, I was afraid to go to anyone to ask him to sell me the articles. It is unlawful in Georgia for a white man to trade with slaves without the master's consent. But, notwithstanding this, many persons will sell a slave any article that he can get the money to buy. Not that they sympathize with the slave, but merely because his testimony is not admitted in court against a free white person.

Therefore, with little difficulty I went to different parts of the town, at odd times, and purchased things piece by piece (except the trousers which she found necessary to make) and took them home to the house where my wife resided. She being a ladies' maid, and a favorite slave in the family, was allowed a little room to herself; and amongst other pieces of furniture which I had made in my overtime, was a chest of drawers; so when I took the articles home, she locked them up carefully in these drawers. No one about the premises knew that she had anything of the kind. So when we fancied we had everything ready the time was fixed for the flight. But we knew it would not do to start off without first getting our masters' consent to be away for a few days. Had we left without this, they would soon have had us back into slavery, and probably we should never have got another fair opportunity of even attempting to escape.

Some of the best slaveholders will sometimes give their favorite slaves a few days' holiday at Christmas time; so, after no little amount of perseverance on my wife's part, she obtained a pass from her mistress, allowing her to be away for a few days. The cabinetmaker with whom I worked gave me a similar paper, but said that he needed my services very much, and wished me to return as soon as the time granted was up. I thanked him kindly; but somehow I have not been able to make it convenient to return yet; and, as the free air of good old England agrees so well with my wife and our dear little ones, as well as with myself, it is not at all

likely we shall return at present to the "peculiar institution" of chains
and stripes.

On reaching my wife's cottage she handed me her pass, and I showed
mine, but at that time neither of us were able to read them. It is not only
unlawful for slaves to be taught to read, but in some of the States there
are heavy penalties attached, such as fines and imprisonment, which will
be vigorously enforced upon anyone who is humane enough to violate
the so-called law.

*   *   *

However, at first, we were highly delighted at the idea of having gained
permission to be absent for a few days; but when the thought flashed
across my wife's mind, that it was customary for travellers to register
their names in the visitors' book at hotels, as well as in the clearance or
Custom House book at Charleston, South Carolina—it made our spirits
droop within us.

So, while sitting in our little room upon the verge of despair, all at
once my wife raised her head, and with a smile upon her face, which was
a moment before bathed in tears, said, "I think I have it!" I asked what
it was. She said, "I think I can make a poultice and bind up my right
hand in a sling, and with propriety ask the officers to register my name
for me." I thought that would do.

It then occurred to her that the smoothness of her face might betray
her; so she decided to make another poultice, and put it in a white handkerchief to be worn under the chin, up the cheeks, and to tie over the
head. This nearly hid the expression of the countenance, as well as the
beardless chin.

The poultice is left off in the engraving, because the likeness could not
have been taken well with it on.

My wife, knowing that she would be thrown a good deal into the
company of gentlemen, fancied that she could get on better if she had
something to go over the eyes; so I went to a shop and bought a pair of
green spectacles. This was in the evening.

We sat up all night discussing the plan, and making preparations. Just
before the time arrived, in the morning, for us to leave, I cut off my

wife's hair square at the back of the head, and got her to dress in the disguise and stand out on the floor. I found that she made a most respectable looking gentleman.

My wife had no ambition whatever to assume this disguise, and would not have done so had it been possible to have obtained our liberty by more simple means; but we knew it was not customary in the South for ladies to travel with male servants; and therefore, notwithstanding my wife's fair complexion, it would have been a very difficult task for her to have come off as a free white lady, with me as her slave; in fact, her not being able to write would have made this quite impossible. We knew that no public conveyance would take us, or any other slave, as a passenger, without our masters' consent. This consent could never be obtained to pass into a free State. My wife's being muffled in the poultices, &c., furnished a plausible excuse for avoiding general conversation, of which most Yankee travellers are passionately fond.

*　　*　　*

When the time had arrived for us to start, we blew out the lights, knelt down, and prayed to our Heavenly Father mercifully to assist us, as he did his people of old, to escape from cruel bondage; and we shall ever feel that God heard and answered our prayer. Had we not been sustained by a kind, and I sometimes think special, providence, we could never have overcome the mountainous difficulties which I am now about to describe.

After this we rose and stood for a few moments in breathless silence— we were afraid that someone might have been about the cottage listening and watching our movements. So I took my wife by the hand, stepped softly to the door, raised the latch, drew it open, and peeped out. Though there were trees all around the house, yet the foliage scarcely moved; in fact, everything appeared to be as still as death. I then whispered to my wife, "Come my dear, let us make a desperate leap for liberty!" But poor thing, she shrank back, in a state of trepidation. I turned and asked what was the matter; she made no reply, but burst into violent sobs, and threw her head upon my breast. This appeared to touch my very heart, it caused me to enter into her feelings more fully than ever. We both saw the many mountainous difficulties that rose one after the other before our view, and knew far too well what our sad fate would have been, were we caught and forced back into our slavish den. Therefore on my wife's fully realizing the solemn fact that we had to take our lives, as it were, in our hands, and contest every inch of the thousand miles of slave territory over which we had to pass, it made her heart almost sink within her, and, had I known them at that time, I would have repeated the following encouraging lines, which may not be out of place here—

> The hill, though high, I covet to ascend,
> The *difficulty will not me offend;*
> For I perceive the way to life lies here:
> Come, pluck up heart, let's neither faint nor fear;
> Better, though difficult, the right way to go,—
> Than wrong, though easy, where the end is woe.

However, the sobbing was soon over, and after a few moments of silent prayer she recovered her self-possession, and said, "Come, William, it is getting late, so now let us venture upon our perilous journey."

We then opened the door, and stepped as softly out as "moonlight upon the water." I locked the door with my own key, which I now have before me, and tiptoed across the yard into the street. I say tiptoed, because we were like persons near a tottering avalanche, afraid to move, or even breathe freely, for fear the sleeping tyrants should be aroused, and come down upon us with double vengeance, for daring to attempt to escape in the manner which we contemplated.

We shook hands, said farewell, and started in different directions for the railway station. I took the nearest possible way to the train, for fear I should be recognized by someone, and got into the Negro car in which I knew I should have to ride; but my *master* (as I will now call my wife) took a longer way round, and only arrived there with the bulk of the passengers. He obtained a ticket for himself and one for his slave to Savannah, the first port, which was about two hundred miles off. My master then had the luggage stowed away, and stepped into one of the best carriages.

But just before the train moved off I peeped through the window, and, to my great astonishment, I saw the cabinetmaker with whom I had worked so long, on the platform. He stepped up to the ticketseller, and asked some question, and then commenced looking rapidly through the passengers, and into the carriages. Fully believing that we were caught, I shrank into a corner, turned my face from the door, and expected in a moment to be dragged out. The cabinetmaker looked into my master's carriage, but did not know him in his new attire, and, as God would have it, before he reached mine the bell rang, and the train moved off.

I have heard since that the cabinetmaker had a presentiment that we were about to "make tracks for parts unknown"; but, not seeing me, his suspicions vanished, until he received the startling intelligence that we had arrived safely in a free State.

# Georgia Baker

## From *Slavery Time: When I Was Chillun down on Marster's Plantation*

I was born on the plantation of a great man. It was Marse Alec Stephens' plantation about a mile and a half from Crawfordville, in Taliaferro County. Mary and Grandison Tilly was my Ma and Pa. Ma was cook up at the big house, and she died when I was just a little gal. Pa was a field hand, and he belonged to Marse Britt Tilly.

There was four of us chillun—me, and Mary, and Frances, and Mack. Marse Alec let Marse Jim Johnson have Mack for his bodyguard. Frances worked in the field, and Mary was the baby—she was too little to work. I was fourteen years old when the war was over. I swept yards, toted water to the field, and played around the house and yard with the rest of the chillun.

The long, log houses what us lived in was called shotgun houses because they had three rooms, one behind the other in a row like the barrel of a shotgun. All the chillun slept in one end room and the grown folks slept in the other end room. The kitchen where us cooked and ate was the middle room. Beds was made out of pine poles put together with cords. Them wheat-straw mattresses was for grown folks mostly because nigh all the chillun slept on pallets. However, there was some few slave chillun what had beds to sleep on. Pillows? Them days us never knowed what

Georgia Baker was interviewed in August 1938 by Sadie Hornsby at 369 Meigs Street, Athens, Georgia, for the WPA Slave Narratives project.

pillows was. Gals slept on one side of the room and boys on the other in the chilluns room. Uncle Jim, he was the bed-maker, and he made up a heap of little beds like what they calls cots now.

Becky and Stafford Stephens was my Grandma and Grandpa. Marse Alec bought them in Old Virginny. I don't know what my Grandma done because she died before I was borned, but I remembers Grandpa Stafford well enough. I can see him now. He was a old man what slept on a trundle bed in the kitchen, and all he done was to set by the fire all day with a switch in his hand and tend the chillun whilst their mammies was at work. Grandpa Stafford never had to holler at them but one time. They knowed they would get the switch.

Marse Alec had plenty for his slaves to eat. There was meat, bread, collard greens, snap beans, 'taters, peas, all sorts of dried fruit, and just lots of milk and butter. Marse Alec had twelve cows and that's where I learned to love milk so good. George and Mack was the hunters. When they went hunting they brought back possums, rabbits, coons, squirrels, birds and wild turkeys. The same Uncle Jim what made our beds made our wooden bowls what they kept filled with bread and milk for the chillun all day. You might want to call that place where Marse Alec had our vegetables raised a garden, but it looked more like a big field to me it was so big. You just ought to have seed that there fireplace where they cooked all us had to eat. It was one sure enough big something, all full of pots, skillets, and ovens. They weren't never allowed to get full of smut neither. They had to be cleaned and shined up after every meal, and they sure was pretty hanging there in that big old fireplace.

Summertime us just wore what us wanted to. Dresses was made with full skirts gathered on to tight fitting waists. Winter clothes was good and warm; dresses made of yarn cloth made up just like them summertime clothes, and petticoats and drawers made out of osnaburg. Chillun what was big enough done the spinning and Aunt Betsey and Aunt Tinny, they wove most every night 'till they rung the bell at ten o'clock for us to go to bed. Us made bolts and bolts of cloth every year.

Us went barefoot in summer, but us had good shoes in winter and wore good stockings, too. It took three shoemakers for our plantation. They was Uncle Isom, Uncle Jim, and Uncle Stafford. They made up holestock shoes for the womans and gals and brass-toed brogans for the men and boys. Holestock shoes had extra pieces on the sides so us wouldn't knock holes in them too quick.

Us had pretty white dresses for Sunday. Marse Alec wanted evvybody on his place dressed up that day. He sent his houseboy, Uncle Harris, down to the cabins every Sunday morning to tell every slave to clean himself up. They warn't never give no chance to forget. There was a big old room set aside for a washroom.

Marse Lordnorth Stephens [cousin of Alexander W. Stephens] was the boss on Marse Alec's plantation. Course Marse Alec owned us and he was our sure enough master. Neither one of them ever married. Marse Lordnorth was a good man, but he didn't have no use for womans—he was a sissy. There weren't no master no where no better than our Marse Alec Stephens, but he never stayed home enough to tend to things himself much because he was all the time too busy on the outside. He was the President or something of our side during the war.

Uncle Pierce went with Marse Alec every where he went. His dog, Rio, had more sense than most folks. Marse Alec, he was all the time having big men visit him up at the big house. One time, out in the yard, him and one of them important men got in a argument about something. Us chillun snuck up close to hear what they was making such a rukus about. I heared Marse Alec say: "I got more sense in my big toe than you got in your whole body." And he was right—he did have more sense than most folks. Ain't I been a-telling you he was the President or something like that, them days?

Ma was Marse Alec's cook and looked after the house. After she died Marse Lordnorth got Mrs. Mary Berry from Habersham County to keep house at the big house, but Aunt Liza done the cooking after Miss Mary got there. Us little Niggers sure did love Miss Mary. Us called her "Mammy Mary" sometimes. Miss Mary had three sons and one of them was named Jeff Davis. I remembers when they come and got him and took him off to war. Marse Lordnorth built a four-room house on the plantation for Miss Mary and her boys. Everybody loved our Miss Mary, because she was so good and sweet, and there warn't nothing us wouldn't have done for her.

Marse Lordnorth never needed no overseer or no carriage driver neither. Uncle Jim was the head man what got the Niggers up every morning and started them off to work right. The big house sure was a pretty place, a-setting up on a high hill. The squirrels was so tame there they just played all around the yard. Marse Alec's dog is buried in that yard. I never knowed how many acres there was in the plantation us lived on, and Marse Alec had other places, too. He had land scattered everywhere. Lord, there was a heap of Niggers on that place, and all of us was kin to one another. Grandma Becky and Grandpa Stafford was the first slaves Marse Alec ever had, and they sure had a parcel of chillun. One thing sure Marse Lordnorth wouldn't keep no bright-colored Nigger on that plantation if he could help it. Aunt Mary was a bright-colored Nigger and they said that Marse John, Marse Lordnorth's brother, was her Pa, but anyhow Marse Lordnorth never had no use for her because she was a bright-colored Nigger.

Marse Lordnorth never had no certain early time for his slaves to get up nor no special late time for them to quit work. The hours they worked was according to how much work was ahead to be done. Folks in Crawfordville called us "Stephens' Free Niggers."

None of Marse Alec's slaves never run away to no North, because he was so good to them they never wanted to leave him. The onliest Nigger what left Marse Alec's place was Uncle Dave, and he wouldn't have left except he got in trouble with a white woman. You needn't ask me her name because I ain't going to tell it, but I knows it well as I does my own name. Anyhow Marse Alec give Uncle Dave some money and told him to leave, and nobody never seen him no more after that.

Most times, when slaves went to their quarters at night, men rested, but sometimes they helped the womans card the cotton and wool. Young folks frolicked, sung songs and visited from cabin to cabin. When they got behind with field work, slaves worked after dinner Saturdays, but that wasn't often. But, oh, them Saturday nights! That was when slaves got together and danced. George blowed the quills, and he sure could blow grand dance music on them. Them Niggers would just dance down. There warn't no foolishment allowed after ten o'clock no night. Sundays they went to church and visited around.

Oh, what a time us Niggers did have on Christmas Day! Marse Lordnorth and Marse Alec give us everything you could name to eat: cake of all kinds, fresh meat, lightbread, turkeys, chickens, ducks, geese and all sorts of wild game. There was always plenty of pecans, apples and dried peaches too at Christmas. Marse Alec had some trees what had fruit that looked like bananas on them, but I done forgot what was the name of them trees. Marse Alec would call the grown folks to the big house early in the morning and pass around a big pitcher full of whiskey, then he would put a little whiskey in that same pitcher and fill it with sweetened water and give that to us chillun. Us called that "toddy" or "dram." Marse Alec always had plenty of good whiskey, because Uncle Willis made it up for him and it was made just right. The night after Christmas Day us pulled syrup candy, drunk more liquor and danced. Us had a big time for a whole week and then on New Year's Day us done a little work just to start the year right and us feasted that day on fresh meat, plenty of cake and whiskey. There was always a big pile of ash-roasted 'taters on hand to go with that good old baked meat. Us always tried to raise enough 'taters to last all through winter because Niggers sure does love them sweet 'taters. Us never knowed nothing about Santa Claus 'till after the war.

There warn't no special cornshuckings and cotton pickings on Marse Alec's place, but, of course, they did quilt in the winter because there had to be lots of quilting done for all them slaves to have plenty of warm covers, and you knows womans can quilt better if they gets a parcel of them together.

Old Marster was powerful good to his Niggers when they got sick. He had them seed after soon as it was reported to him that they was ailing. Grandpa Stafford had a sore leg and Marse Lordnorth looked after him and had Uncle Jim dress that poor old sore leg every day. Slaves didn't get sick as often as Niggers does now days. Mammy Mary had all sorts of teas made up for us, according to whatever ailment us had. The first thing they always done for sore throat was give us tea made of red oak bark with alum. Scurvy grass tea cleant us out in the springtime, and they made us wear little sacks of assfiddy around our necks to keep off lots of sorts of miseries. Some folkses hung the left hind foot of a mole on a string around their babies' necks to make them teethe easier.

I remembers just as good as if it was yesterday what Mammy Mary said when she told us the first news of our freedom. "You all is free now," she said. "You don't none of you belong to Mister Lordnorth nor Mister Alec no more, but I does hope you will all stay on with them, because they will always be just as good to you as they has done been in the past." Me, I warn't even studying nothing about leaving Marse Alec, but Sarah Ann and Aunt Mary, they throwed down their hoes and just whooped and hollered because they was so glad.

Whilst Marse Alec was President or something, he got sick and had to come back home, and it warn't long after that before the surrender. Allen was appointed to watch for the blue coats. When they come to take Marse Alec off, they was all over the place with their guns. Us Niggers hollered and cried and took on powerful because us sure thought they was going to kill him on account of his being such a high up man on the side what they was fighting. All the Niggers followed them to the depot when they took Marse Alec and Uncle Pierce away. They kept Marse Alec in prison off somewhere a long time, but they sent Pierce back home before long. I seed Jeff Davis when they brung him through Crawfordville on the train. They had him all fastened up with chains.

I stayed on with my two good Marsters 'till most three years after the war, and then went to work for Marse Tye Elder in Crawfordville. I seed Uncle Pierce before he died and us sat and talked and cried about Marse Alec. Us sure did have the best master in the world. If ever a man went to Heaven, Marse Alec did. I sure does wish good old Marster was living now.

# Joel Chandler Harris

## From *On the Plantation*

### CHAPTER I.
### Joe Maxwell Makes a Start

The post-office in the middle Georgia village of Hillsborough used to be a queer little place, whatever it is now. It was fitted up in a cellar; and the postmaster, who was an enterprising gentleman from Connecticut, had arranged matters so that those who went after their letters and papers could at the same time get their grocery supplies.

Over against the wall on one side was a faded green sofa. It was not an inviting seat, for in some places the springs peeped through, and one of its legs was broken, giving it a suspicious tilt against the wall. But a certain little boy found one corner of the rickety old sofa a very comfortable place, and he used to curl up there nearly every day, reading such stray newspapers as he could lay hands on, and watching the people come and go.

To the little boy the stock of goods displayed for sale was as curious in its variety as the people who called day after day for the letters that came or that failed to come. To some dainty persons the mingled odor of cheese, camphene, and mackerel would have been disagreeable; but Joe Maxwell—that was the name of the little boy—had a healthy disposition and a strong stomach, and he thought the queer little post-office was one of the pleasantest places in the world.

A partition of woodwork and wire netting cut off the post-office and the little stock of groceries from the public at large, but outside of that was an area where a good many people could stand and wait for their letters. In one corner of this area was the rickety green sofa, and round about were chairs and boxes and barrels on which tired people could rest themselves.

The Milledgeville papers had a large circulation in the county. They were printed at the capital of the State, and were thought to be very important on that account. They had so many readers in the neighborhood that the postmaster, in order to save time and trouble, used to pile them up on a long shelf outside the wooden partition, where each subscriber could help himself. Joe Maxwell took advantage of this method, and on Tuesdays, when the Milledgeville papers arrived, he could always be found curled up in the corner of the old green sofa reading the *Recorder* and the *Federal Union*. What he found in those papers to interest him it would be hard to say. They were full of political essays that were popular in those days, and they had long reports of political conventions and meetings from all parts of the State. They were papers for grown people, and Joe Maxwell was only twelve years old, and small for his age.

There was another place that Joe found it pleasant to visit, and that was a lawyer's office in one of the rooms of the old tavern that looked out on the pillared veranda. It was a pleasant place to him, not because it was a law-office, but because it was the office of a gentleman who was very friendly to the youngster. The gentleman's name was Mr. Deometari, and Joe called him Mr. Deo, as did the other people of Hillsborough. He was fat and short and wore whiskers, which gave him a peculiar appearance at that time. All the rest of the men that Joe knew wore either a full beard or a mustache and an imperial. For that reason Mr. Deometari's whiskers were very queer-looking. He was a Greek, and there was a rumor among the people about town that he had been compelled to leave his country on account of his politics. Joe never knew until long afterward that politics could be a crime. He thought that politics consisted partly in newspaper articles signed "Old Subscriber" and "Many Citizens" and "Vox Populi" and "Scrutator," and partly in arguments between the men who sat in fine weather on the dry-goods boxes under the china-trees. But there was a mystery about Mr. Deometari, and it pleased the lad to imagine all sorts of romantic stories about the fat lawyer. Although Mr. Deometari was a Greek, there was no foreign twang to his tongue. Only as close an observer as the boy could have told from his talk that he was a foreigner. He was a good lawyer and a good speaker, and all the other lawyers seemed to like him. They enjoyed his company so well that it was only occasionally that Joe found him in his office alone. Once Mr. Deometari took from his closet a military uniform and put it on. Joe Maxwell thought it was the most beautiful uniform he had ever seen. Gold braid ran down the sides of the trousers, gold cords hung loosely on the breast of the coat, and a pair of tremendous epaulets surmounted the shoulders. The hat was something like the hats Joe had seen in picture-books. It was caught up at the sides with little gold buttons, and trimmed with a long black feather that shone like a pigeon's breast. Fat as Mr. Deometari was, the lad thought he looked very handsome in his fine uniform. This was only one incident. In his room, which was a large one, Mr. Deometari had boxes packed with books, and he gave Joe leave to ransack them. Many of the volumes were in strange tongues, but among them were some quaint old English books, and these the lad relished beyond measure. After a while Mr. Deometari closed his office and went away to the war.

It would not be fair to say that Joe was a studious lad. On the contrary, he was of an adventurous turn of mind, and he was not at all fond of the books that were in his desk at Hillsborough Academy. He was full of all sorts of pranks and capers, and there were plenty of people in the little town ready to declare that he would come to some bad end if he was not more frequently dosed with what the old folks used to call hickory oil. Some of Joe Maxwell's pranks were commonplace, but others were ingenious enough to give him quite a reputation for humor, and one prank in particular is talked of by the middle-aged people of Hillsborough to this day.

The teacher of the academy had organized a military company among the pupils—it was just about the time when rumors and hints of war had begun to take shape—and a good deal of interest was felt in the organization, especially by the older boys. Of this company Joe Maxwell was the fourth corporal, a position which gave him a place at the foot of the company. The Hillsborough Cadets drilled every schoolday, and sometimes on Saturdays, and they soon grew to be very proud of their proficiency.

At last, after a good deal of manœuvring on the playgrounds and in the public square, the teacher, who was the captain, concluded that the boys had earned a vacation, and it was decided that the company should go into camp for a week on the Oconee River, and fish and hunt and have a good time generally. The boys fairly went wild when the announcement was made, and some of them wanted to hug the teacher, who had hard work to explain that an attempt of this sort was not in accord with military tactics or discipline.

All the arrangements were duly made. Tents were borrowed from the Hillsborough Rifles, and the drum corps of that company was hired to make music. A half-dozen wagons carried the camp outfit and the small boys, while the larger ones marched. It was an entirely new experience for Joe Maxwell, and he enjoyed it as only a healthy and high-spirited boy could enjoy it. The formal and solemn way in which the guard was mounted was very funny to him, and the temptation to make a joke of it was too strong to be resisted.

The tents were pitched facing each other, with the officers' tent at the head of the line thus formed. At the other end of the lane and a little to the rear was the baggage-tent, in which the trunks, boxes, and commissaries were stored. Outside of all, the four sentinels marched up and down. The tents were pitched in an old field that was used as a pasture, and Joe noticed during the afternoon two mules and a horse browsing around. He noticed, too, that these animals were very much disturbed, especially when the drums began to beat, and that their curiosity would not permit them to get very far from the camp, no matter how frightened they were.

It happened that one of Joe's messmates was to go on guard duty at twelve o'clock that night. He was a fat, awkward, good-natured fellow, this messmate, and a heavy sleeper, too, so that, when the corporal of the guard undertook to arouse him, all the boys in the tent were awakened. All except Joe quickly went to sleep again, but this enterprising youngster quietly put on his clothes, and, in the confusion of changing the guard, slipped out of the lines and hid in a convenient gully not far from the camp.

It was his intention to worry if not to frighten his messmate, and while he lay there trying to think out the best plan to pursue, he heard the horse and mules trampling and snorting not very far off. Their curiosity was not yet satisfied, and they seemed to be making their way toward the camp for the purpose of reconnoitering. Joe's mind was made up in an instant. He slipped down the gully until the animals were between him and the camp, and then, seizing a large pine brush that happened to be lying near, he sprang toward them. The mules and horse were ripe for a stampede. The camp itself was an object of suspicion, and this attack from an unexpected quarter was too much for them. Snorting with terror they rushed in the direction of the tents. The sleepy sentinel, hearing them coming, fired his gun in the air and ran yelling into the camp, followed by the horse and one of the mules. The other mule shied to the right when the gun was fired, and ran into the baggage-tent. There was a tremendous rattle and clatter of boxes, pots, pans, and crockery ware. The mule, crazed with fright, made a violent effort to get through the tent, but it caught him in some way. Finally, the ropes that held it down gave way, and the mule, with the tent flapping and flopping on his back, turned and rushed through the camp. To all but Joe Maxwell it was a horrifying sight. Many of the boys, as the saying is, "took to the woods," and some of them were prostrated with fright. These were consequences that Joe had not counted on, and it was a long time before he confessed to his share in the night's sport. The results reached further than the camp. In another part of the plantation the negroes were holding a revival meeting in the open air, preaching and shouting and singing. Toward this familiar scene the mule made his way, squealing, braying, and kicking, the big white tent flopping on his back. As the terrified animal circled around the place, the negroes cried out that Satan had come, and the panic that ensued among them is not easily described. Many thought that the apparition was the ushering in of the judgment-day, while by far the greater number firmly believed that the "Old Boy" himself was after them. The uproar they made could be plainly heard at the camp, more than a mile away—shrieks, screams, yells, and cries for mercy. After it was all over, and Joe Maxwell had crept quietly to bed, the thought came to him that it was not such a fine joke, after all, and he lay awake a long time repenting the night's work. He heard the next day that nobody had been hurt and that no serious damage had been done, but it was many weeks before he forgave himself for his thoughtless prank.

Although Joe was fond of fun, and had a great desire to be a clown in a circus or to be the driver of a stage-coach—just such a red and yellow coach, with "U.S.M." painted on its doors, as used to carry passengers and the mails between Hillsborough and Rockville—he never permitted his mind to dwell on these things. He knew very well that the time would soon come when he would have to support his mother and himself. This thought used to come to him again and again when he was sitting in the little post-office, reading the Milledgeville papers.

It so happened that these papers grew very interesting to both old and young as the days went by. The rumors of war had developed into war itself. In the course of a few months two companies of volunteers had gone to Virginia from Hillsborough, and the little town seemed to be lonelier and more deserted than ever. Joe Maxwell noticed, as he sat in the post-office, that only a very few old men and ladies came after the letters and papers, and he missed a great many faces that used to smile at him as he sat reading, and some of them he never saw again. He noticed, too, that when there had been a battle or a skirmish the ladies and young girls came to the post-office more frequently. When the news was very important, one of the best-known citizens would mount a chair on a dry-goods box and read the telegrams aloud to the waiting and anxious group of people, and sometimes the hands and the voice of the reader trembled.

One day while Joe Maxwell was sitting in the post-office looking over the Milledgeville papers, his eye fell on an advertisement that interested him greatly. It seemed to bring the whole world nearer to him. The advertisement set forth the fact that on next Tuesday the first number of *The Countryman,* a weekly paper would be published. It would be modeled after Mr. Addison's little paper, the *Spectator,* Mr. Goldsmith's little paper, the *Bee,* and Mr. Johnson's little paper, the *Rambler.* It would be edited by J. A. Turner, and it would be issued on the plantation of the editor, nine miles from Hillsborough. Joe read this advertisement over a dozen times, and it was with a great deal of impatience that he waited for the next Tuesday to come.

But the day did come, and with it came the first issue of *The Countryman.* Joe read it from beginning to end, advertisements and all, and he thought it was the most entertaining little paper he had ever seen. Among the interesting things was an announcement by the editor that he wanted a boy to learn the printing business. Joe borrowed pen and ink and some paper from the friendly postmaster, and wrote a letter to the editor, saying that he would be glad to learn the printing business. The letter was no doubt an awkward one, but it served its purpose, for when the editor of *The Countryman* came to Hillsborough he hunted Joe up, and told him to get ready to go to the plantation. The lad, not without some misgivings, put away his tops and marbles, packed his little belongings in an old-fashioned trunk, kissed his mother and his grandmother good-by, and set forth on what turned out to be the most important journey of his life.

Sitting in the buggy by the side of the editor and publisher of *The Countryman*, Joe Maxwell felt lonely indeed, and this feeling was increased as he went through the little town and heard his schoolmates, who were at their marbles on the public square, bidding him good-by. He could hardly keep back his tears at this, but, on looking around after the buggy had gone a little way, he saw his friends had returned to their marbles, and the thought struck him that he was already forgotten. Many and many a time after that he thought of his little companions and how quickly they had returned to their marbles.

The editor of *The Countryman* must have divined what was passing in the lad's mind (he was a quick-witted man and a clever one, too), for he tried to engage in conversation with Joe. But the boy preferred to nurse his loneliness, and would only talk when he was compelled to answer a question. Finally, the editor asked him if he would drive, and this Joe was glad enough to do, for there is some diversion in holding the reins over a spirited horse. The editor's horse was a large gray, named Ben Bolt, and he was finer than any of the horses that Joe had seen at the livery-stable. Feeling a new and an unaccustomed touch on the reins, Ben Bolt made an effort to give a new meaning to his name by bolting sure enough. The road was level and hard, and the horse ran rapidly for a little distance; but Joe Maxwell's arms were tough, and before the horse had gone a quarter of a mile the lad had him completely under control.

"You did that very well," said the editor, who was familiar with Ben Bolt's tricks. "I didn't know that little boys in town could drive horses."

"Oh, sometimes they can," replied Joe. "If he had been scared, I think

I should have been scared myself; but he was only playing. He has been tied at the rack all day, and he must be hungry."

"Yes," said the editor, "he is hungry, and he wants to see his mate, Rob Roy."

Then the editor, in a fanciful way, went on to talk about Ben Bolt and Rob Roy, as if they were persons instead of horses; but it did not seem fanciful to Joe, who had a strange sympathy with animals of all kinds, especially horses and dogs. It pleased him greatly to think that he had ideas in common with a grown man, who knew how to write for the papers; and if the editor was talking to make Joe forget his loneliness he succeeded admirably, for the lad thought no more of the boys who had so quickly returned to their marbles, but only of his mother, whom he had last seen standing at the little gate smiling at him through her tears.

As they drove along the editor pointed out a little log-cabin near the road.

"That," said he, "is where the high sheriff of the county lives. Do you know Colonel John B. Stith?"

"Yes," Joe replied; "but I thought he lived in a large, fine house. I don't see how he can get in at that door yonder."

"What makes you think he is too big for the door?" asked the editor.

"Why, the way he goes on," said Joe, with the bluntness of youth. "He is always in town talking politics, and he talks bigger than anybody."

"Well," said the editor, laughing, "that is his house. When you get a little older you'll find people who are more disappointing than the high sheriff. Boys are sometimes too big for their breeches, I've heard said, but this is the first time I ever heard that a man could be too big for his house. That is a good one on the colonel."

Ben Bolt trotted along steadily and rapidly, but after a while dusk fell, and then the stars came out. Joe peered ahead, trying to make out the road.

"Just let the horse have his way," said the editor. "He knows the road better than I do"; and it seemed to be so, for, when heavy clouds from the west came up and hid the stars, and only the darkness was visible, Ben Bolt trotted along as steadily as ever. He splashed through Crooked

Creek, walked up the long hill, and then started forward more rapidly than ever.

"It is a level road, now," the editor remarked, "and Ben Bolt is on the home-stretch."

In a little while he stopped before a large gate. It was opened in a jiffy by some one who seemed to be waiting.

"Is that you, Harbert?" asked the editor.

"Yes, marster."

"Well, I want you to take Mr. Maxwell here to Mr. Snelson's."

"Yasser," responded the negro.

"Snelson is the foreman of the printing-office," the editor explained to Joe, "and for the present you are to board with him. I hope he will make things pleasant for you. Good-night."

To the lonely lad it seemed a long journey to Mr. Snelson's—through wide plantation gates, down narrow lanes, along a bit of public road, and then a plunge into the depths of a great wood, where presently a light gleamed through.

"I'll hail 'em," said Harbert, and he sent before him into the darkness a musical halloo, whereupon, as promptly as its echo, came a hearty response from the house, with just the faintest touch of the Irish brogue in the voice.

"Ah, and it's the young man! Jump right down and come in to the warmth of the fire. There's something hot on the hearth, where it's waiting you."

And so Joe Maxwell entered on a new life—a life as different as possible from that which he had left behind in Hillsborough.

# Bill Arp [Charles Henry Smith]

## From *Bill Arp's Peace Papers*

### "Fifth Paper: Battle of Rome—Official"

Rome, Ga., May, 1863.

GENRUL JOHNSIN—SUR: So many onreliable pussons will be circulatin spurious akcounts of the "Grand Rounds" tuk by the infernal Yankees in these ROME-antic regions, that I think it highly proper you should git the strait of it from one who seed it with his eyes, and heerd it with his years, and a piece of it fell on his tail.

More than two hundred years ago, Genrul D. Soto had a big fight with the Injins on or about these konsecrated grounds. Since that time a uninterrupted peace hav rained round these klassick hills and hollers. Flowers hav blossomed sweetly, lams hav skipped about, dog fennel hav yellered the ground, and the Coosa River, which was then but a little spring branch, hav grown both wide and deep, until now the magestick steemboat can float upon its buzzum, and the big mud cat gobble up the yearth worms what chanse to fall into its waters.

But rollin years will change a program! Anno domini will tell! Just afore the broke of day on Sunday, the third of May, 1863, the sitizens of the Eternal Sity were roused from their slumbers by the korus of the Marsales him. "To arms, to arms, ye brave; Abe Linkhorn are peggin away; the Yankees are ridin to Rome on a raid." Ah! then were the time to try men's soles; but there were no panic, no skedaddlin, no shaken of kneeze; but one unyversal determinashun to *do sumthin*. The berryal squad organized fust and foremost, and begun to inter their money, and spoons, and four pronged forks, and such like in small graves about the premises. Babys were sent to the rear. Hosses hid in the kane brake. Cows milked onkommonly dry. Kasheers and bank agents carried oph their funs in a pair of saddle bags, which very much xposed their fasilities and the small kompass of their resources. It were, however, a satisfaktory solution of their refusin to diskount for the last 3 months. Skouts wer sent out on evry road to snuff the tainted breze. Kotton bags were piled up akross evry highway and low way. Shot guns and kannon, powder and ball, were brought to the front. The yomanry and millishy jined a squad of confederate troops, and formed in line of battle. They were marched akross the Oustanauly Bridge, and then the plank of the bridge tore up so they couldn't retreet. This were done, however, at their own valyant request bekaus of the natral weakness of the flesh. They determined, jointly and sevrally, by these presents, to *do sumthin*.

Two kracked kannon, that had holes in the ends and 2 or three in the sides, wer proped up atween the kotton bags and pinted strate down the road to Alabam. They wer fust loaded with Buckshot and tax, and then a round ball rammed on top. The ball were to take the rade in the front and the bullets and tax to rake em in the phlank. These latter it were supposed would go through the kracks in the sides, and shute round gen-rully. Everybody and everything determined to die in their tracks or *do sumthin*. The steemboats droped quietly down the river to git out of the thick of the fite. The sharpshuters got on top of semeterry hill with their repeeters and pocket pistuls. The videts dashed with their spi-glasses to the top of the kourt house to see afur off. Dashin komanchy kouriers rode onruly steeds to and fro like a fiddler's elbo. Some went forward to rekonnoiter as skouts—first in the road and then outen the road—some mounted, and some on foot. All were resolved to *do sumthin*.

At this kritikal juncture, and previous and afterwards, reports wer brought into these headquarters, and other quarters, to the effek that 10,000 Yankees were comin, and 5,000 and 2,000, and any other num-ber—that they were ten miles from town, and six miles, and enny other number of miles; that they were on the Alabam road, and the Cave Spring road, and the river road, and eny other road; that they wer krossin the

river at Quinn's ferry, and WmSon's ferry, and Bell's ferry, and eny other
ferry; that they had taken the steamboat "Laura Moore," and "Cherokee," and "Alfaratty," and eny other steamboat; that they had shot a
Kamanchy kourier and had hit him in his koat tale, or his horse tale,
or any other tail; that they had seezed Cis Morris, Bill Morris, or Jep
Morris, or eny other Morris. In fact, a man kould hear enything by gwine
about, and more too.

Shore enuff, however, the important krisis which was to hev arriv did
acktually arriv about ten o'clock in the mornin, a.m., on May the 3rd,
1863. I am thusly partikular, Mr. Editur, bekaus it are to be entered
on next year's almanax as a remarkabel event. The head of the rade did
acktually arriv at the suberben viller of Mr. Myers, and ther it stopped
to rekonnoiter. There they larned that we had six hundred hed of artil-
lery, and six thousin kotton bags, and a permiskuous number of infantry
taktix, and wer only waitin to see the whites of ther eyse. Also that the
history of Genrul Jackson at New Orleans wer read in publik, and that
everybody were inspired to *do sumthin;* whereupon the hed of the rade
turned pail, and sent forward a piket. At this orspishus moment a foot
skout on our side let fly a whistlin bullit, which tuk effek somewher in
them rejuns. It were resunably suposed that one Yankee were killed and
perhaps two, for even to this time sumthin ded kan be smelt in them
parts, though the berryal squad had not been able to find it up to a late
hour yistiddy. After rite smart skummishin the hed of the rade fell bak
down the road to Alabam, and wer pursude by our mounted yomanry at
a respektabul distance.

Now, Mistur Editur, while all these valyant feets wer goin on here-
abouts, Genrul Forrest had been fitin the boddy and tale of the rade
away down at the Alabam line. Finally he proposed to the rade to stop
fitin, and play a game or two of poker, under a seder tree, which they
acksepted. But the Genrul wer not in luck, and had a pore hand, and
had bet his last dollar. The Yankees had a *Strait,* which wood hav taken
Forrest and raked down the pile, but he looked em rite in the eyes and
sed *"he would see em and 4,000 better."* The Rade looked at him, and he
looked at the Rade and *never blinked.* The Rade trimbled all over in his
boots and giv it up. *The Genrul bluffed em,* and ever sence that game were

plade, the little town klose by have been kalled *"Cedar Bluff."* It were *flush* times in Alabam, that day, shore.

Well, Mr. Editur, you kno the sekwel. The Genrul bagged em and brot em on. The planks were put back on the bridge. The river bank infantry kountermarched and fired a permiskuous volly in token of jubilee. One of the side wipin kannon went off on its own hook, and the ball went ded throu a house and tore a buro all to flinders. Sum sed it wer a *Niter Buro,* but a potash man who xamined it sed he rekoned not.

By and by the Kamanchy skouts and pikets all cum in, shuk their ambroshal loks and reseeved the kongratulashuns of there friends. Then begun the ovashun of fare wimmen and brave men. Bokays and teers were mixed up permiskuous. Big hunks of cake and gratitude were distributed genrully and frekwent, strawberries and kream, egs and inguns, pise and pan cakes, all flu round amazingly, for every body were determined to *do sumthin.* Genrul Forrest subsided, and Genrul Jubilee tuk kommand, and Rome were herself again. The 4 pronged forks and silver spunes rose from the ded, and even the old hen that one of our sity aldermen had berried with her *head out,* wer disenterd and sakrifised immegitly for the good of the country.

Thusly have ended the rade, and no loss on our side. Howsomever, I spose that Mr. Linkhorn will keep peggin away.

Yours truly and immensely.

BILL ARP.
*Adjectiv Genrul of Yomanry.*

# From *The Farm and the Fireside*

## CHAPTER III.
### Big John

"Big John" was one of the earliest settlers of Rome, and one of her most notable men. For several years he was known by his proper name of John Underwood, but when another John Underwood moved there, the old settler had to be identified by his superior size, and gradually lost his surname, and was known far and near as "Big John." The newcomer was a man of large frame, weighing about 225 pounds, but Big John pulled down the scales at a hundred pounds more. He had shorter arms and shorter legs, but his circumference was correspondingly immense. He was notable for his humor and his good humor. The best town jokes came from his jolly, fertile fancy, and his comments on men and things were always original, and as terse and vigorous as ever came from the brain of Dr. Johnson. He was a diamond in the rough. He had lived a pioneer among the Indians of Cherokee, and it was said fell in love with an Indian maid, the daughter of old Tustenuggee, a hunted chief, and never married because he could not marry her. But if his disappointment preyed upon his heart, it did not prey long upon the region that enclosed it, for he continued to expand his proportions. He was a good talker and an earnest laugher—whether he laughed and grew fat, or grew fat and laughed, the doctors could not tell which was cause and which was effect, and it is still in doubt, but I have heard wise men affirm that laughing was the fat man's safety-valve, that if he did not laugh and shake and vibrate frequently, he would grow fatter and fatter, until his epidermic cuticle could not contain his oleaginous corporosity.

Big John had no patience with the war, and when he looked upon the boys strutting around in uniform, and fixing up their canteens and haver-sacks, he seemed as much astonished as disgusted. He sat in his big chair on the sidewalk, and would remark, "I don't see any fun in the like of that. Somebody is going to be hurt, and fighting don't prove anything. Some of our best people in this town are kin to them fellers up North, and I don't see any sense in tearing up families by a fight." He rarely looked serious or solemn, but the impending strife seemed to settle him. "Boys," said he, "I hope to God this thing will be fixed up without a fight, for fighting is a mighty bad business, and I never knowed it to do any good."

Big John had had a little war experience—that is, he had volunteered in a company to assist in the forcible removal of the Cherokees to the far west in 1835. It was said that he was no belligerent then, but wanted to see the maiden that he loved a safe transit, and so he escorted the old chief and his clan as far as Tuscumbia, and then broke down and returned to Ross Landing on the Tennessee river. He was too heavy to march, and when he arrived at the Landing, a prisoner was put in his charge for safe keeping. Ross Landing is Chattanooga now, and John Ross lived there, and was one of the chiefs of the Cherokees. The prisoner was his guest, and his name was John Howard Payne. He was suspected of trying to instigate the Cherokees to revolt and fight, and not leave their beautiful forest homes on the Tennessee and Coosa and Oostanaula and the Etowah and Connasauga rivers. He brought Payne back as far as New Echota, or New Town, as it was called, an Indian settlement on the Coosawattee, a few miles east of Calhoun, as now known. There he kept the author of "Home, Sweet Home" under guard, or on his parol of honor, for three weeks, and night after night slept with him in his tent, and listened to his music upon the violin, and heard him sing his own sad songs until orders came for his discharge, and Payne was sent under escort to Washington.

Many a time have I heard Big John recite his sad adventures. "It was a most distressive business," said he. "Them Injuns was heart-broken; I always knowd an Injun loved his hunting-ground and his rivers, but I never knowd how much they loved 'em before. You know they killed Ridge for consentin' to the treaty. They killed him on the first day's march and they wouldent bury him. We soldiers had to stop and dig a grave and put him away. John Ross and John Ridge were the sons of two Scotchmen, who came over here when they were young men and mixed up with these tribes and got their good will. These two boys were splendid looking men, tall and handsome, with long auburn hair, and they were active and strong, and could shoot a bow equal to the best bowman of the tribe, and they beat 'em all to pieces on the cross-bow. They married the daughters of the old chiefs, and when the old chiefs died they just fell into line and succeeded to the old chiefs' places, and the tribes liked 'em mighty well, for they were good men and made good chiefs. Well, you see Ross dident like the treaty. He said it wasent fair and that the price of the territory was too low, and the fact is he dident want to go at all. There are the ruins of his old home now over there in DeSoto, close to Rome, and I tell you he was a king. His word was the law of the Injun nations, and he had their love and their respect. His half-breed children were the purtiest things I ever saw in my life. Well, Ridge lived up the Oostanaula river about a mile, and he was a good man, too. Ross and Ridge always consulted about everything for the good of the tribes, but Ridge was a more milder man than Ross, and was more easily persuaded to sign the treaty that gave the lands to the State and to take other lands away out to the Mississippi.

"Well, it took us a month to get 'em all together and begin the march to the Mississippi, and they wouldn't march then. The women would go out of line and set down in the woods and go to grieving, and you may believe it or not, but I'll tell you what is a fact, we started with 14,000, and 4,000 of 'em died before we got to Tuscumbia. They died on the side of the road; they died of broken hearts; they died of starvation, for they wouldn't eat a thing; they just died all along the way. We didn't make more than five miles a day on the march, and my company didn't do much but dig graves and bury Injuns all the way to Tuscumbia. They died of grief and broken hearts, and no mistake. An Indian's heart is tender, and his love is strong; it's his nature. I'd rather risk an Injun for a true friend than a white man. He is the best friend in the world, and the worst enemy. He has got more gratitude and more revenge in him than anybody."

Big John's special comfort was a circus. He never missed one, and it was a good part of the show to see him laugh and shake and spread his magnificent face.

He took no pleasure in the quarrels of mankind, and never backed a man in a fight; but when two dogs locked teeth, or two bulls locked horns, or two game chickens locked spurs, he always liked to be about. "It is their nature to fight," said he, "and let 'em fight." He took delight in watching dogs and commenting on their sense and dispositions. He compared them to the men about town, and drew some humorous analogies. "There is Jimmy Jones," said he, "who ripped and splurged around because Georgia wouldn't secede in a minute and a half, and he swore he was going over to South Carolina to fight; and when Georgia did secede shore enough, he didn't join the army at all, and always had some cussed excuse, and when conscription came along, he got on a detail to make potash, con-ding him, and when that played out he got him a couple of track dogs and got detailed to catch runaway prisoners. Just so I've seen dogs run up and down the palings like they was dying to get to one another, and so one day I picked up my dog by the nap of the neck and dropped him over on the outside. I never knowed he could jump that fence before, but he bounced back like an Indian rubber ball, and the other dog streaked it down the sidewalk like the dickens was after him. Dogs are like folks, and folks are like dogs, and a heap of 'em want the palings between. Jack Bogin used to strut round and whip the boys in his beat, and kick 'em around, because he knew he could do it, for he had the most muscle; but he couldn't look a brave man in the eye, muscle or no muscle, and I've seen him shut up quick when he met one. A man has got to be right to be brave, and I had rather see a bully get a licking than to eat sugar."

# Eliza Frances Andrews

## From *The War-Time Journal of a Georgia Girl, 1864–1865*

*April 17, Monday. Macon, Ga.*—Up early, to be ready for the train at seven. The Toombses met us at the dépot, where Capt. Greenlaw, Mr. Renaud, and a number of others came to see us off. When the train arrived from Eufaula it was already crowded with refugees, besides 300 volunteers from the exempts going to help fight the Yankees at Columbus. All sorts of wild rumors were flying, among them one that fighting had already begun at Columbus, and that a raid had been sent out towards Eufaula. Excitement on the train was intense. At Ward's Station, a dreary-looking little place, we picked up the train wrecked yesterday, with many of the passengers still on board. They had spent the night there in the cars, having nowhere else to go. Beyond Ward's, the failure of this train to appear had given color to all sorts of wild rumors about the advance of the Yankees into South-West Georgia. The excitement was intense all along the route. At every little station crowds were gathered to hear the news, and at many places we found a report had gone out that both our train and yesterday's had been captured. The excitement increased as we approached Fort Valley, where the Muscogee road (from Columbus) joins the South-Western, and many of the passengers predicted that we should be captured there. At the next station below Fort Valley, our fears regarding the fate of Columbus were confirmed by a soldier on the platform, who shouted out as the train slowed down, "Columbus gone up the spout!" Nobody was surprised, and all were eager to hear particulars. I was glad to learn that our poor little handful of Confederates had made a brave fight before surrendering. The city was not given up till nine last night, when the Yanks slipped over the railroad bridge and got in before our men, who were defending the other bridge, knew anything about it. We had not enough to watch both bridges, and it seemed more likely the attack would be made by the dirt road. Then everybody blundered around in the dark, fighting pretty much at random. If a man met someone he did not know, he asked whether he was a Yank or a Reb, and if the answer did not suit his views he fired. At last everybody became afraid to tell who or what they were. It was thought that our forces had retired towards Opelika. When we reached Fort Valley the excitement was at fever heat. Train upon train of cars was there, all the rolling stock of the Muscogee Road having been run out of Columbus to keep it from being captured, and the cars were filled with refugees and their goods. It was pitiful to see them, especially the poor little children, driven from their homes by the frozen-hearted Northern Vandals, but they were all brave and cheerful, laughing good-naturedly instead of grumbling over their hardships. People have gotten so used to these sort of things that they have learned to bear them with philosophy. Soldiers who had made their escape after the fight, without surrendering, were camped about everywhere, looking tired and hungry, and more disheartened than the women and children. Poor fellows, they have seen the terrors of war nearer at hand than we. As our train drew up at the dépot, I caught sight of Fred in the crowd. He had been in the fight at Columbus, and I concluded was now on his way to Cuthbert to find Metta and me. I called to let him know that we were on board, but he did not hear me, and before I could make my way to the opposite window, the train moved on a few hundred yards and he was lost in the crowd. I was greatly disturbed, for it was said that the train we were on was the last that would be run over the South-Western Road. While I was in this dilemma, Col. Magruder and Marsh Fouché came out of the crowd and hailed me. They said they were on furlough and trying to make their way to Uncle Fouché's plantation in Appling County. I told them my troubles, and they went to hunt up Fred for me, but must have gotten swallowed up in the crowd themselves, for I never saw either of them again. At last I sent for the conductor to unlock the door so that I could get out of the car and begin a search on my own account. Just as I had stepped out on the platform Fred himself came pushing through the crowd and sprang up beside me. He said that some of the passengers who had come with us from Cuthbert, happened to hear him say that he was going to South-West Georgia to get his sisters, and told him that we were there.

From Fort Valley we traveled without interruption to Macon, where the excitement is at its climax. The Yankees are expected here at any moment, from both north and south, having divided their forces at Tuskegee, it is said, and sent one column by way of Union Springs and Columbus, and another through Opelika and West Point. I saw some poor little fortifications thrown up along the line of the South-Western, with a handful of men guarding them, and that is the only preparation for defense I have seen. We are told that the city is to be defended, but if that is so, the Lord only knows where the men are to come from. The general opinion seems to be that it is to be evacuated, and every preparation seems to be going forward to that end. All the horses that could be found have been pressed for the removal of government stores, and we had great difficulty in getting our baggage from the dépôt to the hotel. Mr. Legriel's nephew, Robert Scott, was at the train to take us out to Lily's, but Fred thought it best for us to stay at the hotel, as he wants to leave in the morning by the first train over the Macon & Western. Mulberry Street, in front of the Lanier House, is filled with officers and men rushing to and fro, and everything and everybody seems to be in the wildest excitement. . . . In the hotel parlor, when I came from Lily's, whom should I find but Mr. Adams, our little Yankee preacher! I used to like him, but now I hate to look at him just because he is a Yankee. What is it, I wonder, that makes them so different from us, even when they mean to be good Southerners! You can't even make one of them look like us, not if you were to dress him up in a full suit of Georgia jeans. I used to have some Christian feeling towards Yankees, but now that they have invaded our country and killed so many of our men and desecrated so many homes, I can't believe that when Christ said "Love your enemies," he meant Yankees. Of course I don't want their souls to be lost, for that would be wicked, but as they are not being punished in this world, I don't see how else they are going to get their deserts.

*April 18, Tuesday.*—The first train on the Georgia R.R., from Atlanta to Augusta, was scheduled to run through to-day, and we started off on the Macon & Western so as to reach Atlanta in time to take the next one down, to-morrow. There was such a crowd waiting at the dépot that we could hardly push our way through, and when the ladies' car was opened there was such a rush that we considered ourselves lucky to get in at all. Jenny and Jule were with us, and we were fortunate enough to get seats together. Fred and Mr. Toombs had great difficulty in getting our trunks aboard, and were obliged to leave us to look out for ourselves, while they attended to the baggage. Many people had to leave theirs behind, and some decided to stay with their trunks; they contained all that some poor refugees had left them. The trains that went out this morning were supposed to be the last that would leave the city, as the Yankees were expected before night, and many predicted that we would be captured. There was a terrible rush on all the outgoing trains. Ours had on board a quantity of government specie and the assets of four banks, besides private property, aggregating all together, it was said, more than seventeen million dollars—and there were somewhere in the neighborhood of 1,000 passengers. People who could not get inside were hanging on wherever they could find a sticking place; the aisles and platforms down to the last step were full of people clinging on like bees swarming round the doors of a hive. It took two engines to pull us up the heavy grade around Vineville, and we were more than an hour behind time, in starting, at that. Meanwhile, all sorts of rumors were flying. One had it that the road was cut at Jonesborough, then, at Barnesville, and finally that a large force of the enemy was at Thomaston advancing toward the road with a view to capturing our train. I never saw such wild excitement in my life. Many people left the cars at the last moment before we steamed out, preferring to be caught in Macon rather than captured on the road, but their places were rapidly filled by more adventurous spirits. A party of refugees from Columbus were seated near us, and they seemed nearly crazed with excitement. Mary Eliza Rutherford, who was always a great scatter-brain when I knew her at school, was among them, and she jumped up on the

seat, tore down her back hair and went off into regular hysterics at the
idea of falling into the hands of the Yankees. Such antics would have been
natural enough in the beginning of the war, when we were new to these
experiences, but now that we are all old soldiers, and used to raids and
vicissitudes, people ought to know how to face them quietly. Of course
it would have been dreadful to be captured and have your baggage rifled
and lose all your clothes, but if the Yankees had actually caught us, I
don't think I would have gone crazy over it. So many sensational reports
kept coming in that I finally lost patience and felt like saying something
cross to everybody that brought me a fresh bit of news. Before we left
Macon, Mr. Edward Shepherd gave me the worst fright I almost ever
had, by telling me that my trunk and Jenny Toombs's had been thrown
out of the baggage car and were lying on the track, but this proved to
be a false alarm, like so many others. Then somebody came in and reported that the superintendent of the road had a dispatch in his hand
at that moment, stating that the enemy was already in Barnesville. The
statement seemed so authoritative that Fred went to Gen. Mackall himself, and was advised by him to continue his journey, as no official notice
had been received of the cutting of the road. At last, to the great relief
of us all, the train steamed out of Macon and traveled along in peace
till it reached Goggins's Station, four miles from Barnesville, where it
was stopped by some country people who said that the down train from
Atlanta had been captured and the Yankees were just five miles beyond
Barnesville waiting for us. A council was held by the railroad officials
and some of the army officers on board, at which it was decided that
the freight we were carrying was too valuable to be risked, although the
news was not very reliable, having been brought in by two schoolboys.
There was danger also, it was suggested, that a raiding party might mistake such a very long and crowded train, where the men were nearly all
forced out on the platforms, for a movement of troops and fire into us.
I confess to being pretty badly scared at this possibility, but the women
on board seemed to have worked off their excitement by this time, and
we all kept quiet and behaved ourselves very creditably. While the council was still in session, fresh reports came in confirming those already
brought, and we put back to Macon, without standing on the order of

our going. Helen Swift, a friend of the Toombses, who had joined us at Macon, lives only fifteen miles from the place where we turned back. She was bitterly disappointed, and I don't blame her for nearly crying her eyes out. Mr. Adams undertook to administer spiritual consolation, but I don't think Helen was very spiritually-minded towards Yankees just at that time.

Excited crowds were waiting at all the stations as we went back, and the news we brought increased the ferment tenfold. The general impression seems to be that the Yanks are advancing upon Macon in three columns, and that they will reach the city by tomorrow or next day, at latest. We came back to the Lanier House, and Fred hopes to get us out by way of Milledgeville, before they arrive. When our train got back to Macon, the men on board had gradually dropped off on the way, so that I don't suppose there were more than 200 or 300 remaining of all that had gone out in the morning. The demoralization is complete. We are whipped, there is no doubt about it. Everybody feels it, and there is no use for the men to try to fight any longer, though none of us like to say so.

Just before we reached Macon, the down train, which had been reported captured, overtook us at a siding, with the tantalizing news that we might have got through to Atlanta if we had gone straight on. The Yankees were twelve miles off at the time of its reported capture, and cut the road soon after it passed. There was an immense crowd at the dépot on our return, and when I saw what a wild commotion the approach of the Yankees created, I lost all hope and gave up our cause as doomed. We made a brave fight but the odds against us were too great. The spell of invincibility has left us and gone over to the heavy battalions of the enemy. As I drove along from the station to the hotel, I could see that preparations were being made to evacuate the city. Government stores were piled up in the streets and all the horses and wagons that could be pressed into service were being hastily loaded in the effort to remove them. The rush of men had disappeared from Mulberry St. No more gay uniforms, no more prancing horses, but only a few ragged foot soldiers with wallets and knapsacks on, ready to march—Heaven knows where. Gen. Elzey and staff left early in the morning to take up their new quarters either in Augusta or Washington, and if we had only known it, we might have gone out with them. I took a walk on the streets while waiting to get my room at the hotel, and found everything in the wildest confusion. The houses were closed, and doleful little groups were clustered about the street corners discussing the situation. All the intoxicating liquors that could be found in the stores, warehouses, and barrooms, had been seized by the authorities and emptied on the ground. In some places the streets smelt like a distillery, and I saw men, boys, and negroes down on their knees lapping it up from the gutter like dogs. Little children were staggering about in a state of beastly intoxication. I think there can be no more dreary spectacle in the world than a city on the eve of evacuation, unless it is one that has already fallen into the hands of the enemy. I returned to the hotel with a heavy heart, for while out I heard fresh rumors of Lee's surrender. No one seems to doubt it, and everybody feels ready to give up hope. "It is useless to struggle longer," seems to be the common cry, and the poor wounded men go hobbling about the streets with despair on their faces. There is a new pathos in a crutch or an empty sleeve, now that we know it was all for nothing.

# Mary A. H. Gay

## From *Life in Dixie during the War*

### CHAPTER XVII.

A visit to Confederate lines—A narrow escape—My return—
The fall of Atlanta.

No news from "the front"; no tidings from the loved ones in gray; no friendly spirit whispering words of cheer or consolation. Shut up within a narrow space, and guarded by Federal bayonets! not a ray of friendly light illuminated my environment.

The constant roaring of cannon and rattling of musketry; the thousand, yea, tens of thousands of shots blending into one grand continuous whole, and reverberating in avalanchan volume over the hills of Fulton, and the mountain heights of old DeKalb—told in thunder tones of the fierce contest between Federal and Confederate forces being waged without intermission for the possession of Atlanta.

The haughty, insolent boast of the enemy, now that Joe Johnston was removed from the command of the Army of the Tennessee, that they would make quick work of the rebellion, and of the complete subjugation of the South, had in no way a tendency to mitigate anxiety or to encourage hope. Thus surrounded, I sought and obtained permission to read Federal newspapers. The United States mail brought daily papers to the officers in command of the forces quartered in our yard; and through this medium I kept posted, from a Northern standpoint, concerning the

situation of both armies. While there was little in these dispatches gratifying to me, there was much that I thought would be valuable to my
people if I could only convey it to them; and I racked my brain day
and night, devising ways and means by which to accomplish this feat.
But the ways and means decided upon were, upon reflection, invariably
abandoned as being impracticable.

In this dilemma, a most opportune circumstance offered an immediate solution of the difficult problem. In the midst of a deep study of the
relative positions of the two armies, and of the hopes and fears animating
both, a tall, lank, honest-faced Yankee came to the door of the portico
and asked "if Miss Gay was in."

I responded that I was she, and he handed me a letter addressed to
myself. I hastily tore it open and read the contents. It was written by a
reverend gentleman whose wife was a distant relative of my mother, and
told that she was very ill. "Indeed," wrote he, "I have but little hope of
ever seeing her any better, and I beg you to come to see her, and spend
several days."

I showed the letter to my mother, who was sitting near by, and, like
myself, engaged in studying the situation. She strenuously objected to my
going, and advanced many good reasons for my not doing so; but my reasons for going counteracted them all in my estimation, and I determined
to go.

Taking Telitha with me, I carried the letter to the Provost Marshal, and
asked him to read it and grant me the privilege of going. After reading
the letter, he asked me how I obtained it, and received my statement.
He then asked me if I could refer him to the party who brought it to
me. Leaving the letter with him, I ran home and soon returned with the
desired individual who had fortunately lingered in the yard in anticipa-
tion of usefulness. Convinced that the invitation was genuine, and for a
humane purpose, this usually morose marshal granted me "a permit" to
visit those poor old sick people, for the husband was almost as feeble as
his wife. I told the obliging marshal that there was another favor I should
like to ask of him, if he would not think me too presumptuous. "Name
it," he said. I replied:

"Will you detail one or more of the soldiers to act as an escort for me? I am afraid to go with only this girl."

To this he also assented, and said it was a wise precaution. He asked when I wished to come home.

"Day after to-morrow afternoon," I told him, and received assurance that an escort would be in waiting for me at that time.

It now became necessary to make some important preparations for the trip. A great deal was involved, and if my plans were successful, important events might accrue. A nice white petticoat was called into requisition, and, when I got done with it, it was literally lined with Northern newspapers. "The Cincinnati Enquirer," and "The New York Daily Times"; "The Cincinnati Commercial Gazette," and "The Philadelphia Evening Ledger," under the manipulation of my fingers, took their places on the inner sides and rear of the skirt, and served as a very stylish "bustle," an article much in vogue in those days. This preparatory work having been accomplished, it required but a few moments to complete my toilet, and, under the auspices of a clear conscience and a mother's blessing, doubtless, I started on a perilous trip. The ever-faithful Telitha was by my side, and the military escort a few feet in advance.

After a walk of a mile and a half, I reached my destination for that day. I found the old lady in question much better than I had expected. Nervous and sick himself, her husband had greatly exaggerated her afflictions. By degrees, and under protest, I communicated to these aged people my intention of carrying information to Hood's headquarters, that might be of use to our army. I knew that these good old people would not betray me, even though they might not approve my course, and I confided to them my every plan. Both were troubled about the possible result if I should be detected; but my plans were laid, and nothing could deter me from pursuing them.

The rising sun of another day saw Telitha and me starting on our way to run the gauntlet, so to speak, of Federal bayonets. These good old people had given me much valuable information regarding the way to Atlanta—information which enabled me to get there without conflict with either Confederate or Federal pickets. Knowing the topography of the country, I took a circuitous route to an old mill; Cobb's, I believe, and from there I sought the McDonough road. I didn't venture to keep that highway to the city, but I kept within sight of it, and under cover of breast-works and other obstructions, managed to evade videttes and pickets of both armies. After walking fourteen or fifteen miles, I entered Atlanta at the beautiful home of Mrs. L. P. Grant, at the southern boundary of the city. That estimable lady never lost an opportunity of doing good. The lessons of humanity and Christian grace impressed upon her youthful mind, and intensified by the life-long example of her devoted mother, Mrs. Ammi Williams, of Decatur, had called into action all that is ennobling in woman. On this occasion, as upon every other offering an opportunity, she remembered to do good. She ordered an appetizing lunch, including a cup of sure enough coffee, which refreshed and strengthened me after my long walk. Her butler having become a familiar personage on the streets of Atlanta, she sent him as a guide to important places. We entered the city unchallenged, and moved about at will. The force of habit, probably, led me to Mrs. McArthur's and to Mrs. Craig's on Pryor street; and, by the way, these friends still own the same property, and occupy almost the same homes. The head of neither of these families was willing to accompany me to Confederate headquarters, and without a guide I started to hunt them for myself. What had seemed an easy task now seemed insurmountable. I knew not in what direction to go, and the few whom I asked seemed as ignorant as myself. Starting from Mrs. Craig's, I went towards the depot. I had not proceeded very far before I met Major John Y. Rankin. I could scarcely restrain tears of joy. He was a member of the very same command to which my brother belonged. From Major Rankin I learned that my brother, utterly prostrated, had been sent to a hospital, either in Augusta or Madison. He told me many other things of interest, which I cannot mention now, unless I was compiling a history instead of a series of personal reminiscences. Preferring not to stand upon the street, I asked Major Rankin to return with me to Mrs. Craig's, which he did, and spent an hour in pleasant conversation. Mrs. Craig was a delightful conversationalist, and while she was entertaining the major with that fine art, I retired to a private apartment, and with the aid of a pair of scissors ripped off the papers from my underskirt and smoothed and folded them nicely, and after re-arranging my toilet, took them into the parlor as a trophy of skill in outwitting the Yankee. Telitha, too, had a trophy to which she had clung ever since we left home with the tenacity of an eel, and which doubtless she supposed to be an offering to "Marse Tom," and was evidently anxious that he should receive it. Having dismissed Mrs. Grant's butler as no longer necessary to my convenience, Major Rankin, myself and Telitha went direct to the headquarters of his command. The papers seemed to be most acceptable, but I noticed that the gleanings from conversation seemed far more so. The hopefulness and enthusiasm of our soldiers were inspiring. But alas! how little they knew of the situation, and how determined not to be enlightened. Even then they believed that they would hold Atlanta against Herculean odds, and scorned the idea of its surrender. At length the opening of Telitha's package devolved on me. Shirts, socks and soap, towels, gloves, etc., formed a compact bundle that my mother had sent to our soldiers. Many cheery words were said, and good-byes uttered, and I left them to meet once more under very different circumstances.

I now turned my thoughts to our negroes, who were hired in different parts of the city. Rachel, the mother of King, hired herself and rented a room from Mr. John Silvey, who lived upon the same lot on Marietta street upon which he has since erected his present elegant residence. In order that I might have an interview with Rachel without disturbing Mr. Silvey's family, I went to the side gate and called her. She answered and came immediately. I asked her if she realized the great danger to which she was continually exposed. Even then "shot and shell" were falling in every direction, and the roaring of cannon was an unceasing sound. She replied that she knew the danger, and thought I was doing wrong to be in Atlanta when I had a home to be at. I insisted that she had the same home, and a good vacant house was ready to receive her. But she was impervious to every argument, and preferred to await the coming of Sherman in her present quarters. Seeing that I had no influence over her, I bade her good-bye and left. Telitha and I had not gone farther than the First Presbyterian church (not a square away) from the gate upon which I had leaned during this interview with Rachel, before a bombshell fell by

that gate and burst into a thousand fragments, literally tearing the gate
into pieces. Had I remained there one minute longer, my mortal being
would have been torn to atoms. After this fearfully impressive adventure, unfortified by any "permit" I struck a bee line to Mrs. Grant's,
having promised her that I would go back that way and stop awhile. An
old negro man belonging to Mrs. Williams, who had "come out" on a
previous occasion, was there, and wanted to return under my protection to his home within the enemy's lines. Very earnest assurances from
Mrs. Grant to that effect convinced me that I had nothing to fear from
betrayal by him, and I consented that he should be a member of my
company homeward bound. Two large packages were ready for the old
man to take charge of, about which Mrs. Grant gave him directions, *sotto
voce*. Putting one of them on the end of a walking cane he threw it over
his right shoulder, and with his left hand picked up the other bundle.
Telitha and I were unencumbered. With a good deal of trepidation I took
the advance position in the line of march, and walked briskly. We had
not proceeded very far before we encountered our pickets. No argument
was weighty enough to secure for me the privilege of passing the lines
without an official permit. Baffled in this effort, I approved the action
of the pickets, and we turned and retraced our steps in the direction of
Atlanta, until entirely out of sight of them, and then we turned southward and then eastward, verging a little northward. Constant vigilance
enabled me to evade the Yankee pickets, and constant walking brought
me safely to the home of my aged and afflicted friends, from which I had
started early in the morning of that day. Not being tired, I could have
gone home; but the policy of carrying out the original programme is too
apparent to need explanation. These friends were conservative in every
act and word, and, it may be, leaned a little out of the perpendicular
towards that "flaunting lie," the United States flag; therefore they were
favorites among the so-called defenders of the Union, and were kept supplied with many palatable articles of food that were entirely out of the
reach of rebels who were avowed and "dyed in the wool."

A few minutes sufficed to furnish us with a fine pot of soup (and good
bread was not lacking), of which we ate heartily. The old negro man was
too anxious to get home to be willing to spend the night so near, just for

the privilege of walking into Decatur under Yankee escort, and said he was "going home," and left me.

The next day my escort was promptly on hand, and in due time I was in Decatur, none the worse for having put into practice a favorite aphorism of the Yankees, that "all things are fair in war."

The old man had preceded me, and faithful to the behest of Mrs. Grant, had turned over a valuable package to my mother.

Not many mornings subsequent to the adventure just related, I discovered upon opening the door that the Yankee tents seemed to be vacant. Not a blue-coat was to be seen. What could it mean? Had they given up the contest and ignominiously fled? As if confirmatory of the gratifying suggestion, the booming of cannon in the direction of Atlanta was evidently decreasing. Then again I thought perhaps the wagon train had been sent out to forage upon the country, and as it would now have to go forty-five and fifty miles to get anything, it required an immense military escort to protect it from the dashing, sanguinary attacks of the "rebels." The latter thought was soon dismissed and the former embraced, and how consoling it was to me. Before the sun had attained its meridian height, a number of our scouts appeared on the abandoned grounds; and what joy their presence gave us! But they left us as suddenly as they came, and on reflection we could not think of a single encouraging word uttered by them during their stay. Suspense became intolerable. With occasional lulls, the roaring of cannon was a continuous blending of ominous sound.

In the midst of this awful suspense, an apparition, glorious and bright, appeared in our presence. It was my brother. He had left Madison a few days before, where he had been allowed to spend a part of his furlough, instead of remaining at the Augusta hospital, and where he received the tender ministrations of his estimable cousin, Mrs. Tom Hillsman, and her pretty young daughters, and the loving care of his sister Missouri, who was also at this time an inmate of her cousin's household. How I wished he could have remained there until restored to health. One less patriotic and conscientious would have done so. His mother's joy at meeting her beloved son, and under such circumstances, was pathetic indeed, and I shall never forget the effort she made to repress the tears and steady the voice as she sought to nerve him for the arduous and perilous duties before him. Much of his conversation, though hurried, was regarding his Mary, in Texas, and the dear little boy dropped down from heaven, whom he had never seen. The shades of night came on, and darker grew until complete blackness enveloped the face of the earth, and still the low subdued tones of conversation between mother, son and daughter, mingled with unabated interest. Hark! Hark! An explosion! An earthquake? The angry bellowing sound rises in deafening grandeur, and reverberates along the far-off valleys and distant hilltops. What is it? This mighty thunder that never ceases? The earth is ablaze—what can it be? This illumination that reveals minutest objects? With blanched face and tearful eye, the soldier said:

"Atlanta has surrendered to the enemy. The mighty reports are occasioned by the blowing up of the magazines and arsenals."

Dumbfounded we stood, trying to realize the crushing fact. Woman's heart could bear no more in silence, and a wail over departed hopes mingled with the angry sounds without.

Impelled by a stern resolve, and a spirit like to that of martyred saints, our brother said:

"This is no place for me. I must go."

And then he put an arm around each of us, and kissed us with a fervor of love that knew no bounds, and was quenching itself in unfathomable hopeless tenderness. The quiet fortitude and patriotism of his mother gave way in that dread hour, and she cried aloud in agonizing apprehension of never again clasping to her bosom her greatest earthly joy. No pen can describe the scene of that last parting between mother and son, and in sheer impotency I drop the curtain.

As he walked away from his sobbing mother, through the war-illuminated village, I never beheld mortal man so handsome, so heroically grand. His great tender heart, which I had seen heave and sway under less trying circumstances, seemed to have ossified, and not an emotion was apparent.

# Mary S. Mallard and Mary Jones

## From *The Children of Pride:*
## *A True Story of Georgia and the Civil War*

### XXIII

MRS. MARY S. MALLARD *in her Journal*

*Montevideo, Tuesday, December 13th, 1864.* Mother rode to Arcadia this morning to superintend the removal of household articles and the remainder of library, etc., believing that the Yankees were no nearer than Way's Station, and lingered about the place until late in the afternoon, when she started to return to Montevideo. It was almost sunset, and she was quietly knitting in the carriage, fearing no evil. Jack was driving, and as they came opposite the Girardeau place, now owned by Mr. W. E. W. Quarterman, a Yankee on horseback sprang from the woods and brought his carbine to bear upon Jack, ordering him to halt. Then, lowering the carbine, almost touching the carriage window and pointing into it, he demanded of Mother what she had in the carriage.

She replied: "Nothing but my family effects."

"What have you in that box behind your carriage?"

"My servants' clothing."

"Where are you going?"

"To my home."

"Where is your home?"

"Nearer the coast."

"How far is the coast?"

"About ten miles. I am a defenseless woman—a widow—with only one motherless child with me. Have you done with me, sir? Drive on, Jack!"

Bringing his carbine to bear on Jack, he called out: "No! Halt!" He then asked: "Where are the rebels?"

"We have had a post at No. 3."

Looking into the carriage, he said: "I would not like to disturb a lady; and if you will take my advice you will turn immediately back, for the men are just ahead. They will take your horses and search your carriage, and I cannot say what they will do."

Mother replied: "I thank you for that," and ordered Jack to turn. Jack saw a number of men ahead, and Mother would doubtless have been in their midst had she proceeded but a few hundred yards. (This must have been an officer; he was a hale, hearty man, well dressed, with a new blue overcoat, and well appointed in every respect.) Jack then drove through by Colonel Quarterman's, and not very far beyond met our picket guard.

It was now quite dark. When she came to the junction with the Walthourville road, there she met a company of cavalry commanded by Captain Little. She informed them of the position of the Yankees, and entreated that he would give her an escort if but for a few miles. She told him the distressing circumstances of her family, and that she was compelled to reach her home and her daughter that night. He replied they were ordered to that point, and if she would stay with them or go with them they would protect her, but they could not send anyone with her. She again urged her distressing circumstances. He said: "The Boro bridge is burnt, and you may not go a mile before you meet the enemy. I cannot help you."

"Then I will trust in God and go forward!"

Meeting a servant of Captain Randal Jones's who had been with him in Virginia, he ran along with the carriage. He had been sent from the depot to inform his young mistress of the presence of the enemy. He rendered her very kind service, acting as a scout. He would dart forward, take an observation, and encourage her to proceed. Every moment she expected to meet the Yankees.

Passing from the public road, Mother turned up the crossroad by Tranquil Hill. At the avenue our picket was stationed, who informed her that the bridges on the causeway had been taken up, and her carriage could not cross over. Mother replied: "Then I must get out and walk, for I must reach home tonight if my life is spared!" She rode up to the dwelling house; Dr. and Mrs. Way came to the carriage and pressed her very kindly to remain all night. She had resolved to walk home when Mr. William Winn, one of the picket guard, rode up and informed Mother the bridges had been fixed so as to allow the carriage to pass over.

She hastened forward and met a picket near the crossroads by the Baptist church; saw no one again until reaching the hill above the Boro. Under the crack of the door she discovered a dim light, and taking the reins sent Jack in to inquire if the enemy was near. The reply was: "Yes, the Boro is full of Yankees." Turning up the Darien road, she made her way through an obscure and very rough road through the woods which had been used as a wood road, just back of our encampment. Jack was unacquainted with the way. The old horses completely tired out, so that with difficulty she passed into the old field back of the Boro into the road leading to our enclosure, reaching home after nine o'clock.

I was rejoiced to hear the sound of the carriage wheels, for I had been several hours in the greatest suspense, not knowing how Mother would hear of the presence of the enemy, and fearing she would unexpectedly find herself in their midst at the Boro.

Late in the evening Milton came running in to say a boy had met the oxcarts going to Arcadia and told them they could not pass, for the Yankees were in the Boro. It was a perfect thunderclap. In a few moments the boy was at the door confirming the intelligence; he was sent by Mr. Audley King and Mr. McCollough. Fearing a raiding party might come up, immediately I had some trunks of clothing and other things carried into the woods, and the carts and horses taken away and the oxen driven away, and prepared to pass the night alone with the little children, as I had no idea Mother could reach home.

After ten o'clock Mr. Mallard came in to see us, having come from No. 3, where a portion of Colonel Hood's command was stationed. Upon consultation the trunks were brought back. Mr. Mallard stayed with us until two o'clock A.M. and, fearing to remain longer, left to join the soldiers at No. 4½ (Johnston Station), where they were to rendezvous. He had exchanged his excellent horse Jim with Cyrus Mallard for a mule, as Cyrus was going on picket and he thought he would need a swifter animal. This distressed us very much, and I told him I feared he would be captured. It was hard parting under this apprehension, and he lingered as long as possible, reading a part of the 8th Chapter of Romans and engaging in prayer before leaving. It was moonlight, and Jack was sent forward to see if there was any advance of the enemy upon the place, as there was much open space to be passed over before he could reach the woods. Before parting he went up and kissed his children, charging me to tell them "Papa has kissed them when asleep." I had a fearful foreboding that he would be captured, and we stayed as long as prudence would permit in the front porch.

*Wednesday, December 14th.* Although it had been much past midnight when we retired, Mother and I rose early, truly thankful no enemy had come near us during the night. We passed the day in fearful anxiety. Late in the afternoon Charles came into the parlor, just from Walthourville, and burst into tears.

I asked what was the matter.

"Oh," he said, "very bad news! Master is captured by the Yankees, and says I must tell you keep a good heart."

This was a dreadful blow to us and to the poor little children. Mamie especially realized it, and cried all the evening; it was heartrending to see the agony of her little face when told her papa was taken prisoner. Mr. Mallard was standing in the porch of his own house at Walthourville when Kilpatrick's cavalry rode up and hailed him, demanding his horse. Supposing they were our own men (it being early and a very misty morning), he asked by what authority, when to his surprise he found himself a prisoner. The servants were all in the yard, and say he was dreadfully cursed by his captors, their language being both profane and vulgar. He was taken off upon the mule he had been riding. The servants then took the mules and wagon and in fear and trembling came down here. Mr. Mallard was captured before sunrise.

Mother sent Niger to South Hampton to ask Mrs. King to come to us immediately and to say the enemy was in the county. She was too unwell to come.

*Thursday, December 15th.* About ten o'clock Mother walked out upon the lawn, leaving me in the dining room. In a few moments Elsie came running in to say the Yankees were coming. I went to the front door and saw three dismounting at the stable, where they found Mother and rudely demanded of her: "Where are your horses and mules? Bring them out!"—at the same instant rushing by her as she stood in the door. I debated whether to go to her or remain in the house. The question was soon settled, for in a moment a stalwart Kentucky Irishman stood before me, having come through the pantry door. I scarcely knew what to do. His salutation was: "Have you any whiskey in the house?"

I replied: "None that I know of."

"You ought to know," he said in a very rough voice.

I replied: "This is not my house, so I do not know what is in it."

Said he: "I mean to search this house for arms, but I'll not hurt you." He then commenced shaking and pushing the folding door and calling for the key.

Said I: "If you will turn the handle and slide the door you will find it open."

The following interrogatories took place:

"What's in that box?"

"Books."

"What's in that room beyond?"

"Search for yourself."

"What's in that press?"

"I do not know."

"Why don't you know?"

"Because this is my mother's house, and I have recently come here."

"What's in that box?"

"Books and pictures."

"What's that, and where's the key?"

"My sewing machine. I'll get the key."

He then opened the side door and discovered the door leading into the old parlor. "I want to get into that room."

"If you will come around, I will get the key for you."

As we passed through the parlor into the entry he ran upstairs and commenced searching my bedroom. "Where have you hid your arms?"

"There are none in the house. You can search for yourself."

He ordered me to get the keys immediately to all my trunks and bureaus. I did so, and he put his hands into everything, even a little trunk containing needle books, boxes of hair, and other small things. All this was under cover of searching for arms and ammunition. He called loudly for *all* the keys; I told him my mother would soon be in the house and she would get her keys for him.

While he was searching my bureau he turned to me and asked: "Where is your watch?"

I told him my husband had worn my watch, and he had been captured the day before at Walthourville.

Shaking his fist at me, he said: "Don't you lie to me! You have got a watch!"

I felt he could have struck me to the floor; but looking steadily at him, I replied: "I have a watch and chain, and my husband has them with him."

"Well, were they taken from him when he was captured?"

"That I do not know, for I was not present."

Just at this moment I heard another Yankee coming up the stair steps and saw a young Tennessean going into Mother's room, where he commenced his search. Mother came in soon after and got her keys; and there we were, following these two men around the house, handing them keys (as they would order us to do in the most insolent manner), and seeing almost everything opened and searched and tumbled about.

The Tennessean found an old workbox, and hearing something rattling in it, he thought it was coin and would have broken it open. But Dick, the Kentuckian, prevented him until Mother got the key, and his longing eyes beheld a bunch of keys.

In looking through the bureaus, to Mother's surprise, Dick pulled out a sword that had belonged to her deceased brother and had been in her possession for thirty-one years. Finding it so rusty, they could scarcely draw it from the scabbard, and concluded it would not kill many men in this war and did not take it away.

The Tennessean found a large spyglass which had belonged to Mr. Mallard's father, and brought it out as quite a prize.

I said to him: "You won't take that!"

"No," said he, "I only want to look through it. It's of no use to me."

Dick went into the attic, but did not call for the keys to the two locked rooms. He took up the spyglass, and winking at me said: "I mean to take this to Colonel Jones." (Susan had told him Mary Ruth was Colonel Jones's child.)

Mother said to him: "Is your commanding officer named Jones?"

He laughed and said he meant to take the glass to Colonel Jones.

I said: "You won't take that, for I value it very much, as it belonged to my father."

Said he: "It's of no use to you."

"No, none whatever beyond the association, and you have much finer in your army."

He did not take it, though we thought he would have done so if we had not been present. He turned to Mother and said: "Old lady, haven't you got some whiskey?"

She replied: "I don't know that I have."

"Well," said he, "I don't know who ought to know if you don't!"

Mother asked him if he would like to see his mother and wife treated in this way—their house invaded and searched.

"Oh," said he, "none of us have wives!"

Whilst Mother walked from the stable with one of the Yankees from Kentucky he had a great deal to say about the South bringing on the war. On more than one occasion they were anxious to argue political questions with her. Knowing it was perfectly useless, she would reply: "This is neither the time nor place for these subjects. My countrymen have decided that it was just and right to withdraw from the Union. We wished to do it peaceably; you would not allow it. We have now appealed to arms; and I have nothing more to say with you upon the subject."

Mother asked him if he would like to see his mother and sisters treated as they were doing us.

"No," said he, "I would not. And I never do enter houses, and shall not enter yours."

And he remained without while the other two men searched. They took none of the horses or mules, as they were too old.

A little before dinner we were again alarmed by the presence of five Yankees dressed as marines. One came into the house—a very mild sort of a man. We told him the house had already been searched. He asked if the soldiers had torn up anything. One of the marines (as they called themselves) came into the pantry and asked if they could get anything to eat. Mother told them she had only what was prepared for our own dinner, and if they chose they could take it where it was—in the kitchen. They said they preferred to take it there, and going to the kitchen, they cursed the servants awfully, ordered milk, potatoes, and other things. They called for knives and forks, and having no others Mother sent out those we used; but they ordered Milton to take them immediately back and to tell his mistress to put them away in a safe place, as "a parcel of damned Yankees" would soon be along, and they would take every one from her.

We hoped they would not intrude upon the dwelling; but as soon as they finished eating, the four came in, and one commenced a thorough search, ordering us to get him all the keys. He found some difficulty in fitting the keys, and I told him I would show them to him if he would hand me the bunch.

He replied: "I will give them to you when I am ready to leave the house."

He went into the attic and instituted a thorough search into every hole and corner. He opened a large trunk containing the private papers of my dear father, and finding a tin canister, he tried to open it. Mother could not immediately find the key, and as he spoke insolently to her about getting the key, she told him he had better break it, but she could assure him it contained only the private papers of her husband, who was a minister of the gospel.

"Damn it," he said, "if you don't get the key I will break it. I don't care!"

In looking through the trunk he found a beautiful silver goblet which had been given to Mother by her dear little granddaughter Julia, and which she had valued as a keepsake. His eyes sparkled as he held it up and called out: "Here's something pretty, boys!"

Mother looked at him scornfully and said: "And would you take it?"

He said no, and put it quickly down, although we believe only our presence kept him from pocketing it.

One of the party came in with a secession rosette which Brother Charlie had worn at the great meeting in Savannah when he was mayor of the city. Mother had given it to Jack with a few letters to put away. As they were riding up he took it from Jack, and we were quite amused to see him come in with it pinned on the lapel of his jacket. This one was quite inclined to argue about the origin of the struggle.

One of them had an old cap—the helmet-shaped cap with horsehair plume belonging to the Liberty Independent Troop, and the jacket also, as we afterwards understood were those formerly used by the troop. Being blue with bell buttons, they could very well pass for sailors' jackets. They had rigged themselves from some house they had searched before coming here.

After spending a long time in the search, they prepared to leave with all the horses. Mother told them they were over seventeen years old and would do them no service. They took away one mule, but in a short time we saw it at the gate: they had turned it back.

After they left I found that my writing desk had been most thoroughly searched and everything scattered, and all little articles of jewelry, pencils, etc., scattered. A gold pen was taken from my workbox.

Mother felt so anxious about Kate King that she sent Charles and Niger in the afternoon to urge her coming over to us, and told them if she was too unwell to walk or ride, they must take her up in their arms and let someone help to bring the little children. But they did not reach South Hampton, as they met a Yankee picket which turned Niger back and took Charles with them to assist in carrying horses to Midway, promising to let him return.

*Friday, December 16th.* Much to our relief, Prophet came over this morning with a note from Kate to know if we thought she could come to us. Mother wrote her to come immediately, which she did in great fear and trembling, not knowing but that she would meet the enemy on the road. We all felt truly grateful she had been preserved by the way.

About four in the afternoon we heard the clash of arms and noise of horsemen, and by the time Mother and I could get downstairs we saw forty or fifty men in the pantry, flying hither and thither, ripping open the safe with their swords and breaking open the crockery cupboards. Fearing we might not have a chance to cook, Mother had some chickens and ducks roasted and put in the safe for our family. These the men seized whole, tearing them to pieces with their teeth like ravenous beasts. They were clamorous for whiskey, and ordered us to get our keys. One came to Mother to know where her meal and flour were, insisted upon opening her locked pantry, and took every particle. They threw the sacks across their horses. Mother remonstrated and pointed to her helpless family; their only reply was: "We'll take it!"

They flew around the house, tearing open boxes and everything that was closed. They broke open Mother's little worktable with an andiron, hoping to find money or jewelry; it contained principally little mementos that were valuable only to herself. Failing to find treasure, they took the sweet little locks of golden hair that her mother had cut from the heads of her angel children near a half century ago, and scattering them upon the floor trampled them under their feet. A number of them rifled the sideboard, taking away knives, spoons, forks, tin cups, coffeepots, and everything they wished. They broke open Grandfather's old liquor case and carried off two of the large square gallon bottles, and drank up all the blackberry wine and vinegar which was in the case. It was vain to utter a word, for we were completely paralyzed by the fury of these ruffians.

A number of them went into the attic into a little storeroom and carried off twelve bushels of meal Mother had stored there for our necessities. She told them they were taking all she had to support herself and daughter, a friend, and five little children. Scarcely one regarded even the sound of her voice; those who did laughed and said they would leave one sack to keep us from starving. But they only left some rice which they did not want, and poured out a quart or so of meal upon the floor. At other times they said they meant to starve us to death. They searched trunks and bureaus and wardrobes, calling for shirts and men's clothes.

We asked for their officer, hoping to make some appeal to him; they said they were all officers and would do as they pleased. We finally found one man who seemed to make a little show of authority, which was indicated by a whip which he carried. Mother appealed to him, and he came up and ordered the men out. They instantly commenced cursing him, and we thought they would fight one another. They brought a wagon and took another from the place to carry off their plunder.

It is impossible to imagine the horrible uproar and stampede through the house, every room of which was occupied by them, all yelling, cursing, quarreling, and running from one room to another in wild confusion. Such was their blasphemous language, their horrible countenances and appearance, that we realized what must be the association of the lost in the world of eternal woe. Their throats were open sepulchres, their mouths filled with cursing and bitterness and lies. These men belonged to Kilpatrick's cavalry. We look back upon their conduct in the house as a horrible nightmare, too terrible to be true.

When leaving they ordered all the oxen to be gotten up early next morning.

MRS. MARY JONES *in her Journal*

*Montevideo, Saturday, December 17th, 1864.* About four o'clock this morning we were roused by the sound of horses; and Sue, our faithful woman, came upstairs breathless with dismay and told us they had come upon the most dreadful intent, and had sent her in to tell me what it was, and had inquired if there were any young women in my family. Oh, the agony—the agony of that awful hour no language can describe! No heart can conceive it. We were alone, friendless, and knew not what might befall us. Feeling our utter weakness and peril, we all knelt down around the bed and went to prayer; and we continued in silent prayer a long time. Kate prayed, Daughter prayed, and I prayed; and the dear little children, too, hearing our voices, got up and knelt down beside us.

And there we were, alone and unprotected, imploring protection from a fate worse than death, and that our Almighty God and Saviour would not permit our cruel and wicked enemies to come nigh our persons or our dwelling. We rose from our knees and sat in darkness, waiting for the light of the morning to reveal their purposes, but trusting in God for our deliverance.

New squads were arriving. In the gray twilight of morning we looked out of the window and saw one man pacing before the courtyard gate between the house and the kitchen; and we afterwards found he had voluntarily undertaken to guard the house. In this we felt that our prayers had been signally answered.

MRS. MARY S. MALLARD *in her Journal*

*Montevideo, Saturday, December 17th, 1864.* As soon as it was light Kate discovered an officer near the house, which was a great relief to our feelings. Mother and I went down immediately, when she said to him: "Sir, I see that you are an officer; and I come to entreat your protection for my family, and that you will not allow your soldiers to enter my dwelling, as it has been already three times searched and every particle of food and whatever they wanted taken." He replied it was contrary to orders for the men to be found in houses, and the penalty was death; and so far as his authority extended with his own men, none of them should enter the house. He said he and his squad (there were many others present) had come on a foraging expedition, and intended to take only provisions.

Upon Mother's inviting him to see some of the work of the previous evening he came in and sat awhile in the parlor. Before leaving he discovered a portable desk on a table and walked up and opened it. She said: "That is my private property; it is here for my own use, and has only a little paper in it." He closed it immediately. (It had previously escaped observation and removal.)

The Yankees made the Negroes bring up the oxen and carts, and took off all the chickens and turkeys they could find. They carried off all the syrup from the smokehouse. We had one small pig, which was all the meat we had left; they took the whole of it. Mother saw everything like food stripped from her premises, without the power of uttering one word. Finally they rolled out the carriage and took that to carry off a load of chickens. They took everything they possibly could.

The soldier who acted as our volunteer guard was from Ohio, and older than anyone we had seen; for generally they were young men and so active that Mother called them "fiery flying serpents." As he was going Mother went out of the house and said to him: "I cannot allow you to leave without thanking you for your kindness to myself and family; and if I had anything to offer I would gladly make you some return."

He replied: "I could not receive anything, and only wish I was here to guard you always."

It was not enough that they should insult us by converting our carriage into a chicken-cart and take it away drawn by our own carriage horses; but they sent in to tell Mother if she wanted her carriage to send for it, and when they were done with it she might have it. We afterwards learned it was broken to pieces and left beyond Midway Church.

They took off today June, Martin, George, Ebenezer, Little Pulaski, our house servant Jack, and Carpenter Pulaski. Seeing the two last-named going away, Mother called to the soldier who had them in charge: "Why are you taking my young men away?"

He said: "They need not go if they do not want to."

She then asked: "Boys, do you wish to go or stay?"

They immediately replied: "We wish to stay."

She then said: "Do you hear that? Now, by what right do you force them away?"

They had Pulaski laden down with our turkeys, and wanted Jack to drive one of the carts. So they were all carried off—carriages, wagons, carts, horses and mules and servants, with food and provisions of every kind—and, so far as they were concerned, leaving us to starvation.

A little while after this party started, Mother walked to the smoke-house and found an officer taking sugar that had been put to drip. He was filling a bag with all that was dry. He seemed a little ashamed of being caught in the act, but did not return the sugar, but carried it off on his horse. He was mounted on Mr. Audley King's pet horse, a splendid animal which he had just stolen, and as he rode off said: "How the man who *owns* this horse will curse the Yankee who took him when he goes home and finds him gone!" He had Mr. King's servant mounted on another of his horses, and no doubt knew Mrs. King was with us and would hear the remark.

Immediately we went to work moving some salt and the little remaining sugar into the house; and while we were doing it a Missourian came up and advised us to get everything into the house as quickly as possible, and he would protect us while doing so. He offered to show Mother how to hide her things. She said: "We need instruction from Yankees, for we have never been accustomed to any such mean business." He said he had enlisted to fight for the *Constitution;* but since then the war had been turned into another thing, and he did not approve this abolitionism, for his wife's people all owned slaves. He told us what afterwards proved false—that ten thousand infantry would soon pass through Riceboro on their way to Thomasville.

Soon after this some twenty rode up and caught me having a barrel rolled toward the house. They were gentlemanly. A few only dismounted; said they were from various of our Confederate States. They said the war would soon be over, for they would have Savannah in a few days.

I replied: "Savannah is not the Confederacy."

They spoke of the number of places they had taken.

I said: "Yes, and do you hold them?"

One of them replied: "Well, I do admire your spunk."

They inquired for all the large plantations.

Squads came all day until near dark. We had no time to eat a mouthful. The remaining ox-wagons were taken to the cornhouse and filled with corn.

*Sabbath, December 18th.* We passed this day with many fears, but no Yankees came to the lot; though many went to Carlawter and were engaged carrying off corn, the key of the cornhouse having been taken from Cato the day before and the door ordered to be left open. A day comparatively free from interruptions was very grateful to us, though the constant state of apprehension in which we were was distressing.

In the afternoon, while we were engaged in religious services, reading and seeking protection of our Heavenly Father, Captain Winn's Isaiah came bringing a note from Mr. Mallard to me and one from Mr. John Stevens to Mother, sending my watch. This was our first intelligence from Mr. Mallard, and oh, how welcome to us all; though the note brought no hope of his release, as the charge against him was taking up arms against the U.S. Captain Winn had been captured but released. We were all in such distress that Mother wrote begging Mr. Stevens to come to us. We felt so utterly alone that it would be a comfort to have him with us.

*Monday, December 19th.* Squads of Yankees came all day, so that the servants scarcely had a moment to do anything for us out of the house. The women, finding it entirely unsafe for them to be out of the house at all, would run in and conceal themselves in our dwelling. The few remaining chickens and some sheep were killed. These men were so outrageous at the Negro houses that the Negro men were obliged to stay at their houses for the protection of their wives; and in some instances they rescued them from the hands of these infamous creatures.

*Tuesday, December 20th.* A squad of Yankees came soon after breakfast. Hearing there was one yoke of oxen left, they rode into the pasture and drove them up, and went into the woods and brought out the horsewagon, to which they attached the oxen. Needing a chain for the purpose, they went to the well and took it from the well bucket. Mother went out and entreated them not to take it from the well, as it was our means of getting water. They replied: "You have no right to have even wood or water," and immediately took it away.

*Wednesday, December 21st.* 10 A.M. Six of Kilpatrick's cavalry rode up, one of them mounted on Mr. Mallard's valuable gray named Jim. They looked into the dairy and empty smokehouse, every lock having been broken and doors wide open day and night. They searched the servants' houses; then they thundered at the door of the dwelling. Mother opened it, when one of them presented a pistol to her breast and demanded why she dared to keep her house closed, and that "he be damned if he would not come into it."

She replied: "I prefer to keep my house closed because we are a helpless and defenseless family of women and little children. And one of your officers informed me that the men were not to enter private dwellings. And it is also contrary to the published orders of your general."

He replied: "I'll be damned if I don't come in and take just what I want. Some of the men got wine here, and we must have some."

She told them her house had been four times searched in every part, and everything taken from it. And recognizing one who had been of the party that had robbed us, she said: "You know my meal and everything has been taken."

He said: "We left you a sack of meal and that rice."

Mother said: "You left us some rice; but out of twelve bushels of meal you poured out a quart or so upon the floor—as you said, to keep us from starving."

She then entreated them, on account of the health of her daughter, not to enter the house. With horrible oaths they rode off, shooting two ducks in the yard.

About half an hour after, three came. One knocked in the piazza and asked if Mother always kept her doors locked. She said she had recently done so by the advice of an officer; and Kate King said: "We have been compelled to do so since the house has been so repeatedly ransacked."

He said: "Well, I never do that and did not come for that." Asked if we knew Mrs. S—— of Dorchester, for he had turned some men out of her house who were ransacking it. He demeaned himself with respect, and did not insist upon coming in.

Upon one occasion one of the men as he sat on the bench in the piazza had his coat buttoned top and bottom, and inside we could plainly see a long row of stolen breast pins and jewelry—gallant trophies, won from defenseless women and children at the South to adorn the persons of their mothers, wives, sisters, and friends in Yankeeland!

One hour after, five came. Mother and Kate trembled from head to feet. It appeared as if this day's trials were more than they could bear. They knelt and asked strength from God; went down and found that three had already entered the pantry with false keys brought for the purpose. They immediately proceeded to cut open the wires of the safe and took all they wanted, amongst other things a tin kettle of eggs we had managed to get.

Mother said to them: "Why, you have entered my house with false keys!"

With demoniacal leer they said: "We want none of your keys," and tried to put in one of those they brought into the pantry door.

She told them: "Your soldiers have already broken the key in that lock, and it cannot be opened; but everything has already been taken." When they insultingly insisted the door should be opened, Mother told them: "Very well, break it open just as soon as you please."

She remonstrated against their coming over the house, and told them of the order of the officers. They replied none of their officers prohibited them from coming in, and they would be damned if they would mind any such orders, would be damned if they did not go where they pleased, and would be damned if they did not take what they pleased. Mother remonstrated, and in her earnest entreaty placed her hand upon the shoulder of one of them, saying: "You must not go over my house." Strange to say, they did not go beyond the pantry, and appeared restrained, as we afterwards believed, by the hand of God. They said they wanted pots and buckets, for they were in camp and had nothing to cook in. One asked for whiskey. To our amusement the man who stole the eggs stumbled and fell as he went down the steps and broke them all—but carried off the bucket. (Psalm 27:2—"When the wicked, even mine enemies and my foes, came upon me to eat up my flesh, they stumbled and fell.")

At dinner time twelve more came—six or seven to the door asking for flour and meal. Mother told them she was a defenseless widow with an only daughter on the eve of again becoming a mother, a young friend, and five little children dependent on her for food and protection. They laughed and said: "Oh, we have heard just such tales before!" They wanted to know why the house was kept locked; said it would only make it worse for us. (This had proven false, for when the doors were open it was impossible to keep them out.) Kate observed a large cravat upon the neck of one made of a black silk dress of hers which had been taken by one of them a few days before. Every species of men's clothing in our trunks and bureaus and portmanteaus was taken, but none of our personal apparel, for we generally stood by when they were searching our wardrobes. They took every piece of jewelry they could find.

Twelve sheep were found shot and left in the pasture—an act of wanton wickedness.

Late in the afternoon more came and carried off the few remaining ducks. Going to the Negro houses, they called Cato, the driver, and told him they knew he was feeding "that damned old heifer in the house," and they would "blow out his damned brains" if he gave her another morsel to eat, for they meant to starve her to death. Pointing to the chapel, they asked what house that was. Cato answered: "A church which my master had built for the colored people on the place to hold prayers in the week and preach in on Sunday." They said: "Yes, there he told all his damned lies and called it preaching." And with dreadful oaths they cursed him. To Patience, when they were taking good and valuable books from his library (as they said, to send their old fathers at home), they said, when she spoke with honor of her master and his labors for the good of the colored people: "He was a damned infernal villain, and we only wish he was now alive; we would blow his brains out." To Sue they said, when she spoke of his goodness to the people: "We wish he was now here; we would cut his throat." They stole two blankets from July, and attempted to steal his hat. They took a piggin of boiled potatoes from Sue, and threw the piggin in the marsh when they had eaten them.

After all the day's trials, late at night came Kate's servant Prophet bringing her some clothing and chickens. We were rejoiced to see anyone. He reported South Hampton had been visited by a hundred and fifty men, who had taken all the corn given to the Negroes (three months' allowance), killed forty or fifty hogs and taken seven beef cattle, stolen all the syrup and sugar from the Negroes, and taken their clothing, crawling under their houses and beds searching for buried articles.

MRS. MARY JONES *in her Journal*

*Montevideo, Thursday, December 22nd, 1864.* Several squads of Yankees came today, but none insisted upon coming into the house. Most of the remaining geese were killed by them. One attempted forcibly to drag Sue by the collar of her dress into her room. Another soldier coming up told him to "let that old woman alone"; and while they were speaking together she made her escape to the dwelling, dreadfully frightened and thoroughly enraged. The horrible creature then went to old Mom Rosetta; and she told him he had "no manners," and after awhile got him away. Sue's running into the house sent a thrill of terror into Kate and myself, for we were momentarily expecting them to enter the house. My heart palpitates with such violence against my side that with pain I bear the pressure of my dress.

If it was not for the supporting hand of God we must give up and die. His precious Word and prayer sustains our fainting souls. Besides our morning and evening devotions Kate, Daughter, and I observe a special season every afternoon to implore protection for our beloved ones and ourselves and deliverance for our suffering country. I have often said to the enemy: "I pray not for revenge upon you, but I pray daily for deliverance from you"; and always felt amid my deepest distresses: "Oh, if my country was but free and independent, I could take joyfully the spoiling of my goods!"

MRS. MARY S. MALLARD *in her Journal*

*Montevideo, Thursday, December 22nd, 1864.* About midday the two little boys Mac and Pulaski made their appearance, having escaped from the Yankees at Midway. One of the officers told Pulaski Mr. Mallard was at the Ogeechee bridge, and had been preaching for them and walking at large. They had put no handcuffs on him, and he was walking at large, and they gave him plenty to eat. We are all thankful to hear from him.

Pulaski says he asked for the well chain. They cursed him and said his mistress should do without it.

One squad who came to the house asked Mother when she had seen any rebels, and if there were any around here. She told them her son-in-law had been captured more than a week before, and he was the only gentleman belonging to our household.

Looking fiercely at her, he said: "If you lie to me I will—" The rest of the sentence Mother did not quite understand; it was either "I'll kill you" or "I'll blow your brains out."

She immediately stepped out upon the little porch, near which he was sitting on his horse as he spoke to her, and said to him: "In the beginning of this war one passage of Scripture was impressed upon my mind;

and it now abides with me: 'Fear not them which kill the body and after that have no more that they can do. But fear Him who, after He hath killed, hath power to cast into hell.' I have spoken the truth, and do you remember that you will stand with me at the Judgment Bar of God!"

There were quite a number around. One man said: "Madam, if that is your faith, it is a good one."

She replied: "It is my faith, and I feel that it has power to sustain me."

One of these men threatened Cato with a pistol at his breast that if he did feed his mistress they would kill him; called her an old devil, and applied other dreadful epithets such as are used by the lowest and most profane.

Early in the afternoon the same officer called who had previously been in the house. He immediately inquired if the men had done any injury within since he was here last. Whilst he conversed with Kate and Mother his men were firing and killing the geese in the lot and loading their horses with them.

Before leaving he asked for a glass of water. Mother handed him a glass, saying: "I regret that I cannot offer a glass of fresh water, for you have taken even the chain from my well bucket."

He replied very quickly: "I did not do it. Neither did my men do it."

Having heard nothing from Mr. Stevens, Mother sent Charles to Captain Winn's (where he was staying) to ask him to come to us, as we were all in much distress. Charles returned saying Mr. Stevens would come, but was waiting for Uncle William, who had left Springfield the day before and walked to Dorchester; and they expected him the next day at Captain Winn's.

*Friday, December 23rd.* A day of perfect freedom from the enemy at our dwelling. Five or six rode through the pasture, but none came to the house or Negro houses.

MRS. MARY JONES *in her Journal*

*Wednesday, January 4th.* At daylight my daughter informed me she was sick. She has been in daily expectation of her confinement for two weeks. I sent immediately for the servants and ordered my little riding pony, Lady Franklin, which the Yankees had taken and dragged several miles by the neck (because she would not lead) and finally let go, when she re-turned. And we have tried to keep her out of sight for this very purpose, saddled with my sidesaddle. Prepared a yellow flag for Charles (in case he met the Yankees) and wrote to Dr. Raymond Harris, three miles off and the only physician I know of in the county: "I entreat you to come to the help of my suffering child." Charles started before sunrise, going through the woods.

My heart was filled with intense anxiety and distress, especially as my child had an impression something was wrong with her unborn infant—the consequence of injuries received from a severe fall from a wagon, breaking her collarbone and bruising her severely, as they were making their retreat from Atlanta on the approach of General Sherman.

Dr. Harris, with a kindness and courage never to be forgotten, came without delay and in the face of danger; for the enemy was everywhere over the county. He looked very feeble, having been recently ill with pneumonia. Soon after being in her room he requested a private inter-view, informing me that my child was in a most critical condition, and I must be prepared for the worst. For if he did not succeed in relieving the difficulty, her infant at least must die.

I replied: "Doctor, the mother first."

"Certainly," was his answer.

He returned to her room and with great difficulty and skill succeeded in effecting what he desired. God, our compassionate Saviour, heard the voice of faith and prayer; and she was saved in childbearing, and at eleven o'clock gave birth to a well-formed infant—a daughter.

During these hours of agony the yard was filled with Yankees. It is supposed one hundred visited the place during the day. They were all around the house; my poor child, calm and collected amid her agony of body, could hear their conversation and wild halloos and cursing beneath her windows. Our dear friend Kate King had to meet them alone. She entreated that they would not come in or make a noise, for there was sickness in the house.

They replied: "We are not as bad as you think us. We will take off our spurs and come in." And one actually pushed by her and came in.

She stepped upon the porch and implored if there was one spark of humanity or honor about them that they would not come in, saying:

"You compel me to speak plainly. There is a child being born this very instant in this house, and if there is an officer or a gentleman amongst you I entreat you to protect the house from intrusion."

After a while they left, screaming and yelling in a most fiendish way as they rode from the house.

Dr. Harris returned with Charles as a guide and reached his home safely, having met only one of the enemy.

In the afternoon a very large party rode up; said they wanted to know the meaning of the yellow flag which was placed over the front porch. Had we sick soldiers, or was this a hospital? I told them it indicated sickness in my family: my daughter was ill. One asked for matches; I had none to give. And taking Carpenter Pulaski, they rode to the neighboring plantations. They searched all the Negro houses, within and without and under, taking whatever they wanted. They have taken Gilbert's knife and watch and chain, July's pants and blankets, George and Porter's blankets and clothes, the women's pails, piggins, spoons, buckets, pots, kettles, etc., etc.

# Alexander H. Stephens

## From *Recollections of Alexander H. Stephens*

### CHAPTER I

Fort Warren, Near Boston, Mass., May 27, 1865.—This book was purchased this day of A. J. Hall, Sutler at the Post, by Alexander H. Stephens, a prisoner at the Fort, with a view of preserving in it some regular record of the incidents of his imprisonment and prison life. It may be of interest to himself hereafter, should he be permitted to refer to it; and if his own life should not be spared, it may be of interest to some of his relatives and friends. He knows it will be of interest to his dear and only brother, the Hon. Linton Stephens, of Sparta, Ga., should this brother ever be permitted to see it. He feels sure that all his relatives would be exceedingly glad to peruse it, especially in the event that they never see him again. For these reasons the book has been purchased. In it, he will first transcribe his notes made in pencil from the time of leaving home; that done, he intends to continue it as a daily journal of such things as he may feel disposed to record.

Liberty Hall, Georgia, Thursday, May 11, 1865.—This was a most beautiful and charming morning. After refreshing sleep, I arose early. Robert Hull, a youth, son of Henry Hull, of Athens, Ga., had spent the night at my house. I wrote some letters for the mail, my custom being to attend to such business soon as breakfast was over; and Robert and I were amusing ourselves at casino, when Tim [a negro servant] came running into the parlour saying: "Master! more Yankees have come! a whole heap are in town, galloping all about with guns." Suspecting what it meant, I rose, told Robert I expected they had come for me, and entered my bedroom to make arrangements for leaving, should my apprehensions prove true. Soon, I saw an officer with soldiers under arms approaching the house. The doors were all open. I met him in the library. He asked if my name was Stephens. I replied that it was. "Alexander H. Stephens?" said he. I told him that was my name. He said he had orders to arrest me. I asked his name and to see his orders. He said he was Captain Saint of the 4th Iowa Cavalry, or mounted infantry, attached to General Nelson's command; he was then under General Upton: he showed me the order by General Upton, at Atlanta, directing my arrest and that of Robert Toombs; no charge was specified; he was instructed to go to Crawfordville, arrest me, proceed to Washington and arrest Mr. Toombs, and then carry both to General Upton's headquarters.

I told him I had been looking for something of this kind; at least, for some weeks had thought it not improbable; and hence had not left home; General Upton need not have sent any force for me; had he simply notified me that he wished me at his headquarters, I should have gone. I asked how I was to travel. He said: "On the cars." I then learned that his party had come down on the train arriving just before Tim's announcement. I asked if I would be permitted to carry any clothing. He said, "Yes." I asked how long I might have for packing. He said: "A few minutes— as long as necessary." I set to packing. Harry came in, evincing great surprise and regret, to pack for me. The Captain then said: "You may take a servant with you if you wish." I asked if he knew my destination. He said: "First, Atlanta; then, Washington City." I called in Anthony, a black boy from Richmond who had been waiting on me several years, and inquired if he wished to go; I told him I would send him from Washington to his mother in Richmond. He was willing, so I bade him be ready soon as possible.

In the meantime, Mr. Hidell [his secretary] had come in; he was living with me and had gone out after breakfast. None of my brother John's family residing at the old homestead happened to be with me; however, Clarence, who was going to school at the Academy, hearing of what had occurred (I suppose), came over with some friends from town. It was about 10 A.M. when Captain Saint arrived. In about fifteen minutes—not much over—we started for the depot, Anthony and I with the Captain and squad; friends, servants, and Clarence following, most of them crying. My own heart was full—too full for tears.

While Anthony was getting ready, I had asked Captain Saint if I might write a letter or two to some friends, to my brother and to my sister-in-law's family. He said I might. My brother and his children had left me two days before, after a visit of nearly a week. I wrote him a note in about these words:

*Dear Brother:* I have just been arrested by Captain Saint of the 4th Iowa Cavalry. The order embraces General Toombs. We are both to be carried to Atlanta, and thence to Washington City it seems. When I shall see you again, if ever, I don't know. May God enable you to be as well prepared for whatever fate may await me as I trust He will enable me to bear it. May His blessings ever attend you and yours. My kindest regards to Cosby, Dick Johnston, and all friends. I have not time to say more. My tenderest love to your dear little ones.     Yours most affectionately,
                                                    Alexander H. Stephens.

This I sealed and addressed to Linton and told Harry to send it over to Sparta immediately after I should leave. The Captain said he preferred that I should not send the note then; we should come back, and then I might send it. I told him it simply announced my arrest and destination; he might read it. I opened and handed it to him. He still objected, and I tore it up. Supposing similar objection would be made to my sending any other, I did not write to my sister-in-law's family. I knew that Mr. Hidell, Clarence, servants, and all present would give them full information. At the cars a great many people had assembled. All seemed deeply oppressed and grieved. Many wept bitterly. To me the parting was exceedingly sorrowful. Hidell was to leave for his home in Memphis on this day. He was all packed up and ready to start on the down train.

When we left the depot, the train backed up several hundred yards and took on some soldiers who seemed to have been put out there as scouts. While we were standing, I saw Mr. Singleton Harris and, by the Captain's permission, sent word to Hidell not to leave my house until he should hear from me. When all the soldiers were on the cars the train moved down the road again, not stopping until we reached Barnett, where we took another engine and started to Washington, Ga. About four miles from that town, the train slowed up at a shanty occupied by a track supervisor. Here, I was put off with about twenty soldiers to guard me. The Captain and the others went on to Washington. He said he expected to be back in an hour. He did not return until after dark. During his absence there was a heavy fall of rain, which was much needed as it had not rained for several weeks. The man of the house gave me dinner: fried meat and corn bread. He said it was the best he had. I was not hungry, but to show my gratitude for his hospitality, I shared his homely meal. Night came. The Captain had not returned. The good man asked me to partake of his supper; I accepted as before; his lady was kind, and apologized for having no better fare to offer.

Soon after dark, the engine was heard. I was anxious to know the result of Captain Saint's trip. What we supposed was the train proved to be the engine only: the Captain was bringing his men commissary stores. He went back immediately, but not before I had asked the cause of the detention. What had occurred? was General Toombs at home? He answered evasively, and left me in doubt and perplexity. About nine the engine was heard again. It brought the train. I was put aboard, Anthony looking after the baggage. The ground was wet and I got my feet damp; this, with the chill of the night air gave me a sore throat with severe hoarseness. When the train was under way for Barnett, I asked the Captain if he had Mr. Toombs. "No," he replied, "Mr. Toombs flanked us."[*] This was said in a rather disappointed and irate tone, and I made no further inquires. Reaching Barnett about eleven, we remained for some time and then took the train for Atlanta. Some panes of glass were broken out of the car windows, and I was further chilled.

❊    ❊    ❊

---

[*]Toombs was in his front door when Captain Saint entered his yard; he went out at the back and escaped to the woods.

## CHAPTER III

Thursday, June 1.—Dreamed of home last night. O Dreams! Visions! Shadows of the brain! What are you? My whole consciousness, since I heard of President Lincoln's assassination, seems nothing but a horrid dream.

It is a week since I entered these walls; three weeks since I was arrested at my home; and just four, I think, since all of the Stephens blood and name in Georgia, accidently, or providentially rather, met at the old homestead. That was a remarkable meeting. Linton and his three children were on a visit to me. We went down to the homestead; there, the widow of my brother, John L., and her family reside. Her three sons, John A., Linton Andrew, and William Grier, had just returned from the army. John had just got home from Johnson's Island where he had been a prisoner a long time; had been captured at Port Hudson in 1863. Mr. Lincoln, at my request, had granted him a special parole, for which I was truly obliged; this parole he had promised me at Hampton Roads, and had complied with his promise. He had written me a letter by John which I never saw until after his assassination. I almost wept over the letter when I saw it. He had sent to Johnson's Island for John. Had a personal interview with him [in Washington], treated him very kindly, spoke in kindly terms of his former acquaintance with me, all the particulars of which John gave me in detail. He let John remain in Washington as long as he chose, which was five days, I believe.

Linton A. had just gotten home from the army in North Carolina; William G., wounded in the leg, had been home some days from the same army. James Clarence, 15 years old, was at home; he had never been in the army. Mary Reid, their sister, with her little son, Leidy Stephens Reid, who lived with Sister Elizabeth, my brother John's widow, were at home. So all of our name and blood in the South were met together. All but William walked out to the old burying-ground; we stood by the graves of my father and grandfather. The occasion was a solemn one, and the more so that it was near the anniversary of my dear father's death and the dispersion of his little family circle. Will such a meeting ever take place again? I have often reflected upon the fact that many of the most important events of my life have happened in the early part of May; so much so that I have a sort of superstition on the subject. On the 12th of May, 1812, my mother died; on the 7th May, 1826, my father, on the 14th, my stepmother, and in a few days, the family were dispersed. Now, on the 4th, all who were living and their descendants were gathered together for the first time after the dispersion, thirty-nine years before, on or near the same spot. It seemed ominous.

Rose early. As it is fast day and mourning in memory of Mr. Lincoln, I had requested Mr. Geary, the corporal, to bring me from sutler's nothing but a cup of hot coffee and rolls. These he brought at seven. I noticed he brought the rolls on an earthen plate. This is an improvement in kindness and attention.

On the 7th of May last, Sunday, and the anniversary of my father's death, Harry came into my room about day and told me "The Yankees are here." "Where?" I asked. "All about in the yard and in the lot," he replied. "Well," said I, getting up, "Harry, I expect they have come for me, they will probably take me away; you may never see me after to-day. I want you to take care of my things and to do as I have told you in all particulars as far as you can. Have they asked for me? "No," he replied; "they only said they wanted breakfast and corn for their horses." "Give them what they want," I said, and dressed myself in readiness to leave in case I should be arrested. That dress was unchanged—pants, coat, and vest—until this morning when I put on a thinner suit. But to return to the scenes of that Sunday morning. Harry reappeared and told me that the officer in command said he wished to see me; that I need be under no apprehension of arrest, all he wanted was breakfast and feed for his horses; he expressed high regard for me personally. I went out and met him in the passage. He announced himself as Lieutenant White of the 13th Tennessee, of General Stoneman's command. We talked in a friendly way until breakfast. He and four of his men sat down with me to my table. My brother and his family were also present.

During the day Lieut.-Colonel Stacy, in command of the 13th Tenn. Cav. Reg., came into town with a battalion, and sent his adjutant to say he would be glad to see and take tea with me. My response was for him to "come, I should be glad to see him." In the evening he, his adjutant, and Dr. Cameron, surgeon of the regiment, called, spent some time and took tea. Conversation was agreeable. I invited them to stay all night; they declined but accepted my invitation for breakfast. They gave me to understand that they were in pursuit of Mr. Davis. Monday, after breakfast, they all left by the Sparta road. Monday night, Major Dyer with a battalion arrived; he left Tuesday morning.

Tuesday morning my brother and his three children, and little Emmie Stevens, daughter of Rev. Carlos W. Stevens, of Sparta, left for home. That was my last sight of Linton, perhaps forever. Soon after his departure, considering it most probable that I should be arrested and at an early day, about which we had talked and agreed, I went to the homestead to see my servants there; I gave them all the information I could regarding the condition of public affairs and my own situation. I told them they were now free, at which I was perfectly contented and satisfied; that I might and probably should be taken away from them soon and perhaps hung; that I wished them, if they saw fit, to remain there and finish the crop. I thought this would be best for them; they should have half of what was made and be subsisted out of supplies on hand; at the end of the year, if I were in life and permitted, I would furnish lands to such as wished to remain for the future, dividing the plantation into small farms or settlements which they could occupy, paying rent. I took a parting and affectionate leave of them. That is the last time I have seen them all together.

At home, I called in Harry, my ever true and faithful servant on the lot, and made him a bill of sale for the mules and buggy horses there. He had deposited with me for several years his private earnings; these amounted, I think, with interest to $662. I sold him the mules and horses, to which he was attached, for the debt; he was perfectly willing. They were worth more, but I gave him the difference. I gave him general instructions how to manage, in event of my arrest, until he should hear from me. Subsistence for the summer was the main point. My corn was scarce, not enough on hand. I had some conversation with Mary Reid and John on the same subject but not so full as I wished. We were interrupted by company. The conversation with her, I think, was on Wednesday. I staid at home, not wishing by absence to seem to be avoiding arrest, which from the time I left Richmond, I considered my ultimate fate. I felt distressed and pained at the use made and turn given by the authorities at Richmond to the report of the Commissioners of their conference with President Lincoln and Mr. Seward at Hampton Roads. It seems they were controlled by the genii of fatality. *"Quos Deus vult perdere prius dementat"* seems strongly to apply to them.

At the close of the last sentence, Lieut. W. entered for the usual morning walk. We went on the parapet; looked at target shooting by a company; rested under music-band arbour. He informed me that my room had never been occupied by any prisoner except Captain Webb of the *Atlanta* and some of his men; this in reply to my question prompted by writings on the wall.

A favourite maxim in my life has been, "The world treats a man very much as he treats it," or, "Whoever kicks the world will be apt to be kicked in turn." This was given me soon after my majority, by a man of experience, while I was chafing under some ill usage. I have repeated it to many young persons since. It recurs to me often since I have been here, obtruding itself upon the mind as Job's comforters pressed their consolations on him. The inquiry springs up: "Do you hold to your maxim? If so, must you not admit that you have acted a very bad part toward the world?" With the firmness of Job, I neither make the admission nor repudiate the maxim.

I do know that my acts toward the whole human family have been marked by kindness. In all that I have done from the beginning of the political troubles which have brought me here, I have been governed solely by a sense of duty to do the most good to my fellow men that I could under the circumstances. Personal ambition had no part in anything I have done; nor had prejudice toward the people of the North; I never entertained to them any feeling of unkindness. My earnest desire from the first has been that the conflict might end in the speediest way possible for the interest and well-being of both sections of the country; for their advancement in prosperity and happiness and for the preservation and perpetuation of their Constitutional liberty. This, I thought, and still think, could be better effected by maintenance of the principles of the ultimate, absolute sovereignty of the States, than in any other way. In these principles I was reared. They constitute the polestar of my political life. I am not prepared to admit that I erred in entertaining them, and to govern my conduct accordingly, because I suffer as I do. Why I thus suffer I do not know, but I feel an internal assurance that all will ultimately be right, let the sequel be as it may.

In the Boston *Journal* I see that Gen. Howell Cobb was permitted to visit his family, while Mr. Mallory [Confederate Secretary of Navy] and Senator Hill (B.H., of Georgia, I suppose) had been sent the day before to this place of confinement. I am truly glad Cobb has been permitted to visit his family. Would to God I might be permitted so much as to write and to hear from my dear ones at home! I should be exceedingly gratified to see Mr. Mallory and Mr. Hill when they reach here, but take it for granted that this privilege and pleasure will be denied. It is announced from Washington that though Mr. Davis is about to be removed to the barracks there, his trial is not expected to come off in a month. This I regret. I earnestly wish all trials and results quickly over. Particularly do I wish my own fate determined.

It is a matter of perplexity with me whether or not I should make special application to President Johnson for amnesty. I am willing to comply with the requirements made of others. But how the application might be received, I do not know. Should it be considered as emanating from a desire to evade the responsibility of my acts and to avoid punishment, this would cause me mortification and pain. On the other hand, should I fail to apply, might it not be regarded as evidence of a defiant spirit of protest against the existing state of things resulting from the fate of war? I should regret to be so interpreted. I think I shall wait to hear the result of my request through General Dix for permission to communicate with my relatives and friends.

Much is said in the papers about "loyalty" and "disloyalty," "Union men" and "traitors." What is meant by "loyalty," as thus commonly used, I do not exactly comprehend. No one ever lived with stronger feelings of devotion to the Constitution of the United States and the Union under it than myself. I regarded it as embodying the best system of government on earth. My views on this subject have been often expressed. For the Union barely, without the rights and guarantees secured by the Constitution, I never entertained or professed any attachment.

My devotion and my loyalty were to the Union under the Constitution with the civil and religious rights it secured—not to the Union *per se*. This devotion was felt and expressed by me until the powers that made the Union unmade it; or, at least, until Georgia, one of the parties to the compact, withdrew from it. I opposed that action of the State, in which I was born and of which I was a citizen, to the last. I conformed my conduct to hers not because of less loyalty to the principles of the old Constitution, but because that Power which had transferred the allegiance of its citizens under limitations to the United States had withdrawn this allegiance. It was by Georgia's act as a party to the Compact of Union set forth in the Constitution, that I had owed even a qualified allegiance to the Government of the United States, and it was by her act that I considered that allegiance withdrawn. But my "loyalty" to the principles of Constitutional liberty remained unshaken. My effort was to rescue and save the Constitution—the great principles of self-government therein set forth—to the people of Georgia though the Union had been abandoned by them. Never for one instant has a sentiment of "disloyalty" to these great essential, cardinal principles of American constitutional liberty entered my breast. So much on the point of my "loyalty."

As for the "atrocious rebellion and conspiracy against the life of the Nation" in which I am charged by the press with having taken part, I here state that I always considered the "life" and very *soul* of the "Nation" to be the Constitution and the principles of popular self-government therein set forth and thereby secured. Never did and never can rebel throb enter my breast against these. The "Nation" without these principles never had any proper or legitimate life. The only oath of allegiance the Constitution requires or ever required was and is to itself—to support and defend itself. This, I did to the utmost of my ability *in* the *Union* so long as Georgia acknowledged herself a party to it; and never since her withdrawal have I swerved from the oath, often taken before that event, to support and defend the same sacred principles. This I have done with more hazard and risk and under heavier denunciations than most men are willing to encounter. In doing it, I looked to nothing but the public good, to the welfare of those who without my solicitation had confided high trusts to me.

*   *   *

I admitted that the fathers, both of the North and the South, who framed the old Constitution, while recognizing existing slavery and guaranteeing its continuance under the Constitution so long as the States should severally see fit to tolerate it in their respective limits, were perhaps all opposed to the principle. Jefferson, Madison, Washington, all looked for its early extinction throughout the United States. But on the subject of slavery—so called—(which was with us, or should be, nothing but the proper subordination of the inferior African race to the superior white) great and radical changes had taken place in the realm of thought; many eminent latter-day statesmen, philosophers, and philanthropists held different views from the fathers.

The patriotism of the fathers was not questioned, nor their ability and wisdom, but it devolved on the public men and statesmen of each generation to grapple with and solve the problems of their own times.

The relation of the black to the white race, or the proper status of the coloured population amongst us, was a question now of vastly more importance than when the old Constitution was formed. The order of subordination was nature's great law; philosophy taught that order as the normal condition of the African amongst European races. Upon this recognized principle of a proper subordination, let it be called slavery or what not, our State institutions were formed and rested. The new Confederation was entered into with this distinct understanding. This principle of the subordination of the inferior to the superior was the "corner-stone" on which it was formed. I used this metaphor merely to illustrate the firm convictions of the framers of the new Constitution that this relation of the black to the white race, which existed in 1787, was not wrong in itself, either morally or politically; that it was in conformity to nature and best for both races. I alluded not to the principles of the new Government on this subject, but to public sentiment in regard to these principles. The status of the African race in the new Constitution was left just where it was in the old; I affirmed and meant to affirm nothing else in this Savannah speech.

My own opinion on slavery, as often expressed, was that if the institution was not the best, or could not be made the best, for both races, looking to the advancement and progress of both, physically and morally, it ought to be abolished. It was far from being what it might and ought to have been. Education was denied. This was wrong. I ever condemned the wrong. Marriage was not recognized. This was a wrong that I condemned. Many things connected with it did not meet my approval but excited my disgust, abhorrence, and detestation. The same I may say of things connected with the best institutions in the best communities in which my lot has been cast. Great improvements were, however, going on in the condition of blacks in the South. Their general physical condition not only as to necessaries but as to comforts was better in my own neighbourhood in 1860, than was that of the whites when I can first recollect, say 1820. Much greater would have been made, I verily believe, but for outside agitation. I have but small doubt that education would have been allowed long ago in Georgia, except for outside pressure which stopped internal reform.

*   *   *

## CHAPTER VIII

June 20.—At every reading of Scripture I find something fitting my condition. This morning: "How long will thou forget me, O Lord? Forever? How long shall mine enemy be exalted over me?"

### SCENE IN PRISONER'S ROOM, 19TH OF JUNE

Prisoner intensely interested in a great battle by Cortes, as described by Prescott, with Cortes in the hottest of the fight, when the bugle-blast sounded notice that all lights must be put out. Instantly, prisoner blew out his candle, leaving himself in darkness and in perfect bewilderment as to the result of the battle. He paced his room. Over what regions of time and space did not his thoughts wander? Their flights no walls or bars or bolts could restrain! The treasured meerschaum, gift of Camille E. Girardey, of Augusta, lay upon the table. He picks it up, fills it with some of the weed he brought from home; holds the small end of the poker in the fire until it becomes red, then applies it to the weed. This expedient after the candle is out is usual; he can not resort to match or paper without violating orders, and what might be the consequences of such indiscretion, even in the small matter of lighting a pipe, he does not know. He feels himself subject to rules neither definite nor prescribed. He paces on, indulging his roaming thoughts. On, time also moves. He goes to the wall where hangs his watch; the crystal being broken, he can not wear it in his fob; takes it down, and by the glare from the full grate of anthracite coal all aglow, he sees with the aid of his glasses that an hour has rolled around since he dropped his book and put out his candle. Still not wearied, he lays his meerschaum on the table, and resumes his walk.

He goes to one of his windows facing southeast and looks out upon the heavens. The sky is clear, the stars shine brightly. Prisoner gazes upon them as upon old acquaintances; theirs are the only familiar faces, save the sun's and moon's, that he has seen for many days. His heart is somewhat comforted as he watches the heavenly hosts move on in their far-off nightly courses, just as when he watched them from his own front porch at home. Home, and that porch with its two settees! a thousand thoughts and images of the past rush upon him. There, so many pleasant starlit summer nights have been spent. The refreshing, cooling southern winds seldom failed there. There, the silvery sheen of moonlight on the grass was chequered with the deep shade of cedar, oak, hickory, and other trees. In his mind, as he stood by his prison window, not only images of inanimate things arose, but the well-known forms of persons beloved and dear; among these Linton's.

All around was still; nothing to be seen without save dark outlines of the granite wall; above, the bright luminaries twinkling and sparkling in the high, bending arch of the heavens. Nothing was to be heard save the heavy tread of the guard in his solitary beat on the stone pavement. Prisoner turned and resumed his rounds; on, on, he walks while his thoughts still roam afar. Again, he consults his watch and sees that another hour has passed. He sets the blower as a screen before his grate so as to shut off the heat, takes the end of his bunk and turns it so as to make the length range as nearly north and south as he can guess (this has been done by him ever since he has been here); then spreads before his chair, a newspaper (New York *Herald* as it chanced to be), four sheets double on the stone floor, as is his custom, thus making a mat for his feet; he undresses and stretches himself on his bunk. Here, with soul devout, he endeavours through prayer to put himself in communion with God. To the Eternal, Prisoner in weakness and with full consciousness of his own frailty, commits himself, saying from the heart, "Thy will and not mine be done." With thoughts embracing the well-being of absent dear ones and all the world of mankind besides, whether friend or foe, he sinks into that sweet and long sleep from which he arose this morning.

*　*　*

[August 1—] Night once more upon the earth; and I am alone in these quarters which constitute my present home. Unless the little mouse is eyeing me from his hole, I have no other companion. I think he is about somewhere; he may not be alone, may have plenty of company of his kind for aught I know. The bread I put out for him last night was all gone this morning. In speaking of companions, however, I ought not to omit the flies. I should do them as great injustice by such omission as they do me by their annoyance. I have much more of their company than I like. Perhaps I ought not to omit companions of another sort; whose nature is to stick to you closer than a brother and to keep you awake all night. Since my row with them the other day, I have not seen or heard anything more from them. If they have made any attack, it has been a sly one in small force. I have little doubt that some are about, for the fort is well stocked with them. Of course, I mean bedbugs.

Alone! Did I say? Oh, I am far from ever being alone. Right by my window the sentry or guard is ever walking; by night and day, in rain or shine, his step sounds on the hard stone. Like the ticking of a clock at all hours of the night that step is heard if I chance to be awake. Now, is this not company? The truth is, this is company, and I feel it to be. It is not exactly such as I like best, but prisoners cannot choose their company.

# Frances Butler Leigh

## From *Ten Years on a Georgia Plantation since the War*

On March 22, 1866, my father and myself left the North. The Southern railroads were many of them destroyed for miles, not having been rebuilt since the war, and it was very questionable how we were to get as far as Savannah, a matter we did accomplish however, in a week's time, after the following adventures, of which I find an account in my letters written at the time. We stopped one day in Washington, and went all over the new Capitol, which had been finished since I was there five years ago. On Saturday we left, reaching Richmond at four o'clock on Sunday morning. I notice that it is a peculiarity of Southern railroads that they always either arrive, or start, at four o'clock in the morning. That day we spent quietly there, and sad enough it was, for besides all the associations with the place which crowded thick and fast upon one's memory, half the town was a heap of burnt ruins, showing how heavily the desolation of war had fallen upon it. And in the afternoon I went out to the cemetery, and after some search found the grave I was looking for. There he lay, with hundreds of others who had sacrificed their lives in vain, their resting place marked merely by small wooden headboards, bearing their names, regiments, and the battles in which they fell. The grief and excitement made me quite ill, so that I was glad to leave the town before daylight the next morning, and I hope I may never be there again.

We travelled all that day in the train, reaching Greensborough that night at eight o'clock. Not having been able to get any information about our route further on, we thought it best to stop where we were until we did find out. This difficulty was one that met us at every fresh stopping place along the whole journey; no one could tell us whether the road ahead were open or not, and, if open, whether there were any means of getting over it. So we crawled on, dreading at each fresh stage to find ourselves stranded in the middle of the pine woods, with no means of progressing further.

That night in Greensborough is one never to be forgotten. The hotel was a miserable tumble-down old frame house, and the room we were shown into more fit for a stable than a human habitation; a dirty bare floor, the panes more than half broken out of the windows, with two ragged, dirty calico curtains over them that waved and blew about in the wind. The furniture consisted of a bed, the clothes of which looked as if they had not been changed since the war, but had been slept in, in the meanwhile, constantly, two rickety old chairs, and a table with three legs. The bed being entirely out of the question, and I very tired, I took my bundle of shawls, put them under my head against the wall, tilted my chair back, and prepared to go to sleep if I could. I was just dozing off when I heard my maid, whom I had kept in the room for protection, give a start and exclamation which roused me. I asked her what was the matter, to which she replied, a huge rat had just run across the floor. This woke me quite up, and we spent the rest of the night shivering and shaking with the cold, and knocking on the floor with our umbrellas to frighten away the rats, which from time to time came out to look at us.

At four in the morning my father came for us, and we started for the train, driving two miles in an old army ambulance. From that time until eight in the evening we did not leave the cars, and then only left them to get into an old broken-down stage coach, which was originally intended to hold six people, but into which on this occasion they put nine, and, thus cramped and crowded, we drove for five hours over as rough a road as can well be imagined, reaching Columbia at three o'clock A.M., by which time I could hardly move. Our next train started at six, but I was so stiff and exhausted that I begged my father to wait over one day to rest, to which he consented. At this place we struck General Sherman's track, and here the ruin and desolation was complete. Hardly any of the town remained; street after street was merely one long line of blackened ruins, which showed from their size and beautifully laid-out gardens, how handsome some of the houses had been. It was too horrible!

On Thursday, at six A.M., we again set off, going about thirty miles in a cattle van which brought us to the Columbia River, the bridge over which Sherman had destroyed. This we crossed on a pontoon bridge, after which we walked a mile, sat two hours in the woods, and were then picked up by a rickety old car which was backed down to where we were, and where the rails began again, having been torn up behind us. In this, at the rate of about five miles an hour, we travelled until four in the afternoon, when we were again deposited in the woods, the line this time being torn up in front of us. Here, after another wait, we were packed into a rough army waggon, with loose boards put across for seats, and in which we were jolted and banged about over a road composed entirely of ruts and roots for four more hours, until I thought I should not have a whole bone left in my body.

It was a lovely evening however, and the moon rose full and clear. The air, delicious and balmy, was filled with the resinous scent of the pine and perfume of yellow jessamine, and we were a very jolly party, four gentlemen, with ourselves, making up our number, so I thought it good fun on the whole. In fact, rough as the journey was, I rather enjoyed it all; it was so new a chapter in my book of travels.

Between nine and ten in the evening we arrived at a log cabin, where, until three A.M. we sat on the floor round a huge wood fire. The train then arrived and we started again, and did not stop for twenty-four hours; at least, when I say did not stop, I mean, did not leave the cars, for we really seemed to do little else but stop every few minutes. This brought us, at three A.M., to Augusta, where we were allowed to go to bed for three hours, starting again at six and travelling all day, until at seven in the evening we at last reached Savannah. Fortunately we started from the North with a large basket of provisions, that being our only luggage, the trunks having been sent by sea; and had it not been for this, I think we certainly should have starved, as we were not able to get anything to eat on the road, except at Columbia and Augusta.

The morning after our arrival in Savannah, my father came into my

room to say he was off to the plantation at once, having seen some gentlemen the evening before, who told him if he wished to do anything at all
in the way of planting this season, that he must not lose an hour, as it
was very doubtful even now if a crop could be got in. So off he went,
promising to return as soon as possible, and report what state of things
he found on the island. I consoled myself by going off to church to hear
Bishop Elliott, who preached one of the most beautiful sermons I ever
heard, on the Resurrection, the one thought that can bring hope and
comfort to these poor heart-broken people. There was hardly anyone at
church out of deep mourning, and it was piteous to see so many mere
girls' faces, shaded by deep crape veils and widows' caps.

I can hardly give a true idea of how crushed and sad the people are.
You hear no bitterness towards the North; they are too sad to be bitter;
their grief is overwhelming. Nothing can make any difference to them
now; the women live in the past, and the men only in the daily present,
trying, in a listless sort of way, to repair their ruined fortunes. They are
like so many foreigners, whose only interest in the country is their own
individual business. Politics are never mentioned, and they know and
care less about what is going on in Washington than in London. They received us with open arms, my room was filled with flowers, and crowds
of people called upon me every day, and overwhelmed me with thanks
for what I did for their soldiers during the war, which really did amount
to but very little. I say this, and the answer invariably is, "Oh yes, but
your heart was with us," which it certainly was.

We had, before leaving the North, received two letters from Georgia,
one from an agent of the Freedmen's Bureau, and the other from one
of our neighbours, both stating very much the same thing, which was
that our former slaves had all returned to the island and were willing and
ready to work for us, but refused to engage themselves to anyone else,
even to their liberators, the Yankees; but that they were very badly off,
short of provisions, and would starve if something were not done for
them at once, and, unless my father came directly (so wrote the agent
of the Freedmen's Bureau), the negroes would be removed and made to
work elsewhere.

On Wednesday, when my father returned, he reported that he had found the negroes all on the place, not only those who were there five years ago, but many who were sold three years before that. Seven had worked their way back from the up country. They received him very affectionately, and made an agreement with him to work for one half the crop, which agreement it remained to be seen if they would keep. Owing to our coming so late, only a small crop could be planted, enough to make seed for another year and clear expenses. I was sorry we could do no more, but too thankful that things were as promising as they were. Most of the finest plantations were lying idle for want of hands to work them, so many of the negroes had died; 17,000 deaths were recorded by the Freedmen's Bureau alone. Many had been taken to the South-west, and others preferred hanging about the towns, making a few dollars now and then, to working regularly on the plantations; so most people found it impossible to get any labourers, but we had as many as we wanted, and nothing could induce our people to go anywhere else. My father also reported that the house was bare, not a bed nor chair left, and that he had been sleeping on the floor, with a piece of wood for a pillow and a few negro blankets for his covering. This I could hardly do, and as he could attend to nothing but the planting, we agreed that he should devote himself to that, while I looked after some furniture. So the day after, armed with five hundred bushels of seed rice, corn, bacon, a straw mattress, and a tub, he started off again for the planation, leaving me to buy tables and chairs, pots and pans.

We heard that our overseer had removed many of the things to the interior with the negroes for safety on the approach of the Yankees, so I wrote to him about them, waiting to know what he had saved of our old furniture, before buying anything new. This done, I decided to proceed with my household goods to the plantation, arrange things as comfortably as possible, and then return to the North.

I cannot give a better idea of the condition of things I found on the Island than by copying the following letter written at the time.

April 12, 1866.

Dearest S——, I have relapsed into barbarism total! How I do wish you could see me; you would be so disgusted. Well, I know now what the necessaries of life mean, and am surprised to find how few they are, and how many things we consider absolutely necessary which are really luxuries.

When I wrote last I was waiting in Savannah for the arrival of some things the overseer had taken from the Island, which I wished to look over before I made any further purchases for the house. When they came, however, they looked more like the possessions of an Irish emigrant than anything else; the house linen fortunately was in pretty good order, but the rest I fancy had furnished the overseer's house in the country ever since the war; the silver never reappeared. So I began my purchases with twelve common wooden chairs, four washstands, four bedsteads, four large tubs, two bureaux, two large tables and four smaller ones, some china, and one common lounge, my one luxury—and this finished the list.

Thus supplied, my maid and I started last Saturday morning for the Island; halfway down we stuck fast on a sand-bar in the river, where we remained six hours, very hot, and devoured by sand-flies, till the tide came in again and floated us off, which pleasant little episode brought us to Darien at 1 A.M. My father was there, however, to meet us with our own boat, and as it was bright moonlight we got off with all our things, and were rowed across to the island by four of our old negroes.

I wish I could give you any idea of the house. The floors were bare, of course, many of the panes were out of the windows, and the plaster in many places was off the walls, while one table and two old chairs constituted the furniture. It was pretty desolate, and my father looked at me in some anxiety to see how it would affect me, and seemed greatly relieved when I burst out laughing. My bed was soon unpacked and made, my tub filled, my basin and pitcher mounted on a barrel, and I settled for the rest of the night.

The next morning I and my little German maid, who fortunately takes everything very cheerily, went to work, and together we made things quite comfortable; unpacked our tables and chairs, put up some curtains (made out of some white muslin I had brought down for petticoats) edged with pink calico, covered the tables with two bright-coloured covers I found in the trunk of house linen, had the windows mended, hung up my picture of General Lee (which had been sent to me the day before I left Philadelphia) over the mantelpiece, and put my writing things and nicknacks on the table, so that when my father and Mr. J—— came in they looked round in perfect astonishment, and quite rewarded me by their praise.

Our kitchen arrangements would amuse you. I have one large pot, one frying-pan, one tin saucepan, and this is all; and yet you would be astonished to see how much our cook accomplishes with these three utensils, and the things don't taste *very* much alike. Yesterday one of the negroes shot and gave me a magnificent wild turkey, which we roasted on one stick set up between two others before the fire, and capital it was. The broiling is done on two old pieces of iron laid over the ashes. Our food consists of corn and rice bread, rice, and fish caught fresh every morning out of the river, oysters, turtle soup, and occasionally a wild turkey or duck. Other meat, as yet, it is impossible to get.

Is it not all strange and funny? I feel like Robinson Crusoe with three hundred men Fridays. Then my desert really blooms like the rose. On the acre of ground enclosed about the house are a superb magnolia tree, covered with its queenly flowers, roses running wild in every direction; orange, fig, and peach trees now in blossom, give promise of fruit later on, while every tree and bush is alive with red-birds, mocking-birds, black-birds, and jays, so as I sit on the piazza the air comes to me laden with sweet smells and sweet sounds of all descriptions.

There are some drawbacks; fleas, sand-flies, and mosquitoes remind us that we are not quite in Heaven, and I agree with my laundry woman, Phillis, who upon my maid's remonstrating with her for taking all day to wash a few towels, replied, "Dat's true, Miss Louisa, but de fleas jist have no principle, and dey bites me so all de time, I jist have to stop to scratch."

The negroes seem perfectly happy at getting back to the old place and having us there, and I have been deeply touched by many instances of devotion on their part. On Sunday morning, after their church, having nothing to do, they all came to see me, and I must have shaken hands with nearly four hundred. They were full of their troubles and sufferings up the country during the war, and the invariable winding up was, "Tank the Lord, missus, we's back, and sees you and massa again." I said to about twenty strong men, "Well, you know you are free and your own masters now," when they broke out with, "No, missus, we belong to you; we be yours as long as we lib."

Nearly all who have lived through the terrible suffering of these past four years have come back, as well as many of those who were sold seven years ago. Their good character was so well known throughout the State that people were very anxious to hire them and induce them to remain in the "up country," and told them all sorts of stories to keep them, among others that my father was dead, but all in vain. One old man said, "If massa be dead den, I'll go back to the old place and mourn for him." So they not only refused good wages, but in many cases spent all they had to get back, a fact that speaks louder than words as to their feeling for their old master and former treatment.

Our overseer, who was responsible for all our property, has little or nothing to give us back, while everything that was left in charge of the negroes has been taken care of and given back to us without the hope or wish of reward. One old man has guarded the stock so well from both Southern and Northern marauders, that he has now ninety odd sheep and thirty cows under his care. Unfortunately they are on a pine tract some twelve miles away up the river, and as we have no means of transporting them we cannot get them until next year.

One old couple came up yesterday from St. Simon's, Uncle John and Mum Peggy, with five dollars in silver half-dollars tied up in a bag, which they said a Yankee captain had given them the second year of the war for some chickens, and this money these two old people had kept through all their want and suffering for three years because it had been paid for fowls belonging to us. I wonder whether white servants would be so faithful or honest! My father was much moved at this act of faithfulness, and intends to have something made out of the silver to commemorate the event, having returned them the same amount in other money.

One of the great difficulties of this new state of things is, what is to be done with the old people who are too old, and the children who are too young, to work? One Northern General said to a planter, in answer to this question, "Well, I suppose they must die," which, indeed, seems the only thing for them to do. To-day Mr. J—— tells me my father has agreed to support the children for three years, and the old people till they die, that is, feed and clothe them. Fortunately, as we have some property at the North we are able to do this, but most of the planters are utterly ruined and have no money to buy food for their own families, so on their plantations I do not see what else is to become of the negroes who cannot work except to die.

Yours affectionately,

F.——

The prospect of getting in the crop did not grow more promising as time went on. The negroes talked a great deal about their desire and intention to work for us, but their idea of work, unaided by the stern law of necessity, is very vague, some of them working only half a day and some even less. I don't think one does a really honest full day's work, and so of course not half the necessary amount is done and I am afraid never will be again, and so our properties will soon be utterly worthless, for no crop can be raised by such labour as this and no negro will work if he can help it, and is quite satisfied just to scrape along doing an odd job here and there to earn money enough to buy a little food.* They are affectionate and often trustworthy and honest, but so hopelessly lazy as to be almost worthless as labourers.

My father was quite encouraged at first, the people seemed so willing to work and said so much about their intention of doing so; but not many days after they started he came in quite disheartened, saying that half the hands had left the fields at one o'clock and the rest by three o'clock, and this just at our busiest time. Half a day's work will keep them from starving, but won't raise a crop. Our contract with them is for half the crop; that is, one half to be divided among them, according to each man's rate of work, we letting them have in the meantime necessary food, clothing, and money for their present wants (as they have not a penny) which is to be deducted from whatever is due to them at the end of the year.

---

*N.B. I was mistaken. In the years 1877 and 1880 upwards of thirty thousand bushels of rice was raised on the place by these same negroes.

This we found the best arrangement to make with them, for if we paid them wages, the first five dollars they made would have seemed like so large a sum to them, that they would have imagined their fortunes made and refused to work any more. But even this arrangement had its objections, for they told us, when they missed working two or three days a week, that they were losers by it as well as ourselves, half the crop being theirs. But they could not see that this sort of work would not raise any crop at all, and that such should be the result was quite beyond their comprehension. They were quite convinced that if six days' work would raise a whole crop, three days' work would raise half a one, with which they as partners were satisfied, and so it seemed as if we should have to be too.

The rice plantation becoming unhealthy early in May, we removed to St. Simon's, a sea island on the coast, about fifteen miles from Butler's Island, where the famous Sea Island cotton had formerly been raised. This place had been twice in possession of the Northern troops during the war, and the negroes had consequently been brought under the influence of Northerners, some of whom had filled the poor people's minds with all sorts of vain hopes and ideas, among others that their former masters would not be allowed to return, and the land was theirs, a thing many of them believed, and they had planted both corn and cotton to a considerable extent. To disabuse their minds of this notion my father determined to put in a few acres of cotton, although the lateness of the season and work at Butler's Island prevented planting of any extent being done this season.

Our departure from one place and arrival at another was very characteristic. The house on St. Simon's being entirely stripped of furniture, we had to take our scanty provision of household goods down with us from Butler's Island by raft, our only means of transportation. Having learned from the negroes that the tide turned at six A.M., and to reach St. Simon's that day it would be necessary to start on the first of the ebb, we went to bed the night before, all agreeing to get up at four the next morning, so as to have our beds &c. on board and ready to start by six. By five, Mr. J——, my maid, and I were ready and our things on board, but nothing would induce my father to get up until eight o'clock, when he appeared on the wharf in his dressing-gown, clapped his hands to his head, exclaiming, "My gracious! that flat should be off; just look at the tide," which indeed had then been running down two good hours. Without a word I had his bedroom furniture put on, and ordered the men to push off, which they did just as my father reappeared, calling out that half his things had been left behind, a remark which was fortunately useless as far as the flat was concerned, as it was rapidly disappearing on the swift current down the river.

At three o'clock we started in a large six-oared boat, with all the things forgotten in the morning piled in. The day was cloudless, the air soft and balmy; the wild semi-tropical vegetation that edged the river on both sides beautiful beyond description; the tender new spring green of the deciduous trees and shrubs, mingling with the dark green of the evergreen cypress, magnolia, and bay, all wreathed and bound together with the yellow jessamine and fringed with the soft delicate grey moss which floated from every branch and twig. Not a sound broke the stillness but the dip of our oars in the water, accompanied by the wild minor chant of the negro boatmen, who sang nearly the whole way down, keeping time with the stroke of the oar.

Half-way down we passed the unfortunate raft stuck in the mud, caught by the turning tide. Unable to help it, we left it to wait the return of the ebb, not however without painful reflections, as we had had no dinner before starting, and our cook with his frying-pan and saucepan, was perched on a bag of rice on the raft.

Shortly after five o'clock we reached St. Simon's, and found the house a fair-sized comfortable building, with a wide piazza running all round it, but without so much as a stool or bench in it. So, hungry and tired, we sat down on the floor, to await the arrival of the things. Night came on, but we had no candles, and so sat on in darkness till after ten o'clock, when the raft arrived with almost everything soaked through, the result of a heavy thunder shower which had come on while it was stuck fast. This I confess was more than I could bear, and I burst out crying. A little cold meat and some bread consoled me somewhat, and finding the blankets had fortunately escaped the wetting, we spread these on the floor over the wet mattresses, and, all dressed, slowly and sadly laid us down to sleep.

The next morning the sun was shining as it only can shine in a southern sky, and the birds were singing as they only can sing in such sunlight. The soft sea air blew in at the window, mingled with the aromatic fragrance of the pines, and I forgot all my miseries, and was enchanted and happy. After breakfast, which was a repetition of last night's supper, with the addition of milkless tea, I set about seeing how the house could be made comfortable. There were four good-sized rooms down and two upstairs, with a hall ten feet wide running through the house, and a wide verandah shut in from the sun by Venetian shades running round it; the kitchen, with the servants' quarters, was as usual detached. A nice enough house, capable of being made both pretty and comfortable, which in time I hope to do.

My father spent the time in talking to the negroes, of whom there were about fifty on the place, making arrangements with them for work, more to establish his right to the place than from any real good we expect to do this year. We found them in a very different frame of mind from the negroes on Butler's Island, who having been removed the first year of the war, had never been brought into contact with either army, and remained the same demonstrative and noisy childish people they had always been. The negroes on St. Simon's had always been the most intelligent, having belonged to an older estate, and a picked lot, but besides, they had tasted of the tree of knowledge. They were perfectly respectful, but quiet, and evidently disappointed to find they were not the masters of the soil and that their new friends the Yankees had deceived them. Many of them had planted a considerable quantity of corn and cotton, and this my father told them they might have, but that they must put in twenty acres for him, for which he would give them food and clothing, and another year, when he hoped to put in several hundred acres, they should share the crop. They consented without any show of either pleasure or the reverse, and went to work almost immediately under the old negro foreman or driver, who had managed the place before the war.

They still showed that they had confidence in my father, for when a miserable creature, an agent of the Freedmen's Bureau, who was our ruler then, and regulated all our contracts with our negroes, told them that they would be fools to believe that my father would really let them have all the crops they had planted before he came, and they would see that he would claim at least half, they replied, 'No, sir, our master is a just man; he has never lied to us, and we believe him.' Rather taken aback by this, he turned to an old driver who was the principal person present, and said, "Why, Bram, how can you care so much for your master—he sold you a few years ago?" "Yes, sir," replied the old man, "he sold me and I was very unhappy, but he came to me and said, 'Bram, I am in great trouble; I have no money and I have to sell some of the people, but I know where you are all going to, and will buy you back again as soon as I can.' And, sir, he told me, Juba, my old wife, must go with me, for though she was not strong, and the gentleman who bought me would not buy her, master said he could not let man and wife be separated; and so, sir, I said, 'Master, if you will keep me I will work for you as long as I live, but if you in trouble and it help you to sell me, sell me, master, I am willing.' And now that we free, I come back to my old home and my old master, and stay here till I die.' " This story the agent told a Northern friend of ours in utter astonishment.

To show what perfect confidence my father had on his side in his old slaves, the day after starting the work here, he returned to Butler's Island, leaving me and my maid entirely alone, with no white person within eight miles of us, and in a house on no door of which was there more than a latch, and neither then nor afterwards, when I was alone on the plantation with the negroes for weeks at a time, had I the slightest feeling of fear, except one night, when I had a fright which made me quite ill for two days, although it turned out to be a most absurd cause of terror. The quiet and solitude of the plantation was absolute, and at night there was not a movement, the negro settlement being two miles away from the house.

I was awaked one night about two o'clock by a noise at the river landing, which was not the eighth of a mile from the house, and on listening, heard talking, shouting, and apparently struggling. I got up and called my little German maid, who after listening a moment said, "It is a fight, and I think the men are drunk." Knowing that it could not be our own men, I made up my mind that a party of strange and drunken negroes were trying to land, and that my people were trying to prevent them. Knowing how few my people were, I felt for one moment utterly terrified and helpless, as indeed I was. Then I took two small pistols my father had left with me, and putting them full cock, and followed by my maid, who I must say was wonderfully brave, I proceeded out of the house to the nearest hut, where my man servant lived. I was a little reassured to hear his voice in answer when I called, and I sent him down to the river to see what was the matter. It turned out to be a raft full of mules from Butler's Island, which I had not expected, and who objected to being landed, hence the struggling and shouting. I had been too terrified to laugh, and suddenly becoming aware of the two pistols at full cock in my hands, was then seized with my natural terror of firearms. So I laid them, full cocked as they were, in a drawer, where they remained for several days, until my father came and uncocked them. This was my only real fright, although for the next two or three years we were constantly hearing wild rumours of intended negro insurrections, which however, as I never quite believed, did not frighten me.

I had a pretty hard time of it that first year, owing to my wretched servants, and to the scarcity of provisions of all sorts. The country was absolutely swept; not a chicken, not an egg was left, and for weeks I lived on hominy, rice, and fish, with an occasional bit of venison. The negroes said the Yankees had eaten up everything, and one old woman told me they had refused to pay her for the eggs, but after they had eaten them said they were addled; but I think the people generally had not much to complain of. The only two good servants we had remained with my father at Butler's Island, and mine were all raw field hands, to whom everything was new and strange, and who were really savages. My white maid, watching my sable housemaid one morning through the door, saw her dip my toothbrush in the tub in which I had just bathed, and with my small hand-glass in the other hand, in which she was attentively regarding the operation, proceed to scrub her teeth with the brush. It is needless to say I presented her with that one, and locked my new one up as soon as I had finished using it.

My cook made all the flour and sugar I gave him (my own allowance of which was very small) into sweet cakes, most of which he ate himself, and when I scolded him, cried. The young man who was with us, dying of consumption, was my chief anxiety, for he was terribly ill, and could not eat the fare I did, and to get anything else was an impossibility. I scoured the island one day in search of chickens, but only succeeded in getting one old cock, of which my wretched cook made such a mess that Mr. J—— could not touch it after it was done. I tried my own hand at cooking, but without much success, not knowing really how to cook a potato, besides which the roof of the kitchen leaked badly, and as we had frequent showers, I often had to cook, holding up an umbrella in one hand and stirring with the other.

I remained on St. Simon's Island until the end of July, my father coming down from Butler's Island from Saturday till Monday every week for rest, which he sorely needed, for although he had got the negroes into something like working order, they required constant personal supervision, which on the rice fields in midsummer was frightfully trying, particularly as, after the day's work was over, he had to row a mile across the river, and then drive out six miles to the hut in the pine woods where he slept. The salt air, quiet, and peace of St. Simon's was therefore a delightful rest and change, and he refused to give an order when he came down, referring all the negroes to me. One man whom he had put off in this way several times, revenged himself one day when my father told him to get a mule cart ready, by saying, "Does missus say so?" which, however, was more fun than impudence.

\* \* \*

Mr. James Hamilton Cooper died last week, and was buried at the little church on the island here yesterday. The whole thing was sad in the extreme, and a fit illustration of this people and country. Three years ago he was smitten with paralysis, the result of grief at the loss of his son, loss of his property, and the ruin of all his hopes and prospects; since which his life has been one of great suffering, until a few days ago, when death released him. Hearing from his son of his death, and the time fixed for his funeral, my father and I drove down in the old mule cart, our only conveyance, nine miles to the church. Here a most terrible scene of desolation met us. The steps of the church were broken down, so we had to walk up a plank to get in; the roof was fallen in, so that the sun streamed down on our heads; while the seats were all cut up and marked with the names of Northern soldiers, who had been quartered there during the war. The graveyard was so overgrown with weeds and bushes, and tangled with cobweb like grey moss, that we had difficulty in making our way through to the freshly dug grave.

In about half an hour the funeral party arrived. The coffin was in a cart drawn by one miserable horse, and was followed by the Cooper family on foot, having come this way from the landing, two miles off. From the cart to the grave the coffin was carried by four old family negroes, faithful to the end. Standing there I said to myself, "Some day justice will be done, and the Truth shall be heard above the political din of slander and lies, and the Northern people shall see things as they are, and not through the dark veil of envy, hatred, and malice." Good-bye. I sail on the 21st for the North.

Yours affectionately,

F——

# Henry W. Grady

## "The New South"

"There was a South of slavery and secession—that South is dead. There is a South of union and freedom—that South, thank God, is living, breathing, growing every hour." These words, delivered from the immortal lips of Benjamin H. Hill, at Tammany Hall, in 1866, true then and truer now, I shall make my text tonight.

Mr. President and Gentlemen: Let me express to you my appreciation of the kindness by which I am permitted to address you. I make this abrupt acknowledgment advisedly, for I feel that if, when I raise my provincial voice in this ancient and august presence, I could find courage for no more than the opening sentence, it would be well if in that sentence I had met in a rough sense my obligation as a guest, and had perished, so to speak, with courtesy on my lips and grace in my heart. Permitted, through your kindness, to catch my second wind, let me say that I appreciate the significance of being the first Southerner to speak at this board, which bears the substance, if it surpasses the semblance, of original New England hospitality—and honors the sentiment that in turn honors you, but in which my personality is lost, and the compliment to my people made plain.

I bespeak the utmost stretch of your courtesy tonight. I am not troubled about those from whom I come. You remember the man whose wife sent him to a neighbor with a pitcher of milk, and who, tripping on the top step, fell with such casual interruptions as the landings afforded into the basement, and, while picking himself up, had the pleasure of hearing his wife call out: "John, did you break the pitcher?"

"No, I didn't," said John, "but I'll be dinged if I don't."

So, while those who call me from behind may inspire me with energy, if not with courage, I ask an indulgent hearing from you. I beg that you will bring your full faith in American fairness and frankness to judgment upon what I shall say. There was an old preacher once who told some boys of the Bible lesson he was going to read in the morning. The boys, finding the place, glued together the connecting pages. The next morning he read on the bottom of one page, "When Noah was one hundred and twenty years old he took unto himself a wife, who was"—then turning the page—"140 cubits long—40 cubits wide, built of gopher wood—and covered with pitch inside and out." He was naturally puzzled at this. He read it again, verified it, and then said: "My friends, this is the first time I ever met this in the Bible, but I accept this as an evidence of the assertion that we are fearfully and wonderfully made." If I could get you to hold such faith tonight I could proceed cheerfully to the task I otherwise approach with a sense of consecration.

Pardon me one word, Mr. President, spoken for the sole purpose of getting into the volumes that go out annually freighted with the rich eloquence of your speakers—the fact that the Cavalier as well as the Puritan was on the continent in its early days, and that he was "up and able to be about." I have read your books carefully and I find no mention of that fact, which seems to me an important one for preserving a sort of historical equilibrium if for nothing else.

Let me remind you that the Virginia Cavalier first challenged France on the continent—that Cavalier, John Smith, gave New England its very name, and was so pleased with the job that he has been handing his own name around ever since—and that while Myles Standish was cutting off men's ears for courting a girl without her parents' consent, and forbade men to kiss their wives on Sunday, the Cavalier was courting everything in sight, and that the Almighty had vouchsafed great increase to the Cavalier colonies, the huts in the wilderness being as full as the nests in the woods.

But having incorporated the Cavalier as a fact in your charming little books, I shall let him work out his own salvation, as he has always done, with engaging gallantry, and we will hold no controversy as to his merits. Why should we? Neither Puritan nor Cavalier long survived as such. The virtues and good traditions of both happily still live for the inspiration of their sons and the saving of the old fashion. But both Puritan and Cavalier were lost in the storm of the first Revolution, and the American citizen, supplanting both and stronger than either, took possession of the republic bought by their common blood and fashioned to wisdom, and charged himself with teaching men government and establishing the voice of the people as the voice of God.

My friends, Dr. Talmage has told you that the typical American has yet to come. Let me tell you that he has already come. Great types, like valuable plants, are slow to flower and fruit. But from the union of these colonists, Puritans and Cavaliers, from the straightening of their purposes and the crossing of their blood, slow perfecting through a century, came he who stands as the first typical American, the first who comprehended within himself all the strength and gentleness, all the majesty and grace of this republic—Abraham Lincoln. He was the sum of Puritan and Cavalier, for in his ardent nature were fused the virtues of both, and in the depths of his great soul the faults of both were lost. He was greater than Puritan, greater than Cavalier, in that he was American, and that in his honest form were first gathered the vast and thrilling forces of his ideal government—charging it with such tremendous meaning and elevating it above human suffering that martyrdom, though infamously aimed, came as a fitting crown to a life consecrated from the cradle to human liberty. Let us, each cherishing the traditions and honoring his fathers, build with reverent hands to the type of this simple but sublime life, in which all types are honored, and in our common glory as Americans there will be plenty and to spare for your forefathers and for mine.

Dr. Talmage has drawn for you, with a master's hand, the picture of your returning armies. He has told you how, in the pomp and circumstance of war, they came back to you, marching with proud and victorious tread, reading their glory in a nation's eyes! Will you bear with me while I tell you of another army that sought its home at the close of the late war—an army that marched home in defeat and not in victory—in pathos and not in splendor, but in glory that equaled yours, and to hearts as loving as ever welcomed heroes home! Let me picture to you the footsore Confederate soldier, as buttoning up in his faded gray jacket the parole which was to bear testimony to his children of his fidelity and faith, he turned his face southward from Appomattox in April 1865. Think of him as ragged, half-starved, heavy-hearted, enfeebled by want and wounds, having fought to exhaustion, he surrenders his gun, wrings the hands of his comrades in silence, and lifting his tear-stained and pallid face for the last time to the graves that dot old Virginia hills, pulls his gray cap over his brow and begins the slow and painful journey. What does he find—let me ask you who went to your homes eager to find, in the welcome you had justly earned, full payment for four years' sacrifice—what does he find when, having followed the battle-stained cross against overwhelming odds, dreading death not half so much as surrender, he reaches the home he left so prosperous and beautiful? He finds his house in ruins, his farm devastated, his slaves free, his stock killed, his barns empty, his trade destroyed, his money worthless, his social system, feudal in its magnificence, swept away; his people without law or legal status; his comrades slain, and the burdens of others heavy on his shoulders. Crushed by defeat, his very traditions are gone. Without money, credit, employment, material, or training; and beside all this, confronted with the gravest problem that ever met human intelligence— the establishing of a status for the vast body of his liberated slaves.

What does he do—this hero in gray with a heart of gold? Does he sit down in sullenness and despair? Not for a day. Surely God, who had stripped him of his prosperity, inspired him in his adversity. As ruin was never before so overwhelming, never was restoration swifter. The soldier stepped from the trenches into the furrow; horses that had charged Federal guns marched before the plow, and fields that ran red with human blood in April were green with the harvest in June; women reared in luxury cut up their dresses and made breeches for their husbands, and, with a patience and heroism that fit women always as a garment, gave their hands to work. There was little bitterness in all this. Cheerfulness and frankness prevailed. "Bill Arp" struck the key-note when he said: "Well, I killed as many of them as they did of me, and now I'm going to work." Of the soldier returning home after defeat and roasting some corn on the roadside, who made the remark to his comrades: "You may leave the South if you want to, but I am going to Sandersville, kiss my wife and raise a crop, and if the Yankees fool with me any more, I'll whip 'em again." I want to say to General Sherman, who is considered an able man in our parts, though some people think he is a kind of careless man about fire, that from the ashes he left us in 1864 we have raised a brave and beautiful city; that somehow or other we have caught the sunshine in the bricks and mortar of our homes, and have builded therein not one ignoble prejudice or memory.

But what is the sum of our work? We have found out that in the summing up the free Negro counts more than he did as a slave. We have planted the schoolhouse on the hilltop and made it free to white and black. We have sowed towns and cities in the place of theories, and put business above politics. We have challenged your spinners in Massachusetts and your iron-makers in Pennsylvania. We have learned that the $400,000,000 annually received from our cotton crop will make us rich when the supplies that make it are home-raised. We have reduced the commercial rate of interest from 24 to 6 per cent., and are floating 4 per cent. bonds. We have learned that one northern immigrant is worth fifty foreigners; and have smoothed the path to southward, wiped out the place where Mason and Dixon's line used to be, and hung out latchstring to you and yours. We have reached the point that marks perfect harmony in every household, when the husband confesses that the pies which his wife cooks are as good as those his mother used to bake; and we admit that the sun shines as brightly and the moon as softly as it did before the war. We have established thrift in city and country. We have fallen in love with work. We have restored comfort to homes from which culture and elegance never departed. We have let economy take root and spread among us as rank as the crabgrass which sprung from Sherman's cavalry camps, until we are ready to lay odds on the Georgia Yankee as he manufactures relics of the battlefield in a one-story shanty and squeezes pure olive oil out of his cotton seed, against any down-easter that ever swapped wooden nutmegs for flannel sausage in the valleys of Vermont. Above all, we know that we have achieved in these "piping times of peace" a fuller independence for the South than that which our fathers sought to win in the forum by their eloquence or compel in the field by their swords.

It is a rare privilege, sir, to have had part, however humble, in this work. Never was nobler duty confided to human hands than the up-lifting and upbuilding of the prostrate and bleeding South—misguided, perhaps, but beautiful in her suffering, and honest, brave and generous always. In the record of her social, industrial and political illustration we await with confidence the verdict of the world.

But what of the Negro? Have we solved the problem he presents or progressed in honor and equity toward solution? Let the record speak to the point. No section shows a more prosperous laboring population than the Negroes of the South, none in fuller sympathy with the employing and land-owning class. He shares our school fund, has the fullest protec-tion of our laws and the friendship of our people. Self-interest, as well as honor, demand that he should have this. Our future, our very exis-tence depend upon our working out this problem in full and exact justice. We understand that when Lincoln signed the emancipation proclama-tion, your victory was assured, for he then committed you to the cause of human liberty, against which the arms of man cannot prevail—while those of our statesmen who trusted to make slavery the corner-stone of the Confederacy doomed us to defeat as far as they could, committing us to a cause that reason could not defend or the sword maintain in sight of advancing civilization.

Had Mr. Toombs said, which he did not say, "that he would call the roll of his slaves at the foot of Bunker Hill," he would have been fool-ish, for he might have known that whenever slavery became entangled in war it must perish, and that the chattel in human flesh ended forever in New England when your fathers—not to be blamed for parting with what didn't pay—sold their slaves to our fathers—not to be praised for knowing a paying thing when they saw it. The relations of the Southern people with the Negro are close and cordial. We remember with what fidelity for four years he guarded our defenseless women and children, whose husbands and fathers were fighting against his freedom. To his eternal credit be it said that whenever he struck a blow for his own liberty he fought in open battle, and when at last he raised his black and humble hands that the shackles might be struck off, those hands were innocent of wrong against his helpless charges, and worthy to be taken in loving grasp by every man who honors loyalty and devotion. Ruffians have maltreated him, rascals have misled him, philanthropists established a bank for him, but the South, with the North, protests against injustice to this simple and sincere people. To liberty and enfranchisement is as far as law can carry the Negro. The rest must be left to conscience and common sense. It must be left to those among whom his lot is cast, with whom he is indissolubly connected, and whose prosperity depends upon their possessing his intelligent sympathy and confidence. Faith has been kept with him, in spite of calumnious assertions to the contrary by those who assume to speak for us or by frank opponents. Faith will be kept with him in the future, if the South holds her reason and integrity.

But have we kept faith with you? In the fullest sense, yes. When Lee surrendered—I don't say when Johnson surrendered, because I understand he still alludes to the time when he met General Sherman last as the time when he determined to abandon any further prosecution of the struggle—when Lee surrendered, I say, and Johnson quit, the South became, and has since been, loyal to this Union. We fought hard enough to know that we were whipped, and in perfect frankness accept as final the arbitrament of the sword to which we had appealed. The South found her jewel in the toad's head of defeat. The shackles that had held her in narrow limitations fell forever when the shackles of the Negro slave were broken. Under the old regime the Negroes were slaves to the South; the South was a slave to the system. The old plantation, with its simple police regulations and feudal habit, was the only type possible under slavery. Thus was gathered in the hands of a splendid and chivalric oligarchy the substance that should have been diffused among the people, as the rich blood, under certain artificial conditions, is gathered at the heart, filling that with affluent rapture but leaving the body chill and colorless.

The old South rested everything on slavery and agriculture, unconscious that these could neither give nor maintain healthy growth. The new South presents a perfect democracy, the oligarchs leading in the popular movement—a social system compact and closely knitted, less splendid on

the surface, but stronger at the core—a hundred farms for every plantation, fifty homes for every palace—and a diversified industry that meets
the complex need of this complex age.

The new South is enamored of her new work. Her soul is stirred with
the breath of a new life. The light of a grander day is falling fair on her
face. She is thrilling with the consciousness of growing power and prosperity. As she stands upright, full-statured and equal among the people
of the earth, breathing the keen air and looking out upon the expanded
horizon, she understands that her emancipation came because through
the inscrutable wisdom of God her honest purpose was crossed, and her
brave armies were beaten.

This is said in no spirit of time-serving or apology. The South has nothing for which to apologize. She believes that the late struggle between the
States was war and not rebellion; revolution and not conspiracy, and that
her convictions were as honest as yours. I should be unjust to the daunt-
less spirit of the South and to my own convictions if I did not make this
plain in this presence. The South has nothing to take back. In my native
town of Athens is a monument that crowns its central hill—a plain, white
shaft. Deep cut into its shining side is a name dear to me above the names
of men—that of a brave and simple man who died in brave and simple
faith. Not for all the glories of New England, from Plymouth Rock all
the way, would I exchange the heritage he left me in his soldier's death.
To the foot of that I shall send my children's children to reverence him
who ennobled their name with his heroic blood. But, sir, speaking from
the shadow of that memory which I honor as I do nothing else on earth,
I say that the cause in which he suffered and for which he gave his life
was adjudged by higher and fuller wisdom than his or mine, and I am
glad that the omniscient God held the balance of battle in His Almighty
hand and that human slavery was swept forever from American soil, the
American Union was saved from the wreck of war.

This message, Mr. President, comes to you from consecrated ground.
Every foot of soil about the city in which I live is as sacred as a battle-
ground of the republic. Every hill that invests it is hallowed to you by
the blood of your brothers who died for your victory, and doubly hallowed to us by the blow of those who died hopeless, but undaunted, in

defeat—sacred soil to all of us—rich with memories that make us purer and stronger and better—silent but staunch witnesses in its red desolation of the matchless valor of American hearts and the deathless glory of American arms—speaking an eloquent witness in its white peace and prosperity to the indissoluble union of American States and the imperishable brotherhood of the American people.

Now, what answer has New England to this message? Will she permit the prejudice of war to remain in the hearts of the conquerors, when it has died in the hearts of the conquered? Will she transmit this prejudice to the next generation, that in their hearts which never felt the generous ardor of conflict it may perpetuate itself? Will she withhold, save in strained courtesy, the hand which straight from his soldier's heart Grant offered to Lee at Appomattox? Will she make the vision of a restored and happy people, which gathered above the couch of your dying captain, filling his heart with grace; touching his lips with praise, and glorifying his path to the grave—will she make this vision on which the last sigh of his expiring soul breathed a benediction, a cheat and delusion? If she does, the South, never abject in asking for comradeship, must accept with dignity its refusal; but if she does not refuse to accept in frankness and sincerity this message of good will and friendship, then will the prophecy of Webster, delivered in this very society forty years ago amid tremendous applause, become true, be verified in its fullest sense, when he said: "Standing hand to hand and clasping hands, we should remain united as we have been for sixty years, citizens of the same country, members of the same government, united, all united now and united forever." There have been difficulties, contentions, and controversies, but I tell you that in my judgment,

> "Those opened eyes,
> Which like the meteors of a troubled heaven,
> All of one nature, of one substance bred,
> Did lately meet in th' intestine shock,
> Shall now, in mutual well beseeming ranks,
> March all one way."

# Part Three

The Twentieth Century,
1900–1970

The nonfiction of modern Georgia takes a number of different forms. Autobiography replaces the diary as the predominant form of private writing, and much of the modern writing presented here is autobiographical in some way. Only a few of the selections, however, focus exclusively on the writer's life story. More often, they are concerned with describing life in the past and contrasting it with the present. Or they seek to describe conditions in modern Georgia to an audience at least partially non-Georgian and non-Southern. In some sense this is what the novelist Corra Harris was doing in many of the short articles and essays she wrote for various New York magazines in the early 1900s. The title of her essay "How New York Appears to a Southern Woman" makes clear its purpose and audience. She is not writing for Southerners, and she exploits her regional identity for the purpose of persuading Northern readers to think of their city from an outsider's perspective, subtly seeking to wean them from their urban provincialism. Harris makes few apologies for her Southern origins and views. By explaining to her readers how a Southern woman reacts to New York City, she is also explaining what Southerners are like, pleading in a sense for sympathy and understanding. At the same time, she betrays her own provincialism. Blaming New Yorkers for racial prejudice that results in "local segregations almost incredible to the more liberal-minded Southerner," she overlooks the failures of her own region, whose racial policies she justifies as "simply the duty of preserving the standard and integrity of a higher race from the disintegrating effects of a lower, all the harder to do because we have an affection for the latter." This attitude was characteristic of many white Southerners of her day.

The noted black philosopher, leader, and educator W. E. B. Du Bois, in *The Souls of Black Folk* (1903) and other writings, also sought to understand and explain Southern life. Writing from an African-American perspective, he was capable of a remarkable objectivity. He knew that white Southerners were as much the victims of history as blacks. He viewed the state's history as one of violent economic and physical exploitation. He links the fate of the Cherokee and the Creek to slavery and demonstrates how in the decades following the Civil War other forms of enslavement—sharecropping and absentee landowners among them— caused serious problems for rural blacks and whites alike. Du Bois sees the South as a land without leaders, an economic wasteland of debtors. Unfortunately, he concludes that "The Jew is the heir of the slave-baron" in rural south Georgia. Although in some sense he is mainly referring to Northern moneylenders in general, by making this claim he also falls victim, like many white Southerners of the post-Reconstruction era, to the error of blaming the South's problems on outsiders. He also belies an ethnic prejudice that continues to be an issue in contemporary America.

Explanations are among the most important of motives for modern Georgia writers. Non-Southerners want to know about life in the American South. Moreover, modern Georgia readers, accustomed as they are to urban life, air-conditioning, and the mass media, have little if any knowledge of life in the rural South even half a century ago. But writers are not merely trying to satisfy the curiosity of their readers. They are recording a way of life that has disappeared, or receded so far into the peripheries of the Georgia consciousness that many modern citizens have no awareness of it. They are preserving their pasts and their identities. Katharine Du Pre Lumpkin in *The Making of a Southerner* (1946), Erskine Caldwell in *Deep South: Memory and Observation* (1968), Harry Crews in *A Childhood: The Biography of a Place* (1978), Philip Lee Williams in "Some Things You Can't Pave Over" (1986), Raymond Andrews in *The Last Radio Baby* (1991), and many others have all written with this purpose. Writing about the past does not necessarily mean nostalgic sentimentalizing, however. In fact, most of the writers included in this volume are notably free of sentimentality. But their apprehension that the Georgia they once knew is disappearing motivates them to try to preserve it in their writings.

One of the best examples of such writing is "The Life and Death of Cousin Lucius," by John Donald Wade, one of the twelve Southerners who lent their names to the Agrarian manifesto *I'll Take My Stand* in 1930. Of the twelve essays in that volume, Wade's is the only narrative: an account of the life and times of a fictional man who was born shortly before the Civil War and who lived well into the twentieth century. Despite its narrative structure, Wade's essay is no less purposeful than the other social, political, and cultural commentaries in the volume; it extols the virtues of life in the preindustrial South and mourns their gradual disappearance as industrialism and commerce make their inevitable way across the modern Southern landscape. Wade's essay is one of the most effective statements in *I'll Take My Stand*. Eloquently written, its strategy of using the archetypal figure of Cousin Lucius to exemplify the Old South, and to experience, as well, change brought by the twentieth century, allows it to avoid much of the dogmatism of the other essays. Though on the one hand it suffers from the same racial myopia as the rest of the volume, on the other hand its tone is more elegiac than polemical, a statement more literary than political. It mourns the inevitable loss that accompanies time's passage, and in the process analyzes from a regional perspective the transformation that came to the South in the fifty years following the Civil War.

John Talmadge, one of Wade's colleagues at the University of Georgia, on his retirement in 1967 began to exchange letters with his friend and fellow faculty member William Davidson (the brother of former Fugitive and Agrarian writer Donald Davidson) in which both described their early lives in Georgia and Tennessee. Talmadge's descriptions of Athens in the early 1900s are vivid and detailed. He occasionally comments on the youthfulness of the college students he sees each day and alludes to his own sense of being out of place in a world that has changed much since his childhood. His letters serve him almost as a form of therapy, a way of certifying his identity and experience. Change, and the prospect of personal obliteration, drove him to record his memories in hopes of assuring, in however small a way, their permanence. In a similar vein, Donald Windham's poignant *Emblems of Conduct* (1963) evokes with faint but unmistakable nostalgia the Atlanta of the early decades of the modern century. All of these writers are motivated by an apprehension of change and by a desire to record those scenes and characters that change will soon wipe away.

Reminiscence is hardly the only mode of modern nonfiction in Georgia. Much significant nonfiction has been political in nature, and in fact one can trace the outline of the state's history, of the conflicts that defined it, through many of the writings in this volume. Elias Boudinot's speech to the Georgia legislature, Grady's "New South" address, Alexander Stephens's prison journal, Du Bois's *The Souls of Black Folk*, Ralph McGill's journalism, Walter White's autobiography, Martin Luther King's orations, Alice Walker's essays, and Rosemary Daniell's sexual confessions all address political issues, though they do much else as well. Such writing seeks in some sense to persuade, to mold the opinions of its audience. Boudinot argues for the cultural and territorial rights of the Cherokee; Grady urges the South to adopt a more commercially oriented economy; Stephens defends slavery and the Southern cause; King analyzes the American failure to apply its founding ideals to all races. Such writing is an inevitable product of a society in a constant process of change. It is also a consequence of the fact that life is political, that the modern world is riven with social and political dispute and often turmoil.

One of the most notable examples of political writing from the midcentury is Lillian Smith's *Killers of the Dream* (1949). The discursive nature of this book makes it difficult to describe. The preface to the revised 1961 edition, along with the opening chapter, prepares one for a series of narratives about racism in the South before 1960. The book turns out to be something quite different. The second and third chapters describe a group of children acting out a play in which they stumble upon the meaning of racial equality. One of the older children approaches the narrator, Smith, to express anger that she would be taught the virtues of racial equality in a world that does not practice equality. Smith explains to the girl, in a long, meandering lecture, the meaning of Southern experience, the burdens of history, the sins of slavery and racism. The rest of the book follows in much the same mode, though Smith's discussion of Southern religion, and her own experiences with evangelists and tent meetings, is a pleasant respite from the book's dominant didacticism.

The moral fierceness of *Killers of the Dream* makes it memorable. But its sermonizing grows tiresome, and its author's grasp of history and political theory is weak. Smith talks *about* the South without deeply penetrating to its essence, as such commentators as W. J. Cash and C. Vann Woodward often succeeded in doing, and as Faulkner, Welty, O'Connor, Walker, and others managed to do in fiction. Smith dismisses Southern writers, for the most part, without mentioning a single name. The Vanderbilt Agrarians (whom she misremembers as the Fugitives) she regards as talented men who turned their backs on their region and the moral dilemmas of the present day. In short, her book is not a reliable study of Southern culture. It analyzes without being analytical, and it fails to dramatize the injustices it describes. As a personal testament, however, it is powerful and unsettling. When it was first published, it contributed to the growing consciousness of black and white Americans concerning race relations in the South, and for that reason it remains an important document from the early days of the civil rights movement.

Lillian Smith, Rosemary Daniell, and Alice Walker are all in some sense literary writers. That is, their nonfiction is a by-product of their literary careers (though Smith's *Killers of the Dream* is arguably her most important work). Some of the nonfiction included here was not written by literary authors; rather, it was a by-product of the public vocations these writers chose. Walter White early in his life wrote two novels, *The Fire in the Flint* (1924) and *Flight* (1926), but he soon became so involved in his work for the NAACP that he did not again turn to fiction. His autobiography, *A Man Called White* (1948), barely mentions those novels or his other books and instead dwells on his civil rights work and other aspects of a long public life. Yet his early experience as a novelist serves him well in this book. (The early chapters, for instance, give a harrowing account of an Atlanta race riot in 1906.) Its title is ironic. It refers to his name, of course, but it also refers to his light skin color, which would have allowed him to pass for white had he so chosen, though he makes clear that he is writing the autobiography of a black man. This book is also the history of the struggle for civil rights in the first half of the century, and it is full of vivid, piercing illustrations of the damaging effects of racism (just the sort of illustrations that Lillian Smith's *Killers of the Dream* does not provide). One of his themes is the absurdity of social distinctions based on race or color. He concludes the book by commenting on the ambiguity of his own skin color: "Black is white and white is black. When one shoots the other he kills his own reflection . . . I am one of the two in the color of my skin; I am the other in my spirit and my heart. It is only a love of both which binds the two together in me, and it is only a love for each other which will join them in the common aims of civilization that lie before us."

A quite different sort of writer with many of the same concerns was Ralph McGill, editor of the Atlanta *Constitution* from 1942 to 1969. All of his work was in some way the consequence of a career in journalism, and he became famous while editor of the *Constitution* for his moderate advocacy of the civil rights movement in the 1950s and 1960s. His columns against racism, his analyses of important cultural and political leaders in the South, and his descriptions of many different aspects of Southern life form a remarkable document of the years between 1940 and 1970 in Georgia. He was probably the most influential Southern newspaper editor of his time, and certainly as significant a figure in Georgia history as his predecessor on the *Constitution*, Henry Grady, who lived hardly half as long. One is frequently troubled in McGill's short essays and editorials, however, by the limitations of newspaper writing. He was an intelligent, perceptive man, but too many of his columns stop short just as he seems about to develop a full description or analysis, though he overcame this problem to an extent in some of his books. He remains an important figure in Georgia history, if not so much for what he wrote as for his willingness to risk unpopularity and his stature as an editor in defense of moral and just causes.

The central figure in Georgian and Southern culture of the twentieth century was Martin Luther King, Jr. The facts of King's life and career are well known and need no repeating. He left at his death a relatively large body of work: four books, numerous essays and speeches, and other writings. With a few exceptions, perhaps most notably "Letter from the

Birmingham Jail," his writing is consistently interesting but not especially distinguished. He was too busy with the affairs of the civil rights movement to become a great writer. But he was probably the greatest orator of the century, and his most famous speech, "I Have a Dream," given at the March on Washington in 1963, became a rallying cry for the civil rights movement. It is one of the few speeches in history that in some real sense can be said to have changed the world. The power of King's oratory is apparent in the language and rhythms of his speeches and to an extent in his essays, but these are no substitute for the sound of his voice. The essay included here, "The American Dream," expresses a theme to which King returned often in the 1960s: in order to honor the ideals of the Declaration of Independence, he argued, the United States must guarantee equal rights and opportunities for all its citizens. Only then could the American Dream truly be said to be within reach.

Although King was born in Georgia and spent much of his adult life there, he was hardly a citizen of this state alone. His importance stems from his impact on the South and the United States. The civil rights movement of which he became the prime mover and symbol set in motion changes whose consequences reverberate today. They propelled Georgia and the South firmly into the modern world. One may lament some of the effects of time and change on the state and its heritage, but surely the changes that King symbolizes have made it possible for all citizens of conscience to feel proud of their region at last.

# Corra Harris

## "How New York Appears to a Southern Woman"

New York is a wonderful place, broadening to the mind but confusing to the morals. The people do not reckon life by morals, indeed, but by "conditions." They have a great deal of information, but not much wisdom. They are fresh and appear to be developing a new kind of egregiousness which makes them at once depressingly pessimistic and absurdly optimistic. And I have never seen any place where there was greater need of pure food laws for the mind. They have absolutely no protection against any kind of knowledge, however dangerous. And, all told, they are diabolically intelligent. I did not meet a single person who could not get the best of me in the discussion, no matter how wrong he was. But my only misgiving was one which every Southerner must entertain, of not knowing whether the people were kind to me because they really liked me, or because it was their aggravatingly superior way of bearing with what they considered a narrow-minded, invincibly ignorant person.

A Northern visitor in the South is always more interested in the blacks, the desperately poor and disreputable, than in the rest of us. Personally, I have no doubt that this taste, this curiosity, this morbid sympathy had much to do with the abolition zeal in the North before the war. However that may be, Southerners do not share it; and I was more particularly interested in the respectable people of New York. There were no young ones among them. I did not see a dozen children during the month I was there, except on the Bowery. But, of course, New York is not dependent upon this source for its population. It imports citizens from the ends

224

of the earth, full-grown and work-broken. This accounts in part for the seething mind to be found there. We bring up our own generation here in the South, and so we know what we are getting. It keeps us a trifle behind the times, but we are repaid in peace of mind. When a man is autochthonous he is not so likely to throw bombs or to kick against the pricks. If New York had more babies in its homes there would be fewer "revolutionists" in its streets.

Another thing one misses upon the streets is the cheerfulness of the poor. With us they are still the happiest class as a whole. But in New York they wear a wise, cynical, bitter look, as if they had caught on, and considered that they had been cheated. They have learned the lesson of the new economists. They are not thankful for charity. They want their rights—that is, Wall Street and the fulness thereof, share and share alike. These low-browed, sulky looks contrast strangely with the mercenary formation of the human countenance in the more prosperous parts of the city like Fifth avenue. However, it is no use to put on airs. We are getting the same expression down here as fast as we can. The difference is that on Fifth avenue it is a remote million-dollar stare and with us it is a simple one-dollar look. The former is founded upon financial egotism, the latter upon financial incompetency, and it is hard to tell which is worse for those who come after us.

The finest looking, most intelligent and capable people to be seen in New York are on the ferries and subways in the late afternoons. They have not yet got the ugly money birthmark, and they evidently belong to the achieving class who govern the city, count her change and keep an eye upon the government. But this reminds me to say that for people who have excellent manners at home and in their own social circles, New York men have the worst I ever saw in public. They are as innocent of courtesy as Brobdingnagians. When I complained of this to one of them, he said that it was "due to the shape of Manhattan Island." It was not wide enough to permit business men to carry their politeness around with them. But my own impression is that there is a sentiment against courtesy, especially to women, on the grounds that it is mawkish and that they do not deserve it. Possibly they agree with Schopenhauer, who thought that the notions of gallantry and reverence for women are products of Teutonico-Christian stupidity. He says "these notions have served only to make women more arrogant and overbearing; so that one is occasionally reminded of the holy apes in Benares, who, in the consciousness of their sanctity and inviolable position, think they can do exactly as they please." Certainly this comment cannot apply to the women on the cars and in other public places in New York, but it is the men who remind one of the holy apes of Benares. This may not indicate a reversion to type, of course, but it shows an astonishingly primitive nature impervious to the softer graces of civilization.

I have already intimated a partiality for respectable people, but there is another reason why the stranger does not see all the people in New York, nor even all the different kinds. Race prejudice there is so strong that it results in local segregations almost incredible to the more liberal-minded Southerner. I did not learn, for example, where they keep their negroes, Chinese and Hottentots, except when they invite them to dine— this invitation to dinner now and then is the subterfuge used there in the place of that universal social equality which they advocate for us in the South. As a matter of fact, New York is the home of all the different kinds of race antipathy. The whites, blacks, yellows and browns have a *natural* aversion to one another. We know nothing of these jungle sensations here. With us it is simply the duty of preserving the standard and integrity of a higher race from the disintegrating effects of a lower, all the harder to do because we have an affection for the latter. And this difference illustrates a universal difference between the people of the North and the South which must interest the close observer. The former are more highly developed intellectually, but they are decidedly more primitive and savage and tribal natured every other way. They are not nearly so evenly civilized as Southerners; and they have apparently used their gifted heads to preserve these primitive traits of hardness and ferocity against each other.

But of the people I did see, those on the Bowery showed more monotony of features than any other. The only thing like it is a big negro quarter on a Southern plantation where the same lack of variety exists in the cast and expression of the black faces. And there were fifteen hundred Germans in the Atlantic Garden one afternoon who looked like twins;

but this probably resulted from the fact that they were all half-asleep. A poor young thing who thought she could laugh with her legs was on a stage in front trying to amuse them. This was why they slept. It is impossible to amuse people in New York, because their faculty for amusements is jaded, and most of them have lost the power of illusion. The only way to deceive them is to let them deceive themselves. They go to the theaters and aggravate themselves with an analysis of the play, but they do not come under the spell of it, because they have the decomposing mind.

Evidently there are as many of the people who belong to the eternal order in New York as elsewhere, or the thing would not hold together as it does. But because they do belong to the order, rather than to the disorder, they attract less attention than those who simply make the prevailing noise of the place. These have a consciousness founded upon an egotism so naïve as to be diverting. This accounts in part for their obsession for "world movements." You do not need to be a great or gifted person in New York to lead a "world movement." All you need is the idea and the vocabulary. Even if you do something wrong or queer or foolish, you do not drop out of notice in your embarrassment, but you select the "movement" which corresponds to your dilemma and you give lectures upon your "specialty." Fortunately the wise old world is rarely ever moved. Here are the delegates to the Peace Congress, for example, getting ready to move for "universal peace." It is a grand idea they have got merely in their heads. Nothing in history or experience warrants it. We shall never have universal peace, because we do not want it. A nation may have its little decadent spell for a generation or so when the bankers and tariff-makers get the best of the situation, but it cannot last, because men are not born civilized, and eventually enough of them will escape to make a stand against the bedsores of a too-peaceful civilization.

Down here we are too sane to entertain such illusions; and we think more of ourselves than we do of the world. And even if this is selfish, it is not so bombastic as mistaking a torchlight procession for a "revolution." We are not nearly so clever as the people who make these mistakes, but the kind of sense we have keeps us level-headed. The peculiarity of these thrilling, stirring world errants is that they speak in terms of universality about abridged personal experiences. Besides, they do not mean what they say. They have the most daredevil brain courage, but, observed closely, even the "terrorists" prove to be lambs in wolves' clothing. The most looked-down-upon man I saw in New York was a poor apologetic anarchist who had missed his cue and actually thrown a bomb somewhere. He sustained the same relation to the terrorists that a man who eats with his knife sustains to polite society—an egregious person incapable of understanding the spirit of the thing. And so he was. He thought that these people who talk so threateningly about turning things upside down were in earnest, but they are not. Their forte is to "create public sentiment." Somebody else will do the world moving if it is ever done.

In conclusion, New York is spiritually minded, but not religious. The people do not go to church for the same reason that we do. We go for the sake of convention, or because we are really pious, or because we hope some time to be convicted of our sins. And they do not seem to feel the need as we do of being born again. Most of them are too well fortified with theories of evolution even to bother about repentance, and one almost fears that some of them regard sin as a preliminary stage of virtue. But without exception they are keen humanitarians, and they ask no odds of the will of God. They can do their duty without prayer or fasting, and they visit the widow and the orphan as if the Lord had nothing to do with it. In short, they are academic sentimentalists. They are deeply moved by any kind of abuse, and they will go to admirable lengths to correct it; but there is nothing personal in their championship. They care not at all for the people whom they rescue except to take credit for them in some kind of "report." They have a theory of life which takes the kindness out of charity and which insults gratitude. Having bound up his sores and called an ambulance, a New York humanitarian would coolly turn his back upon a Lazarus and never think of him again. Nothing could be more heartless, but it is what you may expect of people whose civilization is designed chiefly for the head and not the heart.

# "The Circuit Rider's Wife's First Thanksgiving Dinner"

The manner in which the first generation in the South was brought up after the Civil War was as ridiculous as it was honorable. The object was to teach us a tremendous self-respect with a Mason and Dixon's boundary line. I thought the best people landed in Virginia, which forever settled the quality of all other pioneers in this country.

It was a remote historical circumstance recorded in the school history that some immigrants came over in a ship called the Mayflower and settled in that section which afterward became New England. But I did not know there could be any distinction connected with them and had never seen a man or woman indiscreet enough to claim he had an ancestor on that ship.

I knew that these Pilgrim fathers had set aside a day of Thanksgiving in the year 1621 for the harvest which alone saved them from perishing during the following winter, but I was a woman grown and married before I ever participated in a Thanksgiving celebration, or realized that it was a national holiday proclaimed by the President himself.

I grew up during the Reconstruction period in the South, when our people had very little to be thankful for, and would not in any case have permitted themselves to be thankful according to a custom set by New England. New England did not set well with us. We were gallant and conscientious about evading the victories they thought they had won over us, all the laws they made to discipline us, and would have preferred indeed to have another God altogether to praise and worship if this could have been arranged without heresy. As it was, we manipulated the Scriptures according to our pride and peculiar needs and went ahead.

### ELEGANT DISTINCTIONS

This does not mean that we were taught to hate the Northern people. On the contrary pains were taken with every young pauper aristocrat to instill certain elegant distinctions in the use of terms which were more

effective upon our point of view than the most partial interpretation of
history our fathers had just made could have been. The "professional
Southerner" was a later and regrettable product thoroughly despised still
by every Southerner. We might recite patriotic poetry, such as Furl that
Banner; otherwise references to the North were not regarded as suitable
for polite conversation.

The topic was too painful, if not downright offensive. No child would
have called a Southern soldier a rebel. This was blasphemy. Neither must
any well-bred person speak of a Northern man as a Yankee. This name
by an association of memories was so opprobrious that it was in the same
class with profane words used by vulgarians. I was so sternly disciplined
along these lines that to this day I could not possibly call any man a
Yankee. And I still experience a slight sense of embarrassment if someone
applies this name to another in my presence, as if he had committed a
breach of good manners.

Thus, in a thousand ways, we were brought up to carry on the Secession Movement politely and with a great delicacy for the next forty years.
Without being told to do so, we instinctively avoided Northern ideas,
opinions, convictions and customs as being unsuited to our character,
quality and natural conditions—never inspired by positive antagonism,
but for the same reason that we should not adopt the standards and customs of a foreign people, separated from us by some kind of geography
of the mind.

As a young girl I was not nearly so much aware of the North as I
was of China, for by that time there began to be considerable missionary
agitation about the heathen in the uttermost parts of the earth. But after
certain episodes attendant upon the Reconstruction period were properly
closed, forcing upon us duties of discipline extremely distasteful to our
moral nature, we left the North to its fate, without benefit of clergy so
far as we were concerned. What I mean is that we did not even pray for
those people as we did for the heathen.

As near as I can figure it out from my recollections of the men and
scenes during that far-off time, this accounts for our failure to observe
Thanksgiving Day. According to our local calculations the origin of it
was too far North—natural enough in that frost-bitten country of in-

clement weather, but in our warmer, more fertile land we had never been sufficiently astonished at the Lord's mercies to set aside a special day of thanksgiving for an abundant harvest. There were practically no markets except for cotton, but even in a bad crop year everybody raised more foodstuffs than they could sell.

### DAYS OF FEASTING

The whole of November was a gala month on the old plantation where I was born. The harvests had been gathered and the pigs killed. The barns, cribs and smokehouse were filled to overflowing. Quite unconsciously the scenes of Thanksgiving were laid. Mother's kitchen bloomed with garlands of red pepper on the walls, bunches of sage left over from her sausage making—in case a neighbor came short on sage at the last moment and dispatched a messenger for this seasoning—twigs of rosemary tied together and hanging by the stems, used in scenting the lard; strands of link sausage drying above the fireplace; pumpkins and cushaws piled in a corner under the kitchen table.

A dozen splendid ears of very special corn, chosen by father for seed, were tied on a stout cord and hung like the golden pendants of a huge brooch above the door. The work of the year was done. The negroes frolicked. The white planters visited and entertained. The hunters were in the fields. All the dogs in the country were beside themselves with excitement. Foxes took to their holes. So far as food was concerned we passed back into the medieval period of the carnivorous Anglo-Saxons. We lived on game, barbecued rabbit, squirrel pies.

I remember still the stir in the house when my father and uncles went out before day and sometimes returned in the early dawn with a huge wild turkey; the emotion I felt at the sight of this great bird with its dead wings covering the back of the negro who bore him on his shoulders. Another vivid recollection is of a great blue platter on the candlelit table in the evening, filled with broiled birds, which were not laid out skimpily on toast as we do now to cover the bottom of the dish, but piled high. Or it may have been a fat opossum, barbecued with wedges of yellow yams cooked in the fat.

Rice must have been very expensive, for only a little was ever kept in the house, and this to serve when we were ill, with milk and sugar. But mother made her own lye hominy of corn, and there was always a large round bowl of this on the table. There were other dishes, but I have only a child's sweet-tooth recollection of the tall-stemmed glass dish filled with crab-apple preserves, and the low, bright place in the candlelight made by the cherry pickle.

We feasted nearer thirty days than one, but I do not remember any reference to thankfulness beyond the moment at every meal when father bowed his Roman nose and his two-story head very low and asked the Lord to "Make us thankful for what we are about to receive." Still, by the gayety and laughter of these occasions we must have indicated an art-less confidence in the bounties of the Lord more real than any prayers we address to Him on account of the lack of perfect faith.

Meanwhile it turned out that I was never to enjoy the satisfaction a cer-tain class of people take in their prejudices. More knowledge or some kind of good will has long since deprived me of nearly all those convictions with which so many Southerners of that period hallmarked themselves, with burning memories of their misfortunes.

By a mere fluke of circumstance not predicted in my fortunes, I finally strayed far enough North to discover New England and to find among her people the dearer and nearer friends of my lifetime. Their faults, prejudices and limitations have made them easier to love than if they had been as wise and superior as they think they are. And by the getting of knowledge I discovered that the Pilgrim Fathers only revived a custom old as the history of man when they celebrated the harvest in 1621 with a day of thanksgiving.

Whether heathen, pagans or Christians, wherever men have earned their bread on the land by the sweat of their brows, there is a record of thanksgiving after the harvest, made with sacrifices, orgies or prayers to whatever gods they worshiped.

### THE ORIGIN OF THE DAY

The idea can only be inspired by the conscious recognition of Providence. For countless ages these people who live and have lived by sowing and reaping are in the last ditch cut by Providence between the weather and the land. They cannot manipulate the seasons in their favor. They are laborers who pass through hardships and suspense and still must look forever to the heavens for their reward.

This seems to be the real origin of Thanksgiving celebrations. Scientists may prove that there is no God, but still we are the prisoners of His winds and weather. And the wealth we accumulate must crumble without the harvests His mercies afford.

I am only setting down here the history of Thanksgiving Day in the South as I knew it, because while there may have been isolated exceptions where the day was observed, the custom was not general, and it is not to this day in the rural sections.

Thus years passed. I do not know how many before I was brought face to face with my Christian duty to be thankful on a certain day set aside for that purpose, by the President's proclamation. By this time I was the young wife of my Circuit Rider. The suggestion to "keep" Thanksgiving Day was his. He had been brought up more particularly according to the Scriptures, but not so carefully as I had been according to strictly Southern traditions. His prejudices were moral, not sectional. He could not hate even an enemy.

### A GOOSE SAVES THE DAY

We were living then in a little parsonage next door to the church in a very small town. He was for starting off the day with a Thanksgiving service in the church. We would have the dinner in the evening, invite the stewards and their wives. There would be no social competition, because the people of that town had never dreamed of celebrating the day.

We were in straitened circumstances as usual. In those days a parsonage was scantily and eccentrically provisioned. We might have a surplus of dried fruit contributed by the rural members of our congregations, and they were generous with fresh meats and vegetables in season, but they rarely furnished fat fowls and I had never heard of a preacher receiving a turkey.

But when I presented this question of food for the feast my dear husband was equal to the emergency. "How about the goose?" he suggested gayly.

Now it transpired that our fourth Quarterly Conference for the year had been held on Saturday before Thanksgiving Day.

This is always an anxious occasion for any Methodist circuit rider, because it is then that the stewards of the various churches on his circuit pay him whatever moneys and substances they have been able to collect from the members.

I do not recall what we received at this particular conference. It must have been a modest sum since the preacher's salary for the whole year on that charge was four hundred and fifty dollars, but I do remember that a certain widow, being without funds herself, had contributed a goose to be credited on her "quarterage."

I had my misgivings. Mother had raised four fluffy feather beds from her flock of geese at home, but she had never dreamed of serving one as food. Still I felt obliged to take my husband's view that the Lord had miraculously provided us with a goose for the occasion.

He announced services in the church for Thanksgiving. We invited four stewards and their wives to dine with us in the evening; and I gave myself soul and body to planning the feast. This included the borrowing of dishes and silver from the ladies of our congregation.

My neighbors were gracious and helpful. They sent in cakes and other delicacies beyond our means to provide. The old black mammy we had then knew how to prepare a goose for the table; I was destined to learn, however, that it is one thing to cook a goose and a much more strenuous business to carve one. My own gifts shone chiefly in the setting of the table, which fairly glistened with the glass, silver and chinaware of the whole community.

Someone had given us a huge oblong pumpkin with splendidly fluted sides. I cut it in half, scraped it to the golden rind, set it in a wreath of autumn leaves in the middle of the table and filled it with nuts, apples, oranges and bright-colored candies, with a half-shucked ear of red corn sticking up in the middle to give it height and veracity as a harvest manifestation of joy and thankfulness. I swathed the hideous oil lamp that hung from the ceiling above with pumpkin-colored tissue paper, and set two brass candlesticks at either end of the pumpkin bowl.

Thus, I contrived the light of a harvest moon and two little flickering stars of candlelight, and was so entranced with the luminous opulence shed by all this splendor in that dingy parsonage dining room that I was flushed and swollen with pride by the time the guests began to arrive.

The goose lay resplendent on a borrowed silver platter, a very long bird, looking like an inverted golden brown boat, short legs pressed down for oars, and smelling to heaven of the sage and onion dressing with which it was stuffed, no doubt to mitigate the goosiness of its flavor.

Whatever embarrassment connected with that feast was suffered by the Circuit Rider whose duty it was to carve that durable bird. Since the beginning of my ministry as a hostess I have always enjoyed a sort of innocent inebriation at my own table with guests. Whether the meal served was bountiful or meager I do not remember ever being anxious or on the defensive.

This is not a grace with me but some kind of humor inspired by the camaraderie of sharing food with other people, which may have been inherited from a long line of male ancestors who took their liquors with laughter and a flourish. In any case, my first Thanksgiving dinner stands out still in memory as a vivid scene of rosy laughing faces, bewhiskered stewards telling jolly stories. I had never seen so many official Christians merry before. I was in high feather, not consciously thankful, but triumphant.

Many Thanksgiving Days have passed since then, formally kept with other people who have accepted the custom. For the past fifteen years they have gone by like flag days in a nation's prosperity. But they seem now to have lost for me the intimate touch and significance of that first one we achieved nearly forty years ago, with the pumpkin bowl of nuts and corn and fruit sitting in the center of the table, and the two short candles in the brass candlesticks standing by to brighten it with the good little flickering flames of poverty and peace.

# W. E. B. Du Bois

## From *The Souls of Black Folk*

### VII
#### *Of the Black Belt*

I am black but comely, O ye daughters of Jerusalem,
As the tents of Kedar, as the curtains of Solomon.
Look not upon me, because I am black,
Because the sun hath looked upon me:
My mother's children were angry with me;
They made me the keeper of the vineyards;
But mine own vineyard have I not kept.
                    —The Song of Solomon

Out of the North the train thundered, and we woke to see the crimson soil of Georgia stretching away bare and monotonous right and left. Here and there lay straggling, unlovely villages, and lean men loafed leisurely at the depots; then again came the stretch of pines and clay. Yet we did not nod, nor weary of the scene; for this is historic ground. Right across our track, three hundred and sixty years ago, wandered the cavalcade of Hernando de Soto, looking for gold and the Great Sea; and he and his foot-sore captives disappeared yonder in the grim forests to the west. Here sits Atlanta, the city of a hundred hills, with something Western, something Southern, and something quite its own, in its busy life. And a little past Atlanta, to the southwest, is the land of the Cherokees, and there, not far from where Sam Hose was crucified, you may stand on a spot which is to-day the centre of the Negro problem,—the centre of those nine million men who are America's dark heritage from slavery and the slave-trade.

Not only is Georgia thus the geographical focus of our Negro population, but in many other respects, both now and yesterday, the Negro problems have seemed to be centered in this State. No other State in the Union can count a million Negroes among its citizens,—a population as large as the slave population of the whole Union in 1800; no other State fought so long and strenuously to gather this host of Africans. Oglethorpe thought slavery against law and gospel; but the circumstances which gave Georgia its first inhabitants were not calculated to furnish citizens over-nice in their ideas about rum and slaves. Despite the prohibitions of the trustees, these Georgians, like some of their descendants, proceeded to take the law into their own hands; and so pliant were the judges, and so flagrant the smuggling, and so earnest were the prayers of Whitefield, that by the middle of the eighteenth century all restrictions were swept away, and the slave-trade went merrily on for fifty years and more.

Down in Darien, where the Delegal riots took place some summers ago, there used to come a strong protest against slavery from the Scotch Highlanders; and the Moravians of Ebenezea did not like the system. But not till the Haytian Terror of Toussaint was the trade in men even checked; while the national statute of 1808 did not suffice to stop it. How the Africans poured in!—fifty thousand between 1790 and 1810, and then from Virginia and from smugglers, two thousand a year for many years more. So the thirty thousand Negroes of Georgia in 1790 were doubled in a decade,—were over a hundred thousand in 1810, had reached two hundred thousand in 1820, and half a million at the time of the war. Thus like a snake the black population writhed upward.

But we must hasten on our journey. This that we pass as we leave Atlanta is the ancient land of the Cherokees,—that brave Indian nation which strove so long for its fatherland, until Fate and the United States Government drove them beyond the Mississippi. If you wish to ride with me you must come into the "Jim Crow Car." There will be no objection,—already four other white men, and a little white girl with her nurse, are in there. Usually the races are mixed in there; but the white coach is all white. Of course this car is not so good as the other, but it is fairly clean and comfortable. The discomfort lies chiefly in the hearts of those four black men yonder—and in mine.

We rumble south in quite a business-like way. The bare red clay and pines of Northern Georgia begin to disappear, and in their place appears a rich rolling land, luxuriant, and here and there well tilled. This is the land of the Creek Indians; and a hard time the Georgians had to seize it. The towns grow more frequent and more interesting, and brand-new cotton mills rise on every side. Below Macon the world grows darker; for now we approach the Black Belt,—that strange land of shadows, at which even slaves paled in the past, and whence come now only faint and half-intelligible murmurs to the world beyond. The "Jim Crow Car" grows larger and a shade better; three rough field-hands and two or three white loafers accompany us, and the newsboy still spreads his wares at one end. The sun is setting, but we can see the great cotton country as we enter it,—the soil now dark and fertile, now thin and gray, with fruit-trees and dilapidated buildings,—all the way to Albany.

At Albany, in the heart of the Black Belt, we stop. Two hundred miles south of Atlanta, two hundred miles west of the Atlantic, and one hundred miles north of the Great Gulf lies Dougherty County, with ten thousand Negroes and two thousand whites. The Flint River winds down from Andersonville, and, turning suddenly at Albany, the county-seat, hurries on to join the Chattahoochee and the sea. Andrew Jackson knew the Flint well, and marched across it once to avenge the Indian Massacre at Fort Mims. That was in 1814, not long before the battle of New Orleans; and by the Creek treaty that followed this campaign, all Dougherty County, and much other rich land, was ceded to Georgia. Still, settlers fought shy of this land, for the Indians were all about, and they were unpleasant neighbors in those days. The panic of 1837, which Jackson bequeathed to Van Buren, turned the planters from the impoverished lands of Virginia, the Carolinas, and east Georgia, toward the West. The Indians were removed to Indian Territory, and settlers poured into these coveted lands to retrieve their broken fortunes. For a radius of a hundred miles about Albany, stretched a great fertile land, luxuriant with forests of pine, oak, ash, hickory, and poplar; hot with the sun and damp with the rich black swamp-land; and here the corner-stone of the Cotton Kingdom was laid.

Albany is to-day a wide-streeted, placid, Southern town, with a broad sweep of stores and saloons, and flanking rows of homes,—whites usually to the north, and blacks to the south. Six days in the week the town looks decidedly too small for itself, and takes frequent and pro-longed naps. But on Saturday suddenly the whole county disgorges itself upon the place, and a perfect flood of black peasantry pours through the streets, fills the stores, blocks the sidewalks, chokes the thoroughfares, and takes full possession of the town. They are black, sturdy, uncouth country folk, good-natured and simple, talkative to a degree, and yet far more silent and brooding than the crowds of the Rhine-pfalz, or Naples, or Cracow. They drink considerable quantities of whiskey, but do not get very drunk; they talk and laugh loudly at times, but seldom quar-rel or fight. They walk up and down the streets, meet and gossip with friends, stare at the shop windows, buy coffee, cheap candy, and clothes, and at dusk drive home—happy? well no, not exactly happy, but much happier than as though they had not come.

Thus Albany is a real capital,—a typical Southern county town, the centre of the life of ten thousand souls; their point of contact with the outer world, their centre of news and gossip, their market for buying and selling, borrowing and lending, their fountain of justice and law. Once upon a time we knew country life so well and city life so little, that we illustrated city life as that of a closely crowded country district. Now the world has well-nigh forgotten what the country is, and we must imagine a little city of black people scattered far and wide over three hundred lonesome square miles of land, without train or trolley, in the midst of cotton and corn, and wide patches of sand and gloomy soil.

It gets pretty hot in Southern Georgia in July,—a sort of dull, deter-mined heat that seems quite independent of the sun; so it took us some days to muster courage enough to leave the porch and venture out on the long country roads, that we might see this unknown world. Finally we started. It was about ten in the morning, bright with a faint breeze, and

we jogged leisurely southward in the valley of the Flint. We passed the
scattered box-like cabins of the brick-yard hands, and the long tenement-
row facetiously called "The Ark," and were soon in the open country,
and on the confines of the great plantations of other days. There is the
"Joe Fields place"; a rough old fellow was he, and had killed many a
"nigger" in his day. Twelve miles his plantation used to run,—a regular barony. It is nearly all gone now; only straggling bits belong to the
family, and the rest has passed to Jews and Negroes. Even the bits which
are left are heavily mortgaged, and, like the rest of the land, tilled by
tenants. Here is one of them now,—a tall brown man, a hard worker and
a hard drinker, illiterate, but versed in farm-lore, as his nodding crops
declare. This distressingly new board house is his, and he has just moved
out of yonder moss-grown cabin with its one square room.

From the curtains in Benton's house, down the road, a dark comely
face is staring at the strangers; for passing carriages are not every-day
occurrences here. Benton is an intelligent yellow man with a good-sized
family, and manages a plantation blasted by the war and now the broken
staff of the widow. He might be well-to-do, they say; but he carouses
too much in Albany. And the half-desolate spirit of neglect born of the
very soil seems to have settled on these acres. In times past there were
cotton-gins and machinery here; but they have rotted away.

The whole land seems forlorn and forsaken. Here are the remnants
of the vast plantations of the Sheldons, the Pellots, and the Rensons;
but the souls of them are passed. The houses lie in half ruin, or have
wholly disappeared; the fences have flown, and the families are wandering in the world. Strange vicissitudes have met these whilom masters.
Yonder stretch the wide acres of Bildad Reasor; he died in war-time, but
the upstart overseer hastened to wed the widow. Then he went, and his
neighbors too, and now only the black tenant remains; but the shadow-
hand of the master's grand-nephew or cousin or creditor stretches out of
the gray distance to collect the rack-rent remorselessly, and so the land is
uncared-for and poor. Only black tenants can stand such a system, and
they only because they must. Ten miles we have ridden to-day and have
seen no white face.

A resistless feeling of depression falls slowly upon us, despite the gaudy sunshine and the green cotton-fields. This, then, is the Cotton King-dom,—the shadow of a marvellous dream. And where is the King? Per-haps this is he,—the sweating ploughman, tilling his eighty acres with two lean mules, and fighting a hard battle with debt. So we sit mus-ing, until, as we turn a corner on the sandy road, there comes a fairer scene suddenly in view,—a neat cottage snugly ensconced by the road, and near it a little store. A tall bronzed man rises from the porch as we hail him, and comes out to our carriage. He is six feet in height, with a sober face that smiles gravely. He walks too straight to be a tenant,— yes, he owns two hundred and forty acres. "The land is run down since the boom-days of eighteen hundred and fifty," he explains, and cotton is low. Three black tenants live on his place, and in his little store he keeps a small stock of tobacco, snuff, soap, and soda, for the neighborhood. Here is his gin-house with new machinery just installed. Three hundred bales of cotton went through it last year. Two children he has sent away to school. Yes, he says sadly, he is getting on, but cotton is down to four cents; I know how Debt sits staring at him.

Wherever the King may be, the parks and palaces of the Cotton King-dom have not wholly disappeared. We plunge even now into great groves of oak and towering pine, with an undergrowth of myrtle and shrub-bery. This was the "home-house" of the Thompsons,—slave-barons who drove their coach and four in the merry past. All is silence now, and ashes, and tangled weeds. The owner put his whole fortune into the rising cotton industry of the fifties, and with the falling prices of the eighties he packed up and stole away. Yonder is another grove, with unkempt lawn, great magnolias, and grass-grown paths. The Big House stands in half-ruin, its great front door staring blankly at the street, and the back part grotesquely restored for its black tenant. A shabby, well-built Negro he is, unlucky and irresolute. He digs hard to pay rent to the white girl who owns the remnant of the place. She married a policeman, and lives in Savannah.

Now and again we come to churches. Here is one now,—Shepherd's, they call it,—a great whitewashed barn of a thing, perched on stilts of stone, and looking for all the world as though it were just resting here a moment and might be expected to waddle off down the road at almost any time. And yet it is the centre of a hundred cabin homes; and sometimes, of a Sunday, five hundred persons from far and near gather here and talk and eat and sing. There is a school-house near,—a very airy, empty shed; but even this is an improvement, for usually the school is held in the church. The churches vary from log-huts to those like Shepherd's, and the schools from nothing to this little house that sits demurely on the county line. It is a tiny plank-house, perhaps ten by twenty, and has within a double row of rough unplaned benches, resting mostly on legs, sometimes on boxes. Opposite the door is a square home-made desk. In one corner are the ruins of a stove, and in the other a dim blackboard. It is the cheerfulest schoolhouse I have seen in Dougherty, save in town. Back of the schoolhouse is a lodge-house two stories high and not quite finished. Societies meet there,—societies "to care for the sick and bury the dead"; and these societies grow and flourish.

We had come to the boundaries of Dougherty, and were about to turn west along the county-line, when all these sights were pointed out to us by a kindly old man, black, white-haired, and seventy. Forty-five years he had lived here, and now supports himself and his old wife by the help of the steer tethered yonder and the charity of his black neighbors. He shows us the farm of the Hills just across the county line in Baker,— a widow and two strapping sons, who raised ten bales (one need not add "cotton" down here) last year. There are fences and pigs and cows, and the soft-voiced, velvet-skinned young Memnon, who sauntered half-bashfully over to greet the strangers, is proud of his home. We turn now to the west along the county line. Great dismantled trunks of pines tower above the green cotton-fields, cracking their naked gnarled fingers toward the border of living forest beyond. There is little beauty in this region, only a sort of crude abandon that suggests power,—a naked grandeur, as it were. The houses are bare and straight; there are no hammocks or easy-chairs, and few flowers. So when, as here at Rawdon's, one sees a vine clinging to a little porch, and home-like windows peeping over the fences, one takes a long breath. I think I never before quite realized the place of the Fence in civilization. This is the Land of the Unfenced, where crouch on either hand scores of ugly one-room cabins, cheerless and dirty. Here lies the Negro problem in its naked dirt and penury.

And here are no fences. But now and then the criss-cross rails or straight palings break into view, and then we know a touch of culture is near. Of course Harrison Gohagen,—a quiet yellow man, young, smooth-faced, and diligent,—of course he is lord of some hundred acres, and we expect to see a vision of well-kept rooms and fat beds and laughing children. For has he not fine fences? And those over yonder, why should they build fences on the rack-rented land? It will only increase their rent.

On we wind, through sand and pines and glimpses of old plantations, till there creeps into sight a cluster of buildings,—wood and brick, mills and houses, and scattered cabins. It seemed quite a village. As it came nearer and nearer, however, the aspect changed: the buildings were rotten, the bricks were falling out, the mills were silent, and the store was closed. Only in the cabins appeared now and then a bit of lazy life. I could imagine the place under some weird spell, and was half-minded to search out the princess. An old ragged black man, honest, simple, and improvident, told us the tale. The Wizard of the North—the Capitalist—had rushed down in the seventies to woo this coy dark soil. He bought a square mile or more, and for a time the field-hands sang, the gins groaned, and the mills buzzed. Then came a change. The agent's son embezzled the funds and ran off with them. Then the agent himself disappeared. Finally the new agent stole even the books, and the company in wrath closed its business and its houses, refused to sell, and let houses and furniture and machinery rust and rot. So the Waters-Loring plantation was stilled by the spell of dishonesty, and stands like some gaunt rebuke to a scarred land.

Somehow that plantation ended our day's journey; for I could not shake off the influence of that silent scene. Back toward town we glided, past the straight and thread-like pines, past a dark tree-dotted pond where the air was heavy with a dead sweet perfume. White slender-legged curlews flitted by us, and the garnet blooms of the cotton looked gay against the green and purple stalks. A peasant girl was hoeing in the field, white-turbaned and black-limbed. All this we saw, but the spell still lay upon us.

How curious a land is this,—how full of untold story, of tragedy and laughter, and the rich legacy of human life; shadowed with a tragic past, and big with future promise! This is the Black Belt of Georgia. Dougherty County is the west end of the Black Belt, and men once called it the Egypt of the Confederacy. It is full of historic interest. First there is the Swamp, to the west, where the Chickasawhatchee flows sullenly southward. The shadow of an old plantation lies at its edge, forlorn and dark. Then comes the pool; pendent gray moss and brackish waters appear, and forests filled with wild-fowl. In one place the wood is on fire, smouldering in dull red anger; but nobody minds. Then the swamp grows beautiful; a raised road, built by chained Negro convicts, dips down into it, and forms a way walled and almost covered in living green. Spreading trees spring from a prodigal luxuriance of undergrowth; great dark green shadows fade into the black background, until all is one mass of tangled semi-tropical foliage, marvellous in its weird savage splendor. Once we crossed a black silent stream, where the sad trees and writhing creepers, all glinting fiery yellow and green, seemed like some vast cathedral,— some green Milan builded of wildwood. And as I crossed, I seemed to see again that fierce tragedy of seventy years ago. Osceola, the Indian-Negro chieftain, had risen in the swamps of Florida, vowing vengeance. His war-cry reached the red Creeks of Dougherty, and their war-cry rang from the Chattahoochee to the sea. Men and women and children fled and fell before them as they swept into Dougherty. In yonder shadows a dark and hideously painted warrior glided stealthily on,—another and another, until three hundred had crept into the treacherous swamp. Then the false slime closing about them called the white men from the east. Waist-deep, they fought beneath the tall trees, until the war-cry was hushed and the Indians glided back into the west. Small wonder the wood is red.

Then came the black slaves. Day after day the clank of chained feet marching from Virginia and Carolina to Georgia was heard in these rich swamp lands. Day after day the songs of the callous, the wail of the motherless, and the muttered curses of the wretched echoed from the Flint to the Chickasawhatchee, until by 1860 there had risen in West Dougherty perhaps the richest slave kingdom the modern world ever knew. A hundred and fifty barons commanded the labor of nearly six thousand Negroes, held sway over farms with ninety thousand acres of tilled land, valued even in times of cheap soil at three millions of dollars. Twenty thousand bales of ginned cotton went yearly to England, New and Old; and men that came there bankrupt made money and grew rich. In a single decade the cotton output increased four-fold and the value of lands was tripled. It was the heyday of the *nouveau riche*, and a life of careless extravagance reigned among the masters. Four and six bob-tailed thoroughbreds rolled their coaches to town; open hospitality and gay entertainment were the rule. Parks and groves were laid out, rich with flower and vine, and in the midst stood the low wide-halled "big house," with its porch and columns and great fire-places.

And yet with all this there was something sordid, something forced,—a certain feverish unrest and recklessness; for was not all this show and tinsel built upon a groan? "This land was a little Hell," said a ragged, brown, and grave-faced man to me. We were seated near a roadside blacksmith-shop, and behind was the bare ruin of some master's home. "I've seen niggers drop dead in the furrow, but they were kicked aside, and the plough never stopped. And down in the guard-house, there's where the blood ran."

With such foundations a kingdom must in time sway and fall. The masters moved to Macon and Augusta, and left only the irresponsible overseers on the land. And the result is such ruin as this, the Lloyd "home-place":—great waving oaks, a spread of lawn, myrtles and chest-nuts, all ragged and wild; a solitary gate-post standing where once was a castle entrance; an old rusty anvil lying amid rotting bellows and wood in the ruins of a blacksmith shop; a wide rambling old mansion, brown and dingy, filled now with the grandchildren of the slaves who once waited on its tables; while the family of the master has dwindled to two lone women, who live in Macon and feed hungrily off the remnants of an earldom. So we ride on, past phantom gates and falling homes,—past the once flourishing farms of the Smiths, the Gandys, and the Lagores,—and find all dilapidated and half ruined, even there where a solitary white woman, a relic of other days, sits alone in state among miles of Negroes and rides to town in her ancient coach each day.

This was indeed the Egypt of the Confederacy,—the rich granary whence potatoes and corn and cotton poured out to the famished and ragged Confederate troops as they battled for a cause lost long before 1861. Sheltered and secure, it became the place of refuge for families, wealth, and slaves. Yet even then the hard ruthless rape of the land began to tell. The red-clay sub-soil already had begun to peer above the loam. The harder the slaves were driven the more careless and fatal was their farming. Then came the revolution of war and Emancipation, the bewilderment of Reconstruction,—and now, what is the Egypt of the Confederacy, and what meaning has it for the nation's weal or woe?

It is a land of rapid contrasts and of curiously mingled hope and pain. Here sits a pretty blue-eyed quadroon hiding her bare feet; she was married only last week, and yonder in the field is her dark young husband, hoeing to support her, at thirty cents a day without board. Across the way is Gatesby, brown and tall, lord of two thousand acres shrewdly won and held. There is a store conducted by his black son, a blacksmith shop, and a ginnery. Five miles below here is a town owned and controlled by one white New Englander. He owns almost a Rhode Island county, with thousands of acres and hundreds of black laborers. Their cabins look better than most, and the farm, with machinery and fertilizers, is much more business-like than any in the county, although the manager drives hard bargains in wages. When now we turn and look five miles above, there on the edge of town are five houses of prostitutes,— two of blacks and three of whites; and in one of the houses of the whites a worthless black boy was harbored too openly two years ago; so he was hanged for rape. And here, too, is the high whitewashed fence of the "stockade," as the county prison is called; the white folks say it is ever full of black criminals,—the black folks say that only colored boys are sent to jail, and they not because they are guilty, but because the State needs criminals to eke out its income by their forced labor.

The Jew is the heir of the slave-baron in Dougherty; and as we ride westward, by wide stretching cornfields and stubby orchards of peach and pear, we see on all sides within the circle of dark forest a Land of Canaan. Here and there are tales of projects for money-getting, born in the swift days of Reconstruction,—"improvement" companies, wine companies, mills and factories; nearly all failed, and the Jew fell heir.

It is a beautiful land, this Dougherty, west of the Flint. The forests are wonderful, the solemn pines have disappeared, and this is the "Oakey Woods," with its wealth of hickories, beeches, oaks, and palmettos. But a pall of debt hangs over the beautiful land; the merchants are in debt to the wholesalers, the planters are in debt to the merchants, the tenants owe the planters, and laborers bow and bend beneath the burden of it all. Here and there a man has raised his head above these murky waters. We passed one fenced stock-farm, with grass and grazing cattle, that looked very homelike after endless corn and cotton. Here and there are black freeholders: there is the gaunt dull-black Jackson, with his hundred acres. "I says, 'Look up! If you don't look up you can't get up,'" remarks Jackson, philosophically. And he's gotten up. Dark Carter's neat barns would do credit to New England. His master helped him to get a start, but when the black man died last fall the master's sons immediately laid claim to the estate. "And them white folks will get it, too," said my yellow gossip.

I turn from these well-tended acres with a comfortable feeling that the Negro is rising. Even then, however, the fields, as we proceed, begin to redden and the trees disappear. Rows of old cabins appear filled with renters and laborers,—cheerless, bare, and dirty, for the most part, although here and there the very age and decay makes the scene picturesque. A young black fellow greets us. He is twenty-two, and just married. Until last year he had good luck renting; then cotton fell, and the sheriff seized and sold all he had. So he moved here, where the rent is higher, the land poorer, and the owner inflexible; he rents a forty-dollar mule for twenty dollars a year. Poor lad!—a slave at twenty-two. This plantation, owned now by a Russian Jew, was a part of the famous Bolton estate. After the war it was for many years worked by gangs of Negro convicts,—and black convicts then were even more plentiful than now; it was a way of making Negroes work, and the question of guilt was a minor one. Hard tales of cruelty and mistreatment of the chained freemen are told, but the county authorities were deaf until the free-labor market was nearly ruined by wholesale migration. Then they took the convicts from the plantations, but not until one of the fairest regions of the "Oakey Woods" had been ruined and ravished into a red waste, out of which only a Yankee or a Jew could squeeze more blood from debt-cursed tenants.

No wonder that Luke Black, slow, dull, and discouraged, shuffles to our carriage and talks hopelessly. Why should he strive? Every year finds him deeper in debt. How strange that Georgia, the world-heralded refuge of poor debtors, should bind her own to sloth and misfortune as ruthlessly as ever England did! The poor land groans with its birth-pains, and brings forth scarcely a hundred pounds of cotton to the acre, where fifty years ago it yielded eight times as much. Of this meagre yield the tenant pays from a quarter to a third in rent, and most of the rest in interest on food and supplies bought on credit. Twenty years yonder sunken-cheeked, old black man has labored under that system, and now, turned day-laborer, is supporting his wife and boarding himself on his wages of a dollar and a half a week, received only part of the year.

The Bolton convict farm formerly included the neighboring plantation. Here it was that the convicts were lodged in the great log prison still standing. A dismal place it still remains, with rows of ugly huts filled with surly ignorant tenants. "What rent do you pay here?" I inquired. "I don't know,—what is it, Sam?" "All we make," answered Sam. It is a depressing place,—bare, unshaded, with no charm of past association, only a memory of forced human toil,—now, then, and before the war. They are not happy, these black men whom we meet throughout this region. There is little of the joyous abandon and playfulness which we are wont to associate with the plantation Negro. At best, the natural good-nature is edged with complaint or has changed into sullenness and gloom. And now and then it blazes forth in veiled but hot anger. I remember one big red-eyed black whom we met by the roadside. Forty-five years he had labored on this farm, beginning with nothing, and still having nothing. To be sure, he had given four children a common-school training, and perhaps if the new fence-law had not allowed unfenced crops in West Dougherty he might have raised a little stock and kept ahead. As it is, he is hopelessly in debt, disappointed, and embittered. He stopped us to inquire after the black boy in Albany, whom it was said a policeman had shot and killed for loud talking on the sidewalk. And then he said

slowly: "Let a white man touch me, and he dies; I don't boast this,—
I don't say it around loud, or before the children,—but I mean it. I've
seen them whip my father and my old mother in them cotton-rows till
the blood ran; by—" and we passed on.

Now Sears, whom we met next lolling under the chubby oak-trees,
was of quite different fibre. Happy?—Well, yes; he laughed and flipped
pebbles, and thought the world was as it was. He had worked here twelve
years and has nothing but a mortgaged mule. Children? Yes, seven;
but they hadn't been to school this year,—couldn't afford books and
clothes, and couldn't spare their work. There go part of them to the fields
now,—three big boys astride mules, and a strapping girl with bare brown
legs. Careless ignorance and laziness here, fierce hate and vindictiveness
there;—these are the extremes of the Negro problem which we met that
day, and we scarce knew which we preferred.

Here and there we meet distinct characters quite out of the ordinary.
One came out of a piece of newly cleared ground, making a wide detour
to avoid the snakes. He was an old, hollow-cheeked man, with a drawn
and characterful brown face. He had a sort of self-contained quaintness
and rough humor impossible to describe; a certain cynical earnestness
that puzzled one. "The niggers were jealous of me over on the other
place," he said, "and so me and the old woman begged this piece of
woods, and I cleared it up myself. Made nothing for two years, but I
reckon I've got a crop now." The cotton looked tall and rich, and we
praised it. He curtsied low, and then bowed almost to the ground, with
an imperturbable gravity that seemed almost suspicious. Then he continued, "My mule died last week,"—a calamity in this land equal to a
devastating fire in town,—"but a white man loaned me another." Then
he added, eyeing us, "Oh, I gets along with white folks." We turned
the conversation. "Bears? deer?" he answered, "well, I should say there
were," and he let fly a string of brave oaths, as he told hunting-tales of
the swamp. We left him standing still in the middle of the road looking
after us, and yet apparently not noticing us.

The Whistle place, which includes his bit of land, was bought soon
after the war by an English syndicate, the "Dixie Cotton and Corn Company." A marvellous deal of style their factor put on, with his servants

and coach-and-six; so much so that the concern soon landed in inextricable bankruptcy. Nobody lives in the old house now, but a man comes each winter out of the North and collects his high rents. I know not which are the more touching,—such old empty houses, or the homes of the masters' sons. Sad and bitter tales lie hidden back of those white doors,—tales of poverty, of struggle, of disappointment. A revolution such as that of '63 is a terrible thing; they that rose rich in the morning often slept in paupers' beds. Beggars and vulgar speculators rose to rule over them, and their children went astray. See yonder sad-colored house, with its cabins and fences and glad crops? It is not glad within; last month the prodigal son of the struggling father wrote home from the city for money. Money! Where was it to come from? And so the son rose in the night and killed his baby, and killed his wife, and shot himself dead. And the world passed on.

I remember wheeling around a bend in the road beside a graceful bit of forest and a singing brook. A long low house faced us, with porch and flying pillars, great oaken door, and a broad lawn shining in the evening sun. But the window-panes were gone, the pillars were worm-eaten, and the moss-grown roof was falling in. Half curiously I peered through the unhinged door, and saw where, on the wall across the hall, was written in once gay letters a faded "Welcome."

Quite a contrast to the southwestern part of Dougherty County is the northwest. Soberly timbered in oak and pine, it has none of that half-tropical luxuriance of the southwest. Then, too, there are fewer signs of a romantic past, and more of systematic modern land-grabbing and money-getting. White people are more in evidence here, and farmer and hired labor replace to some extent the absentee landlord and rack-rented tenant. The crops have neither the luxuriance of the richer land nor the signs of neglect so often seen, and there were fences and meadows here and there. Most of this land was poor, and beneath the notice of the slave-baron, before the war. Since then his nephews and the poor whites and the Jews have seized it. The returns of the farmer are too small to allow much for wages, and yet he will not sell off small farms. There is the Negro Sanford; he has worked fourteen years as overseer on the Ladson place, and "paid out enough for fertilizers to have bought a farm," but the owner will not sell off a few acres.

Two children—a boy and a girl—are hoeing sturdily in the fields on the farm where Corliss works. He is smooth-faced and brown, and is fencing up his pigs. He used to run a successful cotton-gin, but the Cotton Seed Oil Trust has forced the price of ginning so low that he says it hardly pays him. He points out a stately old house over the way as the home of "Pa Willis." We eagerly ride over, for "Pa Willis" was the tall and powerful black Moses who led the Negroes for a generation, and led them well. He was a Baptist preacher, and when he died two thousand black people followed him to the grave; and now they preach his funeral sermon each year. His widow lives here,—a weazened, sharp-featured little woman, who curtsied quaintly as we greeted her. Further on lives Jack Delson, the most prosperous Negro farmer in the county. It is a joy to meet him,—a great broad-shouldered, handsome black man, intelligent and jovial. Six hundred and fifty acres he owns, and has eleven black tenants. A neat and tidy home nestled in a flower-garden, and a little store stands beside it.

We pass the Munson place, where a plucky white widow is renting and struggling; and the eleven hundred acres of the Sennet plantation, with its Negro overseer. Then the character of the farms begins to change. Nearly all the lands belong to Russian Jews; the overseers are white, and the cabins are bare board-houses scattered here and there. The rents are high, and day-laborers and "contract" hands abound. It is a keen, hard struggle for living here, and few have time to talk. Tired with the long ride, we gladly drive into Gillonsville. It is a silent cluster of farm-houses standing on the cross-roads, with one of its stores closed and the other kept by a Negro preacher. They tell great tales of busy times at Gillonsville before all the railroads came to Albany; now it is chiefly a memory. Riding down the street, we stop at the preacher's and seat ourselves before the door. It was one of those scenes one cannot soon forget:—a wide, low, little house, whose motherly roof reached over and sheltered a snug little porch. There we sat, after the long hot drive, drinking cool water,—the talkative little storekeeper who is my daily companion; the silent old black woman patching pantaloons and saying never a word; the ragged picture of helpless misfortune who called in just to see the preacher; and finally the neat matronly preacher's wife, plump, yellow, and intelligent. "Own land?" said the wife; "well, only this house." Then she added quietly, "We did buy seven hundred acres up yonder, and paid for it; but they cheated us out of it. Sells was the owner." "Sells!" echoed the ragged misfortune, who was leaning against the balustrade and listening, "he's a regular cheat. I worked for him thirty-seven days this spring, and he paid me in cardboard checks which were to be cashed at the end of the month. But he never cashed them,—kept putting me off. Then the sheriff came and took my mule and corn and furniture—" "Furniture?" I asked; "but furniture is exempt from seizure by law." "Well, he took it just the same," said the hard-faced man.

# John Donald Wade

## "The Life and Death of Cousin Lucius"

He remembered all his life the feel of the hot sand on his young feet on that midsummer day. He was very young then, but he knew that he was very tired of riding primly beside his mother in the carriage. So his father let him walk for a little, holding him by his small hand. On went the carriage, on went the wagons behind the carriage, with the slaves, loud with greetings for young master. In the back of the last wagon his father set him down till he could himself find a seat there. Then his father, still holding his hand, lowered him to the road, and let him run along as best he could, right where the mules had gone. The slaves shouted in their pride of him, and in their glee, and the sport was unquestionably fine, but the sand was hot, too hot, and he was happy to go back to his prim station next the person who ruled the world.

That was all he remembered of that journey. He did not remember the look of the soil, black at times with deep shade, nor the far-reaching cotton-fields running down to the wagon ruts in tangles of blackberry bushes and morning-glories. He knew, later, that they had forded streams on that journey, that they had set out with a purpose, from a place— as travelers must—and that they had at last arrived. But all that came to him later. In his memory there was chiefly the hot sand.

What he learned later was this—that in 1850 his father had left his home in lower South Carolina and followed an uncle of his—Uncle Daniel— to a new home in Georgia. His father was then only twenty or so, and when he inherited some land and slaves he decided to go on to Georgia, where land, said Uncle Daniel, was cheap and fresh, and where with thrift one might reasonably hope to set up for oneself almost a little nation of one's own.

The next thing actually in his memory was also about slaves. In South Carolina, Aunt Amanda, an aunt of his mother's, had lately died. What that might mean was a mystery, but one clear result of the transaction was that Aunt Amanda had no further use for her slaves, and, in accordance with her will, they had been sent to him in Georgia. Their arrival his memory seized upon for keeps. They were being rationed—so much meal, so much meat, so much syrup, so much rice. But not enough rice. "Li'l' master," said one of his new chattels to him, "you min' askin' master to let us swap back all our meal for mo' rice?" He remembered that he thought it would be delightful to make that request, and he remembered that it was granted.

Next he remembered seeing the railway train. There it came with all its smoke, roaring, with its bell ringing and its shrill whistle. It was stopping on Uncle Daniel's place to get wood, the same wood that all that morning he had watched the slaves stacking into neat piles. It seemed to him indeed fine to have an uncle good enough to look after the hungry train's wants. That train could pull nearly anything, and it took cotton bales away so easily to the city that people did not have to use their mules any longer, at all, for such long hauls.

But in some things the railroad did not seem so useful. For when it nosed farther south into the state, after resting its southern terminus for a year or two at a town some miles beyond Uncle Daniel's, the town went down almost overnight, almost as suddenly as a blown bladder goes down, pricked.

Then a war came, and near Uncle Daniel's, where the road crossed the railroad and there were some little shops, some men walked up and down and called themselves drilling. That seemed a rare game to him, and he never forgot what a good joke it seemed to them, and to him, for them to mutter over and over as they set down their feet, corn-foot, shuck-foot, corn-foot, shuck-foot—on and on. At last the men went away from the crossroads, and Cousin James and Cousin Edwin went with them— Uncle Daniel's son and his daughter's son. His own father did not go and Lucius was very glad, but very sorry too, in a way. He did not go, he said, because he could hardly leave Lucius's mother and the baby girls—for somehow two baby girls had come, from somewhere. Lucius thought his father very considerate, but he wondered whether the girls were, after all, of a degree of wit that would make them miss their father very much.—But before he had done wondering, off his father went also.

That war was a queer thing. It was away, somewhere, farther than he had come from when he came first to Georgia. He heard no end of talk about it, but most of that talk confused itself later in his mind with his mature knowledge. He clearly remembered that there were such people as refugees, women and children mostly, who had come that far south because their own land was overrun by hundreds and hundreds of men, like Cousin James and Cousin Edwin, who were up there fighting hundreds and hundreds of other men, called Yankees. They were really fighting, not playing merely. They were shooting at one another, with guns, just as people shot a beef down when time came. But after they shot a man they did not put him to any use at all.

One day he went with Uncle Daniel to see a lot of soldiers who were going by, on their way north to help whip the Yankees. Uncle Daniel said that the soldiers were the noblest people in the world, and Lucius understood why it was that he took his gold-headed cane and wore his plush hat, as if he were going to church, when he went to say his good wishes to such noble people. As the train stopped and as he and Uncle Daniel stood there cheering, one of the soldiers called out to Uncle Daniel, boisterously: "Hey," he said, "what did you make your wife mad about this morning?"—"I was not aware, sir," said Uncle Daniel, "that I had angered her."—"Well," the soldier said, and he pointed at the plush hat, "I see she crowned you with the churn." Lucius wished very much that Uncle Daniel would say something sharp back to him, but he did not. He simply stood there looking a little red, saying, "Ah, sir, ah, sir," in the tone of voice used in asking questions but never coming out with any question whatever.

Once Lucius was with his mother in the garden. She was directing a number of negro women who were gathering huge basketfuls of vegetables. The vegetables, his mother told him, were being sent to Andersonville, where a lot of Yankees the soldiers had caught were being kept in prison. He asked his mother why they had not shot the Yankees, but she told him that it would have been very un-Christian to shoot them, because these particular Yankees had surrendered, and it was one's duty to be kind to them.

Years later he searched his mind for further memories of the war, but little else remained. Except, of course, about Cousin Edwin. He was at Cousin Edwin's mother's, Cousin Elvira's. It was a spring morning and everything was fresh with new flowers, and there were more birds flying in more trees, chirping, than a boy could possibly count. And at the front gate two men stopped with a small wagon.

He called to Cousin Elvira and she came from the house, down to the gate with him to see what was wanted. She was combing her hair; it was hanging down her back and the comb was in her hand so that he had to go round and take the other hand. What those men had in that wagon was Cousin Edwin's dead body. Cousin Elvira had not known that he was dead. Only that morning she had had a letter from him. He had been killed. How Cousin Elvira wept! He, too, wept bitterly, and the wagon men wept also. But Cousin Edwin was none the better off for all their tears. Nor was Cousin Elvira, for her part, much better off, either. She lived forty years after that day, and she told him often how on spring mornings all her life long she went about, or seemed to go about, numb through all her body and holding in her right hand a rigid comb that would not be cast away.

He was a big boy when the war ended, nearly fifteen, and the passing of days and weeks seemed increasingly more rapid. As he looked back and thought of the recurrent seasons falling upon the world it seemed to him that they had come to the count, over and over, of Hard Times, Hard Times, Hard Times, more monotonous, more unending, than the count of the soldiers, muttering as they marched, years before, in the town which had before been called only the crossroads.

He went to school to Mr. and Mrs. Pixley, who taught in town, some three miles from his father's plantation. Both of them, he learned, were Yankees, but it seemed, somehow, that they were good Yankees. And he took with him to Mr. Pixley's his two sisters. There was a brother, too, and there was a sister younger still, but they were not yet old enough to leave home.

One day his mother was violently ill. He heard her cry aloud in her agony—as he had before heard her cry, he remembered, two or three distinct times. She was near dying, he judged, for very pain—but they had told him not to come where she was and he waited, himself in anguish for her wretchedness. That day as she bore another child into the world, that lady quit the world once and for all. He thought that he would burst with rage and sorrow. Wherever he turned, she seemed to speak to him, and he cursed himself for his neglect of her. Surrounded by a nation of her husband's kin, she had not always escaped their blame. She had known that times were hard, well, well; but she had insisted that some things she must have while her children were still young. She had saved her round dollars and sent them to Philadelphia to be moulded into spoons; she had somehow managed to find some books, and a piano she *would* have. Well, she was dead now, and it seemed to Lucius that the world would be always dark to him, and that things more rigid, more ponderous, more relentlessly adhesive than combs are, would drag his hands downward to earth all his life.

It would not do, then, he decided, to take anybody quite for granted. Already he had learned, as a corollary of the war, that *things* are not dependable; even institutions almost universally the base of people's lives could not, from the fact that they were existent in 1860, be counted upon to be existent also in 1865. He knew now that people also are like wind that blows, and then, inexplicably, is still.

He examined his father, coldly, impersonally, for the first time—not as a fixed body like the earth itself. His father had obviously many elements of grandeur. He was honest and kind and capable. He was introspective, but not sure always to arrive by his self-analysis at judgments that Lucius believed valid. By the Methodist church, which he loved, he was stimulated wisely in his virtues and led to battle against a certain native irascibleness. But in that church such a vast emphasis is set on preaching, that the church is likely to be thought of as little more than a house big enough for the preacher's audience. Lucius learned before long that

many of the preachers he was expected to emulate might with more justice be set to emulate him, let alone his father. But his father could not be
brought to such a viewpoint, and indeed, if Lucius had dared to suggest
his conclusions very pointedly, it might have proved the worse for him.

Soon Lucius was sent to a college maintained by Georgia Methodists,
and he stayed till he was graduated. The college was in a tiny town remote from the railroad, and it was such a place that if the generation
of Methodists who had set it there some forty years earlier had looked
down upon it from Elysium, they would have been happy. Whatever
virtues Methodism attained in the South were as manifest there as they
were anywhere, and whatever defects it had were less vocal. The countless great oaks on the campus, lightened by countless white columns,
typified, appropriately, in his mind the strength and the disciplined joyousness that light might come to. His teachers were usually themselves
Methodist ministers, like those who had come periodically to his father's
church at home, but the burden of their talk was different. The books
they were constantly reading and the white columns among the oaks and
the tangible memories thereabout of one or two who had really touched
greatness, had somehow affected all who walked in that paradise.

In his studies the chief characters he met were Vergil and Horace and
other Romans, who seemed in that atmosphere, as he understood them,
truly native. More recent than they were Cervantes and Shakespeare,
and the English Lord Byron, the discrepancies of whose life one could
overlook in view of his inspiring words about liberty. Hardly dignified
enough, because of their modernity, to be incorporated into the curriculum of his college, these writers were none the less current in the college
community.

Lucius knew many other boys like himself. In his fraternity, dedicated
to God and ladies, he talked much about their high patron and their
patronesses, and in his debating society he joined in many windy disser-
tations on most subjects known to man. In spite of all the implication
about him regarding the transiency of earth, in spite of the despair evident in some quarters regarding the possible future of the South, Lucius
and his fellows and even his teachers speculated frequently and long on

mundane matters. They were large-hearted men, in way of being philosophic, and they felt a pity for their own people, in their poverty and in their political banishment from a land that they had governed—no one in his senses would say meanly—through Jefferson and Calhoun and Lee.

Once he went as a delegate from his fraternity to a meeting held at the state university, where an interest in this world as apart from heaven was somewhat more openly sanctioned than at his own college. The chief sight he saw there was Alexander Stephens, crippled and emaciated and shockingly treble. As he spoke, a young negro fanned him steadily and gave him from time to time a resuscitating toddy. That man's eyes burned with a kind of fire that Lucius knew was fed by a passionate integrity and a passionate love for all mankind. He was obviously the center of a legend, the type to which would gravitate men's memories of other heroes who had been in their way great, but never so great as he was.

Many young men whom Lucius met at the state university acknowledged the complexities of that legend when they attempted to follow it; when they rose to speak—as people were so frequently doing in those days at such conventions—they behaved themselves with a grandiloquence and declaimed with a gilded ardor that matched the legend of Stephens better than it matched the iron actuality. But Lucius did not know that. He admired the fervid imitations. He regretted that he could never send a majestic flight of eagles soaring across a peroration without having dart through his mind a flight of creatures as large as they, but of less dignified suggestion. He was sure that he could never speak anything in final earnestness without tending to stutter a little. His virtues were of the sort that can be recognized at their entire value only after one has endured the trampling of years which reduce a man to a patriarch.

When Lucius finally had A.B. appended to his name with all the authority of his college, he went home again. Hard Times met him at the train. For indeed the stress of life was great upon his father. Cotton was selling low and the birth rate had been high. Sister Cordelia was already at a Methodist college for girls, and Sister Mary would be going soon. And behind Mary was Brother Andrew. Lucius's father had married again, his first cousin, the widowed Cousin Elvira. And in the house was Cousin Elvira's ward, her sister's daughter, Lucius's third cousin. Her name was Caroline, and she was nineteen, and she had recently, like Lucius, returned home from college.

It was time for Lucius to go to work, and there was not much work one could do. The cities had begun to grow much more rapidly than in times past, and some of his classmates at college had gone to the cities for jobs. The fathers of some of them were in a position to help their sons with money till they could get on their feet, but Lucius felt that it would be unjust, in his case, to his younger brothers and sisters for him to expect anything further from his father. About the only thing left was to help his father on the farm, but his father was in the best of health, and as vigorous and capable an executive as ever. He really did not need a lieutenant, and the thought of becoming a private soldier of the farm no more entered Lucius's mind than the thought of becoming executioner to the Tsar. While he was still undecided where to turn, he heard one day of the death of Mr. Pixley. Temporarily, then, at least, he could be Mr. Pixley's successor.

So with his father's help he took over Mr. Pixley's academy, naming it neither for its late owner nor, as his father wished, for Bishop Asbury. Instead he named it for the frail man with the burning eyes whom he had seen at the state university, Stephens.

All that fall and winter and into the next spring he managed his academy—one woman assistant and some eighty youngsters ranging from seven to twenty-one. And just as summer came round the year following he married Cousin Caroline.

So life went with him, year in, year out. Children came to him and Cousin Caroline in God's plenty, and children, less intimately connected with him, flocked to the academy. He was determined to make all these youngsters come to something. After all, his lines were cast as a teacher. At least he could make a livelihood at that work, and very likely, there, as well as in another place, he could urge himself and the world about him into the strength and the disciplined joyousness which he had come to prize and which he believed would surely bring with them a fair material prosperity. If the children were amenable, he was pleased; if they were dull, he was resolute, unwilling to condemn them as worse than lazy. When night came he was tired—like a man who has spent the day ploughing; but perhaps, he thought, in a little while the situation would become easier.

After the war, nearly all the owners of plantations moved into town, and land that had formerly made cotton for Uncle Daniel gradually turned into streets and building lots. Lucius felt that the thing he had learned at college, and had caught, somehow, from the burning eyes of Mr. Stephens, involved him in a responsibility to that town that could not be satisfied by his giving its youth a quality of instruction that he, if not they, recognized as better than its money's worth. He organized among the citizens a debating society such as he had seen away at school, and he operated in connection with it a lending library. Shakespeare and Cervantes and the English Lord Byron were at the beck of his fellow townsmen—and Addison and Swift and Sterne and Sir Walter Scott, and even Dickens and Thackeray and George Eliot. Lucius managed to make people think (the men as well as the women—he stood out for that) that without the testimony and the comment of such spirits on his life they would all find this life less invigorating.

He found abettors in this work—his father and Uncle Daniel and others of the same mind—but he was its captain. His school, then, affected not merely those who were of an age appropriate for his academy, and it was not long before he was known almost universally in his village as "Cap"—for Captain.

His father turned over about two hundred and fifty acres to him as a sort of indefinite loan, and he became in a fashion a farmer as well as a teacher. That possibly was an error, for when word of his pedagogic ability and energy spread far, and he was offered an important teaching position in a neighboring city, he decided not to accept it because of his farm. But possibly all that was not an error. An instinct for the mastery of land was in his blood, and he knew few pleasures keener than that of roaming over his place, in the afternoons, when school was out, exulting in the brave world and shouting to the dogs that followed him.

There is no doubt that Lucius was gusty. He shouted not only to his dogs, but to himself, occasionally, when he had been reading alone for a long time, during vacations, on his shaded veranda. And he shouted,

too, when the beauty of the red sinking sun over low hills, or of clean
dogwood blossoms in a dense brake, seemed to him too magnificent not
to be magnificently saluted.

Hard Times shadowed him night and day, thwarting in his own life
more generous impulses than he could number. Hard Times also, singly
or perhaps in collusion with other forces, thwarted in the lives of his
neighbors activities that he felt strenuously should be stimulated. What
did people mean, in a land where all delectable fruits would grow for the
mere planting, by planting never a fruit tree? His father had fruit trees,
Uncle Daniel had, all of the older men, in fact, commanded for their
private use, not for commercial purposes, orchards of pears and peaches,
and vineyards, and many a row of figs and pomegranates. But only he of
all the younger men would trouble to plant them.

Lucius pondered that matter. Of course there was the small initial expense of the planting, but it was very small or he himself could not have
mustered it. Of course there was the despair, the lassitude of enduring poverty. He would shake his head violently when talking about this
with his father—like a man coming from beneath water—but for all that
gesture could find no clear vision.

It seemed to him, as he considered the world he was a part of, that common sense was among the rarest of qualities—that when it should assert
itself most vigorously, it was most likely to lie sleeping. The prevalent
economic order was tight and apparently tightening, yet the more need
people had to provide themselves with simple assuagements—like pomegranates, for example—the more they seemed paralyzed and inactive.
The bewildering necessity of actual money drove everyone in the farm
community to concern himself exclusively with the only crop productive of actual money. The more cotton a man grew, the cheaper it went,
and the more it became necessary to sustain one's livestock and oneself
with dearly purchased grain and meat that had been produced elsewhere.
Sometimes when Lucius considered these complexities, and ran over in
his mind the actual want of money of his friends, and the cruel deprivation that many of them subjected themselves to in order to send their
children away to colleges which were themselves weak with penury—at
such times he was almost beside himself with a sort of blind anger.

It was lucky that his anger saved him from despair. He was not built for despair, from the beginning, and he was, after all, the husband of Cousin Caroline, and between her and despair there was no shadow of affinity. In every regard he could think of except money, Cousin Caroline had brought him as his wife everything that he, or any man, might ask for.

She knew how to summon a group of people from the town and countryside, and how, on nothing, apparently, to provide them with enough food and enough merriment to bring back to all of them the tradition of generous living that seemed native to them. He often thought that she, who was at best but a frail creature, was the strongest hope he knew for the perpetuation of that bright tradition against the ceaseless, clamorous, insensate piracies of Hard Times. He was sure that the sum total of her character presented aspects of serenity and splendor that demanded, more appropriately than it did anything else, a sort of worship.

Cousin Caroline had religion. She was made for religion from the beginning, and she was, after all, the wife of Cousin Lucius, and in every regard she could think of except money, Cousin Lucius had brought her as her husband, everything that she, or any woman, might ask for. To many beside those two it seemed that Cousin Lucius, because he never quite accepted the Methodist Church, had no religion whatever, that, having only charity and integrity for his currency, he would fare badly at last with St. Peter as concerned tolls. But Cousin Caroline thought better of St. Peter's fundamental discernment than to believe he would quibble about the admission of one who was so plainly one of God's warriors.

Among the best things Cousin Caroline did for him was to bring him to a fuller appreciation of his father. Always fond of him, always loyal to him, Cousin Lucius had never quite understood his apparent satisfaction with the offerings of Methodism. He was affected inescapably when the Methodists presented his father, on his completing twenty-five years as superintendent of their Sunday school, with a large silver pitcher. Most of the people who had helped purchase it were harried by need, and their contributions were all the fruit of sacrifice.

But it was Cousin Caroline's satisfaction, as well as his father's, with the offerings of Methodism that did most to quiet his misgivings in that quarter. Anything that two lofty souls—or indeed one lofty soul, he conceded—can be fain of, must itself be somehow worthy. And if it is worthy, an adherence to it on the part of one person should never stand as a barrier between that disciple and an honest soul who is unable to achieve that particular discipleship. As Cousin Lucius grew older, then, his love and admiration of his father, while no greater perhaps than they had been formerly, were certainly more active, less hampered by reservations. His father, he knew, had doted on him in a fashion so prideful that it had seemed a little ridiculous, but that surely could be no barrier between them, and the two men loved each other very tenderly.

Occasionally on trips to this or that city, he encountered friends whom he had known at college. Most of them were prosperous, and some of them were so rich and eminent that news of them seeped down constantly to the stagnant community that was his demesne. He was conscious, as he talked with some of them, of a sort of condescension for him as one who had not justified the promise of his youth. Friendly, aware soon that the old raciness and the old scope of his mind were still operative, one and another of them suggested his coming, still, to live in a city, where he might wrestle with the large affairs that somebody *must* wrestle with, and that he seemed so peculiarly fitted to control.

He learned pointedly through these people what was stirring in the great world. All of them recognized that the condition of Georgia, and of all the South, was indeed perilous, for acquaintance with Hard Times had taught them that Hard Times is a cruel master, who will brutalize, in time, even the stoutest-hearted victim. Somehow the tyrant must be cast down.

In the meantime Cousin Lucius saw the Literary and Debating Society, with its library, gradually go to pieces. It had lasted twenty years. People could not afford the bare expenses of its operation. He saw men resort to subterfuges and to imitations for so long that they at last believed in them; and he, for one, while opposed to anything that was not true, was too sorry for them not to be in part glad that they could persevere in their hallucination. He saw the negroes, inescapably dependent on the whites, sag so far downward, as the whites above them sagged, that final gravity, he feared, would seize the whole swinging structure of society and drag it fatally to earth. He saw the best of people, identified with as good a tradition as English civilization had afforded, moving he feared unswervably, toward a despair from which they never might be lifted.

A small daughter of his, one day, chattering to him, said a thing that made him cold with anger. She used the word "city" as an adjective, and as an adjective so inclusively commendatory that he knew she implied that whatever was the opposite of "city" was inclusively culpable. He knew that she reflected a judgment that was becoming dangerously general, and he wondered how long he himself could evade it. For days after that he went about fortifying himself by his knowledge of history and of ancient fable, telling himself that man had immemorially drawn his best strength from the earth that mothered him, that the farmer, indeed until quite recently, in the South, had been the acknowledged lord; the city man most often a tradesman. "But what have history and ancient fable," the fiend whispered, "to do with the present?" Cousin Lucius admitted that they apparently had little to do with it, but he believed they *must* have something to do with it if it were not to go amuck past all remedy.

Some of Cousin Lucius's friends thought that the solution of their troubles was to adopt frankly the Northern way of life; and others thought that the solution was to band themselves with discontented farmer sections elsewhere in the country, and so by fierce force to wrest the national organization to a pattern that would favor farmers for a while at the expense of industrialists. On the whole, philosophically, he hoped that farming would continue paramount in his Georgia. He knew little of the philosophy of industrialism, but he knew some people who had grown up to assume that it was the normal order of the world, and he knew that those people left him without comfort. Yet he doubted the wisdom of fierce force, anywhere, and he disliked the renunciation of individualism necessary to attain fierce force. And he observed that in the camp of his contemporaries who relied on that expedient there were many who favored socialistic measures he could not condone, and more whose ignorance and selfishness he could not stomach. The only camp left for him, in his political thinking, was the totally unorganized—and perhaps unorganizable—camp of those who could not bring themselves to assert the South either by means of abandoning much that was peculiarly Southern or by means of affiliating themselves with many who had neither dignity nor wisdom nor honesty.

Cousin Lucius was nearly fifty by now, but he had not yet reconciled himself to the rarity with which power and virtue go hand in hand, leading men with them to an Ultimate who embodies all that our poor notions of virtue and power dimly indicate to us. When he was at college, among the great oaks and the columns, it had seemed to him that those two arbiters were inseparable, as he observed them along the shaded walks. And he had taught school too long—Euclid and Plato were more real to him than Ulysses Grant and William McKinley.

About 1890 one of Cousin Lucius's friends sent some peaches to New York in refrigerated boxes. They sold well. And slowly, cautiously, Cousin Lucius and all the people in his community began putting more and more of their land into orchards. It took a long time for them to adopt the idea that peaches were a better hope for them than cotton. Old heads wagged sagely about the frequent winters that were too cold for the tender buds, young heads told of the insect scourges likely to infest any large-scale production; and every sad prophecy came true. In spite of all, the industry proceeded. Farm after farm that had been sowed to crops afresh each year since being cleared of the forests was set now in interminable rows of peach trees. In spring, when the earth was green with a low cover-crop and each whitewashed stalk of tree projected upward to the loveliest pink cloud of blossom, Lucius was like a boy again for sheer delight. And in summer, when the furious activity of marketing the fruit spurred many of the slow-going Georgians to the point of pettishness, his own vast energy became, it seemed, utterly tireless. What he saw made him believe that the master compromise had been achieved, that an agricultural community could fare well in a dance where the fiddles were all buzz-saws and the horns all steam-whistles.

An instinct, perhaps, made all of Cousin Lucius's children less confident of that compromise than he was. Without exception they revered him; and persuaded, all of them, of his conviction that the test of a society is the kind of men it produces, they could not think poorly of the system that had him as a part of it. But they could not gain their own consent also to live in that system. And one by one they went away to cities, and they all prospered.

An instinct, too, perhaps, made the people of his community restive under the demands he made of school children. He had yielded to the community judgment to the extent of turning his academy into a public school, but he could not believe that the transformation was more than nominal. That is where circumstance tricked him. The people had lost faith in the classics as a means to better living, or had come to think of *better living* in a restricted, tangible sense that Cousin Lucius would not contemplate. And to teach anything less than the classics seemed to him to involve a doubt as to the value of teaching anything. He wondered why people did not send their children to "business colleges" and be done with it. So he was repudiated as a teacher, after thirty faithful years. The times, he thought, and not any individuals he knew, were responsible and he was in no way embittered. It was, of course, a consideration that he would no longer draw his hundred dollars a month, but the farm was more remunerative than it had been since the Civil War. And before long the village bank was reorganized and he was made its president.

Money was really coming into the community, and it was sweet not to be stifled always with a sense of poverty. But sometimes he felt that money was like a narcotic that, once tasted, drives men to make any sacrifice in order to taste more of it. All around him, for instance, many gentlemen whom he had long recognized as persons of dignity were behaving themselves with a distressing lack of dignity. On the advice of New York commission merchants they were attaching to each of their peach-crates a gaudy label, boasting that peaches of that particular brand were better than peaches of any other brand. There were gentlemen who were actually shipping the same sort of peaches, from the same orchard, under two distinct brands. Cousin Lucius was sure that such conduct was not native with them, and he was at a loss to know what they meant. What if the commission merchants had said that such practice was "good business"? Who were the commission merchants, anyway?

Another by-and-by had come round and Hard Times was no longer knocking at the door. Cousin Lucius saw men and women, whose heads had been held up by a feat of will only, holding their heads high, at last, naturally. He thought they should hold them higher still. By the Eternal, these people were as good as any people anywhere, and it had not been right, he believed, nor in accord with the intent of God, for them to be always supplicants.

It made him glad to see the girls of various families with horses and phaetons of their own. When a group of citizens promoted a swimming club, he exulted with the happiness of one who loved swimming for itself and who loved it in this special case as a symbol of liberation. The water that he cavorted in on the summer afternoons, while he whooped from time to time to the ecstatic shrieks of a hundred children, plopped no more deliciously upon his body than upon his spirit. For forty years he and his kind had wandered through a dense wilderness, with little external guidance either of cloud or fire. He told himself that by the light of their own minds they had wandered indeed bravely, but he was unashamedly glad that help had come, and that other men and cities were at last visible.

His father lived on, hale at ninety. He had become in the eyes of everybody who knew him a benign and indomitable saint. Shortly before his death he was in extreme pain and feebleness, and Cousin Lucius, for one, while he was saddened, could not be wholly sad to have the old man go on to whatever might await him. As he ran over in his mind the events of the long life just ended, one thing he had not before thought of stuck in his memory. His father had continued superintendent of the Methodist Sunday school until his death, and yet when he had rounded out his fifty years, though his flock was less hard pressed by far than it had been twenty-five years earlier, there was no silver pitcher offered in recognition of that cycle of effort. He believed that his father, too, had let the anniversary go unnoticed.

Yet Cousin Lucius felt that the omission meant something, most likely something that the people were not conscious of. To all appearances the Methodists were never so active. Like the Baptists—and as incompletely as he indorsed the Methodists, it truly grieved him for them to execute their reforms Baptistward—they had replaced their rather graceful wooden church with a contorted creation, Gothic molded, in red brick.

Most of their less material defects remained constant. But the church's neglect of his father's fifty years of service made him know that in spite of its bustling works, it was bored upon from within by something that looked to him curiously like mortality. And the most alarming part of the situation was that the church could not be persuaded of its malady. People simply did not look to it any longer as the center of all their real hopes. He felt that for the great run of men the church is an indispensable symbol of the basic craving of humanity for an integrity which it must aspire to, if it can never quite exemplify.

He dimly felt that in its zeal to maintain itself as that symbol it had adopted so many of the methods of the men about it, that men had concluded it too much like themselves to be specially needful. It had become simply the most available agent for their philanthropies. For its continued services on that score they paid it the tribute of executing its ceremonies, but they believed, in their hearts, if they were not aware that they did, that all those ceremonies were quite barren. Cousin Lucius, too, had felt that they were barren, but rather because they understated the degree of his humility than because they overstated it. It seemed to him that most of his contemporaries, who were in fact, by now, almost all his juniors, felt that those ceremonies needlessly belittled creatures who were in fact not necessarily little at all.

He did not solve those questions, but he held them in his mind, to couple them, if occasion came, with facts that he might run upon that seemed related.

So the new day was not altogether cloudless. Cousin Lucius felt that people were going too fast, that, villagers, they were trying to keep the pace of people they considered, but whom he could not consider, the best people in the great cities. He believed that the people who had represented in an urban civilization in 1850 what his family had represented at that time in a rural civilization were most likely as little disposed as he was to endorse the new god, who was so mobile that he had lost all his stability.

Tom and Dick and the butcher and the baker and others were all shooting fiercely about in automobiles, and Europe was trying to destroy itself in a great war—and then America was driven into the war, too. As a banker, he urged Tom and Dick to buy government bonds to sustain the war, but most of them were more concerned to buy something else. Perhaps the older families in the cities were protesting as he protested— and to as little purpose. And people would not read any more. Well-to-do again, they would not listen to his efforts to reorganize the old Library. They would swim with him, they would set up a golf club, but they would not read Cervantes because they were too busy going to the movies.

That war in Europe, with the clamorous agencies that swung to its caissons, woman's suffrage and "socialism" and prohibition, was a puzzle to him. His knowledge of history taught him that most of the avowed objects of any war prove inevitably, in the event, not to have been the real objects. As for woman's suffrage, despite his fervor for justice, he was sure that the practice of a perfectly sound "right" often involves the practicer, and with him others, in woes incomparably more galling than the renunciation of that right.

Socialism meant to him at bottom the desire of the laboring classes for a more equable share of the world's goods, and the laboring classes that he knew were negro farm hands. It seemed to him that in all conscience they shared quite as fully as justice might demand in the scant dole of the world's goods handed down to their white overlords.

For many years Georgia had had prohibition, and he had voted for it long before it was established. He believed that it was mainly an expedient for furthering good relations between the whites and negroes. It was not practical for a rural community to command adequate police protection, and he was willing to sacrifice his right to resort to liquor openly, in order to make it less available to persons who were likely to use it to the point of madness.

But national prohibition, involving the effort to force upon urban communities, and upon rural communities with a homogeneous population, a system designed peculiarly for the rural South, seemed to him as foolhardy and as vicious as the efforts of alien New England to control the ballot-box in the South. The law was passed in spite of him, and for a while—stickler as he was for law—he grudgingly abided by it. But he soon learned that he was alone, with scarcely anybody except women for company, and that made him restless. He remembered his initial objection to the program, and reminded himself of the statute books cluttered with a thousand laws inoperative because people did not believe in them, and at last, so far as he was concerned, repealed the national prohibition law altogether and abided by the prohibition law of Georgia only, as he had before abided by it, with wisdom and temperance.

One day he was sitting in his brother's store, and he heard some men—they had all been students of his—talking lustily among themselves out on the sidewalk. "What this town needs," said one of them, "is looser credit. Look at every town up and down the road—booming! Look at us—going fast to nothing. What we need is a factory, with a big payroll every Saturday. Naturally we haven't got the capital to float the thing from the start, but, good Lord! how would anything ever start if people waited till they had cash enough to meet every possible expense? In this man's world you've got to take chances. The root of our trouble"—and here Cousin Lucius listened earnestly. He was president of the bank, and though he had not thought the town was disintegrating, he recognized that comparatively it was at a standstill—"the root of our trouble," continued his economist, "is old-man Lucius. Fine old fellow and all that kind of thing, but, my God! what an old fogy! I'll tell you, it's like the fellow said, what this town needs most is one or two first-class funerals!"

Cousin Lucius was pretty well dazed. He did not know whether to go out and defend himself, or to hold his peace, and later, when appropriate, to clarify his position as best he could for a race that had become so marvelously aggressive. He was afraid that if he went he would not be able to talk calmly. He had fairly mastered his trait of stuttering, but he felt sure that before any speech he might make just then he would do well to fill his mouth with pebbles and to plant himself by the roaring surf.

He knew well what that bounding youngster had in mind. He wanted, without effort, things that have immemorially come as the result of effort only. His idea of happiness was to go faster and faster on less and less, and Cousin Lucius was bound to admit that that idea was prevalent nearly everywhere. He did not know, for sure, where it had come from, but it was plainly subjugating Georgia, and if reports were faithful, it was lord everywhere in America. He did not care, he told himself, if it was lord everywhere in the hypothecated universe, it should win no submission from him. The true gods might be long in reasserting themselves, but life is long enough to wait. For that which by reason of strength may run to fourscore years, by reason of other forces may run farther. He would not concede that we are no better than flaring rockets, and he would never get it into his old-fashioned head that anything less than a complete integrity will serve as a right basis for anything that is intended to mount high and to keep high.

He would not say all that now. He believed that the peach business would be constantly remunerative, but he remembered that it had been in existence less than twenty-five years, and he knew that many things of longer lease than that, on men's minds, had suddenly crashed into nothingness. For that reason he was glad that his community had undertaken the commercial production of asparagus and pecans as well as peaches and the older dependence, cotton. He did not anticipate the collapse of all those industries. All that he insisted on was that the expansion of his community be an ordered response to actual demands—not a response so violently stimulated to meet artificial demands that it created new demands faster than it could satisfy the old ones.

The peach crop in 1919 was a complete failure—for reasons not yet determined. The fruit was inferior; the costs of production and transportation, high; the market, lax. And in turn other crops were almost worthless. Next year, everybody said, things would be better. And pretty soon it was plain to Cousin Lucius that his faith in the compromise between farming and industrialism had in its foundations mighty little of reality.

He was himself cautious and thrifty and he had not spent by any means all that the fat years just past had brought to him. He had saved money— and bought more land. He blamed, in a fashion, the people who had lived on all they had made, but against his will he had to admit to himself that he did not blame them very much. Gravely impoverished for years, holding in their land a capital investment that in theory, only, amounted to anything, they had toiled to feed and clothe a boisterous nation which had become rankly rich and which had reserved for itself two privileges: to drive such iron bargains with the Southern farmer that he could scarcely creep, and to denounce him from time to time for his oppression of the negro. Seeing all that, Cousin Lucius could hardly blame the grasshoppers for flitting during the short and, after all, only half-hearted summer of the peach industry. But he considered that he was weak not to blame them more, and he was torn to know whether he should promise the people a better day, which he could not descry, or berate them about the duties of thrift.

The towns in the peach area which had committed themselves to the looser credits he had heard advocated were in worse condition now, by far, than his own town. The same people who had called Cousin Lucius an old fogy began now to say that he was a wise old bird. And he accepted their verdict to this extent—he was wise in seeing the folly that a farm community surely enacts in attempting to live as if it were an industrial community. While he conceded that no community could in his day be any longer purely agrarian, he felt—when he heard people urging a universal acceptance of the industrial program—that that program was not suitable even for an industrial community if it was made up of human beings as he knew them. He recognized that his wisdom was only negative, that there were basic phases of the question that lay too deep for his perceiving.

The farmer, it seemed to him, was in the hard position of having to win the suffrage of a world that had got into the industrialists' motor-car and gone riding. He could run alongside the car, or hang on behind the car, or sit beside the road and let the car go on whither it would—with destination unannounced and, one might suspect, unconsidered.

The case was illustrated by some towns he knew. One of them had continued to grow cotton exclusively—and the world had forgotten it. Many of them had run as hard as ever they could to keep up with the world, and they had fallen exhausted. His own town had hung on as best it could, and though the industrialists might grumble, it managed not to be dislodged. That was a half victory indeed.

He thought as a matter of justice to the farmer and as a matter of well-being for the world, that that motor-car should be controlled not always by the industrialists but sometimes by an agency that would be less swift, more ruminative. A truly wise bird would bring *that* about, and Cousin Lucius knew that that lay clean beyond him.

One might speculate on these things interminably, but what Cousin Lucius actually saw was that the economic structure of his community was falling down, like London Bridge, or like the little town which, as a child, he had seen burst, bladder like, when the railroad pushed on beyond it. He heard doctrinaire persons, sent down by the government, explain that the trouble lay wholly in the commitment of the people to one crop only. That infuriated him. His community was not committed to a one-crop system; it had four crops. But he found the doctrinaire persons hopelessly obtuse.

Four crops! They had five crops, worse luck, for the countryside everywhere was being stripped of its very forests, so that the people in the cities might have more lumber. That was a chance of getting some money, and one could not let it pass. Woods he had roamed, calculating—as he had learned to do at college—their cubic content in timber per acre, were to his dismay being operated upon in actuality, as he had often fondly, with no thought of sacrilege, operated on them in fancy. It seemed that people could not be happy unless they were felling trees.

One day the young school superintendent began chopping some oaks on the school grounds, for the high purpose of making an out-of-door basketball court. Cousin Lucius had not a shred of authority to stop the young man, but when he found that the persons who did have authority would not interfere, he interfered himself. At first Cousin Lucius reasoned with him calmly, but the superintendent would not be convinced. There was much talk.

"I have the authority of the Board of Education," said the superintendent, concluding the matter. But Cousin Lucius was determined that that should not conclude the matter. "Authority or no authority," said he, flustered, stuttering a little, "you will take them down, sir, at your peril." Then he walked away.

The superintendent knew that Cousin Lucius had no mandate of popular sentiment behind him, but knew also *one* person who did not mean to risk that old man's displeasure. The trees were spared.

The sacrifice of the forests was a symbol to Cousin Lucius, and a sad one. He knew by it how grave, once more, was the extremity of his friends—how fully it meant the arrival once more of Hard Times as their master. Even now they retained a plenty of most things they actually needed, but lacked the means of acquiring anything in addition. Of course they had wanted too much, and had curbed their desires in general less successfully than he had done, and they were consequently harder pressed. But they were a people not bred to peasant viewpoints. Traditionally they were property owners. They worked faithfully, they maintained holdings upon the value of which was predicated the entire economic structure of the nation. Society would not in either decency or sense deny that value, and it never did. What it did—by some process Cousin Lucius could not encompass—was to make the revenues from that value quite valueless—or at least quite valueless as compared with the revenues from equal amounts of capital invested elsewhere.

Once again he saw inaugurated the old process, checked for a while, of people leaving their farms and putting out for the cities. And he observed that those who went prospered, while those who stayed languished. Formerly, the more or less gradual development of the cities made them incapable of offering work to all who came, and many of his younger neighbors kept to their farms through necessity. Now the cities were growing like mad—precisely, he thought, like mad—and most of the old families he knew were moving off, losing their connection with their old home. Some survived their difficulties, but many, after lapsing deeper and deeper into debt, finally turned over their holdings to one or another mortgage firm, and went away. And the mortgage firms turned over the land to aliens, people from here and yonder, whose grandfathers never owned a slave nor planted a pomegranate.

Even the negroes, conscious at last of the insatiate capacity of the new cities, were moving away. The Southern cities had absorbed as many negroes as they could use, but the Northern cities had much work of the sort they felt negroes were suited for. It saddened Cousin Lucius to see them go. Men and women whose parents had come with his parents from Carolina, and who lived in the same houses all their lives, were going away—to Detroit, to Akron, to Pittsburgh. Well, God help them.

The prospect was not cheerful, but Cousin Lucius thought that as a human being he was superior to any prospect whatever. When he preached that doctrine to some of his friends they taunted him with the idea that his particular bravery was sustained by certain government bonds he had, and it was true that he had the bonds. He and Cousin Caroline had not stinted themselves during the fat years all for nothing, and he had kept out a small share of his savings to go into Liberty Bonds. But he told those who mourned, and he told himself, that even if he had not saved the bonds, he would still have asserted his humanity over the shackling activities of mere circumstance.

It was a fine sight to see him early on a summer morning walking the mile-long street between his home and the bank. On one side there were great oaks bordering his path, and the other side was a row of houses. In front of nearly every house a woman was stirring among her flowers, and Cousin Lucius had some words for nearly all of them. "Nice morning, ma'am," he would say. "I hope you all are well this morning." And then he would pass on, and often he would sniff the cool air greedily into his nostrils. "My, my," he would say, "sweet! How sweet the air is this morning!" And when a breeze blew, he would stretch out his arms directly into it—for of all the good things to have up one's sleeve he considered a summer breeze among the usefulest.

The time came round when he and Cousin Caroline had been married fifty years. And they gave a great party, and all their children came home, and people from all that section came to say good wishes to them. Cousin Caroline sat most of the evening, lovely in her black dress and with her flowers, and Cousin Lucius—sure that Cousin Caroline would pay for the two of them whatever was owing to propriety—sat nowhere, nor was indeed still for a moment anywhere. He looked very elegant, as young, almost, as his youngest son, and he was as vigorous, apparently, as anybody in all that company. Cousin Lucius had never lost a moment in his whole life from having drunk too much liquor, but he had always kept some liquor on hand, and he felt that that night surely justified his touching it a little more freely than was his custom. So he summoned by groups all the gentlemen present into his own backroom, and had a toast with them. Now the room was small and there were many groups and that involved Cousin Lucius's having many toasts, but he used his head and came through the operation with the dignity that was a part of him.

Not everybody was satisfied with his conduct. Some of the ladies especially who had men-folk less well balanced than they might have been, thought the situation scandalous. They had been indoctrinated fully with the dogma which says that life must be made safe for everybody at the cost, if necessary, of shutting the entire world into a back yard with high palings, and they believed that somebody prone to sottishness might be wrecked by Cousin Lucius's example. They did not realize the complexities of life which baffle those who have eyes to see, and make them despair at times of saving even the just and wise—much less the weak and foolish.

Those ladies were not shadowed—nor glorified—by a sense of tragic vision, and they were not capable—not indeed aware—of philosophic honesty, but they were good and angry with Cousin Lucius and they went to Cousin Caroline and told her that she should curb him. That lady was not dismayed. The thought of being angry with Cousin Lucius did not once occur to her, but for the briefest moment she realized that she was having to check herself not to be outraged against the little ladies who had constituted themselves his guardians. "Oh," she said, "you know Lucius! What can *I* do with Lucius? My dear, where *did* you find that lovely dress. You always show such exquisite taste. I am so happy to have you here. No friends, you know, like old ones. I am *so* happy."

The next winter Cousin Lucius and Cousin Caroline both had influenza, and Cousin Lucius's sister, who came to look after them, had it, too. They all recovered, but Cousin Lucius *would* violate directions and go back to work at the bank before he was supposed to go. And as spring came on it was evident that something ailed him, very gravely. It was his heart, but he refused to recognize the debility that was patent to everybody else, and went on.

And when summer came, and the jaded people began again to market the peaches they felt sure—and rightly—would be profitless, he, with the rest, set his operations in motion. One of his sons, Edward, was at home on a visit, and early one morning the father and son went out to the farm, with the intention of coming back home for breakfast. Only the negro

foreman, Anthony, was at the packing-house, where they stopped, and
Edward strolled down into the orchard, leaving Cousin Lucius to talk
over the day's plans with Anthony. A little way down one of the rows
between the peach trees, Edward almost stumbled upon some quail. And
the quail fluttered up and flew straight toward the packing-house.

He heard his father shout at them as they went by, the fine lusty shout
that he remembered as designed especially for sunsets and clean dogwood
blossoms. And then there was perfect silence. And then he heard the
frantic voice of Anthony: "Oh, Mas' Edward! Help, help, Mas' Edward!
Mas' Lucius! Mas' Lucius! O Lord! help, Mas' Edward!" Stark fright
slugged him. He was sick and he could scarcely walk, but he ran, and
after unmeasured time, it seemed to him, he rounded the corner of the
packing-house and saw Anthony, a sort of maniac between grief and terror, half weeping, half shouting, stooping, holding in his arms Cousin
Lucius's limp body. "Oh, Mas' Edward! Mas' Edward! Fo' God, I believe Mas' Lucius done dead!"

He *was* dead. And all who wish to think that he lived insignificantly
and that the sum of what he was is negligible are welcome to think so.
And may God have mercy on their souls.

# John E. Talmadge

## From "Growing Up in Georgia and Tennessee"

*When John E. Talmadge and William Wallace Davidson retired from the Department of English at the University of Georgia, they had the happy idea of swapping reminiscences by letter, the one from Suches in the North Georgia mountains, the other from Georgetown on the South Carolina seaboard.*

January 17, 1972

Dear Bill:

Exchanging reminiscences through a series of letters is a splendid idea. I'll enjoy hearing about the younger William Wallace Davidson and the influences that made him into the man I know. I'm even willing to lead off, but never mind that blarney about "Since you are older and, I think wiser, I must ask you to start." I'm one year older than you; hardly a sizeable gap when we're both past seventy, and as for being wiser—you forget I've played poker with you and am on to your innocent ways.

I'd like to start off by saying, "And this is the way it was," but I can't. The ability—in fact, the desire—to separate fact from fiction has never been a trait of my family. There was an old aunt who could make an adventure story out of a trip to the post office. Another family failing (often pointed out by my wife) is a tendency to tell a story over and over again. So how can I tell whether I saw something sixty years ago or heard about it later? Well, I'll promise this, Davidson: what I tell you either happened, or could have happened, or *should* have happened. O.K.?

279

I was born in October, 1899, in Athens, Georgia, at the home of my grandfather, John E. Talmadge, Sr., whose name I bear. Right here I might as well tell you about Grandpa. The small world I was born into was *his* world; the rest of us merely lived in it under rules he had set up. His program was a simple one. The four sons would, of course, go to work in Grandpa's wholesale grocery. When they married they would bring their wives back to his large house to stay there until after the first child was born or the couple knew there would be no children. If a daughter-in-law did not belong to the Presbyterian Church, she was expected to rectify that mistake as soon as possible. He was generous to his children and grandchildren, but he expected and got obedience from all. Grandpa was an extreme example of those Confederate Veterans who came out of the war penniless, built up prosperous businesses by their own efforts, and came to conduct their families as they did their stores and offices. Other older Athens families were run pretty much along the same lines, as I later learned.

Although we lived at Grandpa's until I entered school, I don't remember seeing much of him in those days. I have a vague mental picture of him and Papa driving up in a buggy with Grandpa sort of sprawled back on the seat and dangling one leg over the dashboard. (He was several inches over six feet.) My older sister claims she used to climb into his lap and stroke his long white moustache. (He had never used a razor on his upper lip, and his moustache was soft and silky, according to my sister.) Unlike my bold, impudent sister I stayed out of Grandpa's way, for, even then, I must have begun to share the family's awesome respect for him. In an early dream of mine it seemed that God, on the top of a high hill, was telling me to proceed to Hell. Suddenly Grandpa appeared and said to God, "Oh let him in. He isn't too bad a boy and I'll see that he behaves." All the while he was nudging me back up the hill. (Confidence can hardly rise any higher than this.)

Females dominate my hazy recollections of those early years: my tiny grandmother, who used to discharge Negro cooks so that she could get back to cooking; her old maid sister, who today would be put in a nursing home; my mother, who lived comfortably with a horde of Talmadges without ever becoming one of them; my two sisters, the older mischievous and imaginative, the younger gentle and placid; and my young Negro nurse, whom I thought almost as beautiful as my mother. I was aware of strange females in the house at various times, but evidently none impressed me enough to remember their names. One, however, a fanatically religious cousin of Grandpa's, indirectly made trouble for me. Hoping to make a better girl of my older sister the cousin warned her of the terrors of Hell. All she accomplished was to furnish my sister with information for frightening me.

There was a rural atmosphere in Grandpa's household. He farmed a hundred acres back of the house, kept a herd of cows and killed a number of hogs every fall. (Once a friendly Negro blew up a hog's bladder for me to play with. I doubt that I ever enjoyed a toy balloon half so much.) I remember Grandpa weighing the cottonpickers' sacks early one morning and how the pickers had to empty their sacks on the ground after they were weighed. Later I learned that he was on to the trick of putting stones in their sacks to up their pay.

Meat, milk and vegetables from a large garden reached the table via the kitchen and pantry where Grandma presided. There was great activity in that area of the house: cooking, churning and preserving. I remember being told more than once that I must not play there. Periodically a dray would arrive from the Store with sacks and boxes to be opened and their contents stored, under Grandma's watchful eye, in the huge pantry bins. With such plenty it was no wonder that most male Talmadges ate too much and developed stomach ailments. It was also not the best upbringing for those of us who years later had to pull in their belts during the Great Depression.

With the house a junction between the Store and the farm we were living in the early transition of the Agrarian into the Industrial South.

I remember nothing about a trip with my parents to Chattanooga at some time during those first six years, but one incident there was told me by Mother. I don't know how old I was, but in the opinion of Uncle Sam, one of Mother's brothers, and my father I was certainly old enough not to be sporting long golden curls. The story goes that after a couple of drinks the two men decided to take the matter in their own hands— or rather to put them into the hands of a local barber. With my sizeable head well-cropped I was presented to my mother with the assurance that "now he looks like a boy." Mother always complained that they might at least have saved one curl as a keepsake. I imagine that most fathers of that period took a dim view of Little Lord Fauntleroys.

I might forget a train trip of those days, but I pleasantly recall rides on Athens streetcars. Mothers found them useful in getting small children from under their feet on long summer afternoons. My nurse and I would board a car in front of our house on upper Prince Avenue and ride leisurely around the loop of the business section to a stop in front of the Hawaiian Ice Cream Parlor on College Avenue. There would be ample time before the next car arrived to enjoy an ice cream in the big Parlor cooled by barbershop fans. The return trip would be via the Boulevard where a steeper incline would cause the car to go at an exciting speed. All this pleasure could be had for the nurse's fare of ten cents and twenty more for our two plates of ice cream. My teen-aged nurse seemed to get as much pleasure out of the adventure as I did.

I suppose that even for a child tragic events appear dramatic and are therefore more clearly remembered. At any rate, I can still picture with some details three unhappy scenes from those days. The first was the death bed of Grandma's elderly sister, whose favorite I was among the children; she probably felt she had to protect me from the pranks of my sisters. One morning I was taken to her room and lifted on the bed for her to kiss. I still remember the wild, startled look on her face. Around her bed the men of the family stood silent and the women were crying. The second scene was a runaway horse and buggy, a common experience, I'm sure, at that time. I was walking with Papa and a cousin of his on Milledge when the horse and buggy with a screaming woman clutching a child came dashing up the street. Papa and his cousin rushed into the street waving their arms, but they had to jump aside when the horse failed to slow down. Then the husband, who had been thrown from the buggy, came running behind it shouting frantically. I never heard the outcome of the runaway. The most frightening of the three scenes came one afternoon when the family were sitting on Grandpa's side porch watching several carpenters working on Papa's new house, which was going up next door. Suddenly a man on the two-story roof lost his footing and fell. I can still see him turning over in the air. I saw one of my uncles vault over the porch banister, but at that point someone must have hurried me into the house because I can't remember any more. A few days later I went with my parents to see the man heavily bandaged but out of danger.

A convenient place to stop my memories of this first period was the night my sisters, several neighborhood children and I were seated on some lumber for the new house watching people move around in the lighted yard of the Hodgsons next door. The wedding reception of Miss Julie Hodgson was in full swing. In a few more days we would leave Grandpa's and move into the house of our own, and in the fall I would begin school.

Now it's your serve, Davidson.

Best regards,
John

\*   \*   \*

February 3, 1972

Dear Bill:

I went through several of the same childhood experiences you told about in your last letter. I wonder how many other Southern boys of those times were taught to read by elderly female relatives, thought more about hell than about heaven, and obligingly recited poetry before "company." Mother read us *Hiawatha*, but I probably was not erudite enough to memorize it. Later, however, I became a whiz on "The Charge of the Light Brigade" and was ready with "Horatius at the Bridge" if an encore was requested.

My mother would have felt at home in your letter. She spent her early childhood on a farm at Pinhook, Tennessee. Before the War, her father, John A. Erwin, had been a not very successful merchant at Cartersville, Georgia. While he was away with Joseph Johnston's army, the family moved very hurriedly to Athens, Georgia, to avoid entertaining William T. Sherman. They lived at Gilmer Hall on the State Normal School campus, and Grandma Erwin and the older children became friends with the nearby Talmadges. Thirty years later Charles Talmadge, my father, married Justine Erwin. In your reply to this letter you are supposed to say that some good came out of Sherman's infamous march.

I refuse to feel any gratitude to Sherman, but I have my mother to thank for getting me as far as high school. The Talmadges didn't set much store by education, and there would be a job at Grandpa's store for me whenever I gave up school. Mother was well-educated for a girl of her day—especially for a girl left an orphan in her teens. When their parents died, the Erwin children were scattered among various relatives. Mother fortunately fell to a spinster aunt, Fanny Beall, who taught Latin and Greek at Atlanta's Girls High, the best female preparatory school in the state. Aunt Fanny couldn't afford a college education for her niece, but she saw that Mother got the most out of Girls High and instilled in her a love of reading she never lost.

In September, 1905, Mother stood on our front porch and watched me trail my sisters up Prince Avenue to the State Normal Practice School. For the past year I had watched my sisters join one of the small groups of children headed in that same direction. These boys and girls came from families pretty much like ours and lived near us. My sisters had talked about their friends and I even got to know a few of them; so, I imagined all the students would be like those I had seen. I was startled to find the school yard filled with large, tough-looking boys and girls shouting, shoving and wrestling. The student body was largely made up of children from nearby farms and from the large cotton-mill district on the Upper Boulevard.

I was in for some rough experiences, which probably taught me more than the teachers did. In time I learned to stay away from centers of disturbances and, fortunately, my older sister changed from a tormentor to a protector and demonstrated she could hold her own in fights with either a boy or girl.

Gradually I became aware that the Principal, a tall, raw-boned country girl, could cope with the rowdiest of the students. Most outbreaks quieted down when she appeared, but I saw her, more than once, grapple with a hulking boy, pin his flailing arms and drag him to her office where it was rumored she kept a "whipping machine." (Later I learned from personal experience that she needed no mechanical aids.) Two older teachers helped maintain law and order. One, a large, imposing-looking woman, seemed to depend upon her bass voice; the other, with snapping black eyes, followed the Principal's tactics of coming to grips with the trouble-makers. It was said she once dragged a boy across the yard by his ear. The rest of the teachers, mostly young graduates from the Normal School across the drive, sometimes had to call for help from the three veterans.

I seem to recall those early classrooms as a world of desks, blackboards and chalk. A graduate of my great-aunt's "head-start" reading program, I had few difficulties with my studies until I encountered more advanced arithmetic in the sixth grade. Since the school was an offshoot of a teachers college, it probably offered more "frills" than the public schools of that day. The teachers read to us a great deal, made us attempt drawing and devoted a large part of the last period to singing. In about the third or fourth grade I became enamored of a pretty blonde girl who was sometimes allowed to carry the chorus of a song alone. In those early grades I think I enjoyed the classrooms more than I did the yards where we spent recesses, although the wooden seat got awfully hard and I looked forward to opening the wicker lunchbox and eating the fat biscuits filled with either ham or sausage—hardly a "balanced diet" but a tasty one.

My major academic problem seems to have been to keep from losing my "homework" assignments before I got home. Carrying it in the side pocket of my trousers didn't prove a safe place. When I got home, Mother would ask for my assignment. If I couldn't produce it, she would phone the teacher that evening and copy it down for me. Once Papa declared that she was pampering me and that the next time I lost an assignment I would go to the teacher's house and get it for myself. "Your teacher," he warned, "won't be as light on you as your mother." When I returned, he asked what the teacher had said. "She didn't get mad," I said. "She gave me a piece of chocolate cake." Papa explained to us what *his* teacher would have said in such a situation.

The only close friend I seem to have made was a peaceable country boy, tall and skinny like me and no better equipped for fistfighting. Some time during my fourth or fifth school year, I was forced into my first real fight. One of the "factory" boys took a dislike to me and used to walk down the other side of Prince Avenue shouting insults and threats at me. Then we took to "rock battles." Fortunately neither of us were accurate at that dangerous pastime. Then one day he must have taken to heart something I yelled at him, for he ran across the street and hit me. The next thing I knew we were trading licks. Suddenly I realized I was stronger. I began to hit harder and then threw him down and sat on him. He began to cry and say that his big brother would "fix" me. If I had read *Tom Sawyer*, I would have said I had an even bigger brother, but I pictured a huge edition of the enemy waiting for me after school the next day. I let him up and he went back across the street. As I went into our yard, a rock whizzed by my head, and I turned to see him running down a side street. The next day I anxiously questioned another factory boy and was told that the brother was a grown man who worked down town.

Still I had fought and won a fight and now felt I could take care of myself. Not long afterwards I met with a reverse. At recess the boys in my class would occasionally gather across the road and throw rocks at the older girls in the front yard. Up until that time I had remained a spectator, but now I moved into the front rank of the embattled males hurling stones and witty taunts at the ladies. I was stooping down for ammunition when something that felt like a brick banged against the top of my head. Bleeding and crying I was hurried into the building. As we passed through the frightened girls I heard them shouting out the name of the girl who "did it." I was far from being fatally injured, as I first thought, but the unlucky girl paid a long visit to the Principal's office and some of the boys brought me the assuring news that they could hear the switches going it inside. After school the girl had to come by home and tell my mother she was sorry.

But the time came when I heard the door of the Principal's office close on me and saw her reach for the switches on top of a cabinet. Our fifth grade teacher had decided to entertain us with some stereopticon slides and darkened the room for the treat. Immediately two boys just in front of me sneaked to the blackboard and began throwing chalk at the teacher. After a brief hesitation I resolved to join in the sport. I reached the board, and located some chalk. Then the lights went up and the only people standing were me and the teacher. The two real culprits managed to look as astonished as the rest of the class. Holding a handkerchief to one eye the teacher escorted me to the Principal and presented the damning evidence. I declared my innocence, but the Principal shook her head and reached for the switches. When she had finished, she said I must apologize to the teacher before the class. I refused. She ordered me to come back after school and to tell her I had apologized. When I told my classmates at recess that I had not apologized, I rose so high in their estimation that I felt I had to take the second whipping as much as I dreaded it. But I had not been prepared for a *third*. The Principal sent a note home which Mother reluctantly showed Papa. He decided that the evidence was too strong against me, but his assault on my rear was far briefer than the lecture he gave me on telling the truth.

Recently I read in a biography where an old gentleman told of being whipped at school "for telling the truth." A friend of his observed, "Well, at any rate, it broke you of *that* habit."

Looking back on those first five years of school, I can't believe they did much for my youthful mind, but they did teach me that the outside world was quite different from life in Grandpa's domain.

I look forward to getting your next installment.

Best wishes,
John

\* \* \*

February 19, 1972

Dear Bill:

Your second letter to hand yesterday and your third today. Both did entertain me mightily as Master Pepys would say.

In your second letter you remarked that in childhood you couldn't cope with the people around you, and, as a result, acquired the habit of listening and watching. That set me to thinking. I wonder if both you and I haven't remained essentially spectators throughout our lives. Now I don't mean we have sat on the sidelines when some lively possibility presented itself, but I believe we have acquired the habit of observing people, especially entertaining characters given to foibles and eccentricities. Maybe if we hadn't spent so much time watching and pondering, we might have got Ph.D.'s and ended up as department heads at Slippery Rock or Ohio Wesleyan. But there have been compensations. I see now that our unbroken friendship of twenty-five years has been, at least largely, the result of this basic trait we share. I understand more clearly why I always enjoyed wandering down to your office in Park Hall, putting my feet on the other side of the desk and telling what we called "lies" to each other. Undoubtedly we did pep up some of our stories, but I'm convinced they were truth to fiction, which means truth to human nature.

One more digression. Recently I read in the newspaper where a scientist prophesied that noise, and not pollution, would eventually crumple our civilization. There were, of course, noises in our boyhood—railroad trains, fire department wagons, circus calliopes, brass bands—but there were also periods of undisturbed quiet in which one could relax and stop thinking. In trying to relive my early days, I recall many such instances, but will describe only two as examples. One Saturday morning I was lying on the grass between our house and Grandpa's. Not a sound came from either house or the yard. Then a cotton mill on a nearby hill began to drone softly. I would probably have fallen asleep if I hadn't wanted the moment to go on. I remember also one fall night when the lights had been put out and all the family was in bed. Gradually I became conscious of the sound of a streetcar laboring up the Boulevard hill. I could trace its progress by the change in sound as it turned the curve and came down Prince Avenue, and I could feel the quietness coming on behind it. Just before I fell asleep a solitary horse clopped steadily up the street. When that noise had also faded, I was conscious of the soft wind in our old oak tree. During bouts of insomnia I sometimes think of that night.

When I was about ten, Saturday became a day to look forward to. If the weather was good and my father wasn't feeling "out of sorts," he would take me to the store for the morning. As we drove down Prince, he exchanged greetings with pedestrians and men in other buggies. Occasionally, however, we would pass someone he didn't know, and Papa would say, either to himself or me, "Must be someone from out of town. I never saw him before." Clayton Street was jammed with buggies, wagons and drays all apparently headed in different directions. On the sidewalks people were threading their way around piles of sacks and boxes before the various stores. "Country come to town," Papa would say. No one seemed in a hurry. Streetcars would wait while some driver backed his wagon across the tracks and up to the curb. The motorman might sound his bell once to announce he was waiting, but he never stuck his head out and swore at the driver as modern taxi drivers will do.

Our store was the building now occupied by S. H. Kress Co. From three large doors in the front, wide aisles ran back to three doors on Washington Street. A busy traffic of hand-trucks pushed by Negroes brought sacks and boxes to the front for delivery or incoming shipments from the back to be stacked in designated areas. Papa and I immediately separated. He went on to the offices half way down the center aisle, and I stopped to talk with the Negroes. I found them always friendly and ready to delay work for a chat. It was from them, and not at church, that I learned those hymns you and I used to sing in the mountains. Tommy Jones would announce the hymn. He was a small, agile Negro whose job was to pitch down sacks and boxes to the truckman below. Perched almost up in the rafters, Tommy would give out the first line, "Brightly beams Our Father's mercy," then from all over that section of the store a full-bodied chorus would come up, "From His lighthouse evermore." I can hear it right now, especially the deep bass of "Big 'Un" Sims who stood an inch or two under seven feet.

Going further down the aisle I would find Grandpa and two other old men seated around a big potbellied stove. Mr. Elder and Mr. Mygatt had served in the same Civil War regiment with Grandpa. They were the first two men he hired when he started the store forty years earlier. Now they did little except to sit and chew tobacco with Grandpa. They were privileged characters; the only employees not afraid to quarrel with him. Papa said he once heard them in a heated argument as to who had spit tobacco juice on one of the store cats.

Grandpa seemed as idle as the other two, but he had an eye or an ear on all that went on. At noon on Saturday my youngest uncle would open a window in his office, and the Negroes would line up for their weekly pay. Each man who came to the window posed a financial problem for Uncle Julius' consideration. "Now look-a-here, Buster," he would say.

"You're twelve dollars behind and you've got the nerve to ask for a full week's pay." Buster always had an answer. "That's right, Mister Julius, but Monday my wife got down. . . ." The debate was finally cut short by Grandpa's voice. He might call out, "Oh give him his money," or, "Five dollars is every dam' cent you gonner get this week, Buster." But whatever the decision announced, Uncle Julius would no more have contested it than Buster would.

It was a paternal administration. Grandpa put the fear of God in both Whites and Blacks, but he paid their medical bills, got them out of jail and at Christmas gave each a bag of fruit and candy and a box of cigars. Also, anyone of them who came to his house to wish him Merry Christmas got a healthy drink of whiskey. The Negroes seldom failed to pay him the courtesy of a Christmas visit.

In those days the wholesale grocery was a necessary link in the chain of a cotton economy. The wholesaler extended credit, at interest, to the retailer, and the retailer, with a high markup, extended credit to the farmer, White or Black. In the fall, when cotton was sold, the money went back down the chain to the wholesaler. Talmadge Bros. & Co. was highly profitable until three staggering blows struck: Grandpa's death, the boll weevil, and the Great Depression. It struggled on as a small business until my brother and I sold it in 1938.

Grandpa had expected it to go on after him. In arranging its sale I had to read his will. Its final codicil expressed his hope that his sons would carry on the business and pass it on to their sons. At the bottom of the safety-deposit box containing his will I found a handful of tarnished buttons bearing the letters C.S.A. They told a tragic little story. When the Confederate soldiers returned home, the occupying Union troops allowed the losers to continue wearing their grey uniforms—many had no other clothes—but the buttons were stripped from their coats. Evidently Grandpa had picked his up and saved them.

Those far-off Saturday mornings were real holidays except when I learned my mother had arranged a visit for me to the dentist. A trip to the barber's wasn't bad. The barbers were Negroes then, and Dick Harris was a kindly fellow who insisted on "mistering" me at the age of ten. But the dentist office loomed as a torture chamber for years to come. That ordeal was partly offset by the coming of Athens' first movie house, conveniently located across the street. On Saturday morning at ten I would be in my seat impatient to learn how Pauline of "The Perils of Pauline" was rescued from her tied-down position on the railroad tracks before the train I had heard blowing in the distance last Saturday passed merrily over her. Papa used to tell an amusing story about the time he took a mountain farmer to his first movie. Suddenly the man sprang from his seat and shouted, "Look out! He's right behind the door."

Papa and I never left the store until almost two, so most people had finished their noonday meal. Several Jewish families lived along both sides of Hancock Avenue, and on every porch we would see a stout Jewish lady in a rocking chair. They would wave at Papa and he would bow and call back, "Good afternoon, Mrs. Levy, good afternoon Mrs. Stern, good afternoon Mrs. Meyers." Then he would say to himself or to me or the horse, "All filled with good goose."

Those were happy Saturdays.

Best wishes,<br>John

\*   \*   \*

February 26, 1972

Dear Bill:

I expect I read more trash in my younger days than you did: *Alger Boys, Tom Swift, Rover Boys*, etc. About the best I did was the G. H. Henty stories, and I recall you said your father thought poorly of them. With encouragement from Mother I got through some Scott and Dickens and a book of Greek myths. But my two favorites were *Two Little Savages* and *The Bears of the Blue River*. They, at least, sent me to the woods to build a tree house and even to dig a cave. Then I got started on a Civil War history of Grandpa's. An aunt sent me a book on the War which seemed to favor the Yankees at every turn. I showed it to Grandpa one evening while he was reading in front of an open fire. He read a few lines, threw the book into the fire and went back to his newspaper.

Two ordeals at that time were the Y.M.C.A. and Sunday School. At the "Y" there was always some boy who threw a softball at your head, ducked you in the pool or flipped a towel at your naked buttocks. Before and after Sunday School well-dressed, loud-mouthed boys from Milledge Avenue treated the few of us from upper Prince as if we had come to a place that belonged to them. On the whole I preferred the roughnecks at the "Y" who came to tolerate me when they found I had some skill at basketball. Church proved worse than Sunday School, in a different way. I thought the preacher would never stop talking, and the hymns sounded flat after hearing them sung by the store Negroes. I built a lively dislike for two dowagers in the front row of the choir who would nod their heads and advise the congregation to "Ask the Savior to help you."

The automobile surely stepped up the tempo of Athens, especially when Miss Bertie Marks came roaring up the street paying little attention to the horses and mules dancing around on their hind feet. Papa loathed automobiles from the first; he was the last of Grandpa's sons to buy one. One Sunday a car drove into our yard with Ned Cohen, a raffish cousin of Papa's generation whom we children affectionately called "Uncle Ned." After considerable persuasion Papa climbed into the rumble seat, and in spite of his protests my friend Asbury Hodgson and I crowded in on either side of him. Out on the Jefferson Road the driver picked up speed. Papa first pled, then cursed and finally promised to knock the driver's and Uncle Ned's heads together if he should reach home alive. But once on the ground he headed for the front door. My pert older sister asked him when we were going to have a car. Papa gave her a dazed, puzzled look.

Circuses always filled the streets with people. Schools were let out, farmers came to town, and Negroes left off work. I enjoyed going with father before daylight to watch the elephants and camels unloaded from the train, and I usually went with Asbury Hodgson or other boys to see the parade go down and up Prince, although we always called it a cheat to keep so many of the cages closed. Eventually, however, I gave up going to the afternoon performance. I didn't like the crowds, noise and smells. But not so Charles, my younger brother, and our wild-eyed Negro maid. They would wait impatiently for Papa's warning that they must not get close to the animals. He had once heard that a rhinoceros had swallowed a Negro baby. Then off they would go to eat fried fish at a food stand and return with a small whip Charles always bought and Papa would find more serviceable than peachtree switches.

Like other Athens families we went on vacations. All I can recollect about a train excursion to Tallulah Falls, then unspoiled by the Georgia Power Company, was that I got a bit frightened at the huge, roaring fall of water and decided to take Uncle Ned's hand instead of Mother's when we started up the path to the top. One summer we went with Uncle Coke's family to a Charleston beach. I remember how strange the world seemed when I waked up in the cool, damp air and heard the ocean pounding away. An older boy got stung by a stingeree, the military band from Fort Moultrie played after supper, and some friendly boys taught me to "cuss"—an accomplishment Papa soon put an end to.

One summer Papa rented a cottage near Cornelia, Georgia, and we went up by train: parents, four children, trunks and bags. I don't think it turned out a happy outing; I'm sure it wasn't for Mother especially after Papa decided he'd better get back to the store. I suppose my sisters got bored; anyway, they began to plague me. One day at the dinner table of the hotel where we ate our noonday meal, they told me the soup plates had animal pictures on their bottoms. I hoisted mine up and spilled soup over the clean table cloth. Mother went back to the cottage, and when the two girls left the hotel I began to "rock" them. The hotel clerk ran out to stop me, but I ran him back inside with some near-hits. For the rest of our stay I was rather unpopular with everyone, but my sisters let me alone.

On our return trip home, with Papa again in charge, we missed the train connection at Lula and were in for a five hour wait. Papa rented a furnished room over a store, and we all stripped to our underclothes and lay down on the two beds. I can remember how hot it was and how someone was always asking Papa how long before our train came.

The most exciting trip I made back then—perhaps the most exciting I ever made—was in 1910 when Papa took me to a Georgia-Georgia Tech football game in Atlanta. On a dark, cold morning Papa, Uncle Ned, Uncle Coke and I, along with what seemed a lot of other people, got on the train, which was running late. The train pounded along in the fog with the engineer blowing the whistle every few minutes, as if urging it to go faster. Across the aisle a man said, "That damn fool is gonner run this thing off the tracks." I looked anxiously at Papa, who shook his head and then went to sleep. Safe in Atlanta we walked towards the middle of town. I felt that all the people on the streets were Tech supporters and, therefore, enemies. An Atlanta food manufacturer took Papa and several others to lunch at the Transportation Club. A couple of boys and I were left on a sofa in a fancy room and immediately brought tall glasses of lemonade by dressed-up Negro waiters. When the men came back, they seemed in mighty good humor, laughing loudly at everything said.

We rode to Piedmont Park on a street car crowded with people I took to be Tech supporters. I wished Uncle Ned would stop predicting loudly a certain Georgia victory. One moment in the game comes back clearly: the line of Georgia players beginning to move into the kickoff. It was a close game. I kept expecting Tech to score, but they never did, and finally Bob McWhorter, Georgia's freshman star, went in for the game's only touchdown. That night at the Atlanta Terminal McWhorter presented the game ball to Captain Kid Woodruff. A perfect ending to a perfect day. I slept on the way back to Athens.

Greater events in the outside world either didn't echo very loudly in Athens, or if they did, I didn't listen. But, as I recall, when my parents and friends rocked and talked on the front porch after supper, they talked about Athens happenings and Athens people. At times, however, world, national or state events would stir local comment which children would sometimes parrot to each other. When Admiral Perry and Captain Cook were arguing as to which had discovered the North Pole, we used to sing a song at school which began with the line, "Captain Cook's in town, turn the damper down." The Jim Jefferies–Jack Johnson heavyweight fight aroused no arguments on the playground; only universal agreement that Jefferies would easily whip the Negro. School was out of session when the fight proved us wrong, but I imagine the boys, like the men in our family, had little to say the following day. The Hoke Smith–Joe Brown gubernatorial race divided the boys at my school into two fighting factions: the factory boys were for Brown; the Prince Avenue boys for Smith. One day my husky friend, Asbury Hodgson, hit a factory boy during a political argument. The boy pulled out a knife, but Asbury stood his ground, and the boy walked away muttering.

The Jefferies-Johnson fight reminds me that I don't recall hearing of any racial trouble in Athens at that time. There were probably isolated incidents, but nothing serious enough to reach the front-porch gossips or the school boys. I do remember Papa saying one night that the Negroes in Atlanta "are getting out of hand," and that Governor Smith, his hero, had been seen buying buckshot shells at a hardware store.

In 1909 (I think) President Taft made a visit to our town and, although a Republican, got a hearty welcome. As the parade passed our house Taft rose to bow to the crowd. Charles, age four or five, was held up by his crony, the eccentric Negro maid, to get a good look. He burst into tears and began to shout, "That ain't Taft. That ain't Taft." Back in the house he explained he had seen a picture of Taft and that "his stummick came way down over his knees and his legs wasn't any longer than mine." He had seen a cartoon in our local paper.

I didn't intend to write so much, but the more I wrote the more I remembered.

Best regards,
John

＊　＊　＊

March 6, 1972

Dear Davidson:

Like you, I find myself thinking more kindly about the up-and-coming younger generation; at least, I've stopped condemning all of them. Recently I began to realize that the only people on the campus who smiled and wished me "good day" were some of the most disreputable-looking boys and girls. The rest of the students and all the professors appeared to be on their way to an appointment with destiny. I am so glad there are still a few young people who aren't wasting their youth on deadly-serious matters.

But on with my story. In this letter I want to tell you about a period, from my eleventh to my fourteenth year, when an abiding interest helped to shape the person I became.

By 1911 the city was becoming more evident in our neighborhood, but the atmosphere in Grandpa's principality remained essentially rural. My father and his two younger brothers were great hunters. The walls of our carriage house sported a row of dried skins from coons my father had shot with his pistol. The three brothers had a pack of hounds which were kept in a pen back of Uncle Coke's. On Sunday afternoons he used to "exercise" the dogs with a walk over the farm. If the dogs insisted on chasing rabbits, he would explain later that it was hardly his fault. Grandpa saw through that dodge and sternly forbade any more Sunday hunting. One Sunday afternoon Uncle Coke offered me a quarter if I would slip down to the pen and leave its gate open. He would blame the Negro boy who fed them every morning. For a quarter I would even risk the wrath of Grandpa. So the dogs went on an unchaperoned "walk" and soon the expected volley of baying broke out on the south end of the farm. Next a big buck rabbit burst into Cobb Street and headed across the Hodgson's front lawn and on to the first of the Talmadge lawns hotly pursued by the hounds and various curs that had joined in the fun. People rose to their feet on front porches, and old Mr. Hodgson shouted un-needed encouragement to the dogs. Grandpa ran out into his yard. Then I heard his bass beller out, "Git him boys, Git him."

I don't know what conferences took place down at the store the fol-lowing day, and I didn't ask. Maybe Grandpa said nothing, and Uncle Coke was afraid to push his luck. Anyway there were no more offers for my services in getting another Sunday hunt started.

On some Saturdays and most holidays during the fall and winter there were larger rabbit hunts further afield. Papa refused to take me on the possum and coon hunts, which came at night, and I don't believe he really wanted me on the rabbit hunts, at least not when I was nine or ten, but he could hardly refuse me. My small mongrel fox terrier was too handy in routing rabbits out of briar patches which the lopeared hounds hesitated to enter. I was as proud of "Tee" as I was of my older son years later when he won a Merit Scholarship.

The hunts were held either at Mr. George Thurmond's on the Jefferson Road or at Mr. Will Lester's on the Mitchell Bridge Road, two big-scale farmers. Papa, Tee, and I would leave home about daylight. Tee would curl up in my lap to keep warm, and I would still be shivering when we arrived. Looking back now on those hunts I can see a resemblance to those in the Anglo-Irish novels of Somerville and Ross, except that we were after rabbits not foxes, and we walked instead of riding horses. The farm yard would be filled with men, Whites and Negroes, and dogs occasionally breaking into brief fights, and a few boys eyeing each other shyly. Off we would go over heavy fields, in and out of bare woods. When the first dog sounded off I could hardly make myself stay at Papa's heels where I had been warned to stay. Then the whole field would come alive with the howls of the dogs and the shouts of the men. I could hear Tee's shrill yapping in the deeper roar of the hounds, and I would feel it was *my* hunt that was being run.

Around noon we ate lunch. Usually each man brought his own food, but occasionally the host, either Mr. Lester or Mr. Thurmond, would lead us to a place where two or three Negroes were unpacking huge baskets from a wagon. There would be sausage, ham, chicken, corn bread, and pies, "enough to feed Coxey's Army," as some guest would be sure to say. Then the men would lie around and smoke and praise various dogs. We would drive home at sundown under a cold, clear sky with a reddish streak in the west. You must excuse me, Davidson, if I grow poetic. Those were days to stir an old man's memory.

Perhaps I should let another type of hunt from those days remain untold. To describe it in these days of acute social consciousness would horrify many people you and I know intimately. But the only condemnation it brought sixty years ago among either the Negroes or Whites in Athens was from a few people who thought it should not have been enjoyed on Sunday. Back then during the summers Sunday afternoons sat heavily upon such active sportsmen as Papa and his hunting friends. One of them came up with a plan. They drove out to the local convict camp and asked the superintendent if one of his "trusties" would be willing, for a five dollar bill, to play hide-and-seek with the camp bloodhounds. According to Papa, all of the trusties volunteered to be the rabbit. The one selected led the dogs on quite a chase until he got tired and was found resting in a safe tree. I don't believe Mother thought highly of the sport, but Papa assured her that the quarry enjoyed the chase as much as the dogs and hunters did, and that he collected far more than five dollars when he was "caught."

I never watched one of those hunts. During those summers I was enjoying myself elsewhere. Papa and his sporting friends had decided to build a lodge out on the Oconee River near Mitchell Bridge. From June to the middle of September the permanent residents there were Uncle Julius, whose wife and son spent the summers in Chattanooga with her parents, and two bachelors, Mr. George Williamson and Mr. Earnest Jester. Married members would drive out for dinner when they could get away and stay for longer spells while their families were away on vacations. My parents were worrying because I seemed to get skinnier every year that went by, so Papa arranged for me to spend the summers there with George Stockley, the lodge's excellent Negro cook.

For four summers I literally "ran wild." There was the river to swim and fish in and an unending woods where Tee and I rambled for hours on end. On nearby farms there were Negro boys always ready to slip off from work or to get their chores done early so they could join me on the river. To hasten their freedom I would help them chop cotton, pull fodder and, in the early fall, pick cotton. On a wide sandbar in the river we would shed our clothes and swim or wrestle with each other. Frank Boyle, one of the boys, taught me some "holts" that came in handy in the few fights I had when I went back, unwillingly, to school in the fall. George Stockley slept on the side porch, so Mr. Williamson let me put my cot out there. I remember waking one night and seeing the stars through the tall pine trees around the lodge. That night came back to me years later when a New Yorker friend was visiting in our summer home in the mountains and said it had been so quiet he couldn't sleep. There was no electricity or plumbing in the lodge. (Forty years later when we bought the mountain house at Bucksnort I felt at home in the outhouse.) The men at the lodge stopped by their Athens' houses for baths on the way out in the evening. George Stockley, when he thought about it, would give me a cake of soap to take to the river, but I would usually lose it once I got in the water. When I reached home on Saturdays, Mother would start running water in the tub as soon as she heard my voice.

Strangely enough, I did some reading at the lodge—and not such bad stuff, either. Mr. Williamson and Uncle Julius brought out magazines— *Cosmopolitan, Saturday Evening Post* and the *American,* but hardly ever opened them. On hot afternoons when the Negro boys didn't show up, I would leaf through some copies and occasionally find something interesting. I read several Jack London stories, George Randolph Chester's

"Get-Rich-Quick Wallingford," and even John Galsworthy's "Man of Property."

During those summers, however, I acquired more knowledge of worldly than of literary matters. The older Negro boys kept me up to date on sexual affairs in the neighborhood. At times George Stockley evidently got bored with solitude (he considered himself superior to the Negro farmers), for he would tell me about the goings on at the hotel where he cooked in the winters. Occasionally Uncle Julius and the two bachelors would assume that I had gone to sleep around the corner of the porch and would talk rather freely about current rumors in the city. Once, by accident, I had a front row seat at a bit of active love-making. Uncle Julius and I were hidden in some bushes along the river road waiting for rabbits to come out and play when a buggy with a young couple drove up and stopped just in front of us. Immediately the boy seized the girl and began trying to kiss her. She put up a stout resistance, and after a brief struggle he picked up the reins and drove furiously back the way they had come. Uncle Julius told me on our way back to the lodge that the couple was from prominent Athens families and that we must never tell what we had seen. But that night from my cot I could hear him giving the two bachelors a blow-by-blow description.

During a summer two or three small barbecues were cooked in front of the lodge, and in late August Grandpa gave a grand one for the employees at the store. George Stockley had to step aside for a famous barbecue cook: Clayton Harris, a tall, red-skinned Negro (he was part Cherokee Indian), who was also a prominent figure in all the big rabbit hunts. The morning before the 'cue a store wagon would deliver the carcasses of two lambs, a large pig and various other items, and around noon Clayton would drive up with his own equipment and a couple of his grandsons. George Stockley would have collected a pile of wood, but after a careful examination Clayton would discard most of it and go into the woods for more suitable logs and sticks. The cooking was a slow affair. The carcasses were spitted and placed over a thin bed of coals which Clayton would replenish again and again from a nearby fire. When the sun went down, the fire would throw an eerie light over the clearing. About ten o'clock at a summons from Mr. Williamson, I would go reluctantly to bed. By morning the meat had taken on a faint brown color. The two Negro boys would be asleep on the ground, but Clayton would still be basting the meat and studying it with a critical eye.

Then the cars, buggies, and two wagon loads of Negroes would begin to arrive. The Whites grew more and more jovial after making short trips up into the woods—but not too often, for Grandpa believed that he was the only person who could drink sensibly. Finally, the food reached the long wooden tables. It was a man's meal: meat, bread, and coffee, with some token plates of pickles and sliced tomatoes. When the Whites had stuffed themselves, the Negroes replaced them at the table. Then a quartet, in which Papa sang tenor and Mr. Williamson bass, would render hymns and popular songs. The Spanish-American War was not too far in the past, and among the quartet's numbers were "My Father was a Sailor on the Maine," and another song which told how the sons of Yankees and Confederates had fought together to free Cuba. It was strangely quiet when all the guests had gone.

At the end of my second year in high school, city interests had taken hold, and I gave up going to the lodge. But those summers left an indelible imprint on my memory which, in old age, has been revived in the solitude of our mountain house.

Best regards,<br>John

P.S. You and I have remembered early incidents when we were punished for something we didn't do. Only this morning I read the following sentence in a Kipling story. "The Headmaster always told us that there was not much justice in the world, and that we had better accustom ourselves to the lack of it early." Maybe those miscarriages of justice were a valuable lesson for us to learn.

March 13, 1972

Dear Bill:

In this letter I'll try to cover several years of my schooling. My sixth grade report card brought on a family conference—I had failed arithmetic. My parents decided to move me to a public school, not because they blamed the teacher or the Practice School for my grade. My inability to cope with figures had been evident for some time. But most neighborhood boys had changed to public schools and the girls to Lucy Cobb Institute. My parents decided upon Meigs Street School; there was freedom of choice in those days. Unfortunately busing was not imposed then, so I had a mile walk to my new school.

Meigs Street would probably be considered a slum school today. Classes were held in a sprawling, one-story wooden building. There was no gymnasium or assembly hall. On rainy days the students were given a few breaks to stretch and talk, and the school day was cut shorter. No cafeteria served food, and the students did not bring their own lunches, at least not the seventh graders; when I reached home about two-thirty I was really hungry. The classrooms were heated by stoves. The top of ours blew off one day (a prankish boy would not deny or admit he had inserted a firecracker through the stove door), and we rushed out the door yelling in pretended terror. On the whole, however, the class behaved pretty well. There were several merry-andrews among the boys, but our plump young teacher enjoyed their levity if it didn't go too far.

Two triumphs and one defeat from that year come to mind. I proved to be an unspectacular center on the school's football team, but my day came. In a close game our quarterback decided to pass for a badly-needed touchdown. Looking for a receiver, he saw that our best players were well covered, but I was standing idle over the goal line. Yelling my name he threw, and I managed to hold on to the ball. I prized far more the cheers of my teammates than I did the praise of my teacher when I won second prize, an unreadable book, in the yearly essay contest of the Daughters of the Confederacy. I was a bit disgruntled at not winning the first prize of five dollars. I still didn't have any luck at fighting. One day a sixth grade boy about my size dared me to meet him for a fight up a side street. I was confident I could handle him, so I appeared, threw him down and was bumping his head against the ground when a rock whizzed by mine. He had planted a burly friend of his in the bushes in case of need. I retreated in a shower of rocks.

The following September I walked a half mile further to the high school on Childs Street. There I came under the best teachers I have ever had, not excepting the Harvard Graduate School. Miss Elizabeth Colwell in English read poetry aloud with such obvious enjoyment that, in turn, the students recited with enthusiasm their assigned passages. In history Miss Mary Turnbull, an imposing elderly lady, instilled respect—in, at least, a few of us—for such long-lived institutions as the British Empire and the Christian Church. Mr. Marvin Perry, fresh out of the University and later president of D. C. Heath book publishers, took us carefully, step by step, through German grammar and vocabulary and on into simple stories. But Miss Pattie Hilsman was that rare teacher who can get a maximum of work from dunces and bright students in the same class. It was a bold boy or girl who turned up with an unprepared lesson. Miss Pattie, a tall, red-haired spinster, had only to fix her eye upon the delinquent to make him shudder. She made us see that Latin was a clean, orderly language which we could learn and were *going* to learn. It wasn't enough that our written assignments were correct in substance; they must also be neat and properly spaced. She was as hard as Good Queen Bess (and looked a bit like her), but her sparse praise would set you up for the rest of the day. A few years ago I visited her in the hospital in her last illness. I started to tell her what a wonderful teacher she had been. Miss Pattie nodded and changed the conversation. There was nothing of the sentimentalist in Miss Pattie.

There were, however, a couple of nice, "easy" teachers. Unfortunately they taught my weakest subjects—mathematics and science. The math teacher seemed as bored with geometry as I was; one day she let her lecture gradually fade away and began to ask us riddles. Final examinations could be exempted with an eighty-five average. I had to complain just once that my grade of eighty was my only mark below the exemption level. From then on she gave me an eighty-five. The science teacher was a pathetic oldish man incapable of keeping order. One day he asked the students if they thought life was worth living. After getting a barrage of ridiculous answers, he was asked what he thought. "Yes," he said, "if you have a good digestion." The cynicism in his answer was, of course, lost on his audience.

The high school was admirably administered by Principal Ted Mell, a gentle but firm widower. The students respected rather than feared him.

Most of the teachers could smother misbehavior before it spread, but even the capable faculty would have faced graver problems without the calming influence of Mr. Mell on the student body. Once a couple of muscular brothers let it be known they were going to beat up Mr. Anderson, the science teacher my freshman year. The pair went up to him in the hall one day, and one brother announced their intentions. Mr. Anderson picked him up and slammed him against the wall. Mr. Mell appeared from nowhere. The combatants separated, and Mr. Mell began to talk in an undertone to Mr. Anderson, all the while edging him towards his classroom. Then he put an arm around the weeping boy, and the two disappeared into his office.

Athletics at the high school were largely left up to the students. The school arranged no schedule of games and provided no athletic field or, as far as I know, any paid coaches. In the major sports there were teams which occasionally played other schools at home or abroad, but aroused little interest in the students. (A band, cheerleaders, and parades might have brought out a larger attendance.) Organized social activities were not a part of the school's program. During my four years there I never heard of a school dance or party. However much or little a student got out of his classes, he could only have seen the school as a place where one learned or didn't learn.

Looking back upon the Athens High of my day, I believe it made available a sound, sensible program of education. True, the majority of its students did not go on to college, and many of those who did went only a year or two, long enough to join a fraternity and earn the right to say they had gone to college. But a college education at that time was considered more a luxury than a necessity. A few years earlier the state legislature had tried to pass a bill to appropriate money only for secondary education. Colleges, it was argued, should charge its "rich" students enough tuition to meet all expenses.

The popular idea seems to have been that college could do little or nothing to help a man earn a living. At least one member of my class proved the truth of that philosophy. He began a highly successful business career in high school. At recess when the ice-cream wagon drove up, he would cheerfully lend money to boys who raised pet rabbits and bantam chickens. Then when a debtor couldn't pay up, the young robber baron would kindly take a rabbit or rooster (usually the best) in lieu of payment. His father could afford to send him to college, but after a year he announced that he could not waste any more time on such nonsense; he had to start making money. He became the only millionaire that our class produced.

About the middle of my senior year in high school I underwent what a psychologist would probably call a "personality change." What brought it about I still can't say. Up until that time I had been leading a semi-solitary life. I had few close friends, seldom went to a party, and spent most of my spare time, even in winter, with my Negro friends out near the lodge. I can't remember just when the change took place, but I began to take pains with my appearance, notice girls, and feel hurt if I was not invited to a party. Studying had become a habit, so I finished my last year with reasonably good marks, but it no longer held my interest.

Perhaps the University's fraternity system had much to do with this change. That year the fraternities made a drive to collect local "pledges" before they entered college. I felt highly flattered when three solicited my membership. When I finally settled upon one, I began to spend too much time at its chapter house. I became attracted to the sporting element in the chapter and tried to imitate their dress and manners. But whatever the cause, I looked forward to college as a place where I was going to have a high old time. In a later letter you will learn that I did.

But before I go into my unacademic college career, I want to try in my next letter to describe Athens on the eve of World War I. After that mammoth tragedy my hometown appeared as drastically changed as I was after my last year in high school.

Best regards,

John

March 22, 1972

Dear Bill:

Athens was still a pleasant place when you moved there in the late 1930's. But I believe you would have enjoyed living there more in the years just before World War I. Of course it didn't have the conveniences, comforts, and activities of today, but it did have an atmosphere and a beauty which has gradually disappeared, and, even more important, it had an individuality now completely lost, as far as I can tell.

The large homes, either with white columns or the iron work of the coastal architecture, dominated Milledge and Prince Avenues. Most of them had stood for over a half century, and seeing them, still sturdy and placid, you could only think they would go on standing in the years ahead. If a visitor, however, saw only those two avenues, he would miss some of the loveliest sections of Athens. Up such side streets as Dearing, Pope, Henderson, and Harris were houses usually smaller but built with the same care and taste that had gone into the larger residences.

The businesses of Athens also seemed stable and permanent. The larger institutions—banks, mills, wholesale and department stores—were mostly owned and managed by the older families living in the homes along Milledge and Prince. Few of the sons went elsewhere for greater opportunities, but took over when their fathers stepped down. Smaller retail stores, such as drugs, food, shoes, and others, had been started and continued by local people. A few highly popular ones were run by foreigners: Vanstraten's Market sold the best meat and seafood in town; Costa's Fruit Stand had wonderful grapes and bananas; and Miss Rosa Vonder Leith's Toy shop was a joy to several generations of Athens children. Chain stores with their frozen foods and Japanese-made toys were far in the future.

It would be untrue to claim there was no gradation in Athens society, and most of the prominent families did have comfortable incomes. But the lines were understood rather than proclaimed, and money alone didn't guarantee acceptance in some circles. Nor was there a Junior League or a country club to further the pretentions of the ambitious. As nearly as I can recall, social activities were largely confined to neighborhood groups—with, of course, guests from other parts of the city. Occasionally there were large affairs such as the wedding reception of a daughter of a wealthy family. The largest was probably given at White Hall, several miles out of Athens, for the daughter of Judge John White. Carriages and autos stretched from the end of Milledge to the Whites' front gate, and champagne flowed freely. In later years Mother proudly told how Papa had to help take off her dress when they got back home.

A small, highly-respected Jewish community seemed to fit comfortably into the pattern of Athens life without giving up its racial identity. If someone had asked me what I thought about Jews—and no one ever did—I would probably have said they were, somehow, different from us, but lived the same way we did. My family had every reason to feel friendly towards them. When Grandpa died in 1922, Mr. Buddy Michael wrote a beautiful eulogy of him in the Athens paper, and a little later when Papa was recovering from a heart attack, Mr. Sol and Mr. Sidney Boley brought him a bottle of fine wine. I don't think I used the word *anti-Semitism* until I went to New York in 1928.

Back then the few Catholics in Athens had services in a small frame house where their church stands today. I imagine the congregation was largely made up of Costas, Palmisanos and Posteros, members of a single family of industrious Italians which came to Athens about 1910 to open a fruit store, an ice-cream parlor, and a billiard parlor called "The Q Room," which became almost a club for University students. The first Catholics to attract attention both in the city and University were the French Lustrats. Monsieur Joseph Lustrat became professor of Romance Languages, just when I can't remember. The Gallic frankness, which he and Madame never lost, brightened the social life of the University as when the professor congratulated the wife of a Presbyterian colleague on her obvious pregnancy.

In those days it would have been hard to tell where the University left off and the town began, or so it seemed to me. University professors came to stay—and did stay without benefit of tenure. The Greek and Latin professors were friends of my family and active officers in our Presbyterian church. Their colleagues were prominent in other denominations although one of the science professors was said to be an "infidel" and brazenly worked in his front yard on Sundays. His irreligion, however, seemed to be treated as an eccentricity and no reason for ostracism. Mother told me later that she and Papa always attended the President's reception. The campus buildings looked as native and permanent as the mansions on the avenues. The University was a part of Athens.

If the relations between Athens' Whites and Blacks caused any commotion in the quiet community, I didn't hear of it. The paternalistic attitude of the more privileged Whites was not shared, I'm sure, by Whites in the rougher sections of the city, but I had firsthand knowledge of only one case of callous discrimination against a Negro. One Monday Papa paid a fine for our yardman who admitted in court to disturbing the peace, but on the way home he told Papa that the policeman had made him pay a "fine" of five dollars when he was arrested. Papa stormed back to the City Hall where the burly policeman insisted the Negro had lied. Papa argued, I think logically, that the Negro was a timid fellow and would not have dared to bring a false charge against a White man, especially against a policeman well-known for his freedom with a billy. But the Recorder said it was only the Negro's word against the policeman's, so Papa got nowhere. I think the only time I felt hostile towards Negroes was when a friend and I saw a special showing of *The Birth of a Nation*, but that feeling was gone by the time I got home.

In those days Athens enjoyed a number of "characters" and the stories or legends about them. There was a hulking hot-tempered doctor who appeared frequently in court for knocking someone down. After one such case had gone against him, he floored a spruce little lawyer who had twitted him during the trial. The following day several men phoned the doctor that the lawyer was making out his will in preparation for a duel with him. At first the doctor laughed at the warning, but as the day wore on, he began to have second thoughts and finally wrote an apology which was graciously accepted. On Dearing Street lived a rich, elderly spinster who appeared only after dark in bedroom slippers, with a pistol peeping out of her bag, headed for the movie house. A sad-faced man would wait on Milledge Avenue every Saturday afternoon for the downtown car. When asked by an inquisitive lady why he made the weekly trip, he is said to have replied, "I've got to go to town and get drunk, and God how I hate it." Another citizen went on the same mission to town one afternoon and returned with his mission too well accomplished. Starting up the walk to his house he ran headlong into a solitary tree. He returned to the sidewalk for another try to be blocked again by the same tree. Seating himself on the curb he muttered mournfully, "Lost in an impenetrable forest."

Good whiskey was made available in Athens then by a model dispensary whose successful operation was copied by several other cities.

There is a humorous story, which I can't vouch for, about its closing and a more authentic one which reflects no credit upon my family. Sometime back in those days a rabid temperance movement reached a crest in a church meeting the night before a vote on the dispensary would be taken. An eloquent lawyer, deep in his cups, offered to bet some cronies that he could deliver a winning speech on either side of the question. He was given the temperance side, walked in the church, spoke and awoke the following morning to find he had won his bet.

The sadder story is that my grandfather's name appeared in a newspaper petition to close the dispensary. Not that he intended to forego his toddies. A few days before the closing two of the store's drays drove up to his house loaded with cases and barrels of good drink. He always believed that he was one of the few people who could "handle likker."

Two half-witted Negro beggars conducted active sales campaigns along the streets of Athens. Pope, a huge, fierce-looking Black, always demanded a quarter on the dubious plea that he had just got out of jail. Fiddler, a small engaging fellow, made the more modest demand of a nickel. The procedure was that you would first give him a penny and insist it was a nickel. Fiddler would roll his eyes to heaven and pretend to throw away the coin, knowing well that a larger one was forthcoming. Today Pope and Fiddler would be given the option of jail or welfare. Back then they could practice their profession unmolested.

Two scenes come back to me when I think of Athens and its countryside in those days. One is a dusty road on a quiet, hot Sunday in August with the creaky sound of an organ playing an old hymn in a nearby farmhouse. The other is a drive up Prince one night in spring. From one house behind some sweet-smelling shrubbery the victrola music of a sentimental song came through the quiet darkness.

You would have felt completely at home, Davidson, in the Athens of that time.

Best regards,
John

# Katharine Du Pre Lumpkin

## From *The Making of a Southerner*

### A Child Inherits a Lost Cause

#### I.

Men like my father spoke of the Lost Cause. It was little more than a manner of speaking. Even of the war they would say, "We were never conquered . . ." and of reconstruction, "I'm an unreconstructed rebel!" They would sing in gayer moods:

> *I've not been reconstructed,*
> *Nor tuck the oath of allegiance,*
> *I'm the same old red hot rebel,*
> *And that's good enough for me!*

Seriously, they would say: "We need not and will not lose those things that made the South glorious." If new features must be permitted the Southern edifice, so be it. At least the fundamentals should be kept intact. It became the preoccupation of their kind to preserve the old foundations at all costs.

In my father's case, as far back as 1874 he had launched upon his career in behalf of Confederate veterans. In that year there met in Union Point, Georgia, then his home, the first regimental reunion of Confederates—this was the claim—ever to be held in the South. This was a gathering of his own, the Third Georgia Regiment. Thenceforth, Father was ever at the beck and call of his comrades' interests.

These were the years when in towns and cities throughout Georgia, South Carolina, and all Southern states, men raised a slender shaft, topped by a tall soldier figure—the Confederate soldier. With solemn ceremony, a "rebel yell" from assembled veterans, a band playing *Dixie*, and oratory of a bygone day, these sacred monuments were unveiled. My father soon became a favorite orator on such occasions: he could be counted on to drop everything for them; also, he spoke such things as his audience wanted to hear, and in the way they wanted—feelingly, eloquently. I should hesitate to guess how many of these shafts in the small towns of South Carolina had the veil lifted from them by his devoted hand.

Besides this there were the Confederate reunions, Southwide, statewide, and even on a smaller scale. Father was an inveterate reunion-goer and planner. So were literally hundreds of his kind, men who were also of the Old South's disinherited, who had lost so much and regained so little, materially speaking. It may well be that these men were a mainspring of this "Lost Cause movement," kept it pulsing, held it to fever pitch while they could, firing it with its peculiar fervor. Where but in the past lay their real glory? Who more than they would have reason to keep lifted up the time of their greatness?

Theirs was certainly a tireless effort in behalf of the Lost Cause, and a labor of love if ever there was one. These men expected to get nothing from it save people's warm approbation, perhaps, and the personal satisfaction that comes with performance of a welcome duty; and of course—indeed above everything—their sense that by this means they were serving the paramount aim of preserving the South's old foundations. Father would say: "The heritage we bear is the noblest on earth; it is for us to say whether . . . we will make the home of the South what the home of the South once was—the center of a nation's life; it is for us to keep bright the deeds of the past, and we will do it." For him it was sufficient reward that people could say, as they did on one occasion of my older sister (nor did anyone mind the fulsome language still so dear to the heart of the South at the turn of the century): "Daughter of an eloquent father, reared in a home where the Confederacy is revered as a cause, holy and imperishable. . . ."

We had lived in South Carolina less than five years when I was dipped deep in the fiery experience of Southern patriotism. This was the Confederate reunion of 1903, held in our home town of Columbia.

It was but one in a long line of reunions. In South Carolina they had a way of placing the first in the year 1876—"the grandest reunion ever held in any State, one of the most sublime spectacles ever witnessed," "thrilling the hearts" of the people of Columbia. They called it the first, but "there were no invitations, no elaborate programme, no committees of reception, no assignment of quarters, no reduced rates of transportation, no bands of music, no streamers flying." Of it they said: "The State was prostrate. The people had with marvelous patience restrained themselves from tearing at the throat of the Radical party. Hampton had been elected governor, and yet the tyrannical party would not yield." (Wade Hampton and his "red shirts" had just overthrown reconstruction.) At that moment, the story goes—"It was the supreme moment of the crisis"— there appeared, coming into Columbia from every direction, by all the highways, "men in apparel which had become the most glorious badge of service since the history of the world—those faded jackets of gray." They came, it is said, ten thousand of them, converging on Columbia, making their way straight to the headquarters of the Democratic party. They were resolved, they said, "to make this State one vast cemetery of free men rather than the home of slaves." Their voices shouted hoarsely, "Hampton!" "Forth came the great captain who stilled the tumult with a wave of his hand." He said: "My countrymen, all is well. Go home and be of good cheer. I have been elected governor of South Carolina, and by the eternal God, I will be governor or there shall be none." Men said, "There will never be another such reunion."

It was not a reunion of course in the later sense. Since 'seventy-six the South had seen an exceedingly complex organization of Confederate sentiment. The United Confederate Veterans covered all the Southern states. Each state had its division of the parent organization, and each division its multitude of "camps" honeycombing the counties, each bearing the name of some hero, living or dead. Not only the veterans, but their wives and widows, sons and daughters, children and grandchildren, were organized. My father was an active veteran; my mother and older sister, "Daughters of the Confederacy"; my brothers, as each grew old enough, "Sons of Confederate Veterans"; we who were the youngest, "Children of the Confederacy." Thousands of families showed such a devotion. While yet the old men lived, on whom centered all the fanfare, it was a lusty movement and fervently zealous. I chanced to know it at the peak of its influence.

I remember nothing of the Lost Cause movement before the Confederate reunion of 1903. I may have been drinking it in since the time of my babyhood, but all before that is indistinct, cloudy. In 1903 I was verily baptized in its sentiments. Sooner or later in those three event-packed days we must surely have run the whole marvelous gamut of exuberant emotions. Not the least of the thrill was the Lumpkin part in it—the sense of our complete belonging to this community cavalcade which paraded before us in so many wonderful guises. I was too young myself to have any direct share in it; school children did, but I was just this side of being an old-enough school child. It meant no deprivation, however, for I felt part of it. So absorbed in its planning and execution was our family that we all felt a part, even I, the youngest. I was permitted to see it all, everything, excepting only the balls and receptions to which children did not go but of which they could hear the glowing accounts.

In the air we felt a sense of urgency, as though the chance might never come again to honor the old men. The oratory stressed it: "Ranks of the men who fought beneath the Stars and Bars—the beautiful Southern Cross—are thinner. . . ." "Pathos . . . there cannot be many more reunions for these oaks of the Confederacy. . . ." "Not far from taps . . . for many the ties that bind will soon be severed . . . the high tribute is but their honor due." Hardly a year before, Wade Hampton, Carolina's foremost citizen, had passed away. We must indeed hasten. "Gone is the peerless chieftain, the bravest of them all, the lordly Hampton, that darling *beau sabreur* of whom Father Ryan, the priest-poet of the dead republic, sang. To his stainless memory the reunion is dedicated . . . for him who sleeps under the great oak in Trinity churchyard." I do not remember seeing him ride at the head of the columns, although I may have. Vaguely I can recall the great funeral, the vast throng; and clearly the many times in ensuing years when our family would troop in reverent pilgrimage to his always flower-strewn grave after Sunday services at Trinity.

The grand reunion was held in the month of May. It was the ideal time for it. Earlier would not do, lest we have April showers; later would not have been good, after the summer's heat had set in, and a torrid, sultry spell might mow the old men down like grain under the sickle. If luck held, May was the perfect time, for refreshing breezes could almost certainly be counted on; trees and shrubs were at their deepest green, the great elms and oaks casting cool shade and not yet filtered over with dust as they would be a little later, when horse-drawn vehicles, rolling along broad unpaved avenues, stirred up the hot dry sediment, sifting it onto everything. And when would flowers ever be so bountiful or varied again as in May, letting us literally strew them on the path of the old men and smother our carriages and floats with them in the parade?

Bustle and business of preparation. What child would not love it, when everywhere was unbounded enthusiasm and her own family in the thick of everything? Twenty thousand veterans and visitors coming—almost more people than in the city itself. Committee meetings every day at the Chamber of Commerce. Indeed, the Chamber was in the heart of it. Its president was a Confederate veteran-businessman; its secretary, son of a veteran. Why would not its every facility be poured into this reunion? Good business, to be sure. But much more than this, it was good Southern patriotism. A true Southern businessman's heart was in it.

Besides businessmen, all the leading people, and some not so leading, were drawn into the effort. No, not drawn; they had poured, all anxious to have a part on this paramount occasion—institutions, organizations, whole families, including parents, young people, and children. Entertainment, housing, parades, decorations, meetings—these were men's tasks. Feeding the veterans, in particular manning two free lunch rooms down town, was the ladies'. Social events fell to the young people, the Sons of Veterans—Maxcy Gragg Camp—and the young ladies; they must plan for balls and receptions, and for the good times of over two hundred sponsors and maids-of-honor, "bevy of the State's most beautiful young ladies." Local bands must serve. Local militia—"wearing uniforms as near like the Confederate butternut as U. S. Arsenals afford"; students of

South Carolina College and the two "female" colleges; school children, two hundred of them, to strew flowers, sing in a chorus, execute intricate marches which took hours and days for training; the Cotillon Club, select dancing society; the town's "riding set" for the parade; the Metropolitan Club; the local lodge of Elks; merchants and manufacturers and other businessmen to give their time and money and elaborately decorate their establishments. Everyone must decorate. Stores had stocked their shelves. Everyone must go home loaded down with red and white bunting and Confederate flags.

The day dawned. Tuesday, May 13. A brilliant day. On Monday had come a heavy, prolonged shower, casting us into gloom. But we were quickly comforted. It but laid the dust and sent cool breezes blowing. The paper sang: "Under a sky that was an inverted bowl of sapphire . . . in an air that kissed and caressed them as pleasantly as any zephyr that ever swept across the Southland, the remnants of the thin gray line mustered into Columbia. . . ."

The moment was here. The pageant unfolded. All the way to Main Street, every home festooned in bunting and flags, and Main Street itself, from end to end, red and white bunting, incandescent lights of white and red. By night these lights, in a child's eyes, looked like one's dream of fairyland. Confederate flags. They were everywhere, by the thousands, of every size. People thronging Main Street carried flags. A few might also have South Carolina's banner—a palmetto tree and crescent against a field of blue—but all would have a Confederate flag. Dominating Main Street, at its head, was the State Capitol building, domed and dignified, granite steps mounting to its entrance. From window to window was draped bunting, and spread across its face, a huge Confederate banner. Across from it, both Opera House and City Hall were festooned and flag-draped.

Under the shadow of the State House dome on the Capitol grounds was a huge "bivouac tent"—a circus tent—ninety feet in diameter, they said. Six hundred veterans would be sheltered there, overflow from people's homes. Everyone talked of it; patrolled day and night by militia units; army cots provided from the Armory; only half a block from Convention Hall; information bureau but a stone's throw; General Hampton's grave a hundred yards away. Mr. Gantt, Secretary of State, not being satisfied, had the Negro convicts install a lavatory. General Frost, Adjutant General, pitched some smaller tents like a company street to bring back "old times." They called it Camp Wade Hampton. Hardly a yard, inside and outside the bivouac, but was hung in bunting. On its highest pole floated a grand banner—"of course the emblem of the Lost Cause."

All Tuesday veterans and visitors poured in. Every hour broad Main Street grew more crowded. Committees of men on duty at Union Station from daybreak until midnight. Father's stint was four hours in the afternoon, several men under him, all wearing their conspicuous badges (how proud I was): "Ask Me. Entertainment Committee." Helping the hundreds of old men; assigning them quarters; handing them badges: "Veteran," open sesame to everything, free of charge, nothing excluded, the city theirs. Band music all afternoon on the capitol grounds—martial airs—old Southern songs—and *Dixie!* Ever so often, *Dixie!*

How quaint it seems, but not so then—the veterans' free trolley ride. All over the city on the rumbling, bumping trolleys, for two hours, "to their hearts' content," no nickels called for, special trolleys provided. This to keep them occupied until affairs began.

Parades. Two of them. Best of all the "veterans' parade." The old men marching. Not too long a march; just from post office to State House, half a mile. They were getting so old, more should not be expected. How thronged were the sidewalks—thousands of people—and the windows of buildings—people leaning out to cheer and wave Confederate flags. Men doffing their hats so long as the old men were passing, women fluttering their handkerchiefs. School children ahead of them, spreading the streets with a carpet of flowers, lavishly, excitedly. There in a conspicuous carriage, the surviving signers of the Ordinance of Secession! Bands playing march tunes until it seemed one's spine could not stand any more tingles. But then—the Stars and Bars, dipping and floating and—*Dixie!* From end to end along the route, shouting and cheering, always wild shouting and cheering, at the Stars and Bars and *Dixie.* For me too there was the thrill of looking proudly for Father marching with "the Georgians." These were a special contingent, come from Augusta on their own train and given "the place of honor" in the parade, right behind General Carwile, the Commander. "The band of survivors—come from Augusta in their gray jeans . . . with their old muskets . . . to give an exhibition of Hardee's tactics." Everyone was chuckling over the special permission the Georgians asked, to bring the old firearms across the border, telling the Governor, "If fired the old muskets were more dangerous to the shooter than the men aimed at." Wonderful old muskets! Father, particular host to the Georgians—"Col. W. W. Lumpkin, always solicitous for the Georgians, will have charge of their headquarters, and will superintend their arrangements. . . ." And march with them on parade. Also I was looking for my sister. At the end of the long line rode the sponsors and maids-of-honor in carriages. Here also rode the reunion orators.

Hardly less wonderful, on another day, was the "floral parade." "Most beautiful spectacle of the reunion. . . ." One somber note was permitted. Behind the marshals where on other years had ridden a military figure, now there walked an aged Negro, John Johnson, General Hampton's old coachman, ". . . now led by the bridle an unsaddled horse . . . charger of the dead hero." Sponsors and maids-of-honor on splendid floats elaborately decorated as bowers by institutions and businesses. Mounted escort, "ladies and gentlemen of the city's riding set." Carriages of everyone who owned a carriage, swathed in flowers, graced by their owners and by "beautiful young ladies." Even three motor cars, one a "large French one" smothered in white and pink roses. ". . . A series of spectacles . . . parade of flowers with its living buds. . . ."

The meetings. The speeches. Even a child liked to listen, punctuated as they were every few moments with excited handclapping, cheers, stamping of feet, music. And such great men. All were veterans or sons of men in gray: the Chamber of Commerce head; white-haired clergymen pronouncing invocations; Governor Heyward, a veteran; Judge Andrew Crawford, veteran and "silver tongued orator." Most revered of all, Bishop Capers, "warrior-Bishop," by then a pre-eminent religious leader, who at twenty-eight had become a Confederate general, in all eyes saintly, epitome of the South's best. Who there would not feel his Lost Cause blessed when so noble a man could tell them, "We all hold it to be one of the noblest chapters in our history . . ."?

All but one who spoke were veterans or their sons. The one was a daughter. It was the opening night. She was to welcome them—"a daughter of a Confederate." A child would never forget this particular moment. Bands playing a medley of old war tunes. Crowds pushing, for there was not room for all; orchestra and dress circle crammed with old veterans; aisles and entrances packed long before time for opening. The stage—huge to a child's eyes—massed with human figures: great chorus of trained voices waiting their signal; sponsors and maids-of-honor seated tier on tier and trailing from their shoulders broad sashes of office embossed in gold letters. Old soldiers who had been bidden to the stage—generals, colonels, majors, captains, every rank, in spick-and-span gray uniforms. Somewhere among them the slight figure of a young woman.

Roll of drums; blare of trumpets; then the first high, clear notes of *Dixie!* All the gathering surging, scrambling to their feet—clapping, stamping, cheering, singing. In time it ended. It must end from sheer exhaustion. Then Bugler Lightfoot coming forward to sound the sharp notes of the "assembly," and with its dying away, the chorus beginning, and every voice swelling and rolling it forth, the Long-Meter Doxology—"Praise God from whom all blessings flow. . . ."

There were speeches, but they were as nothing to me that opening night. The newspaper said: "The veterans were waiting." So was I waiting. "Their enthusiasm . . . seemed to have been kept in check until Miss Elizabeth Lumpkin, who addressed them last year, was presented. . . ."

> *There is nothing stronger or more splendid on this wide earth than to have borne the sorrow you have borne, than to have endured the pain that you have endured. . . . You young men in whose veins beat the blood of heroes, uncover your heads, for the land in which you live is holy, hallowed by the blood of your fathers, purified by the tears of your mothers. . . . If I could write . . . I would tell how the private fought. . . . He came back and fought poverty, ruin, sometimes degradation for his dear ones at the hands of brutal men. . . . Men of the South, the day when the rebel yell could conquer a host is past . . . the day when you fought . . . is past. . . . Think you the day for all action is past as well?*

It was a long speech, but how could I find it so? "Eloquent . . . finished." So said the accounts. It was true, I knew. "Frequently . . . made to pause because of the cheering. . . ." "Time and again interrupted by thunderous applause. . . ." I joined in, beating my hands together and jumping to my feet like the others to stamp them on the floor.

Even the least of our participation was of moment to me. So for Father's every smallest duty; and Mother's assisting at the veterans' free lunch rooms; and my school-age sister's share in the children's chorus; and seeing them march or ride in the parades. It was so when a thirteen-year-old brother spoke before the old men—"In recognition of his gift of oratory and of devotion to the dead Confederacy . . . General Carwile, amid much enthusiasm, pinned the badge of 'honorary member, U.C.V.' upon the child's patriotic breast." It was so, also for the last night of the reunion.

Speeches must be listened to again. Finally, they were ended, and the closing moments came. Lights were extinguished. We waited while the curtain descended and rose again. Gleaming through the darkness was a bright camp fire with a kettle hanging from a tripod. Around the fire one could see men in bedraggled uniforms. One soldier lounged up to the fire—"Quaint reminder of long ago as he stood in the half light, pipe in mouth, pants tucked into his socks, coatless and collarless." He began to tell a tale of war. More men slipped out and settled down by the fire. ". . . A hushed house as the tale proceeded . . . lights gradually bright-ened . . . the speaker was recognized . . . Col. W. W. Lumpkin, a soldier of the Confederacy again." After that: bright lights, stacked guns seen in the foreground, tents near by, then stories from other veterans, dear to a child's heart, and to adults' too, apparently. A song begun, joined in by the audience, "We are tenting tonight on the old camp ground," rolling up to the very eaves of the Opera House. Then hilarity, the old soldiers frolicking, young soldiers again, gusts of laughter from the audi-ence urging them on. Quiet again, as a soldier thrummed a banjo and began again to sing, and we to sing with him, one after another, the old Southern ballads, plaintive, nostalgic. On the notes of these the reunion of 1903 "passed away into the land of memories."

2.

Confederate reunions after all came infrequently. At least it was so for us children. We must wait until it was the turn of our town again to welcome the old men. Moreover, reunions could not do everything. They could be counted upon to arouse our Southern patriotism to a fervid pitch and spur us on to fresh endeavors. When all was said and done, however, something continuing and substantial should be going on if we children were indeed to fulfill the part our people had set their hearts upon.

My father put it this way. He would say of his own children with tender solemnity, "Their mother teaches them their prayers. I teach them to love the Lost Cause." And surely his chosen family function in his eyes ranked but a little lower than the angels. He would say: "Men of the South, let your children hear the old stories of the South; let them hear them by the fireside, in the schoolroom, everywhere, and they will preserve inviolate the sacred honor of the South."

Many other men like Father—men of his station and kind, men who like him still lived in the days of their lost plantations—also said such words, said them continually. For my home, I know it did not rest at words. I know that Father not alone preached these things. In very fact he lived them, at the same time impregnating our lives with some of his sense of strong mission.

Nor could it be without weight that ours was a family in most ways of the old school: Father, head and dominant figure, leader, exemplar, final authority, beyond which was no higher court in family matters; one who, even outside our circle, plainly possessed prestige and recognition for the role he played despite his obvious lack of worldly goods; one through whom we could look back to plantation days, and, who knows, maybe look forward to them. A unique man, in our eyes, perhaps in others', even in some sense unique in appearance: Prince Albert coat, stiff-fronted shirt with studs, wing collar, black tie; a clean shaven man, his thick gray hair worn *en pompadour,* sometimes close-cropped, occasionally long and swept back. It was his wont to call himself the "ugliest man in South Carolina"; he could afford to say it; his audience could afford to laugh; he was standing before them. I might feel a bit dubious, being young, wondering if someone might not believe he meant it, despite the evidence of their eyes. I should have understood. I knew even then that his name as a teller of tales was second only to his name as devotee of the Lost Cause; and how profligate he was with his stories, how inexhaustible his store, how invariable his technique—a ludicrously solemn face, never relaxed even to the end, while his audience, be it around our family table or before a large gathering, was convulsed with laughter. In his manners also Father was ever a goal and example. Where other men were courteous, he made an art of courtesy. Who could show so much deference to a lady, and more than any other, to his wife? Who could bow from the hips with more formality and grace than Father? Who could be more strict in the deference children must show to older people? In how many homes, even in that day, did children immediately rise when their parents entered; and Father with us, when our mother came into the room, even if only to join us with her sewing? These were symbols reminiscent in a hundred other ways of a bygone day. Why would they not reinforce my father's authority—make his person in our eyes the epitome of what he stood for?

To be sure, much was handed on to us incidentally. Family customs seemingly remote from the Lost Cause somehow acquired its flavor. Christmas for us was full of pomp and ceremony, gaiety and gifts; overflowing stockings hanging from the mantel; full, rich carol singing. But also, Christmas was reminiscent of the old days; shouts of "Christmas gif' "; Father's childhood rituals—how well we knew from whence they came; and at the day's end the gathering before the blazing logs, and Father's voice in stories of his boyhood Christmases, until we verily felt ourselves living again on the old place.

Or let there come our annual family fishing trips. Leisure was best for hearing the old tales. Here was a leisure Father rarely could give us. The stories would begin even as he was seated on the kitchen porch, sorting tackle, attaching new hooks and lines and corks to the long reed poles we used, a pole for each of us; they went on to the incomparable sound and smell of frying chicken which my mother's expert hand prepared for our lunch baskets. The next day the tales would be picked up again. We might rise at four to get an early start; we might return long after dark had settled in; no time was too early and none too late. Our hired surrey, or perhaps a plain wagon, might be crowded; the dirt highway bumpy; the distance to mill pond or river take us several hours to traverse. It was no matter, but rather an infinitely pleasant thing to listen to the slow thud-thud of leisurely horses' hoofs and my father's voice telling of the old days.

Of course we heard stories from others, too. There were my mother's friends, some older than she, who had been in their late teens in the sixties. How many times I would sit at their feet and ask for the old tales of the plantation but more especially of the war. With all their dignity and white hair, how gay they sounded, or, if need be, how their eyes would fill with fire. It seems there were many young Yankee officers who would have shown them attentions. But *they* let the invader come to call, however handsome and debonair? *They* fail to give him a "piece of their mind" for his uncalled-for presumption? Besides these were stories unnumbered of silver saved, cotton bales hidden, horses driven to the swamps, and almost always interwoven with the help of faithful slaves. The books I read were in the same nostalgic vein. I luxuriated in the school of Thomas Nelson Page and even in the poorly-printed little volumes of Confederate memoirs then coming off many local presses, so appealing in their covers of patriotic gray. Such titles as *Surrey of Eagle's Nest, Black Rock, Diddy, Dumps and Tot,* cling to my memory.

All this was well enough, but it was not my father's way to leave our lessons to chance. Nor yet indeed my mother's, for she too had her part to play, secondary and supplementary though it might be as befitted the Southern lady and helpmeet. Both Father and Mother guided the books we read, but the daily task was my mother's. Then it was we knew the firmness in her gentle hand. Try what devices I would, I could find no relaxation in her strict regime which allotted one hour an afternoon for reading aloud under her tutelage. Sometimes it might be Dickens or Thackeray or Stevenson. But also and often it was Robert E. Lee and "Stonewall" Jackson. Even the incomparable Lee's biography could seem dull and hampering when it kept a child of nine or ten from play. Father was ever in search of books to nurture us. One new set, I can recall, had, to be sure, lives of Lee and Jackson, but to our dismay also brought a life of Grant. We children were especially indignant at this affront to our loyalties; I thought it not at all unmannerly when my sister, but a little older, snatched the Grant book away to hurl it into the woodshed as ignominious trash. Actually, my mother quietly rescued it. Books were precious to her in any case. And Father and Mother, I believe, shared in the generous feeling of many Southerners towards Grant, speaking warmly of his soldierly treatment of Lee at Appomattox. Similarly, they spoke tolerantly of Lincoln, saying, "If he had lived, the South never would have been made to suffer reconstruction."

My father devised one special means for teaching us. The design for it may have harked back to his own young manhood. He had been schooled in something very similar under his law teacher and mentor Alexander Stephens. Occasionally Mr. Stephens would have his pupils put aside their law books, to stand before him to be trained in the art of argument and oratory as it was practiced in the Old South. Father had heard Mr. Stephens more than once in the statesman's prime days, he often told us, thrilled to the strangely piercing voice, the burning eyes, the torrent of eloquent words. With peculiar zest he would remember his training under the aged man, who handed his pupils topics of their fiercely controversial day, which they must argue before him or present in orations, with himself interrupting to criticize mercilessly.

Our "Saturday Night Debating Club" was also a training ground, although to us it seemed much more an absorbing family game. It was serious business, but never solemnly serious, nor would any of us have been left out of it for anything. Even I was allowed a small part in keeping with my tender years. On most weekdays Father must be away from home attending to the task of making a living. Each Saturday night he would announce the topic for the next meeting, but being away, he left much of our advice in preparation to Mother. She was entirely qualified to give it, although of course when Father was there we naturally turned to him. Indeed, Mother turned us, saying, "Ask your father. He knows about that better than I do." Occasionally the subject for debate would be an old-fashioned query—"Is the pen mightier than the sword?" Usually, and these were our favorites, we argued topics of Southern problems and Southern history. I say "we." The most I ever contributed were a few lines which Mother had taught me. After that I was audience.

We would hurry through Saturday-night supper and dishes. A table would be placed in the parlor, Father seating himself behind it, presiding. On either side were chairs for the debaters. Mother and I comprised the audience, although at the proper time she would retire with Father to assist in judging. All being assembled, Father would rap firmly for order, formally announce the subject, introduce the first speaker on the affirmative, and the game was on.

And what a game! What eloquence from the speakers! What enthusiasm from the "audience"! What strict impartiality from the chairman! And how the plaster walls of our parlor rang with tales of the South's sufferings, exhortations to uphold her honor, recitals of her humanitarian slave regime, denunciation of those who dared to doubt the black man's inferiority, and, ever and always, persuasive logic for her position of "States Rights," and how we must at all times stand solidly together if we would preserve all that the South "stood for."

The judges' decision by no means concluded the evening. Then came a truly serious time. Then Father would assume the role of teacher, addressing himself to each child in turn, pointing up delivery, commenting on gestures; always praising where he felt praise was due; always, whatever he had to say, giving it a kindly turn, so that no one felt deflated; and with it all, taking pains to analyze each child's argument, to show its weak points, and wherein it could have been made stronger.

As we grew old enough we expected to be called upon to play some active part. At eight or nine I could join the "Children of the Confederacy." Under a proud parental eye, I could on my own initiative devise a scheme whereby a short-lived neighborhood club of ours held a "benefit" for the newly-built Old Soldiers' Home, purchasing a rocking chair with the proceeds, and in Father's company going to make a personal presentation.

My special assignment in the old men's behalf was a Confederate veterans' camp in a village several miles distant from our home. ("Camp" was the name given to local organizations of old soldiers.) Father would take me there to recite for them at their regular meetings—a patriotic poem, or a little speech he had written for me.

Nothing, it seems, had prepared me, who was but a child, for the humdrum, everyday labor that went into preserving a Lost Cause. Hence my veterans' camp was frankly disappointing. After the first time I went as a duty, but it held no lure for me. Here were no bands, no thrilling songs, no crowds, no excitement of any kind. Here was a slow, dull ride on a trolley car for Father and me; then a long walk across a river bridge; then a sleepy village. The meeting room was above a store on a drab little main street. Gathered there would be fifteen or twenty aged men, droning away at their business and making decorous use of numerous spittoons strategically placed among them. To be sure, when I said my little poem they were gently appreciative. They clapped their hands, and afterward a few of them would say nice things to Father in their slow-spoken way.

They liked my coming. This was plain, for they prepared me a gift and set a day for me to come to receive their offering. Father responded for me. Never had I seen him more gracious, easy, even eloquent in a quiet way as he thanked the old men and spoke for them the old story of the "Lost Cause." When they turned the gift so that I too could see it, I was filled with dismay. It seems they had secured a photograph of me from Father, and here was an enlargement, a huge thing, even tinted, and set in a broad, ornate gilt frame. They had contributed their nickels and dimes to make me the gift.

We did not hang the portrait once we were home again—so much for my heartfelt relief, for I had truly feared that our unbounded loyalty might carry us to this extreme. But no mirth was permitted, no slightest suggestion of disrespect. Father sternly suppressed incipient signs of it in the children, gravely announcing that the picture was too large to hang in our present home.

For many years Confederate reunions had been sounding the slogan, "Educate the children!" This had come to pass in the schoolrooms of my childhood. They had said: "Confederate soldiers, you have made history! See that it is written! Put into our schools history books true to the South!" They would urge: "The South and the cause of the Confederacy have nothing to fear from the truth, but we do not want our children educated out of a book which tries to throw disgrace on their fathers!" They would exhort: "You cannot depend on the alien historian to do you justice. You cannot depend on Yankee school books to tell of the heroism of Lee. You cannot depend on teachers who have not been inspired with the fervor of your active participation in the grand events of the war to properly teach your children what they should know." "Insist," they would cry, "that the truth should be taught your children in their schools. Insist that in . . . your colleges true Confederate history should be daily impressed upon the upgrowing generation—your sons and your daughters."

They told what had been done, how for two decades after the war, histories were written "by those ignorant of the true conditions." Southern people "resented the histories," yet were "powerless to correct the evil." But then Southern writers appeared—true men—who began to tell the "true history of the war." Confederate veterans' camps throughout the South were but waiting for the signal. Without delay, so it was said, they "used their influence with school boards" all over the South. At long last, Lost Cause leaders could say in 1905, "The most pernicious histories have been banished from the school rooms."

# Walter White

## From *A Man Called White*

### I
### *I Learn What I Am*

I am a Negro. My skin is white, my eyes are blue, my hair is blond. The traits of my race are nowhere visible upon me. Not long ago I stood one morning on a subway platform in Harlem. As the train came in I stepped back for safety. My heel came down upon the toe of the man behind me. I turned to apologize to him. He was a Negro, and his face as he stared at me was hard and full of the piled-up bitterness of a thousand lynchings and a million nights in shacks and tenements and "nigger towns." "Why don't you look where you're going?" he said sullenly. "You white folks are always trampling on colored people." Just then one of my friends came up and asked how the fight had gone in Washington—there was a filibuster against legislation for a permanent Fair Employment Practices Committee. The Negro on whose toes I had stepped listened, then spoke to me penitently:

"Are you Walter White of the NAACP? I'm sorry I spoke to you that way. I thought you were white."

I am not white. There is nothing within my mind and heart which tempts me to think I am. Yet I realize acutely that the only characteristic which matters to either the white or the colored race—the appearance of whiteness—is mine. There is magic in a white skin; there is tragedy, loneliness, exile, in a black skin. Why then do I insist that I am a Negro, when nothing compels me to do so but myself?

Many Negroes are judged as whites. Every year approximately twelve thousand white-skinned Negroes disappear—people whose absence cannot be explained by death or emigration. Nearly every one of the fourteen million discernible Negroes in the United States knows at least one member of his race who is "passing"—the magic word which means that some Negroes can get by as whites, men and women who have decided that they will be happier and more successful if they flee from the proscription and humiliation which the American color line imposes on them. Often these emigrants achieve success in business, the professions, the arts and sciences. Many of them have married white people, lived happily with them, and produced families. Sometimes they tell their husbands or wives of their Negro blood, sometimes not. Who are they? Mostly people of no great importance, but some of them prominent figures, including a few members of Congress, certain writers, and several organizers of movements to "keep the Negroes and other minorities in their places." Some of the most vehement public haters of Negroes are themselves secretly Negroes.

They do not present openly the paradox of the color line. It is I, with my insistence, day after day, year in and year out, that I am a Negro, who provokes the reactions to which now I am accustomed: the sudden intake of breath, the bewildered expression of the face, the confusion of the eyes, the muddled fragmentary remarks—"But you do not look . . . I mean I would never have known . . . of course if you didn't want to admit . . ." Sometimes the eyes blink rapidly and the tongue, out of control, says, "Are you sure?"

I have tried to imagine what it is like to have me presented to a white person as a Negro, by supposing a Negro were suddenly to say to me, "I am white." But the reversal does not work, for whites can see no reason for a white man ever wanting to be black; there is only reason for a black man wanting to be white. That is the way whites think; that is the way their values are set up. It is the startling removal of the blackness that upsets people. Looking at me without knowing who I am, they disassociate me from all the characteristics of the Negro. Informed that I am a Negro, they find it impossible suddenly to endow me with the skin, the odor, the dialect, the shuffle, the imbecile good nature, traditionally attributed to Negroes. Instantly they are aware that these things are *not* part of me. They think there must be some mistake.

There is no mistake. I am a Negro. There can be no doubt. I know the night when, in terror and bitterness of soul, I discovered that I was set apart by the pigmentation of my skin (invisible though it was in my case) and the moment at which I decided that I would infinitely rather be what I was than, through taking advantage of the way of escape that was open to me, be one of the race which had forced the decision upon me.

There were nine light-skinned Negroes in my family: mother, father, five sisters, an older brother, George, and myself. The house in which I discovered what it meant to be a Negro was located on Houston Street, three blocks from the Candler Building, Atlanta's first skyscraper, which bore the name of the ex–drug clerk who had become a millionaire from the sale of Coca-Cola. Below us lived none but Negroes; toward town all but a very few were white. Ours was an eight room, two-story frame house which stood out in its surroundings not because of its opulence but by contrast with the drabness and unpaintedness of the other dwellings in a deteriorating neighborhood.

Only Father kept his house painted, the picket fence repaired, the board fence separating our place from those on either side white-washed, the grass neatly trimmed, and flower beds abloom. Mother's passion for neatness was even more pronounced and it seemed to me that I was always the victim of her determination to see no single blade of grass longer than the others or any one of the pickets in the front fence less shiny with paint than its mates. This spic-and-spanness became increasingly apparent as the rest of the neighborhood became more down-at-heel, and resulted, as we were to learn, in sullen envy among some of our white neighbors. It was the violent expression of that resentment against a Negro family neater than themselves which set the pattern of our lives.

On a day in September 1906, when I was thirteen, we were taught that there is no isolation from life. The unseasonably oppressive heat of an Indian summer day hung like a steaming blanket over Atlanta. My sisters and I had casually commented upon the unusual quietness. It seemed to stay Mother's volubility and reduced Father, who was more taciturn, to monosyllables. But, as I remember it, no other sense of impending trouble impinged upon our consciousness.

I had read the inflammatory headlines in the *Atlanta News* and the more restrained ones in the *Atlanta Constitution* which reported alleged rapes and other crimes committed by Negroes. But these were so standard and familiar that they made—as I look back on it now—little impression. The stories were more frequent, however, and consisted of eight-column streamers instead of the usual two- or four-column ones.

Father was a mail collector. His tour of duty was from three to eleven P.M. He made his rounds in a little cart into which one climbed from a step in the rear. I used to drive the cart for him from two until seven, leaving him at the point nearest our home on Houston Street, to return home either for study or sleep. That day Father decided that I should not go with him. I appealed to Mother, who thought it might be all right, provided Father sent me home before dark because, she said, "I don't think they would dare start anything before nightfall." Father told me as we made the rounds that ominous rumors of a race riot that night were sweeping the town. But I was too young that morning to understand the background of the riot. I became much older during the next thirty-six hours, under circumstances which I now recognize as the inevitable outcome of what had preceded.

One of the most bitter political campaigns of that bloody era was reaching its climax. Hoke Smith—that amazing contradiction of courageous and intelligent opposition to the South's economic ills and at the same time advocacy of ruthless suppression of the Negro—was a candidate that year for the governorship. His opponent was Clark Howell, editor of the *Atlanta Constitution,* which boasted with justification that it "covers Dixie like the dew." Howell and his supporters held firm authority over the state Democratic machine despite the long and bitter fight Hoke Smith had made on Howell in the columns of the rival *Atlanta Journal.*

Hoke Smith had fought for legislation to ban child labor and railroad rate discriminations. He had denounced the corrupt practices of the railroads and the state railway commission, which, he charged, was as much owned and run by northern absentee landlords as were the railroads themselves. He had fought for direct primaries to nominate senators and other candidates by popular vote, for a corrupt practices act, for an elective railway commission, and for state ownership of railroads—issues which were destined to be still fought for nearly four decades later by Ellis Arnall. For these reforms he was hailed throughout the nation as a genuine progressive along with La Follette of Wisconsin and Folk of Missouri.

To overcome the power of the regular Democratic organization, Hoke Smith sought to heal the feud of long standing between himself and the powerful ex-radical Populist, Thomas E. Watson. Tom Watson was the strangest mixture of contradictions which rotten-borough politics of the South had ever produced. He was the brilliant leader of an agrarian movement in the South which, in alliance with the agrarian West, threatened for a time the industrial and financial power of the East. He had made fantastic strides in uniting Negro and white farmers with Negro and white industrial workers. He had advocated enfranchisement of Negroes and poor whites, the abolition of lynching, control of big business, and rights for the little man, which even today would label him in the minds of conservatives as a dangerous radical. He had fought with fists, guns, and spine-stirring oratory in a futile battle to stop the spread of an industrialized, corporate society.

His break with the Democratic Party during the '90's and the organization of the Populist Party made the Democrats his implacable enemies. The North, busy building vast corporations and individual fortunes, was equally fearful of Tom Watson. Thus was formed between reactionary Southern Democracy and conservative Northern Republicanism the basis of cooperation whose fullest flower is to be seen in the present-day coalition of conservatives in Congress. This combination crushed Tom Watson's bid for national leadership in the presidential elections of 1896 and smashed the Populist movement. Watson ran for president in 1904 and 1908, both times with abysmal failure. His defeats soured him to the point of vicious acrimony. He turned from his ideal of interracial decency to one of virulent hatred and denunciation of the "nigger." He thus became a natural ally for Hoke Smith in the gubernatorial election in Georgia in 1906.

The two rabble-rousers stumped the state screaming, "Nigger, nigger, nigger!" Some white farmers still believed Watson's abandoned doctrine that the interests of Negro and white farmers and industrial workers were identical. They feared that Watson's and Smith's new scheme to disfranchise Negro voters would lead to disfranchisement of poor whites. Tom Watson was sent to trade on his past reputation to reassure them that such was not the case and that their own interests were best served by now hating "niggers."

Watson's oratory had been especially effective among the cotton mill workers and other poor whites in and near Atlanta. The *Atlanta Journal* on August 1, 1906, in heavy type, all capital letters, printed an incendiary appeal to race prejudice backing up Watson and Smith which declared:

> Political equality being thus preached to the negro in the ring papers and on the stump, what wonder that he makes no distinction between political and social equality? He grows more bumptious on the street, more impudent in his dealings with white men, and then, when he cannot achieve social equality as he wishes, with the instinct of the barbarian to destroy what he cannot attain to, he lies in wait, as that dastardly brute did yesterday near this city, and assaults the fair young girlhood of the south . . .

At the same time, a daily newspaper was attempting to wrest from the *Atlanta Journal* leadership in the afternoon field. The new paper, the *Atlanta News,* in its scramble for circulation and advertising took a lesson from the political race and began to play up in eight-column streamers stories of the raping of white women by Negroes. That every one of the stories was afterward found to be wholly without foundation was of no importance. The *News* circulation, particularly in street sales, leaped swiftly upward as the headlines were bawled by lusty-voiced newsboys. Atlanta became a tinder box.

Fuel was added to the fire by a dramatization of Thomas Dixon's novel *The Clansman* in Atlanta. (This was later made by David Wark Griffith into *The Birth of a Nation,* and did more than anything else to make successful the revival of the Ku Klux Klan.) The late Ray Stannard Baker, telling the story of the Atlanta riot in *Along the Color Line,* characterized Dixon's fiction and its effect on Atlanta and the South as "incendiary and cruel." No more apt or accurate description could have been chosen.

During the afternoon preceding the riot little bands of sullen, evil-looking men talked excitedly on street corners all over downtown Atlanta. Around seven o'clock my father and I were driving toward a mail box at the corner of Peachtree and Houston Streets when there came from near-by Pryor Street a roar the like of which I had never heard before, but which sent a sensation of mingled fear and excitement coursing through my body. I asked permission of Father to go and see what the trouble was. He bluntly ordered me to stay in the cart. A little later we drove down Atlanta's main business thoroughfare, Peachtree Street. Again we heard the terrifying cries, this time near at hand and coming toward us. We saw a lame Negro bootblack from Herndon's barber shop pathetically trying to outrun a mob of whites. Less than a hundred yards from us the chase ended. We saw clubs and fists descending to the accompaniment of savage shouting and cursing. Suddenly a voice cried, "There goes another nigger!" Its work done, the mob went after new prey. The body with the withered foot lay dead in a pool of blood on the street.

Father's apprehension and mine steadily increased during the evening, although the fact that our skins were white kept us from attack. Another circumstance favored us—the mob had not yet grown violent enough to attack United States government property. But I could see Father's relief when he punched the time clock at eleven P.M. and got into the cart to go home. He wanted to go the back way down Forsyth Street, but I begged him, in my childish excitement and ignorance, to drive down Marietta to Five Points, the heart of Atlanta's business district, where the crowds were densest and the yells loudest. No sooner had we turned into Marietta Street, however, than we saw careening toward us an undertaker's barouche. Crouched in the rear of the vehicle were three Negroes clinging to the sides of the carriage as it lunged and swerved. On the driver's seat crouched a white man, the reins held taut in his left hand. A huge whip was gripped in his right. Alternately he lashed the horses and, without looking backward, swung the whip in savage swoops in the faces of members of the mob as they lunged at the carriage determined to seize the three Negroes.

There was no time for us to get out of its path, so sudden and swift was the appearance of the vehicle. The hub cap of the right rear wheel of the barouche hit the right side of our much lighter wagon. Father and I instinctively threw our weight and kept the cart from turning completely over. Our mare was a Texas mustang which, frightened by the sudden blow, lunged in the air as Father clung to the reins. Good fortune was with us. The cart settled back on its four wheels as Father said in a voice which brooked no dissent, "We are going home the back way and not down Marietta."

But again on Pryor Street we heard the cry of the mob. Close to us and in our direction ran a stout and elderly woman who cooked at a downtown white hotel. Fifty yards behind, a mob which filled the street from curb to curb was closing in. Father handed the reins to me and, though he was of slight stature, reached down and lifted the woman into the cart. I did not need to be told to lash the mare to the fastest speed she could muster.

The church bells tolled the next morning for Sunday service. But no one in Atlanta believed for a moment that the hatred and lust for blood had been appeased. Like skulls on a cannibal's hut the hats and caps of victims of the mob of the night before had been hung on the iron hooks of telegraph poles. None could tell whether each hat represented a dead Negro. But we knew that some of those who had worn the hats would never again wear any.

Late in the afternoon friends of my father's came to warn of more trouble that night. They told us that plans had been perfected for a mob to form on Peachtree Street just after nightfall to march down Houston Street to what the white people called "Darktown," three blocks or so below our house, to "clean out the niggers." There had never been a firearm in our house before that day. Father was reluctant even in those circumstances to violate the law, but he at last gave in at Mother's insistence.

We turned out the lights early, as did all our neighbors. No one removed his clothes or thought of sleep. Apprehension was tangible. We could almost touch its cold and clammy surface. Toward midnight the unnatural quiet was broken by a roar that grew steadily in volume. Even today I grow tense in remembering it.

Father told Mother to take my sisters, the youngest of them only six, to the rear of the house, which offered more protection from stones and bullets. My brother George was away, so Father and I, the only males in the house, took our places at the front windows of the parlor. The windows opened on a porch along the front side of the house, which in turn gave onto a narrow lawn that sloped down to the street and a picket fence. There was a crash as Negroes smashed the street lamp at the corner of Houston and Piedmont Avenue down the street. In a very few minutes the vanguard of the mob, some of them bearing torches, appeared. A voice which we recognized as that of the son of the grocer with whom we had traded for many years yelled, "That's where that nigger mail carrier lives! Let's burn it down! It's too nice for a nigger to live in!" In the eerie light Father turned his drawn face toward me. In a voice as quiet as though he were asking me to pass him the sugar at the breakfast table, he said, "Son, don't shoot until the first man puts his foot on the lawn and then—don't you miss!"

In the flickering light the mob swayed, paused, and began to flow toward us. In that instant there opened up within me a great awareness; I knew then who I was. I was a Negro, a human being with an invisible pigmentation which marked me a person to be hunted, hanged, abused, discriminated against, kept in poverty and ignorance, in order that those whose skin was white would have readily at hand a proof of their superiority, a proof patent and inclusive, accessible to the moron and the idiot as well as to the wise man and the genius. No matter how low a white man fell, he could always hold fast to the smug conviction that he was superior to two-thirds of the world's population, for those two-thirds were not white.

It made no difference how intelligent or talented my millions of brothers and I were, or how virtuously we lived. A curse like that of Judas was upon us, a mark of degradation fashioned with heavenly authority. There were white men who said Negroes had no souls, and who proved it by the Bible. Some of these now were approaching us, intent upon burning our house.

Theirs was a world of contrasts in values: superior and inferior, profit and loss, cooperative and noncooperative, civilized and aboriginal, white and black. If you were on the wrong end of the comparison, if you were inferior, if you were noncooperative, if you were aboriginal, if you were black, then you were marked for excision, expulsion, or extinction. I was a Negro; I was therefore that part of history which opposed the good, the just, and the enlightened. I was a Persian, falling before the hordes of Alexander. I was a Carthaginian, extinguished by the Legions of Rome. I was a Frenchman at Waterloo, an Anglo-Saxon at Hastings, a Confederate at Vicksburg. I was the defeated, wherever and whenever there was a defeat.

Yet as a boy there in the darkness amid the tightening fright, I knew the inexplicable thing—that my skin was as white as the skin of those who were coming at me.

The mob moved toward the lawn. I tried to aim my gun, wondering what it would feel like to kill a man. Suddenly there was a volley of shots. The mob hesitated, stopped. Some friends of my father's had barricaded themselves in a two-story brick building just below our house. It was they who had fired. Some of the mobsmen, still bloodthirsty, shouted, "Let's go get the nigger." Others, afraid now for their safety, held back. Our friends, noting the hesitation, fired another volley. The mob broke and retreated up Houston Street.

In the quiet that followed I put my gun aside and tried to relax. But a tension different from anything I had ever known possessed me. I was gripped by the knowledge of my identity, and in the depths of my soul I was vaguely aware that I was glad of it. I was sick with loathing for the hatred which had flared before me that night and come so close to making me a killer; but I was glad I was not one of those who hated; I was glad I was not one of those made sick and murderous by pride. I was glad I was not one of those whose story is in the history of the world, a record of bloodshed, rapine, and pillage. I was glad my mind and spirit were part of the races that had not fully awakened, and who therefore had still before them the opportunity to write a record of virtue as a memorandum to Armageddon.

It was all just a feeling then, inarticulate and melancholy, yet reassuring in the way that death and sleep are reassuring, and I have clung to it now for nearly half a century.

# Lillian Smith

## From *Killers of the Dream*

### I
### When I Was a Child

Even its children knew that the South was in trouble. No one had to tell them; no words said aloud. To them, it was a vague thing weaving in and out of their play, like a ghost haunting an old graveyard or whispers after the household sleeps—fleeting mystery, vague menace to which each responded in his own way. Some learned to screen out all except the soft and the soothing; others denied even as they saw plainly, and heard. But all knew that under quiet words and warmth and laughter, under the slow ease and tender concern about small matters, there was a heavy burden on all of us and as heavy a refusal to confess it. The children knew this "trouble" was bigger than they, bigger than their family, bigger than their church, so big that people turned away from its size. They had seen it flash out and shatter a town's peace, had felt it tear up all they believed in. They had measured its giant strength and felt weak when they remembered.

This haunted childhood belongs to every southerner of my age. We ran away from it but we came back like a hurt animal to its wound, or a murderer to the scene of his sin. The human heart dares not stay away too long from that which hurt it most. There is a return journey to anguish that few of us are released from making.

We who were born in the South called this mesh of feeling and memory "loyalty." We thought of it sometimes as "love." We identified with

337

the South's trouble as if we, individually, were responsible for all of it. We defended the sins and the sorrows of three hundred years as if each sin had been committed by us alone and each sorrow had cut across our heart. We were as hurt at criticism of our region as if our own name had been called aloud by the critic. We knew guilt without understanding it, and there is no tie that binds men closer to the past and each other than that.

It is a strange thing, this umbilical cord uncut. In times of ease, we do not feel its pull, but when we are threatened with change, suddenly it draws the whole white South together in a collective fear and fury that wipe our minds clear of reason and we are blocked from sensible contact with the world we live in.

To keep this resistance strong, wall after wall was thrown up in the southern mind against criticism from without and within. Imaginations closed tight against the hurt of others; a regional armoring took place to ward off the "enemies" who would make our trouble different—or maybe rid us of it completely. For it was a trouble that we did not want to give up. We were as involved with it as a child who cannot be happy at home and cannot bear to tear himself away, or as a grownup who has fallen in love with his own disease. We southerners had identified with the long sorrowful past on such deep levels of love and hate and guilt that we did not know how to break old bonds without pulling our lives down. *Change* was the evil word, a shrill clanking that made us know too well our servitude. *Change* meant leaving one's memories, one's sins, one's ambivalent pleasures, the room where one was born.

In this South I lived as a child and now live. And it is of it that my story is made. I shall not tell, here, of experiences that were different and special and belonged only to me, but those most white southerners born at the turn of the century share with each other. Out of the intricate weaving of unnumbered threads, I shall pick out a few strands, a few designs that have to do with what we call color and race . . . and politics . . . and money and how it is made . . . and religion . . . and sex and the body image . . . and love . . . and dreams of the Good and the killers of dreams.

A southern child's basic lessons were woven of such dissonant strands as these; sometimes the threads tangled into a terrifying mess; sometimes archaic, startling designs would appear in the weaving; sometimes, a design was left broken while another was completed with minute care. Bewildered teachers, bewildered pupils in home and on the street, driven by an invisible Authority, learned their lessons:

The mother who taught me what I know of tenderness and love and compassion taught me also the bleak rituals of keeping Negroes in their "place." The father who rebuked me for an air of superiority toward schoolmates from the mill and rounded out his rebuke by gravely reminding me that "all men are brothers," trained me in the steel-rigid decorums I must demand of every colored male. They who so gravely taught me to split my body from my mind and both from my "soul," taught me also to split my conscience from my acts and Christianity from southern tradition.

Neither the Negro nor sex was often discussed at length in our home. We were given no formal instruction in these difficult matters but we learned our lessons well. We learned the intricate system of taboos, of renunciations and compensations, of manners, voice modulations, words, feelings, along with our prayers, our toilet habits, and our games. I do not remember how or when, but by the time I had learned that God is love, that Jesus is His Son and came to give us more abundant life, that all men are brothers with a common Father, I also knew that I was better than a Negro, that all black folks have their place and must be kept in it, that sex has its place and must be kept in it, that a terrifying disaster would befall the South if ever I treated a Negro as my social equal and as terrifying a disaster would befall my family if ever I were to have a baby outside of marriage. I had learned that God so loved the world that He gave His only begotten Son so that we might have segregated churches in which it was my duty to worship each Sunday and on Wednesday at evening prayers. I had learned that white southerners are a hospitable, courteous, tactful people who treat those of their own group with consideration and who as carefully segregate from all the richness of life "for their own good and welfare" thirteen million people whose skin is colored a little differently from my own.

I knew by the time I was twelve that a member of my family would always shake hands with old Negro friends, would speak graciously to members of the Negro race unless they forgot their place, in which event icy peremptory tones would draw lines beyond which only the desperate would dare take one step. I knew that to use the word "nigger" was unpardonable and no well-bred southerner was quite so crude as to do so; nor would a well-bred southerner call a Negro "mister" or invite him into the living room or eat with him or sit by him in public places.

I knew that my old nurse who had cared for me through long months of illness, who had given me refuge when a little sister took my place as the baby of the family, who soothed, fed me, delighted me with her stories and games, let me fall asleep on her deep warm breast, was not worthy of the passionate love I felt for her but must be given instead a half-smiled-at affection similar to that which one feels for one's dog. I knew but I never believed it, that the deep respect I felt for her, the tenderness, the love, was a childish thing which every normal child outgrows, that such love begins with one's toys and is discarded with them, and that somehow—though it seemed impossible to my agonized heart— I too, must outgrow these feelings. I learned to use a soft voice to oil my words of superiority. I learned to cheapen with tears and sentimental talk of "my old mammy" one of the profound relationships of my life. I learned the bitterest thing a child can learn: that the human relations I valued most were held cheap by the world I lived in.

From the day I was born, I began to learn my lessons. I was put in a rigid frame too intricate, too twisting to describe here so briefly, but I learned to conform to its slide-rule measurements. I learned it is possible to be a Christian and a white southerner simultaneously; to be a gentlewoman and an arrogant callous creature in the same moment; to pray at night and ride a Jim Crow car the next morning and to feel comfortable in doing both. I learned to believe in freedom, to glow when the word *democracy* was used, and to practice slavery from morning to night. I learned it the way all of my southern people learn it: by closing door after door until one's mind and heart and conscience are blocked off from each other and from reality.

I closed the doors. Or perhaps they were closed for me. One day they began to open again. Why I had the desire or the strength to open them, or what strange accident or circumstance opened them for me would require in the answering an account too long, too particular, too stark to make here. And perhaps I should not have the wisdom that such an analysis would demand of me, nor the will to make it. I know only that the doors opened, a little; that somewhere along that iron corridor we travel from babyhood to maturity, doors swinging inward began to swing outward, showing glimpses of the world beyond, of that bright thing we call "reality."

I believe there is one experience which pushed these doors open, a little. And I am going to tell it here, although I know well that to excerpt from a life and family background one incident and name it as a "cause" of a change in one's life direction is a distortion and often an irrelevance. The hungers of a child and how they are filled have too much to do with the way in which experiences are assimilated to tear an incident out of life and look at it in isolation. Yet, with these reservations, I shall tell it, not because it was in itself a severe trauma, but because it became a symbol of buried experiences that I did not have access to. It is an incident that has rarely happened to other southern children. In a sense, unique. But it was an acting-out, a private production of a little script that is written on the lives of most southern children before they know words. Though they may not have seen it staged this way, each southerner has had his own private showing.

I should like to preface the account by giving a brief glimpse of my family, hoping the reader, entering my home with me, will be able to blend the edges of this isolated experience into a more full life picture and in doing so will see that it is, in a sense, everybody's story.

I was born and reared in a small Deep South town whose population was about equally Negro and white. There were nine of us who grew up freely in a rambling house of many rooms, surrounded by big lawn, back yard, gardens, fields, and barn. It was the kind of home that gathers memories like dust, a place filled with laughter and play and pain and hurt and ghosts and games. We were given such advantages of schooling, music, and art as were available in the South, and our world was not limited to the South, for travel to far places seemed a natural thing to us, and usually one of the family was in a remote part of the earth.

We knew we were a respected and important family of this small town but beyond this we gave little thought to status. Our father made money in lumber and naval stores for the excitement of making and losing it— not for what money can buy nor the security which it sometimes gives. I do not remember at any time wanting "to be rich" nor do I remember that thrift and saving were ideals which our parents considered important enough to urge upon us. In the family there was acceptance of risk, a mild delight in burning bridges, an expectant "what next?" We were not irresponsible; living according to the pleasure principle was by no means our way of life. On the contrary we were trained to think that each of us should do something of genuine usefulness, and the family thought it right to make sacrifices if necessary, to give each child preparation for such work. We were also trained to think learning important, and books; but "bad" books our mother burned. We valued music and art and crafts- manship but it was people and their welfare and religion that were the foci around which our lives seemed naturally to move. Above all else, the important thing was what we "planned to do." That each of us must do something was as inevitable as breathing for we owed a "debt to society which must be paid." This was a family commandment.

While many neighbors spent their energies in counting limbs on the family tree and grafting some on now and then to give symmetry to it, or in licking scars to cure their vague malaise, or in fighting each battle and turn of battle of that Civil War which has haunted the southern con- science so long, my father was pushing his nine children straight into the future. "You have your heritage," he used to say, "some of it good, some not so good; and as far as I know you had the usual number of grand- mothers and grandfathers. Yes, there were slaves, too many of them in the family, but that was your grandfather's mistake, not yours. The past has been lived. It is gone. The future is yours. What are you going to do with it?" He asked this question often and sometimes one knew it was but an echo of a question he had spent his life trying to answer for himself. For the future held my father's dreams; always there, not in the past, did he expect to find what he had spent his life searching for.

We lived the same segregated life as did other southerners but our parents talked in excessively Christian and democratic terms. We were told ten thousand times that status and money are unimportant (though we were well supplied with both); we were told that "all men are brothers," that we are a part of a democracy and must act like democrats. We were told that the teachings of Jesus are important and could be practiced if we tried. We were told that to be "radical" is bad, silly too; and that one must always conform to the "best behavior" of one's community and make it better if one can. We were taught that we were superior to hate and resentment, and that no member of the Smith family could stoop so low as to have an enemy. No matter what injury was done us, we must not injure ourselves further by retaliating. That was a family commandment.

We had family prayers once each day. All of us as children read the Bible in its entirety each year. We memorized hundreds of Bible verses and repeated them at breakfast, and said 'sentence prayers" around the family table. God was not someone we met on Sunday but a permanent member of our household. It never occurred to me until I was fourteen or fifteen years old that He did not chalk up the daily score on eternity's tablets.

Despite the strain of living so intimately with God, the nine of us were strong, healthy, energetic youngsters who filled days with play and sports and music and books and managed to live most of the time on the careless level at which young lives should be lived. We had our times of anxiety of course, for there were hard lessons to be learned about the soul and "bad things" to be learned about sex. Sometimes I have wondered how we learned them with a mother so shy with words.

She was a wistful creature who loved beautiful things like lace and sunsets and flowers in a vague inarticulate way, and took good care of her children. We always knew this was not her world but one she accepted under duress. Her private world we rarely entered, though the shadow of it lay heavily on our hearts.

Our father owned large business interests, employed hundreds of colored and white laborers, paid them the prevailing low wages, worked them the prevailing long hours, built for them mill towns (Negro and white), built for each group a church, saw to it that religion was supplied free, saw to it that a commissary supplied commodities at a high price, and in general managed his affairs much as ten thousand other southern businessmen managed theirs.

Even now, I can hear him chuckling as he told my mother how he won his fight for Prohibition. The high point of the campaign was election afternoon, when he lined up the mill force of several hundred (white and black), passed out a shining silver dollar to each one, marched them in and voted liquor out of our county. It was a great day. He had won the Big Game, a game he was always playing against all kinds of evil. It did not occur to him to scrutinize the methods he used. Evil was a word written in capitals; the devil was smart; if you wanted to win you outsmarted him. It was as simple as that.

He was a hardheaded, warmhearted, high-spirited man born during the Civil War, earning his living at twelve, struggling through decades of Reconstruction and post-Reconstruction, through populist movement, through the panic of 1893, the panic of 1907, on into the twentieth century accepting his region as he found it, accepting its morals and its mores as he accepted its climate, with only scorn for those who held grudges against the North or pitied themselves or the South; scheming, dreaming, expanding his business, making and losing money, making friends whom he did not lose, with never a doubt that God was by his side whispering hunches as to how to pull off successful deals. When he lost, it was his own fault. When he won, God had helped him.

Once while we were kneeling at family prayers the fire siren at the mill sounded the alarm that the mill was on fire. My father did not falter. The alarm sounded again and again—which signified the fire was big. With dignity he continued his talk with God while his children sweated and wriggled and hearts beat out of their chests in excitement. He was talking to God—how could he hurry out to save his mills! When he finished his prayer, he quietly stood up, laid the Bible carefully on the table. Then, and only then, did he show an interest in what was happening in Mill

Town. . . . When the telegram was placed in his hands telling of the death of his beloved favorite son, he gathered his children together, knelt down, and in a steady voice which contained no hint of his shattered heart, loyally repeated, "God is our refuge and strength, a very present help in trouble. Therefore will we not fear, though the earth be removed, and though the mountains be carried into the midst of the sea." On his deathbed, he whispered to his old Business Partner in Heaven: "I have fought a good fight . . . I have kept the faith."

Against this backdrop the drama of the South was played out one day in my life:

A little white girl was found in the colored section of our town, living with a Negro family in a broken-down shack. This family had moved in a few weeks before and little was known of them. One of the ladies in my mother's club, while driving over to her washerwoman's, saw the child swinging on a gate. The shack, as she said, was hardly more than a pigsty and this white child was living with dirty and sick-looking colored folks. "They must have kidnapped her," she told her friends. Genuinely shocked, the clubwomen busied themselves in an attempt to do something, for the child was very white indeed. The strange Negroes were subjected to a grueling questioning and finally grew evasive and refused to talk at all. This only increased the suspicion of the white group. The next day the clubwomen, escorted by the town marshal, took the child from her adopted family despite their tears.

She was brought to our home. I do not know why my mother consented to this plan. Perhaps because she loved children and always showed concern for them. It was easy for one more to fit into our ample household and Janie was soon at home there. She roomed with me, sat next to me at the table; I found Bible verses for her to say at breakfast; she wore my clothes, played with my dolls and followed me around from morning to night. She was dazed by her new comforts and by the interesting activities of this big lively family; and I was as happily dazed, for her adoration was a new thing to me; and as time passed a quick, childish, and deeply felt bond grew up between us.

But a day came when a telephone message was received from a colored

orphanage. There was a meeting at our home. Many whispers. All afternoon the ladies went in and out of our house talking to Mother in tones
too low for children to hear. As they passed us at play, they looked at
Janie and quickly looked away again, though a few stopped and stared
at her as if they could not tear their eyes from her face. When my father
came home Mother closed her door against our young ears and talked a
long time with him. I heard him laugh, heard Mother say, "But Papa,
this is no laughing matter!" And then they were back in the living room
with us and my mother was pale and my father was saying, "Well, work
it out, Mame, as best you can. After all, now that you know, it is pretty
simple."

In a little while my mother called my sister and me into her bedroom
and told us that in the morning Janie would return to Colored Town. She
said Janie was to have the dresses the ladies had given her and a few of
my own, and the toys we had shared with her. She asked me if I would
like to give Janie one of my dolls. She seemed hurried, though Janie was
not to leave until next day. She said, "Why not select it now?" And in
dreamlike stiffness I brought in my dolls and chose one for Janie. And
then I found it possible to say, "Why is she leaving? She likes us, she
hardly knows them. She told me she had been with them only a month."

"Because," Mother said gently, "Janie is a little colored girl."

"But she's white!"

"We were mistaken. She is colored."

"But she looks—"

"She is colored. Please don't argue!"

"What does it mean?" I whispered.

"It means," Mother said slowly, "that she has to live in Colored Town
with colored people."

"But why? She lived here three weeks and she doesn't belong to them,
she told me so."

"She is a little colored girl."

"But you said yourself she has nice manners. You said that," I persisted.

"Yes, she is a nice child. But a colored child cannot live in our home."

"Why?"

"You know, dear! You have always known that white and colored people do not live together."

"Can she come to play?"

"No."

"I don't understand."

"I don't either," my young sister quavered.

"You're too young to understand. And don't ask me again, ever again, about this!" Mother's voice was sharp but her face was sad and there was no certainty left there. She hurried out and busied herself in the kitchen and I wandered through that room where I had been born, touching the old familiar things in it, looking at them, trying to find the answer to a question that moaned like a hurt thing. . . .

And then I went out to Janie, who was waiting, knowing things were happening that concerned her but waiting until they were spoken aloud.

I do not know quite how the words were said but I told her she was to return in the morning to the little place where she had lived because she was colored and colored children could not live with white children.

"Are you white?" she said.

"I'm white," I replied, "and my sister is white. And you're colored. And white and colored can't live together because my mother says so."

"Why?" Janie whispered.

"Because they can't," I said. But I knew, though I said it firmly, that something was wrong. I knew my father and mother whom I passionately admired had betrayed something which they held dear. And they could not help doing it. And I was shamed by their failure and frightened, for I felt they were no longer as powerful as I had thought. There was something Out There that was stronger than they and I could not bear to believe it. I could not confess that my father, who always solved the family dilemmas easily and with laughter, could not solve this. I knew that my mother who was so good to children did not believe in her heart that she was being good to this child. There was not a word in my mind that said it but my body knew and my glands, and I was filled with anxiety.

But I felt compelled to believe they were right. It was the only way my world could be held together. And, slowly, it began to seep through me: *I was white. She was colored. We must not be together. It was bad to be together. Though you ate with your nurse when you were little, it was bad to eat with any colored person after that. It was bad just as other things were bad that your mother had told you. It was bad that she was to sleep in the room with me that night. It was bad. . . .*

I was overcome with guilt. For three weeks I had done things that white children were not supposed to do. And now I knew these things had been wrong.

I went to the piano and began to play, as I had always done when I was in trouble. I tried to play my next lesson and as I stumbled through it, the little girl came over and sat on the bench with me. Feeling lost in the deep currents sweeping through our house that night, she crept closer and put her arms around me and I shrank away as if my body had been uncovered. I had not said a word, I did not say one, but she knew, and tears slowly rolled down her little white face. . . .

And then I forgot it. For more than thirty years the experience was wiped out of my memory. But that night, and the weeks it was tied to, worked its way like a splinter, bit by bit, down to the hurt places in my memory and festered there. And as I grew older, as more experiences collected around that faithless time, as memories of earlier, more profound hurts crept closer, drawn to that night as if to a magnet, I began to know that people who talked of love and children did not mean it. That is a hard thing for a child to learn. I still admired my parents, there was so much that was strong and vital and sane and good about them and I never forgot this; I stubbornly believed in their sincerity, as I do to this day, and I loved them. Yet in my heart they were under suspicion. Something was wrong.

Something was wrong with a world that tells you that love is good and people are important and then forces you to deny love and to humiliate people. I knew, though I would not for years confess it aloud, that in trying to shut the Negro race away from us, we have shut ourselves away from so many good, creative, honest, deeply human things in life. I began to understand slowly at first but more clearly as the years passed, that the warped, distorted frame we have put around every Negro child from birth is around every white child also. Each is on a different side of the frame but each is pinioned there. And I knew that what cruelly shapes and cripples the personality of one is as cruelly shaping and crippling the personality of the other. I began to see that though we may, as we acquire new knowledge, live through new experiences, examine old memories, gain the strength to tear the frame from us, yet we are stunted and warped and in our lifetime cannot grow straight again any more than can a tree, put in a steel-like twisting frame when young, grow tall and straight when the frame is torn away at maturity.

As I sit here writing, I can almost touch that little town, so close is the memory of it. There it lies, its main street lined with great oaks, heavy with matted moss that swings softly even now as I remember. A little white town rimmed with Negroes, making a deep shadow on the whiteness. There it lies, broken in two by one strange idea. Minds broken. Hearts broken. Conscience torn from acts. A culture split in a thousand pieces. That is segregation. I am remembering: a woman in a mental hospital walking four steps out, four steps in, unable to go further because she has drawn an invisible line around her small world and is terrified to take one step beyond it. . . . A man in a Disturbed Ward assigning "places" to the other patients and violently insisting that each stay in his place. . . . A Negro woman saying to me so quietly, "We cannot ride together on the bus, you know. It is not legal to be human down here."

Memory, walking the streets of one's childhood . . . of the town where one was born.

# Conrad Aiken

## From *Ushant: An Essay*

Back thus to childhood, and infancy—the first day. And God said, let there be light. And there was light. Light, a "blue" light (if R. could be believed) above one's bassinet—or could it be a memory of sky? Then the lights, of opening doors and balconies; and the difference between indoors and outdoors; the sudden assault of the *whole* light, so dangerous, but found also to be precariously acceptable. Yes, and in the south particularly: the light there that was like the spring of the tiger: the dark there that was like the swarming of cottonmouths round one's eyes. The everywhere critical division between light and shade, demarcation as definite and vivid as the striping of the tiger. And if one must begin somewhere, if somewhere there must be a beginning, nevertheless the more one thought of it the less could one discover with any assurance just where it was:—at most, it may be, possibly, just *there*, in light itself: as if in fact one had lived, to begin with, a long life of which light itself was the sole principle, and one's awareness of light one's sole awareness. To have emerged from that, very much as an exhausted swimmer from a wrecked ship—perhaps in the *Chanel de la Helle*—crawls up on a shore, was already in a sense to have begun the long and vivid process of dying which we call life. To be able to *separate* oneself from one's background, one's environment—wasn't this the most thrilling discovery of which consciousness was capable? and no doubt for the very reason that as it is a discovery of one's limits, it is therefore by implication the first and sharpest taste of death.

Natural enough, in that case, the terror that was light's invariable accompaniment—for it was inevitably the cutting edge of revelation, and of course it was oneself that was being cut. Into what shapes—? Shapes of roundness, flat shapes, dully gleaming squares, sharp diamonds and triangles: the secrecy of the diagonal: illuminated movements of curve or angle, surfaces that glowed or sombred, and then, in altering light, the kinaesthetic and palpable textures altering also, the smooth, the flocked, the veined, the corrugated, the pocked, the pleached—granite surface and ivy surface, the cool or warm wall which found its way to shadow in a corner. But above all, the endless variability in the light itself as it shifted over outlines, or filtered, for instance, a little monstrously, through the hairs of a coarse profile, or became slippery and ophidian as it glided over something extended and smooth. The shadows leaned towards, and then away; bent down or as mysteriously departed; one existed as if at the center of a world of luminaries in orbit, and also as if membranously attached to them: as they approached or receded, one felt one's innermost vitality secretly and deliciously warmed or nurtured, or perilously abandoned. Root and stem, one was consciously a tropism of exquisite response in the very center of one's own world, coiled about the source of one's own delight.

Fascinating, that out of this so elementary and as it were abecedarian experience, these huge globed and golden monosyllables of meaning, an onomasticon in which the living particles were alternately as huge as stars or as minute as atoms, floating separately in the dark galaxies whether of ether-dust or plasma, one should so instinctively and automatically become oneself the onomastic who could organize a language for the *plenum*, and fill it: and that out of these primary simplicities should slowly emerge the complex, the increasingly complex, forms of developing consciousness and memory. The forms were in a way simply congealings of light, whether into shapes or events—? for they seemed to be interchangeable. And upon these later would be imposed some of the "false" memories, the hearsay, which would be incorporated subtly and surreptitiously into memory, and then flung back.

Such, for example, was the drawing of D. as an infant, the drawing by his father, as the sole occupant of the floor in the boarding-house room at Savannah: that deliberately hideous, and actually very funny, drawing, of which nevertheless the many details (the Angelus of Millet on the wall, the whatnot in the corner, the washstand, the large bed with knobbed railing, the amateurish picture of the haystack, known all one's life as painted by father) had been in effect, but deceptively, absorbed by himself. The grotesque infant with one hair standing upright on his head, and grinning to show one tooth, dominated the scene already, in the pen-and-ink drawing which had been sent to grandmother; dominated all. Naked except for his diapers, there he squatted, the new emperor, the new inheritor of the virtues and vices of his ancestors. In this memorable drawing, D.'s father had managed to convey something quite appallingly flagrant, the feeling one has, but most of all when one has just become a father (as D. himself remembered), of life's blatant effrontery, its sheer impudence. The egoism of the ovum is only surpassed by that of the baby; and one unconsciously, or even consciously, begins at once to resent it. And in this crude caricature one could recognize all too easily the contention for mastery of the father's anger and pride. It was as good as an admission that (if the brat only knew it!) he already had the upper hand, and was destined to become a powerful, cunning, and treacherous usurper. That child's father and mother were already as good as dead.

Merrymount Nipmuk: so this somewhat deplorable character was to have been called—indeed, *was* called, in the fragment of narrative which had been given the tentative title of "The Lives and Adventures of Merrymount Nipmuk": the name, like the title, perhaps a trifle labored, but the implications clear. The Nipmuks, had they not been one of the lesser Indian tribes of New England, poor but honest, on the whole unspectacular? but with just, especially in the later generations, a saving dash of the aboriginal naughtiness that could be symbolized by the reference to Merrymount, and to that gay phallic Maypole which Morton, the poet, had somewhat rashly and prematurely dedicated on the seaside hill south of Boston, north of Wessagussett—its "flag to April's breeze unfurl'd"? And suitably enough, D.'s father's drawing still reposed, as it always had, between the pages of grandfather's sermons, sermons which had led his church into the wilderness of comparative unbelief. There it had reposed, on the shelf in that tiny cottage on Cape Cod, which, unknown to D., had long before been lived in by Cousin Abiel, the Quaker, and from which Cousin Abiel had written the famous naughty letter to grandfather, then studying for the ministry at Harvard—it had described with much too much gusto the marital habits—or perhaps premarital— of the local Quakers. Grandfather, the far-seeing liberal; Cousin Abiel, the sly wag and iconoclast; a small faded pamphlet of grandmother's poems, capable but undistinguished; and the drawing of D., rampant in diapers, by D.'s father: here, in brief (for Abiel's letter was folded de- murely in the book, too), was a not wholly accidental symposium of the family. Here they slept together more securely, more memorably, and more intimately, than in the prim Quaker graveyard at South Yarmouth, or the suburban cemetery at New Bedford, or under the moss-streamered live-oaks and telephone wires beside the Thunderbolt River at Savan- nah. Here, they spoke in chorus, with one voice; and said one thing: *the ancestors.*

These forms, these coagulations of light, into scenes or events, the shapes of experience, which gradually became the shape of oneself (like the telegram at Savannah, on the sunny morning after Christmas, which announced grandfather's death, and the ensuing walk to the telegraph office—but what was death? this was the first adumbration of death, and it meant a visit with grandfather to Buttonwood Park, sitting there under the trees, and bears in cages, an imaginary tea at a rustic table, and the fragment of a letter from grandfather, which lay, too, in the pages of the volume of sermons, sent from San Francisco, and all about trains)—these shapes of experience were of course to be put together later, and then, like a color of light, or a color of shade, cast back on the simpler forms which had preceded them. But now the immediate shapes were the palmetto leaves which raised dark hands before the windows of the boardinghouse room: the mosquito netting which hung dreamlike over the bed, itself a part of sleep: the bells, that reverberated for meal-times, no doubt some sort of gong which hung in the lower hall, and sent footsteps hurrying up and down on curved stairs round the wide pale stairwell (it was not dissimilar to the bell that rang an alarm on the P. & O. boat, and had been so wonderfully "translated" into fire-bells, or Cathedral bells, from the toy German town in the little story which they had been translating

in a dream, his own dream, itself later to become concept of an artifact):
these were undeniably there, and of their own authority. As, also, the
first really identifiable "scene," or action. This involved the stairwell,
too. There were ladies, there were voices downstairs, at the bottom of
the echoing stairwell, and they were having tea, but this of course must
have been an item of knowledge added later; and into this, down into
this, between the dark banisters of the railing, he had released—now
that he had himself been displaced—his brother K.'s milk-bottle. That
was all. Nothing before, and nothing after. Why did one so particularly
remember this? Because there was so unmistakably an element of calculation in it, a *suppressed* beforeness? Probably. But to suppose that this
was actually one's first recollection of a scene was only superficially, or
in a partial sense, true. For one also remembers, but in a different and
less demonstrable way, much that was inexpressible, and survived only as
the feeling-tone that accompanied certain situations and actions, or even
times of day: when one walked into a field, alone, through the lichened
pasture-gate, in the pale early morning, or thus again past the stone wall
on to the nether slope of a mountain, still in shadow against the east: or
at night in spring along a pitch-dark country lane, the unseen ditches at
either side, the tassels of birches against one's face: or at the moment of
one's waking from a terrible or delicious dream—the execution dream,
for example, of waiting in the chair for the onset of the electricity, then its
profound assault on one's throat and breast and heart, fluctuatingly intrusive, but not at first intrusive enough, so that although one knew that
one was dying, and tried to cry out an appeal for a deeper and more final
intrusion, one succeeded only in a murmur so faint that no one heard
it, and one's dying thought was "even in death I cannot be effectual,
or make myself understood": in such moments, it was from the unconscious memory that the scene took its secret validity. This shapeless but
conforming ever-ready validity of memory was like a cloud which had
always accompanied one, and out of which one had managed, at intervals, but to an always unpredictable degree, to disengage an apparently
separate awareness. It was as much part of oneself as one's body. And
at first for increasingly long periods, like the fish learning to live out
of the sea, one experienced a growing, if spurious, confidence that one

was at last speaking for oneself, without reference to any past, one's own or another, but just the same, one had always known that this was sure to be temporary, and that at length the process would reverse itself; so that then, more and more often, and again too for periods of increasing length, one would sink back into that cryptic cloud, finally to remain there for good. And this cloud, this memory, whether ancestral, or one's own, or both, seemed to extend backward in time forever. More even than one's father and mother, this *was* father and mother.

But theirs too, theirs too.

\* \* \*

And of course the only difference between the early and the late, in experience, was of simple and complex, single and compound, the plain and the ambiguous. The pity being that of these multiples of iridescent complexity one so seldom any longer paused, or had the patience, to ana- lyze back to the still wonderful—(if only one perceived them)—primary units of sense that composed them. If one could still, as at the beginning in Savannah, and in that amazing house that was oneself, set out on that first divine exploration beyond the borders of one's own private sepa- rateness! Just as mobility had first enlarged one's experience, one's map, of the nursery, and then of a whole floor, a story, of the house, with all the marvelous stairs and corners, and the obscure patterns in the carpets, the inviting shadows and caves under tables, or the fringed and fragrant hollows under sofas—for one's earlier adventures were quite absurdly like a dog's or cat's—so in the next phase the sense of one's separateness as an individual (which had been signalized forever, and crystallized, by the walk to the telegraph office with mother) began its own necessary ex- pansions and discoveries. After Wide had been born, and after mother's mysterious illness and seclusion, he had been removed from the nurs- ery, which adjoined her room, and of which the folding-doors had been provokingly kept shut, and given a room of his own.

"Guess you gwine to be a big boy now," Clara had said. "Yes, suh, guess you gwine to be a big boy,"—thrusting her black hands miracu- lously into the flames of the nursery fireplace.

Here was again that flattering overtone as of a newly found impor- tance. A room of his own, with an inside window which looked out into the long "black hall," a bed of white metal, and bright brass knobs which could be unscrewed from the posts; a chair, too, and a small low table, where had stood the red fire-engine, which had for so long smelled of smoke, deliciously, from the fire of excelsior which D.'s father had made in it; and the set of Zouave soldiers, slotted in their box. All this meant a definite and peculiar squaring away of oneself, an acquisition of distance. It was as if one had taken on the dimensions of the new room, or had even come to resemble it. That arranged room was now one's rearranged self, and not only rearranged, but somehow secret. Ah—secret—yea! And this suddenly found secrecy was both attractive and vitalizing. Now for the first time one could do things without being watched. Light matches, for instance! Not everything one did would be known.

It had meant, too, a further expansion of separateness and independence, quite naturally and strategically, down those long back stairs which led first to the pantry, and then, by the outside stairs, to the kitchen and outhouse and yard, and so, again, to the whole outside world, the fascinatingly filthy alley beyond the outhouse, which in turn led to all of secret and subterranean Savannah. This, naturally, was a realm largely unknown to father and mother. If the stoop (and the great beautiful Room) had become a bridge to one sort of world, the official world, now the peach-tree and chinaberry-tree, framing the latticed door to the fetid alley, had become the guardians and symbols of a new birth, a new life: between them he had gone forth to take inevitable possession of his own private world.

# Ralph McGill

## "It Has Happened Here"

James Peters, typical, mild-looking, successful rural banker from Manchester, Georgia was speaking.

He stood on the clerk's rostrum in the House of Representatives in Georgia's state capitol. Immediately below him sat the governor of Georgia, Eugene Talmadge. His scowling face was clamped about a long unlit cigar.

He sat near the head of a table. About it sat fifteen men, members of the board of regents of the state's university system. Days before it had been purged of three members who had refused to vote with the governor in a previous meeting. The new members were somewhat nervous and belligerent.

Regent Peters was one of the new members. Customarily, on that board, the new member is quiet for a period of time. On this day which was, of all days, Bastille Day, Regent Peters, sworn in a brief hour before, was running the show.

Before him where semi-annually sit the members of Georgia's House of Representatives, the seats were filled. Above him, in the gallery, the seats were filled.

The crowd knew what had happened. Also, what would happen. It was history how the governor twice had tried to have Walter D. Cocking, dean of the school of education at the University of Georgia, fired on the charge he had advocated a campus where graduate white and colored students would study the state's educational problems. The statement was alleged to have been made almost two years before at a faculty meeting. One teacher, dismissed from that school and employed in another, had made the charge. More than thirty others, attending the same meeting, did not hear the statement. The dean had denied it.

The governor had tried twice and failed twice. Three regents had been removed. The last vote was eight to seven. On Bastille Day they had come with the three new ones and new "evidence."

The state knew, too, of affidavits made in the last days before the "trial." A representative of the state's gasoline tax department, said one affidavit, had asked a photographer to fake a photograph showing Dean Cocking sitting with Negroes. Another affidavit from Dean Cocking's Negro house servant and yard boy said that he, the boy, had been taken to a tourist camp and told he was in the headquarters of the Ku Klux Klan. There he had been offered a bribe to steal papers from the dean which might have been written by Negro teachers. Or to let them into the house with his key. Finally, he swore, he had been told to sign a typewritten statement which was not given to him to read. A pistol was on a nearby bureau. He signed.

No one ever denied this. None of it appeared in the trial.

On this day Dean Cocking was on trial for the third time. This time the jurors had been changed. With him, also on trial, was Dr. Marvin S. Pittman, president of the South Georgia Teachers' College. The original charge against him had been undue political activity, but that charge was shelved; instead, it was said he, along with Cocking, had sought to promote racial equality.

Hatton Lovejoy, Georgia attorney, appearing for alumni groups of the state university, defended. He asked for time for the gathering of new evidence since the witnesses at the former trial of Dean Cocking had not been called. He had not thought they would be necessary.

The first vote had come. Regent Peters had consulted a typewritten sheet of paper and made the motion that each side would have one hour. The vote was ten to five. The five remaining from the original group of eight to seven were to stand many times that day. No one else was to join them. Always it was ten to five that day.

(All that the crowd knew before it began.)
Regent Peters had begun to speak.

Most of the evidence was from two books, *Brown America,* by Edwin
R. Embree, of the Rosenwald Fund, and *Calling America,* a sympo-
sium published in the magazine *Survey Graphic* and later republished by
Harper.

It has been charged that at Dr. Pittman's school the book *Calling
America* was required reading. Dr. Pittman had said he did not know it
was in the library and it was not required reading. It heatedly was said
to be communistic and to encourage racial equality.

Of *Brown America* it was said that it proposed not merely social
equality but intermarriage and the creating of a brown America. Dean
Cocking, not at all connected with the Rosenwald Fund, was puzzled
as to how it could be evidence against him. The book did not advocate
what was charged, but there was no time for discussion. The typewritten
schedule was rather exact.

Regent Peters went on.

"Pretty soon the Negro will be wanting to sit in the same seats with
us, eat at the same tables with us, and ride in the same train cars with
us," declared Regent Peters.

He paused and, looking down at the governor, waited.

"They ain't a-gonna do it," shouted the governor.

The crowd cheered.

Regent Peters went on. The politicians in the crowd were watching him
closely, cynically. They knew he was being shown to the crowd, without wraps, as a possible candidate for governor in the event the governor
should choose, in 1942, to run for the United States Senate.

Regent Peters slowed down a bit.

"Hit the chair and holler," said the governor.

It went on and on. The crowd was about divided, shocked, angry, and
partisan.

Regent Peters hesitated, fumbling for a word.

"Go ahead, they are listening," said the governor.

The show went on.

Now and then there was testimony of a sort. Witnesses came. The president of the university, Harmon Caldwell, stood with his men. Willis Sutton, superintendent of Atlanta's city schools, testified for Dr. Pittman, saying that if the state of Georgia did not want men like him it was in a bad way.

It was a bit ironic. There had been a flurry by the governor in the weeks before this Bastille Day hearing in which "furriners" had been castigated by the governor. Cocking, from Iowa, was a "furriner." Pittman, from Mississippi, and the son of a Confederate veteran, also was damned as a "furriner" and as promoting a meeting at which whites and colored had met together. The Rosenwald Fund and anyone even remotely connected with it, were damned as favoring "equality."

They came and went. It was not a tense meeting. News reporters had seen the schedule in Regent Peter's hand. It had been known for days what the verdict would be. The governor had announced what it would be ten days before the "trial."

It would have been a pleasant farce, if one could fail to note and feel the vicious undertones. It would have been downright humorous if one could have forgot that it was not just a hearing about the jobs of two men. One might have laughed out loud at it had one not known that this was not just the trial of two men on charges which had no sustaining evidence. It might have been dismissed as political had it not gone so deep.

It was, viewed from one angle, a sort of Gilbert and Sullivan opera, yet from another angle it was a dirty cloud on the skies. It was ironically humorous, even to the defendants, to know that on the night before the hearing a caucus dinner had been held. From that had come the typewritten schedule for the majority to follow.

There was to be, later on, loud laughter. That was when Regent L. W. (Chip) Robert, former assistant secretary of the United States Treasury, stood up and from his pocket produced a typewritten resolution of thanks to the governor for ridding the university of the two men.

Before that act there was some more of "Nigger! Nigger!" some more of the threat to white supremacy, some more talk about your daughter going to school on the same campus as a Negro. No one had advocated all this. It was the old familiar, phoney formula, used for almost half a century by Tom Heflin and others to maintain themselves in office.

It was not all one way on the floor. Part of the crowd cheered the five regents who kept standing up each time the typewritten resolution called for a vote. Now and then this caused a bit of a row. The people saw then, for the first time, the state's new secret police. Men in plain clothes, officers, tried to quiet some of the demonstrations.

Cocking and Pittman were allowed a brief denial and a brief affirmation of and a plea for democracy.

But, at last, Regent Peters had hit the chair for the last time and hollered for the last time. For the last time, that day at least, the vote had been ten to five.

The last line on the typewritten sheet had been reached.

Regent Robert arose, somewhat sheepishly, assuming dignity, and read his resolution praising a verdict arrived at before the hearing. The big-business man, holding millions in government contracts, and with a large state bill collected, had come through.

The two men were dismissed from the university system.

What an almost unanimous roll call of the state's newspapers was to call a "legal lynching," had been accomplished. The newspapers were to keep it up, too, to the great surprise of many. That so many of the weekly newspapers took it up was to cause some worry at the capitol. It was to bring forth a radio speech from the governor and inflammatory editions of his personal political publication.

Three more men were fired from the university system a day later. It was easy then. They were fired for three casual reasons. The governor didn't need reasons.

The whole show was, as everyone knew, not just the trial of two teachers. The farcical trial, the unsupported, unrelated evidence, the typewritten sheet of paper, the deliberate arousing of racial prejudices in a state which had been working hard at cooperation and which had been getting results—all the show sprang from something deeper. The attack on the Rosenwald Fund and the indiscriminate slurs on any who had received one of its fellowships was not merely because it had given money to Negro education in the South. (And more to white education.) It was also an expression of poorly concealed anti-Semitism.

All of them were the chills, the fever, the rash, the high blood pressure, the coated tongue, the sore throat which the doctor finds in sick patients. All were symptoms.

It is best always to begin at the beginning. But, here, it is not easy to find the beginning.

It is easy enough to find the beginnings of the actual "lynching." But it goes deeper.

Before the dictator can strut his not always brief hour upon the stage, someone must build the stage.

Among the ghostly hands which pulled the rope at the lynching were those that had written the freight rates and the tariffs which were to keep the South a tributary section.

The rest of the nation has been very tolerant and easy about the South. They have laughed at the Scopes trial in Dayton, at Heflin, at Bilbo, at Talmadge. They were immensely amused by Huey Long.

Those who work in the South; those who have fought all these men and all they stand for, have long been disturbed by this carefree attitude of the rest of the nation where the South is concerned. The newspaper men and the honest business and professional men of Louisiana knew Huey Long was no clown long before the rest of the nation learned it. They know that the nation which has kept the South a tributary section helped create the lacks and wants which make up the soil in which fascism flourishes. They all are children of the nation, these Heflins, Bilbos, Talmadges, Longs.

Those who work in the South, who work for the South, know that all these things, racial lynchings, chasing off after promises, all this cruelty, spring from the same soil, economic fear. The black man crowds the white man. The eroded fields of small farms give up their boys and girls to come to town and to crowd those who already work there. The poor whites and the poor Negroes resent one another, both wanting the same jobs and food.

One cannot blame them for listening to promises. They have so little.

One cannot be puzzled at their following a Talmadge.

Hitler, like Talmadge, Long, Bilbo, and all the others, arose out of economic failures and poverty, and out of a people with the lacks and wants, despair and doubt, which they produce.

We know it can happen here. The people of Louisiana, of Georgia, and other states, know it has happened here. In Louisiana they already tremble lest the hungry, dispossessed ones fed by Huey Long's hand, turn back to the apostles of Long yet out of jail. There are signs that they may.

The reform moves do not meet the problem. The Talmadges, the Longs, the Bilbos are so much more resourceful and, usually, much more courageous than their foes.

So, Georgia has seen it happen here. And Georgia moves on. There are courageous newspapers, courageous teachers, writers, citizens. They are frightened, now and then, by the ruthless determination of the forces loose in the South and the nation. They wonder how much of a national tie-up there is, how deep go these movements of the demagogues in the South and of all the others in the nation who suppress education, who would burn books, who use slander and smears; who whisper or shout openly anti-Semitic propaganda; who foster a revival of the Klan as a political instrument? How close is the tie-up and who backs them?

No one takes enough time with the red-necked sharecropper, moving his pitiful family and his pitiful belongings each year, going to hear brother Norris preach the good, old-time religion, seeking a better cabin, a better crop, a better landlord, wishing all the while for something easy, something better; looking up to be fed. He has courage and he has convictions. They are often dangerous convictions. But he has them. All this tribe—Bilbo, Long—all had handy convictions.

It is not difficult to understand this soul sickness which listens to promises. Deep-seated, long-standing political and social inequities have created a soul-sickness which no one has solved.

The stage, on which a dictator may strut and from which he may promise food and a surcease from this sickness brought on by lacks and poverty, is plain to see. Its every plank may be named.

The gallows on which Cocking and Pittman were hanged is stark and clear.

Georgia, with other Southern states, remains one of the raw product states, with the accompanying low income which raw product production produces.

The state's per capita income and property values are about half those of the nation.

About two-thirds of the population of Georgia earns its living from the soil, including the timber which grows from it. About two-thirds of that population owns no land. About half that landless two-thirds lacks any tenancy contracts and moves each year.

The average annual income of this farm and lumber group is, across a period of years, about one hundred dollars less than the average individual farm income in the United States. If there are five in a family, and it is interesting to note how often there are five or more, this means there is a family income five hundred dollars less than that of the average farm family of five in the nation.

There are few doctors in the rural section. The politicians fret with proposals such as refusing to admit any student from out of state or with promoting another medical school. They never think that the graduates will keep on leaving the state and leaving the depressed rural areas alone because they, too, must eat and the free samples of vitamins they receive are not enough.

They never think that the reason the depressed rural areas have no doctor is because the people aren't able to pay for them and won't be, no matter if they build a medical school in each section of the state.

Annually there is deploring in all southern states that so many of her young men and women, educated in state universities at the expense of the state, leave the state for work. The legislatures worry themselves with futile thinking about some plan to make them stay at home even though there be no jobs.

The men with skills do the same thing. They leave, going to states with greater industrial developments.

According to the 1930 census almost a million Georgians had left their native state. Only 300,071 had moved in.

The result of all this has been that Georgia, and other southern states, long have found themselves with two high-dependency groups: young people who must be educated and old people who must be supported. Coupled with this are low incomes and low property values.

This has produced another plank in the platform, another prop on the gallows.

Revenue is sorely needed, always. The South is faithful to education. It spends, on education, a larger proportionate share of its income than any other state. It has so little to spend. Today education costs more. And no one can be politically elected who does not promise more and more generous old-age pensions. Business concerns—successful business concerns—literally have been forced into politics.

There must be more and more revenue. The business concerns which are well managed and which produce profits are the targets. They have been forced, and the realist cannot blame them, to buy protection by contributing to political campaigns. They obtain a political, financial interest in people elected to office. It is their only chance for survival. They take it. A poll tax, which is retroactive up to fifteen dollars, is a stumbling block to voting among the low-income farm groups, and also among the low- and medium-income city groups.

The summer political campaigns, especially the campaigns for governor (after 1942 to come only every four years), are the social seasons for the poorest ones of the state. For a whole summer they are given barbecues, free barbecues. The speakers lambaste one another. Names are called. Characters cheerfully and gleefully are blackened. The smear campaigns grow in intensity, the crowds love it.

The landless, hungry, shiftless, half-sick ones become important in the summer campaigns. Many have their poll taxes paid. They suddenly find themselves in front of men standing on platforms promising—promising—the land flowing with milk and honey. A politician might seek to interpret this as saying these people are "bums." This is not to be so interpreted. These are good people, of good stock. If they are landless,

hungry, and half sick, it is because the system has made them so. The
Farm Security Administration has shown in the few hundred cases it
has been able to reach that they have the initiative and the ability to
rehabilitate themselves. Only a few have had the opportunity.

If they lift up their eyes who can blame them?

(Does it still seem easy to say that all one must do is to say to this curious South that really, it must quit lynching Negroes, quit disfranchising
voters? That it really, after all, must come to its senses and get rid of its
foolish demagogues? Does the problem still seem that simple?)

Now and then they provide some entertainment during the off-season.

Georgia's governor brought down to Georgia Dr. Frank Norris. Now
and then Georgia's governor goes up to Detroit "to do a little preaching"
for Dr. Norris. Dr. Norris denies any pro-KKK connection. He merely
goes about preaching the Lord's word in the old-fashioned way.

Georgia's governor had him down recently, preaching in each district.
The governor sat on the pulpit platform and listened while the laborer
in the Lord's vineyard told the crowd they'd nail the hides of newspaper
editors to the fence; assured them they must defend their heritages. It
was the old-fashioned religion. The governor wrote about how pleased it
made him to hear "the great truths of the Bible expounded in the good,
old-fashioned way which our fathers knew."

Georgia's governor has aspirations. He is no fool. He is smart and he
is shrewd. He was an ardent admirer of Huey Long. He obtains the support of businessmen because he promises them—and delivers to them—
a balanced budget and no new taxes. And how he can promise and sway
the ones who love him best—the "wool-hat boys"—eternally waiting for
political promises, bigger and better!

He found the state in debt after four years of administration by his
predecessor who gave to the state a progressive program but lacked the
ability to finance and to direct, and whose friends helped destroy him
and his program.

Georgia's governor, elected not without opposition, but with the support of business and almost all county machines, forced through the
legislature a finance plan which allowed him to do what no other gov-

ernor has been empowered to do—take money from the rich highway department, or from any other department with a surplus, and use it where he willed. The gasoline taxes, heretofore sacrosanct, enabled him to make a really fine showing in paying off the teachers and reducing indebtedness. His predecessor could have financed his program with similar power and with banishment of his "friends."

The point is that Georgia's governor, like others before him and like others who will come after him in the South and in any other states where there are landless, dispossessed farmers and depressed city groups, rose to unusual power out of a state plagued by debt, by despair, and by doubt and confusion.

Only twelve percent of the adult population elected him, eighteen percent of the white adults.

The average Georgia child leaves school in the fourth grade.

More than half the state's farm population are tenants and sharecroppers; of which half are landless, moving from year to year in futile and pitiful search for a better cabin, a better crop, a better landlord.

All this has happened in a state which once was a leader in progress. In this state was established the first Sunday School and the first orphan asylum in the United States. In it was chartered the first state university. In it was established the first women's college in the world, Wesleyan. A graduate of its state university was the first to use ether as an anaesthetic. It was the first state to adopt legislation permitting and allowing married women to own and control their own property, a shockingly progressive piece of legislation at the time of its passing. It was a glowing, gallant history.

When the Civil War was fought and done, there arose the voices of democracy. Henry Grady died, as they said, "literally loving the nation into peace." General John B. Gordon, the general who had covered Robert E. Lee's last retreat, campaigned for governor with a plank for Negro education in his platform. There were voices speaking out.

Even as they spoke the planners of economic inequality were busy building fences. For seventy-five years that inequality has persisted and, as the South well knows, political democracy has been a mockery. It is almost impossible to convince the rest of the nation, even today, that the tributary South is sick because of roots which go back to the writing of freight rates and the tariff laws for a conquered section of the nation. But it is so. The roots go back.

## "Hatred Reaps Its Harvest"

On a dark, cloudy night, symbolic of the callous, hate-filled minds involved, a Negro school in Atlanta senselessly was bombed early Monday morning.

It is too bad the nation could not see the wrecked rooms where the colored Christmas drawings of children, lovingly done, were scattered in such pitiful disorder. These childish doings cry out accusingly with a mute but trumpet-like eloquence.

The big brave men who tossed the explosive in the darkness of the night, and in the deeper darkness of their own minds and souls, have not stopped the processes of education. Their kind have appeared often in history. They were among those who cried, "Crucify Him." Their kind were among those who offered Him vinegar on the cross when He said, "I thirst." Their soul-kin were among those who tended Hitler's gas furnaces. Their kind are among the Communist terror groups. Their kind are related to those who scream filth in the New Orleans demonstrations.

In a time like this, it is fashionable for leaders of those who preach, teach and organize for defiance of law and court decisions to deplore violence and say, "We are not responsible. We do not endorse violence."

But, of course, they do.

*In High Places* Men and women in high places who organize groups to resist court orders, those who urge pledges of never surrendering, and who encourage those of the Klan mentality, did not toss the explosive at the school. But in a very real sense, their hands were there just the same, because, if those who are willing to commit bombings, physical assaults and other crimes of violence were not encouraged by those in established positions who curse the court, who say that American judges are Communists, who reveal their own state of mind to be that of law violators, the lawless would not become so emboldened.

But, as always, when the fruits of their planting are harvested, they recoil and say, "We deplore this. We never meant such things to happen."

And there are always those who try to suggest that perhaps it was done "by the others," by those who want to bring discredit on organizations publicly preaching defiance of law and no surrender to the orders of the government of the United States.

There are always excuses for not doing what is right, for not obeying law and the processes of courts.

So, once again, as in the bombing of the Atlanta Temple—and of schools and churches in other cities—we have a harvest of things sown. It was but a few days ago an Atlanta Klan leader publicly advocated destroying schools.

*Leadership Tested*   Once again, Southern leadership is put to the test.

Here again we have the essence of the Greek tragedy. In the end the decent, civilized people will prevail. In the end there will be education for all children. Bombers prove nothing by bombing, or destroying a school or church. God still lives. Learning remains.

The tragedy is that even though the end of the play is known, there must be needless suffering, violence and ugly lawlessness on the loose.

It isn't always easy to be an American. There are times when we must surrender our own personal wishes, emotions, and preferences for the common good. We have had waves of prejudice move across our country at different periods in its history. They have all broken against the common sense and decency of the American who knows that his country must offer the same great asset to all of its citizens—freedom, liberty, dignity and opportunity. This must be within the reach of all citizens.

The childish drawings of Christmas—of Peace on Earth to Men of Good Will—on the floors of the bombed classrooms have a message for all whose hearts are not ruled by darkness and evil.

# " 'My Old Mule Is Gone' "

On a small farm outside Clinton, N. C., the body of Matt Augustus Usher was recovered from a barn-lot pond near his weather-beaten house. On a deeply worn path from house to pond neighbors found a scrawled pencil note: "My old mule is gone," it said, "I am drowned in this pond." The rest is silence.

Two days before, Matt Usher's old mule had died. For some 20 years they had made crops together. In the process they had shared the experience of growing old.

There had been a communion between them—as there always has been between those who have borne burdens and shared the secret sorrows of life. Mules and small Southern farmers have been closer partners than man and horse or man and dog. For the small farmer the mule was his one indispensable possession.

The wife and children knew that without the mule there would be no furrows plowed, no seed drilled, no wood and water hauled, no cotton taken to the gin, no way to get to the general store. And they knew that on Sundays there would be no church but for the mule hitched to the buggy or, more often, to the wagon in which the straight kitchen chairs had been placed. This was luxury. The family could ride along the lazy serenity of the dirt roads, with an umbrella raised if the sun was hot, and attend church miles away.

*Social Link*   The mule was the social link. Without him there could be no visiting on Sundays or the winter days when the crops were laid by. On a small Southern farm the mule was the center of life.

Matt Usher had only the mule. As others before him have done, he learned, in his loneliness, to talk to the mule as they worked together through the long days of plowing, of cultivating, of harvesting. And there was always communion, even though the mule was silent.

There is something of a mystery about the mule. He is a hybrid, "Without pride in ancestry or hope of posterity," but he has sense like a man. The horse is a silly fool which will run back into a burning barn because it is a symbol of safety. A mule will break down a door to get out.

A horse will work until he breaks down. A mule has sense enough to stop when he is tired and refuse to budge until he feels like it. And those whose daily lives have been shared with a mule know that the mule listens and understands. And though the city dwellers will scoff, such men get back an answer from the mule.

So it was in bygone days, before the boll weevil and the machines came, that men sang and talked to their mules in the fields and there were companionship and mutual trust between them.

*Machines Came*  The machines came . . . the wondrous, miraculous machines. And the mules began to go. Even on the rich Mississippi Delta, with its legends of mules and men and cotton, one began to see the grain elevators on the flat horizon. And here and there were corrals of old mules, with the scars of harness on them, sold to the dog food factories and waiting for death. The machines took over. (We don't know yet whether we shape the machines or they shape us.)

But the little man—the one-gallus farmer, he and his mule held on. They had to. There was nothing else to do. It was a struggle. The economists put their pencils to paper and came up with the conclusion that the mule was obsolete as a unit of energy.

But here and there they hung on—the mules and the obscure Matt Ushers of agriculture in transition. Defeated, lonely, with nothing much ahead of them, they toiled on together.

So when the old mule died, Matt Usher, in his loneliness, thought it over. And having done so he wrote a note, weighted it down with a rock on the path, and walked down to the pond where he so often had taken the mule to drink.

"My old mule is gone, I am drowned in this pond."

# Martin Luther King, Jr.

## "The American Dream"

*Dr. King gave the commencement address at Lincoln University in Pennsylvania on 6 June 1961. This is a transcription of that address.*

Today you bid farewell to the friendly security of this academic environment, a setting that will remain dear to you as long as the cords of memory shall lengthen. As you go out today to enter the clamorous highways of life, I should like to discuss with you some aspects of the American dream. For in a real sense, America is essentially a dream, a dream as yet unfulfilled. It is a dream of a land where men of all races, of all nationalities and of all creeds can live together as brothers. The substance of the dream is expressed in these sublime words, words lifted to cosmic proportions: "We hold these truths to be self-evident, that all men are created equal, that they are endowed by their Creator with certain unalienable rights, that among these are life, liberty, and the pursuit of happiness." This is the dream.

One of the first things we notice in this dream is an amazing universalism. It does not say some men, but it says all men. It does not say all white men, but it says all men, which includes black men. It does not say all Gentiles, but it says all men, which includes Jews. It does not say all Protestants, but it says all men, which includes Catholics.

And there is another thing we see in this dream that ultimately distinguishes democracy and our form of government from all of the totalitarian regimes that emerge in history. It says that each individual has certain basic rights that are neither conferred by nor derived from the state. To discover where they came from it is necessary to move back behind the dim mist of eternity, for they are God-given. Very seldom if ever in the history of the world has a sociopolitical document expressed in such profoundly eloquent and unequivocal language the dignity and the worth of human personality. The American dream reminds us that every man is heir to the legacy of worthiness.

Ever since the Founding Fathers of our nation dreamed this noble dream, America has been something of a schizophrenic personality, tragically divided against herself. On the one hand we have proudly professed the principles of democracy, and on the other hand we have sadly practiced the very antithesis of those principles. Indeed slavery and segregation have been strange paradoxes in a nation founded on the principle that all men are created equal. This is what the Swedish sociologist, Gunnar Myrdal, referred to as the American dilemma.

But the shape of the world today does not permit us the luxury of an anemic democracy. The price America must pay for the continued exploitation of the Negro and other minority groups is the price of its own destruction. The hour is late; the clock of destiny is ticking out. It is trite, but urgently true, that if America is to remain a first-class nation she can no longer have second-class citizens. Now, more than ever before, America is challenged to bring her noble dream into reality, and those who are working to implement the American dream are the true saviors of democracy.

Now may I suggest some of the things we must do if we are to make the American dream a reality. First I think all of us must develop a world perspective if we are to survive. The American dream will not become a reality devoid of the larger dream of a world of brotherhood and peace and good will. The world in which we live is a world of geographical oneness and we are challenged now to make it spiritually one.

Man's scientific genius and technological ingenuity has dwarfed distance and placed time in chains. Jet planes have compressed into minutes distances that once took days and months to cover. It is not common for a preacher to be quoting Bob Hope, but I think he has aptly described this jet age in which we live. If, on taking off on a nonstop flight from Los Angeles to New York City, you develop hiccups, he said, you will hic in Los Angeles and cup in New York City. That is really *moving*. If you take a flight from Tokyo, Japan, on Sunday morning, you will arrive in Seattle, Washington, on the preceding Saturday night. When your friends meet you at the airport and ask you when you left Tokyo, you will have to say, "I left tomorrow." This is the kind of world in which we live. Now this is a bit humorous but I am trying to laugh a basic fact into all of us: the world in which we live has become a single neighborhood.

Through our scientific genius we have made of this world a neighborhood; now through our moral and spiritual development we must make of it a brotherhood. In a real sense, we must all learn to live together as brothers, or we will all perish together as fools. We must come to see that no individual can live alone; no nation can live alone. We must all live together; we must all be concerned about each other.

Some months ago, Mrs. King and I journeyed to that great country in the Far East known as India. I will never forget the experiences that came to us as we moved around that great country, or the opportunity of meeting and talking with the great leaders of India and with people all over in the cities and the villages throughout India. Certainly this was an experience that I will always remember, but there were depressing moments. How can one avoid being depressed when he sees with his own eyes millions of people going to bed hungry at night? How can one avoid being depressed when he sees with his own eyes millions of people sleeping on the sidewalk at night?

In Calcutta alone, more than a million people sleep on the sidewalks every night; in Bombay, more than six hundred thousand people sleep on the sidewalks every night. They have no beds to sleep in; they have no houses to go into. How can one avoid being depressed when he discovers that of India's four hundred million people, more than 365 million make an annual income of less than sixty dollars a year? Most of these people have never seen a doctor or a dentist.

As I looked at these conditions, I found myself saying that we in America cannot stand idly by and not be concerned. Then something within me cried out, "Oh, no, because the destiny of the United States is tied up with the destiny of India—with the destiny of every other nation." And I remembered that we spend more than a million dollars a day to store surplus food in this country. I said to myself, "I know where we can store that food free of charge—in the wrinkled stomachs of the millions of people who go to bed hungry at night." Maybe we spend too much of our national budget building military bases around the world, rather than bases of genuine concern and understanding.

All this is simply to say that all life is interrelated. We are caught in an inescapable network of mutuality; tied in a single garment of destiny. Whatever affects one directly, affects all indirectly. As long as there is poverty in this world, no man can be totally rich even if he has a billion dollars. As long as diseases are rampant and millions of people cannot expect to live more than twenty or thirty years, no man can be totally healthy, even if he just got a clean bill of health from the finest clinic in America. Strangely enough, I can never be what I ought to be until you are what you ought to be. You can never be what you ought to be until I am what I ought to be. This is the way the world is made. I didn't make it that way, but this is the interrelated structure of reality. John Donne caught it a few centuries ago and could cry out, "No man is an island entire of itself; every man is a piece of the continent, a part of the main . . . any man's death diminishes me, because I am involved in mankind, and therefore never send to know for whom the bell tolls; it tolls for thee." If we are to realize the American dream we must cultivate this world perspective.

There is another thing quite closely related to this. We must keep our moral and spiritual progress abreast with our scientific and technological advances. This poses another dilemma of modern man. We have allowed our civilization to outdistance our culture. Professor MacIver follows the German sociologist Alfred Weber in pointing out the distinction between culture and civilization. Civilization refers to what we use; culture refers to what we are. Civilization is that complex of devices, instrumentalities, mechanisms and techniques by means of which we live. Culture is that realm of ends expressed in art, literature, religion and morals for which at best we live.

The great problem confronting us today is that we have allowed the means by which we live to outdistance the ends for which we live. We have allowed our civilization to outrun our culture, and so we are in danger now of ending up with guided missiles in the hands of misguided men. This is what the poet Thoreau meant when he said, "Improved means to an unimproved end." If we are to survive today and realize the dream of our mission and the dream of the world, we must bridge the gulf and somehow keep the means by which we live abreast with the ends for which we live.

Another thing we must do is to get rid of the notion once and for all that there are superior and inferior races. Now we know that this view still lags around in spite of the fact that many great anthropologists, Margaret Mead and Ruth Benedict and Melville Herskovits and others have pointed out and made it clear through scientific evidence that there are no superior races and there are no inferior races. There may be intellectually superior individuals within all races. In spite of all this evidence, however, the view still gets around somehow that there are superior and inferior races. The whole concept of white supremacy rests on this fallacy.

You know, there was a time when some people used to argue the inferiority of the Negro and the colored races generally on the basis of the Bible and religion. They would say the Negro was inferior by nature because of Noah's curse upon the children of Ham. And then another brother had probably read the logic of Aristotle. You know Aristotle brought into being the syllogism which had a major premise and a minor premise and a conclusion, and one brother had probably read Aristotle and he put his argument in the framework of an Aristotelian syllogism. He could say that all men are made in the image of God. This was a major premise. Then came his minor premise: God, as everybody knows, is not a Negro; therefore the Negro is not a man. And that was called logic!

But we don't often hear these arguments today. Segregation is now based on "sociological and cultural" grounds. "The Negro is not culturally ready for integration, and if integration comes into being it will pull the white race back a generation. It will take fifty or seventy-five years to raise these standards." And then we hear that the Negro is a criminal, and there are those who would almost say he is a criminal by nature. But they never point out that these things are environmental and not racial; these problems are problems of urban dislocation. They fail to see that poverty, and disease, and ignorance breed crime whatever the racial group may be. And it is a tortuous logic that views the tragic results of segregation and discrimination as an argument for the continuation of it.

If we are to implement the American dream we must get rid of the notion once and for all that there are superior and inferior races. This means that members of minority groups must make it clear that they can use their resources even under adverse circumstances. We must make full and constructive use of the freedom we already possess. We must not use our oppression as an excuse for mediocrity and laziness. For history has proven that inner determination can often break through the outer shackles of circumstance. Take the Jews, for example, and the years they have been forced to walk through the long and desolate night of oppression. This did not keep them from rising up to plunge against cloud-filled nights of oppression, new and blazing stars of inspiration. Being a Jew did not keep Einstein from using his genius-packed mind to prove his theory of relativity.

And so, being a Negro does not have to keep any individual from rising up to make a contribution as so many Negroes have done within our own lifetime. Human nature cannot be catalogued, and we need not wait until the day of full emancipation. So from an old clay cabin in Virginia's hills, Booker T. Washington rose up to be one of the nation's great leaders. He lit a torch in Alabama; then darkness fled.

From the red hills of Gordon County, Georgia, from an iron foundry at Chattanooga, Tennessee, from the arms of a mother who could neither read nor write, Roland Hayes rose up to be one of the nation's and the world's greatest singers. He carried his melodious voice to the mansion of the Queen Mother of Spain and the palace of King George V. From the poverty-stricken areas of Philadelphia, Pennsylvania, Marian Anderson rose up to be the world's greatest contralto, so that Toscanini could say that a voice like this comes only once in a century. Sibelius of Finland could say, "My roof is too low for such a voice."

From humble, crippling circumstances, George Washington Carver rose up and carved for himself an imperishable niche in the annals of science. There was a star in the sky of female leadership. Then came Mary McLeod Bethune to let it shine in her life. There was a star in the diplomatic sky. Then came Ralph Bunche, the grandson of a slave preacher, and allowed it to shine in his life with all of its radiant beauty. There were stars in the athletic sky. Then came Joe Louis with his educated fists, Jesse Owens with his fleet and dashing feet, Jackie Robinson with his powerful bat and calm spirit. All of these people have come to remind us that we need not wait until the day of full emancipation. They have justified the conviction of the poet that:

> Fleecy locks and dark complexion
> Cannot forfeit nature's claim.
> Skin may differ but affection
> Dwells in black and white the same.
> Were I so tall as to reach the pole
> Or to grasp the ocean at a span,
> I must be measured by my soul,
> The mind is standard of the man.

Finally, if we are to implement the American dream, we must continue to engage in creative protest in order to break down all of those barriers that make it impossible for the dream to be realized. Now I know there are those people who will argue that we must wait on something. They fail to see the necessity for creative protest, but I say to you that I can see no way to break loose from an old order and to move into a new order without standing up and resisting the unjust dogma of the old order.

To do this, we must get rid of two strange illusions that have been held by the so-called moderates in race relations. First is the myth of time advanced by those who say that you must wait on time; if you "just wait and be patient," time will work the situation out. They will say this even about freedom rides. They will say this about sit-ins: that you're pushing things too fast—cool off—time will work these problems out. Well, evolution may hold in the biological realm, and in that area Darwin was right. But when a Herbert Spencer seeks to apply "evolution" to the whole fabric of society, there is no truth in it. Even a superficial look at history shows that social progress never rolls in on the wheels of inevitability. It comes through the tireless effort and the persistent work of dedicated individuals. Without this hard work, time itself becomes an ally of the primitive forces of irrational emotionalism and social stagnation. And we must get rid of the myth of time.

There is another myth, that bases itself on a species of educational determinism. It leads one to think that you can't solve this problem through legislation; you can't solve this problem through judicial decree; you can't solve this problem through executive orders on the part of the president of the United States. It must be solved by education. Now I agree that education plays a great role, and it must continue to play a great role in changing attitudes, in getting people ready for the new order. And we must also see the importance of legislation.

It is not a question either of education or of legislation. Both legislation and education are required. Now, people will say, "You can't legislate morals." Well, that may be true. Even though morality may not be legislated, behavior can be regulated. And this is very important. We need religion and education to change attitudes and to change the hearts of men. We need legislation and federal action to control behavior. It may be true that the law can't make a man love me, but it can keep him from lynching me, and I think that's pretty important also.

And so we must get rid of these illusions and move on with determination and with zeal to break down the unjust systems we find in our society, so that it will be possible to realize the American dream. As I have said so often, if we seek to break down discrimination, we must use the proper methods. I am convinced more than ever before that, as the powerful, creative way opens, men and women who are eager to break the barriers of oppression and of segregation and discrimination need not fall down to the levels of violence. They need not sink into the quicksands of hatred. Standing on the high ground of noninjury, love and soul force, they can turn this nation upside down and right side up.

I believe, more than ever before, in the power of nonviolent resistance. It has a moral aspect tied to it. It makes it possible for the individual to secure moral ends through moral means. This has been one of the great debates of history. People have felt that it is impossible to achieve moral ends through moral means. And so a Machiavelli could come into being and so force a sort of duality within the moral structure of the universe. Even communism could come into being and say that anything justifies the end of a classless society—lying, deceit, hate, violence—anything. And this is where nonviolent resistance breaks with communism and with all of those systems which argue that the end justifies the means, because we realize that the end is preexistent in the means. In the long run of history, destructive means cannot bring about constructive ends.

The practical aspect of nonviolent resistance is that it exposes the moral defenses of the opponent. Not only that, it somehow arouses his conscience at the same time, and it breaks down his morale. He has no answer for it. If he puts you in jail, that's all right; if he lets you out, that's all right too. If he beats you, you accept that; if he doesn't beat you—fine. And so you go on, leaving him with no answer. But if you use violence, he does have an answer. He has the state militia; he has police brutality.

Nonviolent resistance is one of the most magnificent expressions going on today. We see it in the movement taking place among students in the South and their allies who have been willing to come in from the North and other sections. They have taken our deep groans and passionate yearnings, filtered them in their own souls, and fashioned them into the creative protest, which is an epic known all over our nation. They have moved in a uniquely meaningful orbit, imparting light and heat to a distant satellite. And people say, "Does this bring results?" Well, look at the record.

In less than a year, lunch counters have been integrated in more than 142 cities of the Deep South, and this was done without a single court suit; it was done without spending millions and millions of dollars. We think of the freedom rides, and remember that more than sixty people are now in jail in Jackson, Mississippi. What has this done? These people have been beaten; they have suffered to bring to the attention of this nation, the indignities and injustices Negro people still confront in interstate travel. It has, therefore, had an educational value. But not only that—signs have come down from bus stations in Montgomery, Alabama. They've never been down before. Not only that—the attorney general of this nation has called on ICC to issue new regulations making it positively clear that segregation in interstate travel is illegal and unconstitutional.

And so this method can bring results. Sometimes it can bring quick results. But even when it doesn't bring immediate results, it is constantly working on the conscience; it is at all times using moral means to bring about moral ends. And so I say we must continue on the way of creative protest. I believe also that this method will help us to enter the new age with the proper attitude.

As I have said in so many instances, it is not enough to struggle for the new society. We must make sure that we make the psychological adjustment required to live in that new society. This is true of white people, and it is true of Negro people. Psychological adjustment will save white people from going into the new age with old vestiges of prejudice and attitudes of white supremacy. It will save the Negro from seeking to subsitute one tyranny for another.

I know sometimes we get discouraged and sometimes disappointed with the slow pace of things. At times we begin to talk about racial separation instead of racial integration, feeling that there is no other way out. My only answer is that the problem never will be solved by substituting one tyranny for another. Black supremacy is as dangerous as white supremacy, and God is not interested merely in the freedom of black men and brown men and yellow men. God is interested in the freedom of the whole human race and in the creation of a society where all men can live together as brothers, where every man will respect the dignity and the worth of human personality.

By following this method, we may also be able to teach our world something that it so desperately needs at this hour. In a day when Sputniks and Explorers are dashing through outer space, and guided ballistic missiles are carving highways of death through the stratosphere, no nation can win a war. The choice is no longer between violence and nonviolence; it is either nonviolence or nonexistence. Unless we find some alternative to war, we will destroy ourselves by the misuse of our own instruments. And so, with all of these attitudes and principles working together, I believe we will be able to make a contribution as men of good will to the ongoing structure of our society and toward the realization of the American dream. And so, as you go out today, I call upon you not to be detached spectators, but involved participants, in this great drama that is taking place in our nation and around the world.

Every academic discipline has its technical nomenclature, and modern psychology has a word that is used, probably, more than any other. It is the word *maladjusted*. This word is the ringing cry of modern child psychology. Certainly all of us want to live a well-adjusted life in order to avoid the neurotic personality. But I say to you, there are certain things within our social order to which I am proud to be maladjusted and to which I call upon all men of good will to be maladjusted.

If you will allow the preacher in me to come out now, let me say to you that I never did intend to adjust to the evils of segregation and discrimination. I never did intend to adjust myself to religious bigotry. I never did intend to adjust myself to economic conditions that will take necessities from the many to give luxuries to the few. I never did intend to adjust myself to the madness of militarism, and the self-defeating effects of physical violence. And I call upon all men of good will to be maladjusted because it may well be that the salvation of our world lies in the hands of the maladjusted.

So let us be maladjusted, as maladjusted as the prophet Amos, who in the midst of the injustices of his day could cry out in words that echo across the centuries, "Let justice run down like waters and righteousness like a mighty stream." Let us be as maladjusted as Abraham Lincoln, who had the vision to see that this nation could not exist half slave and half free. Let us be maladjusted as Jesus of Nazareth, who could look into the eyes of the men and women of his generation and cry out, "Love your enemies. Bless them that curse you. Pray for them that despitefully use you."

I believe that it is through such maladjustment that we will be able to emerge from the bleak and desolate midnight of man's inhumanity to man into the bright and glittering daybreak of freedom and justice. That will be the day when all of God's children, black men and white men, Jews and Gentiles, Catholics and Protestants, will be able to join hands and sing in the words of the old Negro spiritual, "Free at last! Free at last! Thank God almighty, we are free at last!"

# Donald Windham

## From *Emblems of Conduct*

### "Gentian"

Between the back porch and the chicken yard of Aunt Winnie's house in Gentian, there stood a chinaberry tree. I do not think that I played under it more than elsewhere. But when my brother and I returned from our visit each summer, it was about this chinaberry tree that I thought, more than about Aunt Winnie and Uncle Emmett and the events of the summer. In Mother's family I had experienced many aunts and uncles. And events happened all the time. But this was the first chinaberry tree that I had seen. For me, the small pointed leaves and the green cherry-shaped berries existed only on that one plant, or beneath it on the blackened wood of the boards on two sawhorses that formed a workbench, and on the tarpaper roof of the brooding house, through whose dusty glass windows I could peer and see the baby chickens swarming in the electric brooder inside. A fig tree grew up through the chicken-yard fence a little farther on. The figs were ripe during our visits. I ate them, and it would have been reasonable if I had remembered the fig tree best, or the pecan trees in the front yard. Nevertheless, I forgot these. We had a fig tree at home, and I had often eaten pecans. But the chinaberry tree and its fruit, eaten by neither animals nor men, remained in my mind. And in the middle of winter when I remembered the summer, I would picture the lean branches and the hard green berries, some of which shrivelled and dried up on the tree, others of which dropped to the ground and lay there, ignored even by the birds, until the flesh over their large seeds grew brown and soft like rotten apples, and almost as unpleasant to step on if you were barefooted as were the droppings in the chicken yard.

Aunt Winnie's house, covered in dark shingles and with a large evergreen camphor bush at either end of the front porch, was like a house in a suburb. And despite the fact that all the surrounding country was farm country, the life lived in the house was not farm life. Uncle Emmett went each morning into Columbus, where he worked as superintendent of a textile mill. My three cousins, all older than my brother and I, each went to college and took jobs away from home. But everything about the house tended by my aunt—the sword ferns and geraniums, the maidenhair ferns and forget-me-nots, lining the front porch in lard cans and flowerpots and boxes, and the animals and chickens in the back yard— was as luxuriously rural as those on the surrounding farms.

The food was rural, too, especially in its abundance, and during the last week of our visit, when Mother always came down from Atlanta to join us, every meal was like Sunday dinner. We ate fried chicken twice a day, for dinner and supper, and Aunt Winnie, who raised broilers and fryers, gave me my favorite piece, the brain, which I had learned to like from my Donaldson grandmother but no longer got in the city, where store-bought chickens were headless. Aunt Winnie cooked it the way my grandmother had cooked it—inside the skull—and I cracked the skull the way my grandmother had taught me, by rapping it on the edge of my plate. It broke open, like an English walnut, and the brain, about the size of a large nut meat, came out. Or if it did not, I sucked it out, and although I particularly liked the taste, I am not sure that it was not the complication of getting to it that delighted me most.

The way the evenings were passed was rural, too. Even after Mother came down, there was no entertaining or visiting at Aunt Winnie's. After supper, we sat out beneath one of the two pecan trees in the front yard and watched the sky—so much more brilliant than it ever was in the city—for late-summer showers of falling stars. Uncle Emmett pointed out the Big and Little Dippers, and Venus and Mars, as he smoked his cigar and blew heavy clouds of smoke around us to keep away the mosquitoes. If this did not work, Aunt Winnie burned a bit of rag soaked in kerosene, and the odors of cigar smoke and burning flannel competed as we sat in the dark, talking, listening to the crickets, and watching the sky. Sometimes the conversation touched on my father. We had no contact with any other member of his family except Aunt Winnie, and perhaps it was odd that we were so close to her. But she had been close to my father when they were children, and she was particularly fond of my brother, in whom she saw a strong resemblance to him. My father had disappeared from her life as well as from ours. It was only very occasionally that she had word of him. Silences, more than news, expressed the bond between us; and even when he was mentioned, the conversation usually slipped on to other subjects long before the mosquitoes drove us inside to watch Uncle Emmett twist the dials of his short-wave radio, on which he sometimes picked up broadcasts from England, France, or Germany, or to go upstairs to the big, screened sleeping porch and to bed.

Each day, I spent a good deal of time rolling an automobile tire, either with my brother or by myself. I liked wandering about the yard and the surrounding fields. I was never lonely when I was by myself, only when I was around people of whose affection I was unsure, and in the country rolling an automobile tire had the happy advantage of carrying me alone all through the yard and the surrounding hot, dusty, weed-choked landscape. Each day, I started out from the back yard, where the tire usually lay in the place I had left it the evening before, somewhere beyond the well and near a shed that was full of rusted motor cases and other discarded parts of old automobiles. First I rolled the tire along the smooth earth of the driveway, which left the road and went around the house and came back to the road, making a horseshoe. In my imagination the tire was a vehicle, and when I had driven it to all parts of the yard I would make a long-distance trip, between the rows of the plowed field of cornstalks on the other side of the dirt road, or through the plum orchard and up past the house of an old lady who had been my father's and Aunt Winnie's schoolteacher when they were children, and down the slope on the far side of her house to the creek. With my brother and the youngest of my three cousins I sometimes went swimming there, but it never occurred to me to go swimming alone, and when I reached that far by myself I rolled the tire back to the house and played in the yard or beneath the chinaberry tree.

It was the chinaberry tree, the yard, and the tire that I thought about, but none of these was the important thing in my summers; it was Aunt Winnie. Never having known my father or any other member of his family except her well enough to guess what they were like, I had only her to turn to for traits resembling my own which might have been his or theirs. Aunt Winnie was unique, the way the chinaberry tree seemed to be. But it was through the yard around the chinaberry tree, particularly the chicken yard, that I made contact with her, and even there my interest, I would have said, was not in her but in the eggs. My passion for gathering them was as great as that for rolling the automobile tire, and not even the unpleasantness of the chicken droppings squishing up between my toes was sufficient deterrent against the joy of looking into nests and finding eggs, oval and perfect, lying in the midst of their straw-lined emptiness. I was afraid of the chickens—as I was of cows and horses—and I would not put my hands into the nests that had hens on them, as Aunt Winnie did, and take the eggs out from beneath the hen. But my pleasure in the search overcame my fear. Of all the other entertainments I knew, I enjoyed most the magic shows I was taken to at the Sunday school building of All Saints' Church in Atlanta, and I longed to be a magician. But looking into each of the crates nailed on the back and side walls of the three-room chicken house and finding the previously empty nests with eggs in them was far more absorbing to me than watching a magician pull a rabbit out of a top hat. My disappointment when a nest was empty, or my joy when it contained eggs, was as close as I came to facing the mystery of my dependence on a world beyond my influence or understanding, and today when I look into the mailbox and find that it is empty or that it contains a longed-for letter, the emotions I feel are echoes of the ones I felt then.

Before I went into the chicken yard, Aunt Winnie gave me a large earthenware mixing bowl to gather the eggs in, and when I had been through the chicken house and looked for hidden nests in the grass around the edge of the yard, I took the eggs back to her in the kitchen. She sold eggs as well as fryers and broilers, and if she was ready to make a delivery when I came in from the chicken yard, I sometimes rode with her in her old car. Uncle Emmett bought a new automobile every few years, switching from make to make and endlessly debating their various merits. But Aunt Winnie never abandoned her old square Essex. Day after day, summer after summer, she drove it carefully to the end of the driveway, came to a full stop, looked in both directions, then turned into the dirt road and down to the highway, where she turned once again and drove into town, straddling the white line down the center of the pavement at a steady fifteen miles an hour. Her speed never varied. She only allowed other cars to pass, swerving over to the side of the road at the same steady pace, after they had honked several times, and as they passed she did not glance in their direction but looked straight ahead, her flower-blue eyes as clear as a sailor's, her weathered face as determined, and her thin lips, incurved over her false teeth, as impassive.

This quiet, independent pursuit of her own way was her most characteristic trait, and even her most happy and outgoing expressions were shaded by reserve. When she kissed my mother, my brother, and me on our arrival, she did it as shyly and quickly as a young girl, and that was the last time she kissed us until just before we left. Her reserve and independence were present, too, in the midst of the bounty of the meals she cooked. After having loaded the table with platters of fried chicken and hot biscuits and vegetables from the garden, she liked to serve us and not set a place for herself. When Mother was present this withdrawal in spirit caused too much protest, so she sat down like everyone else, but to a plate on which she took only a single biscuit or piece of corn bread, a wing or a back, and a spoonful of black-eyed peas or beans. Mother accepted Aunt Winnie's explanation that she tasted things in the kitchen and was not hungry; it was a commonplace that cooking spoils the appetite. But even then I felt that this was not the whole reason, and I recognized—with my emotions if not with my thoughts—that turning aside of the will which, finding insufficient outlet, or not the outlet it wants, is forced to exert itself at last in renunciation, especially in a renunciation of what it has itself prepared, and a renunciation no one else can protest or rightfully take offense at.

Her blue eyes and her girl-like kisses were the only clues I had to my aunt's youth. The facts I learned about her and my father's childhood were as sparse and as bare as the south Georgia country was in those years. I was told, when I asked about Aunt Winnie's name, that my grandfather, who was a cabinetmaker and furniture finisher, had been working at the Winnie Joe Willingham Lumber Company in Tennessee when she was born and had named her after it. And I knew that as children they had lived first in Columbus, where my grandfather had owned a house, and that later the whole family had moved to the country. During the years I visited Gentian, my grandfather was still alive— a poor man, and living in Columbus—but he had married again after my grandmother's death, a woman with five children, and Aunt Winnie, who disapproved of the marriage, did not speak to him. I never saw him during our visits, and her disapproving character hid most of the rest of the past of the family as well. She and my father had graduated from St. Elmo Academy, although the other four children in the family had gone to the public schools in Columbus, and there was a photograph in Aunt Winnie's bedroom of her taken at her graduation or on her wedding day soon afterward. But I knew nothing of how the flowerlike schoolgirl I saw in the picture had grown into the quiet and weathered country-woman I visited, and nothing of what her hopes and disappointments had been, but only the energy they had given her.

Uncle Emmett was far more expansive and easy-going, and plump and talkative. In my experience, their marriage was a happy one. Their house was pleasant to visit in, which often was not true of the houses of my uncles and aunts on Mother's side of the family. Still, because I stayed with Aunt Winnie and Uncle Emmett for such long periods of time, I saw some of the friction that is inevitable between people who have lived together and shared each other's existences for twenty years, and there were occasions when I glimpsed beneath the surface of Aunt Winnie's character. One night, after she and Uncle Emmett had crossed each other about something, I saw her withdraw physically as well as spiritually, walk out of the house, no one knew where, perhaps into the chicken yard or the cow pasture or one of the gardens—somewhere, I believe, where she could see and hear what was going on, but in any case somewhere

where she could not be found—and she did not appear again until the next morning, when she was moving about at her usual early hour in the kitchen. Her face was impassive, her work shielding her thoughts as she prepared breakfast for my uncle and my three cousins, my brother and me, the cats and dogs and chickens, then drew water from the well, brought in Mason jars from the garage, and scalded them so they were ready to fill from the big kettles on the stove, where she was already cooking the fig preserves, blackberry shrub, tomato chowchow, pickled peaches, or whatever it was she was preserving that morning. She did not put her thoughts into words. Work provided the outlet for her feelings. And on that occasion as on others, whatever more I saw of her sadness or her joy, beyond what was apparent in the weathered passivity of her face, I saw transformed into the food she prepared, the tablecloths she crocheted, the pot holders she sewed, the wall plaques she made from the tops of cigar boxes, the topiary roosters, baskets, and balls she clipped from the privet hedges in the flower garden. Some of these handicrafts were based on instructions in the pages of *Popular Mechanics* or *Farm & Fireside,* and many of them sold at the Muscogee County Fair, but all of them, even those which were wholly her own, seemed strangely impersonal in comparison with the intensity of her will, which I had glimpsed, and her likes and dislikes, her loyalties and withdrawals.

It is quite possible that Aunt Winnie cared less for all these things she made than she did for the furniture and the other store-bought possessions about the house that resembled those I knew at home but that were made unimpressive in my eyes by the very same country associations that added to the interest of the others—the strange odors of camphor in the bedrooms, of hard-water soap at the faucet on the back porch, and of the outhouse as you approached it through the weeds at the end of the yard. It did not occur to me that she might care most of all for the money her work brought her and for the independence of using it to make her home, and her and her children's lives, into something more like the city life I knew. But wherever the importance lay, she labored over her work with persistent and solitary devotion, and it is impossible not to imagine her feelings the day she was home alone and the house caught fire. Sparks falling from the chimney ignited the roof; in no time at all, the building was a roaring inferno. The only things that she and the neighbors who came to her aid were able to save were a few blistered pieces of furniture from the living room and dining room. The house burned to the ground with everything else in it. In a matter of hours, she was not only homeless but bereft of the slowly accumulated results of her life work, and faced with the equally hard alternatives of a despair as great as her loss and a courage strong enough to go on.

My brother and I did not make our visit that year. But the next summer, when we came down, Aunt Winnie and Uncle Emmett and their son (both their daughters were married by then) were living on the second floor of the double, corrugated-tin garage that Uncle Emmett had built opposite the chinaberry tree. The weight of the sun that summer lay upon the tin building and the yard and the surrounding Chattahoochee riverbed country like the weight of homelessness itself. Each day, the heat fell unbroken over the burned foundation and over the bare driveway and the yard full of wooden frames in which Uncle Emmett and a helper were making white cement bricks. It was too hot to roll an automobile tire, too hot to do anything but go for a swim in the creek, and we went there with our cousin in the afternoons. But in the early mornings, when we got up to join Uncle Emmett in the yard and watch him supervise the pouring of the bricks before he went to the mill, Aunt Winnie was already up and working, having by then calmly accepted what had happened as the continuation of what she knew life to be, and she was still at her tasks when we joined Uncle Emmett again in the evenings, after he came home from work, and helped to empty the white bricks from the frames and add them to the piles stacked at the side of the levelled and cleared foundation.

The new, flat-roofed house was visible from the highway as my brother and I arrived the following summer, driven down by one of Mother's sisters and her husband. At a distance, it possessed an institutional, prison-like look. And after we had turned up the dirt road to the house and parked the car beneath the chinaberry tree in the back yard and gone inside, our highway impression was corroborated. No part of the house was made of a material that would burn. The floors were of poured concrete, the door and window frames of metal. There were bathrooms and running water, and there was a screened porch opening off the driveway porte-cochere, as there had been in the old house. But there was none of the small, shaded, and gardenlike quality I remembered. There was no sleeping porch, either, and the kitchen no longer seemed, as it once had, a more wonderful part of the back yard. All resemblance to the house on whose foundation it was built was missing, just as sometimes in a woman all resemblance to the girl she was will be lost. But if Aunt Winnie regretted the change she did not say so. She had flowers blooming again in boxes and cans on the porch. And she was busy making new tablecloths, new aprons, and new pot holders, and selling more chickens, more eggs, and more butter than ever before.

Aunt Winnie's predilections were no more concealed than her dislikes. I was fully aware that she preferred my brother to me. This did not make me jealous; but the summer that I was eleven, and we were visiting Aunt Winnie in the old shingle house, which was still standing then, his affection for me was already beginning to be much less than mine for him. And I could not yet bear to be excluded. It did not hurt me that Aunt Winnie took his side one day when we had a fight; I was accustomed, when I had a need for intimacy, to turn to her oldest daughter, Vivian. But that day, when I sought out Vivian, I found her cross with me, too. The comfort I wanted was to be told that I deserved to be loved by my brother and that he was wrong not to love me. And when I was dissatisfied with what she offered instead—permission to paint with the poster colors she used at the school where she was a teacher—she lost her temper. With her classroom sharpness, she told me that I was very bad, and that if I could not behave the way my brother did and be the kind of boy he was, I could not expect him or anyone else to like me.

I do not think she imagined the effect her words would have. I shouted that I did not want her or anyone else to like me, and ran down the steps and out of the house. On the porch, where she caught up with me and tried to stop me, I grabbed a flowerpot and would have thrown it at her if it had not been too heavy. Uncle Emmett, who had been reading the Sunday paper on the side screen porch, came to see what was wrong. I broke loose and ran down the steps, past the pecan trees and across the driveway to the road. Uncle Emmett started after me. He was not angry. He did not know what the upset was about. But he was not used to running, and by the time we reached the top of the hill and passed the house where my father's and Aunt Winnie's old schoolteacher lived, he was out of breath. He lost his temper and his wind at the same time. Stopping in the middle of the road, he shouted for me to come back. But his change of mood was clear in his tone, and I ran even faster, gaining for once that speed I longed for in dreams when I was trying to escape from some terror just behind me. When I reached the bottom of the hill, my uncle was out of sight. He called once more for me to come back. Then he was out of hearing.

No destination was in my mind when I ran across the yard or I would have turned in the direction of the Warm Springs highway at the foot of the hill. But as I slowed down, panting to catch my breath, I remembered that the road I was on joined the Hamilton highway two miles farther on. When I reached there, I decided, I would turn in the direction of Atlanta. There were always automobiles on the highway on Sunday going from city to city, and the idea of having to stop one and ask for a ride the hundred miles to home was less unpleasant than the idea of going back.

I had run away once before. That, too, had been when Mother was not present. She was out of the house for the afternoon, and the trouble was my familiar one with my brother. About five o'clock he came down to the back of the yard where I was playing and told me to come inside. I did not obey at once and he grabbed me and tried to drag me. When he did not succeed he said that it did not matter: I would have to come in sooner or later, and when I did I would get a beating. I believed most things my brother said, but one thing was not true: I did not have to go back inside if I did not want to. Reluctantly, I made my way down the bank at the back of the yard to Crescent Avenue, and along it to Fourteenth Street. On Fourteenth, I walked out of the neighborhood I knew, past the vacant lot and the Bar-B-Que drive-in at Spring Street, out of the residential district and through the fields and farms and packing houses along Howell Mill Road. I went several miles into the country before my courage failed. It was long after dark when I returned home. But even then it was not from fear that I turned back so much as it was from my discovery that, away from home, there was no place to go.

There was a place to go from Gentian, however. As I walked I thought of that earlier night when I had reached the house, after my suppertime, after my bedtime, even, and Mother had been so relieved and glad to see me that she had not whipped me, but had wept and kissed me and given me something to eat at the large, round, empty dining-room table, already cleared for the night, before she put me to bed.

I was nearly two miles from the house and almost to the Hamilton highway when I heard Aunt Winnie's Essex coming up the middle of the dirt road behind me at its slow, inevitable speed. When she was beside me she stopped, leaving the motor running, and reached across and opened the door. She was alone in the car. Her face was as calm and gentle as ever, her voice as matter-of-fact.

"Get in," she said.

"No."

"You aren't mad with me, are you?"

"No."

"Then get in. I'm going to Miz David's to deliver some eggs and you can ride with me."

I got in. Aunt Winnie started the car.

"You mustn't pay any attention to Vivi," she said. "She's got a temper like her daddy."

She did not ask me what had happened. She knew; or, at least, she knew how to treat someone who felt as I felt.

"I bet I've forgot the butter," she said. "Look on the back seat in the bowl and see if it's there."

I looked. The butter was in the bowl, wrapped in white paper, balanced on top of the eggs.

"You know that your Aunt Winnie loves you, don't you?" she asked me.

"Yes."

"That's good. But do you know what I've done? I've forgotten the milk. People like that Vivi get you so flustered you don't know what you're doing. But you just have to pay them no mind if they hurt your feelings, and go on about your business."

We returned home the long way around, and just before we got to the house, Aunt Winnie stopped at the store at the bottom of the hill, between the Warm Springs highway and the railroad tracks, and bought us each a Nehi soda. From where we stopped we could see Aunt Winnie's house and the "railway station"—a bench at the side of the tracks with a roof over it and the name of the stop on top of the roof. Between swallows of her soda, Aunt Winnie told me how Gentian had got its name. It had been a long time ago, even before my grandfather had moved nearby. There were no houses and no store, and when the Southern Railway line was built through, the workmen named this obscure stop for the blue flowers they could see growing wild all about them in the woods. The blue flowers had been everywhere, she said, but they were gone now. Driving back to the house, I could see none—only the chinaberry tree.

# Erskine Caldwell

## From *Deep South: Memory and Observation*

### ONE

Being a minister's son in the Deep South in the early years of the twentieth century and growing up in a predominantly religious environment was my good fortune in life.

The experience of living for six months or a year or sometimes longer in one Southern state after another, in cities and small towns and countrysides, and being exposed to numerous varieties of Protestant sects which were Calvinist in doctrine and fundamentalist in practice proved to be of more value to me than the intermittent and frequently-curtailed secular education I received during the first seventeen years of my life.

This fortunate destiny of birth and circumstance could otherwise have been tragic and unrewarding if both my mother and my father had not been wise and tolerant and, consequently, made it possible for me to seek an understanding of life beyond the confines prescribed by prevailing religious beliefs and prejudiced attitudes of mind.

My father was the Reverend Ira Sylvester Caldwell, a North Carolinian, an Associate Reformed Presbyterian ordained minister, a veteran of the Spanish–American War, and a graduate of Erskine College, Erskine Theological Seminary, and the University of Georgia. My mother, Caroline Bell Caldwell, was a Virginian, a teacher, and a graduate of Mary Baldwin College and the University of Georgia. I had neither a brother nor a sister.

Until I was twelve years old, I called my father Bud and my mother was Tarrie. My name for my mother had been derived at an early age from Carrie, which I had been constantly hearing as a diminutive of Caroline. Likewise, by that time, Bud had come to sound to me as befitting and authentic as my own name. Neither parent at any time had ever asked or demanded of me that I call them by names other than Bud and Tarrie.

Aside from the customary formal title of Reverend, my father was known to many of his acquaintances as Ira. In the informal atmosphere of barbershops and on fishing trips with friends it was not unusual for him to be called Preacher.

However, my father's brothers and sisters and other relatives always called him Bud, probably because he was the elder of his parents' six children. Feeling just as closely related to him as anyone else, it had always seemed to me the natural thing to call him Bud, too.

As it happened, though, on my twelfth birthday one of my aunts said it was shocking and disrespectful for me to call my parents Bud and Tarrie, and I was coerced and bribed to promise never again to call them by those names. The bribe I received was a glossy blue bicycle with a bell on the handle-bar and a tyre pump clamped to the frame. I soon became accustomed to saying Mother or *Mère* instead of Tarrie but, while not forgetting the promise I had made, I was never able to think of my father actually having the name Father or *Père*.

There was never a discussion about what I was to call my father instead of Bud but, as if we had found a compromise and had entered into a secret agreement, thereafter when we were together and no other person was present, my name for him was either Ira Sylvester or I.S. We considered this to be a personal matter concerning us alone and therefore did not think of it as being a breach of promise. After all, even though my aunt may have assumed that I would call him by no name other than Father or *Père*, or perhaps Papa or Dad, the only promise I had made was never again to call him Bud.

My father never objected even in later years to my calling him either Ira Sylvester or I.S. and, when I saw him look at me with a blinking of his eyes and an unmistakable smile, it was as if my aunt had never offered to give me a bicycle. However, he undoubtedly realized that it was inevitable that a boy at my age who wanted a bicycle as much as I did would promise anything within reason in order to have one.

It was during this time that I began to be curious about what connection there was between my father and religion. Perhaps it was because he was darkly tall and muscular and always wore starched white shirts and a slightly-askew black bow necktie with his dark suits that he had the appearance of a dignified clergyman. Also, I knew he preached in churches and travelled frequently for religious purposes. However, I did not know why he was a minister and how it had happened that he became one.

When I asked him to tell me the reason for his entering the ministry instead of being a doctor or lawyer or storekeeper, he was evasive and had little to say, probably thinking I was not old enough then to understand a full explanation. The only thing Ira Sylvester would tell me was that he had studied for the ministry because his mother had asked him to do so.

It was not until many years later that I found out the reason why his mother had asked him to become a minister.

At the time I was twelve years old my knowledge of religion and the evidence of its emotional appeal was confined to what I had heard and seen within only the A.R.P. denomination. This was meagre knowledge for a minister's son in those years and, besides, although I had been christened in a religious ceremony at my birthplace in Coweta County in west Georgia, I had never had the experience of being baptized. And more than that, purposely or not, I had never been asked or ordered to attend Sunday-school. When I did go to Sunday-school, it was because my playmates attended and I wanted to be with them.

It was not surprising to me, since it was in keeping with the privilege of being permitted to learn about life as I lived it, that it was not my own father, but a Jewish storekeeper in Charlotte, North Carolina, who made me aware that religious faiths other than that of the A.R.P. existed in the world and that it was possible for human compassion to cross existing religious boundaries. The storekeeper's name was Mr. Goldstein and he owned a family clothing and shoe store on Trade Street in the business centre of Charlotte.

I was riding my bicycle along the street in the summer afternoon and looking for tin foil in discarded cigarette packs. I had already salvaged enough tin foil to make a ball about the size of a small cantaloup and hoped to get enough to be paid a quarter for it when I sold it to a junk dealer in an alley behind Tryon Street.

I stopped in front of Mr. Goldstein's clothing and shoe store to pick up a crumpled cigarette pack from the gutter and he came out to the kerb and asked me if I wanted a job delivering shoes for him. It was the first time I had ever been offered a job in the business world and I must have been too surprised to say anything. He put his hand on my shoulder and gripped it as if afraid I would leave and not take the job. Then again he asked me if I would work for him. He said he would pay me two dollars a week for working every afternoon except Saturday and Sunday.

The certainty of earning two dollars a week was much more appealing than the uncertainty of finding enough tin foil on the streets to earn twenty-five cents occasionally and I eagerly agreed to take the job. Mr. Goldstein took me into the store, handed me a box of shoes, and wrote the delivery address on a slip of paper. I pedalled my bicycle for what seemed like several miles and finally got to the address on Statesville Avenue near the city limits.

After delivering the shoes to the customer, I went back downtown, but it was already becoming dark and Mr. Goldstein had locked the door of his store and gone away. I was late for supper when I got home and I fully expected to be scolded and told that I could not keep my job. However, my parents said that since I had agreed to work by the week for Mr. Goldstein, I should keep my part of the agreement, and so I went back to the store the next afternoon promptly at one o'clock.

The following Friday afternoon, the end of my first week working for Mr. Goldstein, and pay-day, I was given two boxes of shoes to deliver at the same address and instructed to collect two dollars for one pair and to bring the other pair back to the store. Mr. Goldstein explained that the shoes were in two sizes for a boy about twelve years old and that the boy's mother would keep the pair that fitted best.

When I got to the address on South Boulevard where the shoes were to be delivered, I immediately recognized the small, unpainted, weather-greyed house that was in the same neighbourhood where I lived.

It was the home of two of my playmates and I had often gone there to play with them in the back yard. Their mother was a widow and she did sewing and ironing by the day whenever she could find work in the neighbourhood. The three of them lived in the two-room house with little furniture other than two beds, some chairs, and a large oilcloth-covered table in the rear room. The frail, dark-haired woman was a member of the A.R.P. church where my father was the temporary pastor and she attended services almost every Sunday morning. The two boys, however, had not been to Sunday-school for two months or longer.

While the older boy, whose name was Floyd, was in the house trying on the shoes, his brother Pete and I went to the back yard and played with the train and fire engine they kept in a shed they had built with sides of wooden packing-cases and pieces of tin roofing.

In a little while their mother called me to the rear porch and handed me two dollars and one of the boxes of shoes. Then she said that the larger pair fitted Floyd and that I would see him at the picnic the Sunday-school was having in a park the next afternoon. When I asked if Pete would be at the picnic, she said he would have to stay at home because she could buy only one pair of shoes and did not want him to go to the Sunday-school picnic barefooted.

I took the money and the box of shoes and started to get on my bicycle to go back to the store on Trade Street. It was then that I saw Floyd come to the porch wearing his new pair of shoes, and I looked around at Pete. All I could think of was that Mr. Goldstein would give me two dollars in pay when I got back to the store and that the smaller size of shoes would probably fit Pete because he was a year younger than his brother. I went to the porch and put the box of shoes on the steps and then I got on my bicycle and pedalled up South Boulevard as fast as I could.

When I got back to the store, I gave Mr. Goldstein the two dollars I had collected and then began trying to explain why I had not brought back the other pair of shoes as he had told me to do. Before he could say anything, I told him that I wanted him to keep the two dollars he had agreed to pay me and to use it to pay for the shoes I had left for Pete to wear to the Sunday-school picnic the next afternoon.

Mr. Goldstein sat down on a stool and said nothing for a long time. It was late in the afternoon then, and there were no customers in the store. Presently he looked up and beckoned to me with a motion of his head. When I came closer, he pointed for me to sit down on the counter near him.

First, he asked what church I attended, and then he asked what my father did for a living. After that he looked up at me and shook his head back and forth with a solemn expression on his face.

There was a long silence. Then Mr. Goldstein said he would never be able to understand as long as he lived how Christians and gentiles ever made a living in business and kept from going bankrupt. Turning around and looking up at me, he told me that Jewish people were just as kind-hearted and sentimental and human as Christians, but that Jews had learned long ago to earn money first and then give some of it away later for a good cause. He said that I ought to keep that in mind if I expected to make a living in business and keep out of bankruptcy courts when I grew up.

It was closing time for the store. Mr. Goldstein got up from the stool, talking aloud to himself, and began turning out the lights. I could not hear anything he was saying, but just before he was ready to lock the front door, he handed me a dollar. As he did that, he said he owed me two dollars for a week's salary and that I owed him two dollars for the shoes I had given away and that the only thing to do about it was for each of us to contribute a dollar for Pete's shoes.

When I went home and told my father what had happened, he said it proved that a man did not have to be a Presbyterian or a Baptist or a Methodist or anything else, in order to be blessed with the goodness of humanity. Then Ira Sylvester said he had needed a new pair of shoes for a long time and that he was going to Mr. Goldstein's store the first thing Monday morning and buy a pair.

I had to give up my job at Mr. Goldstein's store when we moved from Charlotte to Tampa, Florida, at the end of summer. It was in Tampa that

I became aware for the first time that some white Southern people refused to share religious services with persons whose colour of skin was darker than their own—and including my dark-skinned, black-haired father.

During those years, Ira Sylvester was secretary of the home mission board of the A.R.P. synod, and he frequently went to one of the churches that was in financial difficulty or where there was so much dissension among members of a congregation that the continued existence of that particular church was threatened. At a time like that, he was charged with the responsibility of attempting to readjust the condition that he considered to be the cause of trouble. There were times when he was successful in his efforts to unite two opposing factions and there were times when he was unable to persuade either side to agree to accept or even to discuss the suggestions he offered.

The Tampa church was in the Spanish-speaking neighbourhood of Ybor City where many Cubans lived and worked in the cigar factories. It was a recently-organized mission that had been established by a group of retired farmers and merchants from Mississippi, Alabama, and Georgia and it had a small congregation of less than fifty members at the time. As a means of making the church self-supporting, it was my father's plan to increase attendance and contributions by inviting Cubans who lived near by to come to Sunday services.

After several weeks, Ira Sylvester said he was convinced that it was a mistake to expect Spanish-speaking Cubans to accept Scotch-Irish Protestantism without some introduction to its dogma. Knowing that all Cubans in Ybor City were not committed to Catholicism, he was sure that some of them would be inclined to attend Protestant church services if sermons were shorter and more music provided.

In order that the Cubans would have a better understanding of the words they were singing, the English-language psalms were translated into Spanish and then, so as to enliven the tempo of the music, the organ was exchanged for a piano. It was not long until more than half of the original membership of retired farmers and merchants had stopped attending services and contributing to the support of the church.

However, as the attendance of the original members decreased, the Cuban attendance increased. It was not long until the small wooden church was almost completely filled every Sunday morning and evening. And contributions had increased to such an extent that there was enough money in the church treasury to replace the leaking rusty roof with shiny new tin roofing.

Just a few weeks before we were planning to leave Florida and move to Virginia, two of the elders told Ira Sylvester they wanted him to resign and leave town immediately. When he asked for an explanation, he was told that the white people who had been born and raised in the tradition of the South were not going to violate their principles by attending church with dark-skinned Cubans who resembled half-breed Negroes, that the church had been built for white people only to worship God, and that they would rather see the church closed or burned to ashes than let it be desecrated by people who were not suitably white. They said it was known all over Tampa and that section of Florida that some of the people who passed for Cubans were actually part-Negro, just as there were admitted Negroes who were part-Cuban, and that Southern white people were not going to associate in the same building with people whose colour of skin was just as dark as that of an ordinary mulatto.

When my father asked if they were dissatisfied with him as a minister in any other way, one of the elders admitted that there was one more thing that they wanted to say. He was told that some of the original members felt uneasy about the darkness of his skin, because he was no lighter in colour than some of the Cubans who came to church services.

Ira Sylvester told the elders that he had no way of verifying the purity of his Anglo-Saxon heritage, because his Scottish ancestors had left Scotland and mingled with the Irish and Huguenots—and probably with American Indians, too—but that he did not think his racial mixture had discoloured his religious convictions.

The two men left without shaking hands or saying good-bye when Ira Sylvester told them that he had come to take charge of the church for six months and would not be leaving before the end of that time.

When I was seventeen years old, I had completed the final year of high school in Wrens, Georgia, and I planned to go away to college in the fall. In the meantime, I had been able to get a summer job as a mason's helper in Calhoun, Georgia, not far from Chattanooga, Tennessee. I had been told that my work would be to mix mortar and carry hods of brick for a church under construction. The pay was to be twenty-five cents an hour from seven-thirty to five-thirty and the cost of room and board would be a dollar a day.

By that time, having been with my parents in numerous places in all the states of the South and having lived the life of a minister's son during those years, I had accumulated a considerable amount of religious experience and I felt confident of being able to adjust to life wherever I went. Consequently, I did not expect to be in need of religious advice when I was to live away from home for the first time and I would have been surprised if my father had even mentioned about religion when I was leaving home for the summer job in north Georgia. He knew that my knowledge of the religious side of life was no longer confined to what I had observed in A.R.P. churches.

By that time there had been many memorable occasions in the Southern states from Virginia to Florida to Arkansas when I had been with I.S. in churches of various faiths and denominations. We had gone to Church of God all-night camp-meetings, Holy Roller exhibitions on splintery wooden floors, Primitive Christian baptismal immersions in muddy creeks, Seventh Day Adventist foot-washings, Body of Christ blood-drinking communions, Kingdom of God snake-handlings, Full Redeemer glossolalia* services, Fire Baptized Holiness street-corner rallies, Catholic mass at midnight on Christmas Eve, the rituals of Jewish synagogues, and to philosophical lectures in Unitarian churches.

After attending a calm and dignified religious service performed with a series of songs and prayers, usually there would be favourable comments by I.S. about the architecture of the church or the quality of the choir music. But I.S. rarely had anything to say after taking me to listen to a prolonged and unintelligible babble in the Unknown Tongue, or to see people rolling in the throes of ecstasy on a church floor, or

---

*Glossolalia: an unintelligible litany loudly spoken by members of a congregation uttering individual prayers and not speaking in unison. It is also known as speaking in the Unknown Tongue.

to watch a Sanctified preacher hit his head with an axe handle until he had achieved a state of semi-conscious delirium. However, it is probable that his motive, aside from his own avid interest in the subject, was to provide an educational field course for me in all contemporary religious practices.

Also at this time, after having been in the shadow of the steeple during all those early years, it was unexpected to hear I.S. say that I should know enough about life by then to decide for myself if I ever wished to attend a religious service again or to become a member of a church of any denomination.

Having been offered this freedom of choice, I wondered if I would ever lose interest in observing the spectacle of religious practices as I grew older. I thought not. I had been so close to evangelical religion for so many years that I had the feeling that even if I remained unchurched I would want to continue watching the effect its emotional appeal had on people as time went on.

Now, after forty-odd years, it would seem reasonable to expect that, in contrast, a recollection of the white Anglo-Saxon Protestant religious practices of the historical 'twenties and an observation of those of the contemporary 'sixties would serve to illuminate to some degree the churchly life of the two eras of the Deep South.

# Flannery O'Connor

## "The King of the Birds"

When I was five, I had an experience that marked me for life. Pathé News sent a photographer from New York to Savannah to take a picture of a chicken of mine. This chicken, a buff Cochin Bantam, had the distinction of being able to walk either forward or backward. Her fame had spread through the press and by the time she reached the attention of Pathé News, I suppose there was nowhere left for her to go—forward or backward. Shortly after that she died, as now seems fitting.

If I put this information in the beginning of an article on peacocks, it is because I am always being asked why I raise them, and I have no short or reasonable answer.

From that day with the Pathé man I began to collect chickens. What had been only a mild interest became a passion, a quest. I had to have more and more chickens. I favored those with one green eye and one orange or with over-long necks and crooked combs. I wanted one with three legs or three wings but nothing in that line turned up. I pondered over the picture in Robert Ripley's book, *Believe It Or Not,* of a rooster that had survived for thirty days without his head; but I did not have a scientific temperament. I could sew in a fashion and I began to make clothes for chickens. A gray bantam named Colonel Eggbert wore a white piqué coat with a lace collar and two buttons in the back. Apparently Pathé News never heard of any of these other chickens of mine; it never sent another photographer.

My quest, whatever it was actually for, ended with peacocks. Instinct, not knowledge, led me to them. I had never seen or heard one. Although

405

I had a pen of pheasants and a pen of quail, a flock of turkeys, seventeen geese, a tribe of mallard ducks, three Japanese silky bantams, two Polish Crested ones, and several chickens of a cross between these last and the Rhode Island Red, I felt a lack. I knew that the peacock had been the bird of Hera, the wife of Zeus, but since that time it had probably come down in the world—the Florida *Market Bulletin* advertised three-year-old peafowl at sixty-five dollars a pair. I had been quietly reading these ads for some years when one day, seized, I circled an ad in the *Bulletin* and passed it to my mother. The ad was for a peacock and hen with four seven-week-old peabiddies. "I'm going to order me those," I said.

My mother read the ad. "Don't those things eat flowers?" she asked.

"They'll eat Startena like the rest of them," I said.

The peafowl arrived by railway express from Eustis, Florida, on a mild day in October. When my mother and I arrived at the station, the crate was on the platform and from one end of it protruded a long royal-blue neck and crested head. A white line above and below each eye gave the investigating head an expression of alert composure. I wondered if this bird, accustomed to parade about in a Florida orange grove, would readily adjust himself to a Georgia dairy farm. I jumped out of the car and bounded forward. The head withdrew.

At home we uncrated the party in a pen with a top on it. The man who sold me the birds had written that I should keep them penned up for a week or ten days and then let them out at dusk at the spot where I wanted them to roost; thereafter, they would return every night to the same roosting place. He had also warned me that the cock would not have his full complement of tail feathers when he arrived; the peacock sheds his tail in late summer and does not regain it fully until after Christmas.

As soon as the birds were out of the crate, I sat down on it and began to look at them. I have been looking at them ever since, from one station or another, and always with the same awe as on that first occasion; though I have always, I feel, been able to keep a balanced view and an impartial attitude. The peacock I had bought had nothing whatsoever in the way of a tail, but he carried himself as if he not only had a train behind him but a retinue to attend it. On that first occasion, my problem was so greatly what to look at first that my gaze moved constantly from the cock to the hen to the four young peachickens, while they, except that they gave me as wide a berth as possible, did nothing to indicate they knew I was in the pen.

Over the years their attitude toward me has not grown more generous. If I appear with food, they condescend, when no other way can be found, to eat it from my hand; if I appear without food, I am just another object. If I refer to them as "my" peafowl, the pronoun is legal, nothing more. I am the menial, at the beck and squawk of any feathered worthy who wants service. When I first uncrated these birds, in my frenzy I said, "I want so many of them that every time I go out the door, I'll run into one." Now every time I go out the door, four or five run into me—and give me only the faintest recognition. Nine years have passed since my first peafowl arrived. I have forty beaks to feed. Necessity is the mother of several other things besides invention.

For a chicken that grows up to have such exceptional good looks, the peacock starts life with an inauspicious appearance. The peabiddy is the color of those large objectionable moths that flutter about light bulbs on summer nights. Its only distinguished features are its eyes, a luminous gray, and a brown crest which begins to sprout from the back of its head when it is ten days old. This looks at first like a bug's antennae and later like the head feathers of an Indian. In six weeks green flecks appear in its neck, and in a few more weeks a cock can be distinguished from a hen by the speckles on his back. The hen's back gradually fades to an even gray and her appearance becomes shortly what it will always be. I have never thought the peahen unattractive, even though she lacks a long tail and any significant decoration. I have even once or twice thought her more attractive than the cock, more subtle and refined; but these moments of boldness pass.

The cock's plumage requires two years to attain its pattern, and for the rest of his life this chicken will act as though he designed it himself. For his first two years he might have been put together out of a rag bag by an unimaginative hand. During his first year he has a buff breast, a speckled back, a green neck like his mother's and a short gray tail. During his second year he has a black breast, his sire's blue neck, a back which is slowly turning the green and gold it will remain; but still no long tail. In his third year he reaches his majority and acquires his tail. For the rest of his life—and a peachicken may live to be thirty-five—he will have nothing better to do than manicure it, furl and unfurl it, dance forward *and backward* with it spread, scream when it is stepped upon and arch it carefully when he steps through a puddle.

Not every part of the peacock is striking to look at, even when he is full-grown. His upper wing feathers are a striated black and white and might have been borrowed from a Barred Rock Fryer; his end wing feathers are the color of clay; his legs are long, thin and iron-colored; his feet are big; and he appears to be wearing the short pants now so much in favor with playboys in the summer. These extend downward, buff-colored and sleek, from what might be a blue-black waistcoat. One would not be disturbed to find a watch chain hanging from this, but none does. Analyzing the appearance of the peacock as he stands with his tail folded, I find the parts incommensurate with the whole. The fact is that with his tail folded, nothing but his bearing saves this bird from being a laughingstock. With his tail spread, he inspires a range of emotions, but I have yet to hear laughter.

The usual reaction is silence, at least for a time. The cock opens his tail by shaking himself violently until it is gradually lifted in an arch around him. Then, before anyone has had a chance to see it, he swings around so that his back faces the spectator. This has been taken by some to be insult and by others whimsey. I suggest it means only that the peacock is equally well satisfied with either view of himself. Since I have been keeping peafowl, I have been visited at least once a year by first-grade school children, who learn by living. I am used to hearing this group chorus as the peacock swings around, "Oh, look at his underwear!" This "underwear" is a stiff gray tail, raised to support the larger one, and beneath it a puff of black feathers that would be suitable for some really regal woman—a Cleopatra or a Clytemnestra—to use to powder her nose.

When the peacock has presented his back, the spectator will usually begin to walk around him to get a front view; but the peacock will continue to turn so that no front view is possible. The thing to do then is to stand still and wait until it pleases him to turn. When it suits him, the peacock will face you. Then you will see in a green-bronze arch around him a galaxy of gazing haloed suns. This is the moment when most people are silent.

"Amen! Amen!" an old Negro woman once cried when this happened and I have heard many similar remarks at this moment that show the inadequacy of human speech. Some people whistle; a few, for once, are silent. A truck driver who was driving up with a load of hay and found a peacock turning before him in the middle of our road shouted, "Get a load of that bastard!" and braked his truck to a shattering halt. I have never known a strutting peacock to budge a fraction of an inch for truck or tractor or automobile. It is up to the vehicle to get out of the way. No peafowl of mine has ever been run over, though one year one of them lost a foot in the mowing machine.

Many people, I have found, are congenitally unable to appreciate the sight of a peacock. Once or twice I have been asked what the peacock is "good for"—a question which gets no answer from me because it deserves none. The telephone company sent a lineman out one day to repair our telephone. After the job was finished, the man, a large fellow with a suspicious expression half hidden by a yellow helmet, continued to idle about, trying to coax a cock that had been watching him to strut. He wished to add this experience to a large number of others he had apparently had. "Come on now, bud," he said, "get the show on the road, upsy-daisy, come on now, snap it up, snap it up."

The peacock, of course, paid no attention to this.

"What ails him?" the man asked.

"Nothing ails him," I said. "He'll put it up terreckly. All you have to do is wait."

The man trailed about after the cock for another fifteen minutes or so; then, in disgust, he got back in his truck and started off. The bird shook himself and his tail rose around him.

"He's doing it!" I screamed. "Hey, wait! He's doing it!"

The man swerved the truck back around again just as the cock turned and faced him with the spread tail. The display was perfect. The bird turned slightly to the right and the little planets above him were hung in bronze, then he turned slightly to the left and they were hung in green. I went up to the truck to see how the man was affected by the sight.

He was staring at the peacock with rigid concentration, as if he were trying to read fine print at a distance. In a second the cock lowered his tail and stalked off.

"Well, what did you think of that?" I asked.

"Never saw such long ugly legs," the man said. "I bet that rascal could outrun a bus."

Some people are genuinely affected by the sight of a peacock, even with his tail lowered, but do not care to admit it; others appear to be incensed by it. Perhaps they have the suspicion that the bird has formed some unfavorable opinion of them. The peacock himself is a careful and dignified investigator. Visitors to our place, instead of being barked at by dogs rushing from under the porch, are squalled at by peacocks whose blue necks and crested heads pop up from behind tufts of grass, peer out of bushes and crane downward from the roof of the house, where the bird has flown, perhaps for the view. One of mine stepped from under the shrubbery one day and came forward to inspect a carful of people who had driven up to buy a calf. An old man and five or six white-haired, barefooted children were piling out the back of the automobile as the bird approached. Catching sight of him, the children stopped in their tracks and stared, plainly hacked to find this superior figure blocking their path. There was silence as the bird regarded them, his head drawn back at its most majestic angle, his folded train glittering behind him in the sunlight.

"Whut is thet thang?" one of the small boys asked finally in a sullen voice.

The old man had got out of the car and was gazing at the peacock with an astounded look of recognition. "I ain't seen one of them since my granddaddy's day," he said, respectfully removing his hat. "Folks used to have 'em, but they don't no more."

"Whut is it?" the child asked again in the same tone he had used before.

"Churren," the old man said, "that's the king of the birds!"

The children received this information in silence. After a minute they climbed back into the car and continued from there to stare at the peacock, their expressions annoyed, as if they disliked catching the old man in the truth.

The peacock does most of his serious strutting in the spring and summer when he has a full tail to do it with. Usually he begins shortly after breakfast, struts for several hours, desists in the heat of the day and begins again in the late afternoon. Each cock has a favorite station where he performs every day in the hope of attracting some passing hen; but if I have found anyone indifferent to the peacock's display, besides the telephone lineman, it is the peahen. She seldom casts an eye at it. The cock, his tail raised in a shimmering arch around him, will turn this way and that, and with his clay-colored wing feathers touching the ground, will dance forward and backward, his neck curved, his beak parted, his eyes glittering. Meanwhile the hen goes about her business, diligently searching the ground as if any bug in the grass were of more importance than the unfurled map of the universe which floats nearby.

Some people have the notion that only the cock spreads his tail and that he does it only when the hen is present. This is not so. A peafowl only a few hours hatched will raise what tail he has—it will be about the size of a thumbnail—and will strut and turn and back and bow exactly as if he were three years old and had some reason to be doing it. The hens will raise their tails when they see an object on the ground which alarms them, or sometimes when they have nothing better to do and the air is brisk. Brisk air goes at once to the peafowl's head and inclines him to be sportive. A group of birds will dance together or four or five will chase one another around a bush or tree. Sometimes one will chase himself, end his frenzy with a spirited leap into the air and then stalk off as if he had never been involved in the spectacle.

Frequently the cock combines the lifting of his tail with the raising of his voice. He appears to receive through his feet some shock from the center of the earth, which travels upward through him and is released:

*Eee-ooo-ii! Eee-ooo-ii!* To the melancholy this sound is melancholy and
to the hysterical it is hysterical. To me it has always sounded like a cheer
for an invisible parade.

The hen is not given to these outbursts. She makes noise like a mule's
bray—*hehaw, heehaaw, aa-aaww-w*—and makes it only when necessary.
In the fall and winter, peafowl are usually silent unless some racket disturbs them; but in the spring and summer, at short intervals during the
day and night, the cock, lowering his neck and throwing back his head,
will give out with seven or eight screams in succession as if this message
were the one on earth which needed most urgently to be heard.

At night these calls take on a minor key and the air for miles around
is charged with them. It has been a long time since I let my first peafowl
out at dusk to roost in the cedar trees behind the house. Now fifteen or
twenty still roost there; but the original old cock from Eustis, Florida,
stations himself on top of the barn, the bird who lost his foot in the
mowing machine sits on a flat shed near the horse stall, there are others
in the trees by the pond, several in the oaks at the side of the house and
one that cannot be dissuaded from roosting on the water tower. From
all these stations calls and answers echo through the night. The peacock
perhaps has violent dreams. Often he wakes and screams, "Help! Help!"
and then from the pond and the barn and the trees around the house a
chorus of adjuration begins:

> *Lee-yon lee-yon,*
> *Mee-yon mee-yon!*
> *Eee-e-yoy eee-e-yoy,*
> *Eee-e-yoy eee-e-yoy!*

The restless sleeper may wonder if he wakes or dreams.

It is hard to tell the truth about this bird. The habits of any peachicken
left to himself would hardly be noticeable, but multiplied by forty, they
become a situation. I was correct that my peachickens would all eat
Startena; they also eat everything else. Particularly they eat flowers. My
mother's fears were all borne out. Peacocks not only eat flowers, they

eat them systematically, beginning at the head of a row and going down it. If they are not hungry, they will pick the flower anyway, if it is attractive, and let it drop. For general eating they prefer chrysanthemums and roses. When they are not eating flowers, they enjoy sitting on top of them, and where the peacock sits he will eventually fashion a dusting hole. Any chicken's dusting hole is out of place in a flower bed, but the peafowl's hole, being the size of a small crater, is more so. When he dusts he all but obliterates the sight of himself with sand. Usually when someone arrives at full gallop with the leveled broom, he can see nothing through the cloud of dirt and flying flowers but a few green feathers and a beady, pleasure-taking eye.

From the beginning, relations between these birds and my mother were strained. She was forced, at first, to get up early in the morning and go out with her clippers to reach the Lady Bankshire and the Herbert Hoover roses before some peafowl had breakfasted upon them; now she has halfway solved her problem by erecting hundreds of feet of twenty-four-inch-high wire to fence the flower beds. She contends that peachickens do not have sense enough to jump over a low fence. "If it were a high wire," she says, "they would jump onto it and over, but they don't have sense enough to jump over a low wire."

It is useless to argue with her on this matter. "It's not a challenge," I say to her; but she has made up her mind.

In addition to eating flowers, peafowl also eat fruit, a habit which has created a lack of cordiality toward them on the part of my uncle, who had the fig trees planted about the place because he has an appetite for figs himself. "Get that scoundrel out of that fig bush!" he will roar, rising from his chair at the sound of a limb breaking, and someone will have to be dispatched with a broom to the fig trees.

Peafowl also enjoy flying into barn lofts and eating peanuts off peanut hay; this has not endeared them to our dairyman. And as they have a taste for fresh garden vegetables, they have often run afoul of the dairyman's wife.

The peacock likes to sit on gates or fence posts and allow his tail to hang down. A peacock on a fence post is a superb sight. Six or seven peacocks on a gate are beyond description; but it is not very good for the gate. Our fence posts tend to lean in one direction or another and all our gates open diagonally.

In short, I am the only person on the place who is willing to underwrite, with something more than tolerance, the presence of peafowl. In return, I am blessed with their rapid multiplication. The population figure I give out is forty, but for some time now I have not felt it wise to take a census. I had been told before I bought my birds that peafowl are difficult to raise. It is not so, alas. In May the peahen finds a nest in some fence corner and lays five or six large buff-colored eggs. Once a day, thereafter, she gives an abrupt *hee-haa-awww!* and shoots like a rocket from her nest. Then for half an hour, her neck ruffled and stretched forward, she parades around the premises, announcing what she is about. I listen with mixed emotions.

In twenty-eight days the hen comes off with five or six mothlike murmuring peachicks. The cock ignores these unless one gets under his feet (then he pecks it over the head until it gets elsewhere), but the hen is a watchful mother and every year a good many of the young survive. Those that withstand illnesses and predators (the hawk, the fox and the opossum) over the winter seem impossible to destroy, except by violence.

A man selling fence posts tarried at our place one day and told me that he had once had eighty peafowl on his farm. He cast a nervous eye at two of mine standing nearby. "In the spring, we couldn't hear ourselves think," he said. "As soon as you lifted your voice, they lifted their'n, if not before. All our fence posts wobbled. In the summer they ate all the tomatoes off the vines. Scuppernongs went the same way. My wife said she raised her flowers for herself and she was not going to have them eat up by a chicken no matter how long his tail was. And in the fall they shed them feathers all over the place anyway and it was a job to clean up. My old grandmother was living with us then and she was eighty-five. She said, 'Either they go, or I go.'"

"Who went?" I asked.

"We still got twenty of them in the freezer," he said.

"And how," I asked, looking significantly at the two standing nearby, "did they taste?"

"No better than any other chicken," he said, "but I'd a heap rather eat them than hear them."

I have tried imagining that the single peacock I see before me is the only one I have, but then one comes to join him; another flies off the roof, four or five crash out of the crêpe-myrtle hedge; from the pond one screams and from the barn I hear the dairyman denouncing another that has got into the cow-feed. My kin are given to such phrases as, "Let's face it."

I do not like to let my thoughts linger in morbid channels but there are times when such facts as the price of wire fencing and the price of Startena and the yearly gain in peafowl all run uncontrolled through my head. Lately I have had a recurrent dream: I am five years old and a peacock. A photographer has been sent from New York and a long table is laid in celebration. The meal is to be an exceptional one: myself. I scream, "Help! Help!" and awaken. Then from the pond and the barn and the trees around the house, I hear that chorus of jubilation begin:

> *Lee-yon lee-yon,*
> *Mee-yon, mee-yon!*
> *Eee-e-yoy eee-e-yoy!*
> *Eee-e-yoy eee-e-yoy!*

I intend to stand firm and let the peacocks multiply, for I am sure that, in the end, the last word will be theirs.

# Part Four

Contemporary Georgia,
1970 to the Present

In the last two decades, such humorists as Lewis Grizzard and Roy Blount, Jr., have both satirized and eulogized the virtues of Southern life. Grizzard in many ways carried on the nineteenth-century Southern humor tradition. He attacked those forces of change and corruption that he feared would damage Southern life. Honest analysis of the Southern landscape was not his purpose. Although his columns won him a national readership, he wrote for a primarily Southern audience. His columns and stories are full of tall tales, exaggerations, jokes, pranks, and lampoons. They unabashedly exploit every conceivable stereotype—racial, ethnic, regional—for the sake of comedy. Their posture in this regard is defensive: avowedly anti-North, pro-Southern. Blount, on the other hand, writes for an audience less familiar with the South, and in fact most of his columns, syndicated nationally, are not about the South at all. The incongruities of modern life, of the legacies of the past in contrast to the realities of the present, especially interest him. He entitled his 1980 book *Crackers*—a play on the derisive name for poor white Southerners, to suggest the rich ironies of a white Southern farmer's rise to the White House. Like Grizzard, he often employs exaggeration and tall tales for comic effect. Unlike Grizzard, however, he writes about the South in a manner both sympathetic and adversarial. His typical strategy is to prod the reader toward an understanding of the South by first making fun of comic Southern stereotypes and then by exposing the reality beneath them. Neither Blount nor Grizzard is a "literary" writer, but both exemplify the continuing popularity and vigor of the long-standing tradition of Southern humor. And anyone who has heard either writer read his work becomes instantly aware that the oral quality of that tradition remains vitally alive.

The poet and novelist Rosemary Daniell, in her autobiographical memoirs *Fatal Flowers* (1980) and *Sleeping with Soldiers* (1984), exploits the South with different motives. By portraying the modern South as a gothic miasma of racial and sexual guilt, and as a region oppressive to women in general, she reinforces stereotypical images of the South that have been popularized by pulp fiction and bad movies. Daniell's writing might be described as a form of confessional exhibitionism that describes sometimes in detail (graphic detail in *Sleeping with Soldiers*) her sexual coming of age. She rejects objectivity for the shock value of her analysis of the hostile forces against which Southern women must struggle. Sometimes she is perceptive. In the early chapters of *Fatal Flowers* she movingly describes her mother's struggle to give her a good life and to teach her the finer points of social propriety. In later chapters, and in most of *Sleeping with Soldiers,* sensationalism prevails, though Daniell's writing is never without interest or insight. One might argue that the popular, stereotyped image of the South—the South that Daniell often seems to describe, and which thrives in movies, pulp fiction, and country music— is so pervasive in the popular imagination that it has taken on its own life, parallel and similar to, but distinct from, the South that actually exists.

The black feminist writer Alice Walker (she describes herself as a "womanist") also adopts an adversarial stance toward her Georgia origins. Yet her South is more recognizable. As personal memoir, as cultural and political analysis, her essays provide a biting and unsettling assessment of the region. Walker views the South from a number of perspectives. It is the place of her birth, thus a source of her identity, and she has frequently written about it in her poetry and fiction. It is the region historically responsible for the oppression of her race, yet also the region that produced many of the writers who influenced her. She has written a number of insightful essays, both admiring and critical, on the writers important to her. With Zora Neale Hurston and Flannery O'Connor she discovers a real affinity. In fact, her essay on Hurston, "In Search of Our Mothers' Gardens," became an important document in the literary feminist movement, which has devoted much energy to the recovery of neglected women writers. She is less comfortable with William Faulkner, Carson McCullers, and Eudora Welty, whose fiction she thought "seemed to beg the question of their characters' humanity on every page." For Joel Chandler Harris she expresses contempt: his Uncle Remus tales she criticizes for appropriating African-American folk traditions and for ridiculing black storytellers. Her essay on O'Connor may be the best one she has written. She remarks with uncanny perception on O'Connor's talents, on the bonds of white and black writers to the region of their births, and on her relationship with her own mother and the state of her birth. Walker's essays on O'Connor, Harris, and Hurston are among the most important literary essays by any Southern writer of this century.

Other contemporary Georgians have struggled, like Walker, to come to grips with the paradoxes and mysteries of life in the state. James Kilgo's 1991 essay "Mountain Spirits," an account of a fishing experience in north Georgia, reflects the conflicting forces of the state's changing contemporary landscape. The river he fishes is littered with refuse, the detritus of the modern world. His chance meeting with two north Georgia moonshiners brings the old and the new Georgias together. Kilgo makes no argument for the old-time virtues of the mountaineers. Nor does he ridicule them. But he does vividly illustrate the striking gap between the old Georgia and the new. The mountain men are relics of a day nearly forgotten, while he is a citizen of modern Georgia. They have little in common, though they feel a mutual kinship. Their interest in his fishing, and his relish for their whiskey, briefly unites them. These inhabitants of two Georgias, old and new, urban and rural, affluent and depressed, come to no real understanding. Kilgo suggests, by implication, that such meetings will become increasingly rare as time and change permanently expunge all traces of the old Georgia.

Melissa Fay Greene's 1991 book *Praying for Sheetrock* explores similar themes, though her focus is rural south Georgia rather than the northern mountains. Greene relates in this vivid, often poetic study how the civil rights movement finally made its way into McIntosh County in the early 1970s. In the process she touches on many subjects. She writes of the community of a small south Georgia county and the closeness of the inhabitants to their land, to nature, to history. She is interested in the continuity of history, the unbroken linkages between past and present. She describes the racial heritage of Georgia, and the struggle of rural black Georgians for rights and privileges that urban blacks have had for years. Her book is also about the challenges—moral, political, and personal—that change brings to the state's inhabitants. The failed resolve of the Georgia Trustees, who tried in vain, albeit for all the wrong reasons, to keep slavery from the new colony, continues to echo in the twentieth century as the descendants of slaves struggle against the descendants of the plantation lords who once owned them.

Jimmy Carter's book *Turning Point* offers a similar picture of a society in transition. He relates the history of his first campaign for the Georgia State Senate in 1962, a time when the county unit system allowed sparsely populated rural counties to elect governors and rule the state legislature. Carter makes of his struggle against ballot stuffing and political corruption a parable of the state and the South's struggle to come to grips with its heritage. In *Turning Point* and in *Praying for Sheetrock* history comes full circle—from first settlement in 1733, to Civil War and Reconstruction in the 1860s and 1870s, to the burgeoning technology and social struggle of the last forty years. Life in contemporary Georgia continues to present its citizens with problems and dilemmas that will form the matrix of the history and the life still to come.

# Alice Walker

## "Beyond the Peacock: The Reconstruction of Flannery O'Connor"

It was after a poetry reading I gave at a recently desegregated college in Georgia that someone mentioned that in 1952 Flannery O'Connor and I had lived within minutes of each other on the same Eatonton-to-Milledgeville road. I was eight years old in 1952 (she would have been 28) and we moved away from Milledgeville after less than a year. Still, since I have loved her work for many years, the coincidence of our having lived near each other intrigued me, and started me thinking of her again.

As a college student in the sixties I read her books endlessly, scarcely conscious of the difference between her racial and economic background and my own, but put them away in anger when I discovered that, while I was reading O'Connor—Southern, Catholic, and white—there were other women writers—some Southern, some religious, all black—I had not been allowed to know. For several years, while I searched for, found, and studied black women writers, I deliberately shut O'Connor out, feeling almost ashamed that she had reached me first. And yet, even when I no longer read her, I missed her, and realized that though the rest of America might not mind, having endured it so long, I would never be satisfied with a segregated literature. I would have to read Zora Hurston *and* Flannery O'Connor, Nella Larsen *and* Carson McCullers, Jean Toomer *and* William Faulkner, before I could begin to feel *well* read at all.

I thought it might be worthwhile, in 1974, to visit the two houses, Flannery O'Connor's and mine, to see what could be learned twenty-two years after we moved away and ten years after her death. It seemed right to go to my old house first—to set the priorities of vision, so to speak—and then to her house, to see, at the very least, whether her peacocks would still be around. To this bit of nostalgic exploration I invited my mother, who, curious about peacocks and abandoned houses, if not about literature and writers, accepted.

In her shiny new car, which at sixty-one she has learned to drive, we cruised down the wooded Georgia highway to revisit our past.

At the turnoff leading to our former house, we face a fence, a gate, a NO TRESPASSING sign. The car will not fit through the gate and beyond the gate is muddy pasture. It shocks me to remember that when we lived here we lived, literally, in a pasture. It is a memory I had repressed. Now, for a moment, it frightens me.

"Do you think we should enter?" I ask.

But my mother has already opened the gate. To her, life has no fences, except, perhaps, religious ones, and these we have decided not to discuss. We walk through pines rich with vines, fluttering birds, and an occasional wild azalea showing flashes of orange. The day is bright with spring, the sky cloudless, the road rough and clean.

"I would like to see old man Jenkins [who was our landlord] come bothering me about some trespassing," she says, her head extremely up. "He never did pay us for the crop we made for him in fifty-two."

After five minutes of leisurely walking, we are again confronted with a fence, fastened gate, POSTED signs. Again my mother ignores all three, unfastens the gate, walks through.

"He never gave me my half of the calves I raised that year either," she says. And I chuckle at her memory and her style.

Now we are facing a large green rise. To our left calves are grazing; beyond them there are woods. To our right there is the barn we used, looking exactly as it did twenty-two years ago. It is high and weathered silver and from it comes the sweet scent of peanut hay. In front of it, a grove of pecans. Directly in front of us over the rise is what is left of the house.

"Well," says my mother, "it's still standing. And," she adds with wonder, "just look at my daffodils!"

In twenty-two years they have multiplied and are now blooming from one side of the yard to the other. It is a typical abandoned sharefarmer shack. Of the four-room house only two rooms are left; the others have rotted away. These two are filled with hay.

Considering the sad state of the house it is amazing how beautiful its setting is. There is not another house in sight. There are hills, green pastures, a ring of bright trees, and a family of rabbits hopping out of our way. My mother and I stand in the yard remembering. I remember only misery: going to a shabby segregated school that was once the state prison and that had, on the second floor, the large circular print of the electric chair that had stood there; almost stepping on a water moccasin on my way home from carrying water to my family in the fields; losing Phoebe, my cat, because we left this place hurriedly and she could not be found in time.

"Well, old house," my mother says, smiling in such a way that I almost see her rising, physically, above it, "one good thing you gave us. It was right here that I got my first washing machine!"

In fact, the only pleasant thing I recall from that year was a field we used to pass on our way into the town of Milledgeville. It was like a painting by someone who loved tranquillity. In the foreground near the road the green field was used as pasture for black-and-white cows that never seemed to move. Then, farther away, there was a steep hill partly covered with kudzu—dark and lush and creeping up to cover and change fantastically the shapes of the trees. . . . When we drive past it now, it looks the same. Even the cows could be the same cows—though now I see that they *do* move, though not very fast and never very far.

What I liked about this field as a child was that in my life of nightmares about electrocutions, lost cats, and the surprise appearance of snakes, it represented beauty and unchanging peace.

"Of course," I say to myself, as we turn off the main road two miles from my old house, "that's Flannery's field." The instructions I've been given place her house on the hill just beyond it.

There is a garish new Holiday Inn directly across Highway 441 from Flannery O'Connor's house, and, before going up to the house, my mother and I decide to have something to eat there. Twelve years ago I could not have bought lunch for us at such a place in Georgia, and I feel a weary delight as I help my mother off with her sweater and hold out a chair by the window for her. The white people eating lunch all around us—staring though trying hard not to—form a blurred backdrop against which my mother's face is especially sharp. *This* is the proper perspective, I think, biting into a corn muffin; no doubt about it.

As we sip iced tea we discuss O'Connor, integration, the inferiority of the corn muffins we are nibbling, and the care and raising of peacocks.

"Those things will sure eat up your flowers," my mother says, explaining why she never raised any.

"Yes," I say, "but they're a lot prettier than they'd be if somebody human had made them, which is why this lady liked them." This idea has only just occurred to me, but having said it, I believe it is true. I sit wondering why I called Flannery O'Connor a lady. It is a word I rarely use and usually by mistake, since the whole notion of ladyhood is repugnant to me. I can imagine O'Connor at a Southern social affair, looking very polite and being very bored, making mental notes of the absurdities of the evening. Being white she would automatically have been eligible for ladyhood, but I cannot believe she would ever really have joined.

"She must have been a Christian person then," says my mother. "She believed He made everything." She pauses, looks at me with tolerance but also as if daring me to object: "And she was *right,* too."

"She was a Catholic," I say, "which must not have been comfortable in the Primitive Baptist South, and more than any other writer she believed in everything, including things she couldn't see."

"Is that why you like her?" she asks.

"I like her because she could *write,*" I say.

" 'Flannery' sounds like something to eat," someone said to me once. The word always reminds me of flannel, the material used to make nightgowns and winter shirts. It is very Irish, as were her ancestors. Her first name was Mary, but she seems never to have used it. Certainly "Mary O'Connor" is short on mystery. She was an Aries, born March 25, 1925. When she was sixteen, her father died of lupus, the disease that, years later, caused her own death. After her father died, O'Connor and her mother, Regina O'Connor, moved from Savannah, Georgia, to Milledgeville, where they lived in a townhouse built for Flannery O'Connor's grandfather, Peter Cline. This house, called "the Cline house," was built by slaves who made the bricks by hand. O'Connor's biographers are always impressed by this fact, as if it adds the blessed sign of aristocracy, but whenever I read it I think that those slaves were some of my own relatives, toiling in the stifling middle-Georgia heat, to erect her grandfather's house, sweating and suffering the swarming mosquitoes as the house rose slowly, brick by brick.

Whenever I visit antebellum homes in the South, with their spacious rooms, their grand staircases, their shaded back windows that, without the thickly planted trees, would look out onto the now vanished slave quarters in the back, this is invariably my thought. I stand in the backyard gazing up at the windows, then stand at the windows inside looking down into the backyard, and between the me that is on the ground and the me that is at the windows, History is caught.

O'Connor attended local Catholic schools and then Georgia Women's College. In 1945 she received a fellowship to the Writer's Workshop at the University of Iowa. She received her M.A. in 1947. While still a student she wrote stories that caused her to be recognized as a writer of formidable talent and integrity of craft. After a stay at Yaddo, the artists' colony in upstate New York, she moved to a furnished room in New York City. Later she lived and wrote over a garage at the Connecticut home of Sally and Robert Fitzgerald, who became, after her death, her literary executors.

Although, as Robert Fitzgerald states in the preface to O'Connor's *Everything That Rises Must Converge*, "Flannery was out to be a writer on her own and had no plans to go back to live in Georgia," staying out of Georgia for good was not possible. In December of 1950 she experienced a peculiar heaviness in her "typing arms." On the train home for the Christmas holidays she became so ill she was hospitalized immediately. It was disseminated lupus. In the fall of 1951, after nine wretched months in the hospital, she returned to Milledgeville. Because she could not climb the stairs at the Cline house her mother brought her to their country house, Andalusia, about five miles from town. Flannery O'Connor lived there with her mother for the next thirteen years. The rest of her life.

The word *lupus* is Latin for "wolf," and is described as "that which eats into the substance." It is a painful, wasting disease, and O'Connor suffered not only from the disease—which caused her muscles to weaken and her body to swell, among other things—but from the medicine she was given to fight the disease, which caused her hair to fall out and her hipbones to melt. Still, she managed—with the aid of crutches from 1955 on—to get about and to write, and left behind more than three dozen superb short stories, most of them prizewinners, two novels, and a dozen or so brilliant essays and speeches. Her book of essays, *Mystery and Manners,* which is primarily concerned with the moral imperatives of the serious writer of fiction, is the best of its kind I have ever read.

"When you make these trips back south," says my mother, as I give the smiling waitress my credit card, "just what is it exactly that you're looking for?"

"A wholeness," I reply.

"You look whole enough to me," she says.

"No," I answer, "because everything around me is split up, deliberately split up. History split up, literature split up, and people are split up too. It makes people do ignorant things. For example, one day I was invited to speak at a gathering of Mississippi librarians and before I could get started, one of the authorities on Mississippi history and literature got up and said she really *did* think Southerners wrote so well because 'we' lost the war. She was white, of course, but half the librarians in the room were black."

"I bet she was real old," says my mother. "They're the only ones still worrying over that war."

"So I got up and said no, 'we' didn't lose the war. '*You* all' lost the war. And you all's loss was our gain."

"Those old ones will just have to die out," says my mother.

"Well," I say, "I believe that the truth about any subject only comes when all the sides of the story are put together, and all their different meanings make one new one. Each writer writes the missing parts to the other writer's story. And the whole story is what I'm after."

"Well, I doubt if you can ever get the *true* missing parts of anything away from the white folks," my mother says softly, so as not to offend the waitress who is mopping up a nearby table; "they've sat on the truth so long by now they've mashed the life out of it."

"O'Connor wrote a story once called 'Everything That Rises Must Converge.'"

"What?"

"Everything that goes up comes together, meets, becomes one thing. Briefly, the story is this: an old white woman in her fifties—"

"That's not old! I'm older than that, and I'm not old!"

"Sorry. This middle-aged woman gets on a bus with her son, who likes to think he is a Southern liberal . . . he looks for a black person to sit next to. This horrifies his mother, who, though not old, has old ways. She is wearing a very hideous, very expensive hat, which is purple and green."

"Purple and *green?*"

"Very expensive. *Smart.* Bought at the best store in town. She says, 'With a hat like this, I won't meet myself coming and going.' But in fact, soon a large black woman, whom O'Connor describes as looking something like a gorilla, gets on the bus with a little boy, and she is wearing this same green-and-purple hat. Well, our not-so-young white lady is horrified, out*done*."

"I *bet* she was. Black folks have money to buy foolish things with too, now."

"O'Connor's point exactly! Everything that rises, must converge."

"Well, the green-and-purple-hats people will have to converge without me."

"O'Connor thought that the South, as it became more 'progressive,' would become just like the North. Culturally bland, physically ravished, and, where the people are concerned, well, you wouldn't be able to tell one racial group from another. Everybody would want the same things, like the same things, and everybody would be reduced to wearing, symbolically, the same green-and-purple hats."

"And do you think this is happening?"

"I do. But that is not the whole point of the story. The white woman, in an attempt to save her pride, chooses to treat the incident of the identical hats as a case of monkey-see, monkey-do. She assumes she is not the monkey, of course. She ignores the idiotic-looking black woman and begins instead to flirt with the woman's son, who is small and black and *cute*. She fails to notice that the black woman is glowering at her. When they all get off the bus she offers the little boy a 'bright new penny.' And the child's mother knocks the hell out of her with her pocketbook."

"I bet she carried a large one."

"Large, and full of hard objects."

"Then what happened? Didn't you say the white woman's son was with her?"

"He had tried to warn his mother. 'These new Negroes are not like the old,' he told her. But she never listened. He thought he hated his mother until he saw her on the ground, then he felt sorry for her. But when he tried to help her, she didn't know him. She'd retreated in her mind to a historical time more congenial to her desires. 'Tell Grandpapa to come get me,' she says. Then she totters off, alone, into the night."

"Poor *thing*," my mother says sympathetically of this horrid woman, in a total identification that is *so* Southern and *so* black.

"That's what her son felt, too, and *that* is how you know it is a Flannery O'Connor story. The son has been changed by his mother's experience. He understands that, though she is a silly woman who has tried to live in the past, she is also a pathetic creature and so is he. But it is too late to tell her about this because she is stone crazy."

"What did the black woman do after she knocked the white woman down and walked away?"

"O'Connor chose not to say, and that is why, although this is a good story, it is, to me, only half a story. *You* might know the other half. . . ."

"Well, I'm not a writer, but there *was* an old white woman I once wanted to strike . . ." she begins.

"Exactly," I say.

I discovered O'Connor when I was in college in the North and took a course in Southern writers and the South. The perfection of her writing was so dazzling I never noticed that no black Southern writers were taught. The other writers we studied—Faulkner, McCullers, Welty—seemed obsessed with a racial past that would not let them go. They seemed to beg the question of their characters' humanity on every page. O'Connor's characters—whose humanity if not their sanity is taken for granted, and who are miserable, ugly, narrow-minded, atheistic, and of intense racial smugness and arrogance, with not a graceful, pretty one anywhere who is not, at the same time, a joke—shocked and delighted me.

It was for her description of Southern white women that I appreciated her work at first, because when she set her pen to them not a whiff of magnolia hovered in the air (and the tree itself might never have been planted), and yes, I could say, yes, these white folks without the magnolia (who are indifferent to the tree's existence), and these black folks without melons and superior racial patience, these are like Southerners that I know.

She was for me the first great modern writer from the South, and was, in any case, the only one I had read who wrote such sly, demythifying sentences about white women as: "The woman would be more or less pretty—yellow hair, fat ankles, muddy-colored eyes."

Her white male characters do not fare any better—all of them misfits, thieves, deformed madmen, idiot children, illiterates, and murderers, and her black characters, male and female, appear equally shallow, demented, and absurd. That she retained a certain distance (only, however, in her later, mature work) from the inner workings of her black characters seems to me all to her credit, since, by deliberately limiting her treatment of them to cover their observable demeanor and actions, she leaves them free, in the reader's imagination, to inhabit another landscape, another life, than the one she creates for them. This is a kind of grace many writers do not have when dealing with representatives of an oppressed people within a story, and their insistence on knowing everything, on being God, in fact, has burdened us with more stereotypes than we can ever hope to shed.

In her life, O'Connor was more casual. In a letter to her friend Robert Fitzgerald in the mid-fifties she wrote, "as the niggers say, I have the misery." He found nothing offensive, apparently, in including this unflattering (to O'Connor) statement in his Introduction to one of her books. O'Connor was then certain she was dying, and was in pain; one assumes she made this comment in an attempt at levity. Even so, I do not find it funny. In another letter she wrote shortly before she died she said: "Justice is justice and should not be appealed to along racial lines. The problem is not abstract for the Southerner, it's concrete: he sees it in terms of persons, not races—which way of seeing does away with easy answers." Of course this observation, though grand, does not apply to the racist treatment of blacks by whites in the South, and O'Connor should have added that she spoke only for herself.

But *essential* O'Connor is not about race at all, which is why it is so refreshing, coming, as it does, out of such a *racial* culture. If it can be said to be "about" anything, then it is "about" prophets and prophecy, "about" revelation, and "about" the impact of supernatural grace on human beings who don't have a chance of spiritual growth without it.

An indication that *she* believed in justice for the individual (if only in the corrected portrayal of a character she invented) is shown by her endless reworking of "The Geranium," the first story she published (in 1946), when she was twenty-one. She revised the story several times, renamed it at least twice, until, nearly twenty years after she'd originally published it (and significantly, I think, after the beginning of the Civil Rights Movement), it became a different tale. Her two main black characters, a man and a woman, underwent complete metamorphosis.

In the original story, Old Dudley, a senile racist from the South, lives with his daughter in a New York City building that has "niggers" living in it too. The black characters are described as being passive, self-effacing people. The black woman sits quietly, hands folded, in her apartment; the man, her husband, helps Old Dudley up the stairs when the old man is out of breath, and chats with him kindly, if condescendingly, about guns and hunting. But in the final version of the story, the woman walks around Old Dudley (now called Tanner) as if he's an open bag of garbage, scowls whenever she sees him, and "didn't look like any kind of woman, black or white, he had ever seen." Her husband, whom Old Dudley persists in calling "Preacher" (under the misguided assumption that to all black men it is a courtesy title), twice knocks the old man down. At the end of the story he stuffs Old Dudley's head, arms, and legs through the banisters of the stairway "as if in a stockade," and leaves him to die. The story's final title is "Judgment Day."

The quality added is rage, and, in this instance, O'Connor waited until she saw it *exhibited* by black people before she recorded it.

She was an artist who thought she might die young, and who then knew for certain she would. Her view of her characters pierces right through to the skull. Whatever her characters' color or social position she saw them as she saw herself, in the light of imminent mortality. Some of her stories, "The Enduring Chill" and "The Comforts of Home" especially, seem to be written out of the despair that must, on occasion, have come from this bleak vision, but it is for her humor that she is most enjoyed and remembered. My favorites are these:

Everywhere I go I'm asked if I think the universities stifle writers. My opinion is that they don't stifle enough of them. There's many a best-seller that could have been prevented by a good teacher.
—*Mystery and Manners*

"She would of been a good woman, if it had been somebody there to shoot her every minute of her life."
—"The Misfit," *A Good Man Is Hard to Find*

There are certain cases in which, if you can only learn to write poorly enough, you can make a great deal of money.
—*Mystery and Manners*

It is the business of fiction to embody mystery through manners, and mystery is a great embarrassment to the modern mind.
—*Mystery and Manners*

It mattered to her that she was a Catholic. This comes as a surprise to those who first read her work as that of an atheist. She believed in all the mysteries of her faith. And yet, she was incapable of writing dogmatic or formulaic stories. No religious tracts, nothing haloed softly in celestial light, not even any happy endings. It has puzzled some of her readers and annoyed the Catholic church that in her stories not only does good not triumph, it is not usually present. Seldom are there choices, and God never intervenes to help anyone win. To O'Connor, in fact, Jesus was God, and he won only by losing. She perceived that not much has been learned by his death by crucifixion, and that it is only by his continual, repeated dying—touching one's own life in a direct, searing way—that the meaning of that original loss is pressed into the heart of the individual.

In "The Displaced Person," a story published in 1954, a refugee from Poland is hired to work on a woman's dairy farm. Although he speaks in apparent gibberish, he is a perfect worker. He works so assiduously the woman begins to prosper beyond her greatest hopes. Still, because his ways are not her own (the Displaced Person attempts to get one of the black dairy workers to marry his niece by "buying" her out of a Polish concentration camp), the woman allows a runaway tractor to roll over and kill him.

"As far as I'm concerned," she tells the priest, "Christ was just another D.P." He just didn't fit in. After the death of the Polish refugee, however, she understands her complicity in a modern crucifixion, and recognizes the enormity of her responsibility for other human beings. The impact of this new awareness debilitates her; she loses her health, her farm, even her ability to speak.

This moment of revelation, when the individual comes face to face with her own limitations and comprehends "the true frontiers of her own inner country," is classic O'Connor, and always arrives in times of extreme crisis and loss.

There is a resistance by some to read O'Connor because she is "too difficult," or because they do not share her religious "persuasion." A young man who studied O'Connor under the direction of Eudora Welty some years ago amused me with the following story, which may or may not be true:

"I don't think Welty and O'Connor understood each *other*," he said, when I asked if he thought O'Connor would have liked or understood Welty's more conventional art. "For Welty's part, wherever we reached a particularly dense and symbolic section of one of O'Connor's stories she would sigh and ask, 'Is there a Catholic in the class?' "

Whether one "understands" her stories or not, one knows her characters are new and wondrous creations in the world and that not one of her stories—not even the earliest ones in which her consciousness of racial matters had not evolved sufficiently to be interesting or to differ much from the insulting and ignorant racial stereotyping that preceded it—could have been written by anyone else. As one can tell a Bearden from a Keene or a Picasso from a Hallmark card, one can tell an O'Connor story from any story laid next to it. Her Catholicism did not in any way limit (by defining it) her art. After her great stories of sin, damnation, prophecy, and revelation, the stories one reads casually in the average magazine seem to be about love and roast beef.

Andalusia is a large white house at the top of a hill with a view of a lake from its screened-in front porch. It is neatly kept, and there are, indeed, peacocks strutting about in the sun. Behind it there is an unpainted house where black people must have lived. It was, then, the typical middle-to-upper-class arrangement: white folks up front, the "help," in a far shabbier house, within calling distance from the back door. Although an acquaintance of O'Connor's has told me no one lives there now—but that a caretaker looks after things—I go up to the porch and knock. It is not an entirely empty or symbolic gesture: I have come to this vacant house to learn something about myself in relation to Flannery O'Connor, and will learn it whether anyone is home or not.

What I feel at the moment of knocking is fury that someone is paid to take care of her house, though no one lives in it, and that her house still, in fact, stands, while mine—which of course we never owned anyway—is slowly rotting into dust. Her house becomes—in an instant—the symbol of my own disinheritance, and for that instant I hate her guts. All that she has meant to me is diminished, though her diminishment within me is against my will.

In Faulkner's backyard there is also an unpainted shack and a black caretaker still lives there, a quiet, somber man who, when asked about Faulkner's legendary "sense of humor" replied that, as far as he knew,

"Mr. Bill never joked." For years, while reading Faulkner, this image of the quiet man in the backyard shack stretched itself across the page.

Standing there knocking on Flannery O'Connor's door, I do not think of her illness, her magnificent work in spite of it; I think: it all comes back to houses. To how people live. There are rich people who own houses to live in and poor people who do not. And this is wrong. Literary separatism, fashionable now among blacks as it has always been among whites, is easier to practice than to change a fact like this. I think: I would level this country with the sweep of my hand, if I could.

"Nobody can change the past," says my mother.

"Which is why revolutions exist," I reply.

My bitterness comes from a deeper source than my knowledge of the difference, historically, race has made in the lives of white and black artists. The fact that in Mississippi no one even remembers where Richard Wright lived, while Faulkner's house is maintained by a black caretaker is painful, but not unbearable. What comes close to being unbearable is that I know how damaging to my own psyche such injustice is. In an unjust society the soul of the sensitive person is in danger of deformity from just such weights as this. For a long time I will feel Faulkner's house, O'Connor's house, crushing me. To fight back will require a certain amount of energy, energy better used doing something else.

My mother has been busy reasoning that, since Flannery O'Connor died young of a lingering and painful illness, the hand of God has shown itself. Then she sighs. "Well, you know," she says, "it is true, as they say, that the grass is always greener on the other side. That is, until you find yourself over there."

In a just society, of course, clichés like this could not survive.

"But grass *can* be greener on the other side and not be just an illusion," I say. "Grass on the other side of the fence might have good fertilizer, while grass on your side might have to grow, if it grows at all, in sand."

We walk about quietly, listening to the soft sweep of the peacocks' tails as they move across the yard. I notice how completely O'Connor, in her fiction, has described just this view of the rounded hills, the tree line, black against the sky, the dirt road that runs from the front yard down to the highway. I remind myself of her courage and of how much—in her art—she has helped me to see. She destroyed the last vestiges of sentimentality in white Southern writing; she caused white women to look ridiculous on pedestals, and she approached her black characters—as a mature artist—with unusual humility and restraint. She also cast spells and worked magic with the written word. The magic, the wit, and the mystery of Flannery O'Connor I know I will always love. I also know the meaning of the expression "Take what you can use and let the rest rot." If ever there was an expression designed to protect the health of the spirit, this is it.

As we leave O'Connor's yard the peacocks—who she said would have the last word—lift their splendid tails for our edification. One peacock is so involved in the presentation of his masterpiece he does not allow us to move the car until he finishes with his show.

"Peacocks are inspiring," I say to my mother, who does not seem at all in awe of them and actually frowns when she sees them strut, "but they sure don't stop to consider they might be standing in your way."

And she says, "Yes, and they'll eat up every bloom you have, if you don't watch out."

# Harry Crews

## From *A Childhood:*
## *The Biography of a Place*

### CHAPTER 2

Being as impermanent as the wind, constantly moving, I lost track for thirty-five years of my daddy's side of the family. I remember nothing specific of my paternal grandparents, and my paternal aunts and uncles remained strangers until I was grown. It was not their fault, nor was it mine or anyone else's. It just happened that way.

I saw a good deal of the kin on my mama's side. My Uncle Alton, her brother, was as much as any other man a father to me. He's dead now, but I will always carry a memory of him in my heart as vivid as any memory I have.

I was sitting on the steps of his front porch just after I got out of the Marine Corps in 1956, when I was twenty-one years old, watching him smoking one hand-rolled Prince Albert cigarette after another and spitting between his feet into the yard. He was so reticent that if he said a sentence ten words long, it seemed as though he had been talking all afternoon.

He was probably the closest friend of the longest standing that my daddy ever had. And I remember sitting there on the steps, looking up at him in his rocking chair and talking about my daddy, saying that I thought the worst thing that had happened in my life was his early death, that never having known him, I knew that I would, one way or another, be looking for him the rest of my life.

438

"What is it you want to know?" he said.

"I don't know what I want to know," I said. "Anything. Everything."

"Cain't know everything," he said. "And anything won't help."

"I think it might," I said. "Anything'll help me see him better than I see him now. At least I'd have some notion of him."

He watched me for a moment with his steady gray eyes looking out from under the brim of the black felt hat he always wore and said: "Let's you and me take us a ride."

He started for the pickup truck parked in the lane beyond the yard and I followed. As was his way, he didn't say where we were going and I didn't ask. It was enough for me to be riding with him over the flat dirt roads between walls of black pine trees on the way to Alma. He lived then about three miles from the Little Satilla River which separates Bacon from Appling County and very near two farms that I had lived on as a boy. We drove the twelve miles to the paved road that led into town, but shortly after we turned into it, he stopped at a little grocery store with Pepsi-Cola and root beer and Redman Chewing Tobacco and snuff signs nailed all over it and two gas pumps out front in the red clay lot where several pickup trucks were parked.

We got down and went in. Some men were sitting around in the back of the store on nail kegs and ladder-back chairs or squatting on their heels, apparently doing nothing very much but smoking and chewing and talking.

One of them came to the front where we had stopped by the counter. "How you, Alton?" he said.

Uncle Alton said: "We all right. Everything all right with you, Joe?"

"Jus fine, I reckon. What can I git you?"

"I guess you can let us have two of them cold Co-Colers."

The man got two Cokes out of the scarred red box behind him and Uncle Alton paid him. We went on back to where the men were talking. They all spoke to Uncle Alton in the brief and easy way of men who had known each other all their lives.

They spoke for a while about the weather, mostly rain, and about other things that men who live off the land speak of when they meet, seriously, but with that resigned tone in their voice that makes you know they know they're speaking only to pass the time because they have utterly no control over what they're talking about: weevils in cotton, screwworms in stock, the government allotment of tobacco acreage, the fierce price of commercial fertilizer.

We hadn't been there long before Uncle Alton said casually, as though it were something that had just occurred to him: "This is Ray Crews' boy. Name Harry."

The men turned and looked at me for a long considered time and it again seemed the most natural thing in the world for them to now begin talking about my daddy, who had been dead for more than twenty years. I didn't know it then and didn't even know it or realize it for a long time afterward, but what Uncle Alton had done, because of what I'd said to him on the porch, was take me out in the truck to talk with men who had known my father.

Maybe the men themselves knew it, or maybe they simply liked my father in such a way that the mention of his name was enough to bring back stories and considerations of people who were kin to him. Without making any special thing out of it they began to talk about those days when daddy was a boy, about how many children were in his family, and then about how families were not as big now as they once had been and from that went on to talk about my grandma's sister, Aunt Belle, who had fourteen children, all of whom lived to be grown, and finally to the time one of Aunt Belle's boys, Orin Bennett, was killed at a liquor still by a government man.

"Well," one of them said, "it's a notion most people have nowadays moonshinin was easy work, but it weren't."

"Moonshinin was hard work. Real hard work."

"Most men I known back in them days," said Uncle Alton, "made moonshine because it weren't nothing else to do. They'as working at the only thing it was to work at. I feel like most folks who make shine even today do it for the same reason."

"I'll tell you sumpin else," Joe said. "I never known men back then makin shine that thought it was anythin wrong with it. It was a livin, the only livin they had."

One of them looked at me and said: "It wasn't much whiskey made in your daddy's family, though. I don't know the ins and outs of how Orin come to be killed up at that there still. But your granddaddy didn't hold with none of his own younguns making whiskey or bein anywhere around where it was made. Not ole Dan Crews didn't. He'd take a drink, drunk his full share, I'd say, but he never thought makin it was proper work for a man."

"I've made some and I've drunk some, and I'd shore a heap ruther drink it than make it."

Just as natural as spitting, a bottle of bonded whiskey out of which about a quarter had been drunk appeared from somewhere behind one of the chairs. The cap was taken off. The man who took it off wiped the neck of the bottle on his jumper sleeve, took a sip, and handed it to the man squatting beside him. The bottle passed. Uncle Alton, God love him, didn't have any of the whiskey. Even then his stomach, which finally killed him, was beginning to go bad on him.

The man who had done most of the talking since we came in finally looked up at me and said: "It'll take a lot of doing, son, to fill your daddy's shoes. He was much of a man."

I said: "I didn't think to fill'm. It's trouble enough trying to fill the ones I'm standing in."

For whatever reason they seemed to like that. One of them took a hit out of the bottle and leaned back on his nail keg and said: "Lemme tell you a story, son. It was a feller Fletchum, Tweek we called'm, Tweek Fletchum, and he musta been about twenty-seven years old then, but even that young he already had the name of makin the best whiskey in the county. Makin whiskey and mean enough to bite a snake to boot." He stopped long enough to shake his head over how mean ole Tweek was and also used the pause to bubble the whiskey bottle a couple of times. "Me and you daddy was hired out plowin for Luke Tate and one evenin after we took the mules out we decided to go on back there to Tweek's place to where his still was at. We weren't nothing but yearlin boys then, back before he went off to work down in Flardy, we couldn't a been much more'n sixteen years old, but we *would* touch a drop or two of whiskey from time to time.

"We didn't do a thing but cut back through the field and cross the branch and then up Ten Mile Creek past that place your daddy later tended for one of the Boatwright boys. When we got to Tweek's, his wife, Sarah, pretty thing, a Turner before she married Tweek, she seen us comin and met us at the door and said Tweek was back at the still and me'n your daddy started back there to where he was at. Tweek didn't keep nothin at his house but bonded whiskey an that was just for show in case some government man come nosin around, so we went on back to the still and while we'as kickin along there in the dust, we decided to play us a little trick on Tweek. I cain't remember who thought it up, but it seem like to me it'as your daddy because he was ever ready for some kind of foolishness, playin tricks and such. That ain't sayin a thing agin him, it was just his nature. Coulda been me, though, that thought it up. Been known for such myself.

"Anyhow, that still of Tweek's was set right slap up agin Big Harrikin Swamp. Out in front of the still was the damnedest wall of brambles and briers you ever seen in your life. Musta been twenty acres of them thins, some of'm big as a scrub oak. And it was that suckhole swamp in back of the still. Brambles in front and waist-deep swamp full of moccasins in back, with a little dim woods road runnin in from one side and then runnin out the othern.

"Your daddy went around and come up the woods road from one side, and I went around and come up the other. Everybody was having trouble them days with that govment man come in here from Virginia or sommers like that and given everybody so much trouble before Lummy finally killed him, but in them days, Tweek and everybody else was having trouble with 'm, so when I was sure your daddy had time to git on the other side, I got up close to the still in a clump of them gallberry bushes and cupped my mouth like this, see here, and shouted into my shirt: 'STAY RIGHT THERE!'

"Tweek he was stirrin him some mash, but when I hollered, he taken and thrown down the paddle and jerked his head up like a dog cuttin a rank spoor in the woods. He tuck off runnin down the road the other way, his shirttail standin out flat behind him. I didn't do a thing but cup my mouth agin like this here and holler: 'HEAD'M OVER THERE!' And a course he was runnin straight at your daddy. He waited till ole Tweek got real close and then hollered: 'I GOT'M OVER HERE!'

"Tweek come up slidin soon's he known the road was closed on him at both ends and he tuck him a long look at the Harrikin Swamp behind him and then he tuck'm a long look at them brambles in front of him. And I got to credit ole Tweek, it didn't take'm but about three seconds to make his mind up. He put his head down and charged them briers and brambles.

"We heard'm screamin and thrashin around out there for what musta been fifteen minutes. It was as funny a thing as I ever hope to see, and damn if me and your daddy didn't bout break a rib settin there sippin some mash Tweek'd more'n likely run off that mornin, all the time listenin to Tweek out there screamin and tearin through the brambles.

"Got through and went on back up there to the house and Sarah said, 'No, Tweek ain't come in,' so we set down on the front porch swing to finish off that little mason fruit jar of shine we'd taken from the still. Well, it was damn nigh dark and we'd moved into the kitchen where we'as settin at the table, a kerosene lamp between us, eatin sausage and syrup that Sarah given us, when what do we hear but this te-nine-see *scratchin* at the back door.

"Sarah opened it and I could see Tweek standin down in the yard, but he didn't see us. He was cut from lap to lip, nothin but blood and scratches on his face and neck.

" 'Sarah,' says Tweek, 'put a little sumpin in a sack to eat. Goddamned govment man's after me.'

"She says, 'Tweek, that weren't no govment man. Them's just Ray and Tom that. . . .'

"But we didn't hear the rest of it cause we heard him beller like a bull and seen he was going for the shotgun. Onliest thing that saved us was he had bird shot in it and maybe on account of it was gitten on toward black dark. But he thrown down on us as we'as goin out the fence gate. Your daddy didn't catch none of it, but I'm carryin sign to this day."

He unbuckled his galluses and pulled up his work shirt. His back was full of little purple holes, like somebody had set it afire and then put the fire out with an ice pick.

Uncle Alton and I stayed around for three or four hours talking and drinking—or at least I was drinking a little—and listening to stories and talking about my daddy and his people.

I'd heard the moonshine story sitting around the fireplaces of a dozen different farms. This was the first time I'd ever heard that daddy was there when Tweek had two years of his growth scared out of him, but this was also the first time I ever had the storyteller lift his shirt and show me the sign of the bird shot. Wounds or scars give an awesome credibility to a story.

Listening to them talk, I wondered what would give credibility to my own story if, when my young son grows to manhood, he has to go looking for me in the mouths and memories of other people. Who would tell the stories? A few motorcycle riders, bartenders, editors, half-mad karateka, drunks, and writers. They are scattered all over the country, but even if he could find them, they could speak to him with no shared voice from no common ground. Even as I was gladdened listening to the stories of my daddy, an almost nauseous sadness settled in me, knowing I would leave no such life intact. Among the men with whom I have spent my working life, university professors, there is not one friend of the sort I was listening to speak of my daddy there that day in the back of the store in Bacon County. Acquaintances, but no friends. For half of my life I have been in the university, but never of it. Never *of* anywhere, really. Except the place I left, and that of necessity only in memory. It was in that moment and in that knowledge that I first had the notion that I would someday have to write about it all, but not in the convenient and comfortable metaphors of fiction, which I had been doing for years. It would have to be done naked, without the disguising distance of the third person pronoun. Only the use of *I*, lovely and terrifying word, would get me to the place where I needed to go.

In the middle of the afternoon, Uncle Alton and I left the store and drove out to New Lacy, a little crossroads village where Uncle Elsie and Aunt Gertie lived with their house full of children until Uncle Elsie died. Aunt Gertie was my mama's sister and Uncle Elsie spoke in tongues.

We sat on a little porch with a man who must have been old when daddy died. His eyes were solid and cloud-colored, and his skin so wrinkled and folded it looked like it might have been made for a man twice his size. His mouth was toothless and dark and worked continuously around a plug of tobacco as he told us about chickens with one wing and chickens with one leg gimping about over the first farm my daddy worked on shares.

"Mule was bad to bite chickens," he said, sending a powerful stream of tobacco juice into the yard, apparently without even stopping to purse his old wrinkled lips. "Been your daddy's mule he mought woulda killed it. Horse mule, he was, name of Sheddie."

The old man had withered right down to bone, but his mind was as sharp as a boy's.

"Workin shares like he was, Sheddie come with the crop. But he was bad to bite chickens like I said. Chicken'd hop up on the feed trough to peck a little corn and Sheddie'd just take him a bite. Sometimes he'd git a wing, sometimes a leg. Sometimes the whole damn chicken."

He began to cough and he stopped to spray the porch with black spit.

"Ray he got tired of seein all them chickens hobblin about the place with a wing or a leg missin. So he cured that Sheddie, he did."

Daddy, the old man said, killed a chicken and hung it up to ripen. When it was good and rotten, he blindfolded Sheddie, put on a halter with a jawbreaker bit, and fastened that stinking chicken to the bit with hay wire. It was a full day before the chicken came completely off the bit it had been wired to. Sheddie was never known to bite again. He had lost his taste for chicken.

Before we got through that afternoon, Uncle Alton and I had been all over Bacon County and never once had he said to anybody: "Here is Ray Crews' son and he never knew his daddy and he wants to hear about him." And yet, somehow, he contrived to have the stories told. We finally went back to his house a little after dark and he never mentioned that afternoon again to me nor I to him, but I'll always be grateful for it.

It was through his friendship with my Uncle Alton that daddy first took notice of my mama, whose name is Myrtice. I suppose it was inevitable that he eventually should, because in the same shoebox with his pictures—the pictures of him playing the dandy with half the girls of the county—is a picture of mama just before she turned sixteen. She is sitting in a pea patch, wearing a print dress. And even in the faded black-and-white photograph, you can tell she is round and pink and pretty as she smiles in a fetching way under a white bonnet.

As pretty as she was, though, God knows there were enough children in the family for her to get lost in the crowd. Besides Uncle Alton and mama there was Dorsey, who died when he was four years old from diphtheria. Then there was Aunt Ethel and Aunt Olive and Leon, who died of pneumonia when he was two, and Aunt Gertie and Uncle Frank and Uncle Harley and Aunt Lottie and Aunt Bessie. Grandma Hazelton, whose name was the same as Grandma Crews, Lilly, gave birth to children over a period of twenty years. Nine of them lived to be grown and married. As I write this today, three are still living.

I think he really noticed her for the first time the day her daddy, Grandpa Hazelton, almost killed a man with his walking stick. My daddy had come over to their place for the very reason that he knew there was going to be trouble. He could have saved himself the trip because as it turned out, Grandpa handled the whole thing very nicely and with considerable dispatch.

Uncle Alton, who had just turned seventeen at the time, had managed to get in a row with a man named Jessup over a shoat hog.

"Pa," Uncle Alton said, "Jessup says he's coming over here today and he's gone bring his friends with him."

Grandpa Hazelton was never a man to talk much, probably because he didn't hear very well. He said: "He ain't comin on the place and causin no trouble."

But they did, later that day, three grown men. They stood in the dooryard and called Uncle Alton out, saying they had brought a cowwhip and meant to mark him with it.

Grandpa Hazelton said: "You men git off my place. You on my land and Alton here ain't nothing but a boy. You all git off the place."

Daddy and Uncle Alton were standing on the porch with Grandpa when he said it. The three men, all of whom had been drinking, said they'd go when they got ready, but first they had business to take care of and they meant to do it.

There were no other words spoken. Grandpa Hazelton came off the porch carrying the heavy hickory walking stick he always had with him, a stick he carried years before he actually needed it. He hit the man who had spoken between the eyes with the stick, hit him so hard that his palate dropped in his mouth.

The two men carried their friend, his dropped palate bleeding and his tongue half choking him, to the wagon they had come in and headed off toward town for the doctor. Grandpa followed them all the way to the wagon, beating them about the head and shoulders with his stick.

He stood in the lane shaking with rage and told them: "You come back on the place, I got some buckshot for you."

In that time, a man's land was inviolate, and you were always very careful about what you said to another man if you were on his land. A man could shoot you with impunity if you were on his property and he managed to get you dead enough so you couldn't tell what actually happened. The sheriff would come, look around, listen to the man whose land the killing took place on, and then go back to town. That was that.

In the commotion of the fight, the whole Hazelton family was finally on the porch, and there—daddy's blood still high and hot from watching the old man's expert use of his stick—was my mother standing pink and in full flower under her thin cotton housedress. In that moment, any number of lives took new and irreversible direction.

Once he saw her, he didn't waste any time. Four months later, in November, they were married. She was sixteen, he twenty-three. Immediately there took place in him a change that has been taking place in men ever since they got out of their caves. As soon as he got himself a wife, he took off that white linen suit and put on a pair of overalls. He got out of that Model T Ford and put it up on blocks under Uncle Major's cotton shed because he didn't have enough money to drive it. He drove a mule and wagon instead. And he went to work with a vengeance. More than one person has told me that it wasn't his heart that killed him, that he simply worked himself to death.

Still, he must have cut a fine figure that blustery, freezing day in November of 1928, when he took my mother down to Ten Mile Missionary Baptist Church and married her in a small service attended only by blood kin. They were joined together by Preacher Will Davis, who two years earlier had baptized my mother in Ten Mile Creek, which is just down behind Ten Mile Missionary Baptist Church. They went to the church that day in a mule and wagon, as did most of the other people who came, and after they were married, they spent their wedding night at Uncle Major Eason's house. Uncle Major would one day own the live-stock barn in Alma and become known as one of the best mule traders in Georgia. Uncle Major's first wife had died early and he was then married to my mama's sister Olive.

After spending the night under Uncle Major's tin roof in a deep feather bed, with the ground frozen outside, they got up the next morning and, still in a mule and wagon, went to the first farm they were to live on. Daddy had gone from being a young dandy in a white suit driving a Model T Ford to a married man in overalls sharecropping for a man named Luther Carter. They farmed the place on shares, which meant Luther Carter furnished the seed and the mules and the fertilizer for them to make the crop and at the end of the year they kept half of what they made.

In that little sharecropper's house of Luther Carter's they lived with Uncle John Carter and Aunt Ora, who was daddy's sister. Uncle John Carter was no kin to Luther Carter, but they were in Cartertown, where most people had that last name. The house had a wooden roof that leaked badly, no screens and wooden windows. There were two ten-by-ten bed-rooms and a shotgun hall that ran the length of the house to the kitchen. They put up a partition in the middle of the kitchen, and Uncle John and Aunt Ora had one room to live in and the use of half the partitioned kitchen. Daddy and mama had the same arrangement on their side. Mama had a Home Comfort, Number 8, wood stove to cook on. There was a hot-water reservoir and four eyes on the cast-iron top of the stove, but it was a tiny thing, hardly more than three feet wide and two feet deep.

They brought to the house as wedding presents: a frying pan, an iron wash pot, four plates and as many knives and forks and spoons, an iron bedstead complete with slats and mattress, four quilts, four sheets, and a pillow. Daddy built everything else: a little cook table, a slightly larger table to eat off of, with a bench on each side instead of chairs, a chest of drawers, and an ironing board made from a plank wrapped in striped bed ticking. It was almost a year before they got two flatirons, one of which would be heated on the hearthstone while the other was being used.

The farm had sixty acres in cultivation, and so Luther Carter furnished Uncle John and daddy each a mule. Thirty acres was as much as one man and one mule could tend, and even then they had to step smart from first sun to last to do it. They had no cows or hogs and no smokehouse, and that first year they lived—as we did for much of my childhood—on fatback, grits, tea without ice, and biscuits made from flour and water and lard.

It was on the Luther Carter place that mama—with a midwife in attendance—lost her first child in the middle of August 1929, the year following their marriage. The baby was not born dead, but nearly so, its liver on the outside of its body. Its life lasted only a matter of minutes and mama didn't look at it but once before it was washed and dressed in a cotton gown and put in a coffin not much bigger than a breadbox and hauled in a wagon to Ten Mile Missionary Baptist Church, where it was buried in an unmarked grave. I don't know how wide the practice was or how it originated, but if a child was lost in miscarriage or born dead, or died nearly immediately from some gross deformity, there was never a marker put at its head.

I've tried to imagine what my daddy's thoughts must have been when the child was lost. He had told mama what happened down in the Everglades and in the town of Arcadia, and I know the death of his firstborn son must have hurt him profoundly. It was commonly believed then in Bacon County, and to some extent still is, that a miscarriage or a baby born dead or deformed was the consequence of some taint in the blood or taint in the moral life of the parents. I know daddy must have keenly felt all over again the crippled pleasure of that night so many months before under the palm-thatched chickee with the Seminole girl.

Maybe such thoughts are what drove him to work so hard. The sun always rose on him in the field, and he was still in the field when it set. He worked harder than the mule he plowed, did everything a man could do to bring something out of the sorry soil he worked, but that first year the crop failed. What this meant was that in August at the end of the crop year, he got half of nothing. They stayed alive on what they could borrow against the coming crop and what little help they could find from their people, who had not done well that year either.

Nearly everybody in the county had done worse that year than any of them could remember in a long time. Part of the reason, and probably

the most important, was tobacco. Tobacco had come into the county as
a money crop not many years before, and though eventually it turned
into a blessing of sorts, for a long time it brought a series of economic
disasters. It was a delicate crop, much dependent upon the weather. Most
of the farmers were not yet skilled enough in all that was necessary to
bring in a good crop: sowing the seeds in beds, transplanting from the
beds to the field at the right time, proper amounts of fertilizer (too much
would burn it up), suckering it, worming it, cropping it, stringing it, and
cooking it in barns so that it turned out golden and valuable instead of
dark and worthless.

Before tobacco came into Bacon County, the farmers were self-sufficient in a way they were never to be again. In the days before tobacco
they grew everything they needed and lived pretty well. Since they were
too far south to grow wheat, they had to buy flour. But almost everything
else they really wanted, they could grow. Grandpa Hazelton even grew
rice on a piece of his low-lying land that had enough water to sustain
that crop.

But tobacco took so much of their time and energy and worry that
they stopped growing many of the crops they had grown before. Consequently, they had to depend upon the money from the tobacco to buy
what they did not grow. A failed tobacco crop then was a genuine disaster that affected not just the individual farmer but the economy of the
entire county.

Even if the tobacco crop was successful, all it meant, with rare exceptions, was for one brief moment at the end of summer they had money in
their hands before they had to give it over to whoever supplied the fertilizer to grow the tobacco and the poison to kill the worms, and to those
who helped harvest and cook it, and a hundred other expenses that ate
up the money and put them right back in debt again. Tobacco money was
then and is now an illusion, and growing tobacco became very quickly an
almost magical rite they kept participating in over and over again, hoping
that they would have a particularly good crop one year and they would
be able to keep some of the money and not have to give it all away.

But the tobacco crop was not successful that first year on Luther
Carter's place or anywhere else in the county, and daddy, along with
everybody else, was desperate for money. On top of money worries,

there was great pressure from Grandpa and Grandma Hazelton for daddy and mama to move back to the home place and live with them. Daddy didn't want to do it out of simple pride. Even though he was already a sharecropper, he didn't want to move in with and work for his wife's parents. He had never gotten along very well with Grandpa Hazelton, a man who liked to give much advice and do little work.

Grandpa spent most of his time reading the three newspapers he subscribed to, newspapers brought by the mailman. It didn't bother him that the newspapers were always two or three days out of date; he read them all from the first page to the last, staying up until the small hours of the morning with a kerosene lamp beside him, all the while taking little sips out of a mason fruit jar full of moonshine which he kept on the mantelpiece over the fireplace. He didn't get drunk; he just liked to have little sips while he was awake.

He stopped only long enough to look about now and then to see if anybody was about to do something. If they were, he would explain in great and careful detail just how they should do it. He would do this whether he knew anything about the task at hand or not. Then he would go back to his newspaper.

Daddy was too proud and stubborn and independent for such an arrangement to work. But his wife was the youngest child of the family, still only seventeen years old. She had just lost a baby and the crops had failed, and so, against his better judgment, he went to live with his in-laws.

It was a total and unrelieved disaster that came to the point of crisis, strangely enough, over biscuits one night when they were all sitting at the supper table. Daddy looked up and saw Grandpa Hazelton smiling down the table at him.

Daddy said: "Something the matter?"

Since the old man was bad to bristle and bark himself, he said: "Is it look to be something the matter?"

"What you laughing at?"

"I ain't laughing."

"I seen it."

The old man said: "A man cain't tell me in my own house I was laughing."

Daddy said: "You was. And it was because of them biscuits."

"I don't laugh at biscuits, boy. I ain't crazy yet, even if it's some that think I am."

"You was laughing at how many I et. Was you counting, too?"

Daddy didn't have a very thick skin, and one of the things he was touchy about was how much he ate. Just a little over a month before his run-in with the old man, he was at a church picnic and Frank Porter, a boy from Coffee County, said something about him being Long Hungry, which to the people in that time was an insult. To be Long Hungry meant you were a glutton. A hog at the trough. So Daddy invited Frank Porter—since they were at a church and couldn't settle it there—to meet him the next day on a scrub oak ridge separating Coffee from Bacon.

The next morning at sunup the two men met, daddy and the man who had insulted him, up in the middle of a little stand of blackjack oak on a sandy ridge full of gopher holes and rattlesnake nests. They had each of them brought several of their friends as overseers of the fight, or rather their friends had insisted on coming to make sure that no knives or axes or guns got in the way and resulted in one or both of their deaths.

They set to and fought until noon, quit, went home, ate, patched up as best they could, and came back and fought until sundown. They didn't fight the whole time. By mutual consent and necessity, they took time out to rest. While they were resting, their friends fought. Those that were there said it had been a real fine day. A little bloody, but a fine day. For years after the fight, time was often measured by farmers in both counties by the day the fight took place.

"*It weren't no more'n two months after Ray and Frank met up on the line.*"

"*That girl of mine was born three months to the day before Frank and Ray had the fight.*"

And sitting there now at the supper table still smarting from being called Long Hungry and still carrying sign on his back and chest and head from the fight with Frank Porter, he could not bear what he knew he saw in grandpa's face.

He stood up from the table and said to mama: "Myrtice, git your things. We leavin."

Grandpa said: "Where you going to?"

Daddy stopped just long enough to say, "I don't know where I'm going. It's lots of places I could go. What you don't understand, old man, is if I didn't have anyplace to go, I'd go anyway."

But he had a place to go and he knew it. Uncle Alton had recently been married to a lady named Eva Jenkins and they were sharecropping themselves for Jess Boatwright. Summer was coming on and all the crops had been laid by, which meant they'd been plowed the last time and all that remained was the harvest. Daddy put mama on the wagon seat beside him and started the long slow ride over the dirt roads in the dark to offer Uncle Alton a proposition which in his heart he didn't believe Uncle Alton would take. Since he was sharecropping for grandpa, he meant to trade crops.

"We got to swap," he said when Uncle Alton came to the door.

"Swap what?" Uncle Alton said.

"You take my crop and I'll take yours. You and Eva go and live with your daddy, cause I cain't stand it. Me and Myrtice'll come live here."

Daddy told him what had happened, and Uncle Alton never questioned it, knowing as he did how his daddy was. Also, daddy was his best friend and mama his baby sister. He knew daddy would never consent to going back after leaving in the middle of the night that way. They had to live somewhere. There were no options.

"We'll swap even," Uncle Alton said.

"I ought to give you something to boot," daddy said. "You got ten acres more'n me."

Uncle Alton said: "We'll swap even."

And they did. It made quite a noise in the county. Nobody had ever heard of such a thing. Some of the old folks still talk to this day about that trade, about how daddy and mama moved into the house on the Jess Boatwright place and Uncle Alton and Aunt Eva went over to live with Grandpa Hazelton.

Daddy never set foot in grandpa's house again as long as he lived. He would allow mama to go and visit and after my brother and I were born to take us with her.

After they finished gathering the crop, which was good enough to let them get far enough out of debt to borrow on the next crop, they rented the Jess Boatwright place for one year. But as the world seems to go sometimes when a man's got his back right up against the wall, the tobacco crop that year was so sorry daddy couldn't even sell it, and he ended by putting it in the mule stable instead.

Cotton that year was selling for three cents a pound and you could buy a quarter of beef for four cents a pound. It was 1931. The rest of the country was just beginning to feel the real hurt of the Great Depression, but it had been living in Bacon County for years. Some folks said it had always been there.

But in that year two good things did happen. On the ninth of July, mama gave birth to a healthy baby, who was named after daddy, Ray, but who has always been called Hoyet. The other thing that happened was that daddy somehow managed to buy a mare. A mare, not a mule. Her name was Daisy, and she was so mean that daddy was the only one in the county who could put a bridle on her, much less work her to a plow or wagon. It was the first draft animal he'd owned, and he was almost as proud of the mare as he was of his son.

As mean as she was, Daisy pulled a fine wagon and even a better plow if you could control her. As it turned out, daddy could control her. He had her respect and she had his. They knew what to expect from one another. He knew dead solid certain that she would kick his head off if she got the chance. And she knew just as surely that he would beat her to her knees with a singletree—the iron bar on a plow or wagon to which the trace chains are hooked—if she did not cooperate.

It sounds like a terrible thing to talk about, hitting a mare between the ears with a piece of iron, but it was done not only out of necessity but also out of love. A farmer didn't mistreat his draft animals. People in Bacon County always said that a man who would mistreat his mules would mistreat his family. But it was necessary for daddy and Daisy to come to some understanding before they could do the work that was proper to both of them. And whatever was necessary to that understanding had to be done. Without that understanding, there could be no respect, to say nothing of love. For a man and an animal to work together from sunup to dark, day in and day out, there ought to be love. How else could either of them bear it?

Still, it was unusual for him to have a mare instead of a mule. Horses and mares were playthings. Mules were the workers. Mules bought the baby's shoes and put grits on the table.

I never remember seeing anybody plow a horse in Bacon County, and it wasn't because mules were cheaper than horses. They weren't. Daddy got Daisy for $60. A good young mule even in the depth of the Depression would have cost him $200. So it was not because of cost that farmers plowed mules instead of horses; it was because horses have no stamina in front of a turnplow breaking dirt a foot deep. Worse, a horse doesn't care where he puts his feet. A mule puts his foot down exactly where he means to put it. A mule will walk all day, straight as a plumb line, setting his feet down only inches from young corn, corn that might be less than a foot high, and he'll never step on a plant. A horse walks all over everything. Unless, that is, you can come to some understanding with him, which most men did not seem to be able to do. But daddy made a sweet working animal out of Daisy, and she was ready, if not always willing, to do whatever was required of her. In the shoebox of pictures, there is one of my brother when he was only four years old sitting on Daisy bareback. Nobody is holding her rein and she is standing easy as the lady she became under my daddy's firm, gentle, and dangerous hand.

Maybe it was because of the crops failing or the trouble they'd had with Grandpa Hazelton, but mama remembers the house at the Jess Boatwright place as the worst they ever lived in. It was made out of notched logs, but instead of being mud-sealed, it was board-sealed, which meant the wind had a free way with it in the winter. My brother had a case of double pneumonia that year and almost died. There was no smokehouse, so the little bit of meat they could come by was cured by hanging in the sun during the day and then putting it in the shed at night. They also put some of it in stone jugs of brine to preserve it, but while meat never spoiled in a jug of brine, it took real courage and a certain desperation to eat through all that salt.

But luck fortunately comes in two flavors: good as well as bad. And some good luck came their way at the end of the second year on the Jess Boatwright place. My Grandma Hazelton gave them 120 acres of land. What wealth there was in the Hazelton family at that time came through my grandma. Grandpa Hazelton brought very little to the marriage and what little he brought got away from him somehow while he read his three newspapers every day. But Grandma Hazelton's daddy left her a big piece of land and they—she and grandpa—built the house they lived in out of the sale of part of it. But there was a good bit left, and because mama was the youngest in the family, and because of the tragic circumstances of her firstborn child, and maybe also to try somehow to make up for daddy and mama having to trade crops with Uncle Alton and move out of the house in the middle of the year, she made the land a gift outright, and they went to live on it.

But even good luck rarely comes made out of whole cloth, and theirs had several pretty ragged places in it. For starters, none of the land was in cultivation. It was nothing but pine trees and palmetto thickets and stands of gallberry bushes and dog fennel. Worse than that, if there can be anything worse than a farmer with no land he can farm, there was no house on it, no building of any kind. There was nothing for daddy to do but build one.

And he did. Uncle Randal Jordan and one of my daddy's good friends, Cadger Barnes, helped him. Daddy paid them a wage of a quarter a day. None of the trees on the land they'd been given were big enough to use, so Cadger, who had a heavy stand of big pine on his land, gave daddy enough trees to build the house. And the three of them, using crosscut saws, felled the trees and snaked the logs over to the place with Daisy, and then they cut the trees into lengths they could split for boards. There was no money for a sawmill, so with wedges and mallets and axes they split the pine by hand into boards.

Once it was finished you could smell the turpentine out of that green pine house from a mile away. The whole house cost $50 to build. Mama planted a cedar tree out in the front yard the day they moved in. It was the house in which I would be born. The house is gone now, but I stood in the shade of that cedar tree four months ago.

The first year they were there daddy cleared ten acres for cultivation. The second year he cleared another ten. He and mama did it together with an ax and a saw and a grubbing hoe and Daisy. Daisy pulled what she could from the ground. What she couldn't pull out, mama and daddy dug out. What they couldn't dig out, they burned out. There were a few people, very few, who could afford dynamite to blow stumps out; everybody else dug and burned, burned and dug. An oak stump might cost a man a week of his life.

All through the winter of that second year, the hazy smoke of burning stumps floated over them as they picked up roots and grubbed palmetto and gallberry. Mama had been growing pinker and rounder and seemingly stronger every day with her third and what would prove to be her last pregnancy. She didn't quit going to the field until May, and on the seventh of June, 1935, Daddy got on Daisy and went over to get Emily Ahl, who came racing back behind his galloping mare in her midwifery buggy in which she had gone to farmhouses all over that end of Bacon County.

In the late afternoon, Miss Emily, wearing her black bonnet and black, long dress, a dress and color she considered proper to her calling, cut me loose from mama and tied me off. She was a midwife of consummate skill, and my entrance into the world was without incident.

I am compelled to celebrate the craft and art of the lady who did everything that was required of her so competently. Not only did she make a lovely arrangement of my navel when she cut me free, but she also left me intact, for which I have always been grateful.

Since they had no land to tend while they were taking in the new ground, daddy rented thirty acres from the land bank, a federal agency that controlled a lot of land and let it to farmers at a cost they could afford, which meant practically nothing. In his spare time, when he wasn't farming the acreage he'd rented from the land bank or pulling stumps or working on the stable for Daisy, he hired out to plow for other people. Mama would pack him some biscuit and fatback and maybe a vegetable she might have put up the previous summer, along with a little cold grits; she'd put it all in a tin syrup bucket, and he'd leave the house before sunup and come back after dark, bringing the empty syrup bucket and twenty-five cents for his day's work.

By the time I was born he'd put up a mule barn and a notched log smokehouse sealed with mud. Just when he got the place looking pretty good, he had the chance to sell it at more than he'd thought he'd ever be able to make out of it again, and at the same time the chance to buy a place cheap that he'd been looking at a long time. So he sold out and bought the Cash Carter place, which had a little better than 200 acres of land—about 40 of it in cultivation. He got it at a good price because the land had been allowed to lie fallow until it was rank with weeds. Most of the fences were down, there was no mule lot or smokehouse or tobacco barn, and the dwelling house was nearly as sorry as the one they'd lived in at Jess Boatwright's. But it was 200 acres of land, and daddy knew, or thought he knew, that he could make it into a decent farm on which he could support his family. It wouldn't be easy and it wouldn't be quick, but given five or ten years, he would do it and he would do it right.

# Rosemary Daniell

---

## From *Fatal Flowers:*
## *On Sin, Sex, and Suicide in the Deep South*

*Pictures from my mother's life*—images of the people primary to me hold the power to move me backward into a time before I existed. So deeply do I believe myself to have been there, to have shared the experiences of those whose faces and forms were caught on film before I was born, that I project even those born after me into my multilinear time scheme. Driving from Atlanta to Mother's last home in North Carolina, passing through Clayton and Rabun Gap, Georgia—my disorientation growing with the soft beginnings of the Appalachian Mountains— I turned to my sixteen-year-old daughter, Darcy, in the back seat of the car. Noting again that she had dressed for her grandmother's funeral as flashily as a French whore—orange knit midi, orange suede boots—I asked, "Do you remember what Mother was like when she was three?"

I was thinking of a picture I had seen: Mother, crouched at the base of a thick oak, fat-cheeked, peering sullenly toward the camera, her wide forehead cut squarely across by Dutch-boy bangs that emphasized the body structure Grandmother Lee had always described as "built close to the ground." Her gaze is stubborn, her mien serious, echoing remarkably pictures of myself, and later Darcy, at the same age. Despite the fact that Mother had been slightly curvier and shorter, her breasts a bit fuller, her feet a size or two smaller, we three were sisters, replicas, overlapping paper dolls.

In the hospital after Darcy's birth, I saw a moment of my new daughter's future. Jet-curled, curved, she pumped fat calves down and up, driving her tricycle along the drive of our house. Later, what I had imagined became reality. Though she laughed as the streamers of a red velvet sailor hat sped behind her, her face was determined, an amazing likeness of Mother in the photograph.

"Be careful what you want; you might get it" is a common Southern saying. If one's own or another's future could be so clearly seen, could another's past also? In that moment in the car, speeding toward Mother's last social event, I felt as though the three of us had indeed existed simultaneously. Given the infinity of time, the microcosmic nature of the present, and my sense of my mother's life as simply a fragment of my own, that perception may have been as logical as any. Because of her solemn, almost sad gaze, it would be romantic to believe the picture of Mother beneath the oak tree at three to have been made after what she considered the initial and determining tragedy of her life. But it was a tragedy that occurred later, when she was six—a tragedy that, in Bible Belt tradition, had to do with drink.

"Southerners drink more," a displaced New Yorker observed, "because it's so boring down here." A good ole boy might reply that Black Jack is the perfect companion to the gospel songs, storytelling, and contemplations of mortality of which he is fond. Indeed, drinking oneself to death, according to the lyrics of country music, is an acceptable form of male suicide. (Women, too "good" to drink, are allowed promiscuity and hysteria.) When a great-uncle and his nephew were respectively unable to keep their promises to quit drinking to the good Christian women who were their wives, they promptly shot themselves—acts their widows considered appropriate to the nature of their sin.

Daddy's alcoholism had always seemed to me related to the fundamentalist dictum on total abstinence. In Mother's life, drink-related pain began before she was seven with the early death of her father, Huelet Connell. Huelet, Grandmother Lee's first husband, had been killed at thirty-two in an accident in Leeds, Alabama: a "good man" and nondrinker himself, he had taken a cab driven by a drunken driver.

With her father's death, Mother felt she had permanently lost touch with male gentleness and refinement. She loved to tell my sister, Anne, and me how his family had discussed Milton and Shakespeare at the supper table in Villa Rica, Georgia. In addition, his father had been a circuit-riding Methodist minister, providing a direct line to both propriety and God the Father. Mother had always considered the Methodists to be somehow higher on the social scale, more refined than the openly hellfire-and-damnation-shouting Baptists. The intellectual superiority of the family had been borne out, in her view, when Huelet's brother George was made president of Mercer University in Macon, Georgia.

When I visited Macon and Mercer to give readings from my poetry, I, too, felt a twinge of pleasure as I pointed out to my Yankee lover the inscription of my dead uncle's name on the side of a building erected in his honor. Mother would have been pleased at my pride, though had she known the partly carnal nature of my visit, or the feminist content of the poems I had chosen to read, she would have recoiled in shame.

What Mother revered most—polite society, the Ten Commandments, and the written word—began for her in stories of her father's family. That her grandmother, the Methodist minister's wife, was a habitual snuff dipper was an incongruous detail omitted from her recollections. Even before she was born, Mother was destined, like all white Southern women of her generation, to an allegiance to patriarchy, to what was obviously male superiority.

It was an idea to which she clung for a lifetime, and the one that ultimately destroyed her.

The unknowing carriers of this cultural ideal, Lee Darnell and Huelet Connell, had grown up next door to one another in Villa Rica. Until her mid-twenties, as was the custom in staunch Southern families of Scotch-Irish descent, Lee had remained at home doing the family cooking, cleaning, and sewing along with her younger sister, Bunny.

A picture of Lee taken around that time shows a young woman standing beside the front gate of a white picket fence, her bearing dignified, her face inscrutable. Her hair, I have been told, was a fine pink-red—the color echoed today in that of my older daughter, Laura. Her eyes were—and still are at eighty-seven—a clear blue, her fair skin lightly freckled.

A head shot of Huelet around the same time portrays a boyish, curly-haired young man sporting the raw haircut and gaunt cheeks—almost as though he is sucking them inward—that seem typical of rural Southern men of the period. Yet with the bones, the curls, he is almost pretty—projecting a girlish delicacy that fits Mother's belief in his inherent gentleness and gentility.

When Lee and Huelet married, they moved to Leeds, Alabama, where he had a job with the Southern Railroad. It was 1915, and they began their family, as was customary, immediately. The length of time each child nursed later served as a natural form of birth control, but at the beginning of conjugal life, there was no such protection. Mother—Melissa Ruth Connell—was soon born; within two years came Grace; and in two more, Florance.

Lee says that in spite of being a stranger in the small Alabama town, of giving birth at home with little or no anesthesia, of having no washing machine, air conditioning, or electric refrigeration, she was content. "We didn't have an automobile—not many people did—but I wheeled the babies to the grocery store in their carriage, and sometimes we went somewhere on the streetcar. And there was church once a month, when the local circuit rider came."

After her young husband's sudden death, I envision her moving pragmatically through her grief. The funeral behind her, she must have methodically gathered up the dresses, bloomers, undershirts she had sewn by hand for her three daughters, and the diapers that she washed by hand each day. Though it was common country custom at that time to hang the diapers without washing them, trusting to the sun to bleach out ammonia and urine, Lee undoubtedly washed those of her children. Already, she was deeply imprinted with the stoic patience that was a necessary feminine virtue of her time. Ahead was the long train trip—her three youngsters and all their belongings in tow—back to Villa Rica.

Villa Rica was, and is, typical of many small towns throughout Georgia. Though there *are* towns known for columned mansions, live oaks dripping Spanish moss, magnolia-and-azalea-lined squares, Villa Rica is not one of those. Rather, it is a small community that pours as slowly as the regionally produced sorghum syrup along a stretch of dusty railroad track. There are the ubiquitous Baptist and Methodist churches, a few general stores, and the local drugstore.

Traveling, I've often run into such a pharmacy to ask—as local folk, lemon Cokes in hand, swivel necks and stools beside the soda fountain— for a box of Tampax or a tube of Crest; inevitably, too, the clerk's directions have led me among the narrow counters to a stack of boxes that met my fingertips through a grainy veil of red or gray dust. Inevitably, too, I would suddenly need proof of the continued existence of cities, and as I went out the door, would buy from the bright-yellow box a suddenly exotic *Atlanta Journal* or *Constitution*.

In such a town, even today, the silence of a Sunday afternoon, after the ritual of Sunday school and church, the midday meal of fried chicken, biscuits, and cream gravy, is impermeable, a blanket ruffled only by the rotation of the wooden fan inside the fly-specked drugstore, the occasional screech of tires of a car driven by a local teenager. (In rural Georgia every high school annual has a page dedicated to the "outstanding" senior who died in glory on the football field or was killed that year as he attempted to fly, instead of drive, his old Chevy over bumpy country roads.)

Though a half-hearted attempt at a shopping center, complete with Penney's and Sears, may today rise on the highway leading out of town, life revolved, and still revolves, around Sunday-morning and -evening services, Wednesday-night prayer meetings, Friday-night football games, and meetings of secret men's societies, such as the Elks or Masons. Family and personal pride is based not on lineage or achievement but on the regularity of one's church attendance and one's ability to abstain from drinking, smoking, and telling dirty jokes—all virtue a negation of vice!

It is a society that, for women, holds particularly rigid stipulations. If in Plains, Billy Carter enjoys the role of local bad, or "good ole," boy, the same behavior—belting six-packs of beer, hanging out at the local service station or pool hall—would be unthinkable for his wife. In the teachers' lounge of a consolidated county school where I was poet-in-residence for a week, I noticed that the teachers, mostly women, looked less rested, relaxed, unlined than the urban women I knew who slept less and worked harder. As a guest at a dinner for local teachers at the Holiday Inn, I sat across from the Methodist minister and ate dry roast beef and canned cream corn, washed down with the inevitable iced tea, as a visiting Baptist preacher intoned an anecdote about Sherwood Anderson:

" 'Mr. An-nerson,' he said to him, 'you may have written novels showin' the problems of small-town life in America—the narrowness, the bigotry—but sir, you've failed to show us the so-looshions!' " As he concluded his denunciation of artists and intellectuals—"Sherwood An-nerson may have been a great writer, but he was *not* a great man!"—his voice rose and fell with the evangelistic fervor I had heard since early childhood.

The eyes of the teachers—almost all women—widened: in Bremen, Georgia, the voice of the Baptist preacher is the voice of God. I amused myself by thinking what his response would have been had he known he not only had another unsavory writer in his presence, but a woman who wrote feminist poetry. Yet beneath my uncomfortable amusement, I felt sad. I had been in this town five days; these women never left a place where any unpopular action or assertion could wreck the structure of their lives.

"You do, and we'll run you out of town with a shotgun!" had been my stepfather's immediate, only half-joking response when I suggested, at the height of the women's movement, the instigation of a consciousness-raising group in the North Carolina town where he lived with Mother.

It was to an earlier and more rigid version of such a town that Lee traveled with her three daughters after Huelet's death. For two years, she changed diapers, sewed, washed, and ironed within her parents' house— two years broken only by thrice-weekly church services and the summer evenings when the family gathered on the porch to rock and talk till dark. (It is such endless evenings, such years of talk, that give Southerners— like a kind of verbal hope chest—a head start on a lifelong supply of anecdotes.) Occasionally, a churn filled with salty ice, fruit, cream must have been brought out, turns taken at its handle, until Lee or her mother dished out soup bowls full of homemade Georgia peach ice cream, full of delicious little crystals, juicy chunks of fruit. As a scene my sister, Anne, our numerous cousins, and I later repeated, it flashes before me clearly: Mother, Grace, Florance—perhaps a neighbor child or two— fighting over who would lick the icy dasher, then running with cold, full stomachs after lightning bugs, cupping them in palms or jars, stopping off and on to swing from the rubber tire hung from a great oak near the house, until Lee's voice, cutting the dark, called them in to bed.

When Mr. Carroll began to call, there must have been more of such social evenings. Manager of the Chattahoochee Mills near Atlanta, John Carroll was a widower who had already buried two wives and who had four near-grown children of his own. A man of appetites, energy, and power, he was also a reformed alcoholic. It was *his* brother, *his* nephew who shot themselves because of their fondness for drink. Three of his sons, assisted by "good" wives, repeated his pattern of dissolute youth turned hard-driving businessman and patriarch.

On those summer nights, the brawling, rough, overpowering Irishman must have appealed to the controlled young woman who was my mother's mother. She must have thrilled to the gifts with which he showered her—beaded purses, perfume, jewelry—and to their honeymoon trip by train to New Orleans. At seventy, she confided that she had loved him passionately, though it was a passion that would diminish with the responsibilities of a huge household.

By the time I was five or six, Grandmother Lee and Granddaddy Carroll had moved from the two-story house near the Chattahoochee Mills, from which Mother and her sisters had been driven to school each morning in the limousine. As far back as I can remember, they lived on a working farm in Tucker, outside Atlanta. Granddaddy Carroll had retired from business, bought the farm and much of the surrounding countryside.

There was an enormous one-story white frame house fronted by a verandah and hundreds of feet of lawn; another porch ran along one side of the house, which was organized around a long central hall off which branched broad, high-ceilinged rooms heated by huge fireplaces. Even the beds, the tall four-posters with their double mattresses, seemed extra high—hard for a six-year-old to climb onto. Spending the night, I was afraid to try the climb down, the trip to the bathroom far down the dark corridor, no matter how badly I had to go, and would lie numbly till morning, hoping not to wet my pajamas in my proper grandparents' house.

Out the back door, beyond the main house and the brief yard, was a red-dirt area through which wandered chickens, cats, turkeys, peacocks, dogs; it was bordered by the buildings of household management and farm production—storehouse, chicken house, washroom, curing room, tool shed, barns, and miscellaneous buildings. Behind the buildings began the vegetable gardens, the black people's houses, the cornfields, the railroad tracks, the peach orchard, the creek, and the endless sloping pastures.

Though I feared the snotty peacocks and the mean-eyed gobblers, I loved—in the beginning of an obsession with egg shapes—collecting the shit-smeared eggs from beneath the hens and—until one defecated on my Sunday dress, and the sickening lurch of conscience began—poking the genitals of the endless mewing kittens with twigs. Until I learned it was also full of fleas, I loved the long, cool milking barn with its fat red-and-white cows. When there was a new colt or calf, my cousins and I would chase and try to lasso it as it ran around the barnyard. Beside the barn proper was the hog pen, full of creatures who snorted vociferously as the slops from the kitchen were splashed over the fence; when a sow gave birth, the piglets sliding from her hugely distended vagina looked like toys despite their coating of blood and slime.

I watched as my older, more courageous cousins jumped from the hayloft—which later became a fine place to smooch with my eleven-year-old cousin Bubba. In the storehouse, already in love with family history, I pored through musty boxes of love letters to Mother's half sister, Aunt Billie, from her boyfriend. One afternoon, I hung screaming to the neck of a horse as it galloped undirected up a path; on another, a cow galloped toward me full speed from a distance in the pasture: I barely made it beneath the barbed-wire fence, my new pink angora sweater shredded.

But until adolescence, the farm seemed to me a heaven more vivid, more appealing, than the silly singing, the streets of gold described by the Baptist preacher. Still, during the counterculture sixties, I was immune to the mystique of soap making, the romance of rural communes: unconsciously, I must have observed what the farm meant to Grandmother Lee. Those who have been farm wives rarely wish to go back to the "good old days." Today Lee enjoys her electric sewing machine, washing machine, convenience foods; but then the farm must have formed a kind of prison—inevitably, the sensuality of her chores was lost in their volume.

Spring was the time to plant the vast garden in which she grew the food for the main house. Summer meant canning—tomatoes, beans, field peas, okra, corn. I remember watching her pop the kernels off the cob in three sweet milky layers, her knife moving round and down, almost faster than my eyes could follow. Several vegetables were combined for "soup mix." She made peach preserves, blackberry jam, crab-apple jelly, and the pickles—bread-and-butter, sweet, dill.

Almost every day butter was churned—and churned and churned: a pound of butter could cost an hour of time and energy. Every day there were cows to be milked, hogs to be slopped, milk to be separated, eggs to be collected, chickens to be fed, chicken corpses to be scalded, plucked, eviscerated.

Daily, large meals were to be served: breakfasts included homemade "biscuit" (always referred to in the singular), fried fatback or pork brains, cream gravy, and grits. (When *she* was a girl, she told me, breakfasts meant fried chicken, too.) Promptly at noon on weekdays, Lee dished out "dinner"—chicken and dumplings, country ham or meat loaf, squash soufflé, pole beans, probably collard greens boiled with ham hock, more biscuit and corn sticks, and for dessert, perhaps blackberry cobbler or banana pudding (my first husband's grandmother made it in washtubs).

Sunday lunch—"dinner" again—was at one instead of twelve to allow for church, and was fancier: roast or fried chicken, cream gravy, white rice, canned English peas, perhaps a "salad"—red Jell-O in which hung black cherries, fruit cocktail, chunks of cream cheese, sliced bananas, or pecan halves—plus the ubiquitous dessert of cake or pie. As a child, I loved Sunday dinners at Grandmother Lee's—to stuff myself, then fall asleep on a high bed, until I woke at sunset, with cheeks drool-damp, imprinted by ridges of chenille, ready to chase lightning bugs or my cousins. But for Lee, the dinner had meant rising early—in summer, even on Sundays, the vegetables for the midday meal were to be picked each morning from the garden; the meal must be near-cooked before she could dress herself and the younger children for Sunday school and church.

In late fall, Lee worked overtime. As Thanksgiving and Christmas neared, she seemed continuously to bake: first the fruit cakes, from family recipes—white and dark (which, because of the family's commitment to Christian temperance, were kept wrapped in rags soaked in orange juice rather than the traditional bourbon). Then the layer cakes: Lane cake, thick with raisins and pecans; hickory nut, made from nutmeats laboriously excised from hardwood shells; coconut, made with tediously grated fresh coconut—sometimes her knuckles would abrade and bleed from the effort; lemon cheese, with its tart apple-thickened filling, its snowy-white boiled frosting; and my favorite, caramel, heavy with brown-sugar icing through which marched row after row of handshelled pecan halves. Besides the Bible and her Sunday-school text, Mrs. S. R. Dull's *Southern Cooking,* published in 1928, was the most important book in Grandmother Lee's life; it was her gift to me when I married the first time.

When the great days finally came, with the whole family—aunts, uncles, cousins, grandparents—collected, the feasts commenced with roast turkey (I always hoped it was the one that had rushed, beak aimed, at my bare legs in the yard); dressing (the Southern form of stuffing: not baked within the bird, but in large flat pans, like a savory bread); giblet gravy; sweet potatoes souffléed and stuffed into orange halves, the edges of which had been trimmed into Halloween teeth, and topped with a toasted marshmallow; freshly risen yeast rolls; and for an exotic touch, store-bought stuffed olives and canned jellied cranberry sauce. (When everything fresh was homegrown, what was canned, store-bought, was "fancy.") Besides the cakes and pies, by then decorously arranged on the sideboard, there was ambrosia, a juicy compote of oranges, cherries, coconut, pecans; and maybe a concoction called heavenly hash—a mixture of whipped cream, pineapple, cherries, pecans, and melted marshmallows. It was a cuisine that couldn't have been more carbohydrate-laden. (Years late, in New York, I was taken to dinner in Chinatown by a Chinese artist who hoped to please me with a special dessert: he had found a small watermelon stand and assumed that because I was from Georgia, such an end to our meal would make me feel at home, unaware that in the South, the melon is a snack, not to be confused with "dessert," which contains at least a half pound of white sugar, or "why-at-death," as a displaced Southerner in L.A. put it.)

Besides the production and cooking of food, there was the house to be cleaned, and clothes to be sewn—in addition to her own and her daughters' clothes, Lee made men's shirts and suits. Clothes were still scrubbed by hand on a washboard in a deep black pot heated over an open fire in the red-dirt-floored washroom, then dipped in tubs of thick boiled starch, hung out, and ironed. While Pearl, who lived "on the place," was there from seven to seven, along with occasional "outside" help (black women were often paid less than a dollar a day), the running of the household, with its rituals and necessities, was a seven-day-a-week, fifty-two-week-a-year job that held Lee—and more so, her black servants, who had to do the same jobs at home for their own families—captive.

It was a job that formed her character and attitudes, and her daughters' and grandaughters' idea of what it was to be a Southern woman of a certain class—that was, a woman of physical stamina and endless Christian stoicism. Grandmother Lee *was* the long-suffering Melanie, the Mrs. O'Hara who silently gave birth so as not to disturb a household that Mr. O'Hara instantly disrupted with bellows of pain at a splinter in his finger.

Like Mr. O'Hara and other good patriarchs, Granddaddy Carroll was responsible, paid the bills, but demanded that everything be done just so—the buttermilk into which he liked to dip his cornbread chilled to exactly the right temperature, the "pot likker," a greasy green soup left from the boiling of turnip greens, saved just for him; and as he grew older, the cases of "Co-Cola" to which he had become addicted kept at ready on the "back porch" (a kind of anterior entrance hall common to Southern farmhouses). Most of all, the children and grandchildren were to be kept out of his way as he read the Atlanta papers, or later, when cataracts had developed on his eyes, listened beside the radio for news of World War II. Their mutual young were Lee's responsibility, "to be seen and not heard" the ideal of child behavior. Like Mrs. O'Hara in *Gone with the Wind*, Lee referred to her husband as *Mr.* Carroll.

That her initial passion for him had not survived the years of caretaking was revealed in remarks about the diminishing sexual desire of women as they grow older. "The older you get, the more of a chore it is!" she said, shelling peas as she contradicted an article a daughter had just mentioned from *Good Housekeeping* (the nitty-gritty details of the "chore" were unmentionable, even among the initiated—or married—women). After the long years of her husband's senility and finally his death, she had no desire to remarry: "What? And have another old man to take care of?"

Otherwise, she only obliquely revealed to her daughters her ambivalence about her role. "I never let Melissa or the others help in the kitchen," she says; "they would have just been in the way. Besides, they would have plenty of *that* later. . . ." When her youngest daughter, Billie, married, the young couple, following a common Southern custom, lived in the parental house. When Billie became pregnant, Lee carried trays to her in bed—stewed chicken, scraped beefsteak, chicken broth, milk toast. It was as though Lee's aversion to the implications of motherhood had surfaced in the nine-month-long nausea of the daughter who had seen her work hardest.

Lee's daughters, in their beautiful handmade clothes, enjoying the benefits of a prosperous, if provincial, household, were the rural princesses she had never been. Yet it was she who knew and encouraged the importance of beauty and mystique as measures of feminine worth. As pragmatically, as consistently, as a Chinese mother who knows the value of bound feet in the marriage marketplace, she presented an image of self-restraint that neared self-immolation.

Her values—ladylike passivity, conservative good looks, and the ability to cook—were those she knew with a realistic cynicism to be those sought by the men who could give her daughters the most position and ease. Men who were "good husband material" had their own standards; and though she wouldn't have put it that way, Lee knew that they liked to fuck and eat and didn't want any flack.

If she was rigid in her delineation of proper behavior for her female young, it was a rigidity that seemed as necessary and contradictory as the voluntary infliction of pain by the Chinese mothers on their daughters; and her motivation was the same: she wanted safety for them. All her simplified instructions for the manipulation of men—"Don't let him kiss you until you're engaged. . . . Don't tell him too much about your-self. . . ."—were directed toward the enhancement of one's value as a marriageable object.

Today she wears blue pantsuits and pale-blue turtleneck sweaters that complement her silver-blue hair; but when she wouldn't let my cousins and me into her house with "those pants" (blue jeans) on, she was trying to protect us from what she was sure was destructive behavior.

Though she had never been a princess, Lee seemed to me a queen. Granddaddy Carroll was the owner of most of the ramshackle houses in the local "nigger town." At eight or nine, I stood beside my grandparents on the back steps as the blacks came to pay their rent and ask advice. The obsequious way in which they spoke—"Yes'm, Miz Carroll; yesser, Maser Carroll"—made me feel my grandparents were royalty of sorts, instead of the country equivalent of slumlords.

My view was reinforced by my visits to the small unpainted frame house perched on stilts down in the far pasture. There Pearl and her hus-band, Homer, lived with their five young. Despite the coziness of the two rooms with their fireplace heat, Pearl's rich voice belting out gospel songs as she washed her own children's clothes, and the well out on the back porch into which I liked to let down the old tin bucket to magi-cally raise cool, clear water and sometimes a tiny frog or two, I realized that the simplicity and warmth of Pearl's way of life, especially her out-house, implied inferiority. From my perspective, it was as though she and her husband were children who had children. To be a *real* South-ern woman was to be as responsible, as impenetrable, as unsmiling as Grandmother Lee.

That Mother worshiped, rather than merely loved or admired, her mother, Lee, was made clear to me at seven or eight. As Mother and I walked out to the pen in our backyard in Atlanta to feed our own chickens, she carried a pie pan of cornbread crumbs. She seemed pre-occupied, as she often did when we were alone. I tugged her arm to get her attention—I had a wonderful insight, a gift: "Don't you think that Grandmother Lee looks just like a cow in a pasture?" I asked. I had made what I considered a flattering comparison, equating my grandmother's stoicism with the quiet eyes, the cud-chewing placidity of the cows in her pasture.

I looked at Mother hopefully, then pulled away, surprised: her lower lip had already curled into the downward curve I knew preceded violence. Too late! I felt the stinging *whop* of her open palm against my cheek, heard the clatter of the cornbread pan hitting the gravel. "Don't you evah talk about your grand-pay-rents that way!" she commanded, drawling out the long *a* she habitually inserted into certain words. Retrieving the half-spilled pan, she looked away—as though she had already forgotten my presence—and threw the rest of the crumbs over the fence into the chicken yard.

Neither Anne nor I ever heard our mother question her mother's values, criticize her, or behave any way but submissively toward her. Clearly, Mother considered Lee a model of perfection; within a perfectly patriarchal society, she was indeed the perfect matriarch—subservient, self-denying, self-controlled.

It was a model that for her lifetime, Mother would alternately attempt to evade and embrace. Through her "modern" marriage to Daddy, their urban early married life, and her small family, she sought to remain the little girl, the belle—to escape the pressures with which she had seen her mother deal.

In the last years of her life, remarried to a farmer as patriarchal as Granddaddy Carroll had been, she tried—reluctantly—to fulfill his expectations of summers spent canning beans and corn, hot biscuits for meals as extensive as those cooked by Grandmother Lee, and, most importantly, the consistent exhibition of the stoic temperament proper to a farm wife. In contrast to *her* mother's success, she must have been miserably aware of her own failure.

For Mother, her dream of writing must have meant transcendence of both roles—little girl and matriarch—but here she failed, too. Her fear of her own intelligence, her possible power—and what would surely be the subsequent loss of "love"—was too great. Wary of revealing her repressed rage, the conflicts that were a constant part of her inner life, she confined her writing to self-denigrating stories of struggles with home canning or reverential pieces about visiting male missionaries; even in writing these, she worried obsessively about the response to them of her husband, her mother, the ladies in her garden club.

During the last years of her life, Mother became more and more girlish, whiny, childlike, until, as though her dependency had reached a depth of no return, she turned for a few weeks resigned, as transcendent as Lee had ever been—and killed herself.

When Mother was a small child, there was not much time—or precedent—for the nurturing of females. With her responsibilities, Lee could not have had much energy, even if she had had the desire, for cuddling or coddling. (Though later, when her only son was born, it did seem, magically, to appear.) "Melissa was always hanging on to my skirts," she said, "but I didn't have time to give her any special attention." Wistfully, she added, "I wish I had known how important it was. . . ." Mother told me how she had feared the entrance of John Carroll into a room, his great booming voice, the *shushing* of the little girls by Lee. She wanted, painfully, to cling to her mother. It was as though the sense of isolation we all share was experienced by her earlier, and continued more pronounced.

After Mother's death, Lee mentioned to me that around eleven or twelve, Mother had had a religious crisis: "Melissa had read in the Bible—you know, where it says you cain't be saved if you believe or think a certain thing—I forget what verse it is—" She fumbled in her failing memory, searching for the troublesome commandment. "Well, whatever it was, she thought she had done somethin' wrong in her thoughts. Of course she hadn't, a chile that age, but she thought she had, and worried and worried 'bout it, thought she would surely burn in hell and so on"—I shuddered, recalling my own teenage fears of literal hellfire—"till finely I sent her off to Billy's house in Macon. He was the Baptist preacher, you know, a *fine* man. Well, she stayed a week or two, 'n' when she came back, didn't say eny more about it."

Two pictures of Mother around that time—before she had become the giggling belle, the butterfly—capture on film her frustration. In one, the photographer appears to have snapped her unaware as she meanders down a dirt road in dirndl skirt and white anklets; her brooding sullen gaze focuses unseeingly on the earth near her feet. In the other, a dramatically petulant face is framed by masses of kudzu leaves.

It is the same gaze of cold rage and betrayal that I felt engraved on my own face until beyond adolescence—one borne out by pictures of myself. "Don't stick your lip out at me!" Mother would sneer while curling her own back angrily. "You're the stubbornest chile I evah saw!"

Had she been thinking of her girlhood self? Was I really her replica, as sullen and moody as she had been? Looking at the pictures and at Mother's resentful gaze, I recall the rehearsal of my seventh-grade play: I had been dismissed from the auditorium because of such an expression on my face.

By the time she was fourteen, Mother's roundly indented figure, her natural jet curls and eyes, her creamy magnolia-shaped face, became a picture of full-blown sulky or laughing beauty. She was a girl so pretty that an Atlanta photographer used her image in his shop window as advertisement of his craft.

Lee must have been relieved, certain at last that her erratic older daughter, with her hysterical giggles, her sobs that seemed suddenly to jet from some endless chasm, would be able to find a good man to take care of her; drawn by her lusciousness, held fast by his lust, he would agree to materially care for—with luck, even soothe and pamper—her for a proper Southern lifetime.

Melissa was a product with maximum potential; it made sense to groom her to the hilt. Her clothes, paid for by Granddaddy Carroll, were handmade by Lee and a local seamstress. Dressmaker coats echoed her tiny waist, her full hips. Soft crepe dresses flowed languorously across her plump breasts; scarves, pinned in place by cloth flowers, dripped from her collarbone. Off-the-shoulder evening gowns, bodices held by tiny straps, deep ruffles of ecru lace, clung to her creamy shoulders. Photographs reveal the kind of elegant details called "feminine"—stitched satin lapels, tiny covered buttons, ruching, ruffles, tucks. Dark silk hose, kid slippers that looked like high-heeled Mary Janes—voluptuously curved of heel, fastened by a single silk-covered sphere—emphasized her curvaceous calves, her size-five feet.

Despite her impression of plumpness, she was still smaller than Anne or me. A few months after her death, we each tried on her black velvet evening dress with its fitted bodice and slightly gathered skirt. Neither of us could zip it; nor could we fasten the curved Art Nouveau buckle, the wide mesh belt of sterling silver, circa Mother's sixteenth year. Only my daughter Darcy, with her own "close to the ground" figure, her natural dark curls so like Mother's, could fit into them, creating for a moment a dizzying likeness to the pictures we had spent the morning dividing. It was a likeness to her suicided grandmother that made Darcy quickly pull off the dress, run from the room; months later, I found her silently staring at the picture of Mother that stood framed on the top of my chest of drawers, then into the antique shaving mirror beside it.

In the photograph in which Mother wore these romantically seductive clothes, her complexion is a perfect, if papery, magnolia cream; her cheeks and lips an unnatural Tangee pink, echoing the pink roses she inevitably holds in her arms. Dressed for a dinner or tea dance, she sits still, suspended in time. But even dressed in her school clothes—chemises, middy blouses, pleated skirts—animated and laughing, she is as sexily juicy, a perfect peach, a vamp. "The prettiest girl at Fulton High School," we were told over and over.

Fulton High School was the central-Atlanta school to which students commuted from all over the city and outlying communities. "She could have had any boy she wanted," our aunts told us, emphasizing her choice of our dissolute, if handsome, daddy. Each day Mother and her sisters rode the River car to classes. In Atlanta streetcars of the 1930s, the wicker seats could be slid forward to face the seats behind them. Did the boys jostle and show off, struggling for the seats near her? I can see her holding court among the "popular" boys and girls who were her friends, hear again the giggle that grew more pronounced, more foolish, as she grew older and more disconnected: the giggle of a pretty vivacious girl who thoughtlessly gossiped—with an occasional curl, even then, of her lip—behind a small hand on which the nails were already tinted pink and filed

to the points she liked. As the yearbook stated, she was "pretty, popular, and good-natured"—and undoubtedly accepted her good fortune as
her due.

At sixteen, she was swamped with young men, more than she could
handle. She claimed to have had six dates each weekend. "I had a date on
Friday night, then one on Saturday afternoon for tennis or a movie, and
a date on Saturday night. Then on Sunday, one boy would take me to
church, another for a drive in his daddy's automobile in the afternoon,
and I would get home just in time for my date for church that night."
At fifty, she still craved the kind of excitement she must have had then.
It was as though an addiction to a certain kind of male attention had
begun an inevitable course. For the rest of her life, in whatever group or
situation she found herself, she would defer to the men around her. Yet
there was no reason during that time for her to believe that any of her
fantasies—the handsome blond lawyer, the house with columns, the life
of self-indulgence—would fail to come true. She had no way of knowing
that she was one of those women whose life would peak in the blaze of
high school popularity, that her reign held within it the very seeds of her
exile, her eventual self-destruction.

Yet within a year after high school graduation, Mother was back home
from Georgia State College for Women in Milledgeville. A hundred and
twenty long country miles away, cut off from her sisters, her girl friends,
her beaus, she had suffered her first long-term depression. In spite of
the beauty of the town of Milledgeville, with its Spanish moss–draped
live oaks, magnolia-lit avenues, antebellum mansions, and air of a past
century—the giggling girls from small towns all over the state, and the
forbidden glimpses of the boys from the military school across the way—
she had spent most of her year eating and crying. Even plumper from
the institutional food, her taste for costume frustrated by the required
school uniform, she had had only one social visitor during the year. Boys
were not allowed to visit, even for a Sunday afternoon, without written
parental permission; after Lee had transcribed the proper note, Calvin,
a high school beau, had driven the two hours to Milledgeville in his
newly acquired Ford automobile. For an hour, they sat in the stiff parlor with other girls and their visitors. But Mother must not have given

him much encouragement, or else he may have decided the trip was too long to be worthwhile; back in Atlanta, he was soon engaged to Mother's freckle-faced younger sister Grace.

During that year, she cried so much from homesickness that Lee agreed that she didn't have to go back after summer vacation. But back at home, she was a belle out of her element; her high school court had dissipated; she was a useless component in a well-run household of younger children, busy mother, uninterested stepfather.

By leaving college, she had given up her chance at the respectable profession of teaching. It was a move she always regretted. After years as a clerk-typist—when I had already been married three times, had had three children, and had begun to publish poems and magazine articles—she begged me, if she died, to take whatever money she might leave me to go to the University of Georgia to get a B.A. in journalism. Her regard for credentials was a part of the passivity with which she had early been inculcated. "Being a Southern belle is like being popcorn with no salt, a pizza waiting to be taken home . . . ," wrote one of my students. She might have been describing Mother, who, intimidated by the professors and "smart" girls, had never dared voice her ambition of becoming a writer. (Writer Flannery O'Connor, at the same school, had not been the beauty Mother had been, yet had had more motivation toward achievement. Not allowed to graduate till she had completed her white home-ec. apron, she had made the apron—but, also, aprons for six baby ducks that followed her around the campus. Today the college has a room dedicated to her manuscripts.)

Sensibly, Mother had taken shorthand and typing; but a nine-to-five job must have seemed a dreary alternative to marriage. The clothes, the parties, and her mother's dictum that "you are who you marry" had become imperatives for the immediate future. It was time to look seriously for the man who could replace the gentle father she had lost.

In 1934, Mother was the Sweetheart of Sigma Nu at the University of Georgia in Athens. The rotogravure supplement of *The Red and Black* shows her smiling in a dress that looks as though it has a white lace fichu; on the same page are Miss Dixie Dunbar of Chi Theta and Atlanta, and

Miss Margaret Mitchell of Sigma Chi and Griffin, Georgia. Sigma Nu was Daddy's fraternity, and it was because she was *his* sweetheart that she had been so named.

When Mother and Daddy met, they were ready for "love"—the kind of love described in the songs played by their favorite band leader, Guy Lombardo. Though they had long known of one another—Daddy, an "older man," was the brother of a high school classmate—the combustion didn't take place until Mother was eighteen, Daddy, twenty-four, and they met again on Atlanta tennis courts.

I see Daddy leaping over the net, agile in his tennis whites; over this, an image in which he stands before a bandstand: as he mouths his saxophone, his black eyes close in sensuous pleasure. It is 1934, the midst of the Depression, not long past the time of *The Sheik*—he is dark, Valentino-handsome. (Years later, when I bought a crumbling copy of the romance from a Woolworth's sale counter, I wondered why—until I realized with a wrench that the dashing Arab of the cover, flicking his whip at the haunches of his rearing white horse, brought back my father's early voluptuous beauty.)

Charismatic, ambitious, he has worked his way through the University of Georgia by selling magazine subscriptions, has his own band, and belongs to the same fraternity as Herman Talmadge. And though he isn't blond, a lawyer, doctor, or minister, he plays on his saxophone Mother's favorite dance tunes; his best friend, Claude, has had privately printed a small blue volume of verse; and he has a fine Scotch-Irish, even aristocratic, name—Parker McDonald Hughes. Too, he has a sense of humor—when he invites Mother to a dance, he addresses the envelope to "Mr. Bukowski's Former Girl Friend." Best of all, he has declared her the most beautiful girl he has ever seen, the girl of his dreams—that he wants nothing more in life than to care for her forever!

In a picture taken outside his fraternity house, Daddy wears a dashing felt hat, brim turned jauntily back from his face; his full-lipped mouth seems slightly to tremble. Mother, in her dressmaker coat and satin-faced cloche, has her arm possessively through the elbow that he juts forward. His gaze toward the camera is proud, solemn; hers is pensively radiant; each is triumphant. "Being a Southern boy is like having a dream," wrote another of my students; "a Southern girl is like someone in a Southern boy's dream." Daddy has the belle he has dreamed of; Mother, the promising, appreciative husband-to-be.

Her dreams, garnered from the romantic novels she favored—and not so different from mine fifteen years later—seemed destined for fulfillment. Gone would be the dark moods, the alienation, the tears of longing for the father she had never known. Life with "Donald," as his friends called him, would be one long dance, tennis game, fraternity party, diffusing gradually into the soft focus of babies, cozy meals, the perfect house—the two motifs unified by perpetual kisses and laughter.

How could she foresee that his charisma verged on that of the con man, that the achievements of his college days would become staples, along with boasts of the men he could buy and sell, of dinner-hour ravings that would end only when his face fell into the fried chicken or country steak and gravy she had prepared after her forty-minute bus ride home from her job as a typist in Atlanta. (When they finally separated, after my first marriage at sixteen, Daddy visited a psychiatrist *once*—a visit that concluded with the therapist buying a set of tires from him, then giving him the couch in his office.)

Indeed, how could either know, at the moment in which the tremulous picture was made, that the other was already consumed, eaten away from within, by deficiencies that would keep each forever from giving the total love and nurturing the other needed for survival. Mother didn't know—and probably wouldn't have believed—that Daddy, noticeably sharing his mother Annie's Cherokee blood, was the literal black sheep of his family. Annie profoundly preferred his blond and dimpled younger brother, Bud; the passive, soon-to-pass-away postmaster who was his father had been so depleted by the demands of his imperious wife, the material needs of his family, that he had little to pass on, either materially or emotionally, to his older son.

In certain parts of the Deep South, whole trees, houses, acres are occasionally swallowed by a geological weakness just beneath the earth's surface known as a limestone sinkhole. It is a phenomenon I sometimes think of when I recall my parents' early naïveté. Mother was unaware that Daddy, like herself, was a physically beautiful and intelligent person of sturdy background who, ironically, was as emotionally bankrupt as the eroded red dirt of South Georgia farm country, that each of them ultimately embodied the self-romanticized and self-deluded Southerners described in the works of Faulkner, personified in the life of Zelda Fitzgerald. Neither dreamed that the skeins of their idealized passion would rapidly weave them into a net of mutual self-destruction. Instead, theirs was the courtship of two handsome and promising young people who were made for each other.

It was an illusion of perfect happiness that for a time was maintained. After their elopement, they moved into a garage apartment on Lucille Avenue in West End, a then-fine-old section of Atlanta. Despite the mid-Depression, Daddy had a good job—twenty-five dollars a week at Campbell's Coal Company. In nine months or less, I was born, and named Rosemary after the heroine in the trashy romance Mother was currently reading. My first memories were of the black-and-white puppies in our backyard, and the family of black children who lived beyond the back fence; my parents seemed always to be laughing.

Carried to the terrace or garage apartments of other young married couples, or bachelors from Daddy's fraternity days, I felt glamorous and grown-up in my sunsuits and white high-topped shoes. At neighborhood movies, I sat securely wedged between them—baby-sitters were unknown. At Peacock Alley, their favorite drive-in eating spot, they shared with me a concoction called Hot Fudge Shortcake. At home, too, we enjoyed high-calorie dishes; besides fried chicken and baked sweet potatoes bathed in a pool of margarine, we had sautéed bananas and Spanish pork chops. For a provincial belle, Mother was an imaginative cook who favored the use of oleo and Crisco.

By the time Anne was born when I was five, pictures showed my parents to be two overly nourished, though still-handsome, young people with plump cheeks; it was a plumpness that foreshadowed the puffiness of later years. Six weeks after Anne was born, a friend asked Mother, "Haven't yew had thet baby yet?" She still weighed 186 pounds, 60 pounds above her normal weight, though Anne had weighed only 5. It was an anecdote she told in later years, equating her fullness, her weight, with that brief period of fullness of spirit.

Despite my early memories of the three of us caught in euphoric tableaus, Mother later told me that she had known something was wrong on their honeymoon. As she had listened to a Sunday-night revival meeting on the car radio, Daddy had abruptly snapped it off. The intensity of his response had seemed out of proportion to the ordinary stimulus of a preacher's voice ranting of hellfire and damnation. Indeed, it had been a puzzling reaction in a young man who, like herself, had been brought up in a devout Bible Belt family—though his adamant refusal to discuss his reasons for it was the usual Southern male response to any question raised by an uppity woman.

It was its implications that made the event significant. What if the new husband Mother had thought so ideal did not *believe*? That flaw alone would indicate a Pandora's box out of which could catapult a dozen others, thrusting her not into the life of the pampered Southern wife, but that of one married to a "no good" man, a woman who must make up through prayer and piousness for the sins of her dissolute spouse. It was a role that prescribed that she *never* give up on his salvation, that a bad man can and should be saved by a good woman. At some point— possibly during her crisis of guilt at eleven or twelve—she had decided that alienation from God the Father (or was it patriarchy?) was a psychic separation too painful to again be risked. Yet as a married woman, half of one flesh, her husband's faith was as essential as her own; and she was responsible for that of both. It was a view that would sap her energies for the rest of her life: if she had been good enough, she was convinced until she died, Daddy would have been better.

Ted Hackett, an Atlanta psychotherapist who also practices in rural areas outside the city, observes that Southerners tend to determine behavior by a fixed set of ethics rather than by feeling or relationship. ("Why did you shoot your neighbor's dog?" "Because he peed on mah bushes." "You were angry because he peed on your bushes?" "Nope, just shot 'em 'cause he peed on mah bushes.") Like most Southerners, Mother had rigid ideas about the way things *ought to be*; yet if her fantasy of perfection had been realized and maintained, would she have retained her fragile sanity?

My picture of her life, of my parents' life together is one of extremes of happiness or degradation, placidity or hysteria. At times, reality met the standards set by her fantasies: Mother laughed, the sun shone. When reality failed, the sky opened, hysteria deluged, as though it had been waiting just beneath the sunny surface. For a long time, I felt that her craziness, their misery together, had begun the moment of my birth.

Why else would my beautiful young mother want to kill me?

# Lewis Grizzard

## "Grits Billy Bob"

My name is Billy Bob Bailey, and I live down in Fort Deposit, Alabama, which ain't close to nothing but the ground. Plumbing maintenance is my game—you name it and I can unstop it—but on the side I write a newspaper column for the local weekly.

It's called "The Straight Flush with Billy Bob." My dog Rooster's the one who thought up that name.

Me and Lewis Grizzard go way back. We knew each other before Studebaker went broke. He's a good ol' boy, Lewis, but he's bad to get into what I call one of his sorry spells. Too sorry to work, and too sorry to care if he don't.

If his hind end ever gets any weight on it, they ought to hang the lazy scoundrel.

So here I am bailin' him out again while he takes another day off. I bet his time card's got more empty spaces on it than the doctors saw when they examined the Penn State football team for brain damage after it was run slap over by the University of Aladamnbama in the Sugar Bowl.

We're still celebrating knocking Four-Eyed Joe Paterno out of the national championship. It's true we got us an Auburn man sittin' in the governor's chair in Montgomery now, but it's Mr. Paul Bryant who's still the king, roll Tide.

Football ain't what's on my mind today, though, but I've got something to talk about that's just about as important.

Grits.

You heard me right. G—for "good"—r-i-t-s, grits. This all started a week ago when me and Rooster went down to the diner to have breakfast.

Sittin' in the diner were these two Yankee tourists who got lost trying to find Florida, which ain't exactly hard to locate like Rhode Island or Kansas. You just drive that big black Buick until everybody you see is two years older than Lydia E. Pinkham's hat.

Clovis, the waitress, asked the two Yankees if they wanted grits with their eggs, and they turned up their noses and said they'd rather eat mud first.

Clovis blanched, and it was all I could do to keep Rooster still. I don't know why it is people from up North who come South want to make fun of the way we eat and talk.

Before I got down in my back, I used to have a special way of dealing with riff-raff like that. After they got out of the hospital, they couldn't wait to get back to New Jersey where it smells like what it took me half a day to unclog at the bus station last week.

But Billy Bob ain't as young as he used to be, and I'm learning to be a little more tolerant about ignorance. This is a free country, and if somebody ain't got the good sense God gave a sweet potato, it ain't up to me to move his nose over to the side a little.

The reason Yankees don't like grits is nobody ever told 'em how to eat 'em. If you don't doctor up grits a little, I'll be the first to admit they taste like something I wouldn't even say.

Grits need a little help, and what I'm going to do today is give out my famous recipe for Grits Billy Bob, and if you have anything to do with any Yankees, you might pass it along.

Grits Billy Bob:

First, don't fool with no instant grits. The idiot who invented instant grits also thought of frozen fried chicken, and they ought to lock him up before he tries to freeze-dry collards.

Get yourself some Aunt Jemimas or some Jim Dandys. Cook 'em slow and stir every chance you get. Otherwise, you'll have lumps, and you don't want lumps.

Salt and pepper and stir in enough butter to choke a goat. Fry some bacon and sausage on the side and crumble that in, and then come right on top of that with all the cheese the law will allow.

Grits Billy Bob ought not to *run* out of the pot. They ought to *crawl*. Serve hot. Cold Grits Billy Bob are harder than a steel-belted radial.

Speaking of tires, it was a shame the bad luck those two Yankees had before they could get out of town. All four of their tires blew out right in front of Clovis's brother's service station. His name is Harvey.

Harvey made 'em a good deal on a new set, though. Said he never had seen tires punctured that way. Said they looked like something with real sharp teeth had gnawed right through 'em.

Rooster said he figured they ran over a possum.

# Eugenia Price

---

## From *At Home on St. Simons*

### CHAPTER II
#### *Silence*

Just as dawn began to slip over the small marsh behind my house on a chilly January morning, I opened my garage doors to what represented a near miracle to these once city-deafened ears. I saw nothing but the first sky full of roseate light—pale blue around the edges—as the new wonder broke out of the ocean to the east and hung above the thick miasma still tucked snugly at the marsh margins, but what I heard I will never forget. I was in a hurry to catch the morning flight to Atlanta, but even if I had missed that plane, I would have stopped long enough to listen to the sudden sounds moving swiftly across the misty marsh that special dawn. All sorts of wrong, city-ignorant thoughts flashed through my mind as I stood there. Alligators? Dog over from Harrington hunting in the marshes? No. The sounds were too thin for dogs, and there are no alligators in my marsh anymore. Then I knew what it was I was hearing. Soft, rapid hoofbeats on the black marsh mud, scarcely rustling the dew-drenched spartina grasses, thudding, flying away from me, their beat diminishing, fading, but held to my ears by the unbelievable quiet of a marsh morning—until, unmistakably, one, then two, then three deer, invisible in the mist, splashed into the waters of Dunbar Creek and began to swim steadily to the other side.

I had frightened them, opening my old-fashioned, quite noisy garage doors so suddenly at a time of day no sound disturbs them from my house

486

on its lonely point of land. And even in their flight, they had blessed me. They had given me a set-apart moment of the kind of delight one person can never give to another person. A silence accentuated by their flying hooves and their quick swim across the salt creek—silence I will never forget.

Sudden human actions don't accentuate silence as wild things do. We clutter silence with too much talk, too much crying out when we are afraid. I had only a moment to listen that morning, but I have kept the moment and I am still learning from it.

The deer are almost gone from St. Simons Island. My three invisible marsh travelers would not have been there if the marsh had not been there, if it had been filled and built on and dead forever.

Man needs silence. It is so rare a thing now to find a part of one minute in which we can still "hear" the silence—even on St. Simons Island. I live in a remote place, and in one of those infrequent times when there is not even one plane in the air, not one power saw mutilating a single tree, I stop typing, stop reading, stop whatever I'm doing to listen. It happens so seldom anymore.

The marshes across which my three dawn visitors fled help hold what silence we still possess in coastal Georgia.

I was on my way that morning to Atlanta in order to testify before a Senate hearing for all of us who still care, on behalf of what might be our last chance to save our beloved marshlands: Georgia state Rep. Reid Harris's Wetlands Protection bill. It seems very strange to most of us that anyone would fight a measure like this, but they are fighting it. Otherwise kind, good people are fighting it.

As I stood listening to the miracle of the deer beside my own little stretch of mist-covered marsh that morning, I was glad I had decided to put off my work and go. Glad and grateful that I could go. One or two other Islanders went too. Many people sent letters and telegrams. Maybe we helped a little.

Before beginning to write today, I sat at my desk for fifteen minutes, my doors open to the upstairs porch, listening, still thinking of silence. For exactly twelve seconds of that fifteen minutes, there was no grinding plane motor of any description overhead! This has to be some kind of record. I have tried this before in the years I have lived on St. Simons Island, desperately needing to identify with the Island in the old days before man made his first rackety flying machine. People have been kind enough to say I write rather realistically of the long-gone silences, the sound of bird songs, and the clatter of the marsh hens with only the wind around them. I wonder about this. My little five-to-twelve-second intervals of no roaring in the sky could not possibly give me "research" time on silence, the kind of silence men and women knew in our beloved Golden Isles even as recently as the turn of the century. If I write "silence" realistically, it must be because I am a novelist and not a reporter. I seldom experience it.

Almost no one experiences silence anymore anywhere on the face of the earth. In the West perhaps. I do remember periods of genuine silence in the mountains of Wyoming, on the Mojave Desert. But even there they are broken eventually by a cross-country jet plane, out of sight perhaps, but roaring.

Silence is so rare on St. Simons Island that even in the woods where I live, where no automobile can drive by, when the rare moments come, they are arresting. We would be better people, more aware of one another's needs, if it were possible for us to experience silence just once in a while.

People who manufacture or fly these buzzing little jobs that fill our once-quiet sky will hate me, of course. Will consider me eccentric. I suppose I am, but I am simply overcome now and then with hunger for silence. For silence and time enough to think again—deeply, not off the top of my head between things. Between planes zooming across the sky, cars speeding down our roads; between telephone calls and determined, helmeted people on motorcycles; through the agonized scream of another power saw destroying another tree. (Now and then I'm sure it's the tree that's screaming, not the saw.)

No one told me I was buying land in the flight-path of Glynco Naval Air Station. I suppose I would have been philosophical about it if I had known. I'm as inconsistent as everyone else. I wanted this piece of land— no other. I'm sure I would have bought it regardless. But I doubt that it is all Glynco which causes my longing for silence. True, a plane once jettisoned two bright orange fuel tanks just a stone's throw from the roof of my house. The deafening explosion set the marsh afire, and two helicopters from Glynco shattered the silence, as only helicopters can do, for almost two hours trying to put out the fire in the marsh and pry out the half-buried gas tanks. Of course, I could have been killed. So could my yard man, who tried to hide behind a big oak tree when the screaming "bombs" scattered the birds and shook my house to its foundations.

At Glynco they told me in very polite "public relations" voices that it wasn't one of their planes. It was a jet from God knows where, trying to land at Jacksonville, suddenly becoming bored or overburdened with two fuel-filled tanks, deciding to get rid of them over the ocean missing it only by six miles or so—missing my house by a few hundred feet.

I think maybe only about half of the thunder is from whatever they do at Glynco. The rest is from private citizens hurrying to get wherever they're going, afraid of the silence. Afraid of staying one place long enough to miss making that extra big deal, afraid to miss a round of golf or the glorious opportunity to fire a rifle-blast into the head of an island deer or a marsh hen. Afraid to stop long enough to think. To be alone. Needing to get there. Needing to "hurry up" in order to relax on a beach. "If I hurry—if I buy a plane and fly—I can have a speedy time of rest and relaxation." Aren't we peculiar? And contradictory? And pathetic?

This is not a treatise designed to put down planes or the people who fly them. Some of my best friends fly planes. It is just a small period of musing about how little we think of the other fellow, how lost we are without motors roaring. I'm sure there is a special kind of exhilaration in owning one's own plane, in taking off into the once "wild blue yonder." There must be a genuinely freeing moment of feeling one is leaving earth and all its problems behind. Just a moment, of course, because one is there so soon, back on the troubled earth again. No thought, I'm sure, about what the cherished little plane is doing to nerve-endings on the earth below.

I didn't think of any of this as long as I lived in Chicago. There was so much noise there, so constantly, I was seldom aware of hearing a plane.

St. Simons Island, all of the Golden Isles, is deceptive. One expects it to be different here, and really it was, even in 1960. I remember standing one evening in 1961 on the winding road to the old Island dump, the only one left which looked anything like the roads I was trying to describe in *The Beloved Invader*. For one minute and five seconds, I stood in that narrow, tree-lined sandy road and heard only a cardinal, one wren shouting, and a squirrel barking in the woods behind me. I will never forget that tiny fragment of time.

(I tried "listening" again just now. By my watch, there were seven seconds without a plane overhead. I'm thankful.)

Of course, there is not one thing anyone can or will do about our loss of silence. I hope we will one day see our big industries beginning to do more than talk about their splendid, expensive future plans to stop contaminating our air and our rivers. (Something pouring black smoke into the air from the mainland blocks the view of the sunset from my house every now and then.)

But I doubt that anything can or will ever be done about noise. Those of us who are blessed enough to be living away from metropolitan centers must double our efforts to learn inner balance. Above all, we must not stop being expectant. If I ever grow so callous as not to listen and hope for a moment's real silence, I will hate myself. I will bore myself as do the poor people who have to have noise.

What can we do, those few fringe people among us who still long for quiet and time to think? What can we do? Make the most of the times we are fortunate enough to find. Half a minute—twelve seconds—these are terribly important. Silence holds a quality of life which leaps the limitations of the ticking of our clocks. Eternity will prove this to us, difficult as it is for us to comprehend now.

I learn about God in the silence. Without even trying to concentrate on Him, I find I have experienced a certainty during those five or seven seconds that strengthens my inner self.

These days, I have written month after month about the people who lived on St. Simons Island in the year 1807. This is quite a trick. Our lives are almost totally reversed. The Goulds of New St. Clair and Black Banks wrote of their longing to have something to break the monotony.

On St. Simons Island at Frederica now, I long for just one full minute unfractured by a motor of any kind.

We are peculiar people, meant, I believe, to draw strength from a "still small voice." Our hope is to learn somehow to keep the quiet inside. To refuse invasion. Not to refuse responsibility. Not to refuse people who matter or who need us. But to refuse to waste our own inner quiet, even as the little waspy private planes puncture our efforts, even as the gasoline tanks explode near our houses and as the monster trucks roar by. If we try, if we really concentrate on the values no noise can demolish, we might—oh, we might even reach the place of inner awareness where we will be able to live above the shriek of the power saw and the racket of the helmeted, determined people on motorcycles.

I just tried again. This time seventeen seconds! I am rested inside by it, ready to start writing for the day.

# Roy Blount, Jr.

## "Being from Georgia"

*There on the roads I read Buy your flour meal and meat in Georgia. And I knew that was interesting. Was it prose or was it poetry I knew that it was interesting. Buy your flour meal and meat in Georgia.* —*Gertrude Stein*

For a while after Jimmy arose there was talk about redneck chic, a phrase that reminded me of the expression "nigger heaven." The assumption seemed to be, you weren't going to have to do anything except be Southern to reflect the administration's glory. Persons wearing boots caked with South Georgia slops and pig dung were going to be whooping and rolling and snorting and dancing in the streets of Washington, slaughtering hogs and boiling up big vats of grits out back of the Sans Souci.

I never did think that idea was going to pan out.

"Where are you from?" Northern people ask me socially, with this little glint in their eye.

"Decatur, Georgia, just outside Atlanta," I say in as level a tone as I can.

"I th-o-o-o-*ought* I detected a little accent," they say, and it's the most irritating god damn thing in the world. They get a strange humorous look on their faces.

It's a peculiar sensation. I think I am confessing to something, in their eyes. Something largely amusing, but something which, if they weren't so broad-minded as to feel very nearly complicitous about it, they might feel entitled to describe as low-down.

But it's something they can *handle*—I mean they've seen people on television doing this Southern thing, they know we don't mean half the things we say, just a way we have of talking. ("I love to hear you talk," people have actually said to my *face*.)

I don't know what it is that I am confessing to. If I thought they thought I was confessing to hating niggers, I would tell them I would whip their ass, or get some of my black friends—ask some of my black— some of my friends who happen to be black—to whip their ass if they didn't take it back. If I thought they thought I was confessing to being barefooted, I would get right up there at the dinner table or wherever it is and show them my shoes. Not that I'm wearing shoes for any Northern person's benefit.

But don't worry. I ain't going to complain, that ain't my people's way. We don't let on. (We just send complete fools up to the Congress and let them get even for us.)

*I am talking the way it feels right in my mouth.* "Pore," for instance, is a lot better way of pronouncing the word *poor* than "pooor." When you say "pooor," you purse your lips like a rich person. When you say "pore," you say it the way poor folks and poor old souls and poorhouse residents say it when they say, "This is a pore excuse for living."

Certain Southern vowels are distinguished things. Have you ever heard Jimmie "The Singing Brakeman" Rodgers sing, in "Blue Yodel Number 10":

> *I ain't no shiek man,*
> *Don't try to vamp no girls.*
> *I ain't no shiek man,*
> *Don't try to vamp no girls.*
> *It's my regular grinding*
> *Gets me by in this world.*

Only he don't say "grinding." He says "griiiiiin-din." That long flat pure gristly semi-nasal *i*, like the French ending -*in*, only fuller-bodied, coming from hard up against the right rear corner of the roof of your mouth.

There are notes that can't be struck, things that can't be said, in Northern, because Northern tends to throw a little bit of a long *e* in behind the *i*, so that "Well I be god damn" sounds like "Well i.e. be god damn."

The word "on" *deserves* to be pronounced "own," to rhyme with—
therefore to help counterbalance—"moan," "bone," "alone." What satisfaction is there in crying "Get it *ahn*"? And in the pale lexicon of respectable English there is no such word as "caint." "Caint you see-ee . . .
that evenin sun go down . . ." You want to say "can't" there?

On the other hand. I know. I knew it before I ever left Georgia:
there are Southern vowels that to persons of intelligence are a pain in
the bowels. "Wa'il, *yay*is" for "Well, yes": that kind of thing. However much you can't abide the self-satisfied self-ignorance that crops
up in some Southern vowels, I bet you can abide it better than I can.
You let me worry about that, and you go worry about the self-satisfied
self-ignorance that crops up in some New York, Long Island, Boston,
California, Ohio vowels.

I admit it, I have done some accommodating. I have about quit saying
"faingers" for "fingers," and have gradually modulated a good ways from
"git," on purpose—at least in such expressions as "Perhaps I am missing
the point, but I can't quite put my finger on what you are getting at in
this passage." It's a sad commentary on the way people judge people's
minds, but it's true that if I were to say "my fainger on what you are
gitting at," it might suggest that I actually *was* missing the point.

I have had people back down home accuse me of losing my accent.
And then I get off the plane on the other end and people are saying,
"You're not from the *city*, heeya. I *thot* I heard a little . . ."

Maybe Northern people think I'm trying to sing when I talk. I know
that everywhere I turn, Northern people in their twenties are trying to
sound like Ray Charles or Mother Maybelle Carter. As if it were just a
*sound* you can pick up and use. It used to be, people stood in their par-
lors in evening gowns and sang soprano solos about fairies in the bottom
of their garden. Now they sit around cross-legged with guitars and try
to sound like Southern people—niggers and rednecks, in other words—
complaining that the boll weevil and the pater-rollers are going to get
them. Listen, Northern people. The boll weevil and the pater-rollers
aren't studying you.

And it isn't just amateurs. It's a lot of people you see performing in
public. I'm not talking about the Beatles and the Rolling Stones ripping

off Chuck Berry and all—they filtered it through Liverpool and hallu-cinogens and what have you, and, in a sense, advanced it. I'm talking about people who earnestly pooch their lips out and double their chins and twist their mouths all around so they sOWund lak sumbuddy who knows Jesus—I mean the old tough sweet Jesus—and drinks bad whiskey and has got grit in his or her craw.

Consider Janis Joplin. Janis Joplin didn't start getting good until she stopped trying to be an hysterical Bessie Smith, which was a contradic-tion in terms, and started sounding like her upbringing, brought up to date, on her last album, *Pearl*, notably in "Me and Bobby McGee." You had a real person singing in that album. She started out, you know, in Austin, Texas, singing "Silver Threads and Golden Needles" at Kenneth Threadgill's gas-station bar, which is closed now but where I once had such a good time listening to country music with hippies and professors and men in tractor-company caps, all mixed together, that I nearly got squashed underneath the bare hub of a Hungarian man in the seed busi-ness's car at two o'clock in the morning, helping him change his tire after I'd knocked his glass of whiskey over twice.

*You're supposed to sound like the way you grow up.* Advancing it along and remixing it, up to a point.

But why should I have to explain all that to everybody just because I'm from Georgia? In Harlem, I gather from the novels of Chester Himes, "to send someone to Georgia," or "to Georgia someone," means to take his money and still not fuck him, or to fuck her and still not give her the money. That sounds about right. Georgia is a place you get sent to or you come from or you march through or you drive through. Convicts settled it. It's got some fine red dirt, hills, vegetables, and folks, but I don't believe anybody has ever dreamed of growing up and moving to Georgia.

But now the President of the United States is from Georgia. It's true that he has been snubbed by a freshman congressman from South Dakota, and it's true that he has a pretty mealy-mouth version of a Georgia ac-cent. But he is the President, and he is from Georgia. And here I am in the state of Carter-busters, of Ted Kennedy and Tip O'Neill, of Massa-chusetts—a cold state, settled by Puritans, where it snowed so hard one day in *May* a few years ago that the snow piled up on the green leaves and blossoms and broke off big spring limbs all over town, *boom, boom, boom,* until it sounded like a war.

I missed the war, in Vietnam, the war which Southerners remained steadfastly in favor of, according to the polls, long after the rest of the nation had given up on the idea of destroying something to save it (although that is pretty much what the rest of the nation did to the South during the sixties and seventies of the *last* century). The war which a Texas President and Georgia Secretary of State were able to maintain such an enthusiasm for. The war which was like pro football, in that mostly niggers and rednecks and Slovenians fought it and the rest of us watched.

Well, I say I missed it. I was in the Army when it started building up. I thought I had resisted the draft the only way a healthy American who didn't feel too spiritually pure could, by going through ROTC. I was from Georgia, I didn't know any better at the time. Don't get me wrong: I made bad grades in ROTC, I never shined my brass. But I think anti-military Americans ought to take part in their Army, so they can keep an eye on it.

The closest I came to fighting was in Georgia, Fort Benning, during basic training. We were simulating being on patrol in enemy territory and I was patrol leader. I was having a fairly good time tramping through the piney woods when somebody simulating a local alien farmer jumped out and started yelling in a simulated foreign language. If he kept it up, he'd alert the enemy. It was my job to deal with him. What I did was grab him around the shoulders and shake him, in a largely simulated way. He kept yelling. He looked highly dissatisfied, and probably wished that I were the one yelling and he the one doing the silencing. I tried to think of a way to argue with him. He was a big old country-looking boy with an Adam's apple that jerked.

I guess I was supposed to put my forearm across his throat from behind and throttle off his voice, something like that, but that went against my grain. I don't want to stifle dissent. I always want to hear what people are yelling. I'm afraid I'll miss something. Maybe I was supposed to simulate shooting him, but I hadn't anticipated doing anything like that, on such a personal basis, in the Army. This was a good while before anybody had heard of Lieutenant Calley, the Southern boy who was the GI Joe of his time.

"Well, god damn it, do *something*. Hit him, throw dirt on him, mail him to Houston," my interior voice exclaimed.

"*Sh!*" I said to the simulated farmer, and a disgusted observer appeared out of the bushes.

The next thing I knew I was part of the war effort in New York City, in the Quartermaster Corps, phasing out bases. Then I went back to Georgia to work for the Atlanta *Journal*, which wasn't a real activist institution.

It's true that there was a tradition at the Atlanta papers of anti-redneck editorials. I was proud one afternoon to receive a telegram that said: "COONLOVER [RALPH] MCGILL, COONLOVER [GENE] PATTERSON, COON-LOVER [REESE] CLEGHORN, NOW COONLOVER BLOUNT HELL WILL BURN YOUR TRAITOR SOULS." The old boys in the pressroom were always jib-ing at some of us writers for the liberalism in the slugs of type they had to set, looking us in the eye as one old boy to another and saying, "You know you don't *believe* that shit," sincerely assuming in some cases that we were being duped or bought off by Communists or Rockefellers. But when Reese Cleghorn left the paper to work in civil rights, certain old editorial hands were heard to say, "Well, Reese has got the nigger sickness." Said it sort of tongue-in-cheek but not entirely.

I got a column, and wrote favorably about Tom Hayden and Stokely Carmichael and unfavorably about white sheriffs and Senator Talmadge. I was dimly aware of Jimmy Carter as someone Lester Maddox had brushed off in a Democratic primary.

I wanted to go to New York. Writing for a Georgia outlet is like putting on skits for your parents: you can only go so far. I would sit there at my desk and pound out things which, though I knew they were in-sufficient to the historical moment, I knew would elicit hysterical phone calls anyway. And Mr. Jack Spalding, the editor, who had a whole lot of children, would stop by on his way home and say things in a fatalis-tic vein:

"I've got to go home and take charge of the unit. Marilyn and Charles have gone to the allergist to see what makes Charles sneeze, turn blue, and then purple—I mean John. I hope it's cats. Charles is the one that's down with the virus." And somebody would call up Hugh Park, who wrote columns of local anecdotes, country lore, and criminal-court scenes, and ask him what to do about a howling dog, and Hugh would answer, "Sqwu*eeeeze* his little lar-ynx." Most of us younger *Journal* staffers would chafe at how untroublesome to the white-business, Atlanta power structure the paper was, and it sure was. But some of Hugh Park's columns have held up better over the years than most issue-oriented reporting:

> There was a clean neat woman with her hair drawn tidily back of her head and three of the sweetest-faced, saddest-eyed children you ever saw.
>
> Testimony was that the husband and father, a florid man who wore double-lens glasses, had beaten his shy 16-year-old daughter while drunk and had called them all obscene names.
>
> His wife's voice was broken-hearted as she talked to him. "Will you quit drinking, Daddy?" she asked. "Come back to us. We need you and you need us. You haven't had your medicine for a day and a half now."
>
> She stroked the back of his neck while she talked. He held his head down, his face red with blood and his eyes glassy. He looked like he might suffer from high blood pressure.
>
> "I did wrong," he said in a dead remote voice to no one in particular. "Did wrong . . ." He trailed off, staggered and almost fell. It was as if he had a small stroke.
>
> "I'll let you go this time," said Judge Little hurriedly.

> Paulding Countians became as alert as their pioneer ancestors, particularly at night, after hunters found what doctors believed to be a severed woman's hand.
>
> The hunters, Spurgeon, Ralph and Bobby Lawrence, brought the hand to Sheriff J. K. (Bob) Shipp. "It looked just like the hand of a

medium-sized woman," said the sheriff. "We were disturbed because a girl here . . . had been reported missing."

The sheriff drove to Atlanta . . . where the hand was examined by the state crime laboratory. There it was determined that it was the right rear foot of a bear.

Sounds incredible, doesn't it, that anyone would think for a moment that a bear's paw was a woman's hand? "The hair had come off," explained the sheriff, " and the flesh was pink and natural looking just like a woman's. The claws were also missing. Without claws, a bear's paw is the size and shape of a woman's hand."

Sheriff Shipp believes that the bear may have belonged to a Paulding County farmer who died not too long ago. "He raised them kind of like you would hogs," he said, "although I guess he considered them pets more than anything else. When he died I expect this bear escaped and either hunters shot him or dogs got him. Somebody or something got his claws. There is a little mystery there."

A stout black woman was accused of disrupting the rhythm of a dance floor by standing in the middle of it holding a butcher knife.

She said that people often took advantage of her. "One time," she declared, "my common law husband and his mother caught me when I was asleep and rooted my wig in my head."

Things like that were going on in Georgia during the war. I did walk in some marches and fault the war in the paper. Those activities were easier, and more gratifying and less mysterious, than trying to deal with a yelling simulated alien farmer. Often I felt bad about not having joined the counter-culture. But, I don't know, I had all these Oxford-cloth shirts I didn't want to throw away.

I was twenty-five or twenty-six and owned a forty-five-year-old house with a four- or five-year-old first marriage in it, and the house was up on concrete blocks, and so was the marriage, and I would crawl underneath the whole thing and lie on my back in the Georgia dirt ("I tell you what, boy. You ain't done *diddly* yet") and make up Georgia limericks, which I put in my column. The Georgia limerick proved popular with

all stripes of Georgian. Its first line had to end with a Georgia town—
Meigs, Clyo, Jakin, Gough, Luxomni, Subligna, Leaf, Elmodel, Relee,
Tubize, Plumb, Climax, Glory . . .

*Wade L. McWilliams of Adel*
*Remarked to his wife, "I'm afraid El-*
   *Lenora that you've*
   *Gone too far!" She said "Move*
*Your feet and don't bother me, Wade L."*

*A modern young pastor of Baxley*
*Shepherds his flock rather laxly.*
   *When one of his stewards*
   *Took off for Lourdes,*
*He said, "I don't care what he does, axly."*

*A girl of the Marshes of Glynn*
*Sank in them, as well as in sin,*
   *One day when her boat*
   *Would not stay afloat*
*with one hundred and twenty-four men.*

*There was an old lady of Peach*
*Whose grasp exceeded her reach.*
   *She'd walk down an aisle*
   *Of produce and smile*
*And walk out with three pounds of each.*

*A lonesome old soul of McRae*
*Sat home saying, "There ain't no wae."*
   *Till a lady from Bimini*
   *Slid down his chimini*
*And he granted, "Oh, well, there mae."*

    I was keenly aware that these clouded twenties of mine, more widely
known as the sixties, lacked what people were calling relevance. I *kind
of* got involved in the life of my time every now and then, but it never

seemed to be of a piece with what everybody was sharing nationally in the media. It wasn't *in* the media. It was in *Georgia*.

With fellow Atlanta reporters, including David Nordan (to whom it was, years later, that Jimmy Carter would say about Ted Kennedy, "I don't have to kiss his ass"), I attended what was expected to be an urban disorder, but it didn't work out. I wore somebody's army helmet, the kind you call a steel pot, because all the hard hats were taken. But nobody threw anything at us, anyway. The scene was a housing project, Dixie Hills. I watched a SNCC field worker teach some of the residents how to do the power handshake, and heard him declare that the only good white man was Charles Joseph Whitman, who had shot a bunch of white men.

I admired SNCC. But I felt like a fool just standing there with my mouth hanging open, listening to somebody extol the shooting of a category of people into which I fell. "What about Schwerner and Chaney and Goodman?" was what I wanted to say. But I didn't feel like I deserved to invoke them. And I couldn't remember which two of them were white.

So I started arguing with the SNCC worker about Abraham Lincoln. The SNCC guy himself had brought Lincoln up, saying, "You think *he* was a good white man? He said he'd rather have a union with slavery than no union at all."

"People who get things done are always going to be saying compromising things," was the best I could think of to say.

It wasn't much of an argument, and who was I to be arguing with the Movement, anyway? But I wanted to argue with *somebody* besides white dumb-asses. Right before the rednecks shot Michael Schwerner, one of them asked him, "Are you the nigger-lover?" and he answered, "Sir, I understand how you feel." If I had been there—well, of course I like to think I would have been trying to stop the rednecks and getting shot myself, but I might have seized the opportunity to argue with Schwerner, to say: "You're in the *right* here, of course, but I'm not sure you do know how this old boy here *feels*."

Recently there appeared a TV drama about incidents from those years in the South. After watching this drama, a nine-year-old boy I was sitting with at a Formica table asked me, "Which were you in—the Klan or the FBI?"

"I was just in Georgia," I said.

Then one weekend in 1969 I went to visit my sister Susan—who is about half a generation younger than I am—at the University of Georgia. Word came that kids had been shot at Kent State, and we seized the university.

I didn't want the university. But there I was hunkering in the street outside the chancellor's house, blocking traffic and yelling, "One, Two, Three, Four, We Don't Want Your Fucking War" with everybody else, and having a big time.

When we surrounded the main administration building, the chancellor, who was originally a veterinarian, came out on the balcony to reason with us, and there was this girl student standing right next to him hollering "BULLSHIT" after every sentence he spoke. Right next to me was a youth who regarded me suspiciously because I looked a little old to be doing all this.

"Are you a teacher?" he asked.

I pointed to Susan and said, "No, I'm just a brother."

He said, "We are *all* brothers here."

I enjoyed it. But I didn't feel that it spoke to my needs. To tell the truth, I think anybody who sticks his head up within half a mile of National Guardsmen with rifles is as crazy as anybody who sends National Guardsmen with rifles to a campus in April.

But that's just me, I'm from Georgia. I never did want a revolution. I just wanted to stop feeling so *wrong*.

I wrote only one protest song during the sixties:

> It used to be so nice to be a white man,
> It looked like then the Lord was on our side,
> But I don't think I know a single white man
> Who hasn't recently sat down and cried.
>> Ohhhh. From De-troit to the Fertile Crescent,
>> I am feeling obsolescent.
>> Lift the white man's burden from me, Lord.

*Welfare got Cadillacs*
   *I got to pay for and*
     *I can't pay for my Fooooord:*
*Lift the white man's burden from me Lord.*

*I thank the Lord our President's still a white man,*
*But I don't think that he can pull us through.*
*There must be fifty Nigros in the Congress*
*And there is only one Spiro Agnew.*
  *Ohhhh. From Ocean Hill to Yokohama,*
    *Non-white powr's gonna get my mama,*
    *Lift the white man's burden from me, Lord.*
   *Think about China, all them*
    *millions and millions comin'*
     *at you in a hooooorde:*
*Lift the white man's burden from me, Lord.*

*They've just about took over athaletics,*
*'Cause whites can't run as fast or jump as high.*
*It always used to be we didn't need to,*
*But I'm afraid we're goin' to, by and by.*
  *Ohhhhhh. It started with the Brooklyn Dodgers,*
    *Now we're takin' colored lodgers,*
    *Lift the white man's burden from me, Lord.*
   *My boy Billy played*
    *four years of basket-*
     *ball and never scooooored:*
*Lift the white man's burden from me, Lord.*

*They're all you ever see now on the TV,*
*They've even got them reading us the news.*
*And I thought things was awful on the TV*
*Back when all we ever got was Jews.*
  *Ohhhhh. Bill Cos-by and Diahann Carroll,*
    *They've got white folks over a barrel.*
    *Lift the white man's burden from me, Lord.*

*Lookin' all loosey and goosey and juicy, makin'*
  *whites look*
    *stiff as a booooooard:*
*Lift the white man's burden from me, Lord.*

*In Vietnam they're short and don't wear helmets,*
*And yet it seems we just can't win that war.*
*I think we ought to hit another campus,*
*For there we know just what we're fighting for.*
  *Ohhhh. From Amherst to the Mekong Delta,*
    *Lord, why don't you give me shelta?*
    *Lift the white man's burden from me Lord.*
  *Looks like to me you'd start*
    *comin' on in with that*
      *terrible swift swoooooord:*
*Lift the white man's burden from me Lord.*

It was the best I could do. I was in Georgia.

Then, all of a sudden in the seventies, a Georgian made a real before-God run at the White House, and I had an *interest*.

# Philip Lee Williams

## "Some Things You Can't Pave Over"

I was driving 58 miles an hour down a dirt road just outside Colbert, Georgia, when a red-tailed hawk the size of a coffee table swooped down over the pasture next to me.

"Would you look at that!" I shouted. At that moment, an angular, half-starved bird dog loped across the road not 20 feet from me, and I slammed the Volare into a half spin, winding up in a gritty, blowing cloud of dust.

"Philip, you're going to kill us," the lady next to me said. The lady was Lillie Sisk, my grandmother, now 88, and she held on to the door handle grimly. But a brief smile played across her lips as I straightened out the car and goosed the Slant Six, until once again the tires were scattering red dust over half of north Georgia.

What is it about dirt roads that makes Southerners want to relive *Thunder Road*? No surface was ever less agreeable to speed than a rutted dirt highway, and yet generations have persisted in leaving the asphalt or tar and gravel and spending their adolescence on dirt.

I have this idea that dirt roads are partially responsible for the astounding number of years most Southern boys actually spend in adolescence. Often, we took our sweethearts down those roads to secluded areas. In a rural county, finding secluded spots on dirt roads was ridiculously easy. In our later years, we Southern boys loved to drive those roads, going too fast for anyone with sense, laughing, and drinking cold beer from sweating quart bottles. I confess that when I was in high school my friend Larry Walker and I scattered beer cans all over Morgan County. Larry

had a Corvair. It's a little known fact that the Corvair, otherwise an engi-
neering nightmare, was one of the best dirt road cars ever made. The
engine in the back made it heavy, and so it held the road except when we
came over a hill and all four wheels leapt from the ruts in a glorious rush
toward heaven. (Frankly, I'm surprised we didn't really *get* to heaven.
No one but an idiot drinks and drives, and now, when I console myself
on my deck in the evenings with a glass of my favorite brew, I refuse
even to look at the beasts parked out front.)

Dirt roads are pretty much the same anywhere in the South. They all
choke you with dust. They are all full of dangerous pits, and in winter
you can find yourself in a ditch before you know you've lost control. In
the summer, kudzu lurks in plain sight, twiddling its vines and waiting
for you to slow down so it can race out, grab your tires, and snake you
off to a horrible death in its murky depths.

Passing another car on a dirt road is fun. If you can avoid going into
a ditch or off a bridge that says "Load Limit, Eight Pounds," you will
probably clog your carburetor, run over a Glad bag full of baby food
jars, or fishtail into the kudzu. Then there are possums.

For possums, flat is beautiful. For every round possum I've ever seen,
there have been 40 flat ones. Lemmings have nothing on possums. There
is hardly a Southerner alive who hasn't seen one of the ubiquitous little
beasties waddle in front of the car lights, stop, and Get Flat. Years ago,
most of the flat possums I saw were on dirt roads, but in recent years
they have discovered pavement, though they still seem to prefer tar and
gravel to asphalt.

Around 1958, when I was first beginning to learn the fine art of riding
on dirt, only 29 percent of Georgia's roads were paved. Of the 89,000
miles of roads in the state, some 63,000 were unpaved. It seems strange
now to recall that in the 50s most Southern counties marked their civility
by their miles of paved roads. When county commissions met, when influence was peddled, what was often at issue was whose roads might be
next in line for paving. A hard-surface road meant affluence, easier access
to town, and a mark of distinction.

Housewives hated dirt roads. I know my own mother did. During the long, dusty summers, our house turned a pale red from the north Georgia dirt, and despite frequent dusting, a fine layer of the land often settled on the furniture.

In winter, the road turned into a bog, and my mother recalls getting hopelessly stuck one time. Getting stuck on dirt roads in the winter was an everyday occurrence. Buses were forever late to school because of road conditions.

Like most Southern boys, though, I loved dirt roads. I thought of the Old Buckhead Road as *our* road, though a few other houses were scattered along it. And in the years since, I have talked to dozens of grown men who, though toughened by the wretchedness of life, could lapse into nearly poetic sentimentality about their own dirt roads.

When *I* think of dirt roads now, the images go farther back than high school and the riotous fun we had. It goes back all the way into innocence. I rode my bicycle on the road. I loved to pump as hard as possible and then hit the brakes and slide. It seems now that you could slide forever on a dirt road, the countryside slowly unwinding, before you slowed to a stop, and the dust came waving past you, settling back down.

Convicts would come and work on the road when it became too rutted for safe travel. I loved to hang around with them, and nobody, including the guard, thought it was strange. The men were all black, and they treated me like some kind of mascot. Sometimes, I would ride a couple of miles to see them work, and if one's head hurt from the hot sun, I would ride home and sneak a Goody's headache powder from the bathroom and take it to him.

My friends and I played army in the ditches along the road. Our fathers had all been in the service, and World War II had been over for little more than a decade. We chose up sides and divided into armies, fighting our way up and down the road. Since I was one of the youngest, I spent half my childhood in the Wehrmacht.

Then one summer day, we heard the trucks. I remember going outside and seeing them up the road, spreading a glutinous mixture of tar and gravel. Too soon, they were in front of our house, and the heat and the smell were oppressive.

That night, the tar cooled. That next day was exciting, and I remember the feeling when I put my bike on the tar-and-gravel surface and found how much faster and smoother a ride it was.

But other things changed too. Cars began to roar past us, so I tended not to play as much in the ditches. We moved the Battle of the Bulge to the fields behind our house. Cars, their drivers in love with speed, began to race by in the night. Sometimes, kids heaved watermelons and cantaloupes into our yard.

The road did not need as much maintenance, and the convicts did not come very often. When you hit brakes going as fast as your 9-year-old legs would carry you, all your bike did was burn rubber.

I thought the *world* was changed with the paving of my road. That may be why I have clung all these years—against good sense—to the notion that dirt roads have helped define what it means to be Southern. They meant *Thunder Road* and the pointless and joyful peril of speed; they meant trying to turn away from what was already inexorable. They meant a defiance in the face of technology, an assertion that we were independent and, by God, tough.

By 1986, 63 percent of the roads in Georgia had been paved. But here's the kicker: *There are still 40,000 miles of unpaved roads in the state*. And most other states across the South are veined with similar mileage of dirt lanes, private streets, country roads, and barely passable pig paths. I take comfort in imagining that it takes as long to drive 75 miles on a dirt road as it does to go from Paris to New York on the Concorde.

Why do I feel that way? Is it pure perversity? Is it just dumb nostalgia? Maybe. Maybe.

Or maybe it's this: Dirt roads were a last, fragile thread to the world of our forebears, those men and women who broke the land and planted it. The roads were made from that part of our lives we could not deny: the country. Paved roads were of the city, of a world that was just then breaking, like television, into our lives. Dirt roads were the childhood of the New South, a gift from one way of life to another.

Why else would a grown man feel 17 again after skidding in the dirt to avoid hitting a mangy old dog?

# Raymond Andrews

## From *The Last Radio Baby*

### 5. The Church

Plainview Baptist Church was the community's center. The community's soul. For many years following the end of slavery this community had no church of its own and most folks attended the church of the bordering community of Smyrna. Then in 1898 the community got its own Baptist church, Plainview, the same name the community came to be known by. But this church was built on private land and the preacher was the landlord, who was often accused of acting as if this house of worship belonged solely to him rather than to God and the folks. Then in the early part of this century onto the church grounds strode one Jessie Rose Lee Wildcat Tennessee (before she became Grandmama) who was to create Plainview's "Great Schism" when she had her white man, Mister Jim, donate two acres of land for a new church to be built upon, land given to the people for *their* church that has remained theirs ever since. Built in 1916, this new building became known immediately as the Plainview "Upper Church" because of its location, a quarter of a mile *up* the road from the older Plainview, now "Lower" Church.

The Upper Church started out with mostly the community's young, those who dug Jessie Rose Lee Wildcat Tennessee, who was well known for getting along fabulously with young people. The older heads, believing Jessie Rose Lee Wildcat Tennessee too earthy for the spiritual Lord's taste, stayed with the Lower Church. The "real" Christians would, when the sermons ended at one church, mosey on down, or up, to the other church, thereby being the best sources for God's gossip.

When Jessie Rose Lee Wildcat Tennessee turned into Grandmama, the two churches were still split. Mama had us attend both churches but when the meetings coincided we always went to the Upper Church. Monthly meetings for both churches occurred on the third Sunday of each month (when the preachers preached), with Sunday school being held on all Sabbaths. Whenever a month possessed a rare fifth Sunday, about twice a year, local churches in the area would form a program on what was called "Union Sunday." Plainview was in the same area (conference or league) as Barrows Grove, Smyrna and Springfield and on Union Sunday each of these churches would present its respective program held at one of the four churches on a rotating basis. A program consisted of speeches by grownups, individual and choir singing, and children's recitations. Those were frightening times as a child when you had to learn a "speech" and then walk up to the stage and stand in front of everybody, all of whom were looking at you, and give your speech with enough volume for all (especially your mama and your teacher) to hear without missing a word.

Mama *loved* these Sundays. She was always in charge of Plainview's (Upper Church) program. For herself she always took some section from the Bible and would have us children, usually Benny, Sister and me, get on stage with her and follow her lead by speaking individual, memorized parts. Weeks ahead of time we started rehearsing our Biblical roles and, thanks to Mama's firmness, had them down letter perfect come Union Sunday. These performances always put Plainview's program at the top, but I envied the children who only had to learn a few lines to recite instead of the pages we had to memorize. But we children found it much easier to learn our parts than to try to tell Mama we couldn't do it. We were always telling Mama that she always made us do things other children didn't have to do, to which she always replied, "Don't worry about the 'other' children; that's for their folks to worry about." Mama *always* had an answer.

Plainview's pastor, Reverend Love, was probably in his thirties during the 1940s. But, many felt, he was too young and inexperienced to preach that "old-time religion" the way it was meant to be preached. That is, loud and lively enough to make, throughout the church and within the soul of each individual, the spirit "move." To do this, everyone said, the preacher had to have a voice loud enough for God to hear on high and deep enough to scare Satan down below. Yes, Lord, his dissenters felt Reverend Love was a bit too low-key, or "modern" to make the Bible come "alive" for his congregation. These were the men talking. The women felt fine about the Reverend who was young and good looking and who, many of these same females thought, had a too-fat wife.

One could join the church on any meeting Sunday and get baptized on the following month's meeting Sunday. But nobody worthy of note was ever known to join the church on a meeting Sunday. The time to join the church came at "Revival." In August of every year, during lay-by time, there would be one week, Sunday night through Friday night, of Revival, an old-time religion membership drive that led up to the Third Sunday when all the new members would be baptized. During separate weeks in August a revival was held at both the Lower and Upper churches, thus allowing folks to attend this high holy period at both houses of worship.

To attract as many new members for the church as possible, tradition called for the regular pastor to invite a guest minister to help with the preaching during this special week of the year. Most of these guest preachers were freelancers, those not having their own church or those too old to pastor a church full-time but with plenty enough old-time religion left in their souls to "whup" a week's worth of it on the souls of a congregation. For these younger preachers, the more people they got to join during Revival the bigger grew their own reputations and the better chance they had of getting their own church. Such hungry guest preachers were invited to Revival for one purpose only . . . to kill the devil in the souls of the congregation. We called them "Hired Guns."

Most everyone in Plainview joined the church as a child, many before the age of twelve, the official local age for becoming a "sinner" if not a member of the church. During Revival all non-church members, starting anywhere from ages six to eight, were required to sit in the front row, on the mourners' bench—the seat of the sinner. From there as the night's meeting drew to an end and as an especially-for-the-occasion hymn, "Oh Sinner You Can't Hide," was sung, one stepped forward to join the church by shaking the offered hand of the preacher. In doing so, one left behind forever the mourners' bench and, hopefully, hell. But becoming a Christian consisted of much more than just stepping up and shaking the preacher's extended hand. One first had to get one's soul right with the Lord through constant prayer . . . and no horsing around during Revival week.

I made my way, or was sent, to the mourners' bench at age seven. Not that I was feeling extraordinarily sinful on that particular night, but Harvey and Benny, who had just joined the church themselves and didn't want to be seen sitting next to a sinner, sent me up front with the rest of my sinful kind. Up front on the mourners' bench the rest of the church could see you and give thanks to the Lord that their souls had already been snatched from the gates of hell. Sitting here that night, I, for the first time, began feeling sinful, especially whenever someone said a prayer, they all aimed at the mourners' bench (jammed elbow-to-elbow with us sinners this night). During these prayers the rest of the congregation, the saved, just lowered their heads while we sinners had to get down on our knees with backs bent and heads bowed and lean our elbows on the seat of the bench in order to be prayed over. Enough to make one want to join the church just to get up off your knees and out of the spotlight . . . not to mention saving wear and tear on the knees of your best Sunday pants.

Revival, 1943! After suffering through two years of the mourners' bench blues, I felt I couldn't take being a sinner anymore . . . and decided to join the church on the very first night of Revival. This meant for the rest of the week I would have to sit in the special "holding" section, the front bench of the sacred (and saved) Amen corner, reserved for those who had just joined the church and were awaiting their baptism on the upcoming Sunday. Over here one was "special," sitting safely among the saved deacons and sisters while looking across (and down) with pity upon those poor souls left behind still wallowing in sin on the mourners' bench, "death row." But in order to join the church and for God to forgive me for my nine years of earthly sin I knew I had a whole lot of praying ahead of me.

That Sunday the Andrews children went, as usual, to Sunday school. Afterward, I went up to June's to play . . . and pray. All afternoon we played cowboys and crooks, but having definitely decided to join the church that night I, in between shootouts, fistfights, and horseback chases, would quickly recite the Lord's prayer to myself. When there was little time between the action, I would say beneath my breath the shorter child's prayer, "Now I lay me down to sleep . . ." When the riding, fighting and shooting got fierce, I only had time to mutter to myself the even shorter table blessing. "Lord make us truly thankful for this food . . ."

I cut my visit short with June on this pious day, realizing that if I was going to join the church that night, I had better get serious about my praying. When I got home before sundown it was such a rare occurrence that Mama thought I was sick. While on my way home, bringing up the cows, toting water from the spring, and even en route to church that night, I kept repeating to myself prayers—the Lord's and some of my own creating. Yet from time to time my mind would wander from prayer to wonder what was on the radio or to think about the pictures playing that coming week at the Madison picture show (don'ts with sin written all over them during Revival week). Catching myself, I would quickly ask God's forgiveness and go back to praying . . . to the thundering hooves of the silver screen in the background.

An extremely important step in the process of joining the church came at the end of the "Oh Sinner You Can't Hide" hymn, the last chance for the mourners' bench sinners to be saved that night. Now all attention focused on the newly joined—those (or that one) who took the preacher's hand and sat in the special chair placed for the occasion between the pulpit and the mourners' bench, facing the latter. This was when the preacher would ask the new joinee to please stand and tell the congregation in his or her own words why he or she felt they had religion enough to become a member of Plainview Baptist Church. This was the tough part, tougher than praying, since you prayed to yourself while this stand-up confession had to be said in front of everybody. The thought of having to undergo this public confession, I'm sure, kept many glued to the mourners' bench . . . and sin. Most newly joined who ventured into this public display stood and with heads lowered hurriedly mumbled the old standard, "I prayed and prayed and asked the Lord to forgive me for my sins and I feel he did," before quickly dropping back down in the chair without looking up and around at anybody in the church. Sometimes the girls would just cry and the preacher and congregation felt this was proof enough that God had forgiven them their sins. But boys couldn't, or had better not, cry so they had to think of something to say.

One of the most unforgettable confessions ever spoken in the history of Plainview was delivered one year by Cootney Mapp, our neighbor and Reverend Mapp's oldest son. That historical night Cootney stood up and in a loud voice confessed, "I came to a wall that I couldn't get through. I couldn't go around it, I couldn't climb over it, and I couldn't crawl under it. That's when I knew it was time for me to get myself right with God and that's what I went and did through prayer." This classic confession from such a young person (Cootney was fifteen) drew a long chorus of "Amen!s" and "Bless him Lord's" that had never been experienced before at either an Upper or a Lower Church joining. Unfortunately, following this beautiful confession, Cootney never came back to Plainview Church again, not even to be baptized. But Plainview yet remembered his words.

That night I joined. Mama didn't shout. I was extremely disappointed since I had seen her shout over happenings of much less importance in the church. Some years earlier I had walked out of a meeting because the shouting had scared me. On my way back home I met Mama coming down the road on her way to church (she always sent us children on ahead). I told her that all of those folks shouting had scared me. But when she took me by the hand and led me back into church I felt safe. Then, before the preacher got through with the congregation that day, Mama shouted. I felt deceived. Not able to trust my own mama! Now on the eve of my joining the church—something to shout about—Mama just sat there. I was hoping she would at least cry. She didn't. Later, while standing to confess and with Cootney's classic words ringing in my heard, I hurriedly mumbled, "I prayed and prayed . . ."

The next morning Mama called me aside and asked me if I truly felt I had prayed long and sincerely enough to have gotten a true religion, especially after having spent most of that previous afternoon playing at

June's. Daddy, who was not even a church member, asked me the same thing. I told them both I had religion. Before the week was up, Sister had joined the church, and when she stood to confess she, of all people, couldn't talk. She cried. That next morning she had to go before Mama and Daddy to explain herself and she too told them she had religion. Well, Mama would not allow us to be baptized that following Sunday because she didn't feel our souls were ready, or "ripe," for God. Back to the mourner's bench.

I was both embarrassed and mad. All of that praying going to waste! I seriously thought of *never* joining the church, becoming instead a full-time career sinner. Even though Benny had made heaven sound so wonderful that I just wanted to go without even bothering to die, now I began thinking seriously of remaining a sinner and dying unbaptized and going to hell, which I felt would really fix Mama and Daddy, rather than going through all of that praying again.

But the next year I reran my prayers and, with Sister, I joined the church again. At confession time I stood up with the fullest intention of quoting Cootney . . . chickened out and ended up hurriedly mumbling, "I prayed and prayed . . ." Sister cried. This time Sister and I, along with many others, were baptized on Third Sunday by Reverend Love in a pond down in the woods in the back of the church. Saved, finally!

Through the years there were a few who always managed to squeeze through the Revival net and enter adulthood without joining the church. These grownup, "genuine" sinners rarely came inside the church during Revival, being too embarrassed to walk up front to the mourners' bench and sit among a bunch of youngsters under the limelight of sin and be stared at, looked down upon, and pitied throughout the sermon by the smug saved. Plainview's three oldest living sinners during the 1940s were Mister Coot Durden, Mister Charley Jackson and Daddy. Mister Coot, approaching his nineties, was getting a bit too old to be out at night, so during Revival he stayed home to reserve his energy for daytime sinning. This left Mister Charley and Daddy to represent sin outside the house of God where each Revival night they stood talking, mostly about crops and the weather. Then, Lord, came Revival 1945.

It was that next to last, Thursday, night of Revival when Mister Charley didn't show up and Daddy stood outside talking to a few saved souls about crops and the weather when a storm suddenly came up. When the rain started coming down, the saved souls ran for the only available cover, inside the church. Daddy, preferring rain over religion, remained outside standing under a tree. Then from out of the sky the Lord sent forth to Earth Daddy's greatest fear, a bolt of lightning. Between the long flash of lightning and a heavy explosion of thunder, Daddy streaked through the door of the church. Not wanting to be noticed, he quickly sat down on a bench on the very last row. Too late! For, Daddy, one of Plainview's Big Three Sinners, not to be noticed entering church—even if he was sent in by a streak of lightning—was like God or, better, Satan walking through the church doors trying not to be seen. The preacher stopped in mid-preach. But Grandmama was the first to react. When she stood up everyone thought she was fixing to shout. Instead, Grandmama, from the women's Amen corner up alongside the pulpit and with a now totally stunned and silent preacher and congregation looking on, walked all the way to the back of the church, took Daddy by the hand, and brought him and his bowed head back down the aisle and sat him up front on the mourners' bench.

All this time the only sounds in the church were Grandmama and Daddy's footsteps and the loud overhead claps of thunder resounding from outside. Yes, the Lord does work in mysterious ways. Daddy seated, Grandmama, on her way back to her pew broke out in the hymn, "I Was Lost but Now I'm Found . . . ," which was immediately picked up by the rest of the congregation. The preacher, realizing he had on *his* mourners' bench one of God's "most wanted" sinners, Daddy, went back to preaching with a hellfire-and-brimstone vengeance. Oh, Lord, the congregation immediately answered back in louder song, shouts, hand-clapping and foot-stomping while the outside wind, rain, thunder and lightning stormed on. Mama cried. Rescued by a year from the mourners' bench, I sat watching Daddy's bowed head, thinking this was the first time I'd ever seen him with his cap off in public. His head was shaved clean of any blond hair.

They didn't get Daddy that night but the feeling ran strong that he was "on the edge." Ripe. And with one more night of Revival to go. Lord, have mercy!

Following the services that night, both Grandmama and Mama went up and had separate private sessions with the preacher. Talking about Daddy. In a controlled voice, I heard the preacher say, "We must show patience . . ." Yet while saying this over and over to both Grandmama and Mama, the preacher kept wringing his hands as if he was getting his right one in shaking shape for that Friday, and final, Revival, night. All Plainview went home to wait.

All during the next day, everything was quiet around our house. Even Sister. Early that morning, Mama told us children not to bother Daddy because he was deep in thought . . . prayer. We spent the whole day practically tiptoeing around the house. Mama didn't even argue with Daddy one single time. In fact, when talking to him she spoke softly and would give him kind looks. Having gotten religion twice myself, I knew the hell Daddy must've been going through trying to inwardly pray with only one night left to get saved. And especially while trying to concentrate on those crime magazines he sat reading all day.

All day all of Plainview waited for that night.

With the exception of the white families, everybody in the community, including all the babies, showed up at church that night. All wanted to be there the night of Plainview Revival's biggest sinner catch ever! Honey, hush!

Everybody showed up, that is, except Daddy . . . who stayed home that Friday, final Revival night reading his *True Detective* magazines.

Daddy never went back to church to stand outside when there were signs of a storm brewing.

Children of the community learned early that church was not meant to be a place of fun. Church was serious. It was the *only* place where *all* the colored, both the good and the bad, met as *one*. Sure, the good went inside church and prayed and the bad (unless they wanted to sit on the mourners' bench) stayed outside and played. Yet after services everybody got right back together. At no other place within, or outside, the community could the entire colored family meet like at church; it was the only place we could rightfully call our own where for a few hours each week we conducted our lives our own way. On occasion, Mister McIntire, the white landowner, would come and sit in the back of the church to listen to, or watch, the proceedings. When this happened, the atmosphere instantly changed and the signal "alien in church!" registered within the soul of the congregation, automatically sending up a guard, or "putting on a face," for outsiders. Perhaps this reflex reaction could be traced back to slavery, when the restrictions on blacks congregating were very severe. Whatever the reason, the church, our *only* possession entirely independent of the white world, we only shared with one another . . . and God. Amen.

# James Kilgo

## "Mountain Spirits"

The man who told me how to find Bascomb Creek had lowered his voice to keep from being overheard by the people standing near us. "It's hard to find but it's easy to fish," he'd whispered, "and it's jumping with trout. Just keep it to yourself." That sounded too good to be true, but as soon as I got home I called my friend Charlie Creedmore. At five o'clock the next Saturday morning we were driving north toward Rabun County. At first light we crossed the concrete bridge over Bascomb Creek, pulled over at a wide spot in the gravel road and climbed out. Charlie headed upstream while I made my way south through the dim woods. After walking for perhaps twenty minutes I stepped into the water and began fishing back toward the bridge. My skepticism had been well-founded. The canopy was too low for easy casting, and because of drought the water was warm and shallow, the pools few and far between. I waded fast, eager for a pool I could cast to, and before I knew it I was back at the bridge. It was not yet eight o'clock.

Between me and the bridge, and several terraces above my head, lay a wide inviting pool. Streams of water spilled from it, splashing down to where I stood. I climbed slowly, careful not to spook any fish it might hold. Then, at eye level, on shelved stone around the pool, I saw the trash: styrofoam fast-food containers, empty cans labeled Niblets, beer cans, and the plastic sixpack rings they had come in. I could almost see the crowd that left it, craning their necks at the hatchery truck on the bridge above, eager for its bounty of washed-out rainbows. Keep it to yourself, the man had said.

At least a dozen trout had survived the last onslaught. They were schooled near the bottom—eight- and ten-inchers they looked like—hanging still in the cold lower layer. Tin cans glinted through the depths.

I congratulated myself a little on having the decency not to cast to those harried fish, though in fact I doubted that they would take a fly. I thought of the thermos of coffee in the Blazer, said to hell with fishing, and climbed through the littered woods toward the road. Near the top I came upon a blind TV, set upright among the hemlocks. The road itself looked like a garbage dump. I laid my flyrod across the hood of the Blazer and poured myself a cup of coffee. Amidst the trash across the road fluttered strips of toilet paper.

I did not want to think that mountain people had made this mess. I wanted to believe that mountain people behaved like the stout old craftsmen I had read about in the *Foxfire* books, that treasure of Appalachian lore collected right here in Rabun County by Eliot Wigginton and his high-school students. I knew better than that, of course. The *Foxfire* project was itself a response to the threat of commercial development.

Many years earlier I had taught a young man who had been part of Wigginton's first group of student folklorists. I remembered well a quart jar of white likker he brought me one Monday morning. "That's what they call it," he said. "White likker. And that right there is the best in Rabun County."

The jar had lasted three years because I drank it slowly, saving it for those times when I needed an antidote against the banalities of the world I lived in.

I turned to look again at the broken TV in the woods. Its doleful stare from out of the hemlocks reminded me of a colleague who lost his composure one day over the stupidity of a program his children were watching. Before his rage spent itself, he had hauled the family set out into the country and shot it to pieces with a deer rifle. After the fact he had been a little embarrassed, but he explained to me that he'd had to do it, had to accomplish its destruction with his own hands. In the long run, though, it did no good. By the time he got back home, a neighbor, having heard that his children were deprived of television, had donated one of hers.

I at such times took a ritual sip from the fruit jar. The bite of that mountain corn—like good medicine—reminded me that in Rabun County at least people were still living in a world crafted by their own hands. But that had been fifteen years ago; the jar was long since empty and I had not tasted any since.

As I began to unseat the reel from my flyrod, I heard a car coming, tires on gravel, approaching the bridge. But it wasn't a car. It was an old pick-up, dead-paint blue, and it pulled to a stop directly across the road from me, scattering trash. I became uncomfortably conscious of my fly-fishing vest, Orvis zingers dangling down the front, laminated landing net hanging from the back. I wished I had taken it off. Intent on the rod I ignored the truck.

A door opened, slammed shut. Someone was coming. I glanced—a local it was, sleeveless shirt unbuttoned, black hair greased down solid. Thick glasses magnified his eyes, but the detail that bothered me most was the frames—opaque-green and plastic, dime-store glasses. I had often berated city folks ignorant enough to assume that everyone in Rabun County is as depraved as the two perverts in James Dickey's *Deliverance*, but this fellow at best looked like the kind who would dump his broken TV in the woods. I wondered where Charlie was, what was taking him so long. The man was not walking straight toward me so much as sidling in my direction, and while his face was set my way his eyes seemed fixed, sure enough, on the television set behind me. A bad burn was healing on the back of one hand.

"You going or coming?" he asked.

"Just waiting on my buddy," I said.

"What you fishing with?"

For the first time in my life I hated having to say flyrod.

The man glanced at it, muttered an obscenity.

"I couldn't do nothing with 'em," I said. "Y'all getting ready to try 'em?"

"You ever hear about old Towse?"

The senselessness of the question disturbed me more than anything that had happened yet. "No," I said, "I don't believe I have." I unjointed the sections of my rod, anxious for Charlie.

"I thought you might have heared about old Towse."

The man was close enough now for me to smell the whiskey on his breath. I had a feeling that a lot depended on the answer I gave. "No. You'll have to tell me about him."

"Coon dog. You want a drink?"

As early as it was, I chose what seemed the prudent course. "I believe I might."

The man led me across the road. As we approached the pickup, he spoke to his companion, who was concealed behind the glare of the windshield. "Monroe, reach me that bottle."

While Monroe was bestirring himself, I noticed a revolver on the dash—an unholstered nickel thirty-eight, every visible chamber loaded. I could picture it sliding hard from one side to the other as the truck swung through hairpin curves.

Monroe climbed out on the far side—an older man with a puffy, pocked face, wearing overalls and a soft-looking old baseball cap. Without a word or nod of greeting he offered the bottle across the hood—an old vodka bottle from the looks of what was left of the label and containing a liquid as clear as vodka. A blue and red can of RC Cola followed.

Moonshine can range from real good to toxic. I had no idea what I was on the verge of tasting. But as afraid as I was to drink it, I was more afraid not to. Besides I wanted to hear the story. If this homemade product fell short of my memory of the student's gift, I would say: "That's good, thank you, but I'm afraid it's a little early in the day for me."

It was good. I mean it tasted right as far as I could tell, serious but smooth, no barbed wire in it, and a flavor unlike that of any commercial sourmash I had ever drunk. I declined the RC and took another swallow.

"They's a Church a God preacher over in Walhally put out a bluegrass song on him," the one with glasses said.

On Towse, he meant.

"And they tell me a feller up in Franklin made a ballad about him too, but I ain't heared that one."

"Can you sing the Church of God one?" I asked.

"I ain't got my guitar. You remember the words to it, Monroe?"

"I can't keep 'em straight."

"Damn if he wont a good one. Trail didn't get too cold for Towse."

"I didn't think there were that many coons up here."

"It ain't. Not like it used to be. Where you from?"

I told them I lived in Athens. The one with glasses, whose name was Roy, said they used to hunt around Athens—down in Jackson County— a world of coons down there. He asked was I with the university. Somewhat surprised, I said yes. He figured that must be a good job. Monroe said a cousin of his had a daughter went to the university, he thought I might have known her, named Tami Bascomb, works for a bank in Atlanta now. I started to explain that the university was much larger than most people realized, but Roy passed me the bottle and Monroe said: "They ain't near the game in these mountains they used to be."

"I thought the deer and turkeys were coming back," I said.

"Too much goddam Atlanta," Monroe said. "Used to, a man could feed his family just on hunting and fishing, plant a garden, maybe run a little likker on the side. Right up yonder in that cove one day I killed four pheasants and thirteen gray squirrels."

"Is that right?" I asked, careful to conceal my skepticism. By pheasant Monroe meant ruffed grouse. I had hunted the bird enough to know that four in one day, in these steep wooded hills, required a combination of remarkable luck and exceptional wing-shooting.

"Shore did. Shot three on the ground and one in the air. And thirteen gray squirrels." Monroe held his fist to his face. "I had me a string of stuff this long."

"The thing about Towse," Roy said, "he wouldn't give up on no coon. You take a normal dog, a old coon'll lose him, swim the river on him, run on rock—rock'll not hold his scent, see. But Towse'd stay on his ass—rock, water, what have you. He run a coon one night up in a rock clift." Roy took a pull on the bottle, chased it with RC, passed the bottle to me. "That's what done him in."

I had to ask Roy to explain what he meant by a rock clift.

"Why, it's kindly like a hole."

"A hole in the ground?"

"No. It's where you have a clift in the rock." He paused, then continued, "Hell, it's just a rock clift, is what it is."

I featured a deep cleft in the face of a cliff. "And Towse did what? Ran a coon into the rock clift?"

"That he did. Time we got there, the hole was done caved in, all them dogs a-running round, a-climbing rocks, barking treed. My brother said, 'I don't see Towse.' The old man said, ''Cause he's in there with 'at coon is why.' You remember that, Monroe? And shore 'nough, you could hear him; over all them other dogs, you could hear him way down in that rock clift, a-killing that coon."

Somewhere in Roy's account Monroe had begun to talk. Intent on Roy, I had picked up only snatches, enough to realize that his comments had nothing to do with Towse. He was talking about fishing as far as I could tell, but Roy seemed not to mind; he didn't even slow up. The two men were as oblivious to each other as two radios tuned to different stations, turned up loud. Trying to hear what both were saying was frustrating. If I could stop Monroe with a question, maybe Roy could finish his story. "*What* kind of trout?" I asked.

"Speckled trout."

Roy was saying something about the cave-in, something to do with a slab-sided bitch that was down in there with Towse, but Monroe went right on. "Damn near rare as a chestnut tree any more. Hatchery fish is what done it. Used to, speckled trout was all you'd catch."

Roy was still talking—not competing with Monroe, just telling his story. But I was interested also in this mysterious speckled trout. "I'm not familiar with that fish," I said.

"Generally he'll not go more'n six inches. And real bright. Orange and red and black and white and speckled."

"You mean a brook trout?"

"No. A speckled trout. Old-timey, original fish. Catch him in the morning, he'll not rot on you like these here goddam stocked fish. He's the best eating fish they is. Meat's right pink. I caught forty-three one day, on up Bascomb Creek here."

Roy had stopped to take a drink and had not yet recovered his voice.

"What did you catch them on?" I asked, thinking, corn probably.

"Sawyers. Sawyers and waust grubs."

I had to ask what he meant by sawyers.

"Fat white worms. You find 'em in a old rotten log. Best bait they is. That and waust and hornet grubs."

I wondered how one acquired wasp and hornet larvae, especially during the summer when nests are active, but Monroe did not regard that as a matter requiring explanation.

"You need to cook 'em first. Bake 'em in the oven about forty-five minutes, get 'em right tough. That way they'll stay on your hook. Used to, it'd take my daddy three days to get ready to go a-fishing, three days to gather up his bait. But when he went he by god caught 'em. All speckled trout too.

"It's best to wait for a good hard pour to dingey up the creek. It come up a hell of a rain the day I caught them forty-three. I found me a stooping tree to get up under and waited for it to quit. Time it did I caught the fire out of 'em."

"Was Bascomb Creek named after some of your people?"

"I imagine it was, but I couldn't tell you just exactly who. My granddaddy owned from the bridge here clear up to the headwaters on Hogpen Mountain. But it was Bascomb Creek before his time. They used to be a world of Bascombs all up through here. I reckon we was all kin one way or another."

"Did your granddaddy sell his land to the Forest Service?"

"A right smart of it, he did. And what little bit the government left, goddam developers got. You know Blue Mountain Ski Resort? Got that off my granddaddy's old sister and her not knowing no better."

"It's got to where now a man can't afford to keep his own place," Roy said.

I was afraid the end of his story about Towse had been swallowed up in Monroe's lament for speckled trout, as the dog himself was buried beneath the rock slide. But surely there was more to it than just a dead coon hound, or why would Roy have asked a stranger if he'd heard about old Towse? That might have been the whiskey, of course, but people didn't make ballads out of what I'd heard so far.

"Goddam Atlanta," Monroe said.

"Florida too," Roy added.

"They say these tourists spend a lot of money up here," I suggested.

"Shit." For once they spoke in unison. Roy said he was yet to see the first green dollar of it hisself, and Monroe said: "You want to see that tourist money, look at all this trash strowed up and down the road. People got no self-respect."

I did not believe that tourists from Atlanta and Florida had driven through the National Forest throwing garbage from their windows, and I didn't think Monroe did either, but somewhere in his comment was an association of one with the other that was worth thinking about.

"Same thing with likker. Used to, a man took pride in making whiskey, but this goddam radiator likker they're selling now will kill you. I've seen some would peel the paint off a car. They was a fellow up here at Scaly one night spit out a mouthful against the door of a pickup truck, it run down the side, took the paint right with it."

"How do they use a radiator?"

"Condenser. Instead of a worm. Then they'll put potash in on you, Irish taters, no damn telling what all. Possum fall in and drown, they don't give a damn, run it anyway. I'd not touch a drop that I didn't know who made it. Not like it is now."

I was somewhat comforted by Monroe's implicit endorsement of the product we were drinking. "I guess you know who made this then?"

Monroe paused for a second. Then he said, "Yeah, I do."

"I wasn't asking who. I'm just glad you know it's good."

"I guaran-goddam-tee it's good," Roy said. "This here ain't nothing but pure corn." He thumped the bottom of the bottle to make it bead. "Same as it's always been."

"I guess y'all's ancestors must have passed it down—the right way to make it, I mean—father to son."

Roy said, "That they did."

He took a swallow. "The bitch come out after four days. We thought it was her that caused the slide . . ."

"Generally is," Monroe interjected.

"She was a slab-sided bitch to start with, and after four days in that hole she was poor enough to squeeze through. But Towse was too stout through the shoulders."

"What kind of dog was he?"

"Half redbone and half bluetick and half bulldog. Eighteen days in that hole, he was, and him without nothing but that coon to eat. We like to never got him out."

"What did you do? Dig him out?"

"Blowed him out with dynamite. Case and a half, quarter stick at a time."

I accepted the exaggeration as an appropriate tribute to the dog. I accepted it as I accepted their whiskey, with pleasure. "Good Lord. How much rock did you have to blast through?"

"Forty foot."

"And he was still alive."

"Just barely. You remember when he come up out of there, Monroe? All bowed up and caved in, he was, but he by god walked out on his own. 'Course he never heared too good after that. My daddy just retired him, let him lay up by the stove for as long as he lived, which won't but about another year. But he was one more tough son of a bitch in his prime, won't he, Monroe?"

"He was that. How old was you when your daddy started you at his still?"

"Had me toting jars when I was eight."

It crossed my mind to wonder if Roy's people might have been the ones who had made the whiskey the student had brought me years before. I told them about that—"the best in Rabun County"—and admitted that I'd been curious ever since about the way it was made.

For the first time that morning Monroe laughed. "Why? You ain't aiming to start one up your own self, are you?"

Before I could answer, Roy took over. "Whiskey ain't something you can just lay out the making of like you can a house and expect somebody to come along and read how and then do it. It takes a man that respects corn to do it right. Corn's got it own nature, see. You run it before its time, before them old dogheads go to rising, or sun it too fast or cook it too hot, why it'll not be fit to drink. Making whiskey's more a matter of caring how good instead of how much. A man that don't plan to drink his own likker, I damn shore don't want none of it myself."

"You drink it right," Monroe said, "good likker'll not hurt you. Drink all you want, get up the next morning, eat what they put before you, sausage and eggs and cathead biscuits. I know a preacher drinks it. He don't what you'd call regular drink now, but he will take a sup or two of an evening. Says it makes him rest better. You want some more?"

I decided Charlie could drive us back to Athens.

"They's a Church a God preacher over here to Walhally made up a bluegrass song about old Towse," Roy said. "Put it out on a record. He deserved it too. He was a uncommon dog."

Charlie came walking out of the woods not long after that, as disappointed in Bascomb Creek as I had been. The bottle was almost empty, but we hung around the front end of Roy's pickup long enough for him to have a taste. I asked if they could sell me a bottle to take home, but they said no, the one we'd drunk was all they had.

I rode back to Athens as high on Roy's story as I was on his whiskey. To make the story mine I tried to tell it to Charlie while Roy's words still rang in my head, but it didn't work. In my telling, the story went flat—just another Old Blue tale with appropriate exaggeration. Then it hit me: to tell it right you had to have someone to do Monroe's part. For the two men had been telling the same story all along—I could see it now—two men with nothing better to do that morning than hang around the hood of a pickup truck with a fifth of white likker in a recycled vodka bottle and an audience who must have looked to them like he might understand what they had to tell.

# Melissa Fay Greene

## From *Praying for Sheetrock*

### ONE
### The Old Way

I

U.S. 17 was an old blacktop two-lane running down the Georgia coast at sea level, never straying far from the edge of the continent.

In Savannah it was a dirty liquor street swelling at dusk with honking cars double-parked outside the package stores. Pawnshops closed for the night, dropping latticed chains over their windows, and bail bondsmen opened for business: shirtsleeved men half-seated on desktops waited with crossed arms for the black rotary-dial phones to start ringing. On their walls hung hand-printed signs like, "It's always SPRINGtime at Bulldog Bonding."

Further south, on the outskirts of Savannah, the old highway was lined by mobile home dealerships. Further south still, people *lived* in the mobile homes, set back from the road with chickens and rusty swingsets in the yards, and the nearby businesses were auto junkyards. Further south, used merchandise was sold out of abandoned barns the people called "flea markets." Miss Nellie's Hidden Treasures displayed, at roadside, Mexican vases, shoe boxes of old vacuum cleaner attachments, gold-framed paintings of bullfights or of Elvis on black velvet, dilapidated playpens, and cast-iron black-faced jockeys in their simpering crouch.

In Liberty County and Chatman County, commerce dwindled to the occasional peach or Vidalia onion stand. In midsummer, corn filled the fields and laundered sheets and overalls stiffened on clotheslines outside the sharecropper shacks. One last bit of trade before the road rolled south into the deep country was Mama Harris, Palm Reader. Then Highway 17 dove into the great dark pine forests of McIntosh County.

Wild turkeys, foxes, quail, and deer crunched across a pine needle floor for a hundred miles. Woodpeckers darted among the upper branches like small red arrows in the green light. The old highway lay peacefully abandoned, soft and yellow as a footbridge baking in the summer heat while box turtles scraped across it. Vultures stood on it in a circle like gaunt old card players: tall, cackling cronies with bony shoulders, divvying up the pot.

Occasionally a brontosaurlike lumber truck erupted from a side road, spraying gravel, belching smoke, and brainlessly sashaying down the center line. It drove the felled slash pine north to the port and to the pulp and paper mills of Savannah—Union Camp was the largest paper mill in the world—or south to the turpentine and paper plants of Brunswick. In both cities a sulfurous haze, the industrial rotten-egg odor of jobs, clouded the in-town neighborhoods; but in McIntosh County, where the forests grew, the water tasted like cold stones and the air was clean and piney.

Gradually, to the east, the forest broke open, then disappeared, replaced by vast soft acres of salt marsh. Four hundred thousand acres of marsh stretched between the dry land and the barrier islands of McIntosh County—at some places, a mile wide; at others, ten miles wide. The primeval home of every shy and ticklish, tentacle-waving form of sea life and mud life, the coastal Georgia salt marsh is one of Earth's rare moist and sunny places where life loves to experiment. Because it is flushed out twice daily by the systole of saltwater tide and diastole of alluvial tide, the marsh looks new, as if still wet from creation.

The wetland has been claimed in various epochs by prehistoric Indians, Spanish missionaries, Blackbeard the pirate, French and English explorers, Sir Francis Drake, slaveholders and slaves, Confederates and Yankees, the victorious General Sherman, freed slaves, and unreconstructed

Rebels. Citizens at the edge of the dry land have addressed one another as Monsignor, Excellency, Governor, General, Mistress, Master, Nigger. Furies inspiring men to violence have occurred at the marsh's edge, while in its midst the frogs simply continued to blow their round bass notes. Mastodons once claimed the coast, too, and gigantic pigs and ground sloths the size of elephants; and they all have gone.

Once or twice a century, men stood up on their hind legs beside the swamp and waved their arms—the crown of the evolution of the shy tentacled sea creatures—and swelled with the thought of their own self-importance. A shouted word flew for miles, out to sea, and a gunshot echoed farther than that. The men who raised their voices, flashed their whips, fired their muskets or their revolvers, and imposed their own sense of order on their neighbors found it remarkably easy to do so. Just after the shout or the gunshot, there was silence; then the clicking of the fiddler crabs began again, and the people in their houses scraped their dishes clean and buttoned up their children and chopped wood into logs in their backyard and fed their dogs. So the strong men raised their voices again, fired their weapons, and again, rising to fill the vacuum of silence were not voices of protest or discontent but the sound of clicking, scraping, chopping. Thus, through minor heroics, brashness, and noise on one side, everyday life on the other, local heroes and strongmen arose.

In modern times Sheriff Poppell was the neighborhood head-man who exerted his will and shaped the county, and the people acquiesced as people do when they are not, themselves, hungry for power and when they are permitted to make a nice living far from the rumpus. With Poppell as sheriff, McIntosh County was not the sleepy backwater it ought to have been, nor Darien the homey one-horse town it richly deserved to be. Darien—population 1,800—consisted in 1971 of a few public office buildings, a few All-U-Can-Eat catfish restaurants, the county courthouse, a library, some hardware stores, an eighteenth-century British fort, a car wash, and a wide, hot main street—U.S. 17. But the place was jumping. Expensive cars with unsavory drivers roared through town, jeweled rings sparkled on men's hands as they cracked open their boiled crabs at lunch; gunfire rang out; and one sensed, in sheds off the road, the late-night shuffle of fifty-dollar bills. From the late 1940s through the late 1970s, McIntosh County was a mini–Las Vegas, a mini–Atlantic City, a southern Hong Kong or Bangkok where white men came looking for, and found, women, gambling, liquor, drugs, guns, sanctuary from the law, and boats available for smuggling.

Next door to these fearsome enterprises, just down the road from them, a straight-thinking, churchgoing white community attended to its civic needs in Darien; and a watchful, churchgoing black community made do in nameless hamlets in the pine woods. Sheriff Poppell amiably kept the peace between the black and white communities and between the law-abiding world and the criminals. From his illegal businesses and the looting of trucks, he tossed the occasional bonus to the law-abiding Darien whites and rural blacks. For most of this century, there was a strange racial calm in the county, consisting in part of good manners, in part of intimidation, and in part because the Sheriff cared less about the colors black and white than he did about the color green, and the sound it made shuffled, dealt out and redealt, folded and pocketed beside the wrecked trucks and inside the local truckstop, prostitution houses, clip joints, and warehouse sheds after hours.

Half the population of McIntosh was white and most of the whites lived in Darien. They lived in soft blue, pale green, or yellow wooden houses, with birdbaths and day lilies in the yard. The aluminum of their screen doors was cut in the shape of marsh birds and tall grasses. "People grew up together on these dirt streets fishing and hunting," said Archie Davis. "This was just small-town America. Four or five kids come playing down the street; the grownups knew all of them, knew their daddies."

Emily Varnedoe, a white woman of ninety, had lived in a little house beside the salt marsh most of her life. In the silences after a raised voice or a gunshot flew over the county—as strong men took over McIntosh and steered it this way rather than that—it was such as Emily Varnedoe who shrugged and continued to stir the greens in the saucepan, to repot the geraniums, to tuck in the child, and to settle herself under an afghan in front of the TV, knowing nothing of bullies and race and shoot-em-ups.

She lived quietly and cheerfully, hands crossed in her lap, looking through her windows across the yellow grass sloping toward the water. As she grew old, Emily mused more and more often on one or two things, an old fact and a recent fact, and it consumed a good deal of her day—seated in a chair, clinging to its arms with all her might—just to consider and reconsider these one or two things, not analyze them in their different aspects or wish they had been done differently; no, just bring them to the forefront of thought and make sure that the facts of each case were still arranged correctly.

Mrs. Varnedoe's son, Jesse, went to North Georgia College where he met his wife, Glenda. This was one of the facts of Emily's life which ceaselessly occupied her thoughts. "He went to North Georgia College, he and his wife, but they both told us they would never marry until they graduated," she said. "And so they both graduated before they married. They live in Tampa now. He sells insurance and she worked in the insurance office, and then she left and now she is working in a real estate office. And she says there are forty people working in that office and that's a lot! But they waited to marry, don't you know, until after they could graduate."

When Mrs. Varnedoe finished a statement her jaws moved for a moment more, thoughtfully and silently, and then she looked at you to see what you made of it, offering, in case there had been any misunderstanding: "I sent him. I paid for him to go to North Georgia College. He went there and finished up there, he and the girl he married. And he said they would not marry until they both graduated." A framed photograph of the crewcut college boy leaned backward on the mother's small television, and one would have thought the happy twin events, graduation and marriage (they didn't marry until after they graduated) had just taken place, but Jesse (North Georgia College, 1957) was fifty-four.

Emily Varnedoe's face was like a cream-colored, stained velvet bag, with a drawstring at the pursed lips. Her lips pushed out even in repose, as if to show that this was a garrulous woman who had learned to be silent—had learned that no one out there was available to listen to all her opinions.

"It's quiet over here except for the hummingbird season," she said. What great stillness is possible in a life when a person is distracted from her thoughts by hummingbirds in the yard! Does she lean forward and pound on the glass: "Hey, pipe down out there fellas!"? She sat, lips pursed, hands folded, looking toward the marsh, waiting for the hummingbirds.

There were white people in Darien who knew from which antebellum plantation family they were descended and black people who knew the location of the plantations that had owned their great-grandparents; there were close and long-time connections between the two communities unlike anything in the North. All political discourse and confrontations in McIntosh County would take place between acquaintances: when angry groups of blacks and whites faced each other, everyone would know everyone else's names and addresses, and know their mamas.

Because the whites got to McIntosh first, or "first" in relation to the McIntosh blacks, history itself was laid claim to, as if it were acreage of good bottom land. There were native Americans all along the tangled coast in the sixteenth century when the wooden sailing ships first appeared, but the Europeans killed or converted the local tribes and pushed their way into town long before sending for the Africans.

Permanent settlement first was established along the Altamaha River in 1736 by a troop of Scottish Highland warriors who built a British outpost against the Spaniards in Florida. A second embarkation from Scotland landed in 1742. The name *McIntosh* derived from the leading clan of pioneers.

The colonial history is treasured in Darien. The history of the conquest and settlement of McIntosh is as full of nobility, strife, malaria, starvation, alligators, true love, and Indian wars as any student of history could wish. History, in fact, is what Darien has the way other communities have rich topsoil or a wealth of hidden talent or fine high school athletics. Coastal people understand history personally, the way religious people do, the way ancient people did. They own history in a way lost to most Americans except in a generic, national sort of way, because the rest of us move around so much, intermarry, adopt new local loyalties, and blur the simple narrative line.

Hundreds of direct descendants of the early Scottish settlers of McIntosh still live on the very tracts of land given their families by King George II at the first embarkation in 1736 or at the second in 1742. "We've always known where we were from," said Gay Jacobs, a strong and pretty, black-eyed and amiable liberal Democrat who lived at the waterfront and ran a shrimp business. "I mean this is still part of the original land grant that my—I don't know what, how many greats back—was given. I think my family has always felt a certain responsibility to do right. About politics, about racial issues, to do right and to be right."

The Direct Descendants, as they are actually known, periodically hold reunions at the public library or in one another's homes. They wear corsages and name tags, sip punch, and listen to edifying lectures by speakers dispatched from the Savannah Historical Society. One-hundred-eighty descendants of the two McIntosh clans who landed in 1736 and founded Darien still are living. "One-hundred-eighty if no one was born or died in the last three weeks," piped up Lillian Schaitberger, a sixty-nine-year-old descendant of Donald McIntosh. She is both the treasurer of the Lower Altamaha Historical Society and the person responsible for periodically updating the list of the true and living Direct Descendants from the *first*, not the second, embarkation. "I have had people to get upset," said Schaitberger: " 'If you're *going* to do it, why not do *everybody?*' one woman told me. She was a descendant, you see, of the *second* landing in 1742. I told her, 'If you'd read the booklet closely, you'd have seen it listed the descendants of the first landing only.' "

It *was* a fine and difficult thing the Highland settlers did, living alert and armed against a Spanish enemy mounted on heavy horses (wearing feathers, high boots, and sashes in military gaiety) who charged up the coast toward the Scottish cornfields and cabins, their muskets leveled and the hooves of the horses smashing along the surf. It required physical courage for the Scots to remain on the land, to hoe, to plant, to carry water, to bear children, to believe in the community while, in the distance, there were horses.

It is quite another thing to survive into modern times when a new definition of community is required, to admit that within your town there are households that define themselves—that *you* define—as outsider, alien. Does Darien belong to the Direct Descendants alone (even generously counting the descendants of the second embarkation as bona fide DDs)? Does it belong to the Direct Descendants and their kind (for some had great-great-grandfathers planting fields in Virginia and the Carolinas, after all)? Or does it belong to more people—to more kinds of people— than that? To ask this question requires a moral courage.

But the Direct Descendants and their fellow white citizens prefer to muse on an older and clearer time, a time of wood forts and musketry, of tall ships and cannons, of kilts and bagpipes, of enemies fleeing pell-mell out of the marsh. Contrary to stereotype, they are not nostalgic for the plantation era, though Darien was one of the jewels in the crown of the Confederacy and its planters among the richest and most refined gentlemen in the world. They do not honor slavery or mourn its passing. They honor the time *before* slavery, before Africans touched foot on the land beside the Altamaha River. They wish the question had never come up.

# Jimmy Carter

## From *Turning Point: A Candidate,*
## *a State, and a Nation Come of Age*

### CHAPTER 9
### What Did It All Mean?

Mr. President, I move that the proposed Georgia election code be amended as follows: 'No person may vote either in the Democratic primary or in the general election in the State of Georgia who has been deceased more than three years.'"

It was February 1964, in the Georgia Senate. The amendment was offered by Senator Bobby Rowan from Enigma, a town in south Georgia even smaller than Georgetown or Plains. There followed a lively debate concerning the exact time interval between death and the loss of voting privileges. We assessed how long the spirit and political orientation of dead citizens might still be remembered, applied to current circumstances, and expressed with fair accuracy by survivors as the likely choice of the deceased if they had lived until election day. Although this exchange was humorous, the events leading up to it had been serious indeed.

As was long overdue, the many carefully nurtured loopholes in the Georgia election code, which had kept men like Joe Hurst in power, were now being closed, to the discomfort of some of the statehouse politicians. Many of them owed their high positions to the corrupt and unfair but legal practices that had long been integral facets of our state's election scene.

The year 1962 was a turning point, in that the tides of political history were changed. The combination of white Democratic primaries and rural bias in voting and apportionment that had for generations held the South in thrall were now to be just a fading memory.

Today, three decades after the death of the county unit system, many things are different in Quitman County, the Fourteenth Senatorial District, Georgia, and the South. Georgia political campaigns and elections have, almost invariably, become both open and honest. The votes of urban dwellers have approximately equal weight with those of farmers and residents of small towns. Former Democrats and their children have been able to switch to the Republican party without disappearing into the abyss of political obscurity. For better or worse, there is a strong two-party political system in the state.

The Civil Rights Act of 1964 has slowly been implemented by civil rights workers, federal agents, and state officials liberated from the burden of official racism. Federal judges and other Justice Department officials still monitor election procedures in our region and oversee every reapportionment of congressional and state legislative districts to assure proper racial balance. Black citizens have legal rights to use public facilities, to eat alongside white customers where meals are served to the public, to participate in electing public officials, and to run for office themselves. In many sports and in entertainment, black Americans are ascendant, as they are in the governing bodies of many of our major cities. State legislatures and the U.S. Congress are slowly but inexorably becoming more racially balanced. It seems that the original goals of the civil rights movement have been attained.

However, social and economic barriers to racial equality and better lives are still prevalent. In some ways our society has improved very little since 1962. Political analysts differ on whether the newly empowered urban legislators in the South are significantly more progressive on most issues than were their more rural predecessors. As a state senator and governor, I found that on many subjects the more representative legislature was little changed.

But there is no doubt that there has been significant improvement on the race issue. Just having one forceful black person in any kind of forum has a profound impact. Even without a verbal exchange, white leaders are more likely to accommodate minority sensitivities and needs if a member of that group is present. There was a quick learning process in the state Senate when Leroy Johnson took his seat following the 1962 election. We, his fellow senators, did not know whether to say "colored," "black," or "Negro" in referring to him and his race. South Georgians, in particular, had difficulty in pronouncing the word of his choice, having it come out something like "ni-grur." Patiently, Senator Johnson pointed to his knee, and then made a rising motion with his right hand. We practiced a few times, until finally he nodded his approval. From then on, we carefully enunciated "Knee-grow."

Leroy Johnson quickly became a valued ally for his white colleagues. Many faced for the first time the need to campaign among newly enfranchised black constituents. Senator Johnson was generous with his time and advice, and would visit districts throughout Georgia to assist legislators who earned his confidence. He used this influence with great advantage to black Georgians.

Unfortunately, social and economic factors have counterbalanced the painfully gained legal rights in many ways. With the demise of the county unit system, both rural white citizens and their black neighbors lost political power. Would-be governors, members of Congress, and state legislators changed their campaign strategies to accommodate the shift toward urban power, for they could no longer depend on the rural counties to deliver enough votes to elect them. Folks in the country are consequently not wooed as they used to be, and many of the old personal political relationships are gone. Candidates now realized that their effort is best spent where large numbers of supporters can be sought most efficiently, with the least cost in time and money per vote. Large and expensive appearances in rural county seats, with free barbecues and country music, have become part of history. Not nearly as many hands are shaken or friendships made. Increasingly, slick and impersonal television spots have become the foundation of campaigns, with a few ostentatious visits to small towns thrown in as bucolic media events.

State officials are no longer as willing to concentrate government services such as roads, schools, and job opportunities in the small counties. More important, the end of county bossism has resulted in a more impersonal and less caring relationship between local officials and their constituents. In the old days, everyone knew where to go with a problem, and the local boss had direct access to state officials, who had to be sensitive to his requests in order to get the unit votes he could deliver. Now, it is more difficult to understand the political chain of command or follow it to a favorable decision.

There is little doubt, for instance, that Joe Hurst and his wife, Mary, knew every black and white citizen in Quitman County, having personally delivered monthly welfare checks to the poor families—about half the total population. Whatever criticisms his fellow citizens might level at him, they all acknowledge that "Joe took care of his people." These favors were available even to those who had worked and voted against the Hurst candidates on election day. For those political foes who were willing to request his help, there was at least an implied promise of accommodation in the future. This degree of personal politics rarely exists today, having been replaced for poorer people by encounters with a faceless postal service and a constantly changing cadre of social workers with whom there is little real empathy.

But it is the education system in the South that has borne the brunt of social change. When the public schools were first required to integrate in the wake of *Brown v. Board of Education,* there was a mass exodus of white students whose parents could pay the tuition fees to enroll in the private "segregation academies" that sprang up in almost all communities. A few of these private schools have flourished and developed good academic programs, but most have not been able to compete in terms of quality and have based their continuing existence on parental dedication to racial segregation. Even worse, many public school boards have come to be dominated by affluent members whose children attend the community's private schools. Inevitably, their interests tend to be concentrated more on holding down the property tax rates that finance the public schools than on providing adequate support to enhance the curriculum in the schools their children do not attend.

In the meantime, though, the integrated high school athletic teams have brought black and white fans together in football and basketball stadiums and have made it easier for them to accept biracial classrooms. Over the years, dwindling enrollments in the weaker private academies have caused them to close, and their students have been returning to the public system, at least in the rural communities. In large cities, however, where housing patterns are based on family income, many of the schools are once again almost totally segregated. It is obvious that neither the promised blessings nor the dire predictions of school integration have been realized.

Even under the best circumstances, the degree to which integration is accepted in the schools can be misleading. After spending ten years in public schools, our daughter, Amy, chose to attend a large private boarding school near Atlanta to get advanced college preparatory and art courses. Although fairly expensive and attended mostly by white students, the school had completely integrated programs, with all classes and extracurricular events encouraged to be biracial. The students seemed to be almost totally color-blind. When Rosalynn and I asked Amy how many of her fellow students were black, it was obvious that she had never thought about them in that way. One of her friends was James Forman, Jr., son of the first executive director of the Student Nonviolent Coordinating Committee. When Amy told us that she, James, and other black and white teenagers were going to the graduation dance together, it seemed natural. However, in a few days she called home, angry and distressed. The school officials had informed the student body that no "mixed" couples would be admitted. A social event was different from the campus or the classroom. When she asked us what to do, we encouraged her to use her own judgment. Not surprisingly, she and James informed the school superintendent that they would violate the ruling and go together. They did so and were not stopped at the door. This was in 1985.

Religious congregations also reflect society's ambivalence toward integration. A few formerly segregated Southern churches have been fully integrated, welcoming black members and making them feel that they are brothers and sisters of the white worshipers, but these are the notable exceptions. Even when white church doors are open, differences between black and white congregations in the conduct of religious services form barriers to integration. Our own Maranatha Baptist Church in Plains was formed in 1978 (while we were in Washington) by moderate members who left our mother church, in part because they were willing to have interracial worship. Our congregation exchanges visits on occasion with the black members of Lebanon Baptist Church in Plains, our pastors and choirs share the services, and we welcome black visitors and full-time members. However, of the few nonwhites who have responded to this open invitation, most are from families who have moved into our community from foreign countries. In general, racial segregation is still the norm in Southern churches, which in some communities seems to be what most black and white worshipers prefer.

The 1960s were a time of great hope and expectations. Those of us involved in opening up the political system saw the end of antidemocratic boss rule as the first step in the effort to make our nation live up to its ideals. The "one man, one vote" decision was followed by the Civil Rights Act of 1964, the Voting Rights Act of 1965, and the equal opportunity programs of the Great Society. We did not realize at the time, however, that solving one set of problems does not end all difficulties but, rather, changes their shape. New, unanticipated problems have arisen as the barriers to political participation have fallen—lack of economic progress, insufficient housing, substandard education, and unemployment among our poorest citizens. For two decades, all three branches of the federal government led a steady effort to alleviate these burdens, which fall disproportionately on minorities. However, in the 1980s our national leaders abandoned this commitment, and the ravages of segregation and discrimination (which most of us thought were relics of the past) have once again become prevalent. Our country is growing increasingly polarized along economic lines, and minority citizens suffer most.

When I first ran for the Georgia Senate, there were many black families who owned their own farms and the implements needed to produce a crop. Dozens of them purchased fertilizer, seeds, insecticides, and livestock feed from Carter's Warehouse and brought their cotton to our gin and their peanuts to our storage warehouses. Our competitor across the street had a similar number of these good customers. Now, farms are much bigger and require large investments in sophisticated equipment to make a crop. Federal government policies favoring corporate agriculture, intense economic competition, and the subtle discrimination of banks and other financial institutions have forced black families out of small farm ownership. The warehouse operators in Plains can now name only one active black farmer and landowner left in our community, and this family actually earns a living by manufacturing burial vaults. The interracial sharing of agricultural husbandry and entrepreneurship is rapidly disappearing. A recent study has revealed that rural blacks are losing ownership of about 2,000 acres of Southern farmland every day.

Without farms of their own or the financial ability to work rented land, few of these families can find jobs near their rural homes. Forced to move to urban communities, they are ill equipped for this completely new kind of life. For them and their neighbors, city living can be difficult, and it is growing worse. There is a lack of hope among needy families that their most serious problems will be solved. This hopelessness is often shared by community leaders who have the authority and responsibility for correcting the city's ills. It is easier for city officials and Chamber of Commerce boosters to ignore or deny these problems than to acknowledge and address them forthrightly.

As the social and economic plight of our minority citizens has become more apparent and disturbing, the race issue has crept back into American politics. Even if there is no more talk of a white Democratic primary and few references to the threat of "bloc voting," the political treasure trove of racism is still tapped by some candidates. This was a factor in the 1964 presidential race. Although Barry Goldwater avoided this ploy himself, his campaign managers in the Southern states were less reticent. They understood the subtle euphemisms; one of their most popular bumper stickers read, "I'm against welfare. I work." Goldwater's opposition to Lyndon Johnson's civil rights bills was parlayed into the first victory in history for a Republican presidential candidate in Georgia, a triumph shared only in Alabama, Mississippi, South Carolina, Louisiana, and Goldwater's home state of Arizona.

Playing the race card seems to be a tactic that still wins political contests. It was not a coincidence that Ronald Reagan made his opening "I believe in states' rights" speech of the 1980 presidential campaign in Philadelphia, Mississippi. This was the place where law enforcement officers had murdered three young civil rights workers in 1964 to deter others who were promoting racial integration—the most highly publicized crime of the civil rights era. The 6,200 residents of that town and everyone else involved on both sides of the civil rights movement knew that "states' rights" meant segregation. Subsequently, frequent references from the White House to "welfare queens," public insinuations that Martin Luther King, Jr., was a communist, and a pattern of intercessions by the U.S. attorney general *against* plaintiffs in cases of civil rights abuse were designed to appeal to right-wing constituencies. Likewise, the infamous Willie Horton television spots, with heavy-handed racial overtones, were instrumental in the Republican presidential victory of 1988.

So, what are the overall consequences of the civil rights and electoral reforms of the 1960s? There is no way to know what Southern life would be like now if legal segregation and elections based on rural white supremacy had been perpetuated, but it is beyond question that the new freedoms and equality of opportunity are precious treasures for those who have gained them. Within the reformed legal and political system, there are more opportunities for correcting our social ills; the voices of deprived people can no longer be so easily stilled or their plight ignored. Despite general awareness of these unmet challenges, the tragic fact is that the South and the nation have not succeeded in building a society of justice and equal opportunity on the momentous legal decisions that brought an end to overt racial discrimination.

There is an enormous chasm between the relatively rich and powerful people who make decisions in government, business, and finance and our poorer neighbors who must depend on these decisions to alleviate the problems caused by their lack of power and influence. Even leaders with the best of intentions seldom know personally the families in their communities whose lives are blighted by substandard housing, high crime rates, inferior schools, scarce social amenities, high unemployment, and exorbitant prices in the few nearby stores. In these neighborhoods the average family income is most often less than half the official poverty level. Many students drop out of school, health care and other services are remote or nonexistent, the teenage pregnancy rate is growing, a high percentage of babies are born prematurely and underweight, and the drug culture flourishes. More than 40 percent of America's black babies are born in poverty, often to young mothers who have received little or no prenatal care. Despite some slow progress in reducing the national infant mortality rate, a newborn baby is no more likely to survive in Harlem than in Bangladesh.

The multiplicity of government programs are uncoordinated and poorly designed, administered by top officials who rarely see at first hand why their efforts are so inadequate. Although there are many religious and other benevolent organizations whose workers minister to the poor and attempt to alleviate their problems, these efforts are often confined to one issue or to a very small group of needy families. Little if any overall progress is being made. In fact, conditions in the inner cities are growing worse. In some urban communities, the number of homeless people has increased tenfold in the last decade. The soaring crime rate among our young people is another disturbing indication of this trend. In the five years from 1986 to 1991, offenses involving violence increased 300 percent in the juvenile courts in Atlanta, while crimes involving drugs jumped 1,700 percent!

Our country's history tends to move in cycles, and today we have come to another turning point, as the segregation of our society has become almost as insidious as it was thirty years ago. The division is between rich and poor, but still largely along racial lines. There are now two Atlantas, two Washingtons, two New Yorks, two Detroits, two Americas. Those of us who live in the affluent and comfortable America have homes, jobs, education, health care, and convenient services, while many of our neighbors down the road don't have these things.

The Los Angeles riots in the spring of 1992 revealed the extent of despair and anger implicit in our divided nation, a disturbing state of affairs that Rosalynn and I had already begun to address in our work at the Carter Center. We saw that many families in America's inner cities need attention, as did our black neighbors in south Georgia thirty years ago. Our response has been to help launch a massive effort in Atlanta to address the whole gamut of problems in our most troubled neighborhoods, to coordinate existing private and government services into closer teamwork, and to give needy citizens maximum control over the entire effort. We hope that the successful elements of our Atlanta experience will provide a helpful model for other communities.

Through the Atlanta Project we have targeted the poorest neighborhoods in our own metropolitan area, home to more than 15 percent of our population—about 500,000 people—most of them black or Hispanic. Many of these people, living in areas riddled by crime and the drug culture, have a sense of hopelessness about their future. They don't think the police or the judicial system is on their side, and they don't believe that any decision they make will have an effect, even on their own lives. Tragically, the poor families in our cities are not the only ones who feel that the situation in this country is hopeless. There is an equally troubling belief in the White House, Congress, governors' mansions, city halls, and universities that the best plans and programs cannot make things better.

I do not think the situation is hopeless. We must remember the crises and solutions of the past, build on the achievements, and apply these lessons once again to heal our segregated nation. This is the turning point that we have now reached in the development of our society, when troubled citizens—black and white, poor and rich, liberal and conservative—must seek and find unprecedented ways to work together in solving the challenges of homelessness, unemployment, crime, drugs, and poor education and health care.

Having been caught up in a series of dramatic events, all the way from the Georgetown courthouse to the White House and beyond, I have a sense of the panoramic changes that have occurred since the "one man, one vote" decision was handed down. I am grateful that the millstone of official racism has been removed from the necks of Southerners, both black and white. These reforms have elevated the Southland into equal status with other states for the first time in more than a century. Had this not happened, I could never have been considered as a serious candidate for national office. Overwhelming support from my black neighbors, including the family of Martin Luther King, Jr., helped to alleviate the concerns of voters in other regions about the prospect of electing a Georgia governor to the nation's highest office. I thus became the first president elected from the Deep South in 128 years, since General Zachary Taylor, who made his home in Baton Rouge, Louisiana, won his victory in 1848.

During and since my presidency, I have observed how just laws and democratic procedures in America can offer an end to racial discrimination and human suffering. I have also seen how honest and fair elections in other countries can help end wars and promote democracy. In recent years I have participated personally in helping to arrange and monitor a number of free elections in Latin America and in Africa. I have learned over these years that legal changes and government policies alone are not sufficient to achieve the related goals of justice and freedom. Deprived citizens must help to shape their own destiny. Without a genuine sharing of authority and power, of concerns and fears, of hopes and dreams, little can be done to alleviate human suffering. This unrealized progress remains our challenge for the future.

# Biographical Notes

CONRAD AIKEN (1889–1973) was born in Savannah, Georgia, and lived there until the age of eleven, but his parents were New Englanders and he considered himself one as well. He moved to Massachusetts in 1901 to live with an aunt after his parents' murder-suicide. At Harvard his classmates included Heywood Broun, Walter Lippmann, Van Wyck Brooks, and T. S. Eliot, to whom he gave his poems for criticism. Aiken wrote more than fifty books of fiction, poetry, criticism, drama, and auto-biography. The volume and the difficulty of his work may account for his relative neglect by critics and readers. Nonetheless, he was a significant figure on the modern American literary scene. In 1930 he won the Pulitzer Prize for his *Selected Poems* (1929); his *Collected Poems* (1953) earned the National Book Award in 1954. He was consultant in poetry for the Library of Congress in 1950–51, recipient of the Bollingen Prize in Poetry in 1956, the Academy of American Poetry Fellowship in 1957, the Gold Medal of the National Institute of Arts and Letters in 1958, and the National Medal of Literature in 1969. He spent the last years of his life passing his summers in Cape Cod, Massachusetts, and his winters in Savannah. Governor Jimmy Carter named him Georgia Poet Laureate in 1973. Important works include (novels) *Blue Voyage* (1927), *Great Circle* (1933), *King Coffin* (1935), *A Heart for the Gods of Mexico* (1939), *Conversation; or, Pilgrim's Progress* (1940); (poetry) *The Coming Forth of Osiris Jones* (1931), *Preludes for Memnon* (1931), *Time in the Rock: Preludes to Definition* (1936); (others) *Ushant: An Essay* (1952), *The Short Stories of Conrad Aiken* (1950).

ELIZA FRANCES ANDREWS (1840–1931), though conventional in her pro-Southern sympathies, was an early feminist by example if not by creed; Andrews vowed early in life never to give up the freedom that marriage would cost her. She began writing, sometimes under a male pseudonym, for various national publications after the Civil War. She taught in Yazoo City, Mississippi; Washington, Georgia; and at Wesleyan College in Macon, Georgia. Her three novels are typical domestic stories of the nineteenth century, chronicling how heroines struggle for freedom and happiness before settling for marriage. Late in life Andrews became a botanist and a Marxist. She wrote two botany textbooks and a number of articles on science and botany. She is best known for her Civil War diary, *The War-Time Journal of a Georgia Girl, 1864–1865*, published in 1908. In 1927 she was elected to the Italian Academy of Literature and Science.

RAYMOND ANDREWS (1934–91) was born the son of a sharecropper in Madison, Georgia. He held numerous jobs during his youth, served in the U.S. Air Force from 1952 to 1956, studied at Michigan State University in 1956–57, and worked for KLM Royal Dutch Air Lines from 1958 to 1966. He left the airlines to write in 1966. His central achievement is a trilogy of novels set in the fictional north Georgia county of Muskhogean: *Appalachee Red* (1978), *Rosiebelle Lee Wildcat Tennessee* (1979), and *Baby Sweet's* (1983). All three novels were illustrated by Andrews's brother Benny. Using the oral and tall-tale traditions of Southern and African-American humor, they explore racial interrelationships among the inhabitants of Muskhogean County. They are humorous, sometimes violent and wild, and vividly evocative of the lives of their characters. *Appalachee Red* won the James Baldwin Prize for Fiction. Andrews's memoir, *The Last Radio Baby*, appeared in 1990, and his two novellas, *Jessie and Jesus, and Cousin Claire*, were published in 1991.

ROY BLOUNT, JR. (1941– ) was born in Indianapolis, Indiana, and attended Vanderbilt University (B.A. magna cum laude 1963) and Harvard University (M.A. 1964). He has written for a number of prominent newspapers and magazines, including *Sports Illustrated, Playboy, Rolling Stone*, the *New Yorker, Esquire*, and the *Atlantic Monthly. Crackers* (1980), his collection of essays about the South and the Carter administration, brought him national attention and is his most consistently humorous work. Other books include *About Three Bricks Shy of a Load* (1974), *One Fell Soup, or, I'm Just a Bug on the Windshield of Life* (1982), *What Men Don't Tell Women* (1984), *Not Exactly What I Had in Mind* (1985), *Soup-songs: Webster's Ark* (1987), *Now Where Were We?* (1988), *First Hubby* (1990), *Camels Are Easy, Comedy's Hard* (1992).

ELIAS BOUDINOT (1804–39) was a journalist and a spokesman for the Cherokee Indians. Boudinot vigorously represented his tribe's cause throughout the 1820s and 1830s, as pressure mounted for a solution to the "problem" that many whites believed the presence of the Indians posed. In 1827 he was appointed editor of the *Cherokee Phoenix*, the official newspaper of the tribe, and he used that position to keep the Cherokee informed about tribal culture and local and national events. As pressure for removal mounted, Boudinot traveled and lectured widely, arguing that the Cherokee were civilized and productive and should be allowed to remain on their homeland. Ultimately he came to believe that the tribe could survive only by accepting removal to Oklahoma. He resigned the editorship of the *Phoenix* in 1832, shortly after the Cherokee Council ordered him not to publish his opinions. In 1835 he and a few other Cherokee signed the New Echota Treaty, which authorized the removal of the tribe to Oklahoma, although the treaty contradicted the tribe's stand on the issue. In 1839 Boudinot was killed in Oklahoma by unidentified men.

JOHN BROWN (1820?–?) was, according to Nash Boney, editor of the modern edition of *Slave Life in Georgia*, an illiterate escaped slave "known as Fed or Benford in slavery and renamed John Brown in Freedom" who dictated his narrative to Louis Alexis Chamerovzow, secretary of the British and Foreign Anti-Slavery Society. Brown was born in Southampton County, Virginia. At the age of ten he and his mother were sold away from their family to a slaveowner in Southampton, North Carolina. He was subsequently separated from his mother and taken to central Georgia, where he worked in the fields for many years before escaping, via Louisiana and Mississippi, to the North. Historical records suggest that his narrative gives a largely accurate account of his thirty years as a slave. *Slave Life in Georgia* was one of the last popular slave narratives published prior to the Civil War.


EMILY BURKE (1820?–87) grew up in Boscawen, New Hampshire. In 1840 she arrived in Savannah to teach at the Female Orphan Asylum. During her ten years in the state, she traveled widely, lived and taught on a coastal plantation, and came to know the area well. In 1849 she married the Reverend A. R. Burke, who soon died, and she returned north in 1849 to work as principal of the Female Department of Oberlin College. She was dismissed from her position, however, when she was accused of kissing a male student. After moving to Chicago, she married again and lived much of the rest of her life in a small New Hampshire village. *Pleasure and Pain: Reminiscences of Georgia in the 1840s,* her only book, was published in 1850.


ERSKINE CALDWELL (1902–88) was born a preacher's son in Newnan, Georgia, and grew up in Wrens, Georgia. He attended Erskine College in South Carolina, the University of Virginia, and the University of Pennsylvania, though he never completed a college degree. He was four times married, including once to the photographer Margaret Bourke White, with whom he collaborated on several projects. During the first half of his career, he worked often as a journalist. He spent 1925–26 at the *Atlanta Journal,* served three screenwriting stints in Hollywood, and worked as a foreign correspondent from 1939 to 1944. His first important publication was in *Scribner's Magazine,* edited by Max Perkins. The Scribner's publishing house printed several of his early books, including *American Earth* (1930) and *Tobacco Road* (1932). Caldwell is best and most notoriously known for his portrayal of Southern whites in such novels as *Tobacco Road* and *God's Little Acre* (1933), though whether his portrayals are accurate has been the subject of considerable discussion, including a lawsuit. In style Caldwell worked in the traditions of both American realism and old Southern humor. His best-known writings are about Georgia, though for much of his life he lived elsewhere.

JIMMY CARTER (1924– ) was born in Plains, Georgia, a farming community where he still maintains a home. He studied at Georgia Southwestern College and the Georgia Institute of Technology, graduated from the U.S. Naval Academy in 1946, served under Admiral Hiram Rickover in the U.S. Navy, and returned to Plains, Georgia, to grow peanuts on his farm. In 1962 he was elected to the Georgia senate after a campaign beset by corruption and ballot stuffing, a story he tells in *Turning Point: A Candidate, a State, and a Nation Come of Age* (1992). Although in 1966 his campaign for the office of governor ended in defeat, in 1970 he was elected governor. In 1976 Carter was elected thirty-ninth president of the United States, the first Southerner to hold that office since before the Civil War. A faltering economy and the Iranian hostage crisis were among the most serious issues of his presidency. In 1980 he lost his bid for a second term to Ronald Reagan. Carter has spent much of his time since his defeat working for civic and charitable causes and administering his presidential library in Atlanta. His postpresidential citizenship has won him worldwide acclaim. His books include *Why Not the Best?* (1976), *Keeping Faith: Memoirs of a President* (1982), *The Blood of Abraham* (1985).

WILLIAM CRAFT (1821–1900) and Ellen Craft (1826–91) lived much of their early lives as slaves in Macon, Georgia. They married in a traditional slave ceremony in 1846 and began plotting their escape. In December 1848 they carried out their plan. Ellen, who could pass for white, dressed as a white Southern planter while William masqueraded as her servant. They traveled to Philadelphia, where they settled until the passage of the Fugitive Slave Act in 1850 allowed two slave catchers from Georgia to demand their return. Pressure from abolitionist groups and freed blacks defeated the slave catchers, and the Crafts moved to England, where they worked for abolitionist and other philanthropic causes and attended an agricultural school. Their narrative, *Running a Thousand Miles for Freedom,* appeared in 1860, but the story of the rest of their lives is in many ways as remarkable as that of their escape. William traveled to Dahomey, Africa, in 1861 to persuade the king there to give up human sacrifice and cooperation with the slave trade. After an abortive experience in an import-export business, the Crafts bought a plantation in Hickory Hill,

South Carolina, where they hoped to help freed slaves learn how to become self-sufficient. After night riders destroyed their first crop, they fled to Savannah. Then they leased a plantation in Bryan County and began to seek black tenants to work the land. The opposition of local whites to their activities, and accusations that the Crafts were mishandling charitable funds collected for a school on the plantation, made their lives difficult. Shortly after his wife's death, Craft lost the plantation to creditors.

HARRY CREWS (1935– ) was born a farmer's son in Alma, Georgia. After four years in the marines, where he rose to the rank of sergeant, he left the military and studied writing at the University of Florida under the direction of Andrew Lytle. There he earned his B.A. in 1960 and his M.S.Ed. in 1962 and joined the faculty as a creative writing teacher in 1968. Crews's first novel, *The Gospel Singer,* appeared in 1968, followed by *Naked in Garden Hills* (1969), *This Thing Don't Lead to Heaven* (1970), *Karate Is a Thing of the Spirit* (1971), *Car* (1972), *The Hawk Is Dying* (1973), *The Gypsy's Curse* (1974), *A Feast of Snakes* (1976), *A Childhood: The Biography of a Place* (autobiography, 1978), *Blood and Grits* (1979), *The Enthusiast* (1981), *Florida Frenzy* (essays and stories, 1982), *A Grit's Triumph* (1983), *Two* (1984), *All We Need of Hell* (1987), *The Knockout Artist* (1988), *Body* (1990), and *Scar Lover* (1992). Crews projects a dark, comic, often gruesome vision of life in the modern South. His fiction is marked by frequent violence, a romantic pessimism bordering on the existential, and a remarkable array of dispossessed characters.

ROSEMARY DANIELL (1935– ) was born and raised in Atlanta, Georgia. A dropout from high school at the age of sixteen, and prepared for a career as a mother and housewife, she discovered her passion for writing after a poetry workshop with James Dickey at Emory University. Her books include *A Sexual Tour of the Deep South* (poems, 1975), *Fatal Flowers: On Sin, Sex, and Suicide in the Deep South* (personal memoir, 1980), *Sleeping with Soldiers: In Search of the Macho Man* (personal memoir, 1985), *Fort Bragg and Other Points South* (poetry, 1988), and *The Hurricane Season* (novel, 1992).

W. E. B. DU BOIS (1868–1963) was one of the most important and influential black leaders of the twentieth century. William Edward Burghardt Du Bois earned a Ph.D. from Harvard in 1896 and soon thereafter began to write and campaign on behalf of American blacks. His career traces a path from conservative moderation, like that of Booker T. Washington, to increasing activism, and finally to radicalism. Du Bois founded the NAACP in 1911 and as a leader and writer in that organization campaigned vigorously against segregation and racism. Eventually he found the NAACP too conservative and began to advocate segregation and Pan-Africanism. His influence gradually waned. In 1961 he joined the Communist party and in 1962 became a citizen of Ghana, where he died a year later. Du Bois served on the faculty of Atlanta University from 1897 to 1910 and from 1934 to 1944. He founded two important journals, *Crisis,* a publication of the NAACP, and *Phylon.* Among his important and influential writings are *The Souls of Black Folk* (1903), *Black Reconstruction in the South* (1935), and *Dusk of Dawn* (1940), an autobiography.

MARY A. H. GAY (1829–1918) was born in Jones County, Georgia, to a transplanted Virginia father who died shortly after her birth. Around 1851 she moved with her mother and her half brother and sister to Decatur, Georgia. In 1858 she published a collection of poetry, *Prose and Poetry,* which went through eleven editions in the next thirty years. Gay's half brother, Thomas Stokes, died at the battle of Franklin, Tennessee, in 1864. Using his letters, her sister's journal, and her own memories of the war, Gay wrote *Life in Dixie during the War,* first published in 1892 with an introduction by Joel Chandler Harris. Three more editions were published, somewhat revised and lengthened, in the next nine years. She also published a novel, *The Transplanted,* in 1907.

GEORGE R. GILMER (1790–1859) was born in what is now Oglethorpe County, Georgia, into a family recently settled from Virginia. He studied law in Lexington, Georgia, led an expedition against the Creek in 1812 at a location that later became the site of Atlanta, and in 1818 was elected to the state legislature. He was elected to congressional terms in 1820, 1828, and 1833, though he was not permitted to serve the second term.

Gilmer served twice as governor, from 1829 to 1831 and from 1837 to 1839. He was a vigorous proponent of states' rights and of the removal of the Cherokee, issues he saw as closely related. His memoir, *Sketches of Some of the First Settlers of Upper Georgia*, appeared late in his life, in 1855.

HENRY W. GRADY (1850–89) was born in Athens, Georgia. Grady earned his B.A. at the University of Georgia in 1868 and studied for a year at the University of Virginia. In the late 1860s he began working for a newspaper in Rome, Georgia, and gradually began building a reputation as a journalist. In 1872 he bought interest in an Atlanta newspaper, the *Atlanta Daily Herald*, which later collapsed. He began working in 1876 for the *Atlanta Constitution* and soon convinced the editors to hire another journalist, Joel Chandler Harris. Grady's national reputation began to grow with his coverage of the 1876 Hayes-Tilden election dispute. His 1886 speech "The New South" made him famous. Grady did not actually invent the idea of the New South, but he did become one of its primary spokesmen. As an editor he was notable for his use of modern reporting techniques. As a figure in local, state, and national politics he tended to regard the welfare of the South mainly in terms of the health of its economy. He died of pneumonia in 1889, shortly after his return from a trip to Boston, where he gave a lecture entitled "The Race Problem in the South." Though Grady believed Southern blacks deserved justice, he did not believe they would gain social equality.

MELISSA FAY GREENE (1952– ) was born in Macon, Georgia, and educated at Oberlin College, where she earned a B.A. degree with high honors. She has worked as a paralegal and as a writer. Her book, *Praying for Sheetrock* (1991), was a finalist for the National Book Award and winner of the National Book Critics Circle Award in nonfiction. She has written articles and reviews for a number of journals and is at work on a second book.

LEWIS GRIZZARD (1946–94) was born in Columbus, Georgia. After earning a B.A. in journalism at the University of Georgia in 1968, he worked as a sportswriter and editor for the *Atlanta Journal-Constitution* and then the *Chicago Sun-Times,* but he returned to Atlanta prepared for another kind of writing. His outlandishly comic, exaggerated, and buffoonish columns, unabashed in their regional loyalties and their disdain for outsiders, earned him a national following, and they have appeared in more than three hundred national newspapers. He has published numerous highly popular books since 1980, most of them collections of his columns. Among his many books, the best is a memoir of his father, *My Daddy Was a Pistol and I'm a Son of a Gun* (1986). Others include *Won't You Come Home, Billy Bob Bailey?* (1980), *They Tore Out My Heart and Stomped That Sucker Flat* (1982), *Kathy Sue Loudermilk, I Love You* (1983), *Elvis Is Dead and I Don't Feel So Good Myself* (1984), *Shoot Low Boys—They're Ridin' Shetland Ponies* (1985), *Chili Dawgs Always Bark at Night* (1989), and *I Haven't Understood Anything since 1962* (1992).

CORRA HARRIS (1869–1935) was the prolific and popular writer of fourteen novels and numerous articles, stories, and essays. She was born and educated in Elbert County, Georgia, and after a brief stint as a teacher married Luncy Harris, a Methodist minister, in 1887. Their marriage was not a happy one, for the most part, but they remained together until his suicide in 1910. Worse still, one of her children was stillborn, another died in childhood, and the third died at the age of thirty-one. Three of her novels are loosely based on her experiences as a minister's wife. The first and best known was *A Circuit Rider's Wife* (1910). Harris was conservative and regionalist in her leanings. She wrote for ten years for the New York journal the *Independent* and later was a regular columnist for the *Atlanta Journal.*

JOEL CHANDLER HARRIS (1848–1908) was born in Eatonton, Georgia. He was befriended at the age of thirteen by farmer and newspaper editor Joseph Addison Turner, who introduced him to the worlds of journalism and literature. Harris's life on Turner's plantation gave him much of the knowledge about Georgia plantation life that he later used in his writing. He moved his family to Atlanta in 1873 and began working for the *Constitution,* under the editorship of Henry Grady, with whom he became friends and whose biography he later wrote. He developed the character of Uncle Remus in columns during the mid 1870s, and his first collection of Uncle Remus stories appeared in 1880, followed by three more volumes, in 1883, 1892, and 1905. Harris's Uncle Remus stories, along with his other writings about Southern blacks and plantations, earned him a national following and the respect of no less a writer than Mark Twain. The stories are noteworthy for their relative accuracy in the presentation of African-American folklore, their psychological understanding of the racial situation in the post–Civil-War South, their humor, their variety, and their nostalgia. Harris published a number of often distinguished works on other subjects as well. Although he at first was a strong supporter of Grady's New South movement, he became increasingly disenchanted in his later years with the direction it had taken and worried that the South would lose its cultural distinctiveness to Northern commerce and industry.

HENRY HULL (1798–1881) was the son of Hope Hull, founder of Methodism in Georgia. Hull attended the University of Georgia and graduated in 1815. After earning an M.D. from the University of Maryland, he practiced medicine in Athens, Georgia, while also serving as a trustee of the University of Georgia. In 1829 he was elected professor of mathematics, and from 1830 to 1845 he taught at the University of Georgia. Hull's *Annals of Athens* gives a vivid, sometimes humorous portrait of early life in the northeast Georgia town. His son, Augustus Longstreet Hull, published these sketches along with his own reminiscences as *Annals of Athens, Georgia, 1801–1901* in 1906.

MARY JONES (1808–69), one of the diarists and correspondents in *The Children of Pride*, spent most of her life in Liberty County, Georgia, where her husband, the Reverend Charles Colcock Jones, owned three plantations and attended to his life's vocation: ministry to slaves. They were the parents of four children, three of whom survived to adulthood. After her husband's death in 1863, she struggled to keep their plantations intact but failed. She died in New Orleans shortly after moving there to live with her daughter Mary Mallard.

FRANCES ANNE KEMBLE (1809–93) spent only a few months of her life in Georgia, but during that stay she wrote a detailed, perceptive, and striking account of antebellum plantation life and of slavery. She was born to a famous British family of actors, and though she was not naturally disposed to acting, her parents persuaded her to try it. In 1829 her appearance in a production of *Romeo and Juliet* made her a celebrity. From 1832 to 1834 Kemble toured America with her father, acting in numerous cities on the East Coast. In 1834 she married Pierce Mease Butler of Philadelphia, heir to a large and productive coastal plantation on Butler Island, near Darien, Georgia. She visited there briefly with her husband from January to April of 1839. Her personal disgust for slavery contributed to a growing estrangement from her husband, as her diary makes evident. In 1840 their marriage reached an end, and they lived apart for the next nine years. Divorce was granted in 1849, and custody of their two children went to Butler. Kemble's concern over British support for the Confederacy led her to publish her diary in order to illustrate to British readers the conditions of American slavery. The diary appeared in May of 1863.

JAMES KILGO (1941– ) was born in Darlington, South Carolina. He earned his B.A. in English from Wofford College in 1963, his M.A. from Tulane University in 1965, and his Ph.D. in American literature, also from Tulane, in 1971. He joined the English department at the University of Georgia in 1967, first as an instructor, later as an assistant and then associate professor. At first Kilgo seemed headed toward a conventional academic career. He received numerous awards for his teaching and published several scholarly articles. By the mid-1980s he had begun writing creatively, and in 1988 his book *Deep Enough for Ivory Bills,* a collection of personal essays about hunting, nature, and friendship, was published by the Algonquin Press to widely favorable reviews. Kilgo's nonfiction essays have appeared in such journals as the *Sewanee Review,* the *Georgia*

*Review,* and the *Gettysburg Review.* His second essay collection, *An In-heritance of Horses,* appeared in 1994. He is currently at work on a novel.

MARTIN LUTHER KING, JR. (1929–68) is arguably the most important political figure in modern American history. King was born in Atlanta, Georgia. He earned his undergraduate degree from Morehouse College in 1951, his B.D. from Crozer Theological Seminary in 1951, and his Ph.D. in philosophy from Boston University in 1955. King was a Baptist minister, like his father and grandfather before him. In 1955–56 he organized a year-long boycott of the Montgomery, Alabama, city bus service in protest of its discriminatory practices against blacks. The success of this boycott, and King's own moral force, made him a national figure and helped cement his place as a leader of the civil rights movement. King organized successful voter-registration campaigns and the March on Washington in 1963, and was president of the Southern Christian Leadership Conference. In 1965 he received the Nobel Peace Prize. He was assassinated in 1968 in Memphis, Tennessee. His books include *Stride toward Freedom* (1958), *Strength to Love* (1963), *Why We Can't Wait* (1964), *Where Do We Go from Here?: Chaos or Community* (1968). Selections from these books as well as a number of his essays and speeches are included in *A Testament of Hope: The Essential Writings of Martin Luther King, Jr.* (1986).

FRANCES BUTLER LEIGH (1838–1910) was the daughter of Frances Kemble and Pierce Butler, and she remained loyal to both of her parents after their bitter divorce. Although they disagreed violently on the Civil War, she lived with her mother in Europe for much of the war's duration but returned with her father to his plantation following the Southern defeat, and she undertook management after his death in 1867. She married James Wentworth Leigh, an English clergyman, in 1871. Her diary, *Ten Years on a Georgia Plantation since the War,* was published in 1883.

KATHARINE DU PRE LUMPKIN (1897– ) was born in Macon, Georgia. Lumpkin attended Brenau College in Gainesville, Georgia, and earned an M.A. at Columbia University, followed by a Ph.D. in sociology and economics from the University of Wisconsin in 1928. She served as director of research in industrial studies at Smith College and as research director of the Institute of Labor Studies. She wrote or cowrote a number of studies about the family, child development, and the South, including *The South in Progress* (1940), *The Making of a Southerner* (1947, 1981 rev.), and *The Emancipation of Angelina Grimke* (1974).

HUGH MCCALL (1767–1824) was Georgia's earliest historian; he was born in North Carolina shortly before the Revolutionary War. He served in the Georgia militia for a number of years, at least as early as 1794, rising through the ranks to the level of major by the time of his retirement in 1815. McCall spent much of his life as an invalid and was pulled around town in a cart by a black manservant. He began writing his history of Georgia in 1782. From 1806 to 1823 he served as the jailer in Savannah, though he also worked part of this time as a military storekeeper in Charleston. During these years, and despite frequently bad health, he wrote his two-volume *History of Georgia* (1811, 1816).

RALPH MCGILL (1898–1969) was a writer and longtime editor of the *Atlanta Constitution*. McGill was born in Soddy, Tennessee and studied at Vanderbilt from 1917 to 1922 but was expelled for involvement in a fraternity prank shortly before graduating. Soon afterward he became a sportswriter and then sports editor for the Nashville *Banner*. In 1929 Clark Howell, editor of the *Constitution*, brought McGill to Atlanta as a sports and political writer. McGill was most familiar for the page-one editorial column in which he expressed his opinions on numerous regional, national, and international issues. Although he published in such places as the *Atlantic Monthly* and the *Saturday Evening Post*, his editorial stands during the tumult of the civil rights era earned him national acclaim. Not outspokenly pro-integration, he nevertheless argued that Supreme Court rulings and federal laws should be obeyed and was a strong opponent of the Klan and racist violence. In 1958 he won the Pulitzer Prize for his editorial on the bombing of a black church and a Jewish temple.

MARY S. MALLARD (1835–89) was the daughter of two of the primary figures in the letters collected in *The Children of Pride:* the Reverend Charles Colcock Jones, a Presbyterian clergyman, and Mary Jones. She passed most of her childhood in Liberty County, Georgia, where her parents were prominent plantation owners, and she lived for a time as well in Columbia, South Carolina, and in Philadelphia. She married the Reverend Robert Quarterman Mallard, who was pastor at the Central Presbyterian Church in Atlanta when the city fell to Union forces. They were the parents of five children. Mallard lived out her final years in New Orleans.

JAMES MOONEY (1861–1921) was a gifted ethnographer born in Richmond, Indiana. He taught briefly in Richmond, Virginia, before going to work for a local newspaper. His knowledge of the American Indian was largely self-taught, but it was sufficient to convince the founder of the Bureau of American Ethnology to hire him in 1885. In the succeeding years Mooney wrote numerous articles and monographs about the American Indian. His study *Myths of the Cherokee* (1885–86) is regarded not only as his most important work but also as a major source of information about the Cherokee Indians.

FRANCIS MOORE (fl. 1830–44) is known primarily for two journals. The first was a record of his travels from 1730 to 1735 in Gambia and equatorial Africa, where he worked as a writer and agent for the Royal African Company of England. His account of Africa was published as *Travels into the Inland Parts of Africa* (1738). In 1735 he was employed as a storekeeper by the Georgia trustees and traveled to the colony with Oglethorpe. His narrative of his experiences in the colony was published as *A Voyage to Georgia* in 1744.

FLANNERY O'CONNOR (1925–64) is considered one of the leading writers of short fiction in American literature. O'Connor attended the Georgia State College for Women in Milledgeville, graduating in 1945. She earned her M.A. at the University of Iowa and presented as her master's thesis a collection of stories entitled *The Geranium.* She lived for a time with the translator Robert Fitzgerald and his wife, Sally, in Ridge-field, Connecticut. When she began suffering from lupus in 1950, she returned to her mother's Milledgeville home. In general, except for her illness and her writing, the remainder of her life was uneventful, though her active correspondence with other writers (preserved in *The Habit of Being,* edited by Sally Fitzgerald) reveals a fertile intellectual existence. O'Connor wrote two novels: *Wise Blood* (1952) and *The Violent Bear It Away* (1960). Her first story collection, *A Good Man Is Hard to Find,* appeared in 1955 and the second, *Everything That Rises Must Converge,* in 1965 shortly after her death. O'Connor's fiction blends a fiercely moral, devoutly Catholic vision of a fallen modern world with a comic talent for characterization, description, and dialogue.

JAMES OGLETHORPE (1696–1785) was founder of the colony of Georgia. Elected to Parliament in 1722, in 1729–30 he chaired a committee investigating the conditions of jails. He became convinced that debtors should be given a second chance and conceived the notion of giving them one by sending them to colonies in America. With these reformist ideas, and the support of other English reformists, Oglethorpe organized and led an expedition of British citizens to establish a colony in 1733 at the location of what is now Savannah. Many of the early laws that Oglethorpe and the Georgia Trustees imposed on the colony reflect the reformist ideas of its founding—they prohibited slavery and alcohol, for example, and regulated trade with the Indians. These laws soon came to seem restrictive to many colonists, and by 1752 they had been overturned. Not particularly successful as a governor or military leader, Oglethorpe nonetheless established under difficult conditions a colony that survived to prosper. He returned permanently to England in 1743 and served in Parliament until his defeat in a 1755 election. He remained concerned about the welfare of the colony he founded until his death.

EUGENIA PRICE (1916– ) was born in Charleston, West Virginia. Price attended Ohio University and studied dentistry at Northwestern University. She began writing inspirational books in the 1950s. In 1965 her novel *Beloved Invader* appeared. It was the first of a trilogy of novels about the early history of coastal Georgia. She has also written a tetralogy of novels about Savannah. Largely through the popularity of these Georgia novels, Price is a nationally known novelist who has sold more than twenty million books.

CHARLES HENRY SMITH ("BILL ARP") (1826–1903) was born in Lawrenceville, Georgia. He studied at the University of Georgia for several years, married, and read law with his father-in-law, Judge Nathan Lewis Hutchins, in 1849. In 1851 he set up practice in Rome, Georgia, where he worked until 1861 when he joined the Confederate army, though poor health soon forced his departure. In the same year Smith began writing his satiric Bill Arp letters. He wrote more than two thousand such letters before his death, and at the height of their popularity they appeared in seven hundred weekly newspapers. Smith was friends with Joel Chandler Harris and Henry Grady, both of whom helped popularize his work. Smith's books include *Bill Arp, So Called* (1866), *Bill Arp's Letters* (1868), *Bill Arp's Peace Papers* (1873), *Bill Arp's Scrap Book* (1884), *The Farm and the Fireside* (1891), *A School History of Georgia* (1893), and *Bill Arp: From the Uncivil War to Date* (1903).

LILLIAN SMITH (1897–1966) lived with her wealthy family in Jasper, Florida, until the age of seventeen, when business failures forced her father to relocate to Clayton, Georgia. She attended Piedmont College in Demorest, Georgia, for one year, studied music at Peabody Conservatory in Baltimore on and off for four years, and later attended Teachers College of Columbia University until her father's death in 1930 cut short her schooling. Her three-year experience as a music teacher in China during the early 1920s apparently was a major influence on the development of her liberal attitudes toward race and Southern society. In 1936 she began publishing a literary magazine called *Pseudopodia*, which under various names continued on until 1945. It was the only Southern literary journal of the time to publish black writers. Her first novel, *Strange Fruit*, about a love affair between a black man and a white woman, was published in 1944 and immediately became a controversial best seller. In

1949 she wrote a nonfiction study of Southern culture entitled *Killers of the Dream*. Smith spent much of the rest of her life lecturing, crusading for civil rights, and writing. Later books include *The Journey* (1954), *One Hour* (1959), *Memory of a Large Christmas* (1962), and *Our Faces, Our World* (1964).

ALEXANDER H. STEPHENS (1812–83), a leading antebellum Southern politician, was educated at the University of Georgia, where he graduated first in his class in 1832. He had established a law practice in Crawfordville when he was elected to the Georgia house of representatives in 1836. In 1842 he was elected to the Georgia senate, and in 1843 to the U.S. Congress. A Southern Whig until the party broke apart in 1854, he became a Democrat in 1855. Ardently pro-Southern, he was also ardently anti-secession, but when it was clear that secession was unavoidable he supported it wholeheartedly. One of the writers of the Confederate Constitution, he was appointed vice-president of the Confederacy, but throughout most of the war he was at first privately and then publicly disenchanted with the policies of Jefferson Davis and the Confederate Congress. After brief imprisonment following the surrender, Stephens was elected to the U.S. Senate, but as a former Confederate he was not allowed to take his seat. In the next few years he wrote a two-volume study of the war, *A Constitutional View of the War between the States*, and attempted, unsuccessfully, to edit a newspaper called the *Atlanta Sun*. In 1872 he was elected to Congress again and this time was permitted to serve. He retired in 1882. Almost immediately elected governor, he died after four months in office.

JOHN E. TALMADGE (1889–1978) was born in Athens, Georgia, and educated at the University of Georgia, where he received his B.A. in 1921. After two years of service in the U.S. Infantry (1918–19), he earned his M.A. from Harvard in 1926. He worked for fifteen years in the advertising department of the *New York Times* before joining the journalism faculty at the University of Georgia in 1945. In 1953 he became a member of the English department faculty. Talmadge coauthored with Louis T.

Griffith the *History of Georgia Journalism* (1953) and wrote biographies of the Georgia political figure Rebecca Latimer Felton (1960) and the novelist Corra Harris (1968).

JOHN DONALD WADE (1892–1963) was born in Marshalville, Georgia, and he attended the University of Georgia, earning his B.A. in 1914. He earned his M.A. in English literature from Harvard in 1915 and enrolled in a doctoral program at Columbia University the following year. After serving in the infantry in World War I, Wade taught as an instructor at the University of Georgia (1919–26). He completed his Ph.D. in 1924. His published dissertation, a study of the life and times of Georgia humorist Augustus Baldwin Longstreet, was for many years regarded as a classic study of Southern letters and culture. Wade became a professor at Vanderbilt University in 1928, and in 1930 he contributed an essay ("The Life and Death of Cousin Lucius") to the agrarian manifesto *I'll Take My Stand*. His biography of John Wesley appeared in the same year. Wade returned to the University of Georgia in 1934 and served as head of the English department from 1939 until 1946. He founded the *Georgia Review* in 1947. He retired in 1950.

ALICE WALKER (1944– ) was born into a large sharecropping family in Eatonton, Georgia. She graduated first in her high school class and attended Spelman College in Atlanta for two years before transferring to Sarah Lawrence College in New York. In Atlanta she was active in the civil rights movement, and at Sarah Lawrence she studied writing under Muriel Rukeyser. Her first collection of poems, *Once*, appeared in 1968; her first novel, *The Third Life of Grange Copeland*, followed in 1970. Walker is especially skillful as a writer of short fiction, as her collection *In Love and Trouble: Stories of Black Women* (1973) demonstrates. Two stories from the volume ("Everyday Use" and "The Revenge of Hannah Kemhuff") appeared in *Best American Short Stories* for 1974. Her 1976 novel, *Meridian*, in part concerns the transformative effect of the civil rights movement on one of its participants. In the 1970s Walker served as an editor of *Ms.* magazine and in 1977 won a Guggenheim Fellowship. *The Color Purple*, her widely acclaimed novel about an oppressed young black woman's gradual struggle toward self-discovery, appeared in 1982. It was a best seller and won both the Pulitzer Prize and the American Book Award in 1982. A film based on the novel appeared in 1985. *Living by the Word: Selected Writings, 1973–1987*, appeared in 1988, and another novel, *The Temple of My Familiar*, in 1989.

WALTER WHITE (1893–1955) was born into a middle-class black Atlanta family. He received his B.A. from Atlanta University in 1916 and shortly afterward began working for the recently organized NAACP. Early in his career White did fieldwork for the organization. On occasion, his light skin color allowed him to pose as a white man while he investigated lynchings and Klan activities in Tennessee, Arkansas, and Georgia. In 1929 he became acting secretary of the NAACP, a position that became permanent in 1931 with the retirement of James Weldon Johnson. Among his opponents in the NAACP was W. E. B. Du Bois, whom White pressured to resign from the governing board. As secretary, White lobbied in Washington for various civil rights bills and campaigned vigorously for anti-lynching legislation. White was an important force in the civil rights movement of the pre-1950s. He wrote six books, including *Fire in the Flint* (1924), a well-received novel; *Flight* (1926), his second novel; a study of lynching, *Rope and Faggot: A Biography of Judge Lynch* (1929), written with the support of a Guggenheim Fellowship; *A Rising Wind: A Report on the Negro Soldier in the European Theater* (1948); his autobiography, *A Man Called White* (1948); and *How Far the Promised Land* (1955).

PHILIP LEE WILLIAMS (1950– ) was born in Madison, Georgia, where he has lived for much of his life. He earned a B.A. in journalism from the University of Georgia in 1972 and spent much of the next fifteen years in newspaper work. He was associate editor of the *Madisonian* from 1974 to 1978, and from 1978 to 1985 he edited the *Athens Observer*, a weekly newspaper. He also wrote fiction throughout these years, at first for his own entertainment, then with ambitions to publish. In 1984 his first novel, *In the Heart of a Distant Forest* (the title comes from a line in James Dickey's poem "The Lifeguard"), was published by W. W. Norton. Other novels include *All the Western Stars* (1988), *Slow Dance in*

*Autumn* (1988), *The Song of Daniel* (1989), *Perfect Timing* (1991), and *Final Heat* (1992).

DONALD WINDHAM (1920– ) was born in Atlanta and graduated from Boy's High School in 1937. He worked briefly for Coca-Cola, and at the age of nineteen left for New York City. Though he rarely returned to Atlanta, a number of his works, including *The Dog Star* (1950), *The Warm Country* (1960), and *Emblems of Conduct* (1964), are set there. In New York he became friends with Tennessee Williams. Together they wrote a play, *You Touched Me*, in 1942–43; it was produced on Broadway in 1945. Their friendship is chronicled in Williams's *Memoirs* and Windham's edition of *Tennessee Williams's Letters to Donald Windham, 1940–1965* (1977). Although Windham insists he is a Southern writer, European influences, especially Joyce and Proust, are evident throughout his work. His other novels include *The Hero Continues* (1960), *Two People* (1965), *Tanaquil* (1972, revised 1977), and *Stone in the Hour Glass* (1981).

Further information on these writers can be found in the following volumes, which served as sources for many of these biographical notes: A. L. Hull, *Annals of Athens, Georgia, 1801–1901* (Athens: Banner Job Office, 1906); Edgar A. Toppin, *A Biographical History of Blacks in America since 1528* (New York: McKay, 1971); *Contemporary Authors* (Detroit: Gale Research Co.); Kenneth Coleman et al., *The Dictionary of Georgia Biography* (Athens: Univ. of Georgia Press, 1983); *The Dictionary of Literary Biography* (Detroit: Gale Research Co.); *Dictionary of National Biography;* Frank Magill, *Great Lives from History* (Pasadena, Calif.: Salem Press, 1987); Kenneth Coleman et al., *A History of Georgia* (Athens: Univ. of Georgia Press, 1977); Robert Bain, Joseph M. Flora, Louis D. Rubin, Jr., *Southern Writers: A Biographical Dictionary* (Baton Rouge: Louisiana State Univ. Press, 1979); William L. Andrews, *To Tell a Free Story: The First Century of Afro-American Autobiography, 1760–1865* (Urbana and Chicago: Univ. of Illinois Press, 1986). In addition, individual biographies of many of the writers in this volume also served as sources and are well worth consulting.